The Woods:
A Year on Protection Island

NIGHTWOOD EDITIONS

2016

THE
WOODS

A YEAR ON PROTECTION ISLAND

AMBER
MCMILLAN

Nightwood Editions
P.O. Box 1779
Gibsons, BC VON 1V0
Canada
www.nightwoodeditions.com

COPY EDITOR: Nicola Goshulak
COVER DESIGN: Angela Yen
TYPOGRAPHY: Carleton Wilson
INTERIOR PHOTOS: Amber McMillan, Nathaniel G. Moore, Silas White

Canada

Nightwood Editions acknowledges financial support from
the Government of Canada through the Canada Book Fund and
the Canada Council for the Arts, and from the Province of British Columbia
through the British Columbia Arts Council and the Book Publisher's Tax Credit.

This book has been produced on 100% post-consumer recycled,
ancient-forest-free paper, processed chlorine-free
and printed with vegetable-based dyes.

Printed and bound in Canada.

CIP data available from Library and Archives Canada.

ISBN 978-0-88971-329-1

for Finn and Nathaniel

Contents

"What happens is of little significance compared with the stories we tell ourselves about what happens."

—Rabih Alameddine, *The Hakawati*

PROLOGUE
APRIL 30, 2014, TORONTO

[ONE]

OUR MEAL HAD JUST ARRIVED AT THE STARVING ARTIST ON Lansdowne, just north of Bloor, when our first-floor neighbour texted.

"Look at Kevin's text," I said, handing Nate my phone. "He thinks we left our cat behind and just moved away." Nate read the text and scrolled through a few previous ones from Kevin as well. Arguments between Kevin's phone and mine went back years; it was all time-stamped and saved in chronological order, giving every new argument the full weight of the past—every injustice heavier and heavier on top of old resentments left to fester, feed off and multiply.

"I'm so tired of this," said Nate. "He's ruining my last breakfast in Toronto."

I could feel adrenalin start its course through my veins. My hands were getting clammy and my body temperature was rising. I was tired too, tired of fighting all the time. My muscles felt permanently tight and strained. I was exhausted, having only just arrived at the other side of a record seven-month winter, a winter that annihilated the city of Toronto with rolling power outages, ice storms that felled trees and power lines, four-foot snowbanks and hills of solid ice on every street, sideways sleet and hail, freezing temperatures and the ongoing, unpredictable hassles of travelling through all this: subway delays, traffic jams, overcrowded buses, the layers of necessary extra clothing caught in boots, zippers and jacket arm holes. Everything was wet and cold and heavy. The smallest annoyance was enough to send me into an emotional tailspin.

"He's probably going to let Bernie Mac out the front door now and we'll never see him again. We have to go back," I said and began looking around for our server.

> Me: *We didn't abandon our cat, Kevin. We've hired someone to clean the apartment. We are taking our cat with us tomorrow when we move.*

"I wanted to eat this and have a nice time with you. These people are driving me nuts. I'm gonna lose it, Amber. I'm telling you, if we go back there now, I'm gonna lose it," Nate said as he lifted his plate to our server. "Can you pack this up? Sorry, but we have to leave right away. Sorry."

> Kevin: *Yeah right.*

> Me: *We are coming back to the house now.*

The server brought back our untouched breakfasts in two cumbersome boxes. We left the restaurant to head back to our apartment only a few blocks away. It was still cold, even in April, but the heat of my rage kept my face from freezing against the early spring wind. I began walking faster and faster. I was running through the last conversations I'd had with Kevin: the fight about the shared WiFi password that they changed without telling us; the parties he was always having that inevitably spilled into the lobby at three or four in the morning with drunken rambling and belly laughing; the time they let a film crew of forty people into the house, swarming everywhere; the band rehearsals twice a week ... I was working myself into a frenzy. Twice Nate demanded I ease up on my pace. He was trying to calm down before we got there. I was trying to maintain my edge so I could go through with the confrontation. The last hurrah. Our magnum opus of arguments. I was trying to stay furious.

We stood on the corner of Bloor and Lansdowne for what seemed like forever as cars and buses flew past, spraying our clothes with slush and grit from the street. My skin was becoming numb and tight from the cold as I watched the crosswalk signal, willing it to turn to the flashing stick man. People piled up on the corner, squishing in and pushing their bodies and shopping bags into everything, into my legs and ribs. I instinctively pressed my forearm against my inner pocket to feel that my wallet was still there. I wrapped my scarf tighter around my neck and over my mouth and nose. I stomped my feet to shake off the wet crud soaking into my pants and boots.

"Come on!" I screamed in my head, at the people around me, at Kevin, at the whole city. I needed everything to happen faster. The crosswalk opened and I ran across, manoeuvring myself around the cars that had stopped inside the crosswalk and the people around me, all as frustrated and impatient as me. I saw Nate ahead of me and to the right, his hands jammed hard in his pockets, his head down to block the fierce wind.

As we turned onto our street, I ran ahead and was first to barrel through the front door of the house we shared, for one more night, with Kevin. I stomped past the entrance lobby and knocked as authoritatively as possible on our neighbour's apartment door—the kind of ferocious knock I imagined police trained for to terrify the people inside.

"Kevin, it's us!" I yelled. "Hello! Kevin, hello!"

Nothing. I looked back and could see Nate through the open door, pacing on the front porch and kicking swaths of ice down the stairs to shatter on the sidewalk.

"They're not answering," I said loudly, hoping our neighbours would hear me from inside their apartment.

Nate came through the front lobby and stood beside me. He was breathing slowly and his hands were crossed over his chest, the takeout bag hanging from his fist. He reached out and banged on their door, just once, but louder than I had been able to do.

"Kevin, come out and talk to me," he said, and then stepped back.

We stood there, staring at their door, freezing and outraged, waiting in silence, but there was no movement to be heard from inside the apartment. No voice in reply. Bernie Mac glided down the stairs from our apartment above. He looked happy that we were home and greeted us by nuzzling his face across our boots and purring, his tail waving gracefully in the air.

"Let's go," said Nate.

I turned toward the staircase that led to our apartment above and stomped loudly across the lobby. I sat down on the step and pulled off my hat, beads of water and ice that had collected in the knitted yarn falling to the floor. I pulled off my gloves with my teeth and tossed them into the wicker bin we kept by the stairs. I bent over and pulled open my shoelaces with frozen and stiff fingers, one stitch at a time, red where the laces settled and pulled between my finger joints. I tugged at the knot in my scarf and wrestled it up and over my head, dragging it across the vulnerable, raw skin of my face as I pulled it over.

Upstairs, our apartment was completely empty except for a couple suitcases, a large box and a mattress we planned to sleep on for what would be our last night in the city. With our familiar clutter gone, everything looked strange. Even the light coming in through the windows looked different somehow, looked like the light of someone else's window in someone else's apartment. The kitchen looked pale and unfriendly, the bathroom oddly shaped and unpleasant. The dents and scrapes on the hardwood floor were more apparent than ever and somehow less charming than I had regarded them before. The crack in the plaster wall along the hallway was larger and deeper.

We'd pushed hard those last months preparing to leave:

notifying Lily's school that she wouldn't be finishing her kindergarten year there; registering for a mail-forwarding service; selling all of our furniture in a yard sale in the park across the street.
We'd lain in bed, late into the night, and talked to each other
quietly about our new life out west, about all of our plans, about
how it would all would change for us completely. We imagined
ourselves free of the hassles and troubles we'd accumulated in
Toronto. We imagined a life without rushing, without the subway,
without neighbours at each other's throats, without the noise and
frustration of daily commutes. Life with space. Life without the
massacre of an endless winter, frozen pipes, cracking plaster and
mountains of snow to overcome each morning.

We'd considered many different places to go before settling on
BC. We started first by looking for work and then considering the
places where there were jobs. There was a teaching job for me in
Regina, and another one in the Yukon that paid far above average. There was an attractive opportunity for Nate in Montreal but
that would mean even longer and crueller winters up there. We
realized that nowhere was going to offer us the perfect combination of work and environment so we decided to go all in and aim
for the best environment possible and figure out the money side
when we got there. We finally started to look at the Nanaimo area
on Vancouver Island because it was close to my mother in Victoria, had affordable rentals, was surrounded by water and trees,
and had a low population compared to Toronto. There was also a
university that might have a job for me if I could be patient.

An online forum we'd found described Protection Island as
a small "car-free paradise" in Nanaimo Harbour where residents
got around on bikes or boats to wherever they were going. The
idea of living somewhere without traffic seemed like an impossible fantasy. I thought of the kind of people who would live there,
people who moved around slowly, lived apart in small homes,
hiked through the woods every day, took boat rides in the afternoons, and instead of waiting in thirty-person lineups in oppres-
sively lit grocery stores, grew their own food and ate it out of the

dirt. I wanted to be a person like that. We wouldn't be earning as much as we did in Toronto, but we wouldn't need to because our cost of living would be less. *We'll build a fire every night,* Nate would say. *We'll sleep outside in the summer,* I would say.

Only a few weeks earlier, and after putting down a deposit on a new house we had rented on the distant island, I had cleared out my staff locker at work and best of all, I'd told Humber College I wouldn't be returning to teach the following semester. I was elated to know that I would never again take the 196 Rocket from Kipling Station, the furthest stop west on the Bloor line, to hurtle down Highway 427 at the edge of Toronto at the crack of dawn. I would never again hurry my child out of the house at 6:30 in the morning to a daycare program before school just so I could get to work on time and rush back after to pick her up at the end of the day. Soon I would have time with her, time with Nate and time for myself. We had undone everything we knew, the whole life we'd built, and we couldn't have been more excited to leave.

I walked around the apartment and scanned each room, the way you do during an open house, like a stranger. I was checking to see if we'd forgotten anything, but we hadn't; the place was nothing but walls and floors, a blank slate that didn't belong to me any longer. After a while I joined Nate and our takeout boxes in the living room and sat down on the floor. We ate our cold eggs and toast and listened to Kevin open and close cupboard doors in the kitchen below us. Through the vents we could him singing along to music in another room, trying to keep his voice low.

THE ISLAND

[TWO]

WHEN WE ARRIVED AT THE NANAIMO AIRPORT, FOUR THOU-
sand kilometres from Toronto, we had two suitcases full of clothing and books, a single box of memorabilia and a stack of paintings
we'd collected, protected on the outside by black garbage bags
and wrapped up with duct tape. The new house we had rented
on the island came furnished so we didn't need to bring anything
more, nor did we want to. We saw my mother waiting for us in the
arrivals gate as we came off the plane, her eyes searching and her
smile uncontainable. She had made the one-hour drive up from
Victoria to meet us and help us get ourselves and our belongings
to our new rental on the island. The sky was cloudless and blue
and the spring sun injected everything with vibrant colour. The
trees were greener, birds soared above us, and the water radiated
light.

We stopped at Thrifty's, the downtown supermarket, to pick
up groceries for a few meals before catching the ferry to Protection
Island. Mum parked her car and we carried our bags of groceries, our
boxes and suitcases, and Lily across the Island Highway and down
to the harbour. From there we followed the signs that led us down
a set of stairs and a ramp toward the Protection Island passenger
ferry at the dock. Attached to a blue and white converted lifeboat

was a wooden board with plain, painted letters that read: *Ferry schedule May–October $9.00 round trip for Adults, $6.00 for Children, Extra: Bikes $5.00, Dogs $2.00*. Attached to its top was another rectangular wooden sign that read *Protection Connection* painted in large, red letters. I checked my pockets for change, but came up empty. In the back pocket of my jeans I found a Toronto Transit transfer pass, expired by a day.

"Do you think they take credit cards?" I said to my mum who was standing next to me reading the same sign.

"I hope so. They should, anyway. Let me see if I have any cash, hold on." She pulled open the flap of her purse.

"Cash only," said a man, positioning two large boxes on the bench next to us near the edge of the dock. The small box had a picture of a toaster on the side and the large one showed a black and white drawing of a printer. The man was tall with short greying hair and pale blue eyes. He wore light-coloured jeans and a buttoned-up white shirt with the sleeves rolled up to the elbow. He looked like he'd walked out of an ad for a sailboat. "And it helps if you have exact change."

"Okay, thanks," I replied, and began unzipping one of our suitcases to locate the purse I had stuffed in it earlier that day. I was moving quickly. The ferry was scheduled to depart for the island shortly.

"There's a bank machine over there," he continued, pointing to the other end of the dock, next to a water fountain.

"Thanks again," I said and checked the time. I had about five minutes to get to the cash machine and back before the ferry left.

"Mum, how about you take this box onto the ferry and sit down. I'll run up to the machine and be right back."

"Oh, no," said the man, grinning and rearranging his boxes on the bench so they wouldn't tumble forward. "This boat here is just the waiting room. The ferry isn't here yet. You guys visiting friends on the Island?" he asked.

"In fact, we're moving there. Right now, today," I said and smiled.

"Oh!" he said, resting his arm on top of his boxes. "Well, welcome then. Where are you coming from?"

"Toronto," I said, aware of how surprising that probably sounded.

"Back east, I see. From Toronto to Protection Island. I think it's safe to say you guys are the first I've ever heard of doing that," he said, smiling.

"It'll be a big change," said my mum, still looking through her purse.

"I'm Jim," said the man. "If you need a hand with your stuff on the other side, I can give you a ride. I've got a golf cart over there to get around," he offered and shook my mother's hand, then mine.

"Terrific. Thank you very much. We don't have a lot of stuff to carry, but we'd really appreciate the lift." I looked over at Mum and she smiled.

Mum took Lily's hand and they found a seat in the waiting room. Lily couldn't stop asking questions: *Where are we on a map though? Is this waiting room boat a real boat? Are there sharks under the water here? What if we sink? Are we almost there?*

I checked the time again. Four minutes. I positioned the suitcases against the bench and jogged down the dock and up the ramp toward the cash machine. There was no lineup. When I came back down the ramp a minute or so later, I could see the ferry boat pulling in next to the waiting-room boat and tying up to it. Ten or so people exited the boat, walked through the "waiting room" and out onto the dock. I ran down the dock to catch up to Nate, Lily and my mum, who had already started organizing the boxes and talking with the ferry skipper.

We handed boxes down from the waiting room to the skipper on the ferry, who placed them along the boat's deck. Next we loaded Lily onto the boat, then Mum, Nate and I joined her. We squished into one corner to leave as much room as we could for others getting on the boat, but we quickly saw that our stuff and our bodies were taking up more than our fair share of space.

Thankfully, the ferry skipper was sympathetic to our situation. "It's better to do it this way," he said to us. "My name's Rob. I'll be your skipper most mornings."

"Nice to meet you," I said. I noticed his skin was already dark from spending most days outside on the ferry. The hair on his arms and legs was bleached by the sun.

"You wouldn't want to pay for a barge to get your things to the Island. It's mighty expensive."

The ride was short but chaotic. Lily kept standing up and leaning off the side of the boat, our boxes were shifting beneath us and Bernie Mac was meowing loudly from his cage. The water was bright and blue and the closer we got, the more I could see of the island. Tall trees were packed into its corners and sailboats were cozied along the shore. I had been travelling all day but I was wide awake and excited. I felt disbelief that we'd actually managed to do what we'd done to get here, and I felt gratitude that the island we'd picked sight-unseen from Toronto appeared to be everything I imagined it to be. Within minutes we were docking again and taking the first steps into our new life.

Protection Island is roughly 1.4 kilometres by 1 kilometre in size and divided into 344 residential lots, parks and common areas. A person can walk from one end to the other in less than thirty minutes, but to walk around sightseeing and checking out everything would take more like an hour. The Island is 1.6 kilometres, or a ten-minute motorboat ride, from Nanaimo Harbour. Not all the lots have houses built on them and not all the houses have people living in them. In the summer, the population hits a peak of roughly three hundred people. In the winter months when the colder air, rain and temperamental weather make living and boating more challenging, the population drops to around 150.

Technically speaking, Protection Island is a neighbourhood of the city of Nanaimo and so the water and power supply to the

Island comes from Nanaimo. All the houses are on septic systems and the necessary hookups for internet and cable utilities are available. Many residents use little golf carts to get around and because they are driven on roads with other golf carts and pedestrians, they are required to be insured and driven by licensed drivers. Every once in a while without notice, the RCMP will come over to the Island from Nanaimo and check that drivers are carrying valid licences and that the plates are up to date and match the golf carts they're registered to.

There is no city garbage pickup or recycling collection so Islanders store their waste and transport it to Nanaimo by boat when they need to or hire someone else to do it for them. Two city dumpsters in Nanaimo Harbour are specifically for Protection Island residents to use. Several parks and beaches are open to the public, but there are no public washrooms available. As you exit the ferry and walk up the path onto the Island, signs and notices are nailed to trees warning tourists that the golf carts and bicycles are privately owned and are not to be used by visitors.

Even in the summer, only about twenty residents walk around the dirt roads or pick blackberries from the community garden or swim at one of the swimming spots on any given day. The odds of running into one of those twenty or so is slim. That being said, there were two people I would see every day in the summer besides my daughter Lily and my husband, making it four I could count on. My neighbour to the left, Keith, was the first. He worked nights at the pub and slept during the day, but I saw him before he left for work in his golf cart and occasionally when he drove back. He'd come out during his days off after preparing baked submissions for the seasonal pie contest or gathering supplies to bring to one of the Island's community events—such as the Mad Hatter's Tea Party down at the emergency dock or the "360" bathtub race around the Island's perimeter.

Keith would get out during these festivities and chat up passersby, seemingly to remind them that the pie contest is coming up and that he would, naturally, be entering his best, or to ascertain who would be participating in the bathtub race this year and who is primed to win or lose, depending on past years' outcomes. During these outings, he'd pass the time on his front lawn puttering around with broken machine parts, organizing and reorganizing piles of garbage, and intermittently gazing at the decrepit boat stationed where his lawn meets the arterial road we shared.

Keith would do all this dressed to the nines in heels, a blouse, skirt, cardigan and barrettes holding his long, grey hair from his face. He had a jolting way of moving, all tall and burly, and a bellowing, gruff voice. If I was out on the porch when he rolled around, we'd share a few words. He'd quip about whether rain was coming or ask how we were making out so far, if we needed anything. With a regularity I had begun to depend on, he'd drop off a plate of shortbread cookies or a fruit pie that he'd made for us. Whenever a passing neighbour asked, "How are ya, Keith?" his answer was always, "I'm alive!"

My neighbour to the right, Brad, was a nearly retired contractor in Nanaimo who only used the place as a cabin retreat. I nevertheless saw him more often than Keith as he spent all his available weekend time on the Island outside working on his lot: mowing the lawn, trimming around the trees, pulling moss from his roof, erecting fence posts or painting his porch. He did all this using the loudest power tools possible, shirt off and sweating. His wife was deaf, so there were no sounds of muted conversation between them floating over to my side, only gas-powered, revved-up grinding and chopping. He always took his hand from the lawnmower or Sawzall to wave when he saw me. His lawn was remarkably pretty to look at, with the greenest and tidiest grass, especially compared to Keith's overgrown brush-cave or our own lawn, which we mowed only when the grass became too tall for Lily to run through or when we thought of it, which was rarely.

If it was a day when I'd decided to take our boat over to town, I was sure to run into one of The Commuters, heading back and forth from Mud Bay to town on a daily or twice-daily basis by rowboat, motorboat or sailing dinghy. Mud Bay Dock is operated by the Dock Collective, a small group of dock users who also volunteer to maintain the area. They fix damaged or old dock fingers when needed, or clean up after the seals who throw themselves into open boats or low points in the dock joints to defecate and rest. Occasionally overcrowding occurs and berths are shared by more than one boat, each rafted to the other. The Dock is open to members who pay an annual fee of around a hundred dollars, but allows temporary and overnight tie-ups. At first glance, tying up at the Dock seemed like an affordable and easy option.

After talking over the specifics with a few Protection Islanders about a week after arriving, Nate and I decided to buy a sixteen-foot runabout with a supposedly decent sixty-hp engine for a few thousand dollars. We'd bought it from a guy in town who said he wasn't using it as much as he'd planned and wanted to get rid of it. He added that his wife was putting pressure on him to sell. The guy drove the boat over to us on the Island and let us take it out for a whirl. It worked and was moderately clean, which was good enough for us, so we took it right there on the spot. Before he left, he handed me a two-hundred-page engine manual and told me to read it. We paid the Dock Collective's annual fee and tied it up at Mud Bay.

The Commuters were folks who work in town, in Nanaimo, or have school-aged children in the regular public school system across the water. Most were polite, if a little disengaged. A few of the others were hard-core fanatics, eager to correct abusers of the Dock Code. If a user of the dock misuses or obstructs in any way the function, etiquette or diplomacy of the Dock Code, she can expect harsh retribution. The only way one learns the rules of the Dock Code is to break them unwittingly, and then attempt to uncover the rule based on the punishment rendered.

For example, even though no berths are reserved or ever can be, etiquette applies. If you tie up your boat near the head of the dock, farthest away from land, you must do so only as a regular Commuter. This is prime real estate due to the rising and falling of the tide, and you and your boat are expected to be in, and then quickly back out of that spot. No "camping" at the head. If you are a less frequent Commuter, you ought to park around the belly of the dock, a mid-range location that tends not to disturb others too much.

If you are a Tourist, a term I heard applied with some hostility to all non-residents, you are strongly encouraged to tie up near the foot of the dock or right up against shore. This is the area of the dock most hated and routinely affected by low tide, which causes the boats to be left marooned every morning in thick mud until the tide comes back in and lifts them safely up again.

If you are a Tourist and you park your boat in prime real estate, as I have done, you will soon find one of the following responses: empty beer cans or juice boxes that have been tossed into the hull, your boat lock cut from the dock with a wire cutter, or your boat filled with water until it sinks into the mud for you to rescue later. These punitive measures can seem heavy-handed and frustrating, especially to newcomers, but eventually the point is always made: figure it out or perish.

On the other hand, if it was a day our boat wasn't working, or a time when there was no hope of moorage on the Nanaimo side (which operates on a first-come, first-served basis), I'd take the *Protection Connection* ferry that shuffles people back and forth "every hour, on the hour!" maintained and occasionally driven by the forever-strained Tim, who never laughed at a joke but always nodded hello—a quick downward motion indicating he'd seen you. The ferry was owned and operated by the single commercial outpost, the Dinghy Dock Pub and Restaurant. The pub was the only recognizable form of capitalism on the Island, and therefore the most blatant in its exploitation. The food was deep-fried and expensive, the table service was slow and the ferry cost a working wage to use.

For example, if a person worked in town and needed transportation to and from the Island each day, it would cost three ferry passes (with eleven round trips on each) at two hundred dollars a month. For a couple like Nate and me, it was double. Kids were free while they attended kindergarten, but once they began grade one they had to pay too, which would happen to us come fall when Lily started school again. All told, without a reliable boat we were in for around six hundred dollars a month just to ride the ferry come September.

Calculating this, we figured investing a few thousand upfront in a motorboat, thereby cutting out the cost of the ferry altogether, would save us money in the long run. This might have been true too, if we'd known the first thing about fixing or maintaining a boat, which we didn't. Plus there was the cost of moorage on both sides of the water to think of, which tacked on another few hundred dollars each month. I came to understand quickly that whether we chose to take the ferry or to own a motorboat, the cost of transportation was destined to be second only to rent.

So, typically the ferry was used by Dinghy Dock staff, Islanders without their own working boat, and townspeople coming to PI for the novelty of eating dinner on a floating dock. On days when I had to take the ferry, I could expect to see either Tim or one of the other three skippers driving the boat, and a handful of regular ferry users. One in particular, Rebecca, was a resident who split her travel between the ferry and rowing herself back and forth in a two-person rowboat. She would use the ferry more often during the winter months when the waves got choppy enough to make the short trek terrifying in a little boat. On occasion I have feared my own fate aboard the ferry in a storm. Witnessing a newly hired skipper try to manoeuvre the thirty-foot '66 classic in and out of the dock while pushing and propping throttle levers up and down, amidst a roaring and spitting motor, could set anyone on edge.

Spring was becoming summer though, and the Island was the same every day: sunny, warm and quiet. Things had slowed down, even stopped, since we left Toronto and moved to the smallest, most uninhabited place we could find; since I quit my job at Humber College and took the biggest financial risk of my life. We had moved to a small, distant island in order to escape feeling "trapped" in the city, and we'd found exactly the right place to go: off the grid and far away from Toronto; somewhere that was away from everything else, away from the haste and blitz; somewhere we could stop and rest.

Because of this atmosphere, or perhaps because I was unemployed, Mondays, Fridays and weekends became irrelevant. It also may have been the shock of the move that did away with daily regulators like "lunchtime" or "bedtime." I became lost in thought and found myself struggling to count out weeks or days since something might have happened, or how long ago I paid or didn't pay the phone bill. A surprising consequence of gauzy hours and formless weeks was an unfamiliar focus on my environment: my heartbeat and body temperature; the thin bleached hairs on the knuckles of a man walking past me on the road; the preternatural bat-sense of the Blind Brothers as they raced their dirt bikes down the hill, elegantly dodging each other; the impossible angle of a passing woman's front teeth, horizontal, jutting...

The Murder House

[THREE]

PROTECTION IS SMALLER THAN THE TWO ISLANDS THAT
flank it: Newcastle Island to the northeast and Gabriola Island to
the south. All of which, including Nanaimo, is the traditional land
of the Snuneymuxw, a First Nation of the Coash Salish people with
a territory that spans the mid-island region of Vancouver Island,
the Gulf Islands and the Fraser Valley. The whole of Newcastle is
a provincial marine park with sandy beaches and a great big log
pavilion that can be rented for special events like weddings or
reunions. The pavilion is fully equipped with a dining room, washrooms and a kitchen. In the summer, you can go there and buy
cold drinks and ice cream. No one lives on Newcastle but there is a
popular campground to stay overnight if you bring your own tent.

A ferry shuttles visitors from Nanaimo to Newcastle during
the summer months but is much smaller and runs less frequently
than the *Protection Connection*. Others who come to Newcastle
use kayaks or dinghies and tie up to the public dock that faces the
harbour. Once on my way to town, a ferry skipper told me that
a man who lived on Protection was out late drinking and missed
the last ferry home. Desperate to get back, he swam from town
through the marina and over to Newcastle, walked east along
the beach and then swam over to Protection and walked home. I

could see by looking that it was possible, but would have been a royal pain in the ass.

When the tide is low, you can walk the soggy stretch between PI and Newcastle if you don't mind the mud or that the water level can get up as high as your chest in some parts. When Islanders get bored or their kids are antsy, a common escape is to boat or walk over to one of Newcastle's beaches for the day.

Gabriola, the biggest of the three islands, is highly organized, civilized and economized compared to the others. It has a public school, a bus, a museum, grocery stores, restaurants, a provincially operated ferry system and thousands more residents. It's a town unto itself and even has its own Local Trust Committee and a Director at the Regional District of Nanaimo (who also looks after Mudge and De Courcy Islands) to help govern it.

You hear a lot of traditional stories told about these places. Origin stories, mostly. There's the one about two wolves, probably lovers, that shed their skins and became men, accounting for the split in the Nanaimo River to the west. There's one about Haals, who turned animals and people into stone, accounting for the remarkable and confounding rock shapes scattered along Newcastle's coasts. A story about the red and yellow cedar trees reveals both the curses and gifts of generosity. There's a spot on Gabriola where the rocks along the water rise up and over like a wave and hide deep caves underneath. I've heard stories about old graveyards and treasures buried in those caves.

Stories like these explain how things came to be and truths about human nature. Contemporary stories are just as common here. Most of what I learned about community happenings I got from Nate. He'd been working on the Island doing the occasional handy job since the spring and got to talking to a good deal of people. Every few days he'd tell me a story he knew I'd like.

"Hey, I was over at John's today helping him tear down his shed and he told me the craziest thing. He told me that twice, in the same house but years apart, a man murdered his wife. Here. Up the road," he said and pointed out our front window.

"Two different men killed two different wives in the same house?"

"Apparently." He began putting away his tools, hanging up his ball cap on the coat rack.

"Were they related in any way, these men?"

"Related by evil, I guess." He sat down on the dining chair and untied his boots. His legs were scratched up to where his shorts covered them—small surface cuts from thorny bushes.

"Oh, I forgot to tell you. Someone came over today to tell us about the fire regulations around here. She said no fires are allowed unless it's burn season, which is every weekend in April and October."

"That's eight weekends a year. You mean even a little fire out back?"

"Any fire. If we want to burn things we need a permit or it has to be April or October. On a weekend."

"Shame," he said and headed upstairs to the bedroom.

I gathered up some towels and crammed a bottle of water and a few crackers into a backpack. We were heading to Smugglers Beach for a swim to cool off after a blazing hot morning. Smugglers was the beach that the kids liked to go to because there were miles of bedrock under the water and they could walk far out before the water level reached their chests and they turned back. I'd seen some of the older kids bring surfboards and lie flat on top, paddling with their hands, seeing how far out to sea they could go before they scared themselves and turned back.

"You wanna come for a swim? We're going out now," I yelled up the stairs where Nate had gone.

"Yeah, I could cool off," he called down.

The three of us began the hike toward the beach, but only reached the fork at the top of the road before we heard the rattling of a golf cart behind us.

"Car!" I called, indicating to Lily to choose either the left or the right of the road to walk down instead of the middle.

"Hello there!" boomed Keith as he slowed the cart down

beside us. "You headin' to the beach?"

"Hi Keith," I said. "We are."

"You want a ride?"

"I do! Yes I do! Please, Mum! I DO!" wailed Lily. I turned to Nate, he nodded and we piled in—Lily and me in the front and Nate in the back with our backpack.

"Hey Keith, I was wondering…"

"Yes dear? You'll have to speak up!"

"I was wondering," I said louder, "did a guy murder his wife around here? I mean, is that a true story?" Keith had told me a few weeks earlier that he'd been living on the Island since the sixties, since it became a subdivision and there was a big push to sell land and populate the place. He said he'd bought his house for a couple thousand dollars back then with money he'd gotten unexpectedly and has stayed ever since. If anyone was going to know the facts of this murder-house story, it would be him.

His smile dropped and he shifted his head down slightly. "House is right up here," he said and motioned forward with his chin, both of his hands on the steering wheel. He turned to me momentarily and then back to the road. "I'll show you."

I looked back to Nate but he was only half paying attention to the conversation and didn't seem to notice that our route had changed. We drove for a few more seconds before Keith slowed and then stopped his cart on the road in front of a green and white split-level sitting above a rough patch of rock and tucked in slightly behind some trees.

"Here it is."

I looked past him and toward the house.

"I knew the guy well. He was a carpenter. Built this house himself. One time he and his wife went over to Vancouver for a while and they rented out the place, you know, and the new tenant, this young guy, goes and builds a boat in the living room. Can you believe that? There." He pointed to a window along the side of the house. "Well, when the boat is finished, right, it doesn't fit out the front door!" He laughed and looked around at us crammed into his golf cart. "So when Bill and Eileen come on back, they walk in to find a big ol' boat in the living room. They had to cut a hole in the house to get it out! That's why that window there is so damn big."

"A big boat?" said Lily. "Wow!" She smiled up at me.

"Lily, come back here and sit with me," said Nate.

Lily crawled over my legs to get out of the golf cart, sticking a knee into the side of my guts as she launched herself off the seat.

"Yeah, a carpenter. Friend of mine, actually." Keith dropped his hands from the steering wheel and crossed them in his lap. He wasn't looking at the house or at us anymore.

I looked at the house again. It looked like any other house: white with green window frames along the front and a few stairs from the grass up to the door. A white mailbox. There was a rock garden in the front sprouting new green leaves and a wooden fence leading to what must have been the backyard. Blackberry bushes were growing up along the sides and there was a little shed at the end of the driveway for storing firewood. There was no activity inside and through the windows you could see there was no furniture either. The house was empty and there was a FOR SALE sign at the edge of the property, bent over slightly from the wind. The realtor's name was Jane.

"So what happened? Why'd he do it?" I asked, aware that Lily could hear me but too curious not to know.

"Mum, are we going to the beach now?" called Lily from the back seat.

"Just plum went over the deep end, I guess," said Keith.

"Twice? I mean, did this happen twice in that same house?"

Keith looked at me, confused. "Of course not," he said after a pause.

"Right."

"Oh hell. You must be thinking of the other one. That's around the corner that way over there. I'm not gonna take you up that way, though," he said. His mood lifted to its usual jolly state again. "You can go on up there yourself if you want, I mean. I gotta get to work now."

Keith restarted his golf cart and drove us just ahead to the drop-off at Smugglers Beach and let us all out.

We piled out at the path to the beach and thanked Keith for the ride. From where I stood near the beach, I could see the edge of the murder house and the blackberry bushes that billowed out around it. There was a window, maybe a bedroom window, on the second floor with an unobstructed view of the sea. Whoever stood in that bedroom and looked out the window would see nothing but sky and water in all directions. Nothing but blue.

We walked down the path through the old trees and overgrown grass that led to the beach. At the clearing, Lily ran ahead across the field and down the rocky edge toward the water. From the top of the small cliff I watched her as she joined the other girls in the water flinging seaweed into the air, higher and higher and then falling backwards as they laughed. I watched them dunk each other then resurface wildly seconds later, and I saw the other children too, outliers who ducked under the surface and reappeared a distance from the group, having travelled undetected beneath the water for some time first.

The Book Sale

[FOUR]

IN THE BASEMENT OF BEACON HOUSE, THERE IS A SMALL and thoughtfully stocked library. Beacon House is a modest two-storey house in the shape of a perfect square with white wooden siding, single-pane windows and a red roof. It has a total capacity for sixty-five people and every other weekend there's an event taking place like a craft sale or a pancake breakfast or the Mad Hatter's Tea Party, all as fundraising efforts to cover the costs of running the building and sponsoring more events. Jutting out into the harbour is Gallows Point, originally named Execution Point in recognition of the few but dramatic hangings performed there in the 1800s. It is easily recognizable due to the light-beacon stationed at its farthest reach.

I met Cristine at the library on the third Sunday after we moved to PI. She ran the show by cataloguing books, maintaining the database of borrowers, hauling home and organizing book dona-tions, planning and managing book sales, and scheduling volun-teers. One day on a whim I asked her if she wanted help, if there was a form I should fill out to apply to be a volunteer. In friendly and desperate enthusiasm, she hugged me tightly at the suggestion, smiling and clasping her hands together at her chest. She told me to meet her back at the library entrance every Sunday I could at one o'clock. I did, and quickly became a regular helper. A few months after my initial training began, I was confidently checking books in and out, shelving, and assisting Islanders with book selections.

In the middle of summer, the library was faced with the annual Book Sale, which required weeks of preparation. First there was the job of decataloguing less popular books from the library shelves and relegating them to the Book Sale, thereby making more room for new books. Another task was the extensive sorting through bags of donations to determine which ones would fill the new space on the shelves and which ones would join the library rejects on the Book Sale tables.

Decisions about which books were worthy of the library and which books weren't were based on a set of somewhat intuitive criteria. If a donation was a duplicate of a book already in the library, we chose the better quality of the two copies and kept it for the library; this was the most straightforward of the protocols. The rest of the decision-making system was based on the intrigue of the title, strength of the back cover plot description or blurb endorsements, quality of the binding and general aesthetic of the artifact itself. When it came to children's books in particular, the primary and perhaps only consideration was the beauty of the illustrations. Cristine explained to me that when she read books as a child, the illustrations were her essential priority and that pre-condition has not changed since.

Above all other criteria, however, was the direction that there be no books, children's or otherwise, that Cristine considered wit-less, such as the Gossip Girl series; no books that made any refer-ence, however passing, to angels or other religious symbolism; no books within the spectrum of "spirituality"; and finally no books claiming to have discovered the secret to happiness, a lasting mar-riage, inner peace or the accumulation of abundant wealth. The arranging of the books on the stacks followed a similar sensibil-ity. For example, our biography and autobiography sections were combined and arranged by colour. The cookbooks were sorted by vegetarian on the left and not-vegetarian on the right, with a small but popular baked goods collection distributed at random among the two. There was also a row displaying books of all genres written by Islanders or people who had once lived on the Island, just above the local history shelf.

Having spent weeks arranging and storing every book into either the library catalogue or the Book Sale shelf, organizing display tables and price tags, scheduling sales volunteers and cleaning up, we were prepared for the big day. As I found out upon arriving at the library, the Book Sale that day coincided with a Lions Club meeting, both at Gallows Point. It occurred to me then that my work for the next few hours might be considerable, as the Lions Club meetings were well attended and anticipated by everyone eager to have their voices heard on a range of subjects. The last time I had passed by after a meeting, the laneway was packed with Islanders and golf carts. The meeting had ended and everyone was standing around in groups outside Beacon House rehashing the issues of the day. The conversations covered golf cart licences and restrictions, park and dock maintenance, fundraising and surprisingly, the identity of a woman who was visiting the Island daily and sitting for hours on a bench by Smugglers Beach holding a stuffed dog in her arms:

"She almost missed the last ferry home the other day. I had to get Bill to drive her over so she wouldn't be stranded here."

"Does anyone know her name? Has anyone talked to her?"

"She just sits there all day with that toy in her lap."

"I have some experience with differently abled people and I think she may have some sort of condition."

"She's coming over nearly every day now."

"I'm going to call the crisis line this afternoon. She may have a mental health worker that is looking for her somewhere."

On the morning of the Book Sale, I saw Rebecca and her son on the hill heading to the library ahead of me. "Are you going to the

Book Sale?" I asked when I caught up to her.

"No, I'm just cleaning over there and then heading over to Jim's to clean after. I also need to pick up some crates of apples today. It's Fruit Day," she said, putting the words "Fruit Day" in air quotes.

"Oh, right, the fruit. I don't have summer care for Lily so I have no time to keep on top of everything that's happening."

"Same. It's been really hard to work with my kid all the time. I think people are getting annoyed that I have to bring him 'cause I'm not getting calls for as many jobs as usual. Which sucks. I really need the money."

"I can take care of him if you need to work. I don't have a job so I'm home now all the time."

"Do you mean it? That would really help me out. Can you take him tomorrow? I have a job on the other side of the Island and I could do it so much faster if I did it alone."

"Yeah, tomorrow is fine."

"Thank you. How about we come up with a deal? Like you take mine for a few hours on one day and I'll take yours another day. To be fair."

"Sounds perfect. Let's do that," I said and smiled. As soon as Rebecca and I had banged out a plan, I couldn't help imagining what I would do with a few hours to myself without Lily. I could redo my resumé. I could read a book. I could catch up with friends on the phone. I could take a really long bath.

Moira walked up to us on the hill and stopped.

"Rebecca and I were just complaining about our lives," I said.

"I left my husband two days ago," said Moira, her hair lit by the sun. I couldn't see her eyes past her sunglasses but she smiled ever so slightly. "I'm staying with my daughter now."

Rebecca and I looked at each other.

"You win," said Rebecca.

❖ ❦ ❖

Opening the door to the library, I saw five or six Book Sale volunteers, all women, flitting from one table to the next, pricing book covers and issuing commands to each other. There was an older child, maybe ten or eleven, in the corner with a broom and a dust pan. She was sweeping little piles of dirt under a bookshelf.

"Good, you're here! There's the computer, there's the books that need to be returned, and over here is the pile you need to shelve," greeted Cate, running out of a storage room on my left and toward another on my right. Sensing the no-nonsense atmosphere, I put down my bag and got to work.

Cate was the operator of Beacon House. The grand master. She was small with short brown hair that she tucked behind both ears. She was wearing brown dress pants that were too long and bunched up at the ankles, white sneakers and a blue button-up shirt under a grey cardigan. She had dark glasses with a string attached to each end so that she could take her glasses off and let them hang down around her neck. Multicoloured elastic bands were being stored on her wrists and her fingers were free of jewellery, always outstretched in front of her. She was a very quick-moving, quick-talking hurricane of panic at all times. It took energy just to be around her, even if you did nothing but stood still. This was a good mood but high tension day for Cate, the best anyone could hope for.

"Okay, these books here need to go over on that table. Nicely, in order," she began, speaking to the whole room of volunteers. "And the DVDs on that lower table. Could someone please make a pile of bags in case anyone needs a bag? There's a price list for everything taped to that door there. I made it last night. Anyway, each book will be priced as well, but don't forget it's 50 percent off the price on the cover, okay? Oh, and five dollars for a whole bag. Ask everyone if they just want to fill a bag. It's easier for us and it gets rid of the most books. Oh, I hope we do well this year. Last year we made six hundred dollars at the Book Sale! Or was it five hundred? I have the chart over here." And off she went to locate last year's Book Sale figures.

From the comfort of my corner at the far end of the library, I glanced over at Moira. She met my gaze, rolled her eyes and began stacking books. "I'm sure whatever order I'm putting these in is wrong," she said to the other ladies in the room just before Cate came flying back in from the storage area.

"I found it!" yelled Cate, speed-walking toward us, as she unveiled a four-by-three-foot presentation board, the kind students use to display science fair projects.

"See? Here are the figures for the Book Sale last year. And here are the donations, which were separate. Six hundred dollars in total! And did you know, ninety people showed up that day! That's almost the whole Island! It's terrific." She folded up the presentation board with impossible efficiency and slid it out of sight behind the nearest bookshelf. "Oh, god, someone please sweep the floor!"

A woman I had never seen before appeared on my left. "Hi, you must be Amber. I've heard a lot about you. I'm Wendy," she said and extended her hand. Wendy had a severe bob haircut with bangs, dyed ash-blonde. She wore an ironed pink dress shirt and khaki shorts. She had a warm smile and leaned in when she talked to me.

"It's nice to meet you," I said and shook her hand. Wendy dragged a stray chair next to mine and sat down.

"I'm just thankful you're doing the computer. I can't make heads or tails of it," she said, leaning toward me, whispering. She had a soft, melodic voice.

"Welcome!" Wendy sang, as a small group of women walked into our little space, suddenly changing the dynamic for all of us. "Welcome to the Book Sale. The prices are on the covers, but you can fill a grocery bag for only five dollars," she told them, just as Cate had instructed.

"Thanks," said one. The others had already begun scanning titles.

Behind me, a conversation between some other volunteers caught my attention. "Doug is his name, I think. No, it's Don.

Remember him? He had a shaved head and a big moustache. He was living at Potter's Cottage. Anyway, I told my son, *You are not to go to Don's house for any reason.* My son was only about seven or eight at the time, so it was difficult to explain exactly why I didn't want him there," the woman began in a thick French accent. "Moral complexity arose as I explained that he could visit Keith, decked out in his ladies' garb, but never Don. That Keith was not a threat but Don was," she said and giggled. "Remember he was always taking pictures of the children on the road? I told my boy, *It's not appropriate for a grown man to invite children to his house, or to go 'round taking pictures of them.*"

Wendy turned, having been listening in as well.

"I remember him," Wendy added. "I was raising small children in the eighties the same time Don was here, so I was very much alert to those kinds of things. Kidnappings and stranger danger was all the rage back then."

"Oh yes, you must remember him. I told my son, in French of course, *Don't let him touch your marbles!*" They all laughed. "I say 'marbles' but at the time I used the French word for penis. You have to be explicit with children about these things. Metaphor is completely lost on them."

"I'll take two bags. That's ten dollars, right?" asked a woman from the group who had been searching through the stacks in silence, likely eavesdropping on the conversation as well.

Wendy drew her attention back to me and the customer. "I'll take it," she said. She jiggled the cash box open and gave the woman her change. "Thank you!"

The group shuffled out the library door with two plastic grocery bags filled to the brim with paperbacks.

"I called the police about Don, you know, because my boy ran home one day yelling, *Maman! He grabbed for my marbles! Maman!* The police could do nothing of course, but they said, *Deal with him in any way you see fit.* That is, I believe they were telling me vigilante justice was in order," continued the French woman.

"You never know who is going to come here and stay, what sort of weirdos. It used to be that everyone knew everyone," remarked Cate, uncharacteristically sitting down to rest. "Now, I walk down the street and I don't recognize people. There are a lot of stories that go around too. Who knows what's what. I was just walking along Pirates Lane with Jack the other day, and we passed the Murder House and noticed it had finally sold after so long. Jack told me, *You know, there were two murders in that house, not just that one you know about. I heard there were two!* I said, *Don't be ridiculous, there was only one,* and we were all here for that as you know—well all of us except Amber. Amber, did you hear about that?"

"I did, yes."

"He insisted there had been two, but I think he's mixing it up with that other story, the one about the disabled man."

"Oh, yes," whispered Wendy.

"What story is that?" I asked, trying to sound casual.

"There was a mentally disabled man living here once. He heard voices and hallucinated and so on. He had this little daughter who lived in town across the water and he would visit her there, you know. Well one day, the two of them were sitting on a set of stairs outside and the story goes that he became convinced his daughter was possessed by a demon and he stabbed her in the back. Sitting there on the steps in the middle of the day like that. Just stabbed her and she died," explained Cate.

"My god," I said.

"It didn't happen here on the Island, but he was an Islander, you know. There are a lot of stories. A lot of sick people out there."

Several groups came in and out that day to buy up the discarded library collection: true crime, fantasy, children's picture books, romance and outdated non-fiction, all at bargain prices. A quarter for that, a dollar for this, but somehow the final tally was in the hundreds of dollars and the Book Sale was once again a success.

On the walk home late in the afternoon, I was struck by the still-bright and huge sun squatting between far-off mountain ridges, flooding through the tree branches and setting the sea around it aglow. Past roads and houses I could see Nanaimo across the harbour: a city of tall apartment buildings, street lights and highways, a metropolis of activity. People who lived near stores and office buildings, among pedestrians and cars and late-night liquor stores, rushing off to work, to parties, dates and job interviews—a world contained only a kilometre away, across the water and kept at bay.

THE EXPLOSION

THE
PROTECTION ISLAND
SHAFT

This mural commemorates the coal mining that took place at this site for almost 50 years starting in 1892. Capped now by this concrete block, the Protection Island Shaft was driven down 750 feet to intercept the Douglas and the Newcastle coal seams. The shaft allowed access for 200 or more miners a day, the removal of coal for use on site for shipment abroad and for the downcast of fresh air. The extensive workings stretched under the water, south to the Nanaimo shafts, north to the Newcastle Island shaft and east, far under Northumberland Channel.

In 1913, the nearby explosion of the SS Oscar ravaged the top works. In 1918, the hoist rope broke and 16 miners plunged to their death. However, the mine survived as a mainstay of the local economy until closing in 1938. In celebrations at the end of WWII, the 85 foot high pithead, shown so vividly in this mural, was burned and the surrounding area laid waste.

A walk on the nearby beaches will reveal coal, iron fittings, chimney bricks, sailing ship ballast rocks, Chinese pottery and other and other traces of wealth, hard work and tears that tell the story of this industry.

Owners: Mhindi & Kelly Mayer   Artist: Moss Strom

MARCH 2004

[FIVE]

LILY AND I WAITED AT THE PUB DOCKS TO TAKE THE FERRY to town for groceries and a new propeller. A few days earlier while boating to town, I had failed to recognize a slice of rock below the surface until I dragged the boat clean over it, bending the hell out of one of the three blades. I couldn't use the boat without a new one so I called in the order to the Harbour Chandler, a downtown nautical supply store. The sky was grey and the low-hanging clouds over the harbour made it impossible to see across the water. The ferry was late and we had run out of coffee that morning.

"Listen, when the boat comes, just wait till it stops completely before you jump on it, okay?" I said to Lily, standing beside me. "I always think you're gonna fall in the water when you do that."

"Okay Mum, I promise."

The waiting area was getting crowded with people waiting to board the ferry and talk had begun about what the holdup could be:

"The amount of times they have to fix the ferry, I tell ya."

"It's Thursday. In all likelihood Keith has taken it to refill the kegs."

"I thought that was Fridays."

"It hasn't been Fridays since Cory took over. Now it's Thursdays."

"No no no. It's every Monday now."

Through the fog, the outline of a ferry could be seen in the distance heading for the dock.

"Mum, I just saw a huge spider. There by the benches!" Lily said, running toward me.

"It's okay, don't let it bother you," I said while I searched my wallet for a ferry pass.

"It's the biggest one I've ever seen, Mum. Like this!" she said and stretched her arms out as wide as she could.

The boat was close but pulling in to the berth more slowly than usual due to the limited visibility of the heavy fog.

"*Good, there it is.*"

"*Did you get the flyer for Thrifty's this week? They think a cauliflower for six dollars is a sale.*"

"*Thrifty's has gorgeous pineapple now. I bought two large ones last week. Very large and fresh.*"

A woman I had seen before but couldn't name noticed Lily and I off to the side looking at a spider crawling up the side of the pub. "What have you got there?" she said to Lily, bending down at the waist in order to meet Lily's height.

"A really big spider! He could eat someone!" replied Lily.

"Oh my goodness. Imagine that!" said the woman and looked over at me. "And why aren't you in school today, young lady?" she asked, her face inches away from Lily's.

"I dunno," said Lily, still preoccupied with the spider. Lily reached behind the bench, pulled out a short stick and began poking the spider with the end of it. The spider darted wildly and disappeared into a crevice in the wall.

"We've just moved—arrived in May—and I haven't enrolled her in school here yet," I said. "We'll wait until the fall, it being so late in the school year."

"How, how nice. A little break for you all," the woman said, straightening her posture. She continued to watch Lily poke every crack in the wall with her stick.

The low rumble of the ferry engine caught the woman's attention and she turned from Lily to watch the boat. "Wonderful—

the boat is here." She smiled and turned to stand in the queue.

There was a cumbersome process of unloading boxes of vegetables and other items for the pub before anyone could board the ferry. Tim, the skipper that day, first had to wrangle the heavy boxes off the boat, one at a time, and then took several trips back and forth to wheel them into the pub on a dolly. Each time Tim loaded the dolly with new boxes, Lily tried to hop on the dolly to go for a ride and each time she rolled off the side onto the dock. When we finally loaded the passengers on the boat and left for town, we were severely behind schedule.

Before restarting the motor, Tim handed out small bundles of taffy wrapped in wax paper to all the kids. He said he had bought them for the pub earlier but that he had bought too much and figured the kids would like the leftovers. The older kids put the taffy away in their pockets and continued to stare at their cell phones. The younger ones dumped their collective stash on the deck and crowded around it, deliberating over which pieces were the biggest and who got what colours.

"You can't see, but I painted my toenails blue last night with my granddaughter."

"Did you hear about Lyn's boat?"

"It's awful."

"Star got out of the backyard again and I couldn't find her before I left."

"Grace, I'll need someone to check my mail while we're away."

Lily looked up from where she was sitting among the empty taffy wrappers. "Mum, if there's no school today, what are we going to do?"

"There's Storytime at the library today. You should take her to that," said another woman I recognized but had never spoken to. "Eleven o'clock today. It's wonderful for children to read."

"Yay! The library!" yelled Lily. "Awesome!"

"Yay!" yelled the other kids.

"Well, we have to do some shopping in town first. We'll see if we have time after," I said.

"I've noticed there are still flowers laid at the Number One Mine plaque there in the square from last month," a third woman said, turning to face me. "But some of the children have taken the flowers and tossed them around and they really shouldn't. Be sure Lily doesn't do that if you see some there today."

"Flowers for commemoration?" I asked.

"Each year there's a memorial service in town and people come and bring flowers," the third woman said. "To mourn the miners."

"I'm teaching at the studio full-time now, yeah."

"Tomorrow won't work. She'll be away most of this month, but certainly after."

"Good lord, is it ever hard to see out there."

"I've never tried the pickles. I have tried their onions though."

"I'm sure Star will be waiting for you when you get home."

"The flowers are there to honour the families who lost fathers and husbands in the mine explosion. They're not there for the children to play with," repeated the third woman.

"I understand," I replied.

"Tim, can I drive the ferry?" hollered Lily over the noise. "Pleeease!"

"No," said Tim, glancing over at me momentarily. "It's regulation."

"Lily, pick up the wrappers please and put them in your pockets."

"I brought beautiful flowers to the square last week, on Monday. There were only a few bushels then, but by the end of the week they were everywhere," the third woman said as she stared out the side window of the boat.

"Tim, please? Can I drive the ferry just for one second?"

For the last half of the nineteenth century and well into the next, coal mining was Nanaimo's biggest industry. In fact, Nanaimo's origin as a town owes itself to British coal acquisition efforts. Without coal, there wouldn't have been a Nanaimo. In 1849, Snuneymuxw chief Che-wech-i-kan travelled from the Comox Valley all the way down to Victoria to take his broken rifle to a blacksmith for repair. The story goes that as the blacksmith worked, he kept throwing "black rocks" into the hearth to keep the fire going steadily. Che-wech-i-kan asked what the black rocks were for and so began a conversation with the blacksmith about coal.

Sooner or later Che-wech-i-kan revealed that he had seen black rocks for miles midway between Victoria and Comox, information that was of great value to the blacksmith. The black-smith notified the Hudson's Bay Company in Victoria that there was talk of coal up the island. Che-wech-i-kan showed up at the Hudson's Bay Company in Victoria the following spring with a canoe full of coal. It would take a couple more years for the HBC to stake out what is now Nanaimo to mine for coal, of which there was plenty, just as Che-wech-i-kan had said there was.

Because of dark and often treacherous conditions, mining ac-cidents in Nanaimo were relatively common—everything from collapsing tunnels to premature blasts—but the explosion and fire at the Number One Mine, known as "The Esplanade," was among the worst in BC's history. The Esplanade was an enor-mous underground system of shafts reaching in three directions and as far as Protection Island. Just after six p.m. on May 3, 1887, a few miners standing around the pithead felt a rumble underfoot and took notice. Seconds later the ground quaked violently and erupted, sending rocks, timber and other debris bursting out of the mine and hundreds of feet into the air above. The opened earth revealed smoke and red-hot flames below. Over 150 men were trapped in the burning shafts so deep that the second blast was barely audible to the people above. Word spread quickly and the townspeople rushed to the town's centre to aid in the rescue of the miners trapped underground.

Hopes were raised when seven men escaped within an hour of the explosion, but they were to be the only survivors. The first rescue crew sent below came up shortly after, unable to breathe or see through the thick, deadly smoke. For days, several crews were sent down as far as possible to search for the missing miners, but it wasn't until May 6 that a group finally located the first of dozens of dead miners. In the dust around their bodies, they'd written messages to their families and signed their names before taking their last breaths. One indicated he'd been alive for thirteen hours before expiring, likely asphyxiating from the poisonous gas that the flames and coal dust had created.

It took six days to snuff out the raging fires and more to locate and account for all of the men trapped in the mines that day. The exact tally of the dead changes depending on what documents you consult because many were Chinese men without papers who were not at first counted as either living or dead. Their employers had no legal obligation to report them as dead until 1897. The most common estimate including the Chinese workers is 150, the equivalent of the full-time population of Protection Island today. At the time, the tragedy was blamed on Chinese workers, since it was said they were unable to properly read or follow the safety instructions that were provided in English. The town grieved the tremendous loss of men that left widows and fatherless children all over, but the Esplanade was repaired and continued as a prosperous mine in the years that followed. Every year since, people from Nanaimo and the surrounding area gather around the old pithead to lament the unparalleled disaster that tore through the small community, bringing flowers with them to lay on the ground.

"Mum, look! There's grass stuck to the boat!" Lily shouted, leaning half her body out of the ferry, reaching down into the water to grab hold of a ribbon of seaweed.

I reached out and wrapped an arm around her waist to keep her from tumbling overboard.

"Be careful, she's liable to fall right out behaving like that."

"Bill, did you say you were travelling to Vancouver this weekend or next?"

"I got a piece Mum, look!" Lily cried, her face lit up from the pure achievement of it. "It's so slimy!" She shook the long, green tendril in her hand, spraying water from the plant onto the seats around us.

"Okay, throw that back in now," I said, glancing around at the faces of passengers watching. "Sit down here with me."

"Can I keep it, Mum?" Lily had bunched up the seaweed into her fists and was stuffing it into her front jacket pockets. Most of it fell back out, forming a pile at her feet.

"I don't think so, babe."

"My mother doesn't like to travel with Jack because he smokes in the car."

"I might try the pickles today. They do the onions very well, I must say."

"The reading program at the library is a great place to go on Thursdays. Lily will enjoy it, I'm sure. All the children do," the third woman said.

When the ferry arrived at the town-side berth, I held Lily back and waited for everyone to exit the boat. When the area was clear, I gathered up the seaweed and flung it off the side of the boat into the water. We climbed off and followed the docks to the café at the edge of the harbour to get a coffee and a juice before carrying on to Thrifty's. As we approached, I could see the collections of lilies, carnations, roses and tulips lining the south entrance of Bastion Square and the memorial plaque with the lost miners' names above. Some of the blooms and stray garlands had untangled from the bouquets and were strewn from the square all the way across the harbour and down the bedrock, a rambling mess of petals and baby's breath broadcast across the water.

The Fall

[SIX]

AROUND 2:30 IN THE AFTERNOON, I HAD FINISHED CLEAN-
ing the house, started preparing dinner and finished the first load
of laundry. Lily was playing outside, arranging piles of dirt with
twigs stuck into the tops. She and I had already walked down the
road to the community garden and picked up some rutabaga,
carrots and large green tomatoes. We had also stopped to pick a
handful of wildflowers and a few pocketsful of blackberries. I was
tired like I always was but the sky was blue and clear, and I had the
day's responsibilities more or less under control. I sat down and
checked my email.

> *Amber:*
> *Nate was working on my place and fell off my roof. He's*
> *asked me to email you to let you know what's happen-*
> *ing. I have called the paramedics and they are on their*
> *way. He is still awake and alert—didn't hit his head.*
> *My address is 29 Hispanola Pl.*
> *—Graham*

My stomach dropped. I had the distinct impression that
I might faint—slip from my chair to the ground and just go to

sleep. I looked out the window to the front lawn and saw Lily by the tree swing moving in slow motion. She was holding a bouquet of sticks and kicking a mound of dirt at her feet. *Oh my god,* I thought; I may have even said it out loud.

I stood up and walked out the front door. When I got to end of the driveway I called to Lily to come along. I told her we had to go right now. I told her, "Don't argue." I walked quickly down the road so she could keep up, though I wanted to run.

As we turned the corner to Hispanola Place, I saw Moira on a bicycle riding toward us. She was talking to me but I couldn't hear what she was saying. She was calling me over, waving her hand for me to come to her. She had stopped her bike and was dismounting. "I'll take Lily. Go now. The first responders are there. They'll be leaving for the hospital right away," she said. She was wearing a long, thin dress with a thousand colours on it. Her hair was resting along her shoulders and down her back. She was wearing sandals and one of the buckles had come undone.

"Your dress will get caught in your bicycle spokes," I said.

"You can come and get Lily later at my house. I'll take care of her while you're gone," she said. "Go."

I started to run. I saw the ambulance in a driveway and ran toward it. I felt the tears on my face; I felt them fall from my chin to the ground. I took hard, short breaths. I was getting cold. *Where is he? Where is he?*

"Where is he?" I said in the direction of a man standing near the front door of the house, blocking the entrance.

"Through here," he said, pointing to the back of the house.

I ran through the door and saw the stretcher in the middle of the living room. There were four people around it talking. It must have been Nate who was lying flat upon it on his back, but the people were blocking my view of him. A woman holding a clipboard was writing down the things Nate said to her. She spoke calmly and clearly. The house was open and the walls were painted all white. The light coming in through the windows made everything look bleached, indecipherable.

"Nate," I said and rushed to the side of the stretcher. I put my hand on his arm and he turned his eyes in my direction. His neck was in a white brace and his arms and legs were strapped down by thick, black nylon bands.

"Hi baby," he said. His voice was weak and small.

The paramedics lifted and locked the rails on the sides of the stretcher and began wheeling him out of the house and onto the driveway. Protection Island's only ambulance was waiting in the same place I had seen it when I came in. Someone opened the back doors and the four people pushed Nate and his stretcher into the ambulance.

"I have to go with him," I said, turning to whoever was standing beside me. It was Summer, Moira's daughter, and on the other side Rob, the ferry skipper—in first responders' jumpsuits. *Have they been here all along? What are they doing here?*

"He's going to be okay," Summer said. She put her arm over my shoulders. "He's conscious and lucid. Everything's going to be fine."

I cried uncontrollably and wiped my face with the sleeves of my shirt.

"Rob, I have to go with him," I said, staring, imagining for a moment that I had fainted and was now dreaming—that I was inventing a scenario in which Summer and Rob were paramedics and none of this was really happening.

"Yep. Just get into the ambulance. There's room," Rob said and put his hand on my back. His hand was warm and his eyes were soft and concerned. He was real and this was really happening.

I got into the passenger side of the ambulance and we immediately started driving away. I turned around and watched Nate in the back as we drove. His eyes kept closing and reopening and closing again. He was fighting shock, fighting to stay awake. Within minutes we arrived at the emergency dock where a Coast Guard boat was waiting to take us to the city. Two men and a woman lifted Nate out of the ambulance and wheeled him onto the boat. I jumped on after them and stood beside Nate. The sun was fierce and broiling, reflecting off the water and depositing all its tremendous heat into the black tarmac covering the deck of the boat. It was unthinkably hot; I struggled to see anything, to make out any of the shapes around me. I cupped one hand over my eyes and the other over Nate's. Someone began talking to me.

"Did he fall at his own residence?" said the woman.

"No. He was working." I was squinting to see the person talking to me.

She was tall and dressed completely in black. I couldn't imagine how she was withstanding this heat, this impossible sunshine.

"Does he have worker's insurance?" she asked.

"No. He has regular health coverage. He has a card," I said. My voice sounded far away and not like my own.

Once we left the dock, we moved at a shocking speed, tearing through the water to the other side. It took less than a minute or two to arrive town-side and mere seconds more to manoeuvre Nate into another ambulance, this one heading to Nanaimo General. When we arrived at the hospital, Nate told me to pull out his wallet from his back pocket and hand his health card to the intake nurse. I did. He told me to call his mother in Toronto and explain what had happened. I did that too.

"He didn't hit his head. There's no sign of a concussion."

"Oh my god, my son..."

"The doctor is coming any second. I'll call back soon."

The nurses finished the paperwork and took him into a private room where we waited for the doctor. I told myself everything would be fine. Nate was alive and talking so everything was going to be okay.

"Nathaniel," said an older man in a lab coat as he entered the room. His grey hair was recently cut and styled. He was wearing a bright purple tie. He had a faint tan.

"Yes," I said.

The doctor looked over to me and then back to Nate.

"You've fallen from a roof, about ten or twelve feet?" said the doctor.

"Yes," I said. The doctor looked at me again.

"Okay, Nathaniel, I'm going to lift your shirt and I'm going to press down on your stomach area and abdomen. I want you to indicate to me where you feel pain."

"Okay," said Nate, almost in a whisper.

"How about here?"

"Yes," said Nate.

"And here."

"Yes."

The doctor turned to me. "We need to take some X-rays to determine whether there is any internal bleeding. We will also need a urine sample."

"Okay," I said.

"Nathaniel, I need you to pee into this," said the doctor and handed me a small, plastic container. "I'll be back in a little while." He lifted the corners of his mouth into a simulation of a smile and left the room.

"How the fuck am I supposed to pee into that?" said Nate. "I can't stand up."

"I'm going to hold it." I pulled the hospital sheet down to his knees, undid his pants button as carefully as I could and pulled down the front of his underwear.

"Ow. Fuck. Ow!"

"I'm sorry."

"Do you have it?"

"Just start peeing, I got it."

"Okay," he said and sighed. "Am I peeing?"

"No."

"I can't pee. It isn't working." Panic was invading his voice.

"It's okay. Be patient."

Twenty minutes passed without urine. Nate was beginning to lose hope. A nurse had come in already to collect the sample and I'd had to tell her we weren't ready. In private, away from Nate, she told me that if he couldn't pee into the cup, they would have no choice but to give him a catheter. I went back into the room and told Nate that we needed to find a way to pee. Any way at all. I took out my cell phone and searched for rain and water sounds on YouTube and played them for him, propping the phone on his chest. No dice. I ran the tap water in the sink near his bed. Nothing. I tried to relax him with a video of Adam Sandler singing his Hanukkah song. He laughed a little but didn't pee. My arm was starting to ache because of the odd angle I had to hold the little cup at. After another ten minutes had passed, the nurse came back into the room.

"We need you to pee, okay Nathaniel?" she said. She positioned herself on the opposite side of the bed, facing and addressing me. "Okay, you place the tip in the cup, just like that, good. I'm going to massage his abdomen, his bladder, while you hold it there."

"Okay."

The nurse told Nate to relax, to close his eyes and concentrate on peeing. He closed his eyes. The nurse moved her fingers in firm, slow circles over his abdomen. Two or three times, he jerked unpredictably and it took some concentration to keep the urine container directly underneath. After nearly five minutes of sustained effort on all of our parts, a stream, unsteady at first but gaining in strength, filled the container to nearly three-quarters. We wouldn't need a catheter.

"How are you feeling?" I asked after the nurse left the room.

"You know, that's not how I imagined it in my dream," he said. "In my dream, you and the nurse are naked and at no point am I peeing."

X-rays were taken and came back clear of internal bleeding. Nate would need to stay overnight in the hospital, but overall things looked as good as they possibly could for someone who fell off a roof and landed on a ladder. He had a hairline fracture in his shoulder, several large bruises and scrapes, and a sprained finger on his left hand, but that was it. The doctor said it was amazing. He said Nate would be feeling much better in just a few weeks.

I came back to the hospital the following day to pick him up and take him home. I stood by and listened during his physiotherapy appointment, taking notes. Once the doctor had finished and had handed Nate a prescription for painkillers, I helped him into his shirt and fastened each button. Putting his pants on proved to be more difficult and very time-consuming due to the fact that he needed to bend at the waist to get his legs in. I put on his socks as he sat on the bed. When we'd finished, he looked as good as new. The bruises were covered by his clothes, the tubes had been removed from his hand and chest, and colour was coming back to his face. On the ferry ride back to the Island, Nate was overwhelmed by questions from Islanders aboard the boat. Many of them wanted to know in detail how Nate was feeling, how it had all happened and how he was managing the pain. They told him they were glad to see he was doing well. They told him they would come around soon to drop off a pie, a plate of cookies.

THE POKE

[SEVEN]

IT WAS OCTOBER, THE SCHOOL STRIKE THAT HAD ROCKED
the province since June was over and Lily was starting her first
day of grade one. Our boat had been giving us non-stop problems
since we bought it in May, but over the summer we hadn't needed
it every weekday to get Lily to school and back. All summer we'd
managed to get to town to buy groceries about once a week,
which was all we'd needed. I'd known for months that the pace
would change when school started again, but I hadn't been able to
pull my head out of the fog long enough to conceive a plan.

I woke up before anyone else to get ready. I checked the
school's location on Google Maps and more or less figured out
a route from the ferry drop-off point to École Pauline Haarer in
Nanaimo. It looked like a fifteen-minute walk once we got to the
other side. I had a small stack of Lily's admissions paperwork in
my bag, and I'd packed her lunch the night before. I went outside
and gathered up the trash bags we stored in a wooden box to take
to town that morning as well.

When you make the trek to the other side, there's always a
list to consider: the things you need to take there and the things
you need to bring back. I was able to make coffee and get the garbage ready before Nate and Lily woke up, but it always seemed

like I was forgetting something important, or that there would be something I didn't understand and would have to figure out in the moment. Like angling a motorboat between two others along a short dock. Like remembering to carry cash at all times. Or remembering to pick up things like garbage bags, toilet paper and dish soap, items I used to regard as inconsequential extras.

"I have to head over to Danny's. They're laying the foundation for the new house and they need me first thing," Nate said as he came down the stairs. "Are you taking the boat today or the ferry?"

"I don't know if the boat is going to make it across. If it stalls again, we're going to be late for school," I said, feeling some anxiety rise. Everything I was doing, I was doing for the first time in my life. I was like a baby learning to walk and falling to the floor after every step. "It's only a half-day today. Lily will be out by noon. I should just stay in town and wait for her, right?" I was willing to accept any advice at all, even from Nate, who had the same experience with everything here as I did.

"Yeah, stay. It's too much to go back and forth all morning. Do you have a pass or any money?" he asked. Without a pass, the ferry costs three dollars for locals one way, which meant taking the ferry to town and back with Lily was going to run me twelve dollars in cash.

"Christ. I forgot to take out money when I was in town last week, and remember I washed my pants a few days ago with the pass in one of the pockets?" The resident passes were a small rectangle of heavy paper about the size of a credit card. If they got wet, they disintegrated. "We'll have to take the boat."

"Muuuuum! It's a school day!" hollered Lily, sliding down the hallway in her pajamas. "Can I bring some toys to school? I want to show my teacher my toys," she yelled. "I want to show all the kids too. Can I? What did you put in my lunch? I don't want a sandwich, okay? I don't like sandwiches anymore."

"One toy. Go get dressed—we have to leave soon." I began searching the house for where I left the pants I wore yesterday, where I last put the boat keys, my empty wallet, my cup of coffee.

Lily was first out the door, still pulling her jacket on and forcing her fingers into the gloves she found in the pockets. We waved
goodbye to Nate through the window and walked across the front
lawn to the road. Our dirt driveway was flooded with rainwater,
leaving gaping puddles all over. The trip from our house to Mud
Bay was about a ten-minute walk but seemed extra long that day
as I reviewed the procedure of troubleshooting the boat over and
over in my mind. My frustration with it had frightened Lily in the
past and I didn't want her to develop a fear of riding in boats, so I
tried to keep my panic to myself.

A few days earlier the three of us had gone to town to get some
milk and when we got back in the boat to go home, it wouldn't
start right away. It took nine tries, some swearing and a lot of shot-
in-the-dark attempts at starting the motor before we got it going.
By then a small crowd had gathered along the overlook and were
watching us intently. Midway between town and Mud Bay, the
engine stopped again. I ended up calling over two teenage boys in
a boat nearby and got them to tow us in to the dock. I hadn't tried
to start the engine since.

Lily and I walked the dock, steadying our weight on top of
the undulating fingers. I pulled back the blue tarp covering our
boat and began to fold it up and stuff it into the side of the hull. I
noticed shattered glass across the deck and more gathered on the
farthest seat.

"Stay there Lily," I said and jumped into the boat. The glass
had come from a smashed window on the water side. There were
shards everywhere. I climbed back onto the dock, shook open the
tarp and tossed it over the front of the boat to cover the mess.

"We're going to take the ferry today, okay Lily? I think that
would be more fun, wouldn't it?" I said, already walking away.

"Why? I wanna take the boat!"

I kept walking until Lily gave up the fight and followed. I
didn't want her to see the glass. I didn't understand what had just
happened.

We walked away from Mud Bay toward the pub and the ferry.

At "the Circle," a small parking lot for golf carts, we saw blue herons soar to and from the new nests they'd been building. There were dozens occupying only a few trees. It was early still and they were singing, trying hard to wake up the island. We crossed the Circle and headed down the rock's edge on the other side. The ferry was waiting, as it always was, for the top of the hour when it heads town-side. I checked my pants' pockets for change but came up empty.

"I hope Rob is driving the ferry today," I said to Lily, to myself. Rob was the first ferry skipper we'd met when we got here. Rob had been kind to us, was around the same age as Nate and me, had three young children and seemed like someone who could be our friend. He would also allow me to pay for a ferry trip later if I didn't have any cash on me.

We walked the length of the docks and climbed aboard. There were two other passengers already settled on the middle seats, which housed the life jackets. Rob walked toward us holding a paper coffee cup in one hand and swinging the boat keys in the other. I knew he would be the skipper that day because he was wearing the beat-up fanny pack the skippers tied around their waists to hold change and the hole punch for passes. Rob jumped into the boat and looked around at us. "That's it? Four people?" Rob said and looked at Lily. "Okay, three and a half," he joked and tickled her in the side.

"I'm going to school today! My first day of grade one!" Lily yelled.

"Wow, kiddo! You gonna have fun?" he asked, starting the motor and leaving it to idle.

"I don't have any cash, Rob. Can I pay you on the way back?"

"You bet," he said and moved to the other passengers to collect small bills or to hole-punch a pass. I pulled Lily onto the seat beside me and wrapped my arms around her. Within seconds she wriggled free. She pulled her markers and sketchbook from her backpack and resumed work on the small drawings she had put down days ago. I had chosen one of the port-side seats for the ride, near the exit, and was able to see out to the water with an unobstructed view. If it wasn't too stormy and all the windows were open I could feel the seawater spray up and onto my arms, cold and light. Early in the morning and with only a few passengers on board, the ride was exceptionally peaceful, even through a roaring motor, and halfway through the trip for about two minutes there was a span where it seemed like you were way out to sea, nowhere near land, just sliding along the brim of the planet.

I dropped off Lily at her new school and walked her to the grade one classroom. It was the only public school within walking distance of the PI ferry dock, offered a French immersion program and had a good reputation among the parents I'd spoken to on the Island. We had been on a waitlist for the better part of the year to get her enrolled and according to those I knew, we were very lucky to have gotten in so quickly. As we walked down the halls looking for her room number I noticed the children spoke English until they saw a teacher and then immediately switched to French in mid-sentence. All adults spoke to each other and to students in French at all times. "Are you going to be all right, babe? Do you want me to stay for a while?" I asked.

"You can go. I know that girl," she said, pointing to the corner of the classroom where a few kids had gathered, apparently inspecting art supplies that had been set up at work tables. I recalled seeing the girl with the curly blonde hair around the Island.

"Okay. See you at lunchtime. Love you," I whispered.

"Je t'aime."

I followed the hall back the way we'd come and visited the office briefly to drop off Lily's paperwork and talk with the principal. As I left through the front doors and walked across the parking lot I felt the quake of anxiety. I hoped Lily would make out okay in her new class. I hoped she'd find a way to fit in, get along with the others and come back home more or less unscathed.

In town I stopped at the bank and called Nate to tell him about the broken glass in the boat, about how I owed Rob for the ferry ride.

"So you think someone smashed the window on purpose?"

"I can't know for sure. But even if it was an accident, there's no note or anything. They just did it and left."

"I'm going to call Peter. I heard he's the guy to talk to. The community watch guy or whatever."

"I'll take the rest of the glass out of the window on my way home. It's a real mess right now," I said.

I didn't know what Peter might be able to do about our problem, a problem that was more a social problem than a boat problem. I went to a nearby coffee shop to wait for Lily's half-day to finish. I tried to preoccupy myself with stories in the local newspaper I found in the cafe, but my train of thought kept returning to the broken window. It had been clear to us for a while that we didn't know the first thing about what owning a boat and keeping it at a public dock really entailed. We'd never done it before and we didn't know the Dock Code. We'd pissed people off, without a doubt.

In the six months we'd tied up at Mud Bay, one person had already yelled at us for using the wrong area of the wharf, garbage had been thrown into the hull, our boat lock had been cut in half twice for reasons we still didn't know, and we'd faced several instances of wordless and incomprehensible hostility from others as they passed us. Now there was this broken window. The most frustrating part was less that these things had happened, but that no one wanted to talk about it. No one had explained what the problems were before issuing the punishments, or had offered us any tips for making peace.

After our lock had been cut the second time, Nate wrote a note with our phone number on it and taped it to the windshield of the boat: *Please call if this boat is a problem so we can resolve it.* But no one did. We'd pulled Rob aside in private and asked if he had heard anything, if there was something we should know, but the only thing he could think of was that we should keep our boat as close to shore as possible if it still wasn't working well. He also shared a story about how he had faced similar problems when he first moved to PI. Once, he'd come down the ramp to find his boat filled with water and sinking into the mud. He laughed when he said it; he laughed because unlike us, and several years after the fact, he seemed able to see the humour. We were totally in the dark and without a conceivable way to light. We'd traded the rushed and tiresome subway commute in Toronto for what was becoming an equally pain-in-the-ass situation here.

From inside the cafe I recognized Mike, another regular ferry commuter, crossing toward my side of the street. I got up and made my way around the table to get outside and meet him on the sidewalk. Mike was always on the ferry, often early in the mornings to get to work in town, so I had shared the ride with him several times before. He always sat with Lily and listened to her stories and told her jokes. He was slim with grey hair that he kept pulled back from his face and warm, brown eyes. He wore a plain denim shirt, dark blue jeans and a thick canvas jacket. He looked like a rugged outdoorsman, the kind I remember seeing in cigarette advertisements as a child.

"Mike!" I called and waved in his direction. He nodded back and quickened his walking speed until he reached me.

"How are you?" he said, smiling and calm, happy to stop and chat.

"Fine for now," I said. "I'm just in town waiting to pick up Lily at school and then we'll head back home. Are you off to work?"

"Another day at the office," he said and winked genuinely. Every time I spoke to Mike he was easy and gentle. He had a peace about him that I'd never seen before; it was as if no matter what happened, in any moment, he would accept it with little more than a shrug. He exhibited cooperation with the world, with *things as they are,* that I found mesmerizing and mysterious. It was because of this that I didn't bring up the plaguing issue of the boat window when asked what was up. I kept the mood airy and fine; in that moment, I even experimented with the notion of letting the whole ordeal go for good.

"Oh, before I forget," said Mike, "I've been saving these for Lily." He pulled out a rectangular slip of stickers from his jacket pocket and handed them to me. "I found them in an old box I was rifling through the other day. They must've been left behind by a child visiting the house. I thought Lily might like them."

I took the sheet from his hand. It was three rows of glittering forest animals: birds, ponies, chickens and a dancing bear holding a rainbow.

"She'll love it," I said and slipped the stickers into my purse, careful not to bend the edges.

"Enjoy the beautiful day," Mike said as he reached out, grabbed my hand in both of his and made a gesture like bowing. "Gotta get going to work."

"See you soon, Mike," I said and watched him walk up the hill and around the corner toward the other side of town.

After school, Lily and I returned to the Island, taking the long way home and back through the Mud Bay docks where the boat was exactly where I'd left it that morning. I distracted Lily with the new sheet of stickers and got to work cleaning up the broken glass. I remembered leaving a box of garbage bags in the side somewhere. After a few minutes I located them and began collecting the glass shards and placing them in the bottom of a bag, one by one, as Lily talked to me about the new friends she'd made, where her desk was located and how the playground outside was configured. About halfway through the process, one of the guys Nate had done work for docked about ten feet behind me and climbed out of his boat.

"Looks like you got poked." John pulled his boat toward him by the spring line and tied it up to the dock. I turned to face him. He was filling his backpack with items he'd carried over from town: dish soap, a tube of toothpaste and a stack of white printer paper.

"I guess so," I replied.

"You know, I saw some younger people around here last night or so. Goofing around. Coulda been them put a hole in ya," John said as he walked past us and up the dock toward land.

"Thanks. Could be," I replied.

He made his way up the ramp without looking back.

I filled one corner of the garbage bag with glass, set it on the dock and threw the tarp back over the front of the boat. You could no longer tell the window had been smashed now that the glass was gone from the pane. From where I stood, it looked the same as it always had, like nothing was any different today than it had been yesterday.

It was barely afternoon and I was already exhausted. My muscles hurt and my limbs were heavy from stress and poor sleep. I was paranoid that every person I passed on the dock knew what had happened to my window but no one was going to talk to me about it. I felt terribly alone and frustrated. The first day of real commuting was behind me and we had managed, but I still didn't have a real job I could rely on, our money was getting low and I didn't know what we were actually going to do in any kind of long-term way. The Island was as beautiful as the first day I saw it, but what good was that if I couldn't enjoy it? If I had to inconveniently commute by boat to get to work or school and back? If we had to spend most of our money on transportation? I wondered if it was all worth it, if I would even recognize when the time had come to throw in the towel. I wondered how, with my head down and my will worn to threads, I would notice one way or the other. I lifted the bag of broken glass over my shoulder, picked up Lily's backpack and started on the walk home. The sun was high above us, in the middle of the sky, and was rushing the sea with light. The water looked like it was glowing from underneath and radiating upward. I could hardly see where I was going.

THE PARTY

[EIGHT]

"RESIDENT" OF PI IS NOT TO BE CONFUSED WITH "CITIZEN" in any way, something that was mentioned to us in passing; it was at least once overtly announced on the community listserv when someone called "Steve79" posted something of a manifesto. Steve79's declaration that "There's people who live here and then there's CITIZENS of our paradise island" demonstrated a capacity for both clarity (in this case, a clarity of segregation) and ambiguity (what prompted this statement?) common to many of the posted notices on the listserv giving newcomers like us the sense of never being in on the joke. Even the kinder posts were laced with something other than kindness, giving the whole platform a sense of treachery.

Posts like, "I noticed a fifteen-foot red canoe in Smugglers this morning with a man inside not wearing a life jacket. A life jacket is an essential part of survival out there and not wearing one sets a bad example to our island kids. —J," or, "Don't forget—allowing your unlicensed teenagers at the wheel of your golf cart is dangerous and illegal. —J," tended to come off as meddlesome rather than helpful, and supported the uncomfortable impression that we were all being monitored and reported on daily. The community is so small that most people reading the posts would recognize who the red canoe belonged to and whose teenager was driving a golf cart, which put a rather strong point on the perceived accusations.

Steve79, as it turned out, was a routine commenter, and as became obvious later, was also a hothead about a lot of issues. After a rumour of some kind (I had no idea what) caught fire around the Island, Steve79 posted a long outpouring of fury aimed at his neighbours. He explained that gossip was being spread about him that even involved his mother. He complained about the "dirty looks" he was getting and demanded that those with a problem confront him directly. He swore in all caps and expressed serious disappointment that his "so-called friends" were to blame. He referred to the culprits not by name but as "fucking cunts" and reminded everyone that he hears what goes on in his "community" and that hiding and denying was futile. The replies to Steve79's unspecific outburst took on many of the properties I'd come to recognize as standard for the listserv.

AnnaAndBryce wrote, "Steve I'm sorry you're having trouble, but please refrain from using such profanity." Sunshiner wrote, "I appreciate your concern Steve but perhaps a public forum isn't the right place for it," and GoneFishin wrote, "Steve, these people are all your friends. Be kind and kindness will come back to you tenfold." If anything, the comments against Steve79's outburst seemed to me to only confirm a community divide, a divide that was becoming more and more apparent as the weeks went by. As a result of the listserv, I had begun to notice distinct groups emerging, groups that stuck together: there were the Hotheads, people who reacted loudly to perceived injustices and got attention because of their volume; there were the Busybodies, people who equally loudly attempted to drown out the Hotheads with platitudes of kindness and togetherness, but were only so inspired when the Hotheads publicly threatened their manicured idea of Paradise Island; and finally the Ordinaries, people who didn't involve themselves one way or the other, docked their boats on private docks and carried on contentedly with their own lives, blissfully unconcerned with the affairs of the two rival gangs. I longed to be one of the Ordinaries, to cultivate a life that didn't rely so heavily on the public sphere of the ferry, that didn't require that I get my information from the listserv or down at Mud Bay dock.

An essential characteristic of Steve79's rant eventually came to embody the community as a whole for me. His sign-off read, "I can help you out as a member of the community, OR I can be a Fucking Horrible Cunt and watch you suffer and laugh. Sincerely, I love you, OR I hope you die in a train wreck, Steve (You know which Steve)." Steve79's open animosity running in tandem with the open offer of help to *members* of the community summed up a present and detectable standpoint among my more emboldened neighbours.

I also recognized in Steve79's open letter a hurt at learning that some individuals he considered tribesmen had deceived him, were disloyal and untrustworthy. His letter was the outraged cry of someone forced to face the unlikeable reality that people can be duplicitous and cruel, even people he once trusted, people he regarded as friends. Steve79's letter was a thoroughly painful admission that neighbours on PI had whipped up an unkind scandal, had facilitated cruel gossip, had participated in prejudiced accusations, had been *mean*. It exposed that this place, *his* place, could be troubled by the same malaise and anxiety as the next town—or city.

Here at the heart of Steve79's horror, I recognized something of my own. I too was disappointed and despaired at these contradictions. I too was angry because I had carried expectations, even optimism, that somehow this place was different, was better than other places. I reread Steve79's letter and thought of the time I had stood in a waiting area at the Halifax airport at least four winters ago. The plane that two hundred other passengers and I were scheduled to fly on was grounded due to bad weather and no one was going anywhere. Most of us in that room were tired and eager to go home but we stopped talking and listened to updates over the PA system before we returned to our cell phone screens and paperbacks. We waited.

When I returned from the bathroom for the third time in three hours, I noticed a man and a woman standing far away at the first-class service desk with their carry-on luggage around their feet. The man was yelling and waving his hands in the air. He demanded the plane take off as scheduled, and that it do so immediately. He reminded the woman at the desk that he had paid a large sum of money for this flight and that he was a preferred customer. His expectations of what his membership ought to provide him had been rudely ignored and he wasn't standing for it. He hollered that he was never flying with this airline again. He said he'd been lied to and misled. He told everyone in earshot that he was furious.

I thought again of Steve79 and his "citizenship," the years of work he'd put into establishing a home and community for himself, of the pitfalls of expecting that we can protect ourselves from the world somehow with business-class tickets, exclusive card-carrying benefits and high expectations.

We'd been on PI long enough that others began to recognize us as "residents," even if they didn't know that much about us yet. "Long enough" means longer than a trial period of a few months, something that had happened before with other families who had moved onto the Island only to pack up and move back off a few weeks later. We were regulars on the ferry, we tied up a boat at Mud Bay and we had recently purchased a golf cart, probably the single most obvious signal of an authentic resident. It was making life easier—tasks like getting to the ferry or bringing bags of groceries home could be done with relative ease.

Nate and I had bought the electric golf cart from a retired couple on the other side of the Island for five hundred dollars. It was beige with a dark stripe along the sides. The previous owners had installed Plexiglas doors on tracks to the driver and passenger sides, making it look like a tiny, enclosed car. "My husband's an inventor," the woman had said. "He loves to tinker with things and he had a lot of fun playing with this little car." The couple's second golf cart, which was not for sale, was fashioned to look like a miniature 1926 Bentley Speed Six Tourer. It was dark green with cream accents.

Being recognized as a resident had its benefits: we could access and post on the listserv available to current residents only; we could buy and use the "resident" ferry passes sold at a six-dollar discount below the "visitor" ferry passes; carpooling and boat pooling began to open up as viable travel options; and occasionally, if we found ourselves in the right place at the right time, we might get invited to a party.

It was November, two days after Halloween, when Nate, Lily and I were invited to attend a small get-together at Summer and her husband Steven's place. We were told that it would be a potluck, that we could come whenever we felt like it and that there would be no "end time."

That Saturday, Nate and I bought two six-packs of Old Style Pilsner at the Dinghy Dock, put together a red cabbage and chickpea salad and piled into the golf cart to head to the party. As we approached, we could hear the revelry had already begun: bursting sounds of laughter, dog barks and passionate joke-telling. Summer and Steven's house sat at the end of a short one-way street and was hidden from general view behind a row of non-operational boats and an oversized tool shed. On that day, the large front lawn was crowded with chairs, a barbecue, a table for food and beer, and about twenty or thirty people, dogs and children.

Lily ran ahead of us onto the property and began telling anyone she could about the Halloween candy she'd recently collected, describing in detail the flavours and wrappings of her favourites. Nate went in next, with me only slightly behind him. We carefully approached the group and I held the salad bowl in front of us as an offering.

"Oh, hey guys," Summer said and smiled. "Nate, Amber, this is everyone," she said, moving her outstretched arm toward the group positioned around the firepit.

"Hi," I said and waved a six-pack at them.

"Hey," said Nate.

"The bathroom's not in the house, by the way. We built this last year and tore down the old one inside," Summer said, pointing to a separate, free-standing structure built on the corner of the front porch and decorated with flattened beer caps.

"Oh wow," I said. "That's amazing. You flattened all those beer caps and nailed each one to the walls?"

"Hm-mm," she said and nodded her head. "It was fun."

As I stood there admiring the outdoor toilet, Summer's one-year-old daughter began crawling up the porch steps. "Oh, man. She's going to fall," Summer said and ran to scoop up the girl.

"We don't know anyone here," Nate whispered as soon as Summer was out of earshot.

"I know. What should I do with this salad?"

"I'll get a fork and we can start eating it right here," he said.

"Cut it out!" I said and slapped him on the arm. "Where's Lily?" I asked, still whispering.

"Give me the salad. I'll go find Lily. At least then I'll have someone to talk to," he said in barely audible tones. Nate lifted the salad bowl and one of the six-packs from my clutching arms and started toward the house.

I stood there on the lawn for few seconds before someone's dog came over to smell me. The dog was hyper from being around so many people and was yipping and moving in darting, unpredictable ways. His tail wagged rapidly and slapped against the side of my leg enough times that it began to hurt. I decided to move away from the dog and toward the firepit, even though it meant inserting myself into a group of people I'd never met and a conversation I wasn't yet a part of. I sidled up to a woman who looked about my age, slipped a beer out from one of the plastic rings, placed the five remaining beers on the grass at my feet and took a long sip.

"Did you guys move in beside Keith?" asked the woman.

"Yeah," I said and wiped my mouth.

"How do you like the place?" she asked and looked around at the assembled group, a smirk developing on her lips.

"So far, so good," I said and took another sip. The image of my shattered boat window bobbed on the surface of my mind. I still didn't know what had happened, but I dreaded the fact that someone I regularly walked past on the road, maybe even someone at this party, had done it to teach me a lesson.

"No one's lived there since… let me see, Bruce?" she said and turned to project her voice toward someone on the porch. "Bruce? That log house near Keith's has been empty for how long now?"

"Gotta be four or five years," Bruce said and turned back to his own conversation near the food table.

"Yeah, four years or so, I guess," said the woman.

"How do you like Mona then?" said an older man sitting next to the woman responsible for this line of inquiry.

"Oh, Moni? The landlord?" I asked.

"Right. *Moni*," he said and chuckled.

"Well, she's been putting a lot of pressure on us to buy the house, which we don't want to do. Not yet anyway," I said.

"Huh," said the man. "I bet she is. I wouldn't buy it *ever* if I were you."

Peals of laughter broke out from everyone gathered around the fire.

"Oh yeah? The house is no good?" I asked.

"No good?" said a third person, a man a few years younger than the last and by the looks of it, already several sheets to the wind. "The whole damn place is a mess. Far as I know, there's not even an occupancy permit on it. Prob'ly cause it never passed a single goddamn inspection. I know because I was parta the first crew that built that house. Before *Moni* fired every last one of us for reasons I'll never know."

Laughter all around.

"I can't recall, Steve-o, was that before or after she ran over Danny's dog with her truck?" said a fourth person.

"Oh, well before," replied Steve-o. "It was before she killed the dog, but after she tore up the front lawn with a bulldozer so's to bury the building supplies she didn't wanna pay to haul back to town."

The woman next to me looked over and smiled. I wrestled another beer from the plastic rings.

"I noticed the kitchen isn't totally finished. There's a wall that still has the bare drywall on it," I offered.

"Christ, that's just the beginning of your problems. You know the foundation was poured six times? Six pours 'cause every time the damn inspector came over, y' know, to check on the place, he said the foundation was wrong. Told her to start over," said Steve-o again, his agitation rising. "She got frustrated and I imagine it was costin' her a fortune to keep that up, so she went an' hired herself a crew from the Island. That's when I started on the house. We poured a proper foundation too. That's prob'ly the only damn part of that house which is sound."

"All in an effort to *save* money, she does this," the older man adds. "You do things cheaply, that's what you get. You ever seen someone trip over a ten-dollar bill to pick up a dime?"

The laughing had stopped and everyone now held serious expressions on their faces.

"Anyway," said the woman. "What's done is done."

"She went through at least four or five crews before that house got finished. Each crew worse than the last," continued Steve-o.

There was a silence then with only the sound of a few shuffling feet against the dirt beneath our lawn chairs.

"Well, thanks for the heads up," I said.

"Yeah. Better keep your eyes open is what I'm sayin'," said the older man.

⟡   ❦   ⟡

After an hour or so at the party, I went inside Summer's house to find Nate and Lily sitting on the couch and playing with a litter of black and white baby kittens. Nate balanced on his knees a paper plate filled with a variety of potluck foods: bean salad, cheese squares, crackers and grapes. Beside him, Lily had two kittens on her lap and a third draped over her shoulder. A few of the other Island kids gathered on the carpet and took turns sliding the kittens across the coffee table and trying to stuff them into their pockets when they landed at the other end.

"Look Mum, look how cute they are!" Lily squealed as I walked toward her, frightening the kitten on her shoulder a little.

"Can we go?" Nate said, looking up at me from the couch.

"I want to take this one with us," Lily said, petting the entirely black kitten positioned head-first over her shoulder.

"No one will talk to me so I came to hang out here with the cats and kids," Nate said.

"Okay, let's go if you want," I said. "Listen, I think I might have met Steve79, over by the fire," I whispered as I helped Lily place the kittens back into their basket on the floor.

"Oh yeah? How'd that go?"

"He told me our house was built really badly and that Moni fired everyone who worked on it," I said.

"Huh. Wish I could've been there for that."

"Yeah. He seemed pretty angry. He was one of the people who built our house," I said.

"You sure you got the right guy?" Nate asked.

"No," I replied.

We quickly located Lily's jacket and the sock she'd lost while playing and made our way around the house and yard to say good-bye. Summer was nowhere I could see but her husband was in the kitchen mixing a new bowl of spiked punch. He seemed to tower over the low counter and had the appearance of not belonging in the kitchen where he stood, not knowing where the glasses were, or the mixing spoon, or when he turned around, not knowing which door to take to get back to the outside porch. In spite of his out-of-placeness, he looked happy, smiling all the time, and was casual in his gestures: scratching the side of his leg as he pulled a spoon from a drawer, tossing a stray toy to the edge of the room with a flick of his foot.

We thanked him for having us and headed outside toward the firepit. Steve-o was no longer there, and several new people had replaced the ones I had spoken to only a few minutes before. I decided to keep walking past the firepit and toward our golf cart, waving and yelling out, "See you later!" to the party as a whole. Lily crawled into the back seat holding her shoes and Nate and I took our usual positions in the front.

As we pulled out of the side street and onto the main road, we spotted Danny and Davey on their dirt bikes at the top of the hill, neck and neck, heading directly for us.

"Pull over," said Nate.

"Okay, but they don't hit people when they do this. At least they haven't yet."

"Still. They're blind," he urged.

I drove the golf cart toward the edge of the road and turned it off. Danny and Davey looked around the same age, maybe twenty years old, and were always together. They lived in a big house up the road from us, which they shared with three sisters, two younger brothers, their parents and several roaming cats and dogs. Most of the family members were blind and had been since birth. A few years earlier, Danny invented some kind of Braille system to enhance literacy for the blind and with the help of his family was able to market it and make a bit of money. He was in the process of using the money he'd earned to buy a new lot and build a newer, better, bigger house for his family on the other side of the Island.

Danny often called on Nate to help with the house, but rarely gave much warning—normally no more than ten or twenty minutes. Nate would reschedule his day to be able to go to Danny's because he liked working with him and Danny always paid him on time. Nate often remarked on Danny and his family's intense kindness to everyone and attributed it to the family's overt religiosity. "Christians practise being good to their neighbours. It's the foundation of the doctrine," Nate would say.

Danny and Davey walked all over the Island, and always with their arms linked together. If they passed someone they knew, which was everyone except for the occasional tourist, they would come to a full stop and encourage a conversation, always asking how the other's family was doing, how he spent his weekend, what her plans were for the day. Each time, as they started back down the road after a brief chat, Danny would say, "What a nice person that is, and with such a nice voice."

We watched them race down the hill from inside our golf cart by the side of the road, watched as they weaved their bikes in and out, hurtling toward us and kicking up a tremendous cloud of dirt and rocks behind them as they went. Within seconds, they had sailed past us, missing our golf cart by no more than an inch.

CRISTINE

[NINE]

LATE ONE MORNING, IN SHARP CONTRAST TO THE QUIET OF the Island, the phone rang out through the empty rooms of our house. I tracked it down along the kitchen counter and picked it up.

"Amber, hello. I'm calling because I'd like to know if you're willing to work for the library. The job is cataloguing the books that are given to us by donation. I'll show you how, and then I'll leave you to it. There's an office here at my home you can use to work from. It'll be once a week but there will be remuneration."

Cristine's faint British accent was instantly recognizable, even though we'd only ever spoken to each other in person before. I didn't know much about Cristine, but the few things I knew, I liked. She was planning a trip to Japan and spent hours learning the language from flash cards. She rode her bicycle to and from the library, and kept a little basket in the front to hold books and flowers. She read poetry and had nothing to do with Island gossip. I imagined more than once what she would look like if she took her long, thick hair out of the braid she always put it in; I imagined she would look beautiful that way.

"Sounds great," I said, pleased by the idea of a little extra money. "Do you want me over today?"

I'd been working for the past week as an administrative assistant for a gymnastics studio way across town in Nanaimo and the commute was murder. My hours there were 9:30 in the morning until 4:30 in the afternoon, which at first sounded just fine. After the first few days, however, I learned what it really meant to commute from the Island into town each day for work. It meant catching the 8:00 a.m. ferry to drop Lily off at school on time, then waiting for the 8:45 bus to take me the twenty minutes north I needed to go to get near work. From the bus stop, I needed to walk down the highway for fifteen minutes to get to the gymnastics studio. Getting home was the real challenge, though. Leaving the studio at 4:30 meant missing the 4:25 bus downtown so I'd catch the 5:05, which got me to the ferry's waiting room at about 5:20. I would then wait for the 6:10 ferry back to the Island, arriving at about half past the hour, getting me through the front door at quarter to seven after walking home—half an hour away from Lily's bedtime and eleven hours from when I left in the morning.

I left home in the dark and came back in the dark. I couldn't keep it up. I wasn't seeing my child enough, I was beyond tired and the cost of transportation was eating up most of my pay. The upside was that the sheer intensity of my workdays helped to distract me from the abuse I had to deal with daily from my boss when he showed up to the office late and irritated by everything. Working for Cristine for a few hours a week would mean travelling no more than two blocks from my front door even if I still needed to keep my town job to make ends meet.

"Let's say around two o'clock. I'd like to go for a swim first," Cristine replied and hung up.

The houses on PI are all relatively new builds; none are much older than fifty years or so. What they have in common is the material used (mostly wood) and style (mostly "outback cabin"). None were built with brick or stone since the cost and labour of having to schlep that kind of material over to the Island would be extreme and totally impractical. The building materials contribute to a number of certain similarities among PI homes: they're also often tucked in behind trees, back from the roads, and are mostly brown and green in colour. In some cases, you have to probe through a small forest just to spot one.

The most obvious difference between these houses and those you might find in Toronto's downtown is their overt youth. Houses in Toronto seem to inherit what we associate with ancient brick, stone and Old World architecture: sturdiness, authority, tenure. Aside from a few towering mansions that have been built near the Dinghy Dock Pub, the young houses on the Island are small, unimposing and modest. Cristine's house is not like the others, though. Hers is a white stucco bungalow behind a tidy strip of lawn, a visual anomaly built right on the bedrock.

"Come on this way. I keep an office in the back," Cristine said as she led me past her backyard patio and toward a small garage she'd converted into an office. Even with the door open, there was no sound at all but the waves a few feet away. Cristine carefully pulled out a bag from the desk drawer containing a laptop computer, a power cord, a mouse and a mouse pad, and laid them out on the desk that was pushed against one wall of the room. She placed each item along with the next in an order I could sense was important; I tried to make a mental picture of where things were going so I could adequately perform the same set-up the next time I came over.

Without any chit-chat, Cristine showed me where I could find the computer program for adding new books to the library catalogue and how to enter each title, author and book synopsis. In most cases, the program was able to perform an online search and produce a cover image for the book, automatically adding it to the listing. On other occasions, the cover image wasn't available, or the cover image generated didn't match the edition in our possession. In those instances, I was to search the internet manually for the correct image, copy it and insert it into the new listing.

Cristine entered a couple of new books into the database to show me how the process looked. She was enthusiastic about pointing out grammatical and logical errors she found in the book descriptions online. I was to fix those as well. "There you have it," she said as she stood up from the desk. "I'll come back in two hours and we'll have some whisky."

With Cristine's voice gone from the room and the door closed, there were no sounds except for the ones I made myself: the sound of one book laid on another in a pile, the clicking of keys on the keyboard, my own breathing. Almost right away, my mind started wandering and I noticed myself eagerly anticipating Cristine coming back with whisky. After a while, I'd gotten through the stacks Cristine had organized for me to catalogue, logged out of the program and closed the laptop. I slipped the computer back into its sleeve, wrapped up the power cord, mouse and mouse pad, and returned everything to the bag, trying very hard to remember exactly where each thing was meant to go.

The two-hour work period wasn't up yet so I decided to scan the bookshelves behind me in the office while I waited for Cristine. There were four rows of wooden bookcases along the opposite wall of the office and each had six shelves full of books. Most of the rows were identified by genre and sub-genre in the form of small, masking tape signs at the end of each shelf: FICTION, BIOGRAPHY, ART. Two rows at the bottom of the second bookcase were crammed with children's books of all colours and sizes. No signs were posted there because it was obvious what the books were. All of the spines were bright pink or green or yellow and the covers were covered in big block fonts describing animal and pirate and princess adventures.

I looked back at the desk and noticed a few crumbs of something on top. Doubting that Cristine had left them there herself, I swept them into my hand and then deposited them in my pocket. Moments later, Cristine knocked on the door and opened it soundlessly. "How did it go?" she asked.

"Fine. I catalogued all of these," I said, my hand on a pile of books. The insulation of the surrounding water and the white walls and everything being so quiet made my voice seem like the loudest it had ever been. "And these," I pointed to another, smaller pile, obsessively conscious now of the volume I was speaking at.

"Wonderful." She crossed the room and sat on the daybed in the corner. Her expression and physicality reminded me somehow of a child. When she sat, her feet didn't reach the floor and her hands were clasped together in her lap. She smiled at me in a way that suggested we were sharing a secret. "Time for whisky then."

She reached across the bed to open a drawer in a table next to it. She pulled out two glasses and a half-full bottle of Glenfiddich, filled each glass with a layer of rusty liquid and handed one to me. I sipped, trying to hide my shudder at the taste as the liquor crawled down my throat. I knew I'd have to keep sipping if I wanted to stay, and I wanted to stay.

"So do you think you'll live here for good?" she asked.

"I want to. *We* want to. But we need to get better jobs. I've applied to the university in Nanaimo about twenty times so far but I haven't heard anything. I'm not sure they even get the resumés I send. There's no way of knowing."

"Oh, how burdensome."

"There's no number I can call, no person I can speak with. I just send my resumés out into the abyss and wait," I said and took another sip of the whisky, which went down a little easier the second time.

"Have you spoken with Carol Matthews? Carol used to hire people there. She's retired now, but I'm sure she'd offer you advice. And Frances, of course. Frances commutes by ferry, so you may want to try and catch her in the morning on her way to work. She teaches English at the university, I believe."

"I think I've seen Frances on the ferry. I'll talk to her next time we ride together. Carol lives here on the Island?"

"Three houses that way," Cristine said pointing out the window. "She's just lost her husband and she'll be moving into town to live with her daughter. If you choose to talk with her, you should do so soon."

"I just started this awful job working at an office in town. The owner scares me. To be honest, I feel like he's going to punch me one of these days, he gets so angry. I want to quit but I can't because we need the money. The situation is making me depressed." I took another sip. I hadn't worked there long but the environment was toxic and I spent a good deal of time thinking of ways to escape.

The last time I worked a shift at the town job, I spent forty-five minutes browsing apartment listings in Montreal. If I saw a place I liked, I clicked through and zoomed in on the kitchen, the bathroom, the bedrooms… I imagined walking down the street in the summer and shovelling snow in the winter. Nate and I had started regular conversations about our future lately, about an alternative plan for our lives should this BC thing end up as the full-stop disaster we feared it was becoming. We talked about moving back east if we had to.

Cristine waved her hand in the air. "Oh, that's easy to manage."

"I really don't know what to do," I said and looked her in the face to communicate my sincerity. "The man leans all of his body over me when he wants something done. He verbally intimidates me in front of customers and yells when things go wrong, which is all the time because he has everyone in the place anxious as hell."

"If you want to make things easier," advised Cristine, "ask him for his advice on something and then behave gratefully when he gives it to you. Tell him, *Thank you.*" Her confidence about the way to placate my boss was impressive. I could imagine for a moment how her suggestion might work, but the idea of acting kindly toward this creep, even if I was manipulating the outcome, was impossible to consider. The dread I felt at returning to work on Monday was so sharp that I didn't know how I would cope. I couldn't sleep the nights before my shifts and my appetite was so low that I went most of the day without eating. I took the last sip of my whisky.

"My husband was like that man," Cristine continued. "It was the old days and I did all of the cooking and cleaning and so on, you know. And if I didn't deliver his beer in the precise way he liked it set on the table, well, there was trouble," she said and rolled her eyes as if to say, *Silly man.* "He died, thankfully, and we didn't have any children, so I'm free of all that now."

I poured myself a little more whisky.

"Now I'm going for an artist!" She clapped her hands as she said this, the hands that had been folded in her lap this whole time. "I've always wanted an artist."

"My first marriage was to an artist—a musician," I said. "He drank a lot and I never knew where he was or what the hell was ever going on." I was smiling now too, at the hilarity of it. "I was in my twenties when I married him. He lives in Montreal now. He's a chef."

"I see. An elastically talented artist, then."

"He's very good at those two things, yeah. Those and staying alive no matter what happens to him." We were laughing out loud now.

"A triple threat!"

Cristine had a surprising, full-bodied laugh. When she found something truly amusing, she'd lean backward and lift her face toward the sky. She'd let it all go and then fix herself again right after. You'd be crazy not to like her.

"Have you found an artist yet?"

"I've gotten myself onto a dating website—I forget what it's called—and found a handsome photographer, far away in Vancouver," she said. "He's in his seventies like me and we have terrific sex. Isn't that fantastic?"

"It is fantastic," I said and tipped the last of my whisky into my mouth. "Next time I'll bring beer. Do you like beer?"

"I do," she said, smiling.

✧　❧　✧

That afternoon, I walked as slowly as I could back home. It could have been the whisky buzzing in my brain, but I wanted to hang onto the feeling being with Cristine gave me, the comfort I felt with her. As I walked, I lowered my head to cover my eyes from the descending afternoon sun. I made the turn toward home and heard a high-pitched whistle from above my head. A few feet up soared an enormous eagle coming at a speed I never thought possible. I ducked down out of instinct and covered my head with my arms even though the bird was still far above me. It sailed over me, dipped into a row of blackberry bushes to my left at the side of the road, wrapped its talons around the body of a smaller bird with a yellow belly, lifted and was gone.

In only that partial second, my heart rate quickened and a surge of adrenalin lit up my limbs. If I needed to run faster than ever before, I could've at that moment. My muscles were taut and for a few seconds the lenses of my eyes sharply focused on every object around me. I was able to recognize a structure deep in the woods as a small cabin rather than the bulbous tree trunk I had previously assumed it was. I saw the cabin's window frames, the bronze door handle. I stood on the road without moving for what must have been five minutes. Nothing happened: there were no golf carts or foghorns or even birds. No person came around the corner or called out for their dog. There was only the wind and the sunshine and me.

I got home and found Nate sitting at the dining room table typing something quickly on his laptop while Lily looked on beside him. "Mum, bad news," started Lily as I came in through the door. "There's a little, tiny, baby cat stuck up the tree in the backyard. He can't get down! We tried to get him down but he won't come. He just stays up there and cries." Lily looked at me intently.

"I'm posting on the listserv to see if anyone is missing a cat," Nate said, not looking up from the computer. Nate finished up and we all went outside to where the cat was stuck in the tree. Our ladder was resting against the tree's base, obviously set there in an attempt to get the cat down, but the ladder was no match for the size of the tree and looked pitifully small by comparison. As I stood at the bottom looking up, I heard the faint, infant cry of a kitten. I peered through the branches and could make out what looked like a thin tail gracefully waving back and forth, perhaps thirty or forty feet in the air. Nate's cell phone rang in his pocket.

"Hello. Yeah. I have no idea. Maybe an hour or so? We're here. Quite high. You'll need a very tall ladder. Okay, goodbye."

"Whose cat is it?" I asked.

"Chris and Cora's. The couple with the two kids. You know them, they take the ferry sometimes," he said. "Chris is on his way."

We went inside and began cooking supper while we waited. Lily watched Netflix upstairs and I sat on the kitchen stool while Nate chopped vegetables. Within a few minutes, I saw Chris come down our driveway carrying a ladder far taller than the one we had. From inside the house, I motioned for him to head around back.

"Should we stay in this place?" I said, thinking about the cat stuck in a tree, unable to get down even if it wanted to.

"Yeah. For now. If we just can't do it any longer, we'll go somewhere else."

"Where would we go next?"

"I don't know yet. I don't want to go back to Toronto though."

"That salad looks so good," I said and stuck a fork through the top layer of cilantro and romaine Nate was compiling in a bowl on the counter.

"Patience," he said.

We cooked and mashed some potatoes, baked some whitefish and organized supper on the table. I called up to Lily to come down and eat. As we sat down Chris emerged from the backyard carrying a small cat in his arms. He motioned through the window for me to come outside.

"I'll come by and get my ladder a little later on, if that's alright."

"That's fine," I said. "Is the cat okay?"

"Seems like it. Scratched the hell out of my hand when I pulled her down though," he said as he petted the cat on the top of her head. "I don't know what on earth she was up to. When I got up there I thought she was sleeping in a bird's nest, just because of the way it looked, but she wasn't. She was sitting on top of a dead raccoon."

"A dead raccoon?" It was Lily's voice behind me, shrill and horrified. She must've come out after me without making a sound.

"Go inside, Lily," I said and opened the front door for her. She looked at me with giant eyes and reluctantly turned back through the door.

"A dead raccoon?" I said when I could see Lily was inside and out of hearing range.

"Dead as a doornail and hard as a rock. Must've been running away from something when it went up that tree and couldn't get back down," Chris said, walking back to the road. "Thanks for letting us know about it. The kids will be happy to have this little guy back."

"No problem," I said and watched as Chris leaned into his golf cart and backed out, holding the cat down in the seat beside him.

THE GHOSTS OF
GALLOWS POINT:
PART ONE.

[TEN]

IT IS TOUGH TO UNRAVEL ANY SATISFACTORY HISTORY OF
Protection Island because little has been recorded. What has been
recorded often takes on a mythical life of its own. It is a detective
game to sort out fact from fiction, a game that thoroughly chal-
lenged and confused me during my time there. There are early
logs and other attempts to document what count as major events,
such as the hangings at Gallows Point, the 1913 explosion of the
SS *Oscar* that rocked the city of Nanaimo, and of course the Number One Mine explosion of 1887. But there is little otherwise and
less still about PI specifically.

When you walk up the steep drive toward Gallows Point, you
can tell there's a history there; you can feel there are secrets. Part
of this feeling is due to the ragged shoreline, an obvious danger
to incoming and outgoing boat traffic. It's easy to imagine a ship,
especially in the tosses of a storm, grounding itself on the edges
of this particular jut of land. Standing on the point out near the
beacon, the vastness of the lookout into the strait can make your
heart stop. Just by looking you realize the kind of peril that only
the sea can inspire.

The small, white PI Museum sits right on the boundary of the
land at Gallows Point, almost in the water. Just behind Beacon

House, it was erected as the lightkeeper's cottage in 1912. The museum consists of two rooms inside a wooden bungalow with a small ramp up to the front entrance. The windows are small with red trim. There is a flower garden around the whole perimeter full of purple tulips and yellow daffodils. I never saw anyone come in or go out the door but people were frequently weeding the garden beds and washing the windows.

On January 17, 1853, two Coast Salish men were hanged thirty feet from where the doors now stand, suspects in the 1852 murder of a Hudson's Bay Company shepherd at Christmas Hill near Victoria. One of the men was from the Cowichan area and the other was a chief's son from Nanaimo. When news of the murder and the suspected culprits was heard, Governor James Douglas immediately dispatched a ship to apprehend them and take them north from Victoria to Nanaimo. The story is that the chief's son attempted to escape custody several times between Victoria and Nanaimo, becoming more and more desperate each time he was recaptured.

With little to lose and dangerously close to the hour of his death, the chief's son jumped off the ship just as it passed what he recognized as his home territory along the coast. At first it looked as if he had drowned from the jump, but after several minutes he was spotted in the distance swimming to shore. He swam through the frigid winter water to land and ran through the snowy forests to hide. He was seized hours later for a fourth and final time in an area now referred to as Chase River, just outside of Nanaimo. Little evidence was available to incriminate the two men, but they were tried anyway on the quarterdeck of the SS *Beaver* and hanged at Gallows Point that same afternoon. Both men died in front of an audience of twenty-two, giving the place its original designation of Execution Point.

The first time I came to the museum was in an effort to locate the PI archives I was told were stored there. I was also told that the council of archivists—Beth, June and Mary—were overly protective of their stash and that I was likely to have trouble getting a peek at anything. I walked to Gallows and the PI Museum on a Sunday afternoon and knocked on the door at the top of the ramp.

"Yes?" said an older woman, her hair pulled in a tight ponytail.

"Hi," I said, as friendly as possible.

The woman stood there and looked me over. "We aren't open for visitors today."

"I understand. I was just curious about the history of Protection Island and I heard from a friend that there were some archives stored here. Thought I could have a look sometime." I took a step back.

"Well, not today I'm afraid. Perhaps you could phone ahead next time," the woman said. "Wait here. I'll get you Mary's phone number."

As she cleared the doorway, I was able to glance behind where she'd been standing into what looked like a makeshift office set against the back wall of one of the rooms. Around the desk were boxes of paper stacked on plastic milk crates. There was a lamp on the desk and the desk itself was covered in smaller stacks of documents. The rest of the room was bare.

"Here. Mary is the person to call about the archives." She handed me a torn strip of paper with a phone number written on it. I started to say thank you but the woman was already closing the door.

That week I called Mary three times and only ever got the answering machine. I was told by Islanders that she had taken a vacation, then that she was visiting a doctor, then that she was taking a break from the archives altogether. Once I saw Mary on the commuter ferry. I knew it was her because the man she was speaking with called her Mary and their conversation revolved around her work at the museum. I listened intently to their conversation. As Mary became more and more aware of my eavesdropping, I noticed her body language and general demeanour become guarded. I sensed she knew I was the person who kept calling her and that I was after her archives, archives she didn't want to share.

"Excuse me, Mary?" I said. "I've recently moved here to the Island. I was hoping to get a chance to look at the local archives. I'm interested in the history of this place."

She smiled. "Yes, I'm sorry I didn't return your calls." Mary glanced at her travelling partner, then back to me. "I've been so busy."

"Could I come by the museum next week?"

"Of course. I'll be there Wednesday and can help with whatever it is you're looking for."

I was pleased to have run into Mary and made a plan to sift through the historical documents she kept locked away. I badly wanted to know more about where I was living and what had happened there. I had found some historical books at the library in Nanaimo that helped satiate some of my curiosity, but the fact that Mary seemed to be keeping such a close grip on the archives made them that much more necessary to me.

In fact when I encountered Mary I was carrying *More Shipwrecks of British Columbia* by Fred Rogers, a book cataloguing disasters at sea, many of which took place in the "Graveyard of the Pacific," an area from Tillamook Bay in Oregon to Cape Scott on Vancouver Island. Since European exploration, estimates number in the thousands of vessels and lives lost in this area due to unpredictable weather conditions and tricky coastal patterns. The name is thought to have originated from the early days of fur trading, as a warning that this area was among the most dangerous to travel in and out of. Many of the ships wrecked in this area were totalled to such an extreme degree that salvage attempts were unsuccessful. The Strait of Juan de Fuca, the large body of water emptying the Salish Sea on the east side of Vancouver Island into the Pacific Ocean, is among the deadliest regions in the Graveyard.

In the book I found a small passage about the steamship SS *Oscar*, a floating arsenal that was carrying two thousand cases— approximately fifty tonnes—of dynamite to Vancouver on January 15, 1913 during a snowstorm. Having recently left Nanaimo

Harbour, the captain, Alexander McDonald, noticed smoke coming from the engine area as they passed Entrance Island, a tiny island at the entrance of the Nanaimo Harbour with nothing but a lighthouse on it. The captain and crew of five decided to play it safe and head back to Nanaimo, but before they had a chance to get their bearings, the smoke turned to fire and within minutes the eighty-two-foot ship was engulfed in flames.

The lifeboat was lost in the storm and the *Oscar* itself was adrift. The ship grounded mere moments later near Gallows Point on Protection Island. The six men rushed to get a ladder over the side and climb off the boat to the relative safety of land. They noticed a pithead and began climbing down the mineshaft as far as they could. The spectacular blast when all fifty tonnes of dynamite exploded on the steamer was felt 250 metres below sea level at the lowest point of the mine and all across Nanaimo. Quickly, the mine began to flood as water rushed in through the fractured rock; however, all the men in the mines escaped with their lives.

In town, the windows in every house and store blew out. The mayor at the time, John Shaw, reported that the first thing to catch his eye was a swell of light across the harbour. He told reporters that he got up from where he was sitting in the Windsor Hotel and went over to the window to get a better look. As he squinted to see, glass shattered around him in all directions. The streets filled with people and the town went into panic. Schools and shops closed and all efforts were directed toward repairs. The total damage was around ten thousand dollars, a quarter of that on Protection Island, the area most heavily hit.

When all was tallied, the worst injury was to a blacksmith's eye. No lives were lost but the explosion ended up being the catalyst necessary to consider workers' safety for miners handling coal. New legislation was drafted to cover ships carrying ammunition. The SS *Oscar* was the largest boat explosion Canada had seen until the Halifax Explosion on the opposite coast four years later. Today, during low tide you can see a hole in the beach floor where the ship exploded. Some say parts of the *Oscar* are still visible along the tidal shelf. Metal pieces of the ship have been found by divers in the area between the light-beacon and Smugglers Park along the shore, and I've been told the PI museum has a collection of fittings and other pieces of *Oscar* stashed away in the back room.

The following Wednesday, Lily and I walked over to the museum to meet with Mary again but she wasn't there. I cupped my hands against the window to see into the empty office. It didn't look like anyone had moved a single sheet of paper from the desk since the last time I looked in and I couldn't make out any movement. With nothing else to do, I sat down at a nearby picnic table to wait while Lily played in the empty boat stationed in front of the library on a concrete slab. She picked up a long stick from the ground, climbed into the old boat, and took the sweatshirt from her backpack and tied it around her head. She began swinging the stick in the air like a sword and yelling out commands. She was pretending she was a pirate and the captives aboard her ship were rebelling, daring her to a swordfight.

TABACCA JACK

THIS BE THE SKULL OF A GRAY
THAT DIED OFF UCLUELET ONE DAY
NOW WOULD YOU HAVE BET ~
THAT A DRAGGERMANS NET
MIGHT HAVE SNAGGED IT FOR THIS HERE DISPLAY

[ELEVEN]

SINCE THE FALL FROM THE ROOF, WORK HAD DRIED UP FOR Nate on the Island so he had started working two days a week at a pet store in North Nanaimo. Because of the commute, on those days he would be gone for over ten hours just to work a six-hour shift. The rest of the week he worked over at Danny's digging up earth and pouring concrete for the foundation of the family's new home. The weather was getting colder, the Island was beginning to change and fewer and fewer people remained as autumn turned into winter.

Every year, over a third of the homeowners and renters head off the Island and back into town or to Vancouver for the season. Boat travel becomes uncertain due to weather and the wood stoves present in most homes require a good deal more effort to maintain during those months. On at least a few occasions, the ferry doesn't run at all because of stormy weather and people are forced to make do on the Island with the supplies they have on hand until the ferry can safely operate again. There are also power outages, but they are usually resolved within a few hours so are little more than an inconvenience. If there is snow, it's a spattering and nothing to worry about; the rain and wind tend to cause the travel and electrical issues.

All things considered, Nate and I welcomed what we regarded as an easy winter on the Island. The winter we endured the year before in Toronto was one of the worst on record and lasted for seven months. There were three major ice storms debilitating the city, rolling power outages, and thick, impenetrable ice on sidewalks and roads. No one in Toronto has a wood stove, so many were without heat in the middle of January's sub-zero temperatures. Reports of major disruptions and city-wide emergencies filled the newspapers with headlines like, "300,000 Still Without Power," and "Extreme Weather Alert: Temperatures to Dip Below −20." People desperate for warmth started fires in their homes and garages and as a result, carbon monoxide poisoning reports were in the hundreds. Emergency shelters opened for the homeless, but there wasn't enough space for the amount of people in need, and the cold temperatures sent many to hospital. Some even died.

Police stations moonlighted as warming centres for those without power, heat, food or water and supplied many with overnight sleeping accommodations. Subways were down, daycares and schools were closed and falling trees took out windows, roofs and power lines daily. Overall, the ice storm of 2013–14 left twenty-five dead across Ontario and Quebec, over a million without power and more than two hundred million dollars in damages across Toronto alone. By comparison, winter on PI promised to be a breeze.

Cooler months turned to cold and talk on the ferry revolved around acquiring space heaters and extra wood for warmth. A recent storm felled three titanic Douglas firs along the Newcastle side, and the trunks and branches were swiftly being chopped up and sold on a first-come, first-served basis. In the days that followed, anyone I saw walking along the main roads was also hauling a wheelbarrow or bucket full of newly cleaved firewood. Our rental was one of the few houses outfitted with baseboard heating so we didn't need wood, but we were at a disadvantage if the power were to go out for any reason. Temperatures rarely drop below −6 in this part of the country so even if the power did go out, I was confident we'd survive.

I walked to the library again on Sunday as I had been doing since summer. I looked forward to the time I spent there with Cristine, and to my conversations with Norm, Cristine's long-time friend who was a retired professor of humanities. Each week when I arrived at one in the afternoon, there was a stack of books on my desk that needed to be re-shelved. Norm left this task to me as he found shelving to be extraordinarily frustrating. "I can't be bothered," he'd say. "You're young—you do it."

While I worked, Norm would talk to me about his marriages, his kids, the case for American literature over Canadian, Hobbesian philosophy and his time teaching at the university, a period in his life he regarded with gratitude, saying, "I'm still amazed that my job was to think and talk about all the things I wanted to think and talk about anyway." He kept his hair clipped short, his beard trimmed, and owned a hyper little dog that he took out for walks each day, sometimes past my house. His favourite tea was available only in Taiwan, so he needed to ship it over. He had a reputation for being sarcastic and wry, a quality of his I liked very much.

I walked in and found Norm and Cristine sitting next to each other behind the front desk. There was no one there but the three of us. "A donation of books was dropped off. Look," Cristine said and pointed to a cloth bag near the front door where I was standing. "A rich collection of romance paperbacks."

"I'll drop them off at the Salvation Army," I said, looking into the bag. I saw the telltale signs of broad spines and raised gold lettering on the covers of the books. There must have been about forty crammed side by side. "I'm going to town later today."

"Please do," added Norm.

I hung my coat and scarf on the hat rack and began putting the returned books back on the shelves. Reaching the top of the shelves was easy as the bookcases weren't all that tall, but I had to rattle off the alphabet in my head to find the right spot for each book. *TUVWXYZ. W–A–L–S–H. WATSON. LMNOP, QRST.* A few times I'd been stuck and had to repeat the letters over and over in my head as I stood facing the fiction section, blankly staring at the spines. This week was a light week, though, with only fifteen books to re-stack.

The last in the pile was a recent copy of a scholarly journal named *Biological Psychiatry*. On the cover was a full-sized black and white photograph of twelve children between four and twelve years old taken at the Auschwitz-Birkenau concentration camp in 1942. The children were lined up behind barbed wire, were all facing the camera and were wearing matching striped jackets. The heading along the bottom read, "Holocaust Exposure Induced Intergenerational Effects."

I stood behind the DVDs to read more about Dr. Rachel Yehuda's research into what she referred to as "inherited trauma." It turned out several studies by renowned scientists proposed that experiential trauma, like fear, is passed down from parent to child through DNA, and for generations. These studies went some of the way to addressing questions plaguing thinkers and scientists for decades: what we refer to as everything from paranoia to chronic depression may be something more like ancestral agony manifesting at the behavioural and neuroanatomical levels, passed onto us from Mum and Dad. Factory-installed grief, so to speak.

I thought of some traumas of my own, like the time I was chased around a neighbour's backyard by three dogs, all as big as or bigger than I was. Five at the time, I can recall my terror: the frantic searching for a hiding place or a helping hand; the frenzied cries escaping my throat as I ran, muscles burning; and then my grandmother, eventually noticing my predicament, laughing as she called away the dogs and herded them back to their owner. I thought of Lily too, running as I had from a dog near Dovercourt Park in Toronto last spring. I'd recognized in her face that same preternatural terror for her mortal life.

"What are you reading over there in the corner?" asked Norm, several minutes of silence later.

"This magazine." I held *Biological Psychology* out for him to see. "Good," he said. "You're far better off studying science than anything else." He got up from the chair at the front of the room and sauntered toward the stove at the other end, sidestepping tables and chairs. Everything—all the books, the reading nooks, the DVDs, the children's picture books, the front desk—was stuffed into the cleared-out basement of Beacon House. There were windows, but they were five small rectangular slits equally distributed along the topmost area of three walls. There was a small bathroom and on the other side of it, a full-sized sink and a stove that protruded widely into the children's section, which was decorated with stuffed animals, streamers, coloured posters of book covers and framed photographs of Island kids smiling from the walls.

"Does anyone want tea? I'm going to put the kettle on and go for a smoke outside. If I don't stop smoking, I'm going to get cancer, you know," he said and winked at me.

"No tea for me, thanks." I shifted my weight to the other foot. "Hey Norm, what do you know about Tabacca Jack?" Norm was practically beside me filling the kettle with tap water. "Keith told me he lived here on the Island." I put the journal back in its place on the shelf.

"Yes, I know the story well," Cristine cut in from across the room. "Jack Craig lived here a few years ago, closer to Norm. They called him Tabacca Jack because he could always be found sitting on his porch smoking and playing that guitar. He home-schooled his son, I guess—I forget the boy's name—and his wife worked somewhere in town to bring in money. Anyway, it's accepted fact that he earned what he got."

"He was a bad guy, huh?" I asked.

"He was the worst kind of guy," said Norm, placing the kettle on the burner and setting the stove temperature to high. "He hurt that wife and poor kid. Always yelling and angry, no matter what. You could hear him hollering all the way down the road. We were all pretty satisfied when they left to go back east."

"Someone told me there was a support group for Jack's wife," I said.

"They started that *after* she stabbed him to death," replied Norm.

At some point during the summer of 2005, Jack Craig, then fifty-four, told his wife to get ready to leave their home on Protection Island where they had lived for almost ten years. He had a notion to start fresh in Kemptville, south of Ottawa, where he had grown up. He said they would sell the house, buy a thirty-two-foot RV and hit the road for Ontario. Jack had dreams of starting another business as he had burned a lot of bridges in BC and figured his luck would be better somewhere else. It had been a few years since he'd started and lost a Chinese restaurant in town, and his appetite for entrepreneurship was creeping back into his thoughts.

His wife, Teresa Phochoo Craig, worked days as a cashier at the Salvation Army and their nine-year-old son Martin stayed home, supposedly home-schooled by Jack. There wasn't enough room on the Island or money in the bank for Jack to realize his dreams of wealth and stardom, and he figured Ontario was as good a place to try his luck as anywhere else. He'd been getting disability cheques as a result of a car accident years earlier, but they still had trouble making mortgage payments on the house. Whether neighbours asked or not, Jack told everyone about his dreams of buying a chuckwagon and turning it into a buffalo burger stand—that or he was going to open up a blues bar.

When they arrived in Kemptville after ten days on the road, Jack noticed an advertisement for the sale of a nearby convenience store. He called the agent's phone number and with a little money in the bank from the sale of the house on PI, he bought the store. The next week Jack parked the RV at his new business; a new life had begun. In the weeks that followed, the Craigs worked to fashion themselves the best home they could out of the four-hundred-square-foot RV. Martin had recently turned ten, and Jack found he could use the boy to help with lifting and prepping for the store's opening. Like on Protection Island, Jack spent the evenings writing and playing songs on his guitar, dreaming of superstardom and plowing through cases of beer.

A doctor from Nanaimo sent Teresa an email inquiring why she'd missed her last three appointments with him, noting that he hadn't been able to reach her by phone. Teresa replied by explaining that the family had moved back east and she wouldn't be coming to any more appointments. The doctor thanked her for her message and said he could refer her to another doctor in Ontario that specialized in depression and suicide. Teresa told him it wouldn't be necessary, that she was doing much better even though it had been only less than a year since her suicide attempt and subsequent two-week stay at the Nanaimo General Hospital. The doctor wished Teresa luck and dropped the issue.

Handy's Convenience was situated near the main road but wasn't drawing the customers or the revenue Jack had anticipated. Six months after buying the store, the money from the house sale was gone, the credit cards were maxed and it looked like Handy's was going the way of the Chinese restaurant. Neighbours had originally offered to help but once they saw enough of Jack's violent outbursts, they chose to keep their distance. Jack was on his own; this business was going to succeed or fail because of him alone. Money was tight, but Jack was still optimistic.

There had been fights, with Teresa and with the boy, but lately the arguments had lessened. Then, in the early morning hours of March 31, 2006, just as the long and dark winter season was giving way to new spring blooms, Teresa slid out of the bed she was sharing with her son, positioned herself between the sofa and coffee table where Jack lay asleep, put a pillow over his face and stabbed him four times in the chest with a thirty-centimetre blade. He died in hospital an hour later.

"Did you know them when they lived here?" I asked.

"Sure," said Norm. "Teresa'd come over to talk with my wife and drink tea. I knew she wasn't happy, but I didn't involve myself in her business. My wife was certainly concerned though."

"The sweet boy," added Cristine. "He was very polite, just a little boy then. He was placed in foster care, of course, since his father is dead and his mother was sent to jail for the crime."

✤   ❧   ✤

The library door opened abruptly and Rebecca barrelled through: grocery bags, her child and a handful of flowers hung from her at all sides. The cold air from outside rushed in with a chill. "For heaven's sake, close the door!" Cristine cried.

"Sorry. Here." Rebecca looked exhausted. "Are you still going to town today?" Rebecca said to me, pushing the front door closed with her elbow. She untangled and dumped an armful of groceries on the chair beside her. "I forgot to buy bread. I was hoping you could pick some up for me if you're going."

I looked at the time and then at Norm and Cristine. Both looked as calm as could be. "Okay if I go now?" I asked and Cristine nodded in agreement.

"I'll walk you to the dock. I'm going that way anyway," Rebecca said.

"I want to go home now, Mum," said her son, rubbing his eyes and squishing his face into histrionic strain. The rain was coming in sideways and pelting the front door. It sounded like we were under attack by BB guns.

I put on my coat and picked up the bags Rebecca had dumped on the bench. Now a part of the gust of energy that Rebecca had brought to the tiny room, I headed out of the library's warm cocoon and into the sideways wind and rain toward the docks.

"Are you sure it's okay to pick up bread? Is your boat working?" asked Rebecca as we walked.

"The boat doesn't work. It stalled again the other day in the middle of the ocean. I have to take the stupid asshole ferry until we get it fixed. Which'll cost me, for sure. We have to get rid of the boat, there's no question."

"I'll never get a motorboat. My rowboat is enough for me to worry about. Listen, thanks for your help."

"It's no problem. I was about to go to town anyway. We really need milk and toilet paper."

"When you drop it off, let's have a glass of wine, okay?"

"Absolutely."

We arrived at the ferry dock and I passed Rebecca the bags I'd been carrying. We hugged goodbye and I watched her and her son trek back up the ramp toward her house. The boy was tripping every few feet because his eyes were covered by a hat that kept slipping down his face. From behind and even at the growing distance between us as she walked, I could feel her strain: at parenting, at loneliness, at living here on the Island and all the extra work that it meant. I felt this strain because it was also my own. I sat down on the cold, wooden bench to wait for the ferry. Blue paint from the bench fell off in flakes around my fingers where I gripped its edges, my knuckles white from the cold wind. As soon as Rebecca disappeared behind a row of trees, I saw figures making their way down the ramp toward me on the dock. I could see the group included a small child and a baby strapped to its mother's chest: Summer, Lauren and their children.

Summer was my age. She'd gotten married recently and was the mother of a newly walking toddler. I watched her as others watched me and noticed that she would smile when people were looking, but when they weren't she would keep her head down, preoccupied and sort of somber. Lauren was younger and was also the new mother of a baby. Rebecca told me Lauren was an American ex-pat who visited the Island a couple years ago with friends and never left. She now lives with a man called John, a long-time Island resident, just a few houses away from me. I'd met John only once but he looked to be twice Lauren's age and spoke of his adult children to me over a campfire a few weeks prior. The fact that his daughter was Lauren's age turned the conversation to Lauren's honey-coloured hair, large blue eyes and bright face. Lauren was beautiful and sharp and perennially joyful.

"Hey guys," I said as they approached. I looked up at them quickly and then back down, trying to avoid the wind and sunlight reflecting off the water and into my pupils.

"Hi!" sang Lauren.

They stood beside me and continued a conversation they'd started earlier, which I didn't mind. For me, the most difficult part of relying on the ferry every day was not the exorbitant cost, the long stretches of waiting or even the general inconvenience: it was the talking to other people, all the time. Because I was still pretty new, I felt more intensely scrutinized in the close proximity of the ferry trips. Pressure to be friendly and polite, over time, turned into a burden of positive self-representation in front of an over-involved and probing public.

My previous experiences with commuting had been on city buses and trains in Toronto and in my hometown of London, Ontario. In those cases a bus ride always meant sitting alone or with a friend, merely another passenger among many other passengers, all coming and going throughout the day. When the buses were full and people were sitting immediately next to each other, there was no obligation to strike up conversation with the man or woman next to you. Of course one could if one wanted to, but the pressure to do so wasn't there. Moreover, if you sit down on a Toronto subway and begin talking to the people next to you about the kind of zucchini you picked up at the supermarket, or the argument you just had with your husband, they will think you have lost your mind.

When someone spends a good part of their day in lineups surrounded by loud talking, laughing crowds of strangers and darting, gridlocked traffic just to get to and from work, a bus ride or subway commute becomes a pause in the environmental cacophony, a moment to be left to one's own thoughts—to read a book, listen to music through headphones or quietly read the paper. On an island with few residents and none of the racket of a city, the same commutes become opportunities to catch up and socialize. Of all the culture shocks I had envisioned before moving to the Island, this was one I had failed to imagine, and as a result I was completely unprepared for it.

If I was out of my house, I had to be cognizant of my behaviour, gestures and mood because people were watching—watching and taking note. Some of those observations even made their way to the PI Facebook page. The last few times I had logged in, I'd noticed discussions taking place about the behaviour of others on the Island, including wild accusations and gossip—among the usual photos of sunsets and upcoming event announcements. I felt like I did as a child hiding under the kitchen table during adult parties and listening as the grown-ups talked about us kids and what we were up to, what kind of trouble we were getting into.

"I'm so happy we're finally going!" Lauren squealed, letting out a peal of laughter.

"I've been waiting since we first decided to do it," Summer said, substantially less exuberant than Lauren, as she guided her child to the bench beside me. Her little daughter grabbed my arm and hauled herself into a standing position.

"Where are you going?" I asked—because I felt like I should. Both women exchanged excited looks.

"Naked bungee jumping!" screamed Lauren.

"It's freezing," I said and pulled my jacket tightly around me.

"It's great. I've done it before, last year I think," Summer said, not to me but to the air in front of us.

"Steven will come too, to hold the babies while we jump. And it's for charity, so it's awesome." Lauren looked over at me as she spoke, smiling.

Summer's husband Steven was tall with shaggy blond hair and smooth features that made him look like an adult-sized boy. He was so subtle in his body movements and gestures that it was impossible to know what he was thinking or feeling about anything. He could stand in a group of people for long periods without speaking at all, occasionally grinning to acknowledge a joke. He'd wear shorts over long johns, knitted sweaters, rainbow-coloured hats and mismatched socks every day. In the time I'd known him, I only ever witnessed one facet of his personality: unassumingly pleasant. Nate regarded this as far more bizarre than I did. The hardest part for Nate was Steven's apparent tolerance for everything, never even showing frustration when tourists were drunk and unruly on the ferry he was operating.

Summer's daughter linked her arm to mine and rested her head on my shoulder.

"Don't sleep now." Summer reached over and pulled her child into her arms.

"I hope you have a good time," I said.

"We will."

I looked out on the water for the ferry and saw its tiny outline approaching us in the distance. The sky was the same grey-blue as the ocean, making it impossible to distinguish sky from water. I imagined disrobing and jumping off a bridge in the rain.

"There's a little rickshaw that takes you up to the bridge where you jump," Lauren added. "On the days when jumpers get a discount for getting naked—Sundays—the rickshaw waits at the top so that anyone can watch. Guys'll take the rickshaw up just to look at all the naked ladies," she said and laughed again.

"That figures," I replied.

On the other side, I walked quickly around Thrifty's to gather up supplies for the coming days and get into the checkout line as soon as possible. I had only an hour before the ferry would leave again for Protection, and I didn't like missing it and having to wait around for the next one. By the time I left the shopping centre, I had about six minutes to get down to the ferry dock. I wrapped the handles of the plastic bags around my palms for added stability and ran through the parking lot, across the highway and down the ramp to the docks. When I arrived I was out of breath and there was a crowd of people waiting at the berth. As the ferry pulled up, everyone moved toward it as a single entity in the hopes of ensuring a place on the boat.

These crowds were not Islanders trying to get home; these were mostly town people and their friends hoping to get a table at the Dinghy Dock floating restaurant. These people were our enemies and I had to get a seat before they did. Because the ferry was owned and operated by the pub, its staff and customers were the priority on busy days, which was every day during the summer. If there were too many people and not enough seats on the boat, the skipper had no choice but to force Islanders to wait for the next ferry while the pub customers were shuffled ahead, regardless of who had been waiting the longest. This situation was especially aggravating when Islanders were carrying bags of groceries, or bringing a pet home from the vet, or commuting with small, tired children. Several heated arguments have taken place in the waiting room due to this injustice.

Among the last to board the ferry, I compactly arranged my bags on the boat floor around my feet and plugged my headphones into my ears. I positioned myself outward from the boat to limit attempts at conversation—an intentional strategy for carving out some quiet time that had a poor history of success. On one occasion, I didn't know a woman was talking to me until I noticed her mouth moving in my periphery. When I turned to face her, I realized she was already several sentences into a conversation at me. Thankfully Rebecca lived close to the docks, only a few minutes' walk from the ramp. When I dropped off her bread, I could rest there for a while before heading home with my bags.

THE VISIT

[TWELVE]

IT WAS DECEMBER AND MY MUM WAS COMING FOR A VISIT. At the last minute, she told me she'd be bringing a few things she'd like to unload on me, things like ceramic pots for outside, a dollhouse my grandfather had made, a small bench and a few extra kitchen items. I told her the boat wasn't working so she'd have to haul all this stuff on the passenger ferry, hoping that might discourage her from bringing it.

"I also have a stand-up freezer. It's great for storing food and it's in terrific shape," she said.

"I can't imagine you carrying around a freezer, Mum."

"Well, you guys would have to help me! What a great freezer."

"Thanks, but I can't take it. Bringing things like that onto the Island means getting them off again someday, and that's just such a lot of work." I stared at the puddles of water on my front lawn, the golf cart plugged into a dangling outdoor outlet, the overgrown swamp grass covering the yard.

"Are you sure?" she asked.

"Positive."

I could hear her disappointment through the phone; she was not as convinced as I was that the freezer was a bad idea.

"Please no freezer, okay?"

"Fine."

I had spent hours on the phone talking to my mum about our life on the Island. I told her about the library and Cristine, about Rebecca who was now my best friend for all intents and purposes, and about the exhausting ferry commutes. I talked about Lily and the freedom she'd been afforded, how living here meant she could play unsupervised a lot of time, could freely take walks with the other kids or head down to the basketball court to play hockey, which was a nearly opposite experience to what we'd had in Toronto. I told Mum about the Christmas party down at Gallows Point for the kids, how there were crafts and candy and a dance-off with prizes. I said I was always conflicted, that the minute something good happened, something crappy always seemed to follow. I told her about the damage to our boat and that we didn't know who'd done it. I told her I was tired all the time.

"Small communities can be difficult places and you may never belong," she said. "There are reasons people choose that kind of life. The question is not *why is this so difficult* because of course it is, you knew it was going to be hard; the question you need to ask is why you chose this for yourselves."

I didn't know the answer. Nate and I had stock answers for whenever someone asked us why we'd come. We said to escape the city or to give Lily a better upbringing or to try something new. After a while, none of the answers we gave sounded true anymore. We'd wanted to get away from the city, no doubt, but when we made the choice to come to PI we didn't understand what that really meant. I was lost and angry. I felt like somehow I'd been fooled.

"We need to leave, Mum. There isn't any work here and we're gonna starve to death if we stay past the spring. I've tried everything and followed every lead but I'm getting nowhere."

"I wondered how long you guys were going to hold out. You've been through a lot so far."

"I cry all the time, you know. I cry because of how tired I am."

"I know."

"And because no matter what we do, what we try to do, it doesn't work."

"Yes."

"People walk past our house and stop to stare through the front windows. Did I tell you that? Into the living room while we're sitting on the sofa. There's nowhere to go for privacy."

"I agree that's odd."

"I feel crazy."

"There are things you still like though, right?

"Yeah," I said, pushing against a feeling of despair that grabbed me around the throat and seemed to squeeze the air out of my lungs. "The beach."

There was a long silence. I couldn't get any words past my throat.

"Listen, if you have to leave, you have to leave. That's okay. Just remember that wherever you go, you take yourself with you."

"See you soon, okay?"

"Okay."

A few days later, Mum arrived for her second trip to the Island. She knew what she was in for. She knew she had to bring any necessities with her because there was nowhere to buy anything. She knew there would be little to do besides taking a walk or staying inside and talking. She knew to bring wine. It was early evening in the winter and blind dark outside, but when the ferry was docking I could make her out buried between two large boxes and noticed the handmade dollhouse perched up on the ferry's roof.

"I thought that dollhouse was going overboard," she said as we unloaded her from the boat and pulled it down to safety. "There was no room on the ferry for it."

We borrowed a dolly from the Dinghy Dock to get the stuff up the ramp and onto the golf cart, a process that involved pushing a hundred pounds up a sharp incline now that the tide was low and the ramp's pitch was at its highest. We were out of breath when we got to the top. We loaded everything into the golf cart, returned the dolly back down the ramp and arranged ourselves in the cart among the boxes and bags.

When I turned the key, I noticed the headlights didn't turn on. We fiddled around for a few minutes and finally decided to attach two flashlights, one far bigger and brighter than the other, to the hood on either side with small pieces of rope. The drive home was set to be more treacherous than usual, what with the flashlight headlights and the extra-large dollhouse blocking views on three sides.

"Don't talk. I need to drive and try to see," I said, slowly pulling us out of the Circle and onto the main road.

"Look, there's one coming right for us!" Mum said, pointing.

"I see it," I said and waved at the driver of the oncoming cart. There was no way anyone would be able to make out my friendly gesture through the blackness between us. We probably looked like people walking very quickly holding flashlights, and not like a moving vehicle at all.

"I hope there aren't any kids on the road," Mum said.

"I can't see the road. The flashlights are just illuminating three or so feet ahead. By the time I hit something, it'll be too late."

"I'm going to get out and run beside you. I'll be able to see better from outside. I can guide you," said Nate.

I drove even slower than normal so Nate could keep up beside us. Only once did I have to swerve to avoid hitting something small that leapt across the road. Nate indicated the turns to get us home by yelling out, "Okay, ten feet, left." Fifteen minutes of this and I finally turned into our driveway, marked by a small, plastic pinwheel Lily had stuck into the ground, its metallic edges reflecting the light from the dim glow of the flashlights.

"We're here," I said and wrestled the driver's side door open with my gloved hands. I got out and lifted the hood, careful not to dismantle the flashlight headlights in case I needed them again soon. I pulled out the long cord from the cart's battery and plugged it into the outlet on the side of the house. By then, Nate and Mum had begun unloading things into the house and all that was left for me to carry was the dollhouse teetering on the cart's backside but tied up with rope. I struggled with the knots in the dark but eventually heaved it from its place and up onto my body long enough to get it over the stairs of the deck and through the front door.

"I thought of bringing your oma with me for a visit but she's eighty-eight years old and can't do all this. After having to climb that enormous hill the last time she said she was close to fainting. You'll have to see her next time you go to Duncan," Mum said as she set boxes on the counter and began opening bags. "It's freezing in here."

"I know," I said. "I'll go turn on the heat."

Nate started filling pots with water and searching the fridge for ingredients to make dinner. He poured us each a glass of wine. I took off my boots and jacket, threw them on the chair by the door and went down the hall to the storage closet to find some extra blankets. I was sorting through pillowcases and towels when I heard an abrupt scream.

"Mum?" I said from down the hall.

"Sorry! There's someone at your door," she called back, laughing at herself.

"Coming!" I said and stacked the blankets like a tower to bring back out.

In the doorway huddled an enormous crowd of Islanders. Through the door and front windows, I could see the group stretching the length of the deck and down onto the lawn and driveway. There were children, dogs and at least forty men and women dressed in puffy coats, some with glittering Santa hats on and others with sprigs of holly tucked into buttonholes and fastened on lapels. As I stood in disbelief, my blankets falling out of my arms and to the floor, they began to sing Christmas carols, loudly and in unison, their voices reaching for the dramatic highs and rumbling through the lows. At one point, a baby in the back somewhere began crying and a brown dog walked in circles before settling on the feet of the carollers at the front. When they finished three consecutive hymns, they handed my mother a cookie tin wrapped with ribbons and shouted Christmas greetings into the open door between us. I stared as the group manoeuvred itself off the deck and back onto the road to the next house.

"Well that was a surprise," Mum said as she turned around to face me, a mess of brightly coloured ribbons covering the tin she held and tumbling over her fingers. The gold on the tin was sparkling in the light. It was lettering, probably a holiday greeting, but I couldn't make out the words.

"Wow!" Lily cried, standing on the sofa, still watching the group outside on the road. "I know all those songs!"

"Is the cat still in?" Nate put down his wineglass and starting searching the floor for signs of Bernie Mac.

"I don't know," I said. "The door was open a while. I didn't see."

"I'll look for him."

"Are you okay? Honey, you look upset," Mum said and walked over to where I was standing.

"It was really nice," I managed to get out of my mouth before I cried for what would be the seventh time that week.

"The strangest thing," started Mum as she crossed the kitchen to put the tin of cookies down on the counter, "was that not a single person smiled."

Rebecca

[THIRTEEN]

"I'M FROM GUELPH, BUT I WAS LIVING IN VANCOUVER SELL-
ing fish before I came here," said Rebecca. We were in the sunroom of the house she was renting for herself and her son. Rebecca had long brown-grey hair that she left down in curls way past
her shoulders. She had blue eyes, lovely hands and appeared to
be, and was, in her early forties. She had poured me two glasses of
wine already. We were determined to be friends.

"I was born in Guelph," I said. "It was the nearest hospital to
where my parents were living in Erin at the time. My mum had
to drive herself to the hospital while in labour because my dad
had emptied the medicine cabinet into his throat from the stress
of it all. She left him on the side of the highway after he started
swerving into traffic."

She laughed. "Jesus."

I spent such long periods of time not talking to anyone besides
Nate and Lily that I found it hard to get into the groove of breezy
dialogue. I was overly eager to have a straightforward conversation with someone new.

"I feel like I don't fit in here at all," I said

"I know. So do I. I've been here for longer than you and I still
feel that way. For the first six months I tried really hard to become

a part of things, but no one invited me anywhere or included me in anything so I gave up. You are, like, my only friend."

"It's pretty here, though," I said.

"It's the most beautiful place I've ever lived. I have waterfront property!" We both glanced out the windows behind us and into Rebecca's backyard. There was a big patio off the back and plants everywhere. Large swaths of rosemary and chives led to a tiny gate and then out to the water. Boats were anchored throughout the bays and harbours of PI and Newcastle; a lot of the boats were also homes for people, even year-round. Rebecca's rowboat was tied up to a rock on the beach about a hundred feet from where we sat.

"Maybe I don't want to fit in," I said. "I don't know. I resent the idea that living on an island is somehow a nobler choice than living in a city. I mean, it's just a choice. Both are choices, morally no better or worse than the other."

"Nobler?"

"I mean, part of why I feel this way is because everyone knows I came here from Toronto, which stands for 'city-slicking idiot' I'm pretty sure. I'm a suspicious character because of that. Both Nate and I are."

"And coming from BC stands for 'pot-smoking hippie.'"

I laughed. It was true. Saying these things out loud was so much funnier than saying them in my head, which only seemed to put me in a foul mood. "When I go back to Toronto, I have to practise smiling less so people don't stare at me like I'm insane. I accidently smiled at someone on the subway a few years ago and she rolled her eyes at me. You can't win."

"No winning," said Rebecca.

"Here they're smiling, sure, but my boat lock also gets cut in the middle of the night without explanation. My problem, I think, is that when I go back—to the west or the east—I'm always coming from the wrong direction. I'm always an outsider."

Rebecca put her wineglass down, gathered her hair in her hands and twisted it all up into a bun at the back of her neck.

"When we walked over to the ferry yesterday, someone stopped us to say that my kid's rain boots were on the wrong feet. I said, *Oh, it's okay,* because what does it matter, right? He's three years old! Anyway, she bends down in front of him, takes off his boots and puts them on the right feet before we can go on our way."

We both burst out laughing, wine spraying across the front of our clothes.

"Well I hope you've learned your lesson."

"No, I'm a terrible mother! He had them on the wrong feet all day today too!"

Rebecca's dog came into the sunroom looking for a good place to take a nap. He sniffed at our wineglasses, circled the coffee table a couple of times and collapsed his body into his bed on the floor.

"Your problem," Rebecca continued, pausing for effect, "is that you didn't get permission from everyone to move here from Toronto and have been paying for it ever since. They really would've preferred to have held an Island meeting before you all arrived, to have at least had a say."

"That's totally reasonable, yes. I'm ashamed we thought we could just live wherever we pleased."

"So entitled!"

The dog lifted his head and turned away from us as our voices reached louder and louder volumes.

"Hey, what do you make of the squirrel?" Rebecca asked. For two weeks, the Island's listserv had been lit up with debates and complaints over a black squirrel spotted terrorizing the place: digging up plants, chewing through wires and generally wreaking havoc. It had sent the community into a frenzy. All kinds of plans were being made to locate, abduct and extradite the animal. Photos captured of it were being posted online. All of it was dead serious business.

"At least it's not just us they're after!" I said, laughing.

"It's not just you at all," said Rebecca, no longer laughing. "You hear about Betty?"

Betty was an older Japanese-Canadian woman who lived in a bungalow near Mud Bay dock and had horizontal teeth. Thirty seconds of talking to her would reveal that she had a different handle on reality. She was a hoarder and the whole of her substantial front lawn was covered in doll parts, boat parts, plastic chairs, inflatable tubes, empty plant containers and a variety of broken household furniture. Whenever I'd seen her, she was carrying around jumbo plastic bags crammed full of stuff.

"What happened?"

"A bunch of people secretly got together and planned out how they would load all that junk she has onto a barge and dump it town-side somewhere. They planned to take all her things from her because her front lawn is an eyesore. Steal from her."

"What stopped them from doing it?"

"Enough people eventually figured that was the wrong way to handle it, I guess. There was also concern that Betty would level legal charges if they did. She may be strange but she's not a dummy. She used to be a professor of biology. You should ask her about that sometime."

In fact, I had met her several times when we had run into each other on the road to the ferry and talked with her about various things. I had even seen her a few days earlier at the docks. She was carrying a grocery bag full of stuffed animal toys. She'd adorned her arms with gold and silver bracelets up to the elbows and was sipping a fancy coffee with whipped cream and caramel all over the top. When I rounded the corner and spotted her, she was already talking to the wall, explaining what sounded like a CIA operation in which she was the target and on the run.

When she saw me, she simply shifted the direction of her voice from the wall to me. I saw her eyes move from the water to her bag and then back to me. She made a joke about Russians and I smiled. She put her bag down on the ground and dug through it as she continued in detail about once escaping the grasp of encroaching agents, of hiding out in Bolivia. After a minute or so she pulled out a red and yellow remote-controlled toy car and handed it to me. She told me to give it to my daughter. She said girls like toy cars as much as boys do. She explained that gender is largely a social and cultural construct before puberty. After puberty, she said, hormonal effects prioritize the acquisition of suitable mates and the participation in established gender-sexual roles becomes more complicated. I thanked her and put the car in my backpack.

"Betty told me once that Islanders tried to ban her from riding the ferry," I shared with Rebecca. "She said *because I'm supposed to be crazy*."

"That happened too, yeah. She was disruptive to the passengers and skippers. Thing is, you can't ban a resident from the only public transportation available to and from the Island," said Rebecca.

"So that didn't stick either?"

"Of course not. How could it?"

"I don't know if we're gonna be able to stay," I said.

"I doubt we can, either. As soon as D goes to kindergarten, I won't be able to manage."

"The commute with a kid every day is rough."

"I won't be able to use my rowboat in the winter, so we'll have to go on the ferry. I can't afford the ferry."

"You can't afford the time it takes either."

"It's okay," Rebecca said and sat up a little higher on the sofa. "I've been here a while now. I lived on an island like I wanted to do."

Blackberry bushes lined the sides of Rebecca's house and crowded the area around the sunroom in particular. It wasn't officially summer yet but the plants were already sprouting tiny buds. In a month or so her yard would explode with blooms and fruit, she'd be rowing again and the kids would be blissfully tearing around their kingdom, running or on bikes, swimming at the beaches or picking blackberries by the fistful and stuffing them in their mouths. At night we'd roast hot dogs and corn over the fire, put the limp bodies of our exhausted children to bed and talk late into the night.

As the weeks wore on, Rebecca and I had found in each other something familiar; so to strengthen our odds of survival, we banded together. We would take turns watching the kids when our schedules were strained or to give the other a break. We ate dinners and lunches together, traded resources like fruits and herbs, and time-shared the golf cart. We had similar thoughts and paranoias about life on the Island and were able to confide in each other when we felt overburdened, picked on or just needed someone to split a bottle of wine with. In those days, we were as close as sisters.

I looked down at my watch and saw that it had gotten late. "I have to get on the next ferry to pick up Lily from school."

Rebecca stood up and collected our empty glasses from the table. "I need to pick up D from Amy's too."

"Take the cart. I don't need it today."

"Okay. I'll bring it back tomorrow morning after I load it up with the firewood I bought from Dave."

"No problem," I said and walked toward the front door where I'd left my shoes and jacket. I skipped down the stairs toward the main road and began walking. The air was changing again, becoming lighter and brighter. The water was bluer than it had been in months. I searched my pockets for my cell phone and ear buds. I scrolled through my stored music and played an album I forgot I had. A band from Guelph. The last time I'd remembered hearing them, I'd seen them live at a bar in London, where I grew up. They were screaming love songs and sweating all over their guitars. At one point the keyboard player hit the keys so hard that the keyboard stand came crashing down. They were dirty and tired from touring all over the country and I remember thinking they were beautiful.

The Curious Myth
of Douglas Island

[FOURTEEN]

TELLING STORIES AND SHARING GOSSIP HAS BEEN STUDIED by cultural theorists and psychologists for years. Results from those studies show that this deeply rooted impulse is not only common but beneficial to the group. We use stories to form intimate bonds, to teach or instruct, to interpret the world, to warn against the follies of the past and to establish loyalties. We share them with our children, our friends, our neighbours and our lovers. The stories we tell—everything from the painful to the uplifting—are made up in part from the truth, in part from our perspective of the truth, and in part from what we want the truth to be. They can also reinforce beliefs, provoke us out of old and no-longer-useful patterns, irritate us or ignite fantasy. Whether fact or fiction, the most compelling part of any story is what it tells us about the complicated architecture of the world, what it asks us to consider and what it reveals about who we are in the process.

I picked up an interesting story from Islanders that PI was originally called "Douglas Island" until Frank Ney, later mayor of Nanaimo from 1968 to 1984, purchased the little island in Nanaimo Harbour through his real estate company in 1959 for the sum of $130,000. The story goes that after Ney divided the island into 344 residential lots, he christened it "Protection Island" in

1960 to replace the former "Douglas Island" named after colonial governor James Douglas. This version of history is so prevalent that it is repeated by visitors to the Island, realtors' listings still identifying PI properties as "Douglas Island" and media news outlets (some local and a few published in the US).

One particular broadcast from the local CHEK-TV news channel featured a journalist travelling from Nanaimo Harbour to PI while discussing this naming theory with a passenger aboard the *Protection Connection*. The story sounded odd enough that I decided to investigate its origins: first online and then through archive collections. What I uncovered only confused me further. There is little evidence of the island ever officially being called Douglas Island and I uncovered no reasons why the name Protection Island was ever so unsatisfactory as to require and maintain an alternative.

In 1960, the not-yet-mayor Frank Ney had planned to transform the uninhabited Protection Island into a neighbourhood of Nanaimo. In an effort to draw investment attention to his new project, Ney marketed the island with a pirate theme and gave the streets names like "Captain Morgans Boulevard," "Pirates Lane," "Treasure Trail" and "Captain Kidds Terrace." While Ney is personally responsible for the pirate-themed street names that remain to this day, he is not responsible for coming up with the name Protection Island, which in fact dates back to the origins of the province, over a century prior to his real estate venture.

When I first came across the rumour of Frank Ney renaming the island in 1960, I went to the internet to see what I could uncover. The search revealed several deaths on or near Protection Island between 1896 and the very early twentieth century. The reported deaths were mining accidents, drownings, and one mysterious case of a young woman who suddenly took ill while spending the day walking through the forest, lay down to rest and never woke up. All the resulting paperwork filed by the City of Nanaimo listed the official place of death as Protection Island, as far back as sixty-four years before Ney came around.

This simple revelation was the catalyst for further investigation. I was obsessed with the question of *why*. Why was there any discrepancy at all about the name of the island? Why, if it was so easy to find official death records and thereby determine the place was not renamed "Protection Island" in 1960, did some still insist on calling it Douglas Island? And if we were going to reject the current name for some reason, why not revert back to its original Snuneymuxw name, or even its later Spanish name? I couldn't understand the thinking and set out to find out as much as I could.

I had no access to the secure PI archives collection but I was able to search the BC Archives catalogue. The earliest map of the area on record was published in 1791, having been drafted by the Spanish navy during an eight-day survey of the Georgia Strait. This map was used as the official guide for Pacific coast explorers for more than fifty years after it was published. The map was detailed, but its most obvious failing was its assumption that the Gulf Islands and other islands of the area were attached to Vancouver Island. This was the case for Gabriola Island, indicated on the map as "Punta de Gaviola," as well as Newcastle and Protection Islands, which were presented as offshoots of Vancouver Island in the form of small ridges referred to as "Boca de Winthuysen."

The next and revised map of the area was Admiralty Chart #1917 published in 1849, which took into account the drawings and sketches of Galiano and Valdez in 1792, George Vancouver in 1793 and Henry Kellett in 1847. This was the map that Governor James Douglas had access to for his expedition to Nanaimo in 1852 in search of coal. Some notable changes to the new map were the renaming of the Spanish "Gran Canal de Nuestra Señora del Rosario la Marinera" as "the Strait of Georgia," as well as a far more thorough rendering of the mainland. Little was done, however, to elaborate on central Vancouver Island or the little islands scattered alongside it, least of all Boca de Winthuysen, the area that still lumped together PI, Newcastle Island and Nanaimo Harbour as a single geographical feature.

James Douglas brought along Hudson's Bay Company surveyor Joseph Pemberton on the 1852 coal expedition to sketch the area properly. In a drawing entitled "Report of a Canoe Expedition along the East Coast of Vancouver Island," drafted in 1852 and published in 1854, the HBC distinctly identified and named Newcastle Island (after the British coal centre Newcastle upon Tyne), but still missed the small land mass next to it. However, according to *British Columbia Coast Names* by Captain John T. Walbran, officers of the HBC promptly rectified this situation when they pursued Douglas's confirmation of coal, finally identifying the separate land mass and calling it Douglas Island. It was changed just as quickly to Protection Island in 1853, in recognition of its position sheltering Nanaimo Harbour.

The time frame documented by Walbran suggests that PI was only truly known as Douglas Island for a matter of months between 1852 and 1853. The reason for this confusion may have been that Douglas Island was never actually an official name; rather, it was used informally by officers of the HBC to indicate its position at the end of the "Douglas Vein" of coal found in 1852. The moniker "Douglas Island" was probably only ever intended as an interim way that the HBC used to refer to places that had not yet been given English names, a useful shorthand to provide context for officers and their associates as they staked out the area and began to establish pitheads for coal mining. In all official correspondence, maps and other archival documents dated after 1854 and stored at BC Archives, "Protection Island" is the name used.

It's prudent to note that the naming of Protection Island predates Canadian Confederation and even the establishment of British Columbia as a province. That is to say, the little island in Nanaimo Harbour has been called Protection Island since before there was a province or even a Canada. A history like this raises questions about why there is any contemporary use of the name Douglas Island at all. The community garden on PI is managed by DIGS, which stands for the Douglas Island Gardening Society. DIGS runs a gardening workshop for kids called the "Li'l

Diggers," which certainly has a better ring to it than "Li'l Piggers" if the "P" were to stand for "Protection," but that still doesn't explain why.

I searched for alternative names that could stand in more sturdily as the island's original, but any story beginning with European exploration of course wholly ignores the perspectives of the Snuneymuxw First Nation, the Coast Salish people who lived on these lands before, during and after Europeans sailed over and began pointing at and naming the things they saw. I did learn that in the traditional Hul'q'umi'num language, Newcastle Island is called *Saysutshun*, which translates to "training for running"; *tl'pilus* means "deep going, under water" and was the place people would cleanse and in other ways prepare for a race or a battle. I wasn't able to identify a direct Hul'q'umi'num name for Protection Island, but I learned that names tended to be given to particular uses of areas on the islands rather than to the land masses themselves. *Qulastun*, meaning "backwards," refers to the bay on Newcastle that faces back toward Nanaimo Harbour; similar names were applied to gathering places in and around modern-day Nanaimo.

My fascination with the Island's historical name is less about purist notions of establishing truth and more about considering the system that allows for these problems in the first place: an accepted program of history that oils the squeakiest wheel, practises truth-by-consensus and perpetuates "fact" as defined by the winners. I have resisted the notion that we might invent the past to appease the needs of the present, or to conjure a public image so different from the available facts.

I brought up the name issue once with the web editor for a popular tourism website, Tourism Nanaimo, when I noticed the first paragraph of the description of PI read, "Formerly known as Douglas Island, after James Douglas the first Governor of Vancouver Island and British Columbia, it was renamed Protection Island in 1960." I sent her an email and attached a copy of an early map from the 1850s showing "Protection Island" over a hundred years before Ney bought it. She wrote me back a few days later and thanked me for my message. A year later the tourism website remained unaltered and I never heard from the web editor again.

THE THIRSTY

[FIFTEEN]

WINTER WAS WANING BUT OUR HYDRO BILLS WERE STILL IN the hundreds of dollars, our boat by then was totally broken and we were relying completely on the ferry for getting back and forth. I decided to quit the steady job I had at the gymnastics studio in town because of the impossible travelling time and depression it was causing me. I needed a new one badly but my applications for teaching positions were continuing to go ignored, online job listings were sparse and returned very few leads, and I was running out of confidence. After dropping Lily off at school one morning, I noticed a HELP WANTED sign in a restaurant window on my way back to the dock.

The Thirsty Camel Café was located halfway between Lily's school and the ferry berth, meaning travelling from home to school to work and back would be feasible if I could get a job there. I could ferry us over in the morning, drop Lily off at school and walk the few blocks to work. At the end of my shift, I could walk to pick Lily up and then back down to the ferry to go home. It promised to be an exciting solution to our travel and money problems. I went inside and approached the twenty-something woman at the counter. I told her I'd been a server and a bartender before and she hired me on the spot. I was to begin the following

Monday washing dishes, cooking and managing the till during peak hours.

Working at the Thirsty gave me thirty or so hours a week at minimum wage plus tips, which was enough for us to stay on the Island. Between Nate's jobs and the restaurant, we were just able to pay our utility bills, cover our rent and keep ourselves all in commuter ferry passes, but nothing more. Ashley, the woman who hired me, was the peppiest person I'd ever met. She loved dogs, believed things were either right or wrong, strived to improve herself and the people around her, and was surprised when something senselessly bad happened in the world. For example, Ashley would regularly come to work in the morning preoccupied by something she'd heard in the news, upset that an animal had been found abused or a girl had gone missing. Other times she'd come in and we'd discuss whatever personal issue was on her mind.

Once she told me a story about the ghost of a man who she assumed was a Chinese labourer in her apartment. She said he wrote messages in the condensation on the living room windows that she was never able to read because they were all in Chinese. Then there was the problem of an acquaintance who always invited her out and texted her, but whom she had no interest in knowing; however, she lacked the cruelty to end the friendship.

There was also the time her boyfriend stayed out all night drinking and brought an equally blotto woman home to their apartment at three in the morning. Ashley said the three of them sat on the couch talking for a long time. She said that the drunk woman made a comment about how she didn't like plants, and Ashley had decided then and there that she could never like her. They stayed up until her boyfriend and the woman passed out on the sofa where they sat.

"I mean, what do you think? I'm so mad," said Ashley.

"How long have you and your boyfriend been dating?" I asked.

"Since high school. Six years."

"I think he's trying to tell you something. Bringing a drunk woman home to your girlfriend in the middle of the night is a message."

Ashley was standing very close to me. One of the first things I'd noticed about her is that she stood and talked very close to others. She was tall, so to talk to you she would bend down a little and position herself directly under your face.

"It's a shitty thing to do, is what I'm saying," I continued when she didn't say anything. Her eyes were low and fixed on the garlic she was peeling at the counter.

"It's not that big a deal," she said finally. "I love him, you know. He's really stressed out right now 'cause of his job. They called him in to work early again this morning. He had to drive to Victoria at, like, five a.m."

"That makes sense," I said and dropped it.

A perk of the job was that I got free lunch on the days I worked. I had to prep it, cook it and do the dishes afterward, but it was free. Another perk occurred when Kendra, the teenaged shift manager, cleaned the restaurant with us in the afternoons before they reopened for dinner later in the evening. She'd give her tip money to Atif to buy us off-sale beer at the Cambie across the street. When the last customer left, we'd lock the doors, turn the stereo up as loud as possible, pass out beers and burn through the closing duties: dishes, mopping, food storage and garbage. We were scheduled to take about an hour to do it, but we always finished in half that and spent the remaining thirty minutes hanging out and finishing off the beer.

Atif wasn't a regular, paid employee at the Thirsty but he'd been around since it opened ten years earlier. He'd helped paint the lotus flowers on the exterior walls and still dropped in throughout the week to get a cup of coffee or help us with jobs we couldn't or didn't want to do. For instance, one time Ashley and I noticed that someone had taken a shit in the alleyway beside the restaurant. It was cringingly obvious to anyone walking past in the light of day and had to be cleaned up as soon as possible. When Atif came in for a chat, he offered to do it. Ashley and I were gagging as we explained to him where it was.

"Around that corner," said Ashley, pointing. "God, please don't let me see what you're doing. Don't bring the bag in here or anything. I can't."

"No problem," said Atif.

"Maybe pour this bleach on the spot after." I handed him a pair of plastic gloves, a garbage bag and a bottle of Clorox I found in the storage room.

"No problem," said Atif.

I'd heard through Ashley and Kendra that Atif was a refugee from Iran and that the owner of the Thirsty liked him and allowed him to help out for a bit of money every once in a while. Atif was unusually happy, always coming into the restaurant singing and laughing. He was around almost daily, sometimes even two or three times during my shift. He was short and thin, wore thick-lensed glasses and smoked a pack of cigarettes a day.

One day while I was eating my lunch and sitting at the front window, Atif pulled out a chair beside me. He told me that he once had a family in Iran—a wife and two children—but that was before he'd spoken out about women's rights, an incident that got the attention of a fundamentalist group. Ten years ago he was targeted as a national threat, his wife was raped and killed, and Atif went on the run with his two sons. He told me he had feared for his life and the lives of his sons. Friends and others sympathetic to his situation raised enough money to send his sons to the UK and Atif to Canada.

He arrived in Vancouver in 2005 with no papers, no money and no family, but he was alive. He started making money selling cocaine, but unfortunately developed a cocaine habit himself and quickly owed money instead of making it. He took the little he had, bought a ferry ticket to Nanaimo to escape his predicament in Vancouver, and met Jacob, owner of the soon-to-be Thirsty Camel. Atif explained his situation to Jacob and Jacob let him sleep in the unfinished restaurant at night if he agreed to stop using cocaine and to help out with the renovations, which he did. After a few months, Atif landed a cash-job washing windows, which was enough for him to rent an apartment of his own.

"Where are your sons now?" I asked.

"I don't know. I haven't spoken to them since they were boys, years and years ago. It's still dangerous for me to reach out," he said.

"I'm so sorry."

"It's okay," he said and patted me on the back. "They are alive and safe!"

Atif clapped his hands together, jumped out of his seat, spun around in a circle and danced up to the counter. Ashley laughed and started to make him a coffee to go. Making a cup of coffee at the Thirsty was a precise art and took about four minutes of concentrated labour including grinding, stirring, stirring again and following two different automatic timers. While he waited, Atif sang Ashley a love song in Persian with all the drama of a theatre production. When Ashley passed Atif his fresh coffee, he kissed her on the hand and danced out the front door of the restaurant to his window-washing job five blocks away.

Weeks later and after an especially gruelling shift, Atif joined me while I ate lunch again and told me a story about when he was a child in Iran playing with his brothers and sisters in the woods. He explained that civilians in his country were in constant danger from civil conflict, the Iran–Iraq War or government death squads. One time he and his siblings were playing as they always did—skipping, hide-and-seek—except this day they heard the sounds of militia, obvious by their loud yelling and even louder trucks. The children ran and hid in the woods as they'd been told to do by their parents, but were eventually noticed through shuffling tree branches and rustling leaves.

The soldiers called out, *Hello children! I see you!* as they trudged through the woods, terrifying the kids beyond belief. In an effort to keep up with her older siblings, Atif's six-year-old sister tripped over the exposed root of a tree and broke her leg. The eldest brother ran back, pulled the girl out of the root cage and lifted her over his shoulders. She was heavy, though, and caring for her was slowing everyone down considerably as they tried to get away.

The four children had a grenade that they'd kept and carried in case of emergencies such as this. Their parents had given it to them for protection. Crouched behind a stack of rocks, the children discussed the situation and the injured girl agreed to stay behind with the grenade and allow the soldiers to find her. When they undoubtedly would, she'd pull the pin as she'd been taught to do, and blow them all up, giving the others a chance to get away. They gave their sister the grenade, kissed her and ran for their lives. Atif said it seemed like only a few seconds after they left her that they heard the explosion, but they just kept running, fear and anger the engines of their tiny bodies. He said they ran and ran until they couldn't run anymore.

That evening as I waited for the ferry to go home, I was struck by how quiet the water was, mild and flat. The city lights reflecting off the surface seemed to skim the top, leaving a dense, black basin underneath. There were no sounds of cars or horns at the docks and the wind was warm, a pillow against my face. My body ached and my forearms were sore from the grease burns, which left small, raised welts up to my elbows. I sat down on the dock and put my hands in the water, dragging them back and forth in the cold, soothing the pain. I imagined leaning forward and falling in, the cool water wrapping itself around my limbs, buoyant and light.

I heard a paddle dip into water and then another. I looked up to see Andy and his dog pulling into the berth. Andy lived on PI but I didn't know where. I would only ever see him paddling his boat between the Island and Nanaimo, or playing the flute outside of the library on Commercial Street in town. He'd wear a dark-coloured cap over his long grey hair and had a great big beard going down to the middle of his chest. His bright blue eyes were among the only features of his face that could be seen through all the hair. His dog was his constant companion and looked as old as Andy as they moved around in slow motion. The dog wore its own orange life jacket, which Andy had to put on and take off on a regular basis. I'd never heard Andy speak—not to me or to anyone else.

The wooden boat banged the side of the dock. Andy reached out slowly from inside and grabbed ahold of the edge so he could fasten a line. The dog sat alert but motionless, waiting until Andy had tied up, positioned the paddles inside the boat and organized the contents of his pockets. After what seemed like five minutes of very little activity, Andy picked up the dog and set it on the dock where it again sat waiting, its eyes always on Andy. Andy carefully stood up and one movement at a time, pulled himself out of the boat. I noticed he had brought his flute with him, which stuck out from his back pocket. He knelt down and unzipped the dog's life jacket. He pulled the dog's legs through some system of interlocking straps and tossed the whole thing back into the boat.

"Evening," I said and smiled as Andy and the dog made their way past me and toward the ramp into town. Andy nodded and smiled with his blue eyes, his dog keeping pace beside him. A few minutes later the ferry slid into the mouth of the harbour, slicing through the even surface. The ride at those times, in the evenings like that, was smooth and still. Most of PI's residents were already home so there were only two other people aboard. No one spoke as we sailed in the dark to the Island.

I took my flashlight out of my bag when we docked and turned it on so I could see where I was going. With no street lights, everything on the Island was the same black colour and there was no way to tell the ground from the water. I'd had fears of slipping off the dock in the dark and sliding underwater, unable to find my way around. I pointed the flashlight at the ground to my right so I could keep the edge of the dock in sight. Once I got past the ramp and to solid ground again, I relaxed and made my way comfortably home. Sometimes if I knew I was alone, I'd sing songs out loud as I walked, partly to pass the time and partly to scare off animals I couldn't see but could hear behind trees.

When I got home, Lily was asleep in bed and Nate was upstairs reading. The lamp he had on beside the bed was the only light in the house. I quietly went to the bathroom and washed my face and brushed my teeth. I looked at my arms under the light and saw that the welts had stopped swelling and were less noticeable than I'd expected. I went to Lily's room, pulled the covers to her chin and kissed her on the forehead where her hair was glued down by sweat. I walked up the stairs toward the bed, peeled off my clothes and let them drop to the ground at my feet, naked by the time I arrived at the top. I crawled into bed from the foot and sank my bones into the mattress. I reached an arm across Nate and crammed my head into his armpit. When I closed my eyes, the black became darker. I saw the water again by the docks except now it was rocking back and forth, inky and deep. I let myself slide off and under the surface. I let my body get heavy, let it sink lower and lower. "I love you like crazy," I said.

"I know," he whispered back.

TIM

[SIXTEEN]

MOTORBOATS BREAK DOWN ALL THE TIME, NO MATTER WHAT
preventive measures you take. The very idea that a gas-powered
engine hangs off the back of a boat, half-submerged in salt water
seems like an optimistic oversight of engineering to me. It's not
that I could imagine a better system—I can't—but the fact that
I spent as much time as I did thinking about and worrying about
my boat was a frustrating waste of time.

During the fall season, Nate and I had the added annoyance of
having to bail the rainwater from the hull every few days or so—
and more than once a day on the times that it rained for hours
on end. Because our bilge pump was broken and we couldn't fix
it, we ran the risk of the boat sinking after a heavy rainfall. This
was a problem not only because it would render the boat more
unusable than it already was, but also because it would be our
responsibility to pull it back out from underwater. Before it was
even officially the rainy-winter season, Nate had woken up eleven
times during nighttime heavy rains to go down to the dock to
fill and dump pails of freezing water from the hull back into the
ocean, his hands hypothermic by the time he got back home.

What we knew for sure was that we had to hire someone to
fix the boat as much as possible and sell it. Since the window was

smashed in, I had positioned a large tarp over the damaged side and in so doing, had pissed off the boat owners I shared the dock with. From what I could gather, the optics of a tarp-covered boat meant I was taking up valuable dock space for a vessel I wasn't using. I got wind of just how grim the problem might be one morning on my way to the ferry, when Rob the skipper stopped me on the road and told me I ought to pull my boat out of Mud Bay and keep it on our front lawn. With uncharacteristic urgency, he offered to help me relocate it that very day.

When I asked what the rush was, he replied, "It's gotta go." I remembered about Rob's own sunken boat and could tell he was serious as hell. It was early in the morning and I was on my way to drop off Lily at school then work a shift at the Thirsty. Afterwards, I had planned to pick up a few bags of groceries. The idea of adding a boat haul to the day's itinerary felt insane. Nate was going to have to do it between jobs on the Island; it was the only way.

"Rob says he'll help, but it's going to take both of you to drive it to the launching ramp and get it onto a trailer," I explained to Nate over the phone.

"I have three jobs today. Does it have to be today?"

"Today is when Rob will help. Tomorrow we'll be doing it on our own and with Lily." My hands were damp and I thought I was going to cry. "Also, this weekend's out because my mum is coming to visit again."

"Okay, I'll figure it out. I'll get ahold of Rob. Don't worry, okay? It's going to be fine." He hung up.

When Lily and I arrived at the ferry, I noticed Tim was the ferry skipper that day. Tim fixes boats, mostly the ferry boats, and occasionally drives them as well. We almost never spoke to each other. He was stocky with coarse, wide hands. He had dark hair that he usually covered with a baseball cap and round blue eyes framed by long, dark lashes. He had an awkward way of walking: head down and leaning forward, as if he were always heading into a blizzard. He appeared forever miserable, but on a few instances when the postal lady was delivering mail to the Island, I had

noticed he perked up. He smiled at her and cracked jokes meant
to amuse her alone. He couldn't have been more than forty-five.

"Tim, can I ask you something?" I said as I got on the ferry.
He was startled that I had spoken. "Yeah?" he said.

"As you might know, my boat doesn't work. We want to sell it
and I wondered if I could hire you to fix it a little before we do."

He straightened his posture and avoided eye contact. "I'm
booked up till summer. And even after that, I doubt it," he said as
he rubbed his eyes with the palms of his hands. He was stressed
out by the idea alone.

"Okay. Thanks anyway," I said and got Lily settled in her seat.
Tim didn't speak to me or to anyone else during the ride to town.

A little later, Nate called with details of the boat. "It's done but
it was a total shit show," he said when I picked up. "Rob was busy
so Steven helped me. He also lent us a boat trailer since obviously
we don't have one. I think he wants it back pretty soon though.
We have to sell this fucking thing immediately."

"Steven?"

"Summer's husband. And naturally the boat didn't start right
away, so that was a whole thing. Anyway, it's done. It's on the lawn.
Now everyone can calm down."

"Thank god. See you tonight."

"K. I gotta go. I have to pour concrete for Danny's foundation,
like, now."

I was in a daze for most of my shift at the Thirsty that day. I
burnt a pot full of falafel balls and couldn't balance the till at close.
I felt like I hadn't slept in a week. At the end of the day, the girls
and I opened a beer and sat down to talk.

"Ashley, did I tell you Immigration called me yesterday? Bunti's
papers have been approved. He should be able to come to Canada
in the spring," said Kendra. Kendra had married Bunti a few years
ago in India but hadn't seen him since the wedding.

"That's amazing!" screamed Ashley.

"I'll need to go to India to get him. Can you cover me at work?
Say two weeks?"

"Yes! Oh my god, are you so excited?" squealed Ashley, her enthusiasm outstanding.

Kendra looked down as she finished her beer and fished through her pockets for the door keys, rattling them around in her pocket. "Of course," she said and smiled. "We've been waiting for approval for months." Kendra turned to me directly.

"Congratulations," I said. From pieces of earlier conversations around the restaurant I had learned a little about Bunti. He was a couple years older than Kendra. They had met on one of Kendra's trips to India three years earlier when she was about sixteen and they'd married right away. Kendra told me her marriage was a "love marriage," which was not preferred by her family. Bunti came from a lower economic class and Kendra had to continually insist to her mother that the marriage was a positive thing.

While Kendra and Bunti were having what sounded like an argument on the phone, I learned that Bunti had some unusual ideas about what life was like in Canada and suffered from near-constant anxiety about what his wife was up to over here. For example, Bunti understood that women here were sex-crazed. He told Kendra that he was worried about coming to Canada and not even being able to order a coffee at Starbucks without being assaulted by women trying to bed him. He also regularly questioned his wife about the male customers who came into the restaurant.

On one occasion, Bunti called up the owner of the Thirsty himself and politely asked that no male employees be hired to work alongside his wife as the inappropriateness of Kendra in such close contact with another man was terrorizing to him. To my surprise, the owner agreed, which as it turns out is the reason I was hired over a far more experienced young man who had put in a resumé just before I did. Kendra was sympathetic to Bunti's worries, but she also found them silly and outdated, and often joked about how naive he was. Kendra would share with us many times, through bouts of laughter, the latest concern Bunti had raised about impending life in Canada: *I'm afraid women don't wear shirts outside, Kendra. Is this true?*

We finished the closing duties early that day so I ran to the dock as quickly as I could on the off-chance I could still catch the earlier ferry home. As I ran down the ramp, I saw the ferry pulling away. I waved and yelled. My noise-making caught Rebecca's attention, and she was somehow able to convince the skipper to pull back into the berth to let me on. I couldn't see who was driving through the plastic window coverings. As soon as the boat was close enough to the dock, I stepped on.

"Thanks, Tim. I appreciate that," I said between gasping for air and stepping over grocery bags and building equipment to get to a seat.

He nodded.

I caught Rebecca's eye across the boat, mouthed *Thank you* and rolled my eyes. She smiled and put her hand up to her head in the shape of a gun. I laughed. She mimed drinking from a glass and pointed at me. Wine. I nodded *Yes*. Thumbs up.

"I can only stay for one glass—I have to get home," I said as we got to Rebecca's place.

"The bottle's on the counter." Rebecca sat on the floor in front of her wood stove and began positioning logs inside.

I poured the wine into two small ceramic mugs and sat down with her on the floor.

"What's the story with Tim?" I asked.

"God, I know. I hate taking the ferry with him, especially if I have to pay later," she said, setting the logs and sipping her wine in tandem. "A month ago I didn't have any cash and he wouldn't let me on."

"Is he from here?"

"Yeah. He's Keith's son. Or stepson, I guess," she said and looked at me, amusement all over her face.

"Keith my neighbour?"

"Who else? When Keith married Tim's mum they moved to that house, where Keith still lives. Tim was a little boy then. His mum died several years ago."

"I heard Keith's wife had died—I didn't know that was also

Tim's mum. My landlady told me that as she was building our house, Keith told her his wife had died."

Rebecca lit the logs and closed the door of the stove. The heat was intense and wonderful. Neither of us moved from our spots on the floor.

"Did you also hear about the fire?" asked Rebecca, leaning back on her elbows.

"Keith told me. He said one day he came home and his house was on fire. And afterwards, when it had burned right to the ground, the whole Island chipped in to build him a new one."

"A lot of people think it was arson."

The kindling in the wood stove had caught now and the flames were reaching the logs. I noticed Rebecca had used a few old Christmas cards along the sides of the stove to get the fire going.

"Someone burned down his house?"

"I don't know, I mean I wasn't here at the time, but that's certainly what people say." Rebecca hoisted herself off the ground and plucked the stray shards of wood that had caught on her sweater when she carried the logs in.

"I've never seen Keith and Tim speak to each other," I said, thinking of both men working down at the pub, passing each other on the docks.

"Tim was nice to me when I first moved here," Rebecca said and smiled. "I'd said to someone that I needed a single bed frame and a few hours later, there's Tim at my door with one. I was really grateful. I thanked him and paid him some money for it, but I didn't invite him in, you know. I got the feeling he wanted me to, but I didn't. That was the nicest he's ever been to me."

It was only five o'clock and already dark as I walked home. I pulled out the flashlight I kept in my bag. Because of the tall, dense trees and lack of street lights, it was so dark that I could barely see anything. The flashlight lit only the circular piece of road in front of me and nothing else. I had to go on rote memory, visualize the many walks I'd taken before as there were no other cues to guide me. As I walked, I tripped over a small mound in the dirt, causing me to drop the flashlight. I picked it up and as I did, the light swept over a small blue boat overturned on the side of the road. For a moment, I had thought it was a person bent over, maybe unconscious. I stood pointing the flashlight directly at the upside-down boat for a long while until I felt calm again and could continue to walk the rest of the way.

What was normally a twelve-minute walk from Rebecca's had become twenty-five due to how slowly I had to go. Every turn meant recalling and reconfiguring myself in order to remain on the correct path. Every movement sensed or sound heard in the darkness, from a bird or other small animal, was exaggerated as threatening. By the time I got home, I was frayed again. I walked up my driveway and turned the beam of the flashlight on the front lawn, scanning for the boat. There it was, perched on a trailer, enormous and still. Seaweed and mussels hung off the bottom like clumped hair pulled from a hairbrush. The wetness glistened in the dim light I tossed on it. I stood at the bow and stared up at the looming boat for what felt like an eternity before finally entering the house.

After we had supper, did the dishes and put Lily to bed, Nate and I went upstairs to lie down and watch TV. It was still early in the evening but my body hurt. I was tired and drained. At one point, a commercial came on depicting a woman answering the door to find a police officer on her front porch. There was no dialogue, but the officer delivered news that made the woman cry and then the camera zoomed out to include a young boy erupting in tears. At some point during the commercial, it is revealed that this is an ad for drinking and driving awareness. I thought of Keith, of Atif, of Tim, of the boat pulled from the water, of Kendra and Bunti, of the kitten stuck in the tree, of everything that was wrong with my life.

"Are you okay?" asked Nate as he set the TV volume to mute,

not that it helped. He turned to face me.

"Everything is really hard," I said.

"I know, I know. Listen, we're going to sell the boat. We're going to be okay," he said as he rubbed my ankles, then my calves, then my thighs. I felt myself relax, sinking into the bed covers, my head heavier on the pillow. And then the power went out.

I sat up and looked around. The lights across the street, the ones in our house, the TV, the rattle of the refrigerator, everything was out. Nate let go of my legs and got out of the bed.

"I'll go find candles," Nate whispered. "I hope Lily doesn't wake up."

I heard Nate rummaging through drawers downstairs. The denseness of the dark and the intense quiet were overwhelming. People tend to remember a power outage as mostly a problem of having no working appliances—no stove to cook with, no baseboard heating—but they often forget the quiet that accompanies it. For me, the problem is not the appliances, but the vulnerability of not being able to see anything and being able to hear every single sound instead.

"I found some." Nate climbed back up the stairs, a halo of candlelight around the top half of his ascending body. He put the candle on the bedside table and got back under the covers. The house was already starting to cool down significantly.

"I wonder how long we'll be out. It could take forever to get it back, you know, on this little island," I said.

"I think it's romantic," Nate said. He put his arm around my shoulders and pulled me to him. From our bedroom we could see outside with almost no obstructions through the front windows. The entire world was total darkness except for the phosphorescence of stars across the sky, so bright that they lit the house well enough to distinguish the surface of everything.

Just as the silence had filled the house, a new sound replaced it, as loud as a paint mixer going off next to my head: the shaking, rolling, barking sound of a forty-year-old generator next door in Keith's front yard. Within minutes of the power outage, Keith had set it up and turned it on, filling the air with war-like levels of jarring cacophony. Unable to talk or think through the noise, I motioned to Nate to please go out and talk to Keith. Nate seemed to contemplate other options before finally pulling on his pants, grabbing the flashlight from my bag and heading next door. While he was gone, I went downstairs to check on Lily. She was sitting upright in her bed when I went in. I held her and told her every-thing was going to be fine, the noise would stop soon. I rocked her back and forth and combed her hair with my fingers. As I held her, the lights in the kitchen fluttered back on and the generator stopped. As if on cue, Lily fell back asleep instantly.

"Keith blew all his stuff," Nate said when he came back in the house. "When the power came back on, the surge of the generator and the electricity coming back all at once fried his computer, TV and VCR."

"What? Why didn't he just wait till the power was restored?" I asked.

"He said he was in the middle of a good movie and he wanted to see the end."

THE BOAT

[SEVENTEEN]

I HEARD ON THE FERRY THAT A NEW PERSON HAD MOVED TO PI and his name was Henry. Apparently he was from Sault Ste. Marie and had been staying on the Island at his sister's place for the past month. The important detail to me was that he had his marine technician papers. I began asking around to see if anyone had Henry's phone number or knew where his sister lived. Nate and I had set aside a few hundred dollars to have the boat looked at and hopefully fixed up a bit before we placed an ad to sell it.

"Oh that must be Francine on Pirates Lane. Her brother's just moved in," Rebecca said as we walked off the ferry.

"I'm going to see if I can hire him to fix our boat so we can sell it."

"If you go toward the library from your place, it's the big green house on the corner of Pirates. I hope it works out." She reached out and hugged me, grocery bags and a stroller hanging from her arms.

I loaded the things I had dragged over from town and a pile of wood into the back of the golf cart and began driving toward the library. I turned left where I thought Francine's house might be, and sure enough on the corner of Pirates Lane stood a large green house with red trim. On the front lawn was a well-maintained fish pond that had a filtration system attached to it and elevated rock piles arranged to create a waterfall into one side. In the pond were shimmering little fish and some lily pads. I parked the golf cart in the driveway, walked up the front path and knocked.

Francine opened the door already smiling. She was less than five feet tall and wore her hair short and dyed dark. She was accompanied by a tiny, yipping dog at her feet. The house smelled like sugar and hot blackberries.

"Hi," I said. "I live that way on Captain Morgans. I'm looking for Henry. Is he here?"

"Henry?" she asked with a faint accent. "He's in the garage at the back. Go ahead and find him," she said, indicating I go around the eastern side of the house.

I thanked her and walked in the direction she told me to go. Appearing behind a tall row of cedar was the garage, its front doors open like a barn. It was stocked with a long, handmade worktable, a table saw, tools of all kinds, six or seven industrial power outlets and a bar fridge off to the side. Two cedar strip canoes, attached to the ceiling by pulleys, hung high above. Outside the garage and taking up the whole of the backyard area were boats and boat engines in varying degrees of repair. The largest, at least thirty-five feet long, was missing its motors but the deck and railings were polished and shining as bright as the day they were made. From the far side of the garage came a figure who must have been Henry, short like his sister but with long brown hair tied back at his neck, holding a can of ginger ale.

"Henry?" I asked as he walked toward me.

"Yes," he said and wiped his hands with a cloth from his pocket. He was squinting through the sun in his face.

"I'm here because I heard you could fix boats. I'm Amber. I need to get my boat fixed before I sell it—just a little sixteen-footer with a sixty-horsepower motor."

"Okay," he said and looked behind him at the boats piling up in his backyard. "As you can see, you're not the only one who's asked for help." He laughed and wiped his face again with the cloth. "This one here," he said pointing to the shiny thirty-five-footer, "needs to be done by tomorrow." We both looked at the shiny boat for several seconds in silence. "I can look at yours this weekend though. That okay?"

"That's great. It's on our front lawn right now. We pulled it out of the water a few weeks ago," I said. I noticed that I was hanging my head down when I said this like I was ashamed. I lifted it back up.

"On a trailer? Okay that's good. I can get a look at the hull if it's out of the water." Henry walked toward the small fridge and took out another ginger ale. "Why don't you bring it over Saturday morning. Bring it right here." He opened the can and drained the whole thing in one gulp.

"I don't have a truck to bring it here. I'm just up the road there, next to Keith's. Do you have a truck we could use?" I asked.

"I have one I can bring over to your place then. No sweat," he said and shook my hand. "See you Saturday."

"See you then," I said and walked back to my golf cart.

As I pulled out of the driveway I noticed Francine running out of the house waving at me. I stopped the cart. *Wait!* she was saying. "Here, a pie!" Francine ran around the front of the cart and to my side. She was smiling and holding a great big pie in her hands. I jiggled the door a few times and slid it open.

"Take this pie—I have so many in there!" The pie was hot, right out of the oven. It had little leaves cut out of the crust on the top for decoration.

"Thank you, Francine," I said and returned her smile. I took the pie and put it on the seat next to me. "It looks amazing."

"No, no!" she said, beaming.

I pulled away. In the side mirror I could see Henry and Francine standing on the road waving goodbye.

That Saturday at nine o'clock in the morning, Henry pulled into our driveway in a black pickup truck. He was already hitching the boat trailer to his truck when I saw him. I gulped down the rest of my coffee, kissed Lily on the top of her head, yelled to Nate upstairs that the boat guy was here and ran out the front door. I climbed up and into the cab of Henry's truck and we drove back to his garage.

"First thing we have to do is see if we can get this motor running," Henry said as he hopped out of the driver's seat. His small stature was exaggerated by the enormity of his truck. "Come on this way, you might learn something."

We walked to his garage around back. Everything looked the same as it had the first time I saw it except the big, shiny boat that was there a few days ago was gone, freeing up a remarkable amount of space. I stood outside near the door as Henry went in to search through boxes on the floor. There was the sound of a radio playing quietly but I couldn't see where it was. After searching through three different boxes, Henry had collected what he needed and set the tools and devices on the worktable.

He walked quickly back out of the garage and toward the trailer still attached to his truck in the driveway. He waved for me to follow. He pulled another box out from inside the truck bed and began sifting through that one as well. From the box he pulled out a pair of "earmuffs," a device composed of two round suction cups attached together by a rubber band about four feet long. Henry explained that these allow mechanics to run outboards on dry land without having them overheat. He attached the device to the exterior hose and dragged the whole thing over to the stern of the boat. He affixed the earmuffs to each side of the motor and walked back to the house to turn on the hose. The effect was that water from the hose was now rushing the motor to simulate being at sea.

Henry then climbed the side of the trailer, swung his body into the hull of the boat, and using the keys already in the ignition, started the motor. The sound of the motor spitting and sputtering came at a shocking volume now that it was no longer submerged in the ocean. I jumped back and covered my ears with my hands.

Henry looked over at me and laughed. He listened intently for a few seconds, swung himself back down from the boat and came around to the back so he could get a good look. He waved for me to come toward him. Standing next to the motor like that meant that we couldn't talk to each other without yelling.

"It could be that your carburetor's clogged up—likely the jets need a good cleaning," he yelled over the roaring noise. "I'll clean up your spark plugs while I'm at it. They're probably covered in oil, which is why your motor won't start right away."

"Sounds good," I yelled back.

"It sounds like shit, actually," he joked and jumped back onto the boat to turn off the motor before returning to the ground. He motioned for me to turn off the hose and unhinge the rubber suction cups. He lifted the hood of the motor and pulled out the spark plugs one at a time and put them in his pocket. Back in his garage, he dumped the spark plugs on the worktable and plugged in the blowtorch that was hanging on the wall in front of us. "We're going to torch off all this crud here," he said, pointing to the bases of the spark plugs, which were dark with grime. "Your spark plugs light up the motor. If they're clogged up and covered in oil like this they can't do their job."

Henry fired up the blowtorch and began burning off the oil, smoke billowing from the spark plugs as he did it. After each spark plug was cleaned to its original silver colour, he let them cool off at the side of the worktable. "Don't touch those, they're hot as hell," he warned.

The sun was making its way high in the sky and the garage was heating up. Sweat beaded on my forehead and stung my eyes. One by one, Henry took pieces from the motor and brought them back to the garage. He cleaned each piece with a solution and explained to me its function in the motor, setting each piece aside to get a new one. When all the necessary pieces were dry and reassembled in the engine, Henry suggested we take the boat to the water and "see how she floats," as he put it. "Got enough gas in there for a little spin?" he asked once we were back in the truck and driving to the emergency dock to unload the boat.

"The tank should be almost full," I said. I remembered filling it up the last time we used the boat at the marine gas station in the harbour. At the dock, Henry turned his truck around to back the trailer and boat into the water. He told me to get into the boat while he slowly drove it into the water. Once the trailer was submerged, Henry parked his truck on a sharp angle, jumped out and waded into the water to pull me and the boat off the trailer and into the ocean.

"As soon as you're off, turn on the motor and reverse outta here," he yelled from behind me, waist deep now in the water. "Okay, now. Turn it on!"

I pressed the key in the ignition, but the engine wouldn't turn over. Henry was already stepping back into his truck and pulling the trailer out of the water, leaving me floating near the base of the dock as he drove in the opposite direction. I tried again, and this time raised the choke lever high. The motor spit and chugged. I was drifting backwards toward the side of the dock railing. The current was much stronger than it looked and the boat was being pulled quickly around the side of the dock. "It won't start!" I yelled up to where I imagined Henry probably was.

"Try again!" I heard his voice call back.

I tried twice more. The current was threatening to push my drifting boat out to sea. I was going to have to paddle back to the dock, which would be difficult if I didn't get a handle on things. I pulled the keys from the ignition and grabbed onto the side of the quickly departing dock with both hands, holding on as hard as I could. The boat strained to keep moving but I was eventually able to stabilize it long enough to tie it to the dock with the spring line. I looked down to see my forearms were red and scratched by the force I had to use.

"Up here!" called Henry.

I looked and saw Henry running up the ramp attached to the dock. He was about ten feet above me in the air.

"I'm going to jump onto the boat!" he yelled and slipped his body over the ramp's railings.

I moved toward the back of the boat to give him a place to land and watched as he jumped from the ramp down to the boat.

"It won't start," I said again. He started investigating, trying to see where the problem was. The sun was right above us. I was squinting through it and because of this, was only able to see the sharp refracting light off the water and the infinite blue of the sky. I could not even see Henry.

"Yeah. I don't think the gas lines are open. Let's see," he said. "Okay, try it now."

I wiped my eyes with my arm, poked around to get the key in the ignition and tried again. My hand was shaking but this time the motor thundered back to life.

"Let's go for a ride!" shouted Henry behind me.

I untied the spring line and pushed us away from the dock as hard as I could. When we'd gotten several feet away, I pushed forward hard to move us to stronger and stronger speeds. I wanted to get as far away as I could. I didn't want to be scared like I was back there, tied up to the dock. I didn't want that feeling of helplessness to return, or the opposite terror of being pushed out to sea, pulled farther and farther away by invisible hands below the surface of the water.

Halfway between the emergency ramp we had left and the Mud Bay Dock ahead of us, the motor started failing again. Henry lifted the hood and inspected things, but wasn't able to see right away what the problem was. Closer to Mud Bay than the emergency ramp behind us, we decided to try and push the motor forward and tie up at the community dock until we could figure out what to do next. This time, I made sure to tie up as far away from the head of the dock as I could.

CAROL

[EIGHTEEN]

I WALKED PAST CRISTINE'S AND COUNTED THREE MORE houses as Carol had reminded me to do over the phone. I had never met Carol, but Cristine convinced me that reaching out to her might help with my job search at the university. Carol had, after all, been the dean of community education at the university not long ago so as soon as Carol was free to meet with me, I went over. At the foot of Carol's driveway was a small, stone pathway and several potted plants. I walked along the path, occasionally ducking my head to the left or right to avoid the low-hanging tree branches that reached out like arms into the path. The walkway led to an arched wooden door with a heavy iron handle. I knocked on it and waited.

"Come in!" Carol said as she swung open the door. "I'm moving and there are boxes everywhere. I apologize." She asked me to take off my shoes and meet her in the kitchen. I took my sandals off and slid them over to the side of the doormat. The terracotta floor tiles were cool against the bottoms of my feet as I walked in the direction Carol had indicated a few seconds earlier.

Carol had pin-straight white hair. She kept it in a short bob with long bangs sweeping across her eyes. She wore black framed glasses on the bridge of her nose and looked at me over the top of them, which seemed to magnify the deep brown of her eyes. She wore simple, silver jewellery around her neck and wrists, and a pale linen shirt. The front entrance of the house was wide and white with each room emptying into it so that the entire house could be seen from the front door. There were woven rugs on the floor and comfortable-looking sofas and chairs arranged in every room. There were tall bookcases along a middle wall with several hundred books in boxes on the floor and more still left on the shelves. There were drawings and paintings everywhere, some in frames and some rolled up like maps and leaning against the wall. The back of the house was nearly all windows; it was clear by looking out through them that the house had been built as close to the water as possible, like Cristine's. From the sliding door in the kitchen, the beach was only a few feet away. Also like Cristine's, the house was bright and quiet with only the sounds of waves pushing and pulling against the sand.

"Sit," Carol said and motioned to the dining table by the window. "I'll make some tea and we can talk."

I sat facing the water and glanced around her kitchen. I felt an unusual comfort being there, in a stranger's house, as she made familiar sounds in the kitchen behind me: tearing tea-bag packs open, handling cutlery, pulling tea cups down from the cupboard. She came to the table with our tea mugs and a plate of buttermilk biscuits and sat down across from me.

"So. You'd like to get a teaching job at the university," she started. She took a biscuit from the plate and bit it in half.

"Yes, I think so. I'm not really qualified to do anything else," I said. I stirred the tea bag in the cup before lifting it out and placing it on the saucer between us.

"Have you spoken to Jay? I gave him his first teaching job there a long time ago. He owes me one," she said and winked at me.

"I did. I sent him a copy of my resumé and met with him for a coffee a couple weeks ago. He was very polite about it, but he let me know that working there was a long shot."

"I'm retired now but feel free to let him know you talked to me," she said. "I'll send him an email myself, actually."

"Thank you, Carol. I appreciate that."

Jay and I had stood in the parking lot of the university only a few weeks earlier after we'd been evacuated from his office due to a fire alarm. He explained to me that I could try to apply to teach at ElderCollege while I waited for something more permanent at the university. The benefit of teaching at ElderCollege was small class sizes and total control over the curriculum. The drawback was that you did it for free.

"I guess you've seen these boxes everywhere," Carol said and turned around to have another look herself. "Those are all his books. My husband's books, maybe thousands in total. He died recently of cancer. I plan to donate them to the university." Carol stirred her tea slowly and smiled into the cup.

"I'm sorry."

Carol intertwined her long fingers around her tea mug. "I spent my whole life with him, you know," she said. "I talk to him every day, here at the kitchen table." She talked as though I were an old friend, someone she was used to confiding in instead of the stranger I really was. I took her comfort with me as a sign I could relax.

"Out loud?" I asked.

"Yes, out loud. I sit here at the table with my tea and talk with him. Like this. We used to talk and talk. He loved talking. That box by the door is a box I found a few days ago full of his letters. He would spend hours writing letters to everyone he knew when he was tired of talking."

I looked at the box, the tips of dozens of different-coloured envelopes forming long rows inside.

"There are several in there between my husband and George Bowering. Do you know him?" Carol asked.

"I've heard of him." I looked again at the box.

"They were close friends, Michael and George. George was at my wedding, at the hospital when my daughter was born and so on—a friend of my husband's for decades. Anyway, I found those letters and I called up George to see if he had any interest in having them back. George said, *Not necessary. I have copies of every letter I've ever written.* Carol imitated George's voice as she said this, low and bold. "As it turns out, before George had published his first book, he made carbon copies of each of his letters and mailed them to the National Archives. He would attach a note explaining that in no time he would be the most famous writer in Canada and that copies of his correspondences would be of certain value in the future." Amusement was dancing all over her face.

"You're kidding," I said.

"Not at all."

For three hours, Carol and I sat at the table and discussed the problems of teaching and university administration, the egos of writers, the perils of optimism and the fact that she was soon to move out of the house she'd shared with her husband and off the Island to live with her adult daughter.

"I sold this house to the first people who gave me an offer," she said, pouring us more hot water for tea. "I don't understand people who hold out. Your house is only worth what someone else is willing to pay for it."

She described the conversations she would have with her dead husband, including some of the jokes she would save up to tell him at the kitchen table when she got home. "I tell him strange dreams I have too. I just had a dream that I was swimming farther and farther out to sea and I woke up panicked that I had swum so far out I wouldn't be able to get back to shore."

She said she felt him with her all the time but that she yearned to hear his voice again. Once while she sat at the kitchen table, she began to cry from missing him so badly. She'd said aloud, *Please, I want to hear your voice just once more.* As she said it, she heard her mailbox slam shut outside and went to see what had been left in it. Among the stack of letters and flyers was a small, brown package from a friend in Vancouver. She opened it to find a cassette tape.

She put the tape in the tape player, pressed PLAY, and out came the voice of her husband reading a poem he had written for her and performed many years earlier. She recalled instantly the evening in Montreal, and how she sat at a tiny table by herself while her husband took the stage and read it out to the crowd. "What do you make of that?" she asked.

I looked past her shoulder to the water outside. I saw two freighters positioned near Nanaimo Harbour, probably making a pit stop in town before heading out again. The freighters had been waiting there for days, as I'd seen them do many times. The men aboard were used to long trips away from land, sometimes for months at a time, depending on where they started from and where they were going, so the ships were well-stocked and the men unusually patient.

Because the grocery store was located mere feet from the harbour, the men from those boats could sometimes be found strolling the aisles to restock. You could tell they were the men from the freighter ships, or fishermen up from the US, because of their behaviour. Having been more or less alone for long stretches and unaccustomed to ordinary social life, their gestures become unusual and their speaking patterns odd. Often they were unshaven and wore unwashed clothes. The grime on their hands and beneath their fingernails would be considerable. Waiting in line for the cashier, I once stood behind one of these men and was able to watch him. There was a sense of standing near a ghost, next to someone who was unconvinced of his own presence in the grocery store, let alone anyone else's.

Carol's house rocked and creaked from the force of the wind throwing itself against the exterior. "I think that's a wonderful coincidence," I said, thinking about the cassette tape and the poem. I watched her closely to see if my words had upset her. If they had, I was ready to take them back.

"I'm not suggesting anything supernatural," she said. "Just that it was a gift."

The Ghosts of Gallows Point: Part Two

[NINETEEN]

PETER KAKUA WAS A HAWAIIAN LIVING IN NANAIMO WITH his wife Que-en and her parents. A larger than average man, he had worked as a fur trader for the Hudson's Bay Company since 1853. On December 3, 1868, Peter went to a tavern to drink for a span of several hours, as he was known to do. At home waited his wife, her parents and Peter's newborn daughter.

At this point, two versions of the story of Kanaka Pete are given: one claims that Peter came home late after his night of heavy drinking to find his wife and father-in-law having sex. Flying into a rage, he grabbed an axe from the nearby shed and began swinging in all directions until everyone in the house was dead, including the mother-in-law and his infant child.

A second version posits that Peter and his wife had a terrible fight after he came home from the bar. During the fight, his wife revealed that she had intentions of leaving him and taking their child. As she began packing, Peter seized a nearby axe and hacked his wife, her parents and his infant daughter to death. Whichever story you choose, the results are the same: four members of Peter's family were found in his home hacked to death by an axe.

Staring down at the bodies of his family, Peter suddenly became concerned for his freedom and rounded up a small amount of food, threw on a warm coat and propped the canoe he had made over his head to carry it down to the water. He tossed the bag of food into the canoe and climbed inside. On such a cold and dark night, and still grievously drunk, Peter's initial plans to paddle to Vancouver and escape the law soon became unthinkable. He decided instead to make a pit stop at Newcastle Island to spend the night by a campfire until he was sober and rested enough to carry on to Vancouver the next day. He grounded his canoe on the south side of the island and started building a fire.

Back in town, neighbours eventually responded to the screams that had come from Peter's home an hour before. Two gentlemen found the hacked and bloodied bodies that Peter had left behind, and alerted the local police. A midnight search for the missing husband began immediately and by the next morning, officers had located Peter's makeshift campsite and the sleeping man beside it. It took four men to bind Peter and escort him back to town, first by boat and the rest of the way on foot. Twice Peter attempted to jump out of the boat and twice he was hauled back in. Within six hours of the crime, Peter was taken into the police station and charged with the murder of three adults and a child.

The horrific circumstances of the slayings spread throughout Nanaimo and thoroughly terrified the tiny community. Theories about what must have driven Peter to commit such depravity flourished. Accusations of his temper, alcoholism and likely insanity influenced those in charge of Peter's legal destiny and without much of a trial, Peter Kakua was sentenced to death on February 10, 1869, two months after the bodies of his family were found. His hanging took place on March 10 at Execution Point on the then-uninhabited Protection Island, little more than a decade after the two Coast Salish men were hanged at the very same spot. Peter's body was buried on Newcastle Island, primarily used at the time to contain the dying and infected victims of smallpox.

Decades later, Peter's grave was unintentionally excavated as the Vancouver Coal Mining and Land Company began construction for what would become part of the Number One Coal Mine. His bones were reburied on the far side of Newcastle Island, known later as Kanaka Bay. Since Peter's reburial, many reports of troubling incidents on Newcastle and Protection Islands were blamed on the unruly spirit of Peter Kakua. The mine's explosion shortly after its inception was thought to be the work of Kanaka Pete's spirit until forensic evidence pointed to mislaid dynamite as the likely cause. Mysterious drownings off the beaches of Protection Island up until the late sixties were considered by some to be the work of evil forces inhabiting the land.

Even now, every death or missing person report brings with it the spectre of the past. Campsites on Newcastle Island include signposts and engraved markers describing the circumstances of Kanaka Pete's death. As recently as 2007, a group of university students is rumoured to have toured Newcastle Island in the hopes of uncovering Kanaka Pete's grave, planning to spend the night telling ghost stories to each other over a campfire. It is confirmed that the students arrived on Newcastle, but not that they ever returned home.

Bizarrely, around the time of their alleged disappearance, individual severed feet were found washed up on BC's coast and more along the beaches of Washington state, some of which were identified through DNA analysis as known missing persons. Major news outlets such as the *National Post*, CBC and CNN covered the story as feet were repeatedly found. By the discovery of the fifth foot, international news outlets picked up the story as far away as the *Cape Times* in South Africa. Between August 20, 2007 and February 7, 2016, a total of sixteen human feet were found and scrutinized, all recovered in roughly the same area, and most from the Salish Sea in lower British Columbia.

Investigations linked the feet to the remains of known suicides, missing persons and fishermen purported to have been lost at sea, but speculation continued to range from plane crash debris to evil crime cartels. The second foot, a man's size-twelve right foot, was found by a couple on August 26, 2007 along the shore of Gabriola, a stone's throw from where my house was on Protection. It was waterlogged when they saw it. They said it looked like it had been dragged around the beach by an animal.

Late in the day on a Friday afternoon, after I had worked an early-morning shift at the Thirsty and Lily was home from school, the tide was low enough that it was possible to walk from Protection to Newcastle. I packed Lily a few crackers and a bottle of water and took her over the channel for a hike. In the middle of our trek across, I had to lift her onto my back as her boots were sinking in the thick muck and she was expending a considerable effort just to put one foot in front of the other. After twenty minutes, we were scaling the slippery tide rocks and heaving ourselves onto the solid ground of Newcastle Island. We walked through the public playground, past the picnic tables and past the steel-drum garbage cans. We toured the public path, laid by city workers with tidy mulch, until we finally discovered the plaque indicating the burial area of the infamous Kanaka Pete, a plaque that could only warn of the "most likely" site since the exact location was never determined.

We walked past the sign and off the path into the forest. Pine, maple and fir stretched tall into the sky above us. Rows of fallen trunks, delicately covered in moss and sprouting fern leaves, scattered the ground. Through the trees, the ever-present sight of the even ocean was cutting the straightest of lines across the world. We stopped once to eat a handful of crackers and wipe the mud from the hems of our pants before we headed back across the channel and home to make supper. On the Protection side, Nate met us on the road and suggested we hike home by way of the woods behind our house.

"What the hell is that?" I said as we stepped out of the forest toward the back of our property.

"I can't tell. A tent?" Nate asked.

"It's a house for fairies! Sadie said the fairies live here and have fairy babies and make sparkly fairy dust. You can make wishes on them if you catch one!" squealed Lily.

I walked around the outside of what looked like a tree house on the ground. It was no more than four feet tall and about three feet wide. The walls were made of fibreboard, nailed together badly and decorated with old licence plates. Long strands of coloured twine holding rows of plastic and glass beads were tied around the hole that must have been the doorway. I looked into the hole but I didn't see anyone. "Maybe it's a kid's clubhouse," I said.

Lily tugged on the strings of beads, trying to loosen one to keep for herself.

"How have we never seen this? It's practically in our backyard," Nate said, walking around its perimeter and pushing gently on the walls.

Scattered on the floor of the structure were papers buried under a thin layer of dirt. Upon closer inspection, there were also coins, nails and more strands of beads, all covered in dirt and fallen maple leaves. I pulled on a corner of one of the pieces of paper and lifted it out of the hut. In the light, I could see it was a drawing made with a black ballpoint pen on plain white paper. In the centre of the page was the figure of a wolf-man standing on two legs. It held a large branch in one of its hands and in the other was a rolled-up scroll. It faced forward, bearing its teeth. On its head were two pointed horns.

"Looks like the devil," said Nate, considering the drawing over my shoulder.

"Shut it!" I didn't want to draw Lily's attention to the conversation, to have to explain the devil to her. Lily had managed to pull off a string of beads and was now peering into the devil tent, the beads clutched tightly in her hand.

"Don't go in there, babe," I said after her. "There are nails and other sharp things on the ground and I don't want you to get hurt."

"It's so cool," Lily said pulling her head back out. "It's like a secret fort." She was smiling and her eyes were bright with excitement.

"A weird secret fort in our backyard that no one has seen until now," said Nate.

I placed the picture of the demon wolf-man back on the floor of the devil tent. When I stood back I noticed how starkly white the paper appeared next to the filthy objects around it. I bent back down and swept a layer of dirt over it with my hand.

LEAVING

[TWENTY]

"HOLY SHIT," NATE SAID FROM HIS DESK, SCROLLING through his email. "Remember that job I applied for on the mainland a while ago? I got it. I got the job!"

"Just now?" I asked, kicking the bedsheets off my legs and lifting myself into a sitting position on the bed. It was six in the morning but the sunlight was already tearing through the flimsy blinds and filling the house with daylight.

I remembered when Nate had applied for the job on the Sunshine Coast. We were applying for all kinds of jobs, all the time. A few weeks earlier we had even talked about moving to Montreal, where Nate had once lived, and starting again there. Montreal had affordable housing, several colleges and universities I could work at, and there were lots of people we knew who lived there. We had talked about moving to Vancouver once too. Ideally we wanted to stay in BC but we needed work and were ready for the reality that we'd have to go back east.

"Just a sec," he said, reading through the email. The house was quiet and bright, an unusual combination of stillness and potential.

Downstairs Lily had awoken too and I could hear her quietly talking to her toy penguin. I noticed through the front window that the tarp had blown off the boat and was now draped over the driver's side and into a lake-sized puddle at the base. I could see, too, that there was at least a foot of water inside the hull.

"They offered me a salary and a contract," Nate said, turning around to look at me. "They want me to start next month."

"Holy shit," I said.

"Exactly."

When Nate had applied for the job, they'd interviewed him after flying him to the mainland. Afterwards, Nate had called me and told me about the town we would be living in about a thirty-minute drive from Sechelt, a small community northwest of Vancouver. He said it was a lot like PI, surrounded by water and trees, but that it had a school and a grocery store and a doctor's office. He said it was perfect.

"We need to get rid of the boat. We need to find a new place. We need to move all our stuff across the ocean and into the new place, and we only have a month." I stood up out of the bed. My heart was beating fast and I felt anxious and disoriented.

"We have three weeks," Nate said.

That morning after breakfast, feeling like we had no time to spare, Nate logged onto the Protection Island listserv and posted an ad for the boat: *Fire Sale: Green motorboat with a broken window and (sometimes) working engine: $600 cash*. Six hundred dollars would cover the work we'd paid to have done on the boat, but we would have to eat the cost of the boat itself. I noticed our other posts below the new one, going all the way back to the year before. Posts about looking for someone to fix our boat, a missing cat, asking for a cup of sugar to make peanut butter cookies. I saw the post about the broken window too. *Problem Green Boat at Mud Bay*, it was called. I had sent out a sort of open letter to the Island explaining our history and that our boat had been vandalized at the dock. I asked for help. The post didn't generate any responses but it did incite a couple of phone calls, people eager to know more information about what had happened. While I reread the old posts, a man replied to the new one, asking to come by later that day with his two sons to check out the boat.

I called my mum, excitement replacing my earlier anxiety as I told her about the town we would be living in. I sent her some images of the area that I'd found online. "He's perfect for the job," I said. "It's basically the best thing that could happen."

"I didn't realize he was applying for jobs elsewhere."

"We both have. There's no work here," I explained. I was sure I'd told her. "We've been keeping our eyes open for other options for a while now."

"Eyes open where? Ontario too?"

"All over."

There was silence on the line. After a few more empty seconds I told Mum I had to go, that I had a lot of things to get to, and hung up.

I went downstairs and poured a bowl of cereal for Lily's breakfast and then ran back up to get dressed. To distract myself, I spent the next thirty minutes on the front lawn filling a yogourt container with water from inside the boat and tossing it over the side, filling it and dumping it probably ninety times. I wiped down and dried the seats of the boat, checked the gas, the gas lines, and made sure the keys were easily accessible for when the guy came over to look at it later. When I came back inside, Nate and Lily were dancing wildly in the living room to YouTube music videos. Nate was as happy as I'd ever seen him.

I went into the office and turned on the computer. I searched for listings in or near the area we would be moving to, but the remoteness of this new place meant there were only three available rentals. One was a single-room cabin of three hundred square feet sitting on five acres of land. Part of the lease agreement was to care for the animals that roamed the property: horses, chickens and two goats. The rent was $350 a month but the amount of living space for the three of us wasn't doable by any stretch. The second was a large four-bedroom house about a fifteen-minute drive from the office. The house looked modern and clean but way too big for the three of us.

Near the end of my search I found a two-bedroom house, no more than a kilometre from Nate's work and tucked behind a towering span of trees. It had a great big porch off the side and was available right away. I called Paul, the person listed as a contact. When he picked up the phone, I explained our situation—that we couldn't view the house as we were still living in Nanaimo, that we had to move in three weeks, that we had a daughter who would be going to the local school, that we paid our rent on time and that he could trust us. He asked to speak to Nate and had a long conversation with him. By the end of our chat, we'd secured ourselves as Paul's new tenants.

"I feel like this is a dream. Or like it isn't really happening," I said to Nate.

"I know. Me too. All we really needed was a job. Some money so we aren't struggling as much all the time."

"I can't comprehend it."

"What?"

"That altering one thing, moving the decimal point over as you say, could change everything about everything."

"It's not a decimal point, though. It's a big thing. It's a real job. There's no way we could have kept this up here for much longer. I'm amazed we were able to do it for a year."

"I can't believe we're leaving." I looked around at the house we'd been living in for over a year. I thought of how much I loved it when I first saw it. It was a big log house with lots of space and light in every room. I'd never lived in anything like it before. I looked at it differently now. Now I could see the gaps in the ceiling joists, the crooked staircase, the septic tank hooked up to an extension cord on the front lawn. "Have we been very unhappy here?"

"I don't know how to answer that," Nate said. "Are we going to be happier now that we're moving off this island? Things will become a lot easier, without a doubt."

"Maybe easier *is* happier," I said.

"I don't know. I don't know if those things have that much to do with each other."

The man and his two young boys walked up our driveway, the man holding a folded newspaper over his head to block the rain. He introduced himself, said he lived town-side with his wife and kids but kept a small cabin on the Island to stay in for the summer and as a weekend getaway. He happened to be in need of a motor-boat for occasional travel back and forth.

Sure, we said. *Makes sense,* we said.

He climbed onto the boat and looked around, checking the shape of things as his sons played a game of pirates around the perimeter, waving sticks for swords.

"Can I take it out for a spin?" he asked.

Of course, we said. He inspected the motor with the attention of a man who knew what he was looking at. He pressed in some areas and peered into others. He nodded.

Over the next week, everything fell into place quicker and easier than we ever could have expected. The man and his sons paid for and towed away the boat from our front lawn. We spoke to our landlord and were able to come to an agreement about terminating the lease. We booked a barge and a U-Haul truck for our move. We reserved spots on the two BC Ferries routes that it would take to get us to our new home. We notified Lily's school that she would not be returning the following year.

We packed up the belongings we had and hired someone to take our stuff to town on a barge. I was surprised to see what we had accumulated since moving only a year earlier. Everything we came with fit into the back of a golf cart and now we had stacks of books and lampshades and even a few small pieces of furniture to grapple with. Nate loaded the boxes we had onto the barge and Lily and I cleaned up the house. When we finished, the house looked exactly the way it had when we first stepped through the doors the previous spring. All the furniture that wasn't ours—forming rooms and reading areas and places to hang your coat—looked as strange as it did when I first saw it; strange and out of place and sour.

I wanted to leave the empty house. I took Lily's hand as I walked down the dirt road. We wandered through the woods behind our house and came out near one of the beaches. We ran down the hill and climbed the rocks toward the sand. We scoured the ground for seashells and pieces of sea glass rubbed soft by the ocean and stored them in our pockets. We took off our shoes and ran into the water, splashing each other until we were in up to our chests, salt invading our eyes and mouths. We held hands underwater and yelled to the steamer ships anchored far off in the distance, grey as though they were blending into the sky and visible only by their towering outlines. On the way back to the house we walked slowly to Rebecca's, making sure we noticed as much as we could about the birds, the trees and the boats from all angles and every patch of grass we passed. We knew this was the last time.

"Like I said, I go that way to Savary Island to visit my dad a few times a year. We'll see each other again," Rebecca said when we sat on the sofa together, holding mugs of coffee in our laps.

"I know. And I'll come back this way to visit my mum in Victoria. I can drop in on you then."

"Perfect." She smiled and her eyes were wet.

"The move off the Island is really easy because we only have some boxes and a few other small things. We're going to get some furniture, like beds and stuff, in town. You keep the golf cart."

We couldn't look each other in the eye. I put my coffee cup on the table and picked it back up five or six times as we sat there, not to drink from it but to seem occupied.

"I'm thinking I might move back to Guelph, you know. Maybe go back to school. What do you think?"

"I think it sounds good. I think you can do anything you want to do," I said.

"Doesn't hurt to try, right?"

"Right."

The night before we left the Island, our house and our neighbours, we lay down in bed with a thousand plans, tired and looking ahead off this island. Lily had set up a makeshift bed on the floor next to ours made out of stray pillows and bundled-up bedsheets. The sound of rain on the roof and our nearby conversation had put her to sleep quickly and after a few minutes she was completely still. I recalled a year earlier when Nate, Lily and I boarded the plane to Nanaimo and left our old life in Toronto, pulsing with the inconceivable future that was ahead of us. The plane was delayed, so as I stood waiting in line I scrolled the news coverage on my cell phone. It was only just being made public that a man in Nanaimo had opened fire at a sawmill, killing at least two and sending two others to hospital. The quoted remarks from residents shared their collective shock at learning of the violence that had undone an otherwise ordinary day. They kept saying over and over, *This kind of thing never happens here.*

AFTERWORD

[TWENTY-ONE]

SO FAR IT'S NEVER BEEN TRUE THAT WHAT I THOUGHT WAS
going to happen happened, or how I first perceived a person to be
really was how she or he was. It's never been true that the impression I had of something initially, instantly, was the same impression I had even hours later. Because of this, I don't hear myself
saying things like *I knew right from the start*, or *I saw that coming*,
or *It was so obvious*. I have never known anything from the start
and nothing has ever been obvious.

I am a flawed judge of character and circumstance. I have deep,
maybe permanent, regrets about choices I've made, people I've
trusted and decisions I weighed that balanced on little more than
a feeling. I've learned that my own impulsivity can be dangerous
and has to be mediated by something like clarity, which I've only
ever gotten long after the fact and only sometimes.

Since being old enough to make up my own mind, I have
packed up all my belongings and bought three plane tickets, one
train ticket, countless litres of gasoline and four Greyhound bus
tickets to take me from one side of Canada to the other because
I more or less felt like it. I've lived back and forth between BC
and Ontario, each a few years at a time, since I was ten years old
and my parents first decided to head west from my hometown of

London, Ontario (we were back in London by the time I turned fifteen). I've lived in apartments, houses, spare rooms, tents and motels. Once in my late teens, I lived at a hostel in Victoria that gave me a bed for cleaning a floor of the building in the mornings.

This is to say that when the question of why we moved to an island comes up, which it often does, nothing feels more honest than shrugging my shoulders and saying, *Why not?* We wanted a change and change is good and what's the worst that could happen? I'd left versions of lives behind before, left friends and family, left jobs and a stable income before, and one thing I can say for sure is that not much changes, not really. My friends and family remained and new opportunities for a job or a place to live were available. Whatever fears I had about all the things that could go wrong, all the ways I might fail, never came to pass. The ways I failed and the things that went wrong came as surprises each and every time.

We were excited about the idea of living on an island, especially one that had hydro and WiFi and a septic system. To us, it meant we might be able to hang somewhere between "outback" and "urban." Nanaimo offered schools, grocery stores and other city amenities that would provide job opportunities and conveniences we imagined were necessary, and the city's downtown was only ten minutes away by boat. If we really needed something, we could get it.

At the time, our decision to move from Toronto to Protection felt like a sound one even if it was extreme. Plus the place was called "Protection Island," a name that conjured ideals of the cradle of a mother's embrace and strolls along a warm and unpopulated beach; of the peaceful sounds of seabirds calling to one another across rolling, azure waves; of sunshine, fertile landscapes and an open, sprawling view on all sides; of space; of a new beginning, away from the middle of things, out on our own; of enough privacy and quiet to know our own thoughts again. It was the best idea we had of everything Toronto wasn't, and we weren't afraid because we had each other.

But like I said, not much changes. Not really.

Or if things change, there's a trade sewn into the very seams of the deal because there has to be. There can't be a place to go when the city has exhausted our bodies and shaken the tenderness from our minds. A utopia on Earth, let's say. There can't really be somewhere where the heart is mended to its untroubled beginnings and the chains of living are loosened, and certainly not for the price of a plane ticket; certainly not because we decided there was.

I thought we would fail because we would run out of money, or one of us would be badly injured and unable to make it to the hospital, or we would become so socially isolated that we would see no other option but to return to the city, to what we knew. A few weeks into living on the Island, I spent a week waking up in the middle of the night from nightmares about my child falling into the ocean and being dragged into the whirl of the boat's propeller, or tumbling down our enormous flight of stairs and having to call for an airlift to the nearest hospital, or finding myself alone in the boat at night unable to see where I was going. I worried my daughter would suffer somehow, wouldn't fit in, would miss her friends and become lonely and angry. I worried Nate and I would see a new side to each other out there—and that we wouldn't like what we saw.

I wrote most of this book while still living on Protection Island so I could be close to it, to the people and atmosphere, because I knew even as I was writing it that we would leave that place and that when we left, the stitches holding the thoughts in this book together would begin to unravel. Only twice since I finished this book have I been pulled back into the woods of my memories as I read an email newly landed in my inbox inquiring about whether or not Nate was available to tear down a backyard shed or clear out some neglected eavestroughs.

To look back and say that moving to PI was a mistake wouldn't be the whole truth, nor would reciting a maxim about the great learning opportunities mistakes can bring. It was a mistake and it wasn't. I learned things from that mistake and I didn't. We changed our situation and we didn't change it at all. The long commutes in Toronto were replaced with the long ones on PI; the impossible cost of an apartment in Toronto was replaced with the equally unsustainable cost of ferry passes on PI; the continually surly housemates in Toronto became the meddling community on PI; and the hostile interactions of the big city were swapped out for the tight-lipped passive aggressiveness on the Island. What I learned is that a fantasy is a fantasy, no matter how real the photographs. What I found is what my mother has been telling me my whole life: *Wherever you go, you take yourself with you.*

We all do. And there's nowhere to hide.

ACKNOWLEDGEMENTS

Thanks to Rebecca Isert, Darby Isert, Laila McMillan, Alexis von Konigslow, Laura Nicol, Heather Neale Furneaux, Catherine Stewart and Kevin Chong for your early reading and enthusiasm. Especially, thanks to Silas White and Nicola Goshulak for your editorial wisdom and care.

Finally, thanks to the Ontario Arts Council for its support in the making of this book.

About the Author

Amber McMillan is the author of the poetry collection *We Can't Ever Do This Again* (2015). Her work has appeared in *Arc*, *Contemporary Verse 2*, *PRISM international*, *Best Canadian Poetry* and other publications across North America. She lives and works on BC's Sunshine Coast.

Photo credit: Nathaniel G. Moore

SHARE THE TRAIL

Be nice.
Trails are for everyone.

Calling all trail users! Rails-to-Trails Conservancy
challenges YOU to be the best you can be on America's pathways!
Remember—safe + fun = a great time for everyone!

#sharethetrail

Visit **railstotrails.org/sharethetrail** for more.

Foreword

Welcome to *Rail-Trails: Pennsylvania,* a comprehensive companion for discovering the state's top rail-trails and multiuse pathways. This guidebook will help you uncover fantastic opportunities to get outdoors on the state's trails—whether for exercise, transportation, or just pure fun.

Rails-to-Trails Conservancy's mission is to create a nationwide network of trails, just like these, to build healthier places for healthier people. We hope this book will inspire you to experience firsthand how trails can connect people to one another and to the places they love, while also creating connections to nature, history, and culture.

Since its founding in 1986, RTC has witnessed a massive growth in the rail-trail and active transportation movement. Today, more than 24,000 miles of completed rail-trails provide invaluable benefits for people and communities across the country. We hope you find this book to be a delightful and informative resource for discovering the many unique trail destinations throughout Pennsylvania.

I'll be out on the trails, too, experiencing the thrill of the adventure right alongside you. Be sure to say hello and share your experience with us on social media! We want to hear how you #GoByTrail. You can find us @railstotrails on Facebook, Instagram, and Twitter.

See you on the trail!

Ryan Chao, President
Rails-to-Trails Conservancy

Acknowledgments

Special acknowledgment to Amy Kapp, editor of this guidebook, and to Derek Strout for his work on the creation of the trail maps included in the book. Rails-to-Trails Conservancy also thanks Gene Bisbee and Amy Ahn for their assistance in editing content.

We are also appreciative of the following contributors, editors, and trail managers we called on for assistance to ensure the maps, photographs, and trail descriptions are as accurate as possible.

Milo Bateman

Ken Bryan

Cindy Dickerson

Alan Ibarra

Nancy Kapp

Joe LaCroix

Anthony Le

Laura Stark

Jorge Brito

Ryan Cree

Eli Griffen

Karl Kapp

Willie Karidis

Jake Laughlin

Jimmy O'Connor

The Hanover Junction train station along Heritage Rail Trail County Park (see page 91)

Rail-Trails: Pennsylvania highlights 72 of the top rail-trails and other multiuse pathways across the state. These trails offer a broad range of experiences, from sweeping Appalachian views to narrow wooded ravines, from challenging hiking and biking adventures to relaxing riverside strolls, and from vibrant cities to small towns that thrived in Pennsylvania's heyday in the 19th and 20th centuries as an industrial powerhouse.

Along the 15-mile Mahoning Shadow Trail, you can visit the hometown of Pennsylvania's most famous furry critter—Punxsutawney Phil—who puts the shadow in the trail's name. Or take a majestic trip through Presque Isle State Park on the 13.4-mile Karl Boyes Multi-Purpose National Recreation Trail, featuring majestic views of the Lake Erie shoreline and the Presque Isle Lighthouse.

History buffs may want to explore Greater Philadelphia's Schuylkill River Trail, which currently covers nearly 72 miles and will one day stretch 120-plus miles throughout the Schuylkill River Greenways National Heritage Area. A 30-mile section passes by some of the region's most popular destinations, including the Philadelphia Museum of Art, Valley Forge National Historical Park, and the 2,000-acre Fairmount Park. The trail also helps compose three larger, developing systems, including the 800-mile Circuit Trails network in Philadelphia and Camden, New Jersey; the 3,000-mile East Coast Greenway from Maine to Florida; and the 1,300-mile September 11th National Memorial Trail.

In Cambria and Indiana Counties, the Ghost Town Trail—part of the Trans Allegheny Trails System—allows users to glimpse relics from the region's coal and railroad days, with iron furnaces, disused tipples (equipment that loaded coal onto railroad cars), and other artifacts still visible along its 44.5 miles.

To the west, the Three Rivers Heritage Trail, currently 21.2 miles, features the best of Pittsburgh along the path's namesakes—the Allegheny, Ohio, and Monongahela—with highlights such as Point State Park, Station Square, the Cultural District, the North Side, the 456-acre Schenley Park, and some of the city's most famous bridges. The trail also serves as a hub for a 1,500-mile trail network in development by the Industrial Heartland Trails Coalition, and as a host for the 3,700-plus-mile Great American Rail-Trail.

And don't forget one of the most iconic rail-trails in the United States: the 150-mile Great Allegheny Passage, which is also part of the Great American Rail-Trail and seamlessly connects to the Three Rivers Heritage Trail and the 180-plus-mile Chesapeake & Ohio Canal National Historical Park (also known as the C&O Canal Towpath) to form a 334-mile off-road link to Washington, D.C.

No matter which routes in Rail-Trails: Pennsylvania you choose, you'll experience the unique history, culture, and geography of each, as well as the communities that have built and embraced them.

OPPOSITE: The Montour Trail (see page 157) crosses over the Panhandle Trail (see page 177).

What Is a Rail-Trail?

Rail-trails are multiuse public paths built along former railroad corridors. Most often flat or following a gentle grade, they are suited to walking, running, cycling, mountain biking, in-line skating, cross-country skiing, horseback riding, and wheelchair use. Since the 1960s, Americans have created more than 24,000 miles of rail-trails throughout the country.

These extremely popular recreation and transportation corridors traverse urban, suburban, and rural landscapes. Many preserve historical landmarks, while others serve as wildlife conservation corridors, linking isolated parks and establishing greenways in developed areas. Rail-trails also stimulate local economies by boosting tourism and promoting trailside businesses.

What Is a Rail-with-Trail?

A rail-with-trail is a public path that parallels a still-active rail line. Some run adjacent to high-speed, scheduled trains, often linking public transportation stations, while others follow tourist routes and slow-moving excursion trains. Many share an easement, separated from the rails by extensive fencing. At least 375 rails-with-trails exist in the United States.

What Is the Rail-Trail Hall of Fame?

In 2007 RTC began recognizing exemplary rail-trails around the country through its Rail-Trail Hall of Fame. Inductees are selected based on such merits as scenic value, high use, trail and trailside amenities, historical significance, excellence in management and maintenance of facility, community connections, and geographic distribution. These iconic rail-trails, which have been singled out from more than 2,000 in the United States, have earned RTC's highest honor and represent tangible realizations of our vision to create a more walkable, bikeable, and healthier America. Hall of Fame rail-trails are indicated in this book with a special blue icon; for the full list of Hall of Fame rail-trails, visit **railstotrails.org/halloffame.**

What Is TrailNation™?

At RTC, we believe that communities are healthier and happier when trails are central to their design. Everything we love about trails gets better when we connect them, creating seamless trail networks that link neighborhoods, towns, cities, and entire regions together. That's why we're committed to connecting trails and building comprehensive trail systems that bring people together and get them where they want to go.

We've invested in eight TrailNation™ projects across the country—found in places that are diverse in their geography, culture, size, and scope—to prove

what is possible when trail networks are central to our lives. Two of those Trail-Nation projects can be found in Pennsylvania—the Circuit Trails and the Industrial Heartland Trails Coalition, each with ambitious goals to create vibrant trail systems across the state and the region. Look for the TrailNation project logo throughout the book to find trails that are part of these networks. Learn more about RTC's vision to connect the country by trail at **trailnation.org.**

ABOUT THE CIRCUIT TRAILS

Led by a coalition of dozens of nonprofit organizations, foundations, and agencies, the Circuit Trails are part of a vast trail network that will ultimately include 800 miles of multiuse trails across nine counties in the Greater Philadelphia–Camden, New Jersey, region. More than 350 miles of the network are already complete, and the coalition is working to have 500 miles built by 2025. Learn more at **thecircuittrails.org.**

ABOUT THE INDUSTRIAL HEARTLAND TRAILS COALITION

The Industrial Heartland Trails Coalition is working to establish the region as a premier destination, offering a 1,500-plus-mile multiuse trail network. The network, which will stretch across 48 counties in four states—Pennsylvania, West  Virginia, Ohio, and New York—is spearheaded by the Pennsylvania Environmental Council, the National Park Service, and RTC, along with more than 100 organizations across the area. Visit **ihearttrails.org** for more information.

What Is the Great American Rail-Trail™?

A signature project of RTC, the Great American Rail-Trail is the organization's most ambitious trail project to date and will be the nation's first cross-country multiuse trail, uniting millions of people over its 3,700-mile route between Washington, D.C., and Washington State. This unique journey through the District of Columbia and 12 states—Maryland, Pennsylvania, West Virginia, Ohio, Indiana, Illinois, Iowa, Nebraska, Wyoming, Montana, Idaho, and Washington—will make it possible for travelers to explore some of the country's most renowned geographic and cultural landmarks. Today, the Great American is more than 52% complete, but there are still more than 1,700 miles left to fill in. To get it done, RTC is providing the national leadership and on-the-ground support to bring together the people, plans, and partnerships necessary for completing the Great American Rail-Trail. Learn more at **greatamericanrailtrail.org.**

R*ail-Trails: Pennsylvania* provides the information you'll need to plan a rewarding trek. With words to inspire you and maps to chart your path, it makes choosing the best route a breeze. Following are some of the highlights.

Maps

You'll find two levels of maps in this book: a **state locator map** and **detailed trail maps.**

The trails in this book are located in Pennsylvania, with some trails extending to, or into, Ohio, West Virginia, Maryland, New York, and New Jersey. Use the state locator map to find the trails nearest you, or select several neighboring trails and plan a weekend hiking or biking excursion. Once you find a trail on a state locator map, simply flip to the corresponding number for a full description. Accompanying trail maps mark each route's access roads, trailheads, parking areas, restrooms, and other defining features.

Key to Map Icons

parking | drinking water | restrooms | featured trail | connecting trail | active railroad

Trail Descriptions

Trails are listed in alphabetical order. Each description leads off with a set of summary information, including trail endpoints and mileage, a roughness index, the trail surface, and possible uses.

The map and summary information list the trail endpoints (either a city, street, or more specific location), with suggested points from which to start and finish. Additional access points are marked on the maps and mentioned in the trail descriptions. The maps and descriptions also highlight available amenities, including parking and restrooms, as well as such area attractions as museums, parks, and stadiums. Trail length is listed in miles.

Each trail bears a **roughness index** rating from 1 to 3. A rating of 1 indicates a smooth, level surface that is accessible to users of all ages and abilities. A 2 rating means the surface may be loose and/or uneven and could pose a problem for road bikes and wheelchairs. A 3 rating suggests a rough surface that is only recommended for mountain bikers and hikers. Surfaces can range from asphalt or concrete to ballast, boardwalk, cinder, crushed stone, gravel, grass, dirt, sand, and/or wood chips. Where relevant, trail descriptions address alternating surface conditions.

All trails are open to pedestrians, and most allow bicycles, except where noted in the trail summary or description. The summary also indicates wheelchair access. Other possible uses include in-line skating, mountain biking, horseback riding, fishing, and cross-country skiing. While most trails are off-limits to motor vehicles, some local trail organizations do allow snowmobiles.

Trail descriptions themselves suggest an ideal itinerary for each route, including the best parking areas and access points, where to begin, your direction of travel, and any highlights along the way. Following each description are directions to the recommended trailheads.

Each trail description also lists a local website for further information. Be sure to visit these websites in advance for updates and current conditions. **TrailLink .com** is another great resource for updated content on the trails in this guidebook.

Trail Use

Rail-trails are popular destinations for a range of users, often making them busy places to enjoy the outdoors. Following basic trail etiquette and safety guidelines will make your experience more pleasant.

➤ **Keep to the right,** except when passing.

➤ **Pass on the left,** and give a clear audible warning: "Passing on your left."

➤ **Be aware** of other trail users, particularly around corners and blind spots, and be especially careful when entering a trail, changing direction, or passing so that you don't collide with traffic.

➤ **Respect wildlife** and public and private property; leave no trace and take out litter.

➤ **Control your speed,** especially near pedestrians, playgrounds, and heavily congested areas.

➤ **Travel single file.** Cyclists and pedestrians should ride or walk single file in congested areas or areas with reduced visibility.

➤ **Cross carefully** at intersections; always look both ways and yield to through traffic. Pedestrians have the right-of-way.

➤ **Keep one ear open and volume low** on portable listening devices to increase your awareness of your surroundings.

➤ **Wear a helmet** and other safety gear if you're cycling or in-line skating.

➤ **Consider visibility.** Wear reflective clothing, use bicycle lights, or bring flashlights or helmet-mounted lights for tunnel passages or twilight excursions.

➤ **Keep moving,** and don't block the trail. When taking a rest, turn off the trail to the right. Groups should avoid congregating on or blocking the trails. If you have an accident on the trail, move to the right as soon as possible.

➤ **Bicyclists yield** to all other trail users. Pedestrians yield to horses. If in doubt, yield to all other trail users.

➤ **Check the trail's pet policy.** Dogs are permitted on most trails, but some trails through parks, wildlife refuges, or other sensitive areas may not allow pets; it's best to check the trail website before your visit. If pets are permitted, keep your dog on a short leash and under your control at all times. Discard dog waste in a designated trash receptacle.

➤ **Teach your children** these trail essentials, and be especially diligent to keep them out of faster-moving trail traffic.

➤ **Be prepared,** especially on long-distance rural trails. Bring water, snacks, maps, a light source, matches, and other equipment you may need. Because some areas may not have good reception for mobile phones, know where you're going, and tell someone else your plan.

Key to Trail Use

walking

cycling

wheelchair access

in-line skating

mountain biking

fishing

horseback riding

cross-country skiing

snowmobiling

Learn More

To learn about additional multiuse trails in your area or to plan a trip to an area beyond the scope of this book, visit Rails-to-Trails Conservancy's trail-finder website **TrailLink.com,** a free resource with more than 36,000 miles of mapped rail-trails and multiuse trails nationwide.

Pennsylvania

Trail users appreciate the shade along this section of the Joseph M. McDade Recreational Trail (see page 120).

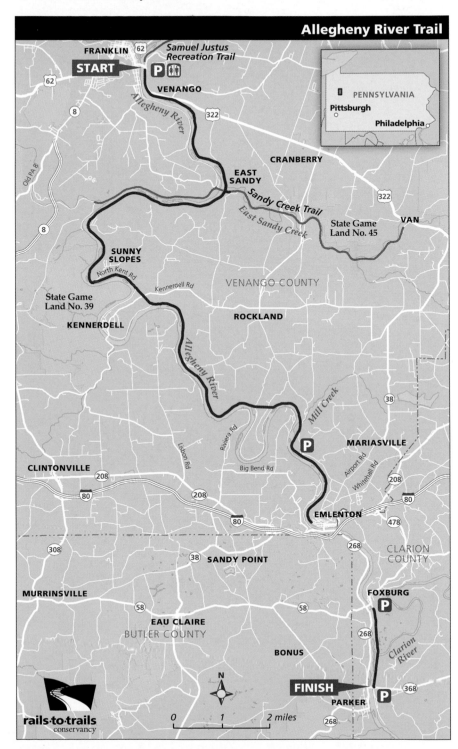

Allegheny River Trail

Keep your eyes open for wildlife when you visit the Allegheny River Trail. This segment of the Allegheny River—once a canoe route for local tribes and French trappers—was designated a national wild and scenic river, and the forests teem with animals. Everything from chipmunks to wild turkeys to deer are frequently spotted along the trail, while eagles rule the sky overhead.

The trail follows the route used by the Allegheny Valley Railroad, later the Allegheny Division of Pennsylvania Railroad, to haul oil. The Scrubgrass Generating Company subsequently acquired it in 1984 and donated it to the nonprofit Allegheny Valley Trails Association.

The trail runs on asphalt between Franklin and Emlenton for 27.5 miles and on an isolated section between Foxburg and Parker for 2.5 miles. It meets the Samuel Justus Recreation Trail (see page 215) in Franklin, crosses beneath

A white split rail fence adds to the trail's bucolic setting.

Counties
Clarion, Venango

Endpoints
Samuel Justus Recreation Trail at US 322/ Lakes to the Sea Hwy. and Bredinsburg Road (Franklin) to Main St. at River Ave. (Emlenton); Main St. at River Road (Foxburg) to Perryville Road at PA 368 (Parker)

Mileage
30.0

Type
Rail-Trail

Roughness Index
1

Surface
Asphalt

the Sandy Creek Trail (see page 218) in East Sandy, and passes through two old railroad tunnels. It is part of the 270-mile Erie to Pittsburgh Trail that one day will link Presque Isle on Lake Erie with Pittsburgh, where it will join the Great Allegheny Passage (see page 82); it's also part of the Industrial Heartland Trails Coalition's developing 1,500-mile trail network through Pennsylvania, West Virginia, Ohio, and New York.

Starting just south of the US 322 bridge into downtown Franklin—also the western endpoint for the Samuel Justus Recreation Trail—you'll pass a couple of riverfront camping sites in the first 4 miles. At 5.2 miles, you'll cross East Sandy Creek and then catch sight of the picturesque Belmar Bridge that carries the Sandy Creek Trail across the Allegheny River. You'll pass beneath the bridge that soars 80 feet overhead, or you can ascend using a stairway.

About 3.2 miles past the bridge, you'll find Indian God Rock, a large boulder at the water's edge with numerous inscriptions, including American Indian

Beautiful foliage abounds along the Allegheny River Trail.

petroglyphs, carved in the soft sandstone. A viewing platform offers a nice panorama, though vandals have destroyed most of the figures on the rock.

Four miles past the viewing platform, the trail veers onto gravelly North Kent Road for 0.75 mile through the Sunny Slopes community. Back on the asphalt trail, you'll pass through the 3,300-foot-long Kennerdell Tunnel and, in another 6 miles, the Rockland Tunnel (2,868 feet long). Both of these tunnels have doglegs and are dark, so you'll need a flashlight.

Emerging from the second tunnel, you'll arrive in Emlenton in 6 miles, the end of this section of trail. You can catch a bite here and soak in the local history at the Pumping Jack Museum with its collection of oil-drilling relics.

A 4.5-mile trail gap exists between Emlenton and Foxburg. Part of the route, a dirt-surfaced pathway that accommodates mountain bikes, travels through private property and is not passable as of 2019.

The trail resumes 4.5 miles downstream in Foxburg, a tourist destination known for its riverfront dining, wine cellars, and historical RiverStone Estate located just uphill from the trail 1 mile south of town. You'll cross the Clarion River in another 0.5 mile and reach the path's end at the PA 368 bridge to Parker.

CONTACT: avta-trails.org/allegheny-samuel-trails.html

DIRECTIONS

To reach the northern trailhead in Franklin from I-80, take Exit 29 to PA 8/Pittsburgh Road. Head north on PA 8, and go 16.4 miles. Turn right onto Liberty St. Go 0.4 mile, and curve right to stay on Liberty St., and then go 0.7 mile, and turn left onto US 322/Eighth St. Go 0.5 mile, and turn right at the sign for Samuel Justus Recreation Trail. Turn right into the parking lot. Access the Allegheny River Trail at the south end of the parking lot.

To reach the trailhead in Emlenton from I-80, take Exit 42 to PA 38/Oneida Valley Road. Head north on PA 38, go 0.3 mile, and turn right onto PA 208/Emlenton Clintonville Road. Go 1.6 miles, and turn left to stay on PA 208/Fifth St., crossing the bridge. Go 0.2 mile, and turn left onto Main St., and then go 0.2 mile to enter the bike-share lane for parking about 0.1 mile ahead. Access the trail at the northern end of the parking lot to head toward Franklin.

To reach the trailhead in Foxburg, follow the directions above to PA 208/Emlenton Clintonville Road. Go 2.2 miles, and continue onto PA 268 S. Go 2.8 miles, and turn left onto PA 58/Foxburg Bridge. Go 0.2 mile, and turn right onto Main St., and then go 300 feet, and look for parking on the right. Access the trailhead at the southern end of the parking lot, on the left side of River Road.

To reach the trailhead in Parker, follow the directions above to PA 268 S. Go 5.5 miles, and turn left onto PA 368. Go 0.3 mile, crossing the bridge, and turn left onto Perryville Road. Go 0.1 mile (heading in a circular direction toward the water), and look for parking on the right.

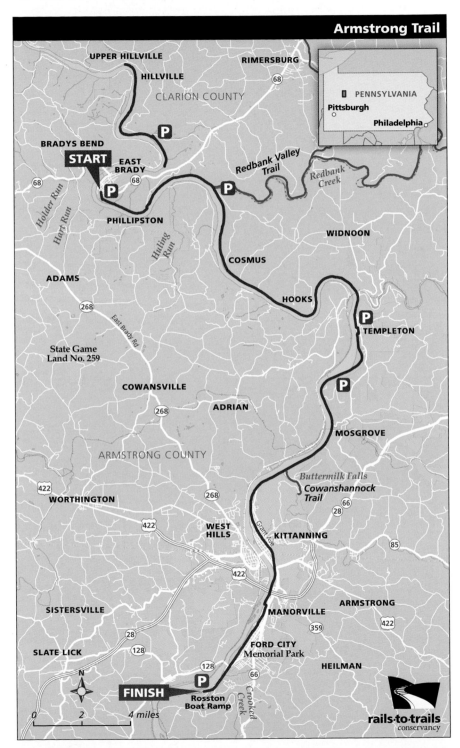

Armstrong Trail

UPPER HILLVILLE

HILLVILLE

RIMERSBURG

68

CLARION COUNTY

PENNSYLVANIA

Pittsburgh

Philadelphia

BRADYS BEND

START

EAST BRADY

68

68

Redbank Valley Trail

Redbank Creek

PHILLIPSTON

Holder Run

Hart Run

Huling Run

WIDNOON

COSMUS

ADAMS

268

HOOKS

East Brady Rd

TEMPLETON

State Game Land No. 259

COWANSVILLE

268

ADRIAN

MOSGROVE

ARMSTRONG COUNTY

422

Buttermilk Falls

Cowanshannock Trail

WORTHINGTON

268

66

28

422

WEST HILLS

Grant Ave

KITTANNING

85

422

SISTERSVILLE

ARMSTRONG

MANORVILLE

422

359

28

FORD CITY Memorial Park

SLATE LICK

128

128

HEILMAN

66

N

FINISH

Rosston Boat Ramp

Crooked Creek

0   2   4 miles

rails·to·trails
conservancy

The Armstrong Trail connects riverfront towns along the east bank of the Allegheny River as it winds through the lush Allegheny Plateau. The flat trail, currently 35.5 miles, follows the river downstream from Upper Hillville to Rosston, passing relics from the area's railroading and industrial past.

The Allegheny Valley Railroad began laying tracks in 1853, and by 1870 the railroad ran between Pittsburgh and Oil City. Absorbed by the Pennsylvania Railroad in 1900, the corridor went through several ownership changes until the Allegheny Valley Land Trust acquired it in 1992 for a trail. Court challenges delayed construction of some trail sections, resulting in today's mix of surfaces, which include asphalt and crushed stone.

The Armstrong Trail is part of the 270-mile Erie to Pittsburgh Trail that will run from Presque Isle on Lake

Counties
Armstrong, Clarion

Endpoints
Just south of Hillville Road at T351 to the end of Riverview Dr., 1.7 miles west of Prospect St. (Rimersburg); Rex-Hide Dr. and Purdum St. (East Brady) to Rosston Boat Ramp at Rosston Cir., 1,000 feet southwest of Ross Ave. (Rosston)

Mileage
35.5

Type
Rail-Trail

Roughness Index
1, 3

Surface
Asphalt, Crushed Stone

The Redbank coaling tower served as a refueling station by dropping coal into the storage bins of locomotives from 1930 to 1957.

Erie to Pittsburgh's connection with the Great Allegheny Passage (see page 82); it's also part of the Industrial Heartland Trails Coalition's developing 1,500-mile trail network through Pennsylvania, West Virginia, Ohio, and New York. In addition, it connects with the Redbank Valley Trail (see page 208), which runs east from the Armstrong Trail for more than 40 miles and includes a 9-mile spur leading to Sligo.

East Brady is the best place to start for an uninterrupted trip down the trail. A closed tunnel the railroad built as a shortcut across a river bend isolates an orphaned 4.5-mile crushed-stone segment upriver. You'll travel on short stretches of gravel road as you leave town.

Just past Phillipston in 2 miles, look for an old railroad turntable left over from the days when the railroad serviced locomotives here. In another 1.2 miles, you'll see the southern entrance to the 0.5-mile 1915 Brady Tunnel; future plans call for renovating and reopening it to connect the northern segment to the rest of the trail. In a little less than 1.5 miles later, you'll pass the coaling tower used to replenish locomotives from 1930 until 1957, when diesel power replaced steam.

The junction for the Redbank Valley Trail and Sligo Spur is just past here, joining the Armstrong Trail at the confluence with Redbank Creek. The Armstrong Trail rolls nearly 2 miles to Allegheny River Lock and Dam 9, built in 1938 as the farthest upstream navigation impoundment (a dam located farther north is for flood control).

Over the next 7.5 miles, the route passes through small communities to Templeton, where you can find a diner and a campground. You'll pass another dam and lock structure a little over 2 miles past Templeton, and 4 miles later you'll come to a junction with the 1.2-mile Cowanshannock Trail, which climbs uphill along a spur line that served a coal mine and brick plant and today passes Buttermilk Falls in Cowanshannock Creek.

In less than 2 miles, you'll enter Kittanning, named for a Shawnee and Lenape village that was destroyed during the French and Indian War. Today it's the largest borough on the trail and home to a wide variety of restaurants, as well as the old train station at Grant and Reynolds Avenues. Continuing south takes you to Ford City, founded in 1887 as the company town for Pittsburgh Plate Glass, at one time the largest glassmaker in the nation. The company left town in the 1990s, but the worker's entrance is preserved at trailside Memorial Park.

The path ends just a couple more miles past Ford City at Rosston Boat Ramp. Beyond the dilapidated bridge over Crooked Creek, the Kiski Junction Railroad continues 9 miles via the old Allegheny Valley Railroad corridor.

CONTACT: armstrongrailstotrails.org or alleghenyvalleylandtrust.org

DIRECTIONS

To reach the Sarah Furnace Road trailhead, which provides the only parking available for the northern section of trail, from I-79, take Exit 99, and turn right to head east on US 422/Benjamin Franklin Hwy. Go 15.9 miles and exit onto PA 68/Chicora Road. Turn left, and go 10.8 miles. Make a slight right to continue on PA 68, and go another 8.4 miles. Just after crossing the Allegheny River, turn right onto PA 68/Kelly's Way. Go 0.4 mile, and turn left onto PA 68/Third St./T581. Go 4.1 miles, and turn left onto SR 3006/Sarah Furnace Road. Go 1.9 miles, and look for on-road parking on the left at the trailhead. The trail dead-ends north and south from this point.

To reach parking in East Brady from I-79, follow the directions above to PA 68/Third St. Go 0.2 mile, and turn right onto Robinson St. Go 0.2 mile, and take a slight left onto Shady Shores Dr. Go 0.1 mile, turn right onto a short access road, and then immediately turn left into the parking lot (adjacent to the East Brady Maintenance Department). Facing the trail from the parking lot, turn right and go 0.3 mile to reach the endpoint.

Additional parking is available at East Brady Playground & Skatepark, which is located at the corner of Robinson St. and Shady Shores Dr. From Third St., go 0.2 mile, and then turn right onto Robinson St., and go 0.2 mile. Take an immediate right turn into the access drive for the park, and look for parking on the left. To reach the endpoint, turn left onto Sixth St. and go 0.1 mile.

To reach the trailhead in Rosston from I-79, take Exit 99, and turn right to head east on US 422 E/Benjamin Franklin Hwy./New Castle Road. Go 36 miles, and take Exit A onto PA 66 toward Ford City. Go 1.2 miles, and bear right onto PA 128/Fifth Ave., and then go 1.8 miles, and turn left onto Ross Ave. Go 0.8 mile, and stay straight onto Ross Cir. Go 0.2 mile, and turn left to stay on Ross Cir.; then go 300 feet, and look for parking to your left at the Rosston Boat Ramp.

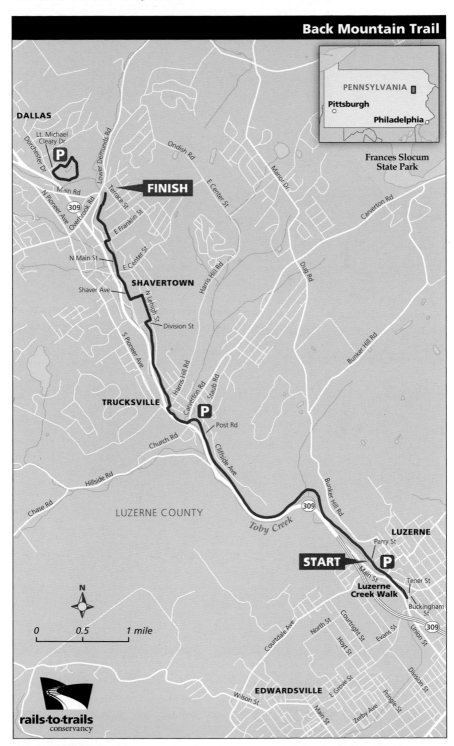

Back Mountain Trail

PENNSYLVANIA

Pittsburgh

Philadelphia

DALLAS

Lt. Michael
Cleary Dr

Dorchester Dr

Lower Demunds Rd

Ondish Rd

Frances Slocum
State Park

Main Rd

309

Overbrook Rd

N Pioneer Ave

Terrace St

FINISH

E Center St

Manor Dr

Carverton Rd

E Franklin St

E Center St

N Main St

E Center St

SHAVERTOWN

Harris Hill Rd

Dug Rd

Shaver Ave

N Lehigh St

Division St

S Pioneer Ave

Harris Hill Rd

Carverton Rd

Staub Rd

Bunker Hill Rd

TRUCKSVILLE

P

Post Rd

Church Rd

Cliffside Ave

Hillside Rd

Chase Rd

LUZERNE COUNTY

Toby Creek

309

Bunker Hill Rd

LUZERNE

Parry St

START

P

Main St

Tener St

Luzerne
Creek Walk

Buckingham
St

N

309

Union St

0   0.5   1 mile

Courtdale Ave

North St

Courtright St

Evans St

Hoyt St

Division St

EDWARDSVILLE

E Grove St

Pringle St

Wilson St

Main St

Zerby Ave

rails·to·trails
conservancy

The Wilkes-Barre and Harveys Lake Railroad—the rail corridor that is now the Back Mountain Trail—was acquired from lumber magnate Albert Lewis by the Lehigh Valley Railroad in 1887. Lumber, ice, leather goods, and anthracite coal produced in the Endless Mountains and Susquehanna River Basin were transported to urban markets and steel mills well into the 1940s. The corridor fell into disuse in 1963.

In 1996 the Anthracite Scenic Trails Association, together with Luzerne County, began work to open the corridor to public use; a planned 14-mile route will eventually extend from Riverfront Park on the Susquehanna River in Wilkes-Barre to the town of Harveys Lake. Today this 5.6-mile rail-trail winds through scenic woodlands punctuated by a meandering creek, a lovely waterfall, and

Despite sections of the Back Mountain Trail running close to the highway, it evokes a feeling of an escape into nature.

County
Luzerne

Endpoints
Buckingham St. and
Tener St. (Luzerne) to
Lower Demunds Road
and Terrace St. (Dallas)

Mileage
5.6

Type
Rail-Trail

Roughness Index
3

Surface
Crushed Stone

expanses of wildflowers. Although sections of the trail run close to the highway, they don't compromise the feeling of escaping into nature.

The trail currently begins at the Luzerne Creek Walk, at Buckingham and Tener Streets behind the Luzerne Fire Department. Plans are in the works for a trail connector linking this section to a segment of the Luzerne County Levee Trail at Rutter Avenue south of PA 309; the connector remains closed for development at the time of this writing, however.

After traveling northwest on the Luzerne Creek Walk for 0.3 mile, you'll meet and cross over Main Street just before it intersects Kelly Street. The trail continues along Parry Street and past a large parking lot to the Parry Street trailhead, where you'll find parking and a trail kiosk. This is the best place to start your journey.

Note: The Luzerne Creek Walk is the only section of the larger Back Mountain Trail that is wheelchair accessible.

The trail winds northwest briefly through dense woods; it then curves south over a small bridge and past a picturesque waterfall before heading north again through Trucksville. Here you'll find additional parking at Carverton Road and South Memorial Highway, as well as trail-access points at Post, Carverton, and Harris Hill Roads. At Carverton Road, you access the trail on a set of stairs south of the road near where it intersects South Memorial Highway.

Continuing north, the route takes a short detour in Shavertown on local roads. Turn right onto Division Street for 250 feet, left onto North Lehigh Street for 0.2 mile, left onto Vine Street for 0.1 mile, and then right onto Shaver Avenue, which becomes North Main Street once you pass East Center Street. After going 0.5 mile, turn right onto East Franklin Street for 225 feet, and then turn left back onto the main trail. The trail continues briefly through woods for another 0.4 mile to its northern terminus at Lower Demunds Road and Terrace Street in Dallas.

In 2016 a local landowner granted an easement—later expanded to a 13-acre donation—to the Anthracite Scenic Trails Association to create a 0.6-mile loop trail near the northern end of the Back Mountain Trail at Dorchester Drive and Lt. Michael Cleary Drive. The new trail boasts a crushed-stone surface as well as several boardwalk sections; its natural highlights include wetlands, woods, abundant wildlife, and a central pond. Future plans include connecting the two trail segments as part of the larger effort to extend the Back Mountain Trail to Harveys Lake.

CONTACT: course.wilkes.edu/bmt

DIRECTIONS

To reach parking at the southern endpoint from I-81, take Exit 170B for PA 309 N toward Wilkes-Barre, and go 0.3 mile. Continue onto PA 309 N, and go 4.4 miles. Take Exit 6 toward Luzerne, go 0.3 mile, and then turn right at a signal at the end of the ramp onto Union St. Go 0.3 mile, and turn right at a signal onto Main St. Take an immediate left onto Parry St., and look for parking immediately to your right.

Additional on-street parking is available just farther north at the Parry St. trailhead. To reach the trailhead from Main St., turn left onto Parry St., and go 0.1 mile. As you approach the trailhead, look for parking along the street immediately to your right; you can access the trail straight ahead where Parry St. makes a hard right turn.

To reach parking at the northern loop section from I-81, take Exit 170B for PA 309 N toward Wilkes-Barre. Continue onto PA 309 N for 9.6 miles, and turn right onto Dorchester Dr. Take an immediate right onto Dorchester Dr. and another immediate right onto Lt. Michael Cleary Dr. Parking is in a cul-de-sac at the end of Lt. Michael Cleary Dr. Additional parking is available just less than 0.1 mile to your left along Lt. Michael Cleary Dr.

Note that the disconnected main Back Mountain Trail segment has no dedicated parking at its northern end.

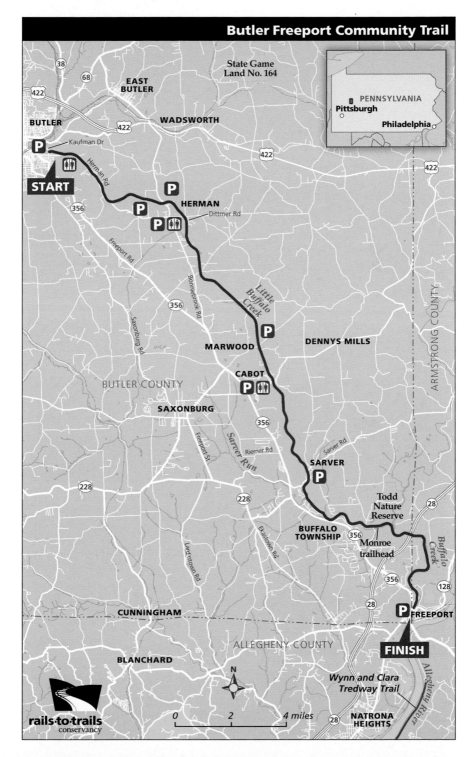

Butler Freeport Community Trail

Built in 1871 to transport the region's high-quality limestone to support Pittsburgh's growing steel industry, the Butler Branch of the Pennsylvania Railroad was the first railroad in Butler County. After a two-day celebration of the opening, the railroad conducted a mock funeral for the stagecoach that ran between the two towns. A branch of the Western Pennsylvania Railroad, the line became part of the Pennsylvania Railroad system in 1903 and discontinued service in 1987. After a volunteer effort organized by the local community, the Butler Freeport Community Trail officially opened in 1992 and was formally completed in 2015. The all-volunteer Butler Freeport Community Trail Council manages and maintains the trail, which is owned by Buffalo Township.

Located about 30 minutes northeast of Pittsburgh, the trail is nestled in the scenic wooded valley that follows

Counties
Armstrong, Butler

Endpoints
Kaufman Dr. just north of Zeigler Ave. near Father Marinaro Park (Butler) to just south of Main St. near Old Pike Road (Freeport)

Mileage
21.0

Type
Rail-Trail

Roughness Index
1

Surface
Asphalt, Crushed Stone

The Butler Freeport Community Trail serves as a pleasant transportation corridor about 30 minutes northeast of Pittsburgh.

Little Buffalo Creek to Buffalo Creek and on to the Allegheny River at Freeport. The surface of the trail comprises mostly crushed stone, with about a mile of asphalt south of the Monroe trailhead and the Buffalo Township Municipal Authority. Mile and 0.5-mile markers line the trail, and restroom facilities along the trail are open seasonally, May–October. Cross-country skiing is permitted—as is horseback riding in designated areas during dry weather (see the Facebook page for updates: **facebook.com/groups/butlerfreeporttrail**).

Keen observers will spot old stone foundations and the remainders of brick kilns, and small dams and waterfalls also appear along the route.

The path begins on the east side of the town of Butler on Kaufman Drive, where a large sign greets trail users. Just a mile northeast on Main Street, you'll find restaurants, shops, hotels, and gas stations. Heading south from Butler, you'll immediately cross over a small bridge as you make your way out of town, with the route on a slight incline for 7 miles to Cabot.

The trail travels southeast along Herman Road for the first couple miles, and then veers left through wooded farmland on the outskirts of Herman. You'll pass multiple road crossings and then cross over Herman Road on a small overpass. About 5.4 miles along the trail at Dittmer Road, just past Herman Road, you'll find a trailhead, restrooms, and parking to your right, and a small bike shop and café to your left. From here the route begins to head directly south, passing a golf course with a café and clubhouse in about 0.7

Trees shade the trail in summer and carpet the path with their leaves in autumn.

more mile, and then several more road crossings, before reaching Marwood, where you'll pass Freehling Lumber Company at the site where a post office and railroad station from earlier days once stood.

From Cabot, the trail heads 13 miles on a downhill trajectory, passing through rural landscapes in Sarver. At miles 14 and 14.5 along the trail, you may notice the remains of two dams along Buffalo Creek that served sand plants in the area. At the Bear Creek Road trailhead, at around 14.9 miles, fishing is permitted.

At around mile 16.8, you'll come to the Monroe trailhead; just a few hundred feet south along Monroe Road is Buffalo Township Audubon Park, managed by the Audubon Society of Western Pennsylvania, where a community park and recreation area—anticipated for completion by 2021—are being developed. You can cast a line for fish on the adjacent property here.

The route passes under PA 28/Alexander H. Lindsay Memorial Highway. At mile 19, look for the ruins of brick kilns along the trail, a reminder of the area's 19th-century brickmaking days. The path ends in about another 2 miles, just south of Main Street in Freeport.

Here, you can opt to take a 0.1-mile shared-road section northwest along Main Street and then south along Old Pike Road to a dedicated bike and pedestrian path that takes you along the east side of the PA 356 bridge to River Landing Drive. From here, you can connect to the Wynn and Clara Tredway Trail that extends a few miles south along the Allegheny River.

CONTACT: butlerfreeporttrail.org

DIRECTIONS

To reach the northern trailhead in Butler from I-79, take Exit 99, and turn right to head east on US 422/Benjamin Franklin Hwy. Go 15.9 miles and exit onto PA 68/Jefferson St. Turn right onto PA 68 W/E. Jefferson St. Go 1.2 miles, and turn left onto S. Monroe St. Go 0.4 mile, and turn left onto Center Ave. Go 0.1 mile, and turn left onto Zeigler Ave. Go 0.3 mile, and turn left onto Kaufman Dr. Go 0.1 mile, and turn right into the trailhead parking lot.

To reach the southern trailhead in Freeport from I-79, take Exit 99, and turn right to head east on US 422/Benjamin Franklin Hwy. Go 18.8 miles and turn right onto Bonniebrook Road. In 6.2 miles turn left onto PA 356, and go 9.8 miles. Turn left onto Old Pike Road, and go about 400 feet, and then turn right onto Main St. Take a sharp right to stay on Main St., and turn left into the trailhead parking lot.

To reach the southern trailhead in Freeport from I-76, take Exit 48, and keep right for PA 28/New Kensington. Merge onto Freeport Road, and go 0.8 mile. Turn right onto PA 910, and in 0.2 mile turn right to merge onto PA 28 N. Go 13.5 miles, and take Exit 17 for PA 356. Turn right onto PA 356 S/Butler Road, and go 1.5 miles, and then follow the directions above from Old Pike Road to the trail.

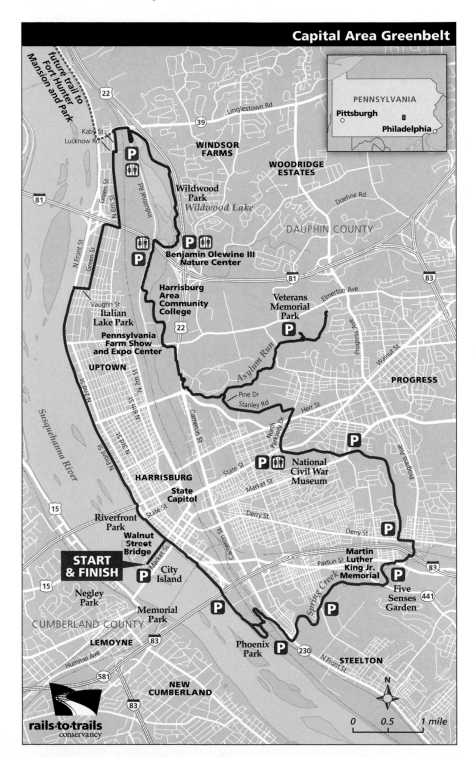

Capital Area Greenbelt

PENNSYLVANIA

Pittsburgh

Philadelphia

Every year, tens of thousands of people take to the Capital Area Greenbelt looping around Harrisburg to play, exercise, and commute. The greenway completely encircles Pennsylvania's capital city as it connects parks, museums, and a stretch of gardens and woods along the Susquehanna River.

Originally conceived by landscape architect Warren Manning in the early 1900s to improve livability in what was a gritty steel town, the greenbelt project was forgotten as more pressing matters arose and many residents migrated to the suburbs. Then in 1991, volunteers with the Capital Area Greenbelt Association (CAGA) resurrected the spirit of those plans and began building trails using wood chips and gravel. Today, private foundations and local and state agencies have adopted the greenbelt, which benefits from state grants totaling millions of dollars.

Trail users can take Walnut Street Bridge from Riverfront Park to City Island.

County
Dauphin

Endpoints
Loop: PA 39/Linglestown Road and Industrial Road to S. Cameron St. and S. 13th St. (Harrisburg)

Mileage
21.2

Type
Greenway/Non-Rail-Trail

Roughness Index
1

Surface
Asphalt, Cinder, Concrete, Crushed Stone

The Capital Area Greenbelt's 20.6-mile main loop comprises paved and crushed-rock paths, wide sidewalks next to streets, low-traffic streets, and road shoulders; the greenbelt also includes a small spur and loop within two parks. Wayfaring signs with mileage markers direct visitors throughout. In 2018 CAGA paved or repaved four sections of trail, and in early 2019, CAGA completed safety upgrades on six intersections, with work including pedestrian-activated flashing beacons, improved crosswalks, and curbs and buffers to separate pedestrians from traffic. Additionally, the Susquehanna Area Mountain Bike Association (SAMBA) has added novice- to expert-level singletrack throughout the greenbelt that can be accessed from many points.

A central place to start is City Island in the Susquehanna River. You'll find parking here, as well as recreational activities. The eastern half of the circa 1890 Walnut Street Bridge carries pedestrians to the greenbelt's Riverfront Park; ice floes washed away the western span in 1996.

Cross the bridge and turn left to head upstream through Riverfront Park. In just 0.3 mile, you can turn right onto State Street to head to the Pennsylvania State Capitol and historic South Capitol Park; however, your route continues north. In about 1.4 miles from the start point, you'll come upon the waterfront Sunken Garden to your left, followed by the Peace Garden in another 0.9 mile. Just past 3 miles, follow the signs taking you through neighborhoods north of downtown to Linglestown Road: turn right onto Vaughn Street, left onto Green Street, left onto North Sixth Street, right onto Lucknow Road, and left onto Kaby Street. Here, CAGA is working to complete a 1.5-mile side trail that heads to the left and upriver to Fort Hunter Mansion and Park overlooking the Susquehanna River; it's expected to open mid-2020. To stay on the main greenbelt, turn off Linglestown Road, taking a right onto Industrial Road, and look for the Wildwood Park entrance on the left. The trail takes the east shore of the lake through the woods, eventually curving west past the Benjamin Olewine III Nature Center.

Heading south underneath I-81, you'll enter the Harrisburg Area Community College campus at about 8 miles, and then the Pennsylvania Farm Show and Expo Center grounds at 9.5 miles. The left fork at 10.5 miles takes you on a side trail for nearly 2 miles up Asylum Run, a tributary of Paxton Creek, with a section that breaks off and heads north to Veterans Memorial Park just after you pass the Susquehanna Soccer Club complex. The right fork continues alongside and on Pine, Stanley, and North Parkway Drives to the grounds of the National Civil War Museum.

The path follows a creek and takes a couple of short side streets to the Five Senses Garden at mile 15. As you continue, watch on the right for the Martin Luther King Jr. Memorial, accessible only from the trail. You'll return to the Susquehanna River in another 2.5 miles through the woods surrounding Spring

The Capital Area Greenbelt commands a view of the Market Street Bridge, which spans the Susquehanna River.

Creek. Note the extra loop in the trail that takes you around Phoenix Park. The Walnut Street Bridge is less than 3 miles from here.

If you'd like to experience the trail with a large group, the Tour de Belt mass bike ride is held in June. Groups of four or more bicyclists or hikers can arrange for a private tour with CAGA.

CONTACT: caga.org

DIRECTIONS

To reach parking on City Island from I-83 S, take Exit 43 onto Second St. Go 0.8 mile, and turn left onto Market St., crossing the bridge. Go 0.5 mile, and turn right to exit the bridge at the City Island sign. Follow the ramp to parking. Facing Harrisburg, the Walnut Street Bridge is to the left. Cross the Walnut Street Bridge to access the Capital Area Greenbelt.

To reach parking on City Island from I-83 N, take Exit 41B for Lemoyne. Turn left onto Lowther St., and go 0.2 mile. Turn left onto S. Third St, and go 0.5 mile, and then turn right onto Market St., and go 0.6 mile. Continue onto the bridge, go 0.1 mile, and turn left to exit the bridge at the City Island sign. Facing Harrisburg, the Walnut Street Bridge is to the left. Cross the Walnut Street Bridge to access the Capital Area Greenbelt.

To reach the north trailhead at Wildwood Park from I-81, take Exit 67B to US 322/US 22. Keep right to merge onto US 22 W, and go 1.8 miles. Exit toward PA 39 toward Linglestown/Rockville, and turn left onto PA 39/Linglestown Road. Go 0.1 mile, and turn left onto Industrial Road. Go 0.2 mile, and look for trailhead parking on the left.

Chester Valley Trail

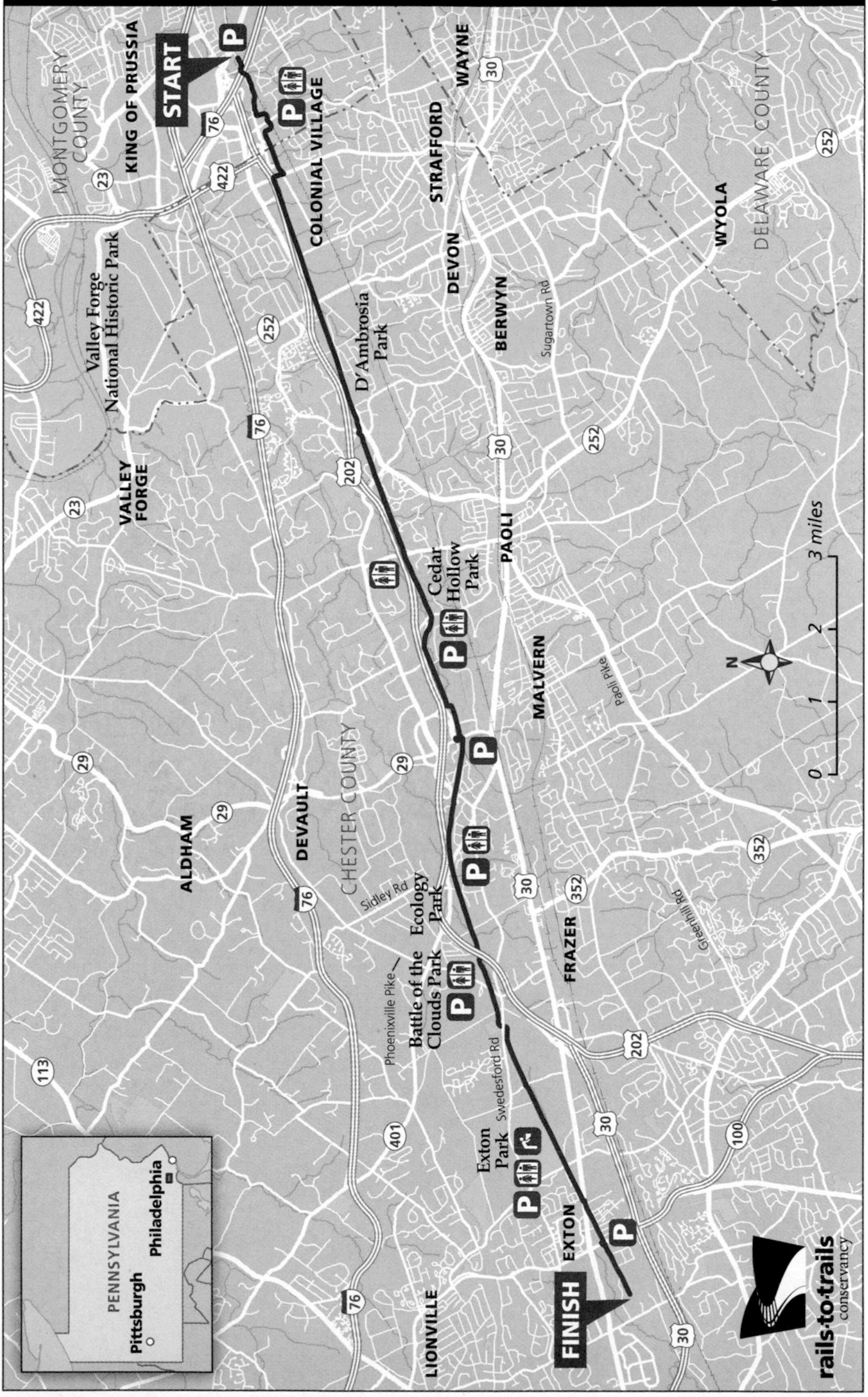

MONTGOMERY COUNTY

KING OF PRUSSIA

START

P

P

76

23

422

COLONIAL VILLAGE

WAYNE

30

STRAFFORD

DELAWARE COUNTY

252

252

WYOLA

Valley Forge National Historic Park

422

252

D'Ambrosia Park

76

DEVON

BERWYN

Sugartown Rd

VALLEY FORGE

23

202

76

Cedar Hollow Park

P

PAOLI

252

30

N

3 miles

2

1

0

ALDHAM

29

29

DEVAULT

CHESTER COUNTY

29

P

MALVERN

Paoli Pike

P

76

Sidley Rd

Ecology Park

P

30

352

352

Greenhill Rd

Battle of the Clouds Park

P

Phoenixville Pike

FRAZER

202

113

Swedesford Rd

401

Exton Park

P

30

100

PENNSYLVANIA

Philadelphia

Pittsburgh

76

LIONVILLE

FINISH

EXTON

P

30

rails-to-trails
conservancy

The Chester Valley Trail provides opportunities for recreation and alternative transportation in the congested commercial center at the northern edge of Greater Philadelphia. The paved rail-trail rolls for just under 15 miles between King of Prussia and Exton, encouraging a variety of users, such as stroller-pushing parents, colleagues on a walking meeting, or cyclists seeking a quick 30-miler.

The trail uses the corridor of the Chester Valley Branch of the Reading Railroad, which was completed between Bridgeport and Downingtown in the 1850s; the line hauled freight into the late 20th century (passenger traffic ended in 1935). Work by Chester and Montgomery Counties began in 2009 to convert the railbed into a trail. Plans call for extending it westward to Downingtown. A planned extension eastward to Bridgeport, which includes a connection to the Schuylkill River Trail (see page 221), will create access to Valley Forge National Historical Park to the north and Philadelphia to the south. The Chester Valley Trail is also part of the Circuit Trails, a developing 800-mile urban network of trails in Greater Philadelphia, of which about 350 miles are complete.

Counties
Chester, Montgomery

Endpoints
King of Prussia Road between S. Gulph Road and US 202/W. Dekalb Pike (King of Prussia) to 0.3 mile west of Indian Run St. and Commerce Dr. (Exton)

Mileage
14.8

Type
Rail-Trail

Roughness Index
1

Surface
Asphalt

Woodlands screen the Chester Valley Trail from adjacent US 202.

The 10- to 12-foot-wide asphalt path, which is open daily, 8 a.m.–sunset, has a slight uphill grade from King of Prussia to Exton. A couple of mild, short hills face travelers in Malvern and just past PA 29. The trail parallels US 202, which you'll barely notice as you travel through a wooded corridor that opens up to farmland approaching Exton.

The route starts near a cluster of hotels in King of Prussia, a community named for a local Colonial-era inn built in 1719. The renovated and relocated inn, which contains offices for the local chamber of commerce, stands 0.3 mile from the current trailhead. The future path of the trail extension to Bridgeport will pass by the old inn named for Frederick the Great.

The current trail immediately crosses I-76 on a pedestrian bridge and heads west past retail centers and office parks along US 202. The rail-trail takes a straight shot across the landscape, except for turns to accommodate busy road crossings. In the less congested western end, the trail utilizes short tunnels to cross US 202 and Swedesford Road.

There's no lack of fast food and restaurants in the retail centers along the eastern segment. You'll pass several small parks with picnic tables: D'Ambrosia Park at 4 miles, Cedar Hollow Park at 6.6 miles, and Ecology Park at 10.1 miles. The landscape opens up beyond here, with more farms and less congestion.

While Valley Forge is located north of the trail, other historic locations of the Revolutionary War are closer by. One of those is Battle of the Clouds Park, located 1 mile past Ecology Park, where the trail crosses Phoenixville Pike. The park commemorates a Revolutionary War attack in 1777 that was foiled by a horrific thunderstorm that drenched the soldiers' gunpowder.

Another 1.3 miles ahead is Exton Park, which covers 727 acres and features a pond, picnic sites, and trails. The rail-trail ends in another 2.4 miles after passing through the community of Exton.

CONTACT: chesco.org/1239/chester-valley-trail or chestervalleytrail.org

DIRECTIONS

To reach the eastern endpoint in King of Prussia from I-76, take Exit 328B. Merge onto US 202/W. Dekalb Pike. Go 180 feet, and turn right onto King of Prussia Road. Then go 0.2 mile, and turn left into the King of Prussia park and ride lot. The trail starts across the street.

To reach the western endpoint in Exton from I-76, take Exit 320, and turn left onto PA 29. Go 1.3 miles, and turn right onto Swedesford Road. Go 0.3 mile, and merge onto US 202 W. Go 2.9 miles, and exit toward US 30 W. Go 0.7 mile, and merge onto US 30/Exton Bypass. Go 1.6 miles, and exit toward PA 100 to Exton. Go 0.4 mile, and turn right onto Pottstown Pike. Then go 0.3 mile, and turn left onto PA 100/Commerce Dr. Go 0.1 mile, and turn left onto Main St. Look for parking on either side of the street. Sidewalks backtrack to the trail next to Commerce Dr.

The Clarion-Little Toby Trail lets you venture on the wild side for 18 miles as it traverses remote state hunting grounds adjoining the Allegheny National Forest. You'll likely see deer and other wildlife as you follow the Clarion River and Little Toby Creek. There are ghost towns to explore and an off-trail swinging bridge you can cross.

The trail consists of fine, well-packed gravel and is flat with the exception of a short hill near Ridgway. Although motorized use is prohibited, motorized wheelchairs are allowed.

The crushed-stone trail connects Ridgway and Brockway, two towns with historic districts that grew out of the early-19th-century logging industry. Both towns offer restaurants and grocery stores to stock up for your travels. The trail follows the former Ridgway and Clearfield Railroad, built in 1883 between Ridgway and Falls Creek to develop coal deposits in the area; the Pennsylvania Railroad acquired the line in 1911. The route fell into disuse between 1968 and 1972, and the Tricounty Rails to Trails Association completed the trail in 2003.

Counties
Elk, Jefferson

Endpoints
Water St. and Center St. (Ridgway) to Seventh Ave. just south of McCullough Ave. at Taylor Memorial Park (Brockway)

Mileage
18.0

Type
Rail-Trail/Rail-with-Trail

Roughness Index
1

Surface
Crushed Stone

A center section of the Clarion-Little Toby Trail becomes rail-with-trail as it runs alongside active railroad tracks for almost 2 miles.

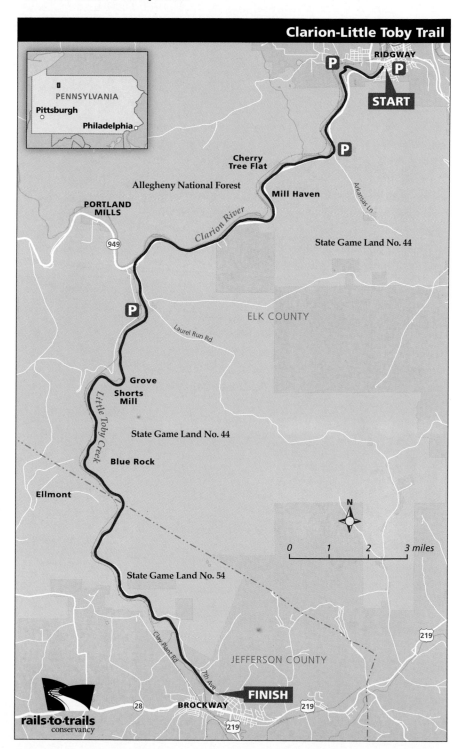

Clarion-Little Toby Trail

Because the trail passes through state game lands (Nos. 44 and 54), it's a good idea to stay on the trail and wear brightly colored clothing during hunting season. At other times you might want to explore the sites of several ghost towns and other landmarks that are described by historical markers.

Starting in Ridgway, the trail soon joins the Clarion River, which was used to transport lumber downstream in the 1800s. In 1996 the Clarion River was named a national wild and scenic river, quite an accomplishment considering that it was once known as the state's most polluted river due to acid-mine runoff and tannery pollution. At 2.5 miles, a 0.2-mile gap puts you on Portland Mills Road/PA 949.

One of the first trailside attractions—at mile 4.1—is the ruins of a dam destroyed by a flood in 1936. Just 0.1 mile beyond this point, you'll find the ghost towns of Cherry Tree Flat and Mill Haven. At the 5-mile mark, you'll see the trestle for the Buffalo & Pittsburgh Railroad that crosses the river, and in another mile, you'll ride alongside those tracks for 1.8 miles.

At 7.8 miles along the route, you'll veer away from the tracks and the Clarion River, as you follow a barely perceptible slope upstream along Little Toby Creek toward Brockway. For the next 9 miles, you travel through state game lands.

Over the next 5 miles, you'll pass old railroad abutments, the site of a Depression-era public jobs camp, ruins of a quarry and rock crusher, and the ghost towns of Grove and Shorts Mill.

The off-trail Blue Rock Swinging Bridge connects to another ghost town across Little Toby Creek at 12.2 miles. The footbridge, once the site of a road crossing between Blue Rock and Ellmont, has cables to steady yourself as you cross. You'll pass a couple more ghost town sites over the last 6 miles before you arrive in Brockway.

CONTACT: tricountyrailstotrails.org/trails/clarion-little-toby-trail

DIRECTIONS

To reach the trailhead in Ridgway from I-80, take Exit 97 for US 219/Pittsburgh-Buffalo Hwy. Head north on US 219, and go 7.6 miles; then make a sharp right onto US 219 N/Main St. Go about 13.4 miles, and bear left to remain on US 219 N/PA 948. Go 4 miles, and turn left onto Water St. Go 400 feet, and turn left onto Center St. Turn left into the trailhead parking lot. The trail starts directly across Center St.

To reach the trailhead in Brockway from I-80, take Exit 97 for US 219/Pittsburgh-Buffalo Hwy. Head north on US 219, and go 7.6 miles. Turn left onto PA 28/Main St. Go 0.4 mile, and turn right onto Seventh Ave. Go 0.3 mile, and turn left into the parking lot, which sits adjacent to the Frank Varischetti Football Field and across the street from Taylor Memorial Park.

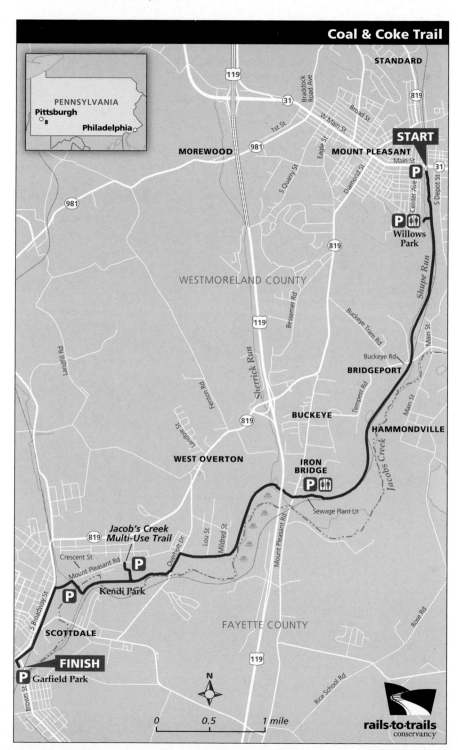

Coal & Coke Trail

PENNSYLVANIA
Pittsburgh
Philadelphia

STANDARD

119

31

Braddock Road Ave

819

Broad St

W Main St

1st St

MOREWOOD

981

Eagle St

START

MOUNT PLEASANT

Main St

31

P

981

S Quarry St

Diamond St

Center Ave

S Depot St

P

Willows Park

819

WESTMORELAND COUNTY

Shupe Run

119

Bessemer Rd

Buckeye Tram Rd

Main St

Landfill Rd

Fenton Rd

Sherrick Run

Buckeye Rd

BRIDGEPORT

Tempest Rd

819

BUCKEYE

Landenberg St

HAMMONDVILLE

WEST OVERTON

IRON BRIDGE

P

Jacobs Creek

Sewage Plant Ln

Jacob's Creek
Multi-Use Trail

819

Lou St

Mildred St

Overholt Dr

Mount Pleasant Rd

Crescent St

Mount Pleasant Rd

P

Kendi Park

P

S Broadway St

FAYETTE COUNTY

Rose Rd

SCOTTDALE

119

FINISH

P   Garfield Park

Brown St

Rice School Rd

N

0   0.5   1 mile

rails·to·trails
conservancy

The scenic Coal & Coke Trail connects the communities of Mount Pleasant and Scottdale in Westmoreland County, offering samples of the picturesque nature and friendly suburban feel of the area. The 6.1-mile trail lies on the old Pennsylvania Railroad corridor, and sections of it parallel an active Southwest Pennsylvania Railroad line.

In the early 1900s, the old railroad corridor was used to transport coal and coke from the many coal-mining companies in the county. Opened in 2007 after eight years of planning and development—and maintained by the Coal & Coke Trail Chapter—the trail allows you to walk along the same paths once taken by the country's most renowned industrialists, including Henry Clay Frick and Andrew Carnegie, among others.

The northern endpoint for the trail is at Main Street/ PA 31 in Mount Pleasant, which was first settled in the 1700s, making it one of the oldest towns in southwestern

Ponder the trail's industrial history as you travel along this secluded path.

County
Westmoreland

Mileage
6.1

Endpoints
W. Main St./PA 31
between Center Ave.
and S. Depot St. (Mount
Pleasant) to Garfield Park
at Church St. and Garfield
Ave. (Scottdale)

Type
Rail-with-Trail

Roughness Index
1–2

Surface
Asphalt, Crushed Stone

Pennsylvania. Half-mile markers line the route, creating a convenient path for exercise and active transportation, as well as recreation.

Just a block west from the endpoint, a series of shops, restaurants, convenience stores, and other services begins to line Main Street for about a mile to Braddock Road Avenue.

Heading south, you'll come to the trailhead at Willows Park in about 0.3 mile, where you'll find parking, restrooms, a children's play area, soccer and baseball fields, and picnic pavilions. From Willows Park, a 1.3-mile on-street bike route is marked to take riders up to Veterans Park at West Main Street and Diamond Street, where you'll find a granite veterans monument in the form of a life-size U.S. Army doughboy from World War I. Several restaurants are nearby. Although there are more direct routes to the park, the bike route avoids major uphill climbs.

Running along the active Southwest Pennsylvania Railroad line, the crushed-stone path passes through scenic wooded areas for about 1.2 miles to the town of Bridgeport, where it crosses over Shupe Run and Buckeye Road/SR 2001 in quick succession. Here, the surface switches to asphalt. Beyond Bridgeport, the trail quickly dips into woodlands again, passing by Buckeye and Hammondville at about 2 miles.

At the East Huntingdon Sewage Treatment Plant in Iron Bridge, about 2.8 miles from your starting point, the trail leaves the former railroad corridor and shares Sewage Plant Lane for about 0.1 mile. You'll then switch back to off-road trail, crossing under US 119 and over Sherrick Run. In this nicely shaded area, note the placard on the stone platform placed in memory of Duane Wolley, founding board member of the Coal & Coke Trail.

This area contains some wetlands and vegetation that impart a remote feel as you make your way to Mildred Street in North Scottdale. Here, you'll switch to on-road trail once again. In about five blocks, the route takes a left onto Overholt Drive, becomes a narrow pathway paralleling the road to the left, and then turns right into a wooded area adjacent to a large salvage yard (Jacobs Creek will be to your left). Upon reaching Kendi Park, a large community soccer and baseball complex, at 4.5 miles, you can opt to cut right toward the trail's first official termination point on Mount Pleasant Road near the park's playground.

At Kendi Park, the paved trail widens, with benches and trash cans lining the route. Here, the path also shares a 0.6-mile corridor with the Jacob's Creek Multi-Use Trail. The rail-trail then turns right, and the separate path ends at around 5 miles on Mount Pleasant Road in Scottdale. An approximately 1-mile on-street route, completed in 2019, leads to the center of town and terminates at Garfield Park on Church Street.

CONTACT: co.westmoreland.pa.us/1006/coal-coke-trail

Travelers will enjoy the trail's scenic views of Jacobs Creek.

DIRECTIONS

To reach the northern endpoint from I-76, take Exit 75 for US 119/PA 66 toward Greensburg, and then keep left to merge onto PA 66 Bus. N. Go 0.2 mile, and take Exit 1 to merge onto US 119 S. Go 5.3 miles, and take the exit for PA 31. Turn left onto PA 31 E, and go 1.6 miles. Turn right into the parking lot.

To reach the trailhead at Willows Park just farther south, follow the directions above to PA 31 E, and go 1.5 miles. Turn right onto Center Ave., and go 423 feet. Turn left to stay on Center Ave., and go 0.3 mile. Turn left into the trailhead parking lot. The endpoint for the trail is 0.5 mile farther north. (Take the short spur at the back of the parking lot, and turn left to head toward the endpoint.)

To reach parking at the southern endpoint from I-76, take Exit 75 for US 119/PA 66 toward Greensburg, and then keep left to merge onto PA 66 Bus. N. Go 0.2 mile, and take Exit 1 to merge onto US 119 S. Go 7.6 miles, and take the exit toward PA 819 S. Turn left onto PA 819, and head south 0.7 mile. Take a slight left onto Overholt Dr., and go 0.5 mile. Turn right onto Mount Pleasant Road, go 0.8 mile, and turn left into the small access road. Look for the parking lot on the left in 400 feet.

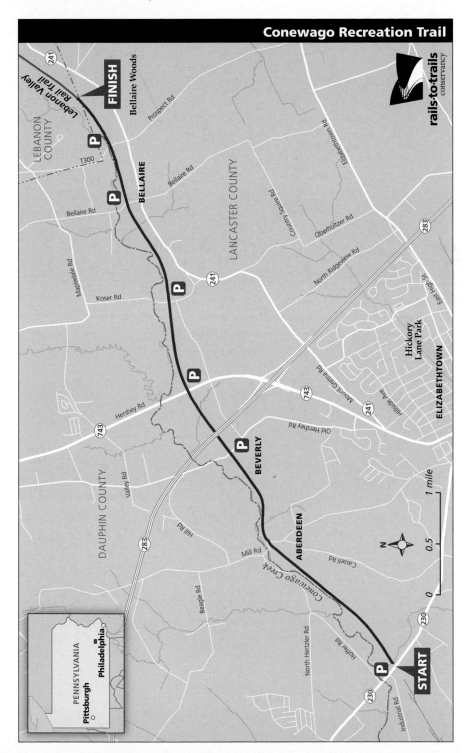

Conewago Recreation Trail

Farms and pastures surround the Conewago Recreation Trail, but it was the discovery and mining of iron ore that led to the development of the railroad that eventually resulted in this trail. The path rolls northeast from the outskirts of Elizabethtown for about 5 miles to a seamless connection at the Lancaster–Lebanon County line with the Lebanon Valley Rail-Trail (see page 139). The connecting trail continues nearly 15 miles to Lebanon. Both trails are part of the September 11th National Memorial Trail that connects the World Trade Center, Flight 93, and Pentagon Memorials, and both occupy the former railbed of the Cornwall & Lebanon Railroad, built in 1883 as a private venture to compete with a railroad that already served the iron ore mines in Cornwall. To challenge an established railroad was risky enough; now consider that the new railroad's owner was Robert Coleman, one of the richest men in Pennsylvania and a cousin of the existing railroad's president. Lawsuits ensued, and the newcomer's railroad tracks were torn up at least once.

County
Lancaster

Endpoints
PA 230/N. Market St. just south of Industrial Road to Lebanon Valley Rail-Trail near PA 241/ Mount Gretna Road and T326/Milton Grove Road (Elizabethtown)

Mileage
5.0

Type
Rail-Trail

Roughness Index
2

Surface
Crushed Stone

The Conewago Recreation Trail offers a delightful mix of lush foliage and open pastures.

As it turns out, there was enough business for everyone. Coleman, however, made bad investments elsewhere and eventually lost his railroad; the Pennsylvania Railroad ended up with it in 1918. After Hurricane Agnes washed out portions of the line in 1972, the route fell into disuse, and Lancaster County bought it in 1979 and soon thereafter turned it into a rail-trail.

The Conewago Recreation Trail follows a creek of the same name for its entire length. Its crushed-limestone surface (renovated in 2007) is hard packed and flat enough to make it wheelchair accessible, except for the Mill Road crossing about 1.4 miles from the Elizabethtown trailhead. Open dawn–dusk, the trail is shaded in the summer, although the Pennsylvania Department of Conservation and Natural Resources has been removing trees infested with emerald ash borer beetle.

You can pick up supplies for your trip in Elizabethtown, called E-town by the locals and located about 2 miles southeast of the trailhead. The town's population has ballooned since the early days of the 20th century, when it was home to a shoe factory and Klein Chocolate (now owned by Mars and making Dove brand chocolate).

A bend in the trail near its southern terminus offers a sweeping vista.

The path is wooded for a short distance, and then passes some fields before plunging back into the woods. There's a steep slope at the Mill Road crossing at 1.4 miles where a trestle has been removed; note that this specific intersection is not conducive to wheelchairs. Other road crossings along the trail are at level, except for the passage under PA 283.

Crossing Hershey Road/PA 743 (use caution at this busy road) at 2.7 miles, you'll pass Rails to Trail Bicycle Shop, which offers rental bikes, snacks, and a place to fill your water bottles. A couple of road crossings later you'll pass through Bellaire, which has an old mill that's now used as a carpentry shop. Not long after passing Prospect Road, you'll see that the trail becomes the Lebanon Valley Rail-Trail.

CONTACT: co.lancaster.pa.us/268/conewago-recreation-trail or lvrailtrail.com/conewago.pdf

DIRECTIONS

To reach the Elizabethtown trailhead from I-283 coming from Harrisburg, take Exit 1A onto PA 283 E. Go 6.4 miles east, and take the exit toward PA 230/PA 341/Toll House Road. Turn right onto Toll House Road, go 0.1 mile, and turn left onto E. Harrisburg Pike/PA 230. Go 3.1 miles, and turn left into the trailhead parking lot.

To reach the trailhead at Prospect Road/T300 from I-283, take Exit 1A onto PA 283 E. Go 11.5 miles east, and exit toward PA 743 for Hershey/Elizabethtown. Turn left onto PA 743 N/Hershey Road, go 0.5 mile, and turn right onto Beverly Road. Go 0.7 mile, and turn right onto Koser Road. Then go 0.2 mile, and bear left to stay on Koser Road. Go 0.1 mile, and turn left onto PA 241/Mount Gretna Road. Go 1.1 miles, and turn left onto Prospect Road/T300. Go 0.1 mile, and look for parking on either side of Prospect Road, where it intersects with the trail.

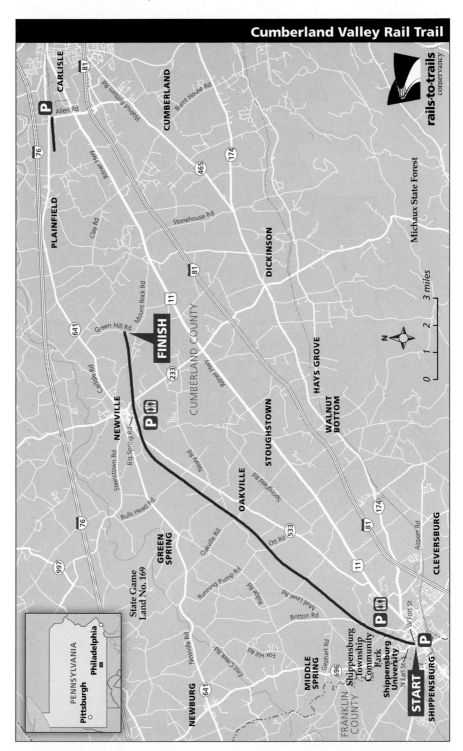

Cumberland Valley Rail Trail

The Cumberland Valley Rail Trail rolls 13.7 miles through a bucolic valley that's hemmed in by the Blue and South Mountains in south-central Pennsylvania. Running from Shippensburg to east of Newville, with a 1-mile segment in Carlisle, the trail will eventually extend seamlessly all the way to Carlisle, the county seat, for a distance of 20 miles. The pathway is part of the September 11th National Memorial Trail that connects the World Trade Center, Flight 93, and Pentagon Memorials.

The route roughly follows travel corridors first used by American Indians and then Scotch-Irish settlers in the mid-1700s. The trail traces the former Cumberland Valley Railroad, which launched service between Harrisburg and Chambersburg in 1837 and grew south all the way to Winchester, Virginia. The railroad became contentious during the Civil War as it delivered Union troops and supplies

Equestrians are welcome to ride in the grassy shoulder alongside the Cumberland Valley Rail Trail.

County
Cumberland

Endpoints
W. Fort St. and N. Earl St. (Shippensburg) to Green Hill Road between Wagners Lane and Mount Rock Road (Newville); Allen Road just south of Cooper Cir. to just south of Newville Road between McAllister Church Road and Rockey Lane (Carlisle)

Mileage
13.7

Type
Rail-Trail

Roughness Index
1

Surface
Asphalt, Concrete, Crushed Stone

into Southern territory; Confederates destroyed a section of tracks in Chambersburg, but the Union had the train running again in a week.

The last operator, Conrail, donated the railroad right-of-way to the Cumberland Valley Rails to Trails Council in 1995. The nonprofit finished nearly 10 miles of trail by 2006 and then set about acquiring the segment that extends to Carlisle in 2011. A 1-mile section in Carlisle, beginning at Allen Road, was completed in 2017, and 2018 saw an additional 2 miles open in Newville, with a goal of eventually connecting to Carlisle.

The path is mostly crushed limestone, though sections in Shippensburg and Newville are asphalt, as are numerous road crossings along the way. The trail is open dawn–dusk, and bicyclists are required to wear helmets. Also, equestrians must keep to the grass alongside the trail, except at road crossings.

If you start in Shippensburg, visit the railroad museum in an old boxcar at the trailhead. Or take advantage of several restaurants and diners located near Shippensburg University. For history buffs, a dozen Civil War and agricultural history signs are posted along the route.

Shippensburg, settled in 1730, was the first community in the Cumberland Valley and was home to a fort during the French and Indian War. Three blocks from the trailhead in downtown, which was occupied by Confederate forces, Civil War historical markers are common.

The Blue and South Mountains of south-central Pennsylvania flank the trail's namesake valley.

Leaving town, you'll pass the Shippensburg University campus and arrive at another trailhead at Shippensburg Township Community Park in 1 mile. The trail is wooded for the next 2 miles and then opens up for wide-ranging views of farms and pastureland on the way to Newville. You might see an Amish family with a horse and buggy as you cross roads along the way. Also, the trail council is known for employing goats to consume invasive weeds growing along the path.

At 6.3 miles, you'll pass through Oakville, a stop on the Cumberland Valley Railroad and now a shady picnic spot. Another 3.8 miles of travel takes you to the Newville trailhead, after which you'll pass the borough of Newville on the south side. If you want a bite to eat, turn left onto Big Spring Road and head a few blocks into the old downtown, settled in 1790, where you'll find a diner and pizzeria.

The path then continues another 1.7 miles to its endpoint on Green Hill Road. A 1-mile section of trail also runs west from Allen Road in Carlisle through trees and farmland. Plans call for connecting to that segment in the future.

CONTACT: cvrtc.org

DIRECTIONS

To reach the Shippensburg trailhead from I-81 N, take Exit 24 and turn left onto PA 696/Olde Scotland Road. Go 2.1 miles, and turn left onto S. Fayette St. Then go 0.6 mile, and turn right onto Orange St. Go 0.2 mile, and turn left onto N. Earl St. Go 0.3 mile, and turn right onto W. Fort St. Look for parking immediately to your left, after passing the starting point for the trail.

To reach the Shippensburg trailhead from I-81 S, take Exit 29, and turn right onto PA 174/Walnut Bottom Road. Go 1.5 miles, and turn left onto US 11/E. King St. Go 0.8 mile, and turn right onto N. Earl St. Then go 0.3 mile, and turn right onto W. Fort St. Look for parking immediately to your left, after passing the starting point for the trail.

To reach the Newville trailhead from I-81, take Exit 37 onto PA 233. Head north, go 3.9 miles, and turn left onto Vine St. Go 0.2 mile, and continue straight to stay on PA 533/Fairfield St. 0.4 mile. Turn left onto Rich St., go 0.1 mile, and turn left onto McFarland St. The trailhead parking lot is immediately to your right.

To reach the Carlisle trailhead from I-81, take Exit 44, and head northwest on PA 465/Allen Road. Go 1.1 miles. Turn right into the parking lot, just after passing Ross Stores Distribution Center. To reach the trailhead, turn right out of the parking lot onto Allen Road, and go about 0.2 mile. Look for the trailhead on your left.

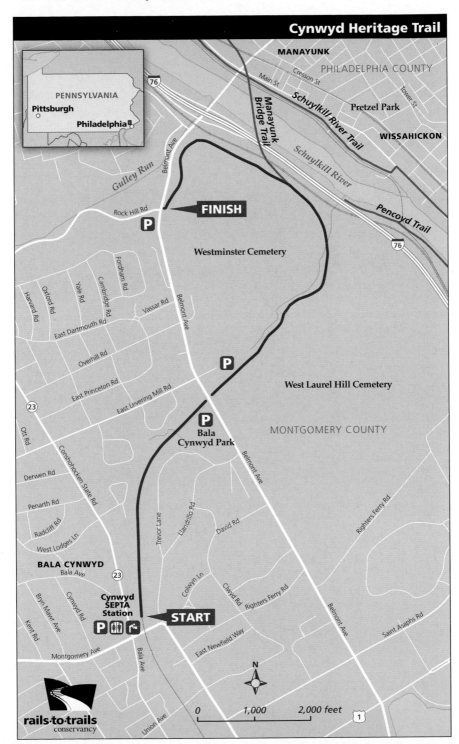

Cynwyd Heritage Trail

MANAYUNK

PHILADELPHIA COUNTY

PENNSYLVANIA

Pittsburgh

Philadelphia

76

Main St

Cresson St

Schuylkill River Trail

Pretzel Park

Tower St

Manayunk Bridge Trail

Schuylkill River

WISSAHICKON

Gulley Run

Belmont Ave

Rock Hill Rd

FINISH

P

Westminster Cemetery

Pencoyd Trail

76

Fordham Rd

Cambridge Rd

Yale Rd

Oxford Rd

Harvard Rd

Vassar Rd

East Dartmouth Rd

Belmont Ave

Overhill Rd

East Princeton Rd

East Levering Mill Rd

23

Olt Rd

P

West Laurel Hill Cemetery

P

Bala
Cynwyd Park

MONTGOMERY COUNTY

Conshohocken State Rd

Derwen Rd

Penarth Rd

Radcliff Rd

West Lodges Ln

BALA CYNWYD

Bala Ave

23

Trevor Lane

Llandrillo Rd

David Rd

Belmont Ave

Righters Ferry Rd

Cynwyd
SEPTA
Station

P

START

Bryn Mawr Ave

Cynwyd Rd

Kent Rd

Montgomery Ave

Bala Ave

Colwyn Ln

Clwyd Rd

Righters Ferry Rd

East Newfield Way

Belmont Ave

Saint Asaphs Rd

N

0   1,000   2,000 feet

1

Union Ave

rails·to·trails
conservancy

The Cynwyd Heritage Trail connects the Southeastern Pennsylvania Transportation Authority's (SEPTA's) Cynwyd Station to Bala Cynwyd Park, the historic West Laurel Hill Cemetery, and Westminster Cemetery, as well as a pedestrian bridge across the Schuylkill River. Though only 1.8 miles long, the trail is part of the Circuit Trails, a developing 800-mile urban network of trails in Greater Philadelphia, of which about 350 miles are currently complete.

The trail takes its name from the Bala Cynwyd community, which was settled by Welsh Quakers who named the area for villages they left behind in Wales in the late 1600s. The trail traces the former route of Pennsylvania Railroad's Schuylkill Branch, which ran from Philadelphia to Norristown beginning in 1884. SEPTA took over the commuter line in 1983 but closed the segment north of the Cynwyd station in 1986. SEPTA leased the section to Lower Merion Township, which created the paved rail-trail in 2011.

Starting at SEPTA's Cynwyd station, the trail passes through a residential neighborhood and arrives at Bala Cynwyd Park.

County
Montgomery

Endpoints
SEPTA station at Montgomery Ave. between Conshohocken State Road and Bala Ave. to Belmont Ave. and SR 3052 (Bala Cynwyd)

Mileage
1.8

Type
Rail-Trail/Rail-with-Trail

Roughness Index
1

Surface
Asphalt, Gravel

The Cynwyd Heritage Trail connects with the Manayunk Bridge Trail that crosses the Schuylkill River to Philadelphia's trendy Manayunk neighborhood. A connection to another trail that crosses the river, the Pencoyd Trail, was in the planning stages in 2019. Interpretive signs tell about the cemeteries, former train stations (Cynwyd and Barmouth), and an old cotton mill along the route. A gravel footpath parallels the asphalt trail at various points, where you will find benches and Adirondack chairs overlooking the river.

Starting at SEPTA's Cynwyd station, you'll find a small coffee shop and restrooms. The trail slopes downhill from here. It passes through a residential neighborhood and arrives at Bala Cynwyd Park in 0.5 mile.

Crossing under Belmont Avenue, you'll pass the historical site of the Barmouth station on the left and the 187-acre West Laurel Hill Cemetery on the right, where notable figures from the 19th and 20th centuries are buried. During the warmer months you'll see wildlife and possibly goats, as the cemetery keeps them on hand to help consume the growth on the ridge between the trail and cemetery. The Westminster Cemetery appears on the left.

At 1 mile, you'll pass the future site of a short spur route down the embankment that will connect to the Pencoyd Trail, which goes across the Schuylkill River to the Wissahickon neighborhood. At 1.3 miles, the Cynwyd Heritage Trail connects with the Manayunk Bridge Trail, which also crosses the river. Both bridges are pedestrian only.

The trail continues another 0.5 mile to circle back to Belmont Avenue.

A 0.5-mile extension from the Cynwyd station south to the Philadelphia city limits is slated to open in 2020.

CONTACT: cynwydtrail.org

DIRECTIONS

To reach the southern trailhead at the Cynwyd SEPTA Station from I-76, take Exit 339 to US 1 S/ City Ave. Merge onto US 1, heading southwest, and go 0.8 mile. Turn right onto Conshohocken State Road/PA 23. Go 0.5 mile, and turn right toward Cynwyd Station parking as Conshohocken State Road turns left. A pathway connects to the trail.

To reach the northern endpoint from I-76, take Exit 338 and head southwest on Belmont Ave./SR 3045. Go 0.3 mile, and turn right into the trailhead parking lot just past Rock Hill Road. The trail starts across Belmont Ave. from the parking lot.

The 38-mile D&H Rail-Trail traces the former corridor of the Delaware & Hudson Railway, a line that primarily carried anthracite coal out of the Lackawanna Valley in the second half of the 19th century. The D&H Railway corridor's early claim to fame: it was on its predecessor—the D&H Gravity Line—that the first steam locomotive in America, the *Stourbridge Lion,* made its one and only run in August 1829.

A good starting point at the southern terminus is the Morse Avenue trailhead, west of the Lackawanna River. Here the trail connects seamlessly with the 32.4-mile Lackawanna River Heritage Trail (see page 132), which leads south to Taylor and north along a shared corridor with the D&H Rail-Trail for 10 miles to Stillwater Dam in Clifford.

Heading north on the D&H on an improved crushed-stone surface, the trail follows the Lackawanna River,

The Starrucca Viaduct along the D&H Rail-Trail in Lanesboro Borough is an engineering wonder of the world that's still in operation today as a railroad.

Counties
Lackawanna, Susquehanna, Wayne

Endpoints
Morse Ave., 1 block northwest of N. Main St./PA 171/Lackawanna River Heritage Trail (Simpson), to 0.5 mile north of Riverview Dr. and Damascus Road (Susquehanna)

Mileage
38.0

Type
Rail-Trail

Roughness Index
2–3

Surface
Crushed Stone, Cinder

D&H Rail-Trail

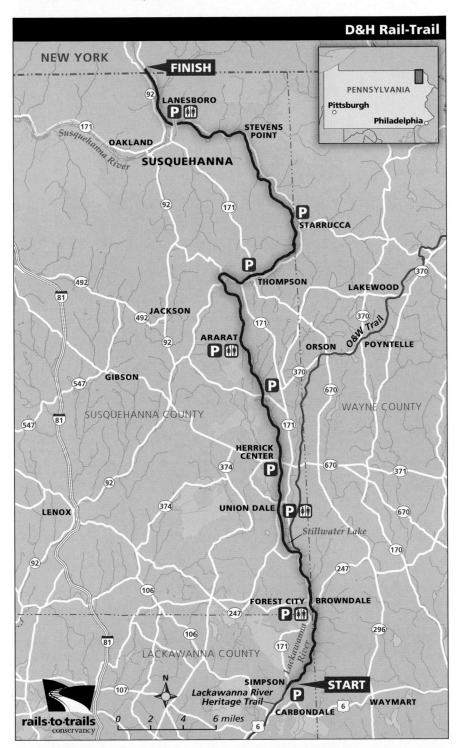

crossing it four times in the first few miles. The scars of coal mining are evident in the beginning, but after passing Forest City, about 5 miles along the route, the trail passes into the scenic Endless Mountains Region, known for farmlands, stone walls, and forests.

At Forest City you'll reach the largest trailhead and parking area on the D&H. Forest City is a welcoming trail town with many goods and services, including restaurants and markets, located just two blocks west of the trail on Main Street. Heading north, you'll cross two more bridges before being treated to views of Stillwater Dam at Stillwater Lake.

The D&H also loosely parallels the unimproved O&W Rail-Trail for its first 8 miles, from Simpson to Stillwater Dam, and loop trips are possible with a mountain bike.

At about 10.2 miles along the trail in Union Dale, at the corner of South Main Street and Norton Hill Boro Street, you'll reach a trailhead with parking and a portable restroom. Also at this location are an original D&H pusher caboose, under renovation (expected to be complete by summer 2020), and the office for the Rail-Trail Council of Northeastern Pennsylvania, which manages the trail. Stop in for trail information, or grab a sandwich at the deli next door (open 6 a.m.–6 p.m.; closed Wednesdays).

Continuing north, the route passes through the rural areas of Herrick and Burnwood, where stone walls line the route. You'll pass three lakes before reaching Ararat at about 19 miles; this is the high point of the trail's grade, which can be challenging. An ADA-accessible trail ramp is located near the Ararat Road trailhead. Here many trail users opt to turn around and enjoy the downgrade back to Forest City or Simpson.

North of the Ararat Road trailhead, the trail surface reverts to original cinder, which has been graded with drainage improvements and is conducive to mountain biking. The route makes a sharp north-south loop before heading east to Thompson, where a seasonal ice cream shop inhabits the only original, still-standing railroad station along the route. North of Thompson, you'll come to a deep ravine and the former site of a 500-foot railroad bridge that has been removed and replaced with switchback trails on either side of the ravine.

The trail continues north, hugging the mountainside—with scenic views of the village of Starrucca below—and then traveling through immense tree cover to Stevens Point in Harmony Township, where the route heads west. The trail intermittently parallels or crosses Starrucca Creek three times between Stevens Point and Lanesboro. Just north of the Brandt Bridge, trail users can bypass a creek washout by utilizing the Upper D&H, the original railbed that connected to the Erie Railroad, for about 300 yards. To continue on the D&H Rail-Trail, stay to the right as a ramp descends back to creekside. (The Upper D&H continues as a gentle upgrade about 1 mile to the active railroad, where it ends.)

Stay on the lower D&H Rail-Trail to reach Lanesboro's Luciana Park, in the shadow of the Starrucca Viaduct. An official trailhead for the route, the park has picnic tables, grills, restrooms, and a large parking area. The trail then passes beneath the railway viaduct—an engineering wonder of the world, with its 17 bluestone arches—which is part of a railroad that is still operating today. It's not uncommon to meet railroad buffs here from around the globe. Interpretive signage about the viaduct and the area's railroad history is located in Luciana Park.

The last few miles of the D&H parallel the mighty North Branch of the Susquehanna River before the trail ends at the New York border. Here the trail is overgrown, but the trail section from Stevens Point to the state line is scheduled for major improvements in 2020.

CONTACT: neparailtrails.org

DIRECTIONS

To reach the southern trailhead in Simpson from US 6, head north onto US 6 Bus. W (Roosevelt Hwy.)—if heading east on US 6, turn left, if heading west on US 6, turn right—and go 0.9 mile. Turn right onto Canaan St., go 0.2 mile, and then turn left onto Morse Ave. Go 0.1 mile, and take a slight left to stay on Morse Ave. for 0.5 mile. Look for a small trailhead parking lot to your right just after you cross the Lackawanna River. Additional parking is available about 400 feet southwest at the intersection of Morse Ave. and Enterprise Dr.

To reach the trailhead in Lanesboro from I-81, take Exit 230 for PA 171 toward Great Bend and Susquehanna. (If heading south on I-81, turn left onto PA 171; if heading north, turn right onto PA 171.) Go 8.1 miles on PA 171 S/PA 92 S, and turn right onto Exchange St. Go 0.2 mile, and turn left onto W. Main St. Go 1.8 miles, take a slight left onto S. Main St., and go 0.1 mile. After crossing Starrucca Creek, take the second right onto Depot St., and then go about 480 feet to pass under the Starrucca Viaduct. Veer left and then immediately right to reach the parking area at Luciana Park.

The D&L Trail runs for more than 140 miles through Eastern Pennsylvania, from Philadelphia's northern metro area to Mountain Top in the Appalachians. It follows historic canal and railroad routes at the core of the Delaware & Lehigh National Heritage Corridor, where natural resources and human ingenuity combined to power the nation's Industrial Revolution.

The trail follows the Delaware and Lehigh Rivers through Bucks, Northampton, Lehigh, Carbon, and Luzerne Counties. After several gaps are closed, it will be the longest rail-trail in the state at more than 160 miles. This national recreation trail is included in five regional trail system projects: the Circuit Trails, which will connect 800 miles of trail in Greater Philadelphia and New Jersey; THE LINK trail network in the Lehigh Valley, working to connect more than 500 miles of trails; the Northeastern Pennsylvania Trails Forum; the September 11th National Memorial Trail; and the East Coast Greenway, which will run from Maine to Florida.

It's a good idea to visit the official trail website (**dela wareandlehigh.org**) before heading out to check on local conditions. You'll find valuable information on detours, lodging, dining, shuttles, and other services. While directions to and from on-road sections of the trail are marked in many cases, it's best to refer to the website's detailed collection of maps and detour information for each trail gap before making a long-distance trip. A portable GPS device is also recommended.

Delaware Canal State Park Segment: 59.0 miles

The southern section of the D&L Trail from Bristol to Easton passes through the linear Delaware Canal State Park for nearly 60 miles. This is the longest section of trail, with only minor interruptions. The crushed-gravel surface follows the towpath that dates to the early 1800s, when

Counties
Bucks, Carbon, Lehigh, Luzerne, Northampton

Endpoints
Jefferson Ave. between Prospect St. and Canal St. (Bristol) to Lehigh St. at Woodlawn Ave. (Mountain Top)
Note: This developing route is not yet fully contiguous; please refer to the interactive maps on the websites listed on page 59 to bridge the gaps.

Mileage
143.8

Type
Rail-Trail/Canal Towpath

Roughness Index
2

Surface
Asphalt, Ballast, Crushed Stone, Dirt, Gravel

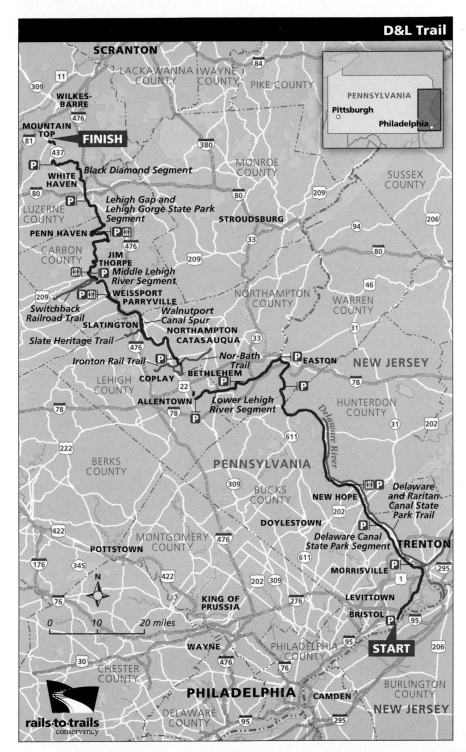

D&L Trail

Bristol was chosen as the terminus of the canal that carried huge shipments of anthracite coal to drive regional industries.

Travelers through here will find canal locks, aqueducts, and other historical structures and homes. Between Bristol and Morrisville the trail passes near Levittown, an early example of the modern American suburb. Dining and lodging are available in many towns along this route. The tree-lined waterway supports bald eagles, herons, and ospreys, as well as smaller bird species and other wildlife. Walleye, bass, and shad thrive in the Delaware River.

Technically, the starting point for the trail begins at Bristol Lions Park (100 Basin Park, Bristol, Pennsylvania); however, a gap currently exists between the park and the trailhead at Jefferson Avenue (near Prospect Street), making the Jefferson Avenue trailhead the best place to begin your journey.

One short gap, requiring some general route finding and road crossings, occurs in the first 3 miles. At Lincoln Highway/Bridge Street in Morrisville, about 9 miles along the route, a blockage on the trail requires a detour. Three former gaps—at Tullytown by the Levittown Town Center, at Tyburn Road in Morrisville, and at the CSX rail corridor just farther north of Tyburn Road—were resolved and formally opened in 2019 through efforts by the Delaware & Lehigh National Heritage Corridor and partners.

Washington Crossing Historic Park marks the site where George Washington gathered troops before embarking on the famous crossing of the Delaware River during the Revolutionary War.

A side trip across the Calhoun Street Bridge in Morrisville leads to New Jersey and the Delaware and Raritan Canal State Park Trail, which runs along the Delaware River for almost 73 miles. Back on the D&L Trail, Washington Crossing Historic Park, a major attraction, lies 8 miles up from Morrisville. It marks the spot where General George Washington and his troops crossed the Delaware on Christmas night in 1776 for a successful surprise attack on British forces.

As you arrive in New Hope, cross PA 32/River Road/Main Street, and take a sidewalk for about 300 feet to a short flight of steps back up to the canal path. The trail goes through downtown, which features dining and specialty shops. A popular stop here for exploring local history is the Locktender's House (which serves as an interpretive center) and Lock 11.

From downtown New Hope, the trail follows the canal 35 miles to Easton, where it turns to head up the Lehigh River from its confluence with the Delaware.

Lower Lehigh River Segment: 16.7 miles

The D&L Trail follows the path of the Lehigh Canal from Easton to Bethlehem and Allentown, the most populated section of the trail. Barges primarily hauled coal and iron from mines and foundries upriver beginning as early as 1818.

The pathway is paved at the beginning of this stretch but later is surfaced with crushed stone. Just before crossing the Lehigh River on the Hill Road

The Mansion House Bridge provides a pedestrian crossing over the Lehigh River leading into Jim Thorpe.

bridge 2.3 miles past Easton, history buffs might enjoy continuing straight to Hugh Moore Park, home of the National Canal Museum, where visitors can ride a mule-drawn canalboat.

About 6 miles farther down the trail from the bridge, you'll find the Freemansburg Canal Education Center, located in a restored mule barn from 1829. The historical site features a canal lock, lock tender's house, and the ruins of a gristmill. Passing through neighboring Bethlehem, you'll have a clear view of the towering Bethlehem Steel chimneys across the river. Once a major steelmaker, the site is now home to an entertainment and cultural events venue named SteelStacks. This section of trail ends at Canal Park in Allentown.

Following the bend in the river north begins an 8-mile gap in the trail, where most of the route, except for a 0.5-mile path through Allentown's Overlook Park, is on shared roads.

Middle Lehigh River Segment: 31.7 miles

An unimproved, but open, 1.4-mile section of the D&L Trail runs along the east side of the Lehigh River in Catasauqua and North Catasauqua. The path resumes at the intersection of Canal Street and West 10th Street in Northampton at a trailhead it shares with the 6-mile Nor-Bath Trail (see page 166). (An interesting side trip is the Ironton Rail Trail [see page 107], across the river in Coplay, where nine towering obsolete cement kilns are preserved in Saylor Park.)

From the Northampton trailhead, the D&L Trail is paved for 1.3 miles through Canal Street Park and crosses the Lehigh River on the PA 329/West 21st Street bridge (bicyclists are encouraged to walk). On the west riverbank, the crushed-stone pathway—which follows the former railbed of the Lehigh Valley Railroad—travels upstream around a few bends through lush forests and towering cliffs with breathtaking views of the river. In 11 miles you'll reach Slatington, where you'll find the Slate Heritage Trail junction; both are named for the abundant slate deposits mined here.

Across the Lehigh River via the PA 873/Main Street Bridge is the 3.9-mile Walnutport Canal Spur that passes through Walnutport, where old locks, a lock tender's house and museum, and ruins of an aqueduct are visible.

Lehigh Gap and Lehigh Gorge State Park Segment: 24.9 miles

Staying on the main D&L Trail for 2 miles after the Main Street Bridge, you'll enter the narrow Lehigh Gap. The Lehigh River and a highway also squeeze through the Kittatinny Ridge water gap, and the Appalachian Trail crosses the river here too. You'll pass the Lehigh Gap Nature Center, which sits on a 750-acre toxic cleanup site left behind by a zinc processing company. This area represents

an environmental success story, as it has been revegetated and returned as a habitat for native birds and wildlife.

From the nature center, it's another 7 miles to Weissport. Note the 1-mile-long section of shared roadway on Riverview Road between East Penn Township and PA 895. Lehighton to Weissport has another 1-mile on-road segment that heads north on Lehigh Drive and then east across the river at Bridge Street to a section of trail heading 1.7 miles south to Parryville or 3 miles north toward the borough of Jim Thorpe. Just before crossing the river, you can also head 0.5 mile north to Lehighton on a spur that provides access to the downtown area, where you'll find a variety of restaurants and the headquarters for the Lehighton Outdoor Center, a biking and whitewater rafting outfitter.

On the east side of the river, the route from Weissport formerly ended just before Jim Thorpe, requiring local shuttle services to serve trail users passing through. Through a partner effort, a new pedestrian bridge, completed in the summer of 2019, enables users to seamlessly cross from Weissport west over the Lehigh River into Jim Thorpe on off-road trail, where trail users can head north along the river to Lehigh Gorge State Park and beyond.

Jim Thorpe, formerly named Mauch Chunk, is the burial site of the legendary Olympic athlete. It's also home to an 1888 train station that's the base of operations for the Lehigh Gorge Scenic Railway. Mountain bikers will enjoy the rugged Switchback Railroad Trail nearby.

The trail picks up again in Jim Thorpe on the west side of the river, just south of the North Street bridge. Dramatic river gorge views greet D&L Trail users as they cross the Nesquehoning Trestle and continue the next 25 miles on crushed stone through Lehigh Gorge State Park and state hunting grounds. (There are no services for 22 miles on this stretch, so stock up in Jim Thorpe.) You'll likely see kayakers and rafters in the river and scattered waterfalls in the steep rock face.

The next borough is White Haven, a former transportation hub during the coal-mining era and a good place to find food or lodging. Snowmobiling is allowed on the segment between Penn Haven and White Haven. At White Haven, a 0.3-mile section shares the road with Main Street and travels by restaurants, stores, and a bike rental shop.

Black Diamond Segment: 11.5 miles

The on-road segment in White Haven leads to the next section of the D&L, known as the Black Diamond Trail due to the region's coal mining heritage. The trail climbs a slope for the next 10 miles, parting company with the Lehigh River along the way, to the Black Diamond Trailhead on Woodlawn Avenue south of Glen Summit. Most riders end (or start) their long-distance rides at the Black Diamond Trailhead, as this is the current end of the main section of trail.

There's about a 4-mile gap from this trailhead north to the isolated 1.2-mile last section of the D&L Trail in Mountain Top. Studies are underway to find the best route through the mostly forested landscape. If you must continue to Mountain Top, consider a shuttle, as PA 437 has narrow shoulders.

The trail's eventual destination is the river commons of the Susquehanna River in Wilkes-Barre. The Delaware and Lehigh National Heritage Corridor is working with multiple partners to complete this trail.

CONTACT: **delawareandlehigh.org** or
trails.dcnr.pa.gov/trails/trail/trailview?trailkey=305

DIRECTIONS

To reach the southern trailhead in Bristol from I-95, take Exit 42 to merge onto US 13 S/Bristol Pike toward Bristol. Go 1.4 miles, and turn left onto Beaver St./Beaver Dam Road. Go 0.2 mile, and turn left onto Jefferson Ave. Go 0.2 mile, and turn right onto Prospect St. Make an immediate right into the parking lot.

To reach the Canal Street trailhead in Northampton from I-78 E, take Exit 59, and turn left onto W. Rock Road. In 0.2 mile turn left onto PA 145, and go 2 miles. Continue straight another 2.1 miles, as the road changes names from S. Fourth St., Basin St., S. Third St., and finally American Pkwy. Turn left onto Sumner Ave., and go 0.8 mile. Turn right onto N. Sixth St., which merges into MacArthur Road in 0.2 mile. Continue on MacArthur, which rejoins PA 145, for 2.7 miles. Turn right onto Lehigh St., go 1.2 miles, and then continue onto Eugene St., which turns into Cypress St. Turn left onto Fourth St., and go 1.3 miles (note that Fourth St. turns right and becomes Main St.). Turn left onto W. 10th St., which turns right and becomes Canal St. Look for the small parking lot at the endpoint, immediately to your left. Another larger parking lot is available just 0.3 mile farther along Canal St., to your left.

To reach the Northampton trailhead from I-78 W, take Exit 60B to merge onto PA 145 N. In 2.8 miles, continue straight onto S. Fourth St., and follow the directions above from there.

To reach the northern trailhead in Mountain Top from I-81 N, take Exit 165A to merge onto PA 309 S. (From I-81 S, take Exit 165, and turn left onto PA 309. Go 1 mile to start the following directions.) Go 3 miles, and turn left onto Woodlawn Ave. Go 0.1 mile, and turn left onto Lehigh St. Look for parking on the right.

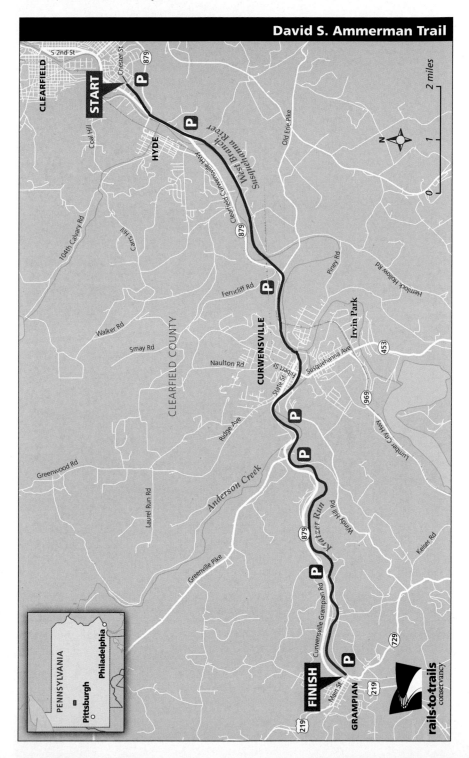

David S. Ammerman Trail

The David S. Ammerman Trail rolls through Pennsylvania coal country for nearly 11 miles between Clearfield and Grampian, skirting the West Branch of the Susquehanna River and two of its tributaries. Originally dubbed the Clearfield to Grampian Trail, the path was renamed in 2011 to memorialize local resident David S. Ammerman, who played a huge role in getting the trail built.

The trail runs in the old railbed of the Tyrone & Clearfield Railroad, which extended to Curwensville in 1874 and Grampian after that. The Pennsylvania Railroad leased the line to serve the extensive lumber and coal industries in the Appalachian Plateau. More than 100 years later, Ammerman, a local attorney, pushed the idea of using the unused railway as a recreation corridor. The Clearfield County Rails to Trails Association subsequently bought the unused right-of-way from Conrail in 1992 and completed the first trail segment in 1996.

The crushed-limestone trail runs slightly upslope from Clearfield to Grampian, allowing bicyclists to coast long stretches downhill from Grampian. With Curwensville situated about halfway, there are many opportunities for enjoying refreshments or for picking up provisions for covered picnic tables.

County
Clearfield

Endpoints
Chester St. and Linden St. (Clearfield) to PA 729/ Grandview Road and W. Stronach Road (Grampian)

Mileage
10.6

Type
Rail-Trail

Roughness Index
2

Surface
Crushed Stone

The David S. Ammerman Trail features a handful of picturesque stream crossings, such as this one over Anderson Creek.

At the trail's eastern end, early settlers near the West Branch of the Susquehanna River named the town Clearfield for the open spaces in the woods where bison browsed and American Indians had farmed. The village, originally named Chinklacamoose, had been settled for more than a thousand years. It was located along the Great Shamokin Path that connected tribal settlements on the Susquehanna and Allegheny Rivers.

The path stays close to Clearfield Curwensville Highway for the first 1.5 miles before it enters a more wooded stretch alongside the West Branch of the Susquehanna River. An early canoe route through the Appalachians, the river was later used to float timber downstream from clear-cutting operations. At 3.4 miles, a renovated railroad bridge spanning the river offers views of the watercourse and surrounding woods.

As you enter Curwensville at 5 miles, the West Branch turns south, but the trail follows its tributary, Anderson Creek, a popular kayaking stream. As the trail crosses Filbert Street, it passes by the Curwensville Feed Store (look to your right), an old Pennsylvania Railroad depot. During the same 1889 storms that caused the Johnstown Flood, floodwaters lapped at the depot's foundation. On the way out of town, you'll pass a former brickmaking plant now used to make cement for high-tech applications.

The trail gets a more remote feel after Curwensville. The route crosses Anderson Creek twice and then follows a still smaller tributary, Kratzer Run, through a forest that becomes denser. In about 5 more miles, you'll reach Grampian, named after the Grampian Mountains of Scotland. From here, it's all downhill back to Clearfield.

CONTACT: facebook.com/clearfieldrailstotrails

DIRECTIONS

To reach the trailhead in Clearfield from I-80, take Exit 120 to PA 879/Clearfield Shawville Hwy. Head south, and go 3.7 miles. Turn right onto Spruce St., go 0.2 mile, and turn left onto Chester St. Go 0.2 mile, and turn left onto Linden St. Look for trailhead parking immediately on your left.

To reach the trailhead in Grampian from I-80 E, take Exit 97 to US 219 S toward DuBois/Brockway. Keep right at the fork, follow signs for US 219, and merge onto US 219 S. Go 0.2 mile, continue on US 219 S, and go 2.2 miles. Turn right onto Liberty Blvd., go 0.6 mile, and continue onto US 219 S. Go 15.9 miles, and stay straight on PA 729/Grandview Road. Go 300 feet, and look for trailhead parking on the left.

To reach the trailhead in Grampian from I-80 W, take Exit 120. Turn left onto PA 879 W (signs for Clearfield), and go 4.3 miles. Turn left to stay on PA 879 W, go 9.9 miles, and turn left onto Grandview Road. Go 300 feet, and look for trailhead parking on the left.

The East Branch Trail is a rare dual-lane rail-trail. The 8-foot asphalt lane serves walkers, bicyclists, in-line skaters, and people in wheelchairs. Horses, specifically horses pulling Amish buggies to and from markets in Spartansburg, use the adjacent 8-foot gravel path. When built in 2010, it was the first dual-lane trail in Pennsylvania, created to help Amish avoid dangerous roads as they travel.

The Amish community in this part of Crawford County is quite large, comprising nine communities. Spartansburg, at the center of the trail, has also become a center for the sale of Amish furniture, country crafts, and baked goods. When encountering Amish on the trail, in accordance with their preference, please refrain from taking photos.

This trail follows the route of the Oil Creek and Allegheny River Railway, built in the early 1860s to connect the oil fields springing up around Titusville at that time to the Atlantic & Great Western Railway and the Philadelphia & Erie Railroad junctions in Corry. Passing through a number of owners, it became the Pennsylvania Railroad's Chautauqua Line and ran trains until 1978, when Conrail discontinued using it. Ten years later, the Clear Lake Authority in Spartansburg acquired the 15.4 miles of disused rail corridor.

The East Branch Trail crosses a dam at Clear Lake, a popular spot for fishing.

County
Crawford

Endpoints
PA 89, 0.4 mile south of Earnest Road, to PA 89 and Blakeslee Road (Spartansburg)

Mileage
3.0

Type
Rail-Trail

Roughness Index
1

Surface
Asphalt, Gravel

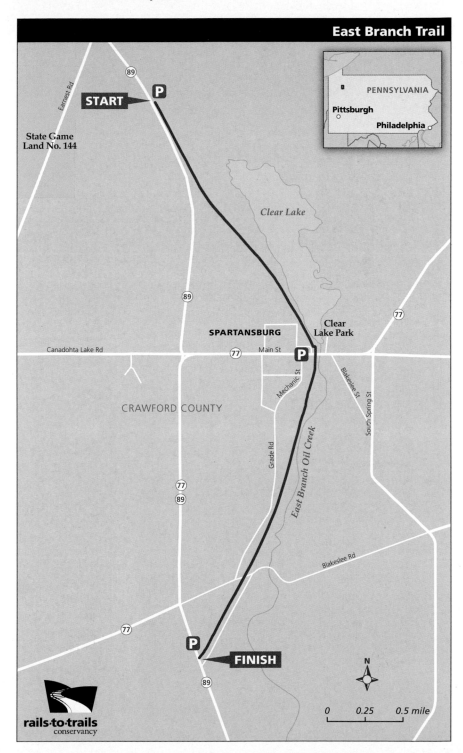

This 3-mile trail makes up one piece of the Erie to Pittsburgh Trail, which is connecting existing trails to create a 270-mile off-road route from Lake Erie's Presque Isle to Pittsburgh. When finished, a person will be able to travel off-road from Lake Erie to Washington, D.C., using the Erie to Pittsburgh Trail, the Great Allegheny Passage (see page 82), and the C&O Canal Towpath. Before that can happen, though, a number of gaps—such as the East Branch Trail's connection to the Corry Junction Greenway Trail in the north and the Queen City Trail (see page 205) in Titusville in the south—need to close. The trail is also part of the Industrial Heartland Trails Coalition's developing 1,500-mile trail network through Pennsylvania, West Virginia, Ohio, and New York.

In the north, the trail starts at a turnoff from PA 89, where you'll find two parking spaces, one reserved for people with disabilities. This is Amish farm country, and many inhabitants eschew modern conveniences. No electric or telephone wires are strung to the houses, where you'll see laundry drying in the breeze and cords of wood stacked for the stove and winter heating.

About 0.5 mile down the trail, you'll see Clear Lake to the left. The man-made lake is popular for fishing from the shore or boats. You'll reach Clear Lake Park in 1.4 miles. An old railroad trestle passes over the dam to family-owned Clear Lake Lumber.

Heading south, the trail passes through Spartansburg, crossing Main Street. Note that several stores in town feature Amish furniture and other artifacts, and several restaurants are noted for Pennsylvania Dutch cuisine. The first week of September is devoted to the community fair.

The trail follows East Branch Oil Creek out of town and rejoins PA 89 in 1.6 miles.

CONTACT: spartansburg.org/east-branch-rails-to-trails

DIRECTIONS

To reach the northern endpoint from I-79, take Exit 147A onto US 322 E/US 19 N/Conneaut Lake Road. Go 1.7 miles, take a slight right onto Park Ave., and turn right onto Linden St. Go 0.2 mile, and turn left onto Liberty St./Liberty St. Ext. Go 0.8 mile, and turn right onto North St. Go 0.1 mile, veer left to continue onto State St., and then go 0.2 mile. Take a slight right onto Washington St. Go 0.2 mile, and turn left onto PA 77 E/Hickory St. Go 25.6 miles, and turn left onto PA 77 E/PA 89 N. Go 1.2 miles, take a slight left to stay on PA 89 N, and go 1.3 miles. Parking is on the right.

To reach the Main St. trailhead in Spartansburg from I-79, follow the directions above to PA 77 E/PA 89 N, and go 1.2 miles. Turn right onto PA 77 E, and go 0.6 mile. Turn left into the trailhead parking lot. The trail runs 1.4 miles north and 1.6 miles south from here.

To reach the southern endpoint from I-79, follow the directions above to PA 77 E/Hickory St. Go 25.6 miles, and turn right onto PA 89 S. Go 0.3 mile, and turn left into the parking lot.

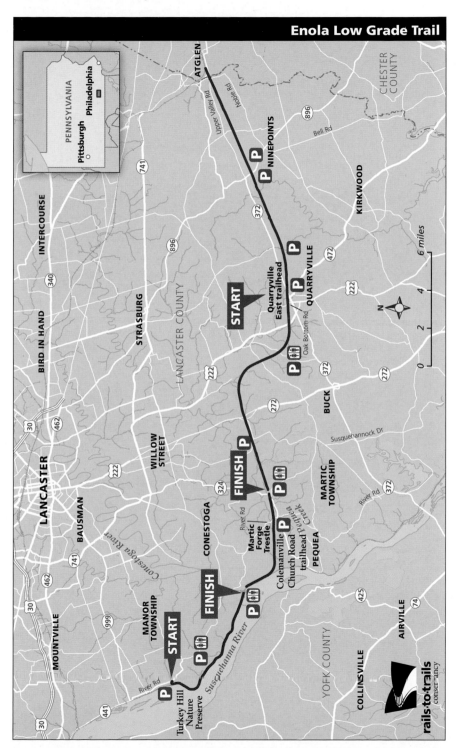

Enola Low Grade Trail

Running east-west through southeastern Pennsylvania, the Enola Low Grade Trail is remarkably flat, even for a rail-trail—it says so right there in the name! Even across hilly terrain, the trail's grades never exceed a 1% slope due to a feat of civil engineering.

Built between 1903 and 1906 by the Pennsylvania Railroad (PRR), the Low Grade Line significantly changed the landscape through wide-scale cuts and fills that were needed to create a level pathway for trains. At the time it was built, it was second only to the Panama Canal in terms of the amount of earth moved—some 22 million cubic yards that provided the PRR with a superhighway of freight rail linking western markets to the ports of Philadelphia, New York, and Baltimore.

Today, the trail is under the auspices of several townships that acquired ownership and responsibility for the

Counties
Lancaster, Chester

Endpoints
Turkey Hill Nature Preserve at River Road between Anchor Road and Letort Road to Safe Harbor Dam at Powerhouse Road and Warehouse Road (Conestoga); River Road near Colemanville Church Road to just north of Brenner Hollow Road, 0.5 mile west of Green Hill Road (Conestoga); Main St. between Zion Hill Road and Valley Ave./PA 372 (Atglen) to PA 324 and Red Hill Road (Pequea)

Mileage
28.9

Type
Rail-Trail

Roughness Index
1–3

Surface
Crushed Stone, Ballast

The Martic Forge Trestle over Pequea Creek and River Road is being rebuilt after a 2018 fire.

sections within their boundaries. With management divided between several municipalities, trail conditions can differ from one to the next, though the overarching elements—including trail regulations, signage, style of benches, and the like—remain consistent. The trail is open sunrise–sunset.

Western Section (Manor Township): 5.5 miles

With ample parking available, the westernmost trailhead in Manor Township is a good choice to start a quick trail excursion. The crushed-stone and clay-aggregate surface makes for a smooth and easy nearly 5.5-mile ride along the north bank of the Susquehanna River to the point where the Conestoga River empties into it. As of 2019, the segment ends here, though Manor Township is currently working to bridge the Conestoga River and connect its portion to the rest of the Enola Low Grade Trail. The project has been identified by the state as one of the priority trail gaps to resolve; with federal, state, and county funds secured, the project is underway, and the bridge is expected to be completed in 2022.

At the eastern end of the Manor Township section, you'll see the Safe Harbor Dam, a Great Depression–era hydroelectric public works project. Also visible from the path are active Norfolk Southern tracks, situated downslope from the trail close to the water's edge; the elevation difference between tracks and

You can catch a glimpse of the Safe Harbor Dam, a Great Depression–era project, along the Manor Township section.

trail puts the top of passing trains nearly at your feet. With a restored 1947 Norfolk Southern caboose near the trailhead—as well as picnic shelters, restrooms, observation platforms overlooking the Susquehanna, and signage that explores the history of the railroad—this section of the trail is extremely popular with families and is wheelchair accessible.

Middle Section (Conestoga): 3.4 miles

A currently disjointed section of trail extends along the Susquehanna River from River Road near Colemanville Church Road to Safe Harbor. This section is currently accessible via a trailhead from Colemanville Church Road and passes through a wooded route, terminating just before a closed trestle crossing the Conestoga River.

Eastern Section (Atglen to Martic Township): 20.0 miles

The best place to begin your journey on the eastern segment of the Enola Low Grade Trail, which provides a longer, 20-mile journey, is the Quarryville East trailhead along PA 372/East State Street. The trail quickly deteriorates east of here, turning into unimproved ballast with a sharp, rocky path suited only to hikers and the most dedicated of mountain bikers. Head west instead, where you'll ride along crushed stone and pass by Quarryville; the town, with food options, is accessible on its west end by heading south on Oak Bottom Road. Shortly after Oak Bottom Road, you'll pass over US 222, a recent addition that quite literally bridged a gap in the trail.

The trail in this section is far removed from the Susquehanna, so river views are replaced with expansive farm country—when you're not riding through a cut. You may see snakes, turtles, deer, foxes, turkeys, hawks, falcons, and bald eagles along the way. The crushed-stone path you'll follow westward is nominally downhill, but with such a slight grade, coasting is not an option. The trail offers little shade and no drinking fountains, so come prepared with sunscreen and water.

About 9.5 miles from your starting point, you'll approach what was considered by many to be the jewel of the trail: the Martic Forge Trestle over Pequea Creek and River Road. Unfortunately, the bridge was heavily damaged in a 2018 fire that has closed this section of the trail indefinitely; as of 2019, access to the trail stops more than 0.5 mile shy of the trestle, at the PA 324 parking lot. Martic Township is working to rebuild the bridge, though the time line for completion is uncertain. Officials hope to have the bridge back in use at some point between 2021 and 2023.

CONTACT: enolalowgradetrail.com

DIRECTIONS

To reach the River Road trailhead in Manor Township from I-83, take Exit 21A. Merge onto US 30 E, go 12.9 miles, and take the exit toward PA 441 immediately after crossing the Susquehanna River in Columbia. Turn right onto Linden St., and go 0.2 mile. Turn left onto N. Second St., and go 0.2 mile. Turn right onto Bridge St., and go 0.1 mile. Turn left onto PA 441 S/N. Front St., and go 3.6 miles. Continue on Water St., go 0.1 mile, and then veer left onto Herr St. and right onto River Road. Go 1.8 miles, and turn right into the Turkey Hill Nature Preserve parking lot, where the trail begins, just after passing out of farmland and into a forested area.

To reach the River Road trailhead from the intersection of US 30 and US 222 in Lancaster, head west on US 30 for 1.6 miles, and keep right at the fork to remain on US 30 W. Continue 10.7 miles, and take the PA 441 exit toward Columbia/Marietta. Continue straight onto PA 441 S, go 4.2 miles, and continue on Water St. Follow the directions above from Water St. to the Turkey Hill Nature Preserve.

To reach the Quarryville East trailhead along E. State St./PA 372 from the intersection of US 222 and US 30 in Lancaster, head east on US 30, and go 3.9 miles. Keep left to continue on US 30 E, and go another 2.4 miles. Turn right to head southbound on PA 896/Hartman Bridge Road, and go 9.3 miles (as you progress, the road becomes Decatur St. and then May Post Office Road). Turn right onto PA 372 W/Valley Road, and go 1.7 miles. Turn left into the trailhead parking lot.

To reach the Quarryville East trailhead along E. State St./PA 372 from the intersection of US 322 and US 30 in Downingtown, head west on US 30 for 10.8 miles, and continue another 2.5 miles on US 30 W. Turn left onto Swan Road, and go 2.7 miles. Turn left onto Green St., and take the first right onto Valley Ave. In 1.2 miles turn left onto SR 2009, and in 0.2 mile turn right onto Upper Valley Road. Go 2.3 miles and continue straight onto Valley Road, going another 6.6 miles. Continue on E. State St. 0.2 mile, and turn left into the trailhead parking lot.

To reach the trailhead on PA 896/Georgetown Road in Quarryville from Lancaster, follow the directions above to PA 896/Hartman Bridge Road, and go 2.4 miles. Turn left to stay on PA 896 S/Historic Dr., and go 7 miles. Turn left onto PA 896/Georgetown Road, and go 0.3 mile. Turn right onto PA 372 W/PA 896 S, and go 1.3 miles. Turn right into the parking lot, and look for spaces immediately to your left.

To reach the trailhead on PA 896/Georgetown Road in Quarryville from Downingtown, follow the directions above to Upper Valley Road. Go 2.3 miles and continue straight onto Valley Road, going another 2 miles. Turn left onto PA 896, and go 0.3 mile. Turn right into the parking lot, and look for spaces immediately to your left.

Starting in Meadville, known as the home of the zipper, the 7.2-mile Ernst Trail closes the gap between the city and surrounding forests and farms for visitors. The trail is named for Calvin Ernst, who owned the unused right-of-way of the Meadville and Linesville Railway and donated it to French Creek Recreational Trails in 1996 for trail development.

One of the first towns settled in Northwestern Pennsylvania, Meadville became a destination for Revolutionary War veterans in the early 1800s, who received land grants for their service. Farming, logging, and iron production thrived, and the Meadville Railway Company laid tracks in 1881 to the Pennsylvania Railroad connection in Linesville to bring rail service to the area. That became the Meadville & Linesville Railway three years later.

By 1900, the railway operated as the Bessemer & Lake Erie Railroad, with passenger service to the summer resort at Conneaut Lake until 1934. Service on the Meadville branch ended in 1977. This period also saw the rise and fall

The Ernst Trail traverses a rich array of natural habitats, from creek bottomlands to meadows, marshes, and forests.

County
Crawford

Endpoints
Mary Gable Memorial Park at Shippen St. near Park Row to just east of Krider Road and Franklin St. or to Bailey Road near S. Watson Run Road (Meadville)

Mileage
7.2

Type
Rail-Trail

Roughness Index
1–3

Surface
Asphalt, Gravel, Dirt

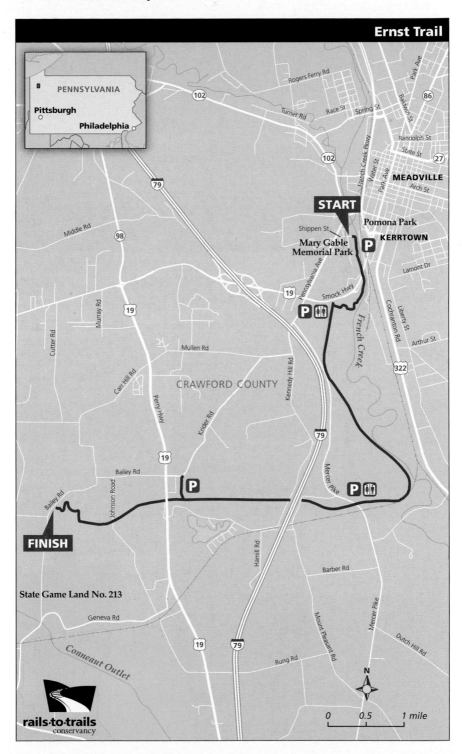

of the local zipper industry operated by the Hookless Fastener Company, which was renamed Talon. Although developed in the 1890s, a good use for the zipper wasn't found until 1923, when B. F. Goodrich used the fastener on rubber galoshes called Zippers. The galoshes are long forgotten, but zippers survive today.

The old railroad corridor starts on Shippen Street across French Creek from downtown, taking a flat route. It heads south along French Creek before turning west around the base of a hill. You'll roll along the meandering creek for the first 3.4 miles of your visit. French Creek is considered one of the most biologically diverse streams in the state, as it's home to more than 80 species of fish and 26 species of mussels. Geologists explain that French Creek used to flow north to Lake Erie, but it changed course during the most recent ice age to flow south as a tributary of the Allegheny River. That allowed the river to adopt species from both the Great Lakes and the Ohio River.

Begin in Mary Gable Memorial Park (look for a small park sign at the entrance to the access driveway for the trail); dirt and gravel comprise the trail surface of the first mile to the trailhead on US 19/US 322/Smock Highway. About 1.3 miles down the path, you'll cross a recently built covered bridge. The route then passes through a short stretch of cropland and forest alongside French Creek.

After 3.2 miles, the trail swings to the right and then heads west, crossing over Mercer Pike at 3.8 miles. Use caution here. The path then crosses under I-79, with the paved section ending at 5.5 miles (before the US 19/Perry Highway underpass). Turn right here, and go 0.2 mile to reach a trailhead and parking at Krider Road. The final 1.5 miles to Bailey Road is on a more recent extension covered in gravel. Like the first mile, the surface is fine for walkers and mountain bikers but dicey for road cyclists and not conducive to in-line skaters and wheelchair users.

CONTACT: ernsttrail.org

DIRECTIONS

To reach the endpoint at Mary Gable Memorial Park from I-79, take Exit 147A to US 6 E/US 322 E/US 19 N. Turn left onto Pennsylvania Ave., go 0.5 mile, and merge onto Pennsylvania Ave./PA 102. Go 0.4 mile, and turn right onto Shippen St. Go 0.2 mile, and look for trailhead parking directly ahead.

To reach the Bailey Road trailhead from I-79, take Exit 147B to US 6 W/US 322 W/US 19 S. Go 1.3 miles, and turn left onto US 19 S/Perry Hwy. Go 1.9 miles, and turn right onto Bailey Road. Go 0.7 mile, and turn left to stay on Bailey Road/T431. Go 0.6 mile, and turn left into the trailhead parking lot.

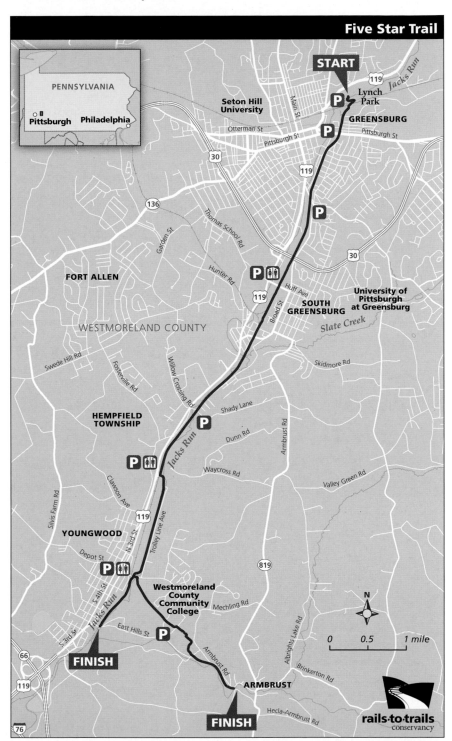

Five Star Trail

The stars in the Big Dipper and Little Dipper help navigators locate the North Star. Following the five stars in the Five Star Trail—the municipalities of Hempfield Township, Youngwood, South Greensburg, Southwest Greensburg, and Greensburg—takes travelers on a more northeastern tack. All five towns in the constellation partnered to create the nearly 7.8-mile trail southeast of Pittsburgh.

The route travels a transportation corridor shared with a major highway and an active railroad through the Laurel Highlands. It's used for recreation and exercise, but the trail is also useful for alternate transportation, as it connects five towns, a community college campus, and a city park. Most of the path is crushed stone, though a 0.9-mile segment in the southern portion runs along a street.

The trail follows the former path of the Southwest Branch of the Pennsylvania Railroad. The Westmoreland

This trailside bench is in Youngwood, one of five towns linked by the Five Star Trail.

County
Westmoreland

Endpoints
Lynch Field just east of Scott Blvd. and Roosevelt Way (near US 119/New Alexandria Road) (Greensburg) to E. Hillis St. just east of S. Third St. (Youngwood) or Armbrust Road, 0.15 mile west of Old Homestead Ln. (Armbrust)

Mileage
7.8

Type
Rail-with-Trail

Roughness Index
1

Surface
Crushed Stone

County Industrial Development Corporation bought the corridor from Conrail in 1995. Today the rail-with-trail shares the route with the Southwest Pennsylvania Railroad, a short-line railroad that runs trains from Greensburg south to Smithfield.

Plenty of parking is available at the Lynch Field trailhead in Greensburg. The town got its start soon after the Revolutionary War, when an inn was built here on the road between Fort Pitt and Philadelphia. Later, universities (Seton Hill University and the University of Pittsburgh at Greensburg) and museums, such as the Westmoreland Museum of American Art, helped make it a cultural center.

Stay on the Five Star Trail in Lynch Field, as bicycles are prohibited on side paths. You'll cross a bridge over Jacks Run, which accompanies the trail south to Youngwood. Then the path enters a tunnel to cross a set of railroad tracks and emerges in a residential and commercial neighborhood. There are establishments for food and drink as you pass through Greensburg, as well as the other four stars on the trail.

Hugging the tracks of the Southwest Pennsylvania Railroad, you'll pass through commercial zones in Southwest Greensburg and South Greensburg until you finally escape the sprawl at about mile 2.8. For the next 1.6 miles, you'll share a valley with the railroad and US 119.

The aptly named Depot Street showcases a blue caboose and the 1902 Pennsylvania Railroad depot, which serves as the Youngwood Historical Museum.

The trail is interrupted at Trolley Line Avenue, mile 4.4, and you'll have to take the shoulder for 0.9 mile. Reaching Depot Street, you'll see an old railroad station and blue caboose across the tracks. This 1902 Pennsylvania Railroad depot is the Youngwood Historical Museum, which has exhibits on railroad history as well as a gift shop and restaurant.

From the end of Trolley Line Avenue, you can go straight ahead for 0.6 mile to East Hills Street. To the left, 200 feet east on Depot Street, the trail heads 1.6 miles through the Westmoreland County Community College Campus to Armbrust Road in the community of Armbrust.

The annual Five Star Trail Poker Run is a walk/run/bike event in July that raises money for the trail.

CONTACT: co.westmoreland.pa.us/1007/five-star-trail

DIRECTIONS

To reach the Lynch Field trailhead in Greensburg from I-76, take Exit 75 for US 119/PA 66 toward Greensburg, and then keep left to merge onto PA 66 Bus. N. Go 0.7 mile, and continue straight onto PA 66 Bus. N/US 119 N/S. Third St., and go 6 miles. Turn right onto E. Pittsburgh St., and go 0.2 mile. Turn left onto Arch Ave., go 0.3 mile, and then turn right onto Beacon St. Almost immediately turn right again onto Roosevelt Way. In 0.1 mile turn right onto Scott Blvd. Turn right into the trailhead parking lot just before you reach Lynch Field Path (across from the aerobic center).

There are no parking lots on the southern endpoints of the trail. The best place to start at the southern end is the Youngwood trailhead on Depot St., near the Youngwood Historical Museum. To reach the trailhead from I-76, take the directions above to PA 66 Bus. N/US 119 N/S. Third St., and go 1.3 miles. Turn right onto Depot St., and go 0.1 mile. Turn right into the trailhead parking lot, just after passing the Youngwood Historical Museum and the train tracks. The trailhead is at the southeast corner of the lot. To reach the endpoint at E. Hillis St., access the trail at the southeast corner of the lot, and head southwest 0.6 mile down the trail. To reach the southernmost endpoint in Armbrust, turn right onto Depot St., go 250 feet, and turn right onto the Five Star Trail. The southernmost endpoint is 1.6 miles farther south.

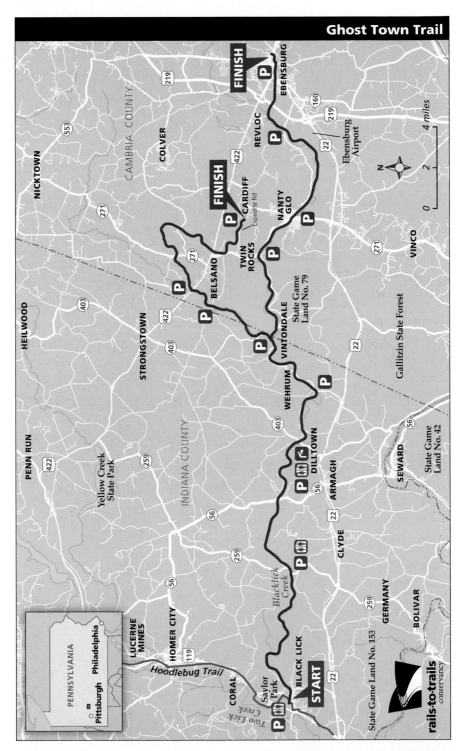

Ghost Town Trail

Part of a larger system in Western Pennsylvania known as the Trans Allegheny Trails, the Ghost Town Trail was named for the long-abandoned towns strung along the tracks of the Ebensburg & Black Lick Railroad and Cambria and Indiana Railroad. When the coal-mining industry started declining in the early 1900s, so too did the towns along the rail route, eventually fading into the ghost towns of today. Established in 1991, the Ghost Town Trail is a designated national recreation trail. The pathway is also part of the Industrial Heartland Trails Coalition's developing 1,500-mile trail network through Pennsylvania, West Virginia, Ohio, and New York.

The crushed-limestone trail winds through the scenic Blacklick Creek watershed east of Pittsburgh and offers a 32.3-mile main stem from the small community of Black Lick eastward to Ebensburg, as well as a 12.2-mile spur.

Counties
Cambria, Indiana

Endpoints
Saylor Park, just north of Burrell St. and Sycamore St. (Black Lick), to Rowena Dr. and Tanner St. (Ebensburg) or North St. just south of Expedite Road (Cardiff)

Mileage
44.5

Type
Rail-Trail

Roughness Index
1

Surface
Crushed Stone

The Ghost Town Trail also passes by boroughs that are not abandoned, such as Vintondale.

You'll pass massive iron furnaces, long-disused tipples (equipment that loaded railroad cars with coal), slag (a by-product of mining), old railroad ties, and other artifacts attesting to the path's rich rail history. Coexisting with these industrial castoffs is a variety of wildlife; hit the trail early enough and you're likely to encounter deer and more than a few chipmunks. Once the sun gets high, watch out for the occasional snake sunning itself on the warm pathway. Black bears have even been spotted crossing the trail!

The trail rises a bit more than 1,000 feet from west to east, so if you're planning a one-way trip, it might be tempting to start at the eastern trailhead and ride downhill; resist the urge and make an uphill ride instead. Spread over 32 miles, the overall slope is negligible, and you'll end in the town of Ebensburg, the largest along the route, with dining and brewery options available after the ride.

Note that Saylor Park, where you begin your ride, is also a trailhead for the 10.5-mile Hoodlebug Trail (see page 95). You'll soon make one of several crossings over Blacklick Creek—your near-constant companion along the route—and encounter a salvage yard of discarded rail cars, their rusted hulks seeming to bloom among the trees.

Interpretive markers along sections of the trail provide information about the long-gone mining towns, as well as some of the historical features you'll pass. Restrooms and a drinking fountain are available at the Dilltown trailhead, 12.5 miles from your start.

As you approach the town of Vintondale, 18.5 miles from your start, the trail will split; to the left (north), a spur of a little more than 12 miles travels along the former rail line of the Cambria and Indiana Railroad. The segment loosely parallels the North Branch of Blacklick Creek and then Elk Creek before curving south toward, and then away from, the small community of Twin Rocks, ending at North Street in Cardiff. Two miles of this trail were completed in late 2018, and plans are in the works to add another 5.5 miles, transforming this spur into a loop that meets back with the main trail at the community of Revloc. Interestingly, the surface of this extension is crushed slag—the otherwise-unusable remnants of the iron smelting process.

Bear right (east) at the fork before Vintondale, and you'll cross over Blacklick Creek and see the remains of the Eliza Furnace on your left. This hot-blast iron furnace, one of the first in the region, produced more than 1,000 tons of iron annually at its peak in the late 1840s. It's one of Pennsylvania's best-preserved iron blast furnaces and is listed on the National Register of Historic Places.

A four-paneled mural at the US 219 underpass celebrates the rail-trail's history and signals that your ride is almost over. In another 1.5 miles, you'll roll in to the Ebensburg trailhead. While the railroad's demise created many ghost towns, the reborn rail-trail has, in a fitting bookend to the region's history,

helped breathe new life into towns such as Ebensburg, with restaurants catering to the trail crowd.

The path extends another 0.5 mile to the eastern edge of Ebensburg before terminating at Rowena Drive; future plans call for extending the trail another 6 miles to Saint Francis University in Loretto.

Short portions of the trail run through state game lands; users are advised to wear orange year-round, particularly in the fall. Bring your camera along to capture the historical features and natural beauty that you'll encounter during your visit: mountain streams, stands of rhododendrons, dozens of wildflower species, and riparian woodlands.

CONTACT: indianacountyparks.org/trails/ghosttown_trail.aspx or transalleghenytrails.com

DIRECTIONS

To reach the Black Lick trailhead at Saylor Park (1284 Old Indiana Road, Blairsville) from the intersection of US 22 and US 119 in Blairsville, head north on US 119. Go 2.3 miles, and turn right onto Main St./SR 2017. Go 0.5 mile; as the road curves left, it becomes Old Indiana Road. In 0.2 mile turn left into the parking lot at Saylor Park. The trailhead is located at the southwest side of the parking lot; head south on the spur, past the baseball field, and turn left onto the Ghost Town Trail.

To reach the Black Lick trailhead from the intersection of US 422 and US 119 in Indiana, head south on US 119. Go 7 miles, and turn left onto Old Indiana Road. Go 1.3 miles, and turn right into the parking lot at Saylor Park. Access the trail by following the directions above from Saylor Park.

To reach parking near the endpoint in Cardiff from the intersection of US 22 and US 119 in Blairsville, head east on US 22. In 21 miles take the exit for PA 271, and turn left. Go 1.7 miles, and turn left to continue on PA 271/Second St. In 3.1 miles turn right onto Expedite Road, and go 1.6 miles. Turn right onto North St., and go 0.1 mile to the parking lot.

To reach parking near the eastern endpoint in Ebensburg from the intersection of US 22 and US 119 in Blairsville, head east on US 22. Go 27.8 miles, and turn left onto S. Center St. (you'll curve left at S. Locust St. to stay on S. Center St.). In 0.3 mile (near the curve) turn left onto Prave St., and look for parking immediately on your left.

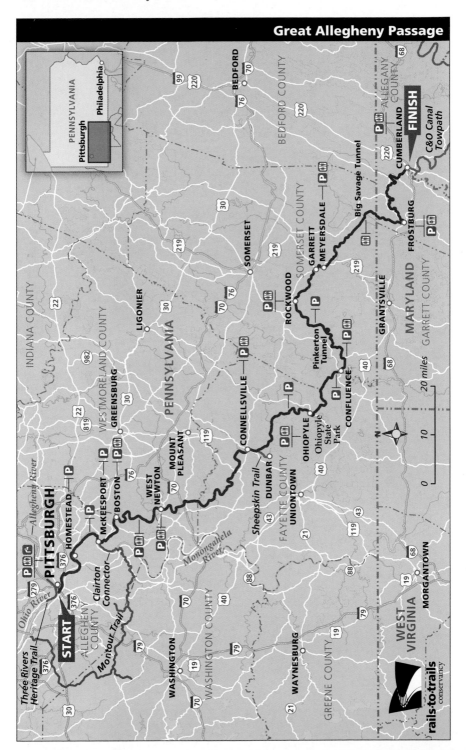

Great Allegheny Passage

20   Great Allegheny Passage

rail-
trail
Hall of Fame

GREAT
AMERICAN
RAIL-TRAIL

Ever since the Great Allegheny Passage (GAP) (**gap trail.org**) opened in 2007, overnight bicycle riders and backpackers have flocked to the 150-mile rail-trail in Western Pennsylvania. The welcoming small towns along the route lure travelers with lodging, camping, markets, and dining. Trail users marvel at the awesome scenery along one of the longest rail-trails in the United States. The biggest allure might be the ability to travel off-road for 334 miles all the way from Pittsburgh to Washington, D.C., when combining the GAP with the Chesapeake & Ohio Canal National Historical Park (C&O Canal Towpath) in Cumberland, Maryland.

The GAP is also a host trail for the 3,700-plus-mile Great American Rail-Trail—which will one day form a seamless connection between Washington, D.C., and Washington State—and is part of the September 11th National Memorial Trail that connects the World Trade Center, Flight 93, and Pentagon Memorials.

East of Meyersdale, you'll cross the curved Keystone Viaduct; in the fall, it provides extensive views of the surrounding land.

Counties
Allegany (MD); Allegheny, Fayette, Somerset, and Westmoreland (PA)

Endpoints
Point State Park near Commonwealth Pl. and Liberty Ave. (Pittsburgh, PA) to Chesapeake & Ohio Canal National Historical Park at Canal St. and Harrison St. (Cumberland, MD)

Mileage
150.0

Type
Rail-Trail/Rail-with-Trail

Roughness Index
1

Surface
Asphalt, Crushed Stone

The route mainly follows old railbeds between Pittsburgh and Cumberland, in many cases alongside scenic rivers and streams. There's a slight but steady grade from Pittsburgh to the Big Savage Tunnel at mile 126; westbound travelers will experience a steeper grade in the 24 miles they have to reach the tunnel from Cumberland. Abundant historical sites from the French and Indian Wars, as well as from the era of western expansion, can be found.

While most users are on foot or bike, equestrians are allowed on grassy adjacent paths between Boston and Connellsville, Rockwood and Garrett, and the Pennsylvania–Maryland state line to Frostburg, Maryland. Cross-country skiing and snowshoeing are popular wintertime pursuits. Before setting out, it's a good idea to check the GAP website (**gaptrail.org**) for local trail conditions, as well as for opportunities for dining, lodging, and shuttle services.

The GAP got its start in 1978 when a local nonprofit bought a segment of unused railroad, and the first section of trail was completed in 1986. The Allegheny Trail Alliance formed in 1995 and spearheaded the piece-by-piece completion of the route. It was the first rail-trail in the country to be inducted into Rails-to-Trails Conservancy's Rail-Trail Hall of Fame in 2007.

Pittsburgh Area

In the north, the trail starts on the Three Rivers Heritage Trail (see page 243) at Point State Park at the confluence of the Allegheny, Monongahela, and Ohio Rivers. The park marks the historic sites of Fort Duquesne and Fort Pitt that now sit among skyscrapers and professional sports venues in downtown Pittsburgh. The trail sticks to the Monongahela River waterfront for 4.5 miles and crosses the river at Hot Metal Bridge, which once carried molten iron from blast furnaces on the south side to steel furnaces on the north.

If you're starting from the park, note that an awkward merge point for I-279 and I-376 used to require an on-road detour, but the completion in 2018 of an off-road segment of trail, including the switchback ramp at the Smithfield Street Bridge, now allows a seamless trail experience to South Oakland. Heading east on the trail, you'll pass a trailside bike rental shop in one block.

The GAP shares the Three Rivers Heritage Trail for 10 miles to Homestead, where modern retail centers with offices and restaurants have replaced the steel factories here. The GAP follows the Monongahela another 8 miles into McKeesport to an old Pennsylvania Union Railroad bridge that dates back to 1928; it replaced a previous bridge built in 1891.

McKeesport

Tons of coal still pass by rail or barges through McKeesport, which sits at the confluence of the Monongahela and Youghiogheny (yawki-gay-nee) Rivers. A

trail junction after the bridge marks the Clairton Connector, which links to the Montour Trail (see page 157) via 5 miles of roadway. The GAP from here to Connellsville follows the former route of the Pittsburgh, McKeesport and Youghiogheny Railroad, known locally by its initials as the P Mickey. A subsidiary of the Pittsburgh & Lake Erie Railroad, the rail line carried coal and coke to Pittsburgh steel mills until it fell into disuse in 1991.

Heading south 44 miles to Connellsville, the GAP passes lush hillsides and once-booming coal towns. The first of these towns, in 4 miles, is Boston, where the trail surface becomes crushed limestone. In 15 miles, you'll arrive in the former paper mill town of West Newton, where a prior train station houses a visitor center. A bike shop, a brewery, and a row of bed-and-breakfasts along the path make this a favorite stop.

Just west of Connellsville, you'll see beehive-shaped ovens in the woods, left over from the early 20th century, that burned coal into coke for use in the steel-making industry. Today the town offers parks, cafés, and lodging to travelers. In 2 miles, the GAP passes the Sheepskin Trail, which goes about 4 miles to Dunbar.

Ohiopyle and Laurel Highlands

For the next 17 miles, the trail passes through an isolated section of the Laurel Highlands in southwestern Pennsylvania. The region is known for the highest mountains in the state, though the trail picks a level course along the Youghiogheny River. Near mile 75, the halfway point, architect Frank Lloyd Wright's famous Fallingwater house sits across the river. You can arrange visits to the house, which is open to the public, through the website (**fallingwater.org**) and catch a shuttle from Ohiopyle.

Arriving in the borough of Ohiopyle, you'll cross two high trestles across the Youghiogheny rapids below. Along this stretch of the GAP—which was the first section of the trail to open after acquisition of the corridor from the Western Maryland Railway—Ohiopyle State Park serves as a big draw for hikers, campers, and whitewater rafters.

Nine more miles along the meandering river bring you to Confluence, aptly named for the meeting of the Youghiogheny River, Casselman River, and Laurel Hill Creek. Confluence has plenty of great places to eat or catch a good night's rest. The GAP crosses the Youghiogheny River and then follows the Casselman River as it leaves town.

The trail swivels and swings northeast for 19 miles toward camping, lodging, dining, and other services in Rockwood. About halfway along this stretch, you'll pass through the 849-foot Pinkerton Tunnel positioned between two trestles over the Casselman River. The tunnel was reopened in 2015 after extensive renovations.

Big Savage Tunnel

The trail takes a southeast heading after Rockwood and follows a grade to Big Savage Mountain. You'll cross the 1,900-foot Salisbury Viaduct that crosses 100 feet above the Casselman River, US 219, and railroad tracks before you arrive in Meyersdale in 12 miles. Leaving this former coal-mining town, you'll cross the iron Bollman Bridge in less than 2 miles, followed by the curved Keystone Viaduct. Both offer scenic views of surrounding farmlands and forests, especially in the fall.

In 9 miles, you'll catch sight of the 3,294-foot Big Savage Tunnel that marks the high point of the trail and the Eastern Continental Divide. Closed late November–early April, the lighted tunnel provides welcome relief on hot summer days. Note that during the closure period, there are no safe road detours around the tunnel. It is recommended that cyclists turn around here and drive to another point on the trail to continue.

Maryland

From the tunnel, it's mostly downhill to Cumberland. Crossing the old Mason–Dixon Line—the traditional border between North and South—into Maryland, you'll roll in to Frostburg in 5 miles. You can visit downtown via a series of uphill switchbacks to a regional museum and a restored 1891 train station that serves as a restaurant. If you're here in mid-September, you can enjoy local music and crafts at the Appalachian Festival (**frostburg.edu/annual-events/afestival**).

Cross high above the Casselman River, a US highway, and railroad tracks on the 1,900-foot-long Salisbury Viaduct.

On the last 16 miles to Cumberland, you'll parallel the Western Maryland Scenic Railroad (**wmsr.com**), which runs steam locomotive excursions on weekends and many weekdays. In fact, 9 miles past Frostburg, the trail shares the 900-foot Brush Tunnel with the train. It's recommended to avoid entering the tunnel with the noisy and smoky train; the locomotive emerging from the tunnel makes a better photo anyway.

Past the tunnel is Cumberland Narrows, where the GAP squeezes through a water gap created by Wills Creek between Wills Mountain and Haystack Mountain. The old National Freeway (US 40), the scenic railroad, and CSX share this historic passage.

The C&O Canal Towpath begins where the GAP ends at the confluence of Wills Creek and the North Branch of the Potomac River in downtown. Here, you'll find the Cumberland Visitor Center for the towpath (**nps.gov/choh**).

The C&O continues another 184 miles along the Potomac River to Washington, D.C. You'll find food, lodging, and entertainment in the vicinity of the junction.

CONTACT: gaptrail.org

DIRECTIONS

Short- and long-term parking suggestions are listed at **gaptrail.org/plan-a-visit/directions-parking.**

To reach parking near Point State Park in Pittsburgh from I-376 E, take Exit 71A on the left for Grant St., and go 0.1 mile. Continue onto Grant St., take a sharp right onto Second Ave., and go 0.6 mile. Turn right into the parking lot, and look for parking on the right.

To reach parking near Point State Park in Pittsburgh from I-376 W, take Exit 73A for PA 885 S toward Glenwood. Turn right onto PA 885 S/Bates St. Go 0.1 mile, turn right onto Second Ave., and go 1.6 miles. Turn left into the parking lot, and look for parking on the right.

To reach the endpoint at the Cumberland Visitor Center from I-68/US 40 W, take Exit 43C toward downtown. Turn left onto W. Harrison St., and go 0.1 mile; turn right onto Canal St. Turn right into the parking lot, which is across from the Cumberland Visitor Center for the Chesapeake & Ohio Canal National Historical Park. To access the trail, turn right onto Canal St., go one block, and follow signs to the visitor center. You'll cross Baltimore St. to access the Great Allegheny Passage on your left.

To reach the endpoint at the Cumberland Visitor Center from I-68/US 40 E, take Exit 43A for Johnson St. toward WV 28 Alt. Continue onto S. Johnson St., go 0.2 mile, and turn right onto Greene St. Go about 450 feet, turn left to stay on Greene St., and go 0.1 mile. Greene St. turns right and becomes Baltimore St. Turn right onto Canal St., go 0.1 mile, and turn left into the parking lot. To access the trail, turn right onto Canal St., go one block, and follow signs to the visitor center. You'll cross Baltimore St. to access the Great Allegheny Passage on your left.

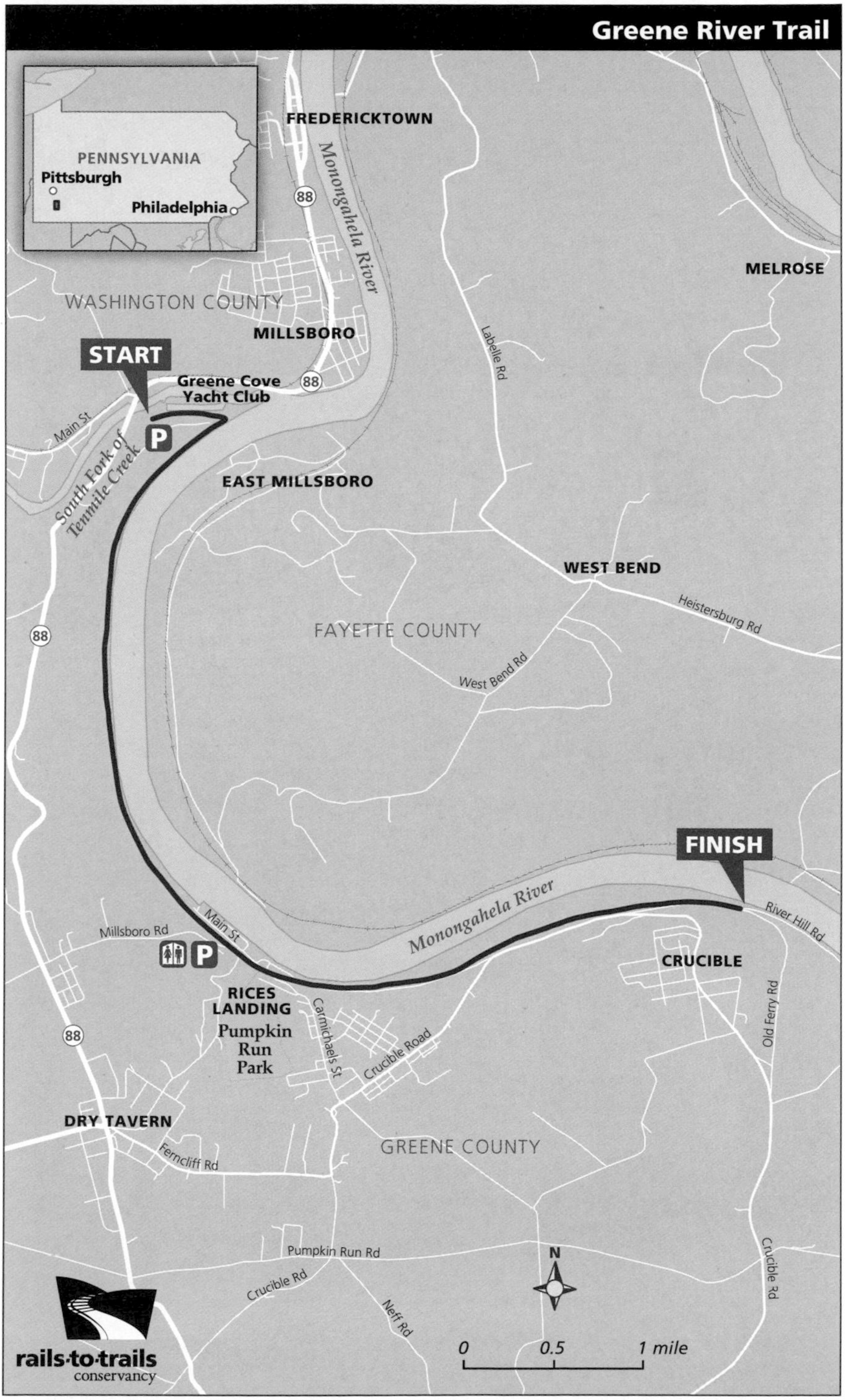

Greene River Trail

FREDERICKTOWN

PENNSYLVANIA
Pittsburgh
Philadelphia

Monongahela River

MELROSE

WASHINGTON COUNTY

MILLSBORO

START

Greene Cove
Yacht Club

88

Main St

South Fork of
Tenmile Creek

EAST MILLSBORO

Labelle Rd

WEST BEND

Heistersburg Rd

88

FAYETTE COUNTY

West Bend Rd

FINISH

Monongahela River

River Hill Rd

Millsboro Rd

Main St

CRUCIBLE

RICES
LANDING

Pumpkin
Run
Park

Carmichaels St

Crucible Road

Old Ferry Rd

88

DRY TAVERN

Ferncliff Rd

GREENE COUNTY

Crucible Rd

Pumpkin Run Rd

Crucible Rd

Neff Rd

N

Crucible Rd

rails·to·trails
conservancy

0   0.5   1 mile

The Greene River Trail provides an up close tour of riverside communities whose histories are steeped in the coal industry. You can see remnants of coal mining along the trail, as well as chipmunks, woodpeckers, and deer. The 5.1-mile crushed-stone path is named for the county, Greene, and not the river it runs alongside, the Monongahela.

The trail grew out of an idea to boost interest in the old coal company towns along the river and resuscitate their economies with tourism, while giving local residents a safe place to exercise. Greene County acquired the unused rail corridor on the west shore of the Monongahela from Conrail. Founded as the Monongahela Valley Railroad in the 1860s, the line was renamed the Pittsburgh, Virginia and Charleston Railway in 1870 and merged with the Pennsylvania Railroad in 1905.

County
Greene

Endpoints
Greene Cove Yacht Club at PA 88 near Main St. (Millsboro) to Old Ferry Road and River Hill Road (Crucible)

Mileage
5.2

Type
Rail-Trail

Roughness Index
1

Surface
Crushed Stone

The Greene River Trail links communities that border the Monongahela River and share a history in the coal industry.

The first trail segment opened in East Millsboro in 2000, and the trail was completed through Crucible in 2008. Plans call for extending the route another 2.5 miles south to a proposed trailhead with parking in Cumberland Township near Jacobs Ferry Road and Stringtown Road. Eventually, the trail could go as far south as Nemacolin on PA 21 for a total distance of 13 miles.

The trail starts on the south shore of the South Fork of Tenmile Creek at the Greene Cove Yacht Club marina. The path makes a sharp right turn at 0.3 mile to enter the steep, wooded valley of the Monongahela River. You'll be heading upriver, as The Mon flows north to Pittsburgh—the destination for frequent barge traffic in previous days.

As you travel along the base of a cliff overlooking the river, look for a welded sculpture of a hiker shortly before you reach Rices Landing trailhead at 2.8 miles. For a taste of the town's industrial past, turn left at Carmichaels Street and head toward the waterfront. The W. A. Young and Sons Foundry, built in 1900, shows the ingenuity of the founders, who could run 25 pieces of machinery off a single motor using belts and pulleys. It's open for tours on summer Sunday afternoons.

A major impediment to completing the final 2 miles to Crucible was the abandoned Crucible Mine, closed in 1961, located next to the trail. Mine shafts had to be sealed, dilapidated buildings razed, and waste coal piles reclaimed. The trail veers away from the river in the final mile, passing the former coal company town on the right. It ends at Old Ferry Road and River Hill Road.

CONTACT: co.greene.pa.us/secured/gc2/depts/rec/trails.htm

DIRECTIONS

To reach the trailhead in Millsboro from I-70, take Exit 37A to merge onto PA 43 S. Go 5.4 miles, and join PA 88/PA 43. Go 1.5 miles, and take Exit 28 to stay on PA 88/Low Hill Road. Go 2.8 miles, and stay straight to go on PA 88/Front St. Go 3.5 miles, cross the bridge over the South Fork of Tenmile Creek, and then turn left into Greene Cove Yacht Club.

To reach the trailhead in Rices Landing, follow the directions above to PA 88/Front St. Go 6 miles, and turn left onto Millsboro Road. Go 0.9 mile, and turn left onto Rices Landing Road. Go 150 feet, and turn left onto Main St. Go 0.1 mile, and turn left into the trailhead parking lot. From here, the trail heads southeast 2.3 miles to the endpoint in Crucible.

Heritage Rail Trail County Park (HRT), along with the connecting Torrey C. Brown Rail Trail that continues south through Maryland, are in Rails-to-Trails Conservancy's Hall of Fame. Both trails follow the former Northern Central Railway corridor, which once connected Harrisburg, Pennsylvania, to Baltimore, Maryland. Built in the 1800s, the railway was used during the Civil War to provide supplies to Northern troops heading south. The route remained in operation until a hurricane washed out a section in 1972.

The longer, southern segment of the trail goes from the Pennsylvania–Maryland state line up to York, Pennsylvania. This portion has a crushed-stone surface and is open to horses. In winter months, the path is also popular among cross-country skiers and snowshoers. Starting at the state line, the trail travels 1.3 miles to New Freedom— the southernmost parking point—where railroad enthusiasts can explore a restored 1940s train station. The New

County
York

Endpoints
Torrey C. Brown Rail Trail just south of Orwig Road, 0.1 mile west of Sorrel Ridge Road, at the PA–MD state line (New Freedom) to John C. Rudy County Park at Mundis Race Road between Dellinger Road and PA 24/N. Sherman St. Ext. (York)

Mileage
25.5

Type
Rail-with-Trail

Roughness Index
2

Surface
Asphalt, Crushed Stone

In addition to bountiful natural beauty, the Heritage Rail Trail County Park experience includes eye-catching public art.

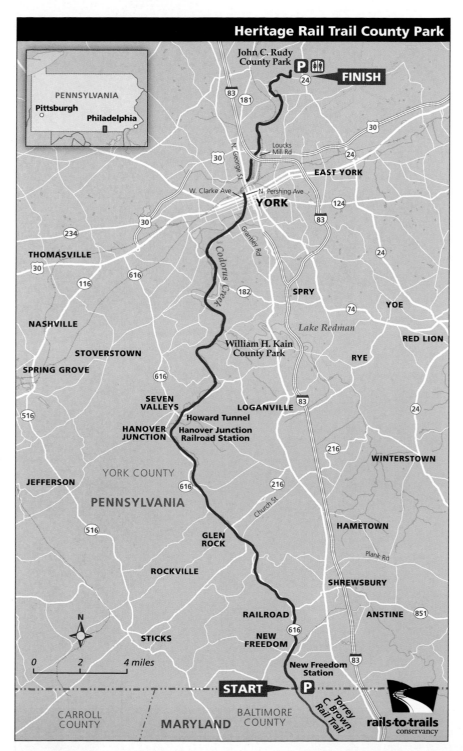

Heritage Rail Trail County Park

PENNSYLVANIA
Pittsburgh
Philadelphia

John C. Rudy
County Park
FINISH

83
181
30
30
24
Loucks
Mill Rd
N. George St
EAST YORK
W. Clarke Ave   N. Pershing Ave
YORK
124
30
234
83
Grantley Rd
THOMASVILLE
30
24
616
116
182
SPRY
Codorus Creek
NASHVILLE
74   **YOE**
Lake Redman
RED LION
STOVERSTOWN
William H. Kain
County Park
RYE
SPRING GROVE
616
**SEVEN
VALLEYS**
516
LOGANVILLE
83
24
Howard Tunnel
**HANOVER
JUNCTION**
Hanover Junction
Railroad Station
216
WINTERSTOWN
JEFFERSON
YORK COUNTY
616
216
PENNSYLVANIA
Church St
516
HAMETOWN
**GLEN
ROCK**
Plank Rd
ROCKVILLE
SHREWSBURY
N
RAILROAD
ANSTINE   851
STICKS
616
**NEW
FREEDOM**
83
0   2   4 miles
New Freedom
Station
START
Torrey C. Brown Rail Trail
rails·to·trails
conservancy
CARROLL
COUNTY
BALTIMORE
COUNTY
MARYLAND

Freedom station also features a railroad museum, an actual-size K-4 engine diorama, and an original working freight scale and safe.

The trail continues about 9 miles through farmland and along the banks of Codorus Creek before arriving at Hanover Junction Railroad Station. During the Civil War, the station served as a telegraph office and a major source of communication between Gettysburg and Washington, D.C.; President Abraham Lincoln also changed trains here on his way to deliver the Gettysburg Address. History and railroad buffs can learn more about these and other Civil War events at the station's museum, which has been restored to its 1863 appearance.

For a more immersive historical experience, trail users can board a replica 1860s steam locomotive from New Freedom to Hanover Junction. Visit **steam intohistory.com** for more information on this unique experience, complete with performances by costumed historical figures and musicians. Trail users: Note that this excursion train parallels the rail-trail, so expect to see a train at any time between New Freedom and Hanover Junction. Where the trail crosses the railroad tracks, check both directions before proceeding.

Leaving Hanover Junction, head 5 miles north to the 370-foot-long Howard Tunnel in Seven Valleys. Built in 1838, the stone-arch tunnel is one of the oldest in the country. Following Codorus Creek, the HRT continues north to the city of York. In 5 miles, you'll cross Grantley Road in York. From here through the remainder of the trail, the surface is paved and does not allow

From New Freedom to Hanover Junction, a replica 1860s steam locomotive chugs along tracks adjacent to the trail.

horses. Continue another mile to a parking lot at North Pershing Avenue and West Philadelphia Street.

In early 2019 a 1.2-mile greenway was completed between North George Street at Hamilton Avenue and Loucks Mill Road near US 30 to connect to the trail's existing Northern Extension. A four-block section of on-road trail remains between West Philadelphia Street and North George Street; however, plans are in the works to move this segment off road in 2020.

The connector follows the west side of Codorus Creek until it reaches US 30, where it then crosses over the creek via a pedestrian walkway that leads to a trail parking lot just south of US 30. The path passes underneath US 30 and then heads north 4.5 miles, ending at York's 150-acre John C. Rudy County Park, which has parking, restrooms, sports fields, pavilions, a dog park, and a variety of other outdoor amenities.

CONTACT: yorkcountytrails.org/trails/heritage-rail-trail-county-park

DIRECTIONS

To reach parking near the southernmost endpoint, take I-83 toward the Maryland–Pennsylvania state line. If heading northbound, take Exit 36 for MD 349 toward Maryland Line/Bel Air, and turn right onto MD 349 W. Go 0.3 mile, take a slight right toward MD 45 N, and continue on MD 45 N to enter Pennsylvania. Go 1.2 miles, and continue onto Main St./Susquehanna Trail S. Go 1.6 miles, and turn left onto Campbell Road. Go 1.1 miles; Campbell Road turns slightly right and becomes E. Main St. Go 0.2 mile and turn left onto Constitution Ave. Immediately turn right onto School Alley, and turn left into the trail parking lot at Marge Goodfellow Park. If heading southbound, take Exit 4 for PA 851 toward Shrewsbury in Pennsylvania. Turn right onto PA 851 W/E. Forrest Ave., and go 0.7 mile. Turn left onto S. Main St., and go 1.1 miles. Turn right onto Constitution Ave., and go 1.7 miles. Turn right onto School Alley, and turn left into the trail parking lot at Marge Goodfellow Park. Head to the southern endpoint by heading 1.2 miles south on the trail to the Maryland–Pennsylvania state line.

To reach parking at the northern endpoint in downtown York from I-83, take Exit 22 and head south on PA 181/N. George St./I-83 Bus. toward US 30 W. Follow N. George St. south 2.1 miles, and turn right onto W. Philadelphia St. Go two blocks, and turn right onto N. Pershing Ave. for street parking.

To reach the northern trailhead at John C. Rudy County Park from I-83, take Exit 22. Head north on PA 181/N. George St. Go 2 miles, and turn right onto Emig Road. In 0.6 mile, turn left onto Mundis Race Road, and go 1 mile. Turn left onto the access road to the park (you'll see signs for both John C. Rudy County Park and Heritage Rail Trail County Park). Go 0.2 mile to the parking lot, on your left.

If you have a tendency to tootle along when you walk or bicycle, then consider taking the Hoodlebug Trail. You'll find many diversions in and around the college campus in the borough of Indiana and other trailside towns, or perhaps you'd prefer to loiter in the woods alongside Stoney Run or Two Lick Creek. You could pause at the trail's historical sites, or time your visit to coincide with September's annual Hoodlebug Festival in Homer City.

The 11.3-mile crushed-stone path is named for the self-propelled passenger coach that traveled the Indiana Branch of the Pennsylvania Railroad between Blairsville and Indiana. Known by the nickname Hoodlebug, it

The Hoodlebug Trail offers several stream crossings over its 11.3-mile length.

County
Indiana

Endpoints
Rose St. and S. 13th St. Ext. (Indiana) to Burrell St. and Sycamore St. (Black Lick); Blaire Road and US 119/Pittsburgh–Buffalo Hwy. (Burrell Township) to Cornell Road and US 119/Pittsburgh–Buffalo Hwy. (Blairsville)

Mileage
11.3

Type
Rail-Trail

Roughness Index
2

Surface
Crushed Stone

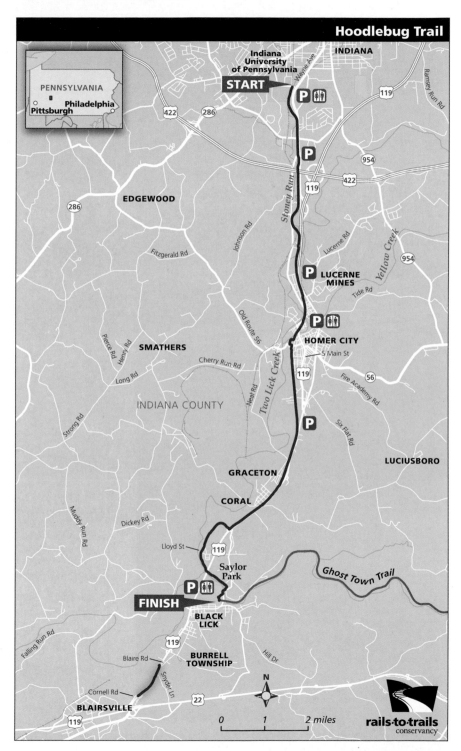

traveled the line until 1940, and the railway ceased to operate in 1977. The first section of trail opened in 2000.

Although not hilly, the trail has steeper grades than most rail-trails. Indiana marks the trail's high point, and the path dips to Homer City and then climbs again to Graceton before terminating at Black Lick, the low point. An isolated 0.8-mile section, located farther south, runs adjacent to US 119 in Burrell Township. The Hoodlebug Trail connects with the 44.5-mile Ghost Town Trail (see page 78) in Black Lick. Both are part of the Trans Allegheny Trails system, comprising 13 rail-trails that stretch across west-central Pennsylvania.

Starting at the southern edge of the Indiana University of Pennsylvania campus, the trail heads south alongside Wayne Avenue, then beside US 119 south to Black Lick. Although it parallels busy highways, the trail is often screened by woodlands.

Just before you cross US 422 at 1.5 miles, you'll pass an A-frame church building on the right that used to be the Red Rooster, a rock-and-roll venue of the 1960s. At 3 miles, you'll pass the old Lucerne Mines coal-mining complex, which included ovens that created coke into the 1970s. Arriving in Homer City at 4.6 miles, at the trailhead on North Main Street you'll see the old depot site that houses a museum in a caboose. After you cross Yellow Creek, the cemetery (rumored to be haunted) to your right dates from the mid-1800s.

You'll pass through Graceton at 7.3 miles, followed quickly by Coral. Both had coke ovens to convert coal for use in the steel industry. To the right of the path, you'll likely see Homer City Generating Station's 1,216-foot tower, reportedly the tallest in the United States. The trail veers off along Lloyd Street at 8.9 miles, then crosses under US 119 and enters Saylor Park in Black Lick. Just before the park, you'll see slag piles left over from an iron furnace that closed in the 1920s.

The trail ends in the park at the junction with the Ghost Town Trail, which heads left toward Ebensburg, 32 miles away. An isolated section of trail begins at Blaire Road and US 119/Pittsburgh–Buffalo Highway and heads south 0.8 mile, terminating at Cornell Road in Burrell Township, near Blairsville's middle school and senior high school complex.

CONTACT: indianacountyparks.org/flipbooks/hoodlebug-trail-flipbook.aspx

DIRECTIONS

To reach parking at the northern endpoint in Indiana from US 422 and PA 28 in Kittanning, head east on US 422, and go 4.4 miles. Exit to stay on US 422 E, and go 20.1 miles. Continue straight to stay on US 422 E, and go 2.2 miles. Take the PA 286/Oakland Ave. exit, and then take a sharp left onto PA 286 E/Oakland Ave., and go 0.9 mile. Turn right onto US 422 Bus., and go 0.6 mile. Turn left onto Rustic Lodge Road, and go 0.2 mile. Turn right onto Kolter Dr., and go 0.5 mile. Turn right onto University Dr., and go 0.1 mile. Turn left into the parking lot.

To reach the parking at the northern endpoint in Indiana from the intersection of US 219 and US 422 in Ebensburg, head west on US 422, and go 23.3 miles. Exit toward Sixth St./PA 954, turn right onto PA 954 N/S. Sixth St., and go 1.3 miles. Turn left onto Indiana Springs Road, and go 1.4 miles. Turn right onto University Dr., and go 0.9 mile. Turn right into the parking lot, which is surrounded on two sides by sports fields.

To reach the Black Lick trailhead at Saylor Park (1284 Old Indiana Road, Blairsville) from the intersection of US 22 and US 119 in Blairsville, head north on US 119. Go 2.3 miles, and turn right onto Main St./SR 2017. Go 0.5 mile; as the road curves left, it becomes Old Indiana Road. In 0.2 mile turn left into the parking lot at Saylor Park. The endpoint is located 2.8 miles farther south.

To reach the Black Lick trailhead at Saylor Park from the intersection of US 422 and US 119 in Indiana, head south on US 119. Go 7 miles, and turn left onto Old Indiana Road. Go 1.3 miles, and turn right into the parking lot at Saylor Park. The endpoint is located 2.8 miles farther south.

Stretching 12.6 miles through south-central Pennsylvania, this rail-trail follows the route of the former Huntingdon and Broad Top Mountain Railroad, a standard-gauge railroad founded in 1852 to carry coal—the black diamonds of Pennsylvania—to eastern markets. By the end of World War I, coal mining on Broad Top Mountain reached its peak, and the need for the railway began a slow decline; the Huntingdon and Broad Top Mountain Railroad declared bankruptcy in late 1953 and shuttered its operations early the following year. History buffs take note: The Everett Railroad Station Museum, 3 on-road miles from the southern trailhead, offers more on the railroad and history of the surrounding area (Saturdays, April–October).

Tracing a relatively flat path from the community of Tatesville, located in Everett in the south, to Riddlesburg in the north, the upper half of the trail closely parallels

A 1930s-era railroad bridge takes trail users across the Raystown Branch and serves as the visual centerpiece of the rail-trail.

County
Bedford

Endpoints
Plank Road between Methodist Church Road and Greensboro Road (Everett) to the Red Cut Picnic Area, just less than 2 miles north of Six Mile Run Road and Riverview Road (Saxton)

Mileage
12.6

Type
Rail-Trail

Roughness Index
1

Surface
Crushed Stone

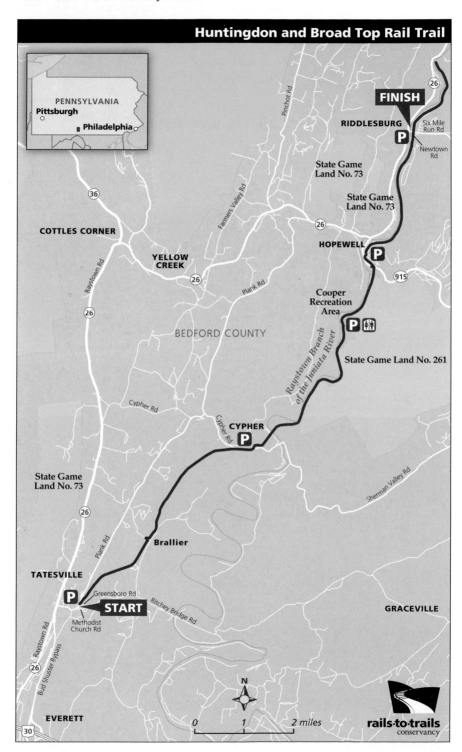

Huntingdon and Broad Top Rail Trail

PENNSYLVANIA
Pittsburgh
Philadelphia

FINISH

RIDDLESBURG

Six Mile Run Rd

Newtown Rd

Pinchot Rd

State Game Land No. 73

State Game Land No. 73

COTTLES CORNER

Farmers Valley Rd

HOPEWELL

YELLOW CREEK

Raystown Rd

Plank Rd

Cooper Recreation Area

BEDFORD COUNTY

Raystown Branch of the Juniata River

State Game Land No. 261

Cypher Rd

Cypher Rd

CYPHER

Sherman Valley Rd

State Game Land No. 73

Brallier

Plank Rd

TATESVILLE

Greensboro Rd

START

Methodist Church Rd

Ritchey Bridge Rd

GRACEVILLE

Raystown Rd

Bud Shuster Bypass

N

EVERETT

0   1   2 miles

rails·to·trails
conservancy

the Raystown Branch of the Juniata River as it too flows north. There are no water fountains along the trail, and only one permanent restroom is available at approximately the midway point, so plan ahead.

From the trailhead at Tatesville, the pathway quickly plunges into a forested canopy that provides shade in the summer. A little more than 4 miles of pedaling along the crushed-stone path brings you to a 1930s-era railroad trestle spanning the Raystown Branch. The bridge, about 250 feet long, is perhaps the visual centerpiece of the Huntingdon and Broad Top Rail Trail, delivering lovely views of the river that you'll be following for the final 6 miles of the ride to the northern endpoint.

Shortly after crossing the bridge, state game land will be on your right. Hunters can use the trail, though they are not allowed to discharge firearms from it. Nevertheless, you may hear gunshots year-round, particularly in late fall and winter. Wildlife in the area include deer, turkeys, and even bald eagles.

As you leave the state game land behind and approach the small town of Hopewell, the surface changes to a coarser stone pathway that you'll share with cars accessing the Coopers Recreation Area. Primitive restrooms are available here. Camping is allowed, as is RV parking, though there are no facility hookups available (call the Hopewell Township administrative office at 814-928-5253 to arrange camping). A large concrete pad is all that remains of the Cooper Sawmill, once a major industry in the area and a producer of the creosote used to preserve railway lumber. This spot offers easy fishing access to the river.

The trail is entirely on road through the small town of Hopewell (population less than 250), but the route is well marked. In town you'll pass by the Hopewell Train Station, the original train depot. While the station is not open for tours, the nearby Keystone Foundry Museum is (June–September, Saturdays and Sundays, 1–4 p.m.). The foundry, which served as a production and repair shop for the Huntingdon and Broad Top Railroad, features a collection of tools and equipment seemingly frozen in time the day the facility shut its doors for good in 1935. In an area once brimming with blast furnaces, foundries, and other iron industry sites, the Keystone Foundry alone has survived. *Note:* The museum is operated by volunteers from the nearby senior citizen center; call ahead to ensure the museum is open and staffed: 814-928-5111.

The trail picks up again on the north end of Hopewell with smooth crushed stone underfoot once more. With fairly consistent views of the river, you may well see kayakers and canoeists in warmer weather. A 2-mile extension north from Riddlesburg, completed in October 2019, leads to the new Red Cut Picnic Area, which includes, in addition to picnic tables, interpretive signage memorializing a famous 1909 train accident involving two steam locomotives.

The trail is open 30 minutes before sunrise until 30 minutes after sunset.

CONTACT: railstotrailsofbedfordcounty.org

The bridge across the Raystown Branch makes a great vantage point to savor the views of the river that the trail follows on its journey northward.

DIRECTIONS

To reach the southern trailhead in Everett, take I-70 W to its end in Breezewood, past mile marker 148. Turn left onto US 30 W, go 7.5 miles, and take the exit toward PA 26 N/Huntingdon/ Raystown Lake, and go 0.7 mile. Continue onto the Bud Shuster Bypass, and go 1.9 miles. Bear right to stay on the Bud Shuster Bypass, turn right onto SR 1009, and go 0.2 mile. Continue on Plank Road, go 0.1 mile, and take a sharp left into the trailhead parking lot. The trail begins just across the street from the parking lot on Plank Road.

To reach the northern trailhead in Riddlesburg from I-99 N, take Exit 7 for PA 869 toward St. Clairsville/Osterburg, and turn right onto PA 869 E. Go 3.5 miles, turn right to stay on PA 869 E, and go 5.1 miles. Turn right onto PA 36 S, and go 3.8 miles. Then turn left onto PA 26 N, and go 6.8 miles. Turn right onto Six Mile Run Road, and then take an immediate right onto Newton Road. Look for parking immediately on your left.

To reach the northern trailhead in Riddlesburg from I-99 S, take Exit 23 for PA 164 toward PA 36/Roaring Spring/Portage, and go 0.7 mile. Continue onto PA 164 E, and go 3.3 miles. Then turn left to stay on PA 164 E, and go 10.9 miles. Turn right onto PA 26 S, and go 3.7 miles. Turn right to stay on PA 26 S, and go 4.7 miles. Turn left onto Six Mile Run Road, and then take an immediate right onto Newton Road. Look for parking immediately on your left.

The Indian Creek Valley Bike and Hike Trail winds through the rugged hills in the former coal-mining region of southwestern Pennsylvania. Although remote, the trail passes through several small towns, where travelers can find food and drink at country markets and cafés.

The trail traces the Indian Creek Valley Railroad corridor that got its start primarily hauling timber out of the mountains in 1906. The railroad soon added passenger cars to serve communities along the line. By the time the Baltimore & Ohio Railroad acquired it in 1926, lumbering had declined, but coal mining and coke production boomed.

As those industries dwindled, B&O stopped using the line in 1969, and Saltlick Township acquired the section between Champion and Indian Head for use as a trail, known today as Indian Creek Valley Bike and Hike Trail. The nonprofit Mountain Watershed Association later

The northern section of the trail borders the Roaring Run Natural Area and heads to Champion on the Westmoreland–Fayette County line.

Counties
Fayette, Westmoreland

Endpoints
PA 31 and PA 381 (Jones Mills) to T723, 0.25 mile north of Roger Mill Road/Pitts Road (Normalville); Killarney Road and Bottom Road to Indian Creek Gorge at the confluence of the Indian Creek and the Youghiogheny River (Mill Run)

Mileage
13.7

Type
Rail-Trail

Roughness Index
2

Surface
Crushed Stone, Dirt

Indian Creek Valley Hike and Bike Trail (Indian Creek Valley Trail)

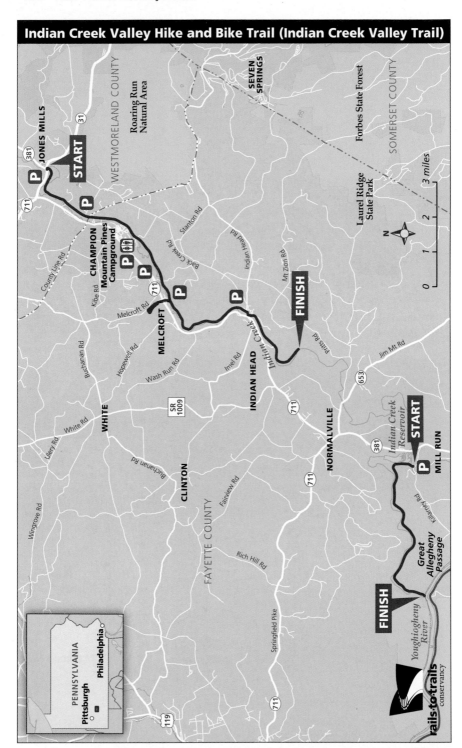

acquired other segments, which became the Indian Creek Valley Trail, explaining why the trail has two names.

Several miles of private property separate the two segments that comprise the 13.7-mile trail. The older northern section runs about 8 miles alongside Indian Creek between Jones Mills and Indian Head. The isolated southern segment passes through scenic Indian Creek Gorge to the confluence with the Youghiogheny River. Long-range plans call for connecting these two segments and building a river crossing to link with the Great Allegheny Passage (see page 82).

Beginning at the PA 31/PA 381 intersection in Jones Mills, the trail runs southwest at the foot of the Roaring Run Natural Area on Laurel Ridge for about 1.5 miles to Champion on the Westmoreland–Fayette County line. Along the way it passes a facility operated by Babcock Lumber, which was established during the timber-cutting boom.

In less than a mile, you'll likely see families from the Mountain Pines Campground enjoying Indian Creek on the opposite shore. The creek also draws kayakers and rafters to its stretches of whitewater. At the old station stop of Melcroft

Indian Creek, which the trail parallels, attracts kayakers, rafters, and other water enthusiasts.

(named for two mining executives), a 1-mile spur heads north and loops around a series of ponds used to treat polluted mine drainage.

Both Melcroft and Indian Head (2.3 miles down-trail) have trailheads and markets. The path follows the creek through a wooded area 1.8 miles past Indian Head before it dead-ends. There's no parking here.

The newest section of trail resumes at Killarney Road about 0.5 mile from PA 381. From the trailhead, the path rolls downhill through dramatic scenery in Indian Creek Gorge for 4.3 miles to the confluence with the Youghiogheny River. Plans are in the works to resurface this dirt stretch with crushed gravel. There are no services along this segment.

CONTACT: indiancreekvalleytrail.com and mtwatershed.com/indian-creek
-valley-trail

DIRECTIONS

To reach the parking at the northeast trailhead in Jones Mills from I-70/I-76, take Exit 91 for PA 31 toward PA 711/Ligonier. Turn left onto PA 31 E, and go 2.8 miles. Turn left onto PA 381 N, and go just under 0.1 mile. Look for a small pull-off to your left. The trailhead is located 0.1 mile south along PA 381, where the road intersects with PA 31.

To reach the parking in Indian Head from I-70/I-76, take Exit 91 toward Donegal. Go through the toll plaza, and turn left onto PA 31 E toward Ligonier. Go 0.3 mile, and continue straight onto PA 31/PA 711. Go 1.8 miles, and turn right to stay on PA 711/PA 381. Go 6.2 miles, and turn left onto Indian Head Road. Go 0.1 mile, and turn left at C. W. Resh Memorial Park Lane. Go about 500 feet, and look for parking on the left. The trail heads south 1.8 miles to a dead end.

To reach parking for the southern segment through Indian Creek Gorge from I-70/I-76, take Exit 91 toward Donegal. Go through the toll plaza, and turn left onto PA 31 E toward Ligonier. Go 0.3 mile, and continue straight onto PA 31/PA 711. Go 1.8 miles, and turn right to stay on PA 711/PA 381. Go 9.7 miles, and turn left to stay on PA 381/Whites Bridge Road. Go 2.1 miles, and turn right at Camp Christian Road/Killarney Road. Go 0.5 mile, and look for parking on the left. The trail ends on the north shore of the Youghiogheny River in 4.2 miles.

The Ironton Rail Trail connects nearly a dozen parks and two dozen historical sites in east-central Lehigh County. The rail-trail comprises a 5-mile loop around Coplay and Hokendauqua on the Lehigh River north of Allentown and a 4-mile spur west toward Ironton.

The trail follows the route of the Ironton Railroad, which obliged the future trail makers by creating a lasso-shaped corridor to connect iron mines in the ore-rich county to iron foundries along the river and the Lehigh Valley Railroad. Built in 1860, the railroad survived the local iron industry decline by serving the growing cement-making industry, which left behind some of the most striking artifacts along the trail. Certain segments fell into disuse starting in 1955, until the last section was discontinued in 1984.

Whitehall and North Whitehall Townships and the borough of Coplay jointly acquired the corridor in 1996. All but 1.4 miles of trail are paved. The 142-mile D&L Trail (see page 53) is just across the Lehigh River from Coplay.

The north side of the loop on Chestnut Street is a good place to start, with parking and restrooms. Heading

County
Lehigh

Endpoints
Chestnut St. near N. Ruch St. (Coplay) to Water St. near Eberhart Road/ SR 1010 (Hokendauqua) to Levans Road/SR 4008 and Mauch Chunk Road/ SR 1017 (North Whitehall)

Mileage
9.0

Type
Rail-Trail

Roughness Index
1

Surface
Asphalt, Concrete, Crushed Stone

A highlight of the Ironton Rail Trail is its passage through Saylor Park, with its 90-foot-high brick cement kilns built in 1893.

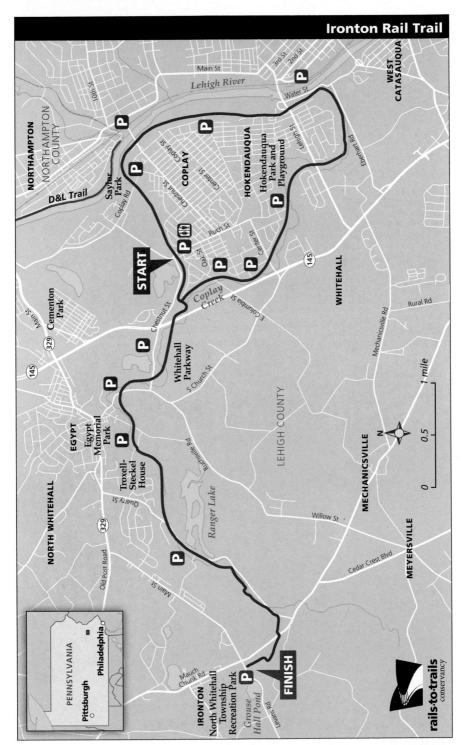

Ironton Rail Trail

east, clockwise around the loop, you'll arrive at Saylor Park in 0.7 mile. From a distance, you might think you've stumbled into Hogwarts on the set of a Harry Potter movie. What you're seeing are the nine 90-foot-high brick cement kilns built for the Coplay Cement Company in 1893. They only operated 11 years before they became obsolete, but the kilns survive today as an open-air museum of the cement industry. The Coplay community pool sits across the trail from the kiln.

The trail bends right at the Lehigh River, a Pennsylvania Scenic River. Heading south, you can see some of the deteriorating buildings of the Thomas Iron Company on the riverfront. Beginning in the 1850s, the company ran hot blast iron furnaces using locally mined iron ore until it went out of business in 1921. The community of Hokendauqua grew up around it.

The trail's riverside run ends 2.1 miles from the trailhead as you turn right and arrive at the athletic fields at the Hokendauqua Park and Playground. The route heads north along Coplay Creek and comes to a junction 1.4 miles past the park. Turn right to finish the loop, or turn left for the 4-mile spur toward Ironton.

The spur trail rolls through the 110-acre Whitehall Parkway for 0.5 mile, where you'll find dirt trails heading into the forest, as well as ruins of kilns and other historical buildings. The path then passes along the shoreline of Ranger Lake for about 0.5 mile before you come to the Troxell-Steckel House and Farm Museum. The stone farmhouse here was built in 1756, and the red barn dates from the 1800s.

You'll spy more evidence of the cement industry along the last 2 miles of trail before you arrive at the western trailhead at North Whitehall Township Recreation Park, which has baseball/softball fields and three lighted basketball courts.

CONTACT: irontonrailtrail.org

DIRECTIONS

To reach the northside trailhead in Coplay from I-78, take Exit 57, and head north on Lehigh St. Go 1.9 miles and veer right onto St. John St. In one block, turn left onto S. Eighth St. In 1.7 miles, turn right onto Greenleaf St., and go 0.1 mile. Turn left onto PA 145 N/N. Seventh St./ MacArthur Road. Go 4.6 miles, and take a sharp right onto Chestnut St. Go 0.5 mile, and turn right into the parking lot.

To reach the eastern trailhead on Water St. from I-78, follow the directions above to PA 145 N/N. Seventh St./MacArthur Road. Go 2.5 miles, and take a slight right toward Eberhart Road. Go 0.1 mile, turn right onto Eberhart Road, and go 0.9 mile. Turn left onto Water St., and go 0.2 mile. Turn left into the parking lot.

To reach the western trailhead in North Whitehall from I-78, take Exit 55, and head north on S. Cedar Crest Blvd. Go 6.4 miles. Turn left onto Mauch Chunk Road, go 0.8 mile, and turn left onto Levans Road. Turn left into the parking lot for North Whitehall Township Recreation Park.

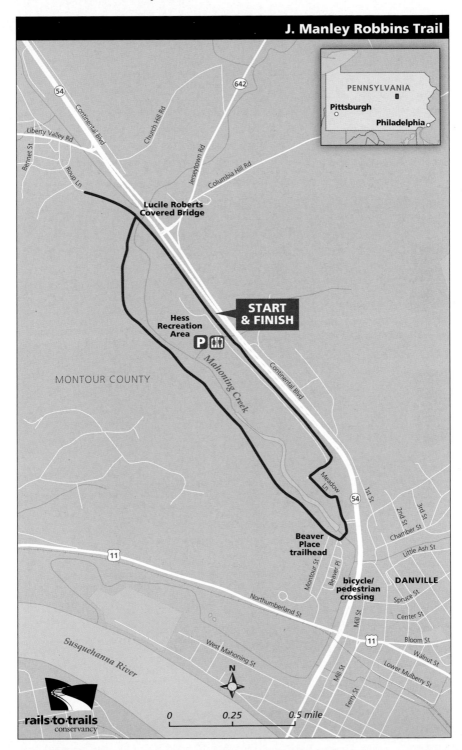

J. Manley Robbins Trail

Although the J. Manley Robbins Trail spans only 2.5 miles, its rich history and natural beauty make a stop in the rural Pennsylvania borough of Danville worthwhile. The rustic trail—forming a loop of hard-packed gravel tucked among the trees north of downtown—is best suited for hikers and mountain bikers.

In the mid-19th century, Danville became a boomtown: iron mines peppered the surrounding hillsides, bustling iron mills were located in town, and local company Montour Iron Works was a major producer of T-rails, a key technological advancement in the flourishing railroad industry. Visit in July when the town celebrates its past with the Danville Heritage Festival; many of the event's activities take place in the Hess Recreation Area, which the rail-trail traverses.

The Robbins Trail, also referred to as the Danville Bicycle Path and the Old Reading Line Trail, is built along a former narrow-gage railroad that once carried iron ore to furnaces for smelting. Fortuitously, just as use of the railroad was declining, bicycles were booming. In the 1890s, when the tracks were no longer in use, a local bicycle club converted the old railroad corridor into a pathway.

To journey through this piece of history, a good place to begin is the Hess Recreation Area, where you'll have access to parking, restrooms, and other park amenities. From there, a counterclockwise direction of travel will whisk adventurers into the solitude of the woods and away from PA 54/Continental Boulevard, which parallels the east side of the park. Near the top of the loop, you'll encounter a delightful covered wooden bridge over Mahoning Creek, a crossing once used by the Reading Railroad. (Note that road construction is planned to begin in 2021 to realign PA 642/Jerseytown Road with PA 642/Liberty Valley Road at PA 54 near the northern point of the trail loop.)

Heading southward, you'll be traveling along a slope overlooking Mahoning Creek, a popular trout-fishing stream and tributary of the Susquehanna River. The deciduous forest that envelops the trail makes this an

County
Montour

Mileage
2.5

Endpoints
Lucile Roberts Covered Bridge at the dead end of Roup Lane, 0.4 mile south of Liberty Valley Road, to the Beaver Place trailhead at Montour St., 150 feet west of Beaver Pl. (Danville)

Type
Rail-Trail

Roughness Index
2

Surface
Gravel, Grass

enchanting place to view autumn's colors. For those who want to linger, additional nature trails are available in the park.

After 1.5 miles, you'll approach the Beaver Place trailhead in a residential neighborhood. You're not far from downtown at this point, so you could take an on-street side excursion down the quiet Beaver Place roadway to the bicycle/pedestrian crossing over Mahoning Creek and Continental Boulevard to reach central Danville. At the end of the bridge, turn right to head southwest on Mill Street to enter the business district, where you'll find many dining and shopping options, as well as the opportunity to see decorative ironwork on some of the town's historical buildings.

In the rural borough of Danville, the deciduous forest along the J. Manley Robbins Trail puts on a brilliant show in autumn.

If you stayed on the trail, as you round the southern end of the loop, the route becomes on road for 0.4 mile. You'll cross over Mahoning Creek on Montour Street, which becomes Meadow Lane shortly after the creek crossing; trail signage is absent here, but you'll see a blue sign pointing to Hess Fields to know you're headed in the right direction. Soon you're back on the trail, paralleling Continental Boulevard northward. Although you will hear road noise, trees screen the pathway. Soon, you'll arrive back at the Hess Recreation Area parking lot, where you can end your journey, perhaps with a packed lunch in the picnic pavilion.

CONTACT: montourrec.com/hess-fields

DIRECTIONS

To reach the Hess Recreation Area from I-80, take Exit 224 to PA 54/Continental Blvd. toward Danville. Head south 2.5 miles, and turn right onto Montour St.; the road is unmarked, but the turn is located at the Perkins Family Restaurant. Take an immediate right onto Meadow Lane. Go 0.2 mile (the road veers left in 400 feet and then turns right in another 0.1 mile), and you'll have the option of turning right into a trailhead parking lot here. To reach the Hess Recreation Area, continue on Meadow Lane an additional 0.7 mile north to the park's main parking lot, and look for parking immediately to your left, adjacent to the sports fields.

To reach the Beaver Pl. trailhead from I-80, take Exit 224 to PA 54/Continental Blvd. toward Danville. Head south 2.5 miles, and turn right at Perkins Family Restaurant onto Montour St., and then immediately turn left to stay on Montour St. Go 0.1 mile, and look for parking on your right, where the road bends.

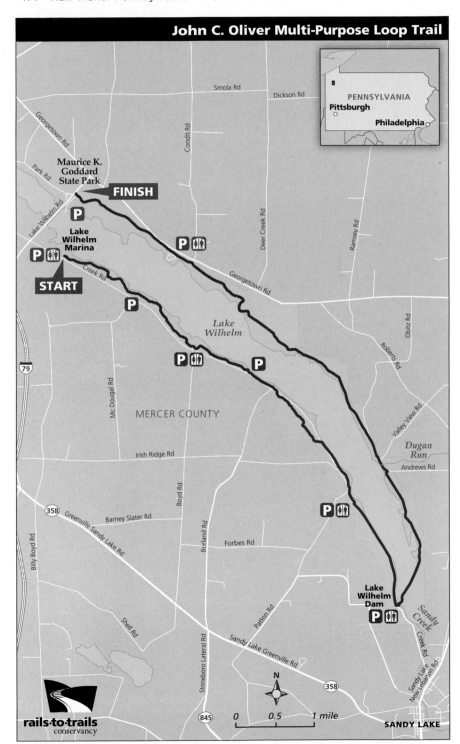

John C. Oliver Multi-Purpose Loop Trail

The 11.7-mile John C. Oliver Multi-Purpose Loop Trail is a centerpiece of Maurice K. Goddard State Park, which spans 2,856 acres in northwestern Pennsylvania. The mostly shaded, paved, off-road trail traces the northern and southern shores of Lake Wilhelm, a popular spot for both anglers and boaters; on-road connections at either end complete a pleasant, largely wooded loop around the lake. In 2015 the trail was named in honor of the first secretary of the state's Department of Conservation and Natural Resources.

Open every day of the year sunrise–sunset, trail users can engage in a variety of activities, including snowmobiling along the north shore and cross-country skiing along the south shore. The state park grounds are also open to hunters, and trail users are advised to wear orange during hunting season. Tree canopy over much of the route can result in moss and moist surfaces, so bicyclists should take caution and use safe speeds at all times.

Begin your journey at the Lake Wilhelm Marina. Here, you'll find plenty of parking and restrooms, as well as opportunities to rent kayaks, boats, and paddleboats. Note

County
Mercer

Endpoints
Lake Wilhelm Marina at Lake Wilhelm Road and Creek Road to Lake Wilhelm Road and Park Road (Sandy Lake)

Mileage
11.7

Type
Greenway/Non-Rail-Trail

Roughness Index
1

Surface
Asphalt

The trail forms a loop around Lake Wilhelm, which is enjoyed by both anglers and boaters.

that while there is a snack shop at the marina and restrooms at various points along the trail, there are no public water fountains, so plan accordingly.

Heading east on paved trail, you'll wind through forest, with the lake on your left and Creek Road to your right. In about 1.7 miles, you'll pass Boat Launch 2, which has restrooms, a picnic shelter, and beautiful views of the lake.

Heading a couple more miles down the trail takes you across Creek Road, after which you'll approach the first of two very steep hills at Jordan Shelter. Upon your descent on the second hill—the steeper of the two—a sign warns of a sharp bend to the right. After the bend, you'll see a sign that says to stop ahead.

Before approaching Boat Launch 1 at 4.1 miles, the trail becomes on road, sharing a pathway with Creek Road to Lake Wilhelm Dam, a stopping point for the southern segment. Here, you can take the path on top of the dam left toward the northern trail section or head down the hill to the dam parking lot.

As you head northwest along the lake now, the woods open up to lake views for a brief period, after which small rolling hills lead you back under tree canopy.

You'll soon come to an opening where Dugan Run flows into the lake, and you'll briefly travel right along the water over large rocks. Just ahead at about 6.9 miles along the trail, there is a fishing area. In the summertime, look for wild berries, which litter the side brush.

The trail switches back and forth between open fields and trees, approaching Boat Launch 4 at 10 miles. Picnic tables and plenty of green space make this an ideal spot for family gatherings.

Continuing west, the route takes a sharp curve left and then right before reaching a parking lot at Lake Wilhelm Road at 11.2 miles, near Park Road. A 2-mile detour off the trail on Park Road—which is accessible across Lake Wilhelm Road and to the left—leads to Boat Launch 3. To reach the marina and close the loop of the main trail, turn left onto Lake Wilhelm Road, go 0.5 mile, and turn left onto the access road for the marina, which is straight ahead in another 0.2 mile.

CONTACT: dcnr.pa.gov/stateparks/findapark/mauricekgoddardstatepark

DIRECTIONS

To reach the trailhead at Lake Wilhelm Marina from I-79, take Exit 130 for PA 358 toward Greenville/Sandy Lake. Head northwest on PA 358 W, and go 0.5 mile. Take a slight right onto Sheakleyville Road, and go 1.1 miles. Then turn right onto Lake Wilhelm Road, and go 1.7 miles. Turn right into the access road for the marina, which is straight ahead in another 0.2 mile.

To reach the endpoint at Lake Wilhelm Dam from I-79, take Exit 121, and head east on US 62 N. Go 2.1 miles, and turn left onto US 62 N. Go 6.0 miles, and turn left to continue on US 62/Main St. Go about 0.4 mile, and continue onto Sandy Lake New Lebanon Road. Go 0.3 mile, and turn left onto Creek Road. Go 0.8 mile, and turn right into the parking lot.

The John Heinz Refuge Trail and various footpaths at John Heinz National Wildlife Refuge at Tinicum stand in stark contrast to the urban setting that surrounds this refuge. At different points on this flat and hard-packed trail, you have views of the Philadelphia skyline, while your immediate surroundings encompass 1,000 acres of water, marsh grasses, and trees.

Expect to see lots of migratory birds here as this freshwater tidal marsh—the largest in Pennsylvania—is a resting and feeding spot for some 300 species of birds, as well as 80 nesting species. Deer, coyotes, raccoons, beavers, and otters are among the mammals that also make their home here, along with many fish and reptiles.

The marshland at the southwest corner of Philadelphia became the first urban refuge in 1972 after local citizens protested the proposed routing of I-95 through the area. Later, the refuge was named after late U.S. Senator John Heinz to honor his commitment to preserving the refuge. The refuge trail is part of the Circuit Trails, a developing 800-mile urban network of trails in Greater Philadelphia, of which about 350 miles are currently complete. It's also on the East Coast Greenway that will eventually extend 3,000 miles from Maine to Florida.

The refuge is open sunrise–sunset; check the exact times for the season at the entrance gates. Bicycles are allowed only on designated service roads in the refuge. All visitors must remain on the trails, which comprise service roads and footpaths. While the refuge has an estimated 10 miles of trails and footpaths, about 9.4 miles are multiuse or maintained for hikers. Pets are allowed, but must be on a leash and must stay out of the water. Fishing is allowed with a Pennsylvania fishing license.

You can reach the refuge by bicycle on the Circuit Trails (**circuittrails.org/find-trails**); by public transportation on bus line 37, 108, or 115; or by car. Starting at the main parking lot off Lindbergh Boulevard in southwestern Philadelphia, you'll find the Cusano Environmental Education Center, where you can learn more about the refuge or take hikes led by volunteer naturalists. You'll also find maps

Counties
Delaware, Philadelphia

Endpoints
Lindbergh Blvd. and S. 86th St. (Philadelphia) to PA 420/Wanamaker Ave. near I-95 Exit 9A (Tinicum Township)

Mileage
9.4

Type
Greenway/Non-Rail-Trail

Roughness Index
2

Surface
Crushed Stone, Gravel

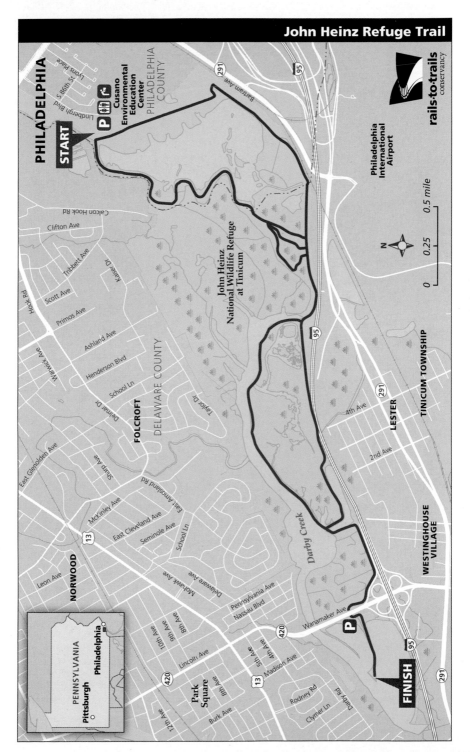

John Heinz Refuge Trail

On the John Heinz Refuge Trail, you'll have unparalleled views of the largest freshwater tidal marsh in Pennsylvania.

displaying the trails and footpaths, as well as wildlife observation areas and fishing platforms.

The main trail forms a figure eight along the shoreline of the impoundment lake and along Darby Creek, which flows into the Delaware River. Footpaths intersect along the way. Taking the right fork after leaving the parking lot (counterclockwise around the lake), you'll encounter a boardwalk at 0.2 mile that crosses the lake. In 0.5 mile past the boardwalk, you'll come to a two-story wildlife observation platform on the shoreline.

The southern side of the figure eight's lower lobe passes alongside I-95 in the vicinity of the Philadelphia International Airport. At the extreme western end, a section of trail dead-ends at the point of a jetty beyond PA 420/Wanamaker Avenue.

CONTACT: fws.gov/refuge/john_heinz

DIRECTIONS

To reach the eastern trailhead at the main entrance of John Heinz National Wildlife Refuge at Tinicum from I-95 N, take Exit 10 toward PA 291 E/ Bartram Ave. Merge onto PA 291 E/Gov. Printz Blvd., go 0.6 mile, and turn left to stay on PA 291/ Bartram Ave. Go 2.2 miles, and turn left onto S. 84th St. Go 0.7 mile, and turn left onto Lindbergh Blvd. Go 0.2 mile, and turn right into the refuge. The parking lot is 0.2 mile ahead.

To reach the eastern trailhead at the main entrance of John Heinz National Wildlife Refuge at Tinicum from I-95 S, take Exit 14 toward Bartram Ave./PA 291. Merge onto Bartram Ave., go 1.1 miles, and turn right onto S. 84th St. Go 0.7 mile, and turn left onto Lindbergh Blvd. Go 0.2 mile, and turn right into the refuge. The parking lot is 0.2 mile ahead.

To reach the western trailhead from I-95, take Exit 9B toward PA 420 N. Go about 0.1 mile north on PA 420 N/Wanamaker Ave., and look for parking on either side of Wanamaker Ave.

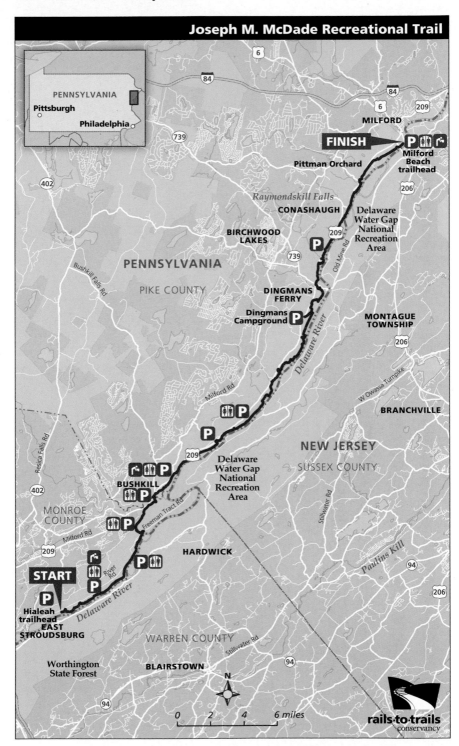

Joseph M. McDade Recreational Trail

PENNSYLVANIA
Pittsburgh
Philadelphia

MILFORD

FINISH
Milford
Beach
trailhead

Pittman Orchard

Raymondskill Falls
CONASHAUGH

Delaware
Water Gap
National
Recreation
Area

BIRCHWOOD
LAKES

PENNSYLVANIA

PIKE COUNTY

DINGMANS
FERRY

Dingmans
Campground

MONTAGUE
TOWNSHIP

Bushkill Falls Rd

Milford Rd

BRANCHVILLE

Delaware River

NEW JERSEY

SUSSEX COUNTY

Delaware
Water Gap
National
Recreation
Area

BUSHKILL

Resica Falls Rd

Freeman Tract Rd

Stillwater Rd

Paulins Kill

MONROE
COUNTY

Milford Rd

HARDWICK

START

River Rd

Delaware River

Hialeah
trailhead
EAST
STROUDSBURG

Worthington
State Forest

WARREN COUNTY

Stillwater Rd

BLAIRSTOWN

N

0   2   4   6 miles

rails·to·trails
conservancy

The Joseph M. McDade Recreational Trail runs nearly the length of the Delaware Water Gap National Recreation Area on the Pennsylvania side of the Delaware River across from New Jersey. The protected area preserves the flora and fauna, as well as historical and archaeological sites, in a steep gorge that the river carved through a ridge in the Appalachian Mountains. Several waterfalls crash off the cliffs.

The federal government acquired the land through which the trail runs in the 1950s to the 1970s for a flood-control dam. The government officially abandoned the dam project in the 1990s, though it was voted down in 1975 due to opposition from scientists and displaced residents. The National Park Service then acquired the 40-mile-long corridor for the recreation area. It named the trail along the river for the late Joseph M. McDade, a congressman who represented the district.

The trail traverses the Delaware Water Gap National Recreation Area, set in a river-carved gorge in the Appalachian Mountains.

Counties
Monroe, Pike

Endpoints
Hialeah trailhead in Delaware Water Gap National Recreation Area on River Road/SR 2028, 1.5 miles east of Shawnee Church Road (East Stroudsburg), to Milford Beach trailhead in Delaware Water Gap National Recreation Area at Milford Beach Road/SR 2013 near Metcalf Lane (Milford)

Mileage
31.3

Type
Greenway/Non-Rail-Trail

Roughness Index
2

Surface
Crushed Stone

The crushed-stone path is mostly flat along its 31.3-mile course along the river, except for a nearly mile-long section that climbs from the river to the visitor center on a ridge overlooking the southern section. Trailheads are less than 5 miles apart and are connected by a free bus shuttle that runs on weekends through the summer. A 2.5-mile section below the cliff face between the Conashaugh and Pittman Orchard trailheads (miles 26 to 28.5) is closed December 15–July 15 every year to avoid disturbing nesting eagles.

Starting at the Hialeah trailhead in East Stroudsburg, the trail runs along a fairly flat segment through the woods along the river for about 6 miles to the Owens trailhead, where it climbs a ridge on switchbacks for 0.7 mile to the park's visitor center. Observation platforms here allow visitors to see the river below and wildlife.

The next 3.5 miles cross rolling terrain into the Bushkill area, once a busy resort and farming community. Archaeological studies here also reveal American Indians once thrived in this area. The trail runs between US 209 and the Delaware River over the next several miles, arriving at the former site of the Egypt Mills.

The trail variously passes through cropland and forests to a good view of the river at Eshback Access, a boat launching site. The woods north of here teem with wildlife, and you may see bears and deer along with squirrels, chipmunks, and raccoons. The longest stretch between trailheads—5.3 miles—occurs between Jerry Lees trailhead and Schneider Farm trailhead at mile 21.4.

In another 1.1 miles you'll reach the Dingmans Campground, which has 133 campsites. (No backcountry camping is permitted west of the Delaware River, and river campsites are reserved for boaters.) The trail and US 209 follow a narrow band between the river and cliffs for much of the remaining 9 miles. You'll come to the popular Raymondskill Falls about 6 miles past the campground.

CONTACT: nps.gov/dewa

DIRECTIONS

To reach the Hialeah trailhead from I-80, take Exit 310 for PA 611/Delaware Water Gap. If coming from I-80 W, continue on the ramp 0.5 mile and exit to the right to merge onto River Road. If coming from I-80 E, turn left onto River Road (part of this road is closed in winter). Go 4.0 miles, and turn right onto the access road for the Delaware Water Gap National Recreation Area. Go about 490 feet, and turn left onto another access road, and then go 0.1 mile to the trailhead.

To reach the northern endpoint at Milford Beach trailhead from I-84, take Exit 46 for US 6 toward Milford, and head southeast on US 6 E. Go 2.2 miles, and continue straight onto E. Hartford St. Go 0.5 mile, and turn left onto Milford Beach Road/SR 2013. Go 0.5 mile, and look for parking in the lot.

The 13.4-mile Karl Boyes Multi-Purpose National Recreation Trail loops around the picturesque Presque Isle State Park, a peninsula in Lake Erie. Considered Pennsylvania's only seashore, the 3,200-acre park features 11 sandy beaches that are open daily in the summer. The park is open year-round, sunrise–sunset, and offers recreational opportunities from fishing, boating, and swimming to cross-country skiing, snowshoeing, ice-skating, and ice fishing. Located along the Atlantic Flyway, the park is known for its diverse ecology and bird population.

Along the trail, you will find easy access to parking, restrooms, picnic tables, and pavilions. Bikes, surreys, and in-line skates are available to rent in the park in season near the Waterworks area. The park also offers seasonal bike tours.

Starting at the park entrance on Peninsula Drive, you'll follow the flat, paved path along its eastern side overlooking the Presque Isle Bay shoreline. This stretch of trail is separated from traffic and offers water views, observation decks, picnic facilities, and a marina as you head toward the Perry Monument in 5.1 miles. Built in 1926,

Climb the steps of the Presque Isle Lighthouse, built in 1872, for a vista of Lake Erie.

County
Erie

Endpoints
Presque Isle State Park entrance on Peninsula Dr. and Old Lake Road (Erie)

Mileage
13.4

Type
Greenway/Non-Rail-Trail

Roughness Index
1

Surface
Asphalt

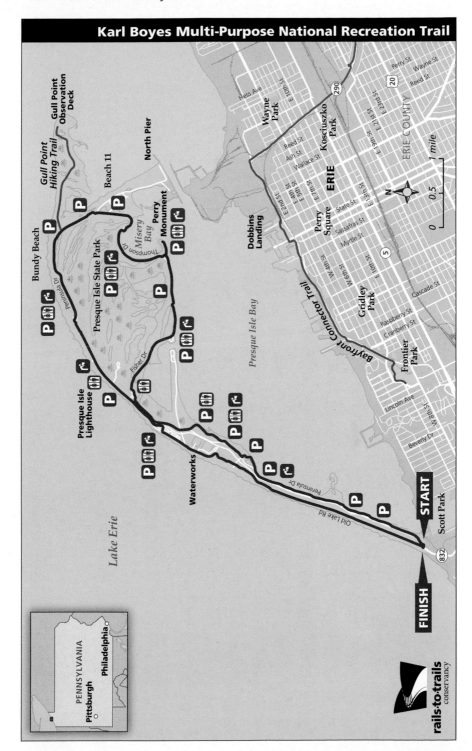

Karl Boyes Multi-Purpose National Recreation Trail

the monument commemorates the victory of Commodore Oliver Hazard Perry in the Battle of Lake Erie during the War of 1812.

Continuing the loop toward the park's 11 beaches, this section of trail features long stretches of on-road bike lanes that are not fully separated from traffic along Thompson and Peninsula Drives. Bicyclists should still find the experience comfortable, as the vehicular speed limit is low. After crossing a small bridge, you'll pass Misery Bay, where you can rent a canoe or take a boat tour exploring the nature and ecology of the bay. Trail users can sign up in advance for these tours.

After the bay, you'll approach the first beach. To access Beach 11 and a scenic lighthouse on the North Pier, leave the trail and turn right onto Coast Guard Road. Back on the trail for another 0.5 mile, you'll pass an access road to your right that leads to the Gull Point parking area, just before access to Bundy Beach, on the northern side of the peninsula. From here, bird lovers can take a detour to the Gull Point Observation Deck via the Gull Point Hiking Trail. Check with the park before your visit, as this area has seasonal restrictions.

For the remainder of the route, which loops south, beach dunes obstruct full views of Lake Erie, making for a good excuse to explore the beaches, take a dip, or catch a sunset. In 1.5 miles from the Gull Point parking area, you'll pass the Presque Isle Lighthouse, built in 1872, to your right, open on weekends for tours. For a fee, you can climb its 78 steps for an expansive view of the lake.

Leaving the lighthouse, you'll pass five beach access points in quick succession before the trail bears right in 2 miles onto a separate unnamed road with no vehicular traffic. Be mindful of cross streets that intersect this road for car access to the beach parking lots. In 1.4 miles, the trail leads to the park's interpretive center and once again follows vehicular traffic along Old Lake Road. The trail passes two more beach access points and travels through a short wooded area before completing the loop back to the park entrance. From here, the western endpoint of the 8.9-mile Bayfront Connector Trail is only 2.7 miles east.

CONTACT: dcnr.pa.gov/stateparks/findapark/presqueislestatepark/pages /default.aspx

DIRECTIONS

To reach Presque Isle State Park from I-79 N, take Exit 182, and keep left to merge onto US 20 W. Go 1.3 miles, and turn right onto PA 832 N/Peninsula Dr. Follow PA 832 for 2.1 miles to the park entrance. There is a parking lot just inside the park entrance, and ample parking lots are available throughout the park. The trail parallels Peninsula Dr. and is easily accessible from all lots.

During the summer, a water taxi service travels to the park from Dobbins Landing in Erie. For the water taxi schedule and pricing, visit **porterie.org/watertaxi.** To reach Dobbins Landing, take I-79 N to its end (near mile marker 183), and continue straight onto Bayfront Pkwy. In 2.7 miles, turn left onto Holland St. Go 0.2 mile to the port.

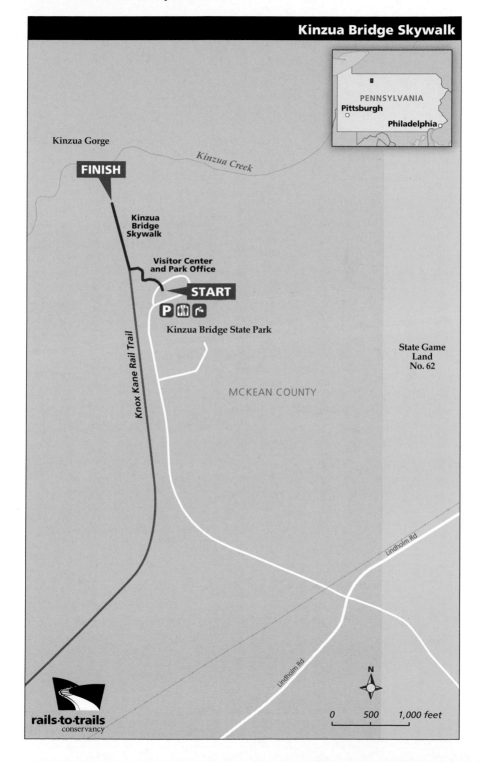

Kinzua Bridge Skywalk

Kinzua Gorge

Kinzua Creek

FINISH

Kinzua
Bridge
Skywalk

Visitor Center
and Park Office

START

Kinzua Bridge State Park

Knox Kane Rail Trail

State Game
Land
No. 62

MCKEAN COUNTY

PENNSYLVANIA
Pittsburgh
Philadelphia

Lindholm Rd

Lindholm Rd

N

0   500   1,000 feet

rails·to·trails
conservancy

Though it may only be 600 feet long, the Kinzua Bridge Skywalk is a special treat for history buffs and thrill seekers alike. Situated within Kinzua Bridge State Park in the township of Mt. Jewett, the steel trestle bridge was once touted as the eighth wonder of the world before a disaster in 2003 changed its fate forever.

At 301 feet high and 2,053 feet long, the Kinzua Bridge—also known as the Kinzua Viaduct—was the tallest and longest railroad bridge in the world when it was built in 1882. The bridge served the Erie Railroad and occasional excursion trains until 1959, when access to a nearby Baltimore & Ohio Railroad line made the aging bridge obsolete. In 1970 the Commonwealth of Pennsylvania opened Kinzua Bridge State Park to the public, preserving the famous trestle, adjacent land, and stunning views of the Kinzua Gorge in perpetuity. From 1987 until

After a 2003 tornado, the remains of the 1882 Kinzua Bridge were salvaged to create a pedestrian walkway.

County
McKean

Endpoints
Kinzua Bridge State Park Visitor Center and Park Office off of SR 3011/ Lindholm Road between Penns Ave. and PA 59/ Mt. Alton-Ormsby Road (Mt. Jewett)

Mileage
0.2

Type
Rail-Trail

Roughness Index
1

Surface
Boardwalk

the bridge closed for restoration in 2002, the Knox and Kane Railroad operated sightseeing steam-train trips over the trestle and through the Allegheny National Forest.

In 2003 a tornado struck the Kinzua Bridge at speeds of nearly 100 miles per hour, leaving a large part of the historic trestle in ruins. Due to the high cost of repairing the 121-year-old bridge, the state decided to use the remaining structure to create a pedestrian walkway that would allow visitors to view the breathtaking gorge below. Remnants and wreckage of the bridge remain in the gorge, allowing users to imagine the scale and length of the bridge in its heyday.

Ever since the skywalk was constructed in 2011, users have explored the history of the bridge and tornado at the Kinzua Bridge State Park Visitor Center and Park Office. From here, users can access the 600-foot pedestrian walkway, with the track still intact. A glass-bottomed section at the end of the walkway provides views of the gorge below.

Users can also walk to a picture-taking platform, adjacent to the bridge, that delivers stunning views of the bridge in its entirety. It's also not as high up, so this is a great spot for those who are not fond of dizzying heights. Note that while the skywalk itself is wheelchair accessible, the viewing platform is only accessible by stairs.

A 3.8-mile section of the Knox Kane Rail Trail, opened in 2018, now provides a seamless, mostly forested, crushed-stone connection between Mt. Jewett and Kinzua Bridge State Park. The Kinzua Valley Trail Club is working to extend the 6.5-mile Kinzua Valley Trail (see page 129)—which currently connects the Red Bridge Bank Fishing Area along PA 321 in Kane to Westline—to Kinzua Bridge State Park and the skywalk for an eventual 21-mile trail.

CONTACT: visitanf.com/kinzua-state-park-sky-walk

DIRECTIONS

To reach parking at the Kinzua Bridge State Park Visitor Center and Park Office from the intersection of US 219 and US 6 in Kane, head east on US 6/E. Main St. Go 4.4 miles to Mt. Jewett, and turn left onto Lower Lindholm Road. Go 0.7 mile, and turn right onto SR 3011/Lindholm Road. Go 2.3 miles, and turn left onto the park access road. Follow signage for Kinzua Bridge. In 0.8 mile, the road dead-ends at the parking lot for the Kinzua Bridge State Park Visitor Center and Park Office.

Deep within the Allegheny National Forest lies a rail-trail with a past. The Kinzua Valley Trail follows the route of the former Kinzua and Hemlock Railroad (later Valley Railroad) near the town of Westline. The railroad fueled the economic vitality of the area from the early to mid-1900s, transporting harvested wood to local lumber mills. As more trees were felled, lumber production slowed, and removal of the Valley Railroad tracks began in the late 1930s.

In the 1970s, people began using the route informally as a cross-country ski trail. After forming in 1999, the Kinzua Valley Trail Club transformed the popular route into what's now known as the Kinzua Valley Trail. Today, nearly 6 miles of the path provide users a calm, well-maintained trail experience that follows the Kinzua Creek west to Kane. A hilly, on-road, 0.6-mile extension on Forest Road now connects users to the Red Bridge Bank Fishing Area in Kane.

The Allegheny National Forest surrounds the Kinzua Valley Trail, offering a secluded experience.

County
McKean

Endpoints
Pine Trail and Kinzua Road (Mt. Jewett) to Red Bridge Bank Fishing Area at PA 321/Kane-Marshburg Road and County Road 122/Forest Road (Kane)

Mileage
6.5

Type
Rail-Trail

Roughness Index
1–2

Surface
Crushed Stone

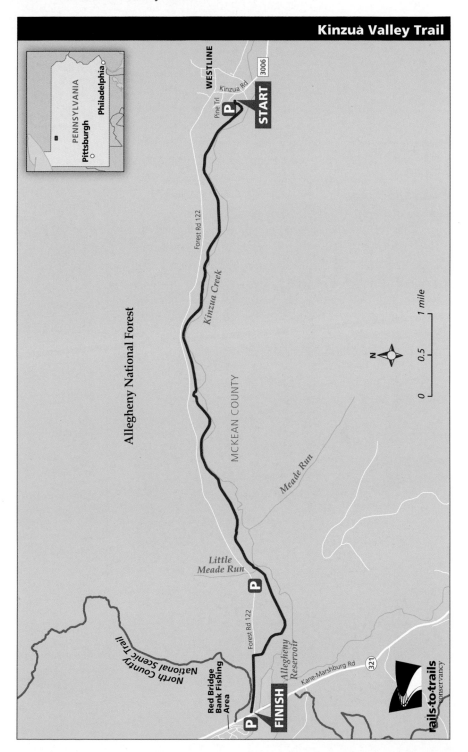

Parking is available at the eastern trailhead in Westline, a community in Mt. Jewett, the best place to begin your trail experience. From here, you'll traverse through the Allegheny National Forest on a crushed-stone pathway following the Kinzua Creek. Whether you're biking, hiking, or resting on one of the benches lining the trail, you can enjoy the sights and sounds of wetland areas along the creek and a full canopy of mature trees bordering the path. Wildlife, including deer and local birds, also frequent the trail.

In approximately 5.5 miles, after passing Little Meade Run to your right, you'll reach a trailhead with a small parking area at Forest Road 122. From here, adventurous trail users can continue 1 mile to PA 321/Kane-Marshburg Road, where the trail ends. The last 0.7 mile, between Root Run and the final trailhead, is an on-road gravel-surfaced section that is lined with SHARE THE ROAD signage and features more grade changes than the rest of the trail. The payoff, however, is exquisite. From PA 321/Kane-Marshburg Road, cross the road to the Red Bridge Bank Fishing Area overlooking the Allegheny River. There is limited parking at this drop-off area, with room for only a few cars.

The Kinzua Valley Trail Club is working to extend the Kinzua Valley Trail to Kinzua Bridge State Park and the Kinzua Bridge Skywalk to create a 21-mile trail. Note that motorized vehicles are prohibited along the Kinzua Valley Trail, with the exception of handicapped scooters and power chairs.

CONTACT: kinzuavalleytrail.org

DIRECTIONS

To reach the eastern trailhead in Westline from the intersection of US 6 and US 219 in Kane, head north on US 219/Pittsburgh-Buffalo Hwy., and go 5.1 miles. Turn left onto SR 3006/Westline Road, keeping an eye out for directional trail signage. Go 3.2 miles, turn right onto Kinzua Road, and then take the first left onto Pine Trail. Parking is available 150 feet ahead at the end of Pine Trail.

To reach parking at the Red Bridge Bank Fishing Area from the intersection of US 6 and US 219 in Kane, follow the directions above to Kinzua Road, and go 0.3 mile. Continue onto Forest Road 122/CCC Road, and go 1.9 miles. Turn left to stay on Forest Road 122, and go 4.2 miles. Turn right onto PA 321 N/Kane-Marshburg Road, and then immediately turn left onto Red Bridge Bank Fishing Road. Go 0.1 mile to the end of the road, which dead-ends into a parking lot. To find the western trailhead, head back out along Red Bridge Bank Fishing Road for 0.1 mile, and turn right onto PA 321 N/Kane-Marshburg Road. Look for the trailhead endpoint on your left in less than 400 feet.

Lackawanna River Heritage Trail

PENNSYLVANIA
Pittsburgh
Philadelphia

D&H
Rail
Trail
171

FINISH

Morse Avenue
trailhead
Stillwater Lake

SUSQUEHANNA COUNTY

LENOXVILLE   247

CLIFFORD
TOWNSHIP

247

374   81

FOREST
CITY
247   P

VANDLING

171

WAYNE COUNTY

106   SIMPSON
P   P

107

*Carbondale
Riverwalk*
CARBONDALE

6

6   WAYMART

Lackawanna
State Park

SCOTT   247

LACKAWANNA COUNTY

438

P
P

407   81

State Game
Land No. 307

JERMYN
P

MAYFIELD

632

State Game
Land No. 300

347

6
P
Laurel St
P

11
CLARKS
SUMMIT

CHINCHILLA

ARCHBALD

Lackawanna River

P
P   JESSUP

476
P

DICKSON
CITY
347

P
P

Dick & Nancy
Eales Preserve

Nay Aug
Avenue
Natural
Play Area

81   P
THROOP

476   307
Scranton
Expy
P   *Scranton
Riverwalk*

E Market St

6

247   MOUNT
COBB

348

Olive St   P
SCRANTON

P   Steamtown
National
Historic Site

START   81   84

84

Depot St   307

590

TAYLOR   11

81

P

N

0   2   4   6 miles

380   435

rails·to·trails
conservancy

The Lackawanna River Heritage Trail follows its namesake waterway along the former New York, Ontario and Western Railway, as well as the Central Railroad of New Jersey in the south and the Delaware and Hudson Railway in the north. These railroads variously carried tourist traffic to the Catskills and agricultural products and anthracite coal throughout the region.

Scranton—the geographic and cultural center of the Lackawanna River Valley—anchors the trail in the south, but future plans call for extending the trail about 7 miles south to the Susquehanna River, eventually connecting to the Luzerne County Levee Trail (see page 147). In the north, the trail overlaps with the D&H Rail Trail for 10 miles, ending at Stillwater Lake in Clifford. From there, you can continue another 30 miles to the New York border.

The trail is mostly paved, crushed stone, or gravel, although several sections share on-road routes. Horseback riding and snowmobiling (with a permit) are allowed on the trail north of Simpson. The Lackawanna River is a popular fishing destination, and a fishing pier is located at the Laurel Street trailhead in Archbald. Consider carrying a trail map, as wayfinding on streets between the trail segments can be confusing.

Though the trail technically begins at Depot Street in Taylor, a great place to begin your journey is about 2.4 miles north along the trail at the Broadway Street trailhead/South Side Sports Complex, which has plenty of parking. Nearby attractions include Steamtown National Historic Site and the Electric City Trolley Museum, for those who wish to explore rail history.

Turning left onto the trail from the parking lot will lead you to the current southern endpoint at Depot Street in Taylor, about 2.5 miles away. Turn right from the parking lot and head north across Broadway Street along the forested pathway that takes you along the banks of the Lackawanna River. This 0.8-mile portion is known as the Scranton Riverwalk, popular with local runners, walkers, and bicyclists.

Counties
Lackawanna, Susquehanna, Wayne

Endpoints
Depot St. near N. Main St. (Taylor) to D&H Rail Trail at Stillwater Lake, about 0.5 mile southeast of SR 2031 and Main St. (Clifford)

Mileage
32.4

Type
Rail-Trail

Roughness Index
1–2

Surface
Asphalt, Crushed Stone, Gravel, Grass

Don't miss the murals as you pass under the Scranton Expressway or the trailside sculptures lining the connecting pathway to Providence Road.

Crossing over Olive Street, the trail proceeds atop a flood-control levee for approximately 1.8 miles on a combination of grass and gravel pathways. You'll cross the river at Albright Avenue and continue along the levee a short distance on the east bank of the river.

After passing the Nay Aug Avenue Natural Play Area, a neighborhood playground with a circular pathway just below the levee, you'll cross back over the river by taking a left onto East Market Street. Turn right onto the paved trail immediately after crossing the bridge. The trail continues on a rough pathway through the woods for about 0.4 mile.

Upon reaching Depot Street, you'll take a short jaunt onto shared roads back to a grassy levee trail. Turn right onto Depot Street, and then right onto Amelia Street and left onto Race Street. Cross Sanderson Avenue, and head up the levee—again on off-road trail—to Parker Street. Turn right, go 0.4 mile, and then turn left onto Boulevard Avenue.

A 4-mile on-road section of trail takes you through Dickson City to Olyphant. Note that in Dickson City, Main Street can be busy, and the sidewalk along the street is not continuous. Plans call for rerouting the trail to the nearby levee trail along the Lackawanna River and bypassing Main Street.

In Olyphant, you'll pick up a 9-mile segment of asphalt trail, with a few on-street sections, stretching through Jermyn. This pleasant segment mostly

Murals, sculptures, and other public art add pops of delight along the Lackawanna River Heritage Trail.

winds through the forested natural areas where you may see otters, eagles, and other wildlife. As you journey through Carbondale, the trail becomes part of the Carbondale Riverwalk, which heads through the heart of downtown and north to Simpson, where the trail meets the D&H Rail Trail at the Morse Avenue trailhead.

The next 10 miles, newly paved and opened in the fall of 2018, continue along the D&H Rail Trail corridor, which becomes increasingly rural through the thickly forested mountains. After passing through Forest City's downtown, the Lackawanna River Heritage Trail officially ends at milepost 40 at Stillwater Lake, but you can continue an additional 30 miles along the D&H Rail Trail to the New York border. Portions of the D&H Rail Trail are newly laid crushed gravel, while some segments are more rustic and challenging.

CONTACT: lhva.org/HeritageTrail.php

DIRECTIONS

To reach parking at the Broadway Street trailhead/South Side Sports Complex in Scranton from I-81, take Exit 185 toward the Central Scranton Expy. Go 0.9 mile, and exit toward Cedar Ave. At the end of the ramp, turn right onto Cedar Ave., go 390 feet, and turn left onto Mattes Ave. Go 0.2 mile, and continue right onto Hickory St. Go 0.2 mile, and the road becomes Broadway St. at the bridge. Go 0.1 mile, and look for parking on the left. The endpoint is located 2.5 miles farther south in Taylor (facing the trail, turn left to head south).

To reach parking near the northern endpoint at Stillwater Lake in Clifford from I-81, take Exit 202 and head east on PA 107. Go 3.5 miles, and turn left onto PA 247. Go 5.7 miles, and turn right to stay on PA 247. Go 1.4 miles, and turn left to stay on PA 247. Then go 1.1 miles, and turn right to stay on PA 247. Go 1 mile, and turn left onto PA 247/Dundaff St. Go 2 miles, and turn right onto PA 247/Main St. Then go 0.4 mile, and turn left to stay on PA 247/Main St. Go 0.2 mile, and turn right onto Commerce Blvd. Go 0.2 mile, and turn right into the entrance to the D&H Rail Trail/Lackawanna River Heritage Trail. Look for parking on your right. The endpoint is located 4.3 miles farther north along the trail—at the junction with the D&H Rail Trail toward New York.

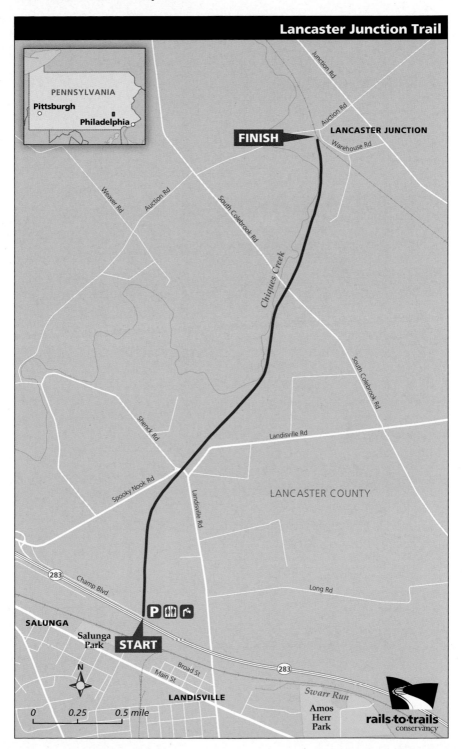

Lancaster Junction Trail

The popular Lancaster Junction Trail follows the former Reading and Columbia Railroad, which transported iron ore and coal from Reading to the Chesapeake Bay via the Susquehanna and Tidewater Canal for more than 120 years. The line eventually expanded into the Pennsylvania towns of Marietta and Lancaster, carrying as many as 10 passenger trains a day. The railroad declined after World War II and ceased to operate in 1985. Lancaster County purchased the right-of-way and opened it as a trail in 1987.

Today, the 2.3-mile rail-trail runs from Lancaster north to the hamlet of Lancaster Junction. Trail users can expect to pass fields, meadows, and the meandering Chiques Creek, a tributary of the Susquehanna River. As there is no parking at the northern endpoint, many trail users choose to begin at the southern trailhead in Lancaster and make a round-trip journey of 4.6 miles. The trail is open dawn–dusk.

People on foot, bicycles, horses, or skis now navigate this former railroad corridor that once hauled iron ore and coal.

County
Lancaster

Endpoints
End of Champ Blvd.,
0.5 mile southeast of its
intersection with Spooky
Nook Road (Lancaster),
to Auction Road and
Warehouse Road
(Manheim)

Mileage
2.3

Type
Rail-Trail

Roughness Index
2

Surface
Crushed Stone

Plentiful parking and restrooms are available at the southern trailhead, located at the end of Champ Boulevard, just off PA 283. Following the shaded trail north along the old railroad tracks, you'll pass farmland on your right. In 0.7 mile, cross Spooky Nook Road with caution, as cars from the left will be coming around a bend in the road.

Trees cover the next portion of trail, creating shaded relief in the summer months. With Chiques Creek to your left, you'll cross South Colebrook Road in a mile and then continue another 0.7 mile to the northern endpoint at Auction Road. To your right is the still-active rail line to which the rail-trail used to connect.

As you enjoy this scenic ride, keep in mind that the properties bordering the trail, including a picnic pavilion near South Colebrook Road, are privately owned. Equestrians are asked to ride at a walking pace.

CONTACT: co.lancaster.pa.us/279/lancaster-junction-recreation-trail

DIRECTIONS

To reach the southern trailhead from I-283, take Exit 1A to merge onto PA 283 E. In 22.3 miles, take the exit toward Salunga, turn left onto Spooky Nook Road, and go 0.3 mile. Turn right onto Champ Blvd., and go 0.5 mile. Turn left into the trailhead parking lot.

While the Lebanon Valley might be best known for its chocolate and distinctive bologna, iron ore is what put the region on the map in the 1700s. The 18-mile Lebanon Valley Rail-Trail—and the connecting Conewago Recreation Trail (see page 38)—trace the route of the Cornwall & Lebanon Railroad and its successors, which served the iron mine and foundry until the tracks and mine were wiped out by Tropical Storm Agnes in 1972.

Constructed by millionaire industrialist Robert Coleman in 1883, the Cornwall & Lebanon Railroad competed directly with a railroad that was already serving the Cornwall iron mine and foundry. In the 1890s, Coleman built a vacation resort at Mount Gretna to augment his passenger business. You can still visit these landmarks, which are minutes from the trail.

Coleman's empire collapsed, and the Pennsylvania Railroad gained control of his rail line in 1918. After it fell into disuse in the wake of Tropical Storm Agnes, neighboring Lancaster County acquired its corridor segment in 1979 and created the 5-mile Conewago Recreation Trail. In 1996 a nonprofit began efforts to develop the trail in Lebanon County and completed the current trail in 2009 (a wood chip side path is for horses, which are only permitted south of Rocherty Road). Future plans call for closing the 10-mile gap to the Swatara Rail-Trail (see page 239); crews completed two segments totaling 3 miles in 2018. The Lebanon Valley Rail-Trail—along with the Conewago Recreation Trail and others—is part of the September 11th National Memorial Trail that connects the 9/11, Flight 93, and Pentagon Memorials.

Starting in Lebanon, you're in a good spot to sample Pennsylvania Dutch cooking—from Lebanon bologna to scrapple (pork trimmings) to schnitz and knepp (ham, dried apples, and dumplings). You'll pass through Lebanon for 2.2 miles from US 422 until you're out of town and following a utility corridor to Zinns Mill Road. From here, it's another 1.7 miles to the Cornwall trailhead, where you'll find a snack stand in the shape of a barrel.

County
Lebanon

Endpoints
US 422 between S. 16th St. and S. 12th St. (Lebanon) to Conewago Recreation Trail, 0.5 mile northeast of PA 241/ Mt. Gretna Road and Prospect Road (Elizabethtown); N. 25th St. near Church St. to Long Lane and Emma Road (Lebanon); Hickory Dell Lane and PA 72 to US 22/ William Penn Hwy. and PA 72 (Jonestown)

Mileage
18.0

Type
Rail-Trail

Roughness Index
2

Surface
Crushed Stone

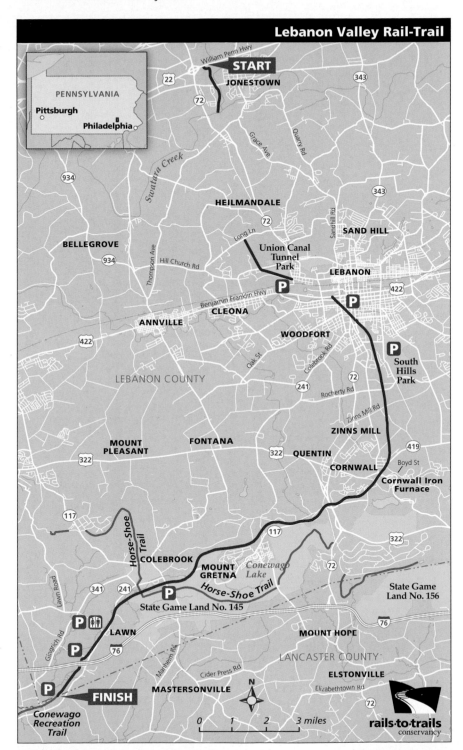

Lebanon Valley Rail-Trail

Cornwall was home to the mine and the Cornwall Iron Furnace, which operated 1742–1883. The brick Gothic Revival iron furnace building, part of a National Historic Landmark District, stands today much as it did the day it closed. To visit from the trailhead, turn left onto Cornwall Road/Boyd Street, and then turn right onto Boyd Street and follow it to the end—a total distance of 0.6 mile.

Leaving the Cornwall trailhead, the route trends uphill to Mount Gretna in about 4 more miles, where Conewago Creek meets Conewago Lake. Mount Gretna is also the site of Coleman's vacation resort and Chautauqua-style arts and education retreat. Much of the town's architecture and flavor remains. Look for a side trail on the left to take a jaunt into town. Check the Mount Gretna website (**mtgretna.com**) for such events as a homes tour, art show, and theater productions.

Continuing downhill 2.5 miles, the trail passes through Colebrook, where you'll find a drive-in and tavern within a couple of blocks of the trail. In another 0.5 mile, the path crosses the Horse-Shoe Trail, an equestrian and pedestrian trail that runs 140 miles between Valley Forge and Harrisburg. Another 4 miles through farmland takes you to the county line, where the trail becomes the Conewago Recreation Trail.

A focal point of the trail in Cornwall is a former railroad bridge spanning 130 feet.

Two short, isolated sections of trail totaling 3 miles have also been constructed north of the main segment. The first segment in Lebanon begins at Union Canal Tunnel Park, where parking and picnic benches are available, and extends north just less than 2 miles to Long Lane. The second segment begins in Bunker Hill near PA 72 and Swatara Creek and extends through Jonestown to US 22.

CONTACT: lvrailtrail.com

DIRECTIONS

To reach the Lebanon trailhead from I-81, take Exit 85 (and keep left, then turn left) or 85A to PA 934 S. Head 0.8 mile south, and turn left to merge onto US 22 E/William Penn Hwy. Go 4.3 miles, and exit onto PA 72 S toward Lebanon. Turn right onto PA 72 S, and go 6.3 miles. Turn right onto N. 10th St., which is also PA 72, and go 0.9 mile. Then turn left onto Walnut St., and go 0.2 mile. Turn right onto S. Eighth St., go 0.4 mile, and turn right into the trailhead parking lot. Access the endpoint by turning right onto the trail and heading north 0.6 mile.

To reach the Lebanon trailhead from I-78 W, take Exit 8 for US 22 W toward PA 343/Lebanon/Fredericksburg. Keep right at the fork, follow signs for Fredericksburg, and merge onto US 22 W. Go 2.4 miles, turn left onto PA 343 S, and go 6.6 miles. Turn right onto Maple St., go 0.1 mile, and turn left at the first cross street onto N. Eighth St. Go 1.4 miles, and turn right into the parking lot. Access the endpoint by turning right onto the trail and heading north 0.6 mile.

To reach the southern trailhead at Eckert Road from I-76, take Exit 266 toward PA 72. Turn right onto PA 72 S, and go 0.9 mile. Turn right onto Cider Press Road, and go 3.8 miles. Turn right onto N. Colebrook Road, and in 0.8 mile, turn left onto Sunnyburn Road. Go 0.3 mile, and turn right onto Lawn Road. Go 1.8 miles, and turn left onto PA 241 S. Go 0.8 mile, turn right onto Eckert Road, and go 0.1 mile. Turn right into the small parking lot, just after passing the trail crossing. The endpoint and the junction with the Conewago Recreation Trail are located 1.2 miles farther south along the trail.

The Lower Trail ranks high on the list of many Central Pennsylvania residents when they're searching for a remote path with a woodsy feel. The Lower (rhymes with *flower*, and named in memory of trail benefactor R. Dean Lower) Trail traces the meandering Frankstown Branch of the Juniata River as it meanders through the water gaps that the river cut through the Allegheny Mountains. The trail, with a mostly crushed-stone surface, rolls 17 miles between trailheads near Canoe Creek State Park and Alexandria. How remote is it? One segment goes 11 miles without a road crossing.

Pennsylvania's canal and railroad eras intersect on the Lower Trail. Originally a path used by local tribes, the corridor in the 1830s became part of the Pennsylvania Canal, a system of waterways connecting Philadelphia to Pittsburgh. Mules slogged on adjacent towpaths and pulled barges through numerous locks. Some of the canal locks and channels, as well as remnants of the lock tenders' houses, can be seen through the thick vegetation.

This section of canal ceased operations in the 1850s but survived until the late 1870s, when a flood washed it away, and the Pennsylvania Railroad built a spur—the Petersburg Branch—to serve limestone quarries in the area. In 1989 the right-of-way came under control of the nonprofit Rails to Trails of Central Pennsylvania, which built the trail.

The Lower Trail is part of the Trans Allegheny Trails System, a group of rail-trails in western Pennsylvania. The trail is also part of the September 11th National Memorial Trail that connects the 9/11, Flight 93, and Pentagon Memorials, as well as the Industrial Heartland Trails Coalition's developing 1,500-mile trail network through Pennsylvania, West Virginia, Ohio, and New York.

Starting at the Alfarata Station trailhead near Alexandria, the trail follows the river upstream through a water gap at Tussey Mountain. Just 0.8 mile from the trailhead, a short turnoff on the right leads to a diner with soft-serve ice cream.

Counties
Blair, Huntingdon

Endpoints
SR 4014 and Brick Yard Road (Alexandria) to Beaver Dam Road and Flowing Springs Road (Williamsburg)

Mileage
17.0

Type
Rail-Trail

Roughness Index
1

Surface
Asphalt, Crushed Stone

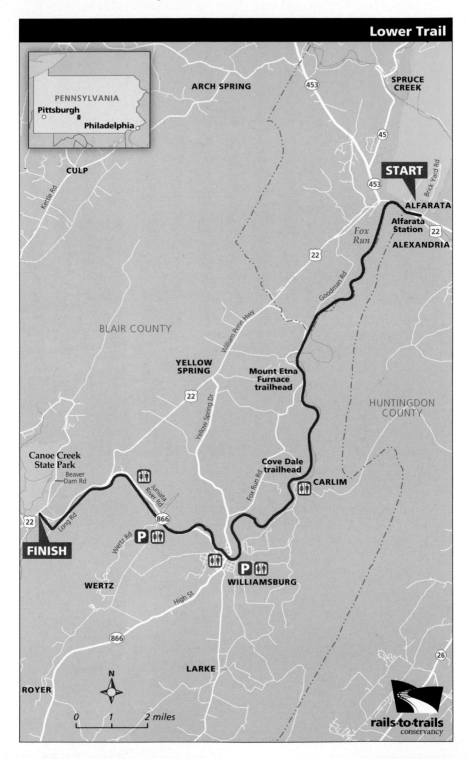

Lower Trail

PENNSYLVANIA
Pittsburgh
Philadelphia

ARCH SPRING
453
SPRUCE
CREEK
45
CULP
Kettle Rd
453
START
Brick Yard Rd
ALFARATA
Alfarata
Station 22
Fox
Run
ALEXANDRIA
22
Goodman Rd
BLAIR COUNTY
William Penn Hwy
YELLOW
SPRING
Mount Etna
Furnace
trailhead
HUNTINGDON
COUNTY
22
Yellow Spring Dr
Canoe Creek
State Park
Beaver
Dam Rd
Cove Dale
trailhead
CARLIM
Juniata River Rd
Fox Run Rd
22
866
Long Rd
FINISH
Wertz Rd
P
WILLIAMSBURG
WERTZ
High St
866
LARKE
26
ROYER
N
0 1 2 miles
rails·to·trails
conservancy

About 3 miles from the trailhead, you'll see dam abutments left behind from the canal. Your first bridge, 4.3 miles from the trailhead, is a stone-arch bridge across Fox Run. Then in 0.5 mile, you'll cross the river twice on bridges the railroad built to avoid a river bend. After the second bridge, you'll come to the Mount Etna Furnace trailhead, named for a pig iron furnace that predates the canal. The ironmaster's residence still stands as a burned-out mansion here.

Continuing 2.6 miles, you'll pass through the remains of Carlim, an old limestone-mining town, near the Cove Dale trailhead. The surface improves to asphalt here for the next 3.5 miles through Williamsburg, where you can catch a bite at a general store or diner. The trail crosses Juniata River Road a little less than 2 miles past Williamsburg and ends 3.5 miles later.

Deer, rabbits, squirrels, turtles, black bears, turkeys, bobcats, and more inhabit the surrounding woods, and the Audubon Society recommends the area to birders for its variety of feathered inhabitants.

The trail used to end at Flowing Springs Road and Long Road, but a project, completed in early 2019, extended the trail to Beaver Dam Road and Flowing Springs Road at the edge of Canoe Creek State Park. From the original terminus, continue 1,500 feet on a shared on-road section (with bike lanes on either side) heading over the Frankstown Branch of the Juniata River. The route then curves left onto a new segment of off-road trail (formerly T444), paralleling US 22 for a short period before looping left and then under US 22 to Beaver Dam Road and

Keep an eye out for the wildlife that inhabits the surrounding forest.

the state park. Future plans call for another section of trail that links the Lower Trail to the main beach and camping area inside the park.

For a unique side trip, check out a small white church on Turkey Valley Road on the way to the park's main entrance; a conservation group bought this circa 1800s building to protect thousands of brown bats that roost here.

Additional long-range plans call for extending the trail southwest toward Hollidaysburg.

CONTACT: rttcpa.org/lower.shtml

DIRECTIONS

To reach the Alfarata Station trailhead from I-99/US 220, take Exit 48 toward PA 453/Tyrone. From I-99 S, turn left toward PA 453 S (signs for Water St./PA 550/PA 453 S). From I-99 N, turn left, then right onto PA 453 S. Go 0.5 mile. Then take a slight right to stay on PA 453 S, and go 8.3 miles. Turn left onto US 22 E, and go 0.7 mile. Turn left onto Logging Road 31101, go 0.1 mile, and continue onto State Route 4014. Go 0.2 mile, and turn right into the trailhead parking lot.

To reach the parking area at Flowing Springs Station from I-99/US 220, take Exit 32 for Frankstown Road toward PA 36. Head southeast on Frankstown Road, and go 3.7 miles. Turn left onto US 22, go 5.0 miles, and turn right onto Flowing Springs Road/T444. Go 0.2 mile, continue straight onto Long Road, and go another 0.2 mile. Turn left into the trailhead.

The history of Pennsylvania's Wyoming Valley is tied to the mighty Susquehanna River. From American Indian cultures and early European settlers to the cities that line the river's shores today, people have depended on the waterway and its fertile banks for transportation, food, and recreation. But living alongside this major river requires enduring the natural ebb and flow of flooding—often with disastrous effects.

The communities built a system of miles-long levees beginning in the 1930s. In the 1990s, the levees were raised an additional 3–5 feet after Tropical Storm Agnes, which raised the river level to 40 feet and inundated 48 square miles in 1972. The four sections of the paved Luzerne County Levee Trail atop the Wyoming Valley Levee System

County
Luzerne

Endpoints
Wyoming Ave. and Swetland Lane (Wyoming) to River St. and Fort St. (Forty Fort); Church St. and Rutter Ave. to Plymouth St. and Main St. (Kingston); W. Union St. and N. River St. to W. South St. and S. River St. (Wilkes-Barre); Riverside Dr. and Locust St. (Wilkes-Barre) to Solomons Creek, 1.1 miles southwest of the end of Fellows Ave., 0.25 mile northwest of Wilcox St. (Hanover Township), or Flat Road and Krest St. (Plymouth)

Mileage
12.8

Type
Greenway/Non-Rail-Trail

Roughness Index
1

Surface
Asphalt

With its historical markers and interpretive signage, the Luzerne County Levee Trail can also be a learning experience.

Luzerne County Levee Trail

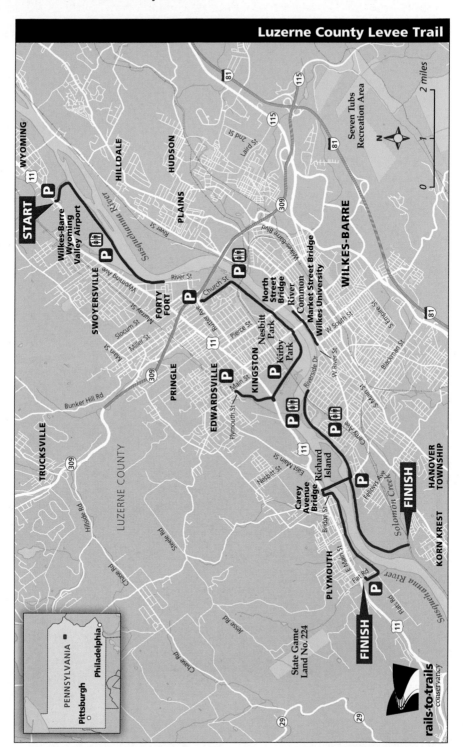

now allow visitors to ride, walk, or hike for a pleasant journey along the river. Historical markers and interpretive signs are posted along the trail.

Beginning at the northern endpoint near the Wilkes-Barre Wyoming Valley Airport, this 2.5-mile section of trail makes its way between the river on your left and the airport and recreational fields on your right. As the route bends south, you'll enter a residential area just beyond the levee wall. The trail leaves the levee and makes its way on shared roadways through the community of Forty Fort.

To reach the next trail section, turn left onto River Street, go 0.4 mile, and turn right onto Rutter Avenue. Go 0.2 mile, and follow the bike lane on Rutter Avenue to the left. Go 0.3 mile, turn left onto Church Street, and pick up the levee trail from the parking lot on the left.

Entering the community of Kingston, this section of trail travels south atop the levee with views of the forested banks of the Susquehanna to the left and neighborhoods to the right. In about 1.4 miles, you'll pass under the North Street Bridge. A pathway to the left takes you through the riverside Nesbitt Park, with fishing access, a boat ramp, disc golf, and other amenities.

The pathway splits at the Market Street Bridge. Staying on the west bank of the 1.8-mile segment, you'll pass by Kirby Park—home to the city's Fourth of July celebration and annual Cherry Blossom Festival, and the location of ample recreational opportunities, including tennis and foot paths. The trail crosses US 11/South Wyoming Avenue and ends at Plymouth and Main Streets behind a home improvement store.

If you choose to cross the Susquehanna River via the Market Street Bridge, you'll follow a wide sidewalk under the magnificent arched pylons topped with stone eagles to River Common, a park on Wilkes-Barre's waterfront. A short section of the Luzerne County Levee Trail parallels River Common, which also has a separate waterfront pathway that is accessible from multiple points along the main trail.

Head left on the Luzerne County Levee Trail for 0.4 mile to pass the park's Millennium Circle, a civic space, and a riverfront amphitheater. The trail segment here terminates at a small building just west of the Luzerne County Courthouse near West Union Street.

A right turn from the Market Street Bridge takes you along the southwestern portion of this section of the trail—past museums and Wilkes University—to another gap beginning at West South Street. At the southern end of River Common, turn right onto West South Street and then left onto West River Street. Turn right onto Riverside Drive, and look for the trail in 0.6 mile.

After 1.4 miles of riverfront travel, the trail branches off at the Carey Avenue Bridge. To remain on the east bank, take the branch under the bridge. This 1.8-mile segment is prone to flooding in the spring and after heavy rains. More

secluded than other sections, it rolls through an open field bordered by trees. It ends as a flood-control facility at Solomon Creek.

If you cross the Susquehanna River on the Carey Avenue Bridge's wide shoulders, you'll pass over Richard Island. After crossing, turn left onto East Main Street and use the sidewalk on the south side for one block. Turn left onto Bridge Street, and the trail begins in 0.1 mile. The trail continues 1.6 miles, ending at a small parking lot on Flat Road.

CONTACT: susquehannagreenway.org/luzerne-county-levee-trail

DIRECTIONS

To reach the northern endpoint in Wyoming from I-81, take Exit 170B toward Wilkes-Barre on PA 309 N. Go 0.3 mile, and merge onto PA 309/N. Cross Valley Expy. Go 3.3 miles, and take Exit 4 for Forty Fort. Go 0.2 mile, and turn right to merge onto Rutter Ave. Go 0.2 mile, and turn left onto River St., and then go 0.8 mile, and turn right onto US 11/Wyoming Ave. Go 1.8 miles, just past a strip mall on the right, and then turn right onto an access road to the parking lot.

To reach the southern endpoint in Plymouth from I-81, take Exit 164 to PA 29 toward Nanticoke. Go 0.5 mile, and merge onto PA 29. Go 4.8 miles, and merge right onto US 11. Go 2.0 miles, and turn right onto Flat Road. Go about 360 feet, and turn right into the parking area.

The Lycoming Creek Bikeway parallels a creek of the same name from Hepburnville to Williamsport in Central Pennsylvania. The 5.3-mile paved trail connects a village formerly named Eeltown due to the preponderance of slimy critters found in the creek there to a city once called the Lumber Capital of the World. Along the way, it passes the site of sandlots where organized Little League Baseball was first played.

It's no surprise that the Williamsport and Elmira Railroad chose the Lycoming Creek valley for a segment of railway begun in 1839. The route, which the Lycoming Creek Bikeway now follows, was originally used by American Indians and early settlers as a shortcut through the mountains between two branches of the Susquehanna River. The rail line later became part of the Northern Central Railway and the Pennsylvania Railroad, the Penn Central, and its successors until it fell into disuse in 1972.

Although it runs through the hilly Appalachian Plateau, the Lycoming Creek Bikeway is generally flat. Plans call for extending the nearby Susquehanna River Walk to the Third Street trailhead. The trail follows alongside US 15 most of the way, and there are several road crossings along the route.

County
Lycoming

Endpoints
W. Creek Road near
Bair Dr. (Hepburnville)
to W. Third St. between
US 15 and Rose St.
(Williamsport)

Mileage
5.3

Type
Rail-Trail

Roughness Index
1

Surface
Asphalt

Leaving Hepburnville, the trail cuts through a coppice of trees shortly after crossing Lycoming Creek.

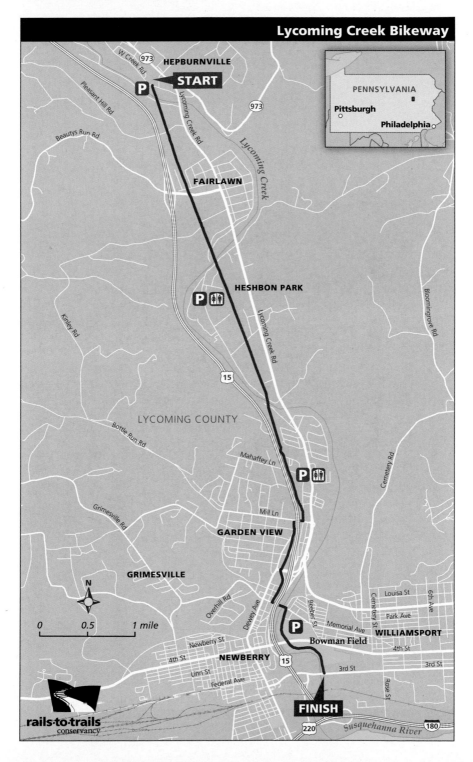

Lycoming Creek Bikeway

Beginning at the athletic fields in Hepburnville, the trail immediately crosses Lycoming Creek and passes through a short stretch of cropland and the village of Fairlawn before crossing another railroad trestle that dates to 1901.

Passing through residential Heshbon Park, you'll cross a pedestrian bridge over the creek and roll along at the base of a sound wall that separates the highway from the neighborhood on your left. At 3.3 miles, the trail passes a sports park in the Garden View community; fast food and markets are nearby.

A bit farther, the trail turns right at Mill Lane to pass underneath US 15 and trace the highway on the west side for 0.8 mile to Memorial Avenue. There it turns left, goes underneath US 15 again, and crosses Lycoming Creek one last time before heading south atop a levee. Flooding in 1996 caused property damage and loss of life in Williamsport.

The trail passes the home field of the Williamsport Crosscutters minor league baseball team, the name an homage to the city's lumber industry heritage. A sandlot baseball diamond in this area gave rise to organized Little League Baseball in 1939. The annual Little League World Series is held nearby in South Williamsport.

Many Victorian-era mansions can be found on Millionaires Row, a National Register of Historic Places site about a mile east of the trail's end on Third Street.

CONTACT: visitpa.com/pa-biking/lycoming-creek-bikeway

DIRECTIONS

To reach the northern trailhead in Hepburnville from US 220, take Exit 29 and head north on US 15 toward Mansfield. Go 5.0 miles. Take the exit toward Hepburnville, and turn right onto Beautys Run Road/Marshall Ave. Go 0.3 mile, and turn left onto PA 973/Lycoming Creek Road. Go 1.1 miles, and turn left onto Bair Dr./Eckard Road. Go 0.1 mile, and turn right onto W. Creek Road. Look for parking immediately on the left.

To reach the northern trailhead from I-180 W in Williamsport, go to the end of the interstate, near mile marker 29; head right onto US 15 N; and follow the directions above.

To reach parking near the southern endpoint at Memorial Park in Williamsport from US 220, take Exit 29 and head north on US 15. Go 0.6 mile, and take the exit toward W. Third St. Turn right onto W. Third St., and go 0.6 mile. Turn left onto Rose St., go 0.1 mile, and turn left onto W. Fourth St. In 0.7 mile turn right into the parking lot. *Note:* The lot shares space with the parking lot for Historic Bowman Field. To find the trail after parking, return to the sidewalk on Fourth St., turn right, and go 500 feet to the trail. Turn left on the path and go 0.5 mile to the southern endpoint; turn right to go north to Hepburnville.

To reach parking near the southern endpoint at Memorial Park from I-180 W, go to the end of the interstate, near mile marker 29, and head right onto US 15 N. Follow the directions above from US 15 to Memorial Park.

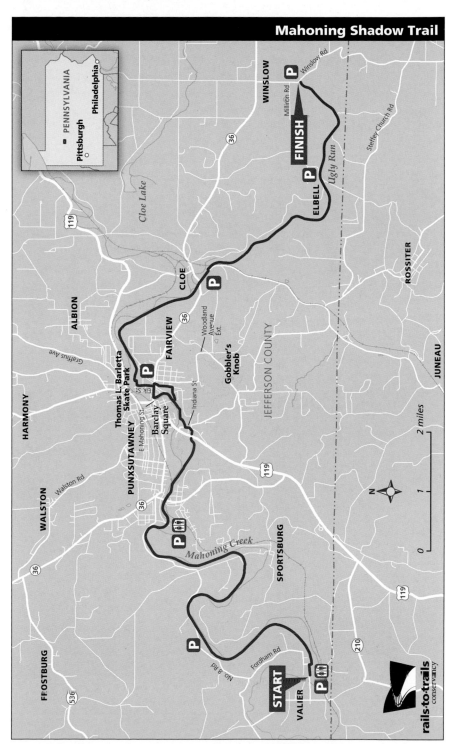

Mahoning Shadow Trail

If Punxsutawney Phil sees his shadow on Groundhog Day, Mahoning Shadow Trail users expect six more weeks of winter before spring arrives. The 15-mile Central Pennsylvania trail passes through the hometown of the groundhog meteorologist, so the forecasts he makes when he emerges from his burrow might be more accurate here than elsewhere.

Phil puts the *shadow* in the trail's name, and Mahoning Creek supplies the other part of the moniker. The path follows Mahoning Creek and Ugly Run as it travels through old coal-mining country that now supports forests and farm lots.

The trail traces a Pennsylvania & North Western Railroad line (later Pennsylvania Railroad) built in the 1890s to haul coal out of mines that honeycomb the region, and which fell into disuse in the 1980s. The Punxsutawney Area Rails to Trails Association formed in 1995 to create the trail, which opened in two segments in 2002 and 2004. Two sections in town—0.2 mile and 0.4 mile—are on neighborhood streets. The western two-thirds is level, but the eastern section has an uphill grade.

Just west of Punxsutawney, the Mahoning Shadow Trail passes under a railroad bridge.

County
Jefferson

Endpoints
Fordham Road/SR 3015 between SR 3013 and Bowers Lane (Valier) to Winslow Road/SR 2001 near Milliron Road (Winslow)

Mileage
15.0

Type
Rail-Trail

Roughness Index
1

Surface
Asphalt, Crushed Stone

Beginning near the old coal-mining town of Valier in the west, the trail travels through woods and past farms for more than a mile before it catches up to Mahoning Creek, a tributary of the Allegheny River. The trail follows the creek closely to Punxsutawney, except for taking a shortcut across a couple of bends.

About 5.5 miles down the trail, you'll see abandoned ovens nearby that burned coal into coke for iron furnaces. You can explore these if you like. The trail crosses Mahoning Creek at 6.1 miles and runs alongside tracks of the Buffalo & Pittsburgh Railroad for a short distance until the active train tracks cross Mahoning Creek on a picturesque railroad trestle. There are views of downtown Punxsutawney in this section.

The trail passes underneath US 119 at 7.3 miles, after which you'll turn left onto Indiana Street and right onto South Gilpin Street (total 0.2 mile) to rejoin the trail at South Penn Street, which uses the levee for about 0.6 mile to East Mahoning Street.

Turn left onto that street to cross the creek for the annual Groundhog Festival (late June or early July) in Barclay Square. To reach the groundhog's year-round residence at Gobbler's Knob, turn right onto East Mahoning Street, and then go south on Woodland Avenue Extension for 1.3 miles.

If you don't take either side trip, you can regain the trail in 0.4 mile by turning right onto East Mahoning Street and then left onto Elk Street. The trailhead is located on the right at Thomas L. Barletta Skate Park.

At South Penn Street, an alternative route originally created for a now-defunct elementary school takes riders off the trail to the right on Penn Street, left onto State Street, left onto Oakland Avenue, and then left onto East Mahoning Street, where it rejoins the trail. This route is marked by signage.

About 2 miles past the skate park, the trail joins Canoe Creek, which it follows for a mile, and then picks up Ugly Run, which it follows upstream—and uphill—for 3.3 miles to the trailhead on Winslow Road.

CONTACT: mahoningshadowtrail.org

DIRECTIONS

To reach the western trailhead in Valier from I-80, take Exit 78, and head south on PA 36 S/Allegheny Blvd. Go 0.4 mile, and turn left onto US 322/PA 36/W. Main St. Go 0.8 mile, and turn right onto PA 36/S. White St./Col. Drake Hwy. Go 18.4 miles, and turn right onto Perry St. Go 0.4 mile, and bear right onto No. 8 Road/SR 3008. Then go 3.2 miles, and turn left onto Fordham Road/SR 3015. Go 1.2 miles, and look for parking on the left.

To reach the eastern trailhead in Winslow from I-80, take Exit 78, and head south on PA 36 S/Allegheny Blvd. Go 0.4 mile, and turn left onto US 322/PA 36/W. Main St. Go 0.8 mile, and turn right onto PA 36/S. White St./Col. Drake Hwy. Go 25.1 miles, and turn right onto Winslow Road/SR 2001. Go 0.6 mile, and look for parking on the right.

The 61.5-mile Montour Trail follows most of the former Montour Railroad's main line west and south of Pittsburgh. This little short line was incorporated during the late 19th century and, despite its small size, became very profitable thanks to the many coal mines once located along its main line. It also benefited from having interchanges with most of the region's notable railroads. In later years, the Montour became a subsidiary of other larger systems. When coal mines closed over the years, the railroad found itself in a difficult position and was finally forced to shut down during the mid-1980s.

Forming a semicircle around Greater Pittsburgh, the corridor now helps host one of the longest suburban rail-trails in the United States, featuring a selection of bridges, trestles, viaducts, and tunnels framed by colorful Western Pennsylvania landscapes and vegetation. The Montour Trail

The Montour Trail provides a quintessential rail-trail experience with former railroad bridges, viaducts, and tunnels dotting the route.

Counties
Allegheny, Washington

Endpoints
Montour Coketown Road and PA 51/Coraopolis Road (Coraopolis) to Pittsburgh International Airport at Airport Blvd. or Hornhead Road near Meadow St. (Westland) or Logan Road between Irishtown Road and Patterson Road (Bethel Park) or PA 837/N. State St. and Mendelsohn Ave. (Clairton)

Mileage
61.5

Type
Rail-Trail/Rail-with-Trail

Roughness Index
1–2

Surface
Asphalt, Crushed Stone

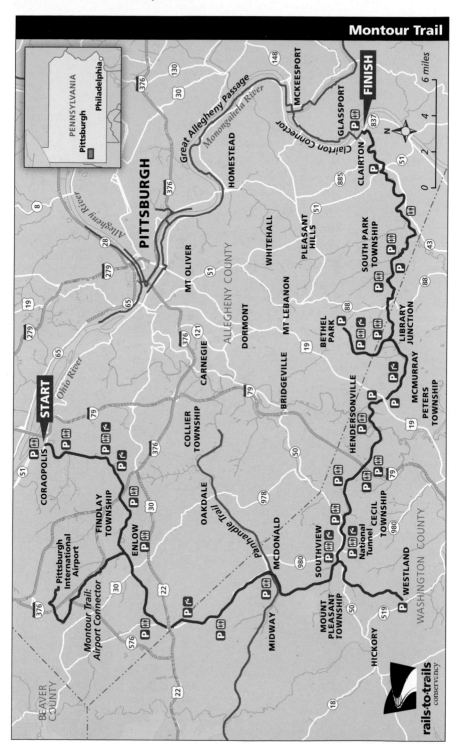

Montour Trail

is also a host trail for the 3,700-plus-mile Great American Rail-Trail—which will one day form a seamless connection between Washington, D.C., and Washington State—and is part of the Industrial Heartland Trails Coalition's developing 1,500-mile trail network through Pennsylvania, West Virginia, Ohio, and New York. The surface is primarily crushed limestone, with small sections of paved trail in Peters Township and Clairton, some on-road trail between South Park Township and Clairton, and a mostly on-road spur to Pittsburgh International Airport. Horses are permitted on the shoulders of the trail in Cecil Township between Morganza Road and the crossing of PA 980 and PA 50. Cross-country skiing is also permitted.

Coraopolis to Enlow: 7.8 miles

Both the trail and the railroad are named for the creek that runs alongside them; you'll follow the waterway for the trail's first 7.8 miles beginning in Coraopolis. Views will primarily be of leafy green neighborhoods sprinkled with wildflowers. A highlight of the trip includes the Enlow Tunnel in Findlay Township, about 7.2 miles along the trail. Not only is its 575-foot expanse fun to traverse, but the journey on either end is a treat as the path winds through a scenic wooded valley here.

Enlow to Airport Connector: 6.4 miles

Just farther south past the Enlow trailhead on Main Street, the trail branches north for about 6.3 miles to Pittsburgh International Airport, mostly along quiet roadways restricted for airport service vehicles. To take this spur, turn right onto Enlow Road. After 0.8 mile, the trail bears left onto a gated, restricted airport access roadway. You'll continue on this wide, asphalt roadway about 3 miles to another gate near a residential area on McCaslin Road. Continue on the shared roadway, and then turn right onto the striped shoulder of the moderately busy Clinton Road. Use caution here, as the roadway crosses over I-376 with merging traffic exiting and entering the highway.

After crossing the interstate, the roadway soon becomes a restricted-traffic roadway to where the trail meets Airport Boulevard. Crossing signals allow trail users to navigate across the often-busy roadway into the airport's extended parking lots, where sharrows (shared-lane markings) guide you to the end of this segment. Bike parking is available here.

Enlow to Southview: 13.4 miles

From Enlow, the trail heads southwest through Imperial and then south under US 22 toward McDonald. As the trail approaches the town of McDonald, it splits. To the left is a connector section to the 29.2-mile Panhandle Trail (see page 177), which travels east to Collier Township and west to Weirton, West Virginia. This connector leads to just across Noblestown Road, where a parking area for the Panhandle Trail is located.

Veering right to stay on the main trail, you'll come to one of the trail's highlights, the beautiful 900-foot McDonald trestle, which crosses over the Panhandle Trail. The Montour Trail continues on through wooded surroundings, and then curves back south and runs next to a large golf course and several farms to the small neighborhood of Southview.

Westland Branch Spur: 4.1 miles

One of the newest segments of the trail splits off from the main route near Southview and heads southwest to Mount Pleasant Township. At just over 0.3 mile past the Galati Road trailhead, the relatively flat, crushed-gravel pathway turns southwest, continuing along 3.5 miles of rail line that were reactivated in 2012 to support the shale gas industry, before terminating at a parking area in the community of Westland.

Southview to Hendersonville: 6.6 miles

Heading out of Southview to the east, you'll cross over PA 50/PA 980/Millers Run Road over a long bridge. The trail then returns to woods as it curves back and forth

The curvature of the 600-foot National Tunnel means that you can't see the other end, but lights guide the way.

on the way to Cecil Township. You'll travel along the southern edge of Cecil and through the National Tunnel—the trail's longest tunnel at 600 feet—named for the nearby National Coal Company mines that the former railroad once served.

It's curved, so you can't see the other end; lights and pavement with guiding reflectors along the trail edge help ease navigation. The tunnel's cool, damp interior is a welcome respite in summer, but in winter, the dripping water can cause beautiful (though dangerous) icicles along the ceiling and mounds of ice on the tunnel floor. The trail then bends right and crosses over Tarr Heights Drive to a parking area and the Cecil-Henderson Montour Trail Campground.

Continuing southeast, you'll pass Henderson Park and reach another trailhead, where you'll find restrooms, parking, and a large bicycle shop.

Hendersonville to Library Junction/Venetia: 6.7 miles

From Hendersonville, the trail skirts the Valley Brook Golf Course, crosses Valley Brook Road twice, and then passes under US 19/Washington Road, where it becomes the Arrowhead Trail. It then passes through McMurray and travels on a mostly rural route to Library Junction.

Just past Hendersonville, you'll cross a two-for-one attraction, the Chartiers Creek High Bridge—offering some of the prettiest vistas on the trail—and the adjacent 235-foot-long Greer Tunnel, both built in the early 1900s. On the other (east) side of the tunnel is another bridge, which crosses over a railroad.

Library Junction/Venetia to Bethel Park Spur: 3.4 miles

At Library Junction, you have the option of continuing east or taking a spur to Bethel Park that curves left and northward (on a triangular junction of the trail), skirting mostly residential neighborhoods on a relatively new and well-maintained section of trail. A small trestle bridge crosses over the intersection of Clifton Road and Highfield Road. Just after this trestle you can head left down a small spur to cross Highfield Road to George Washington Elementary School and a small café.

Library Junction/Venetia to Clairton: 13.1 miles

Heading eastward from Library Junction, the trail passes through more rural landscapes (note that parts of the trail in this section may be washed out, so take caution) before entering Library, where you'll find several restaurants and eateries. At Pleasant Street in Library, an on-road section begins. Turn right onto Pleasant Street, and then turn left onto Brownsville and Library Road. Go 0.9 mile, and turn left onto Stewart Road. In just less than 400 feet, turn right to return to off-road trail.

The trail loosely follows Peters Creek, winding through rural backdrops for 1.6 miles to Piney Fork Road, where it becomes on road once more. The route winds south as it follows Piney Fork Road, which becomes Peters Creek Road shortly after heading north—just after the confluence of Piney Fork and Peters Creek. You'll pass another campground as you travel north along Peters Creek and through the outskirts of Clairton, where the trail turns into Oak Road.

At PA 51, note that the trail turns right onto the busy highway with no shoulders and follows this road 0.2 mile. Use extreme caution here. Upon reaching Peters Creek Road, turn left at the traffic light to cross PA 51, and head north onto Peters Creek Road for about 0.5 mile. The trail then returns off road and heads north through Clairton Resident Park, formally ending at a large parking lot at North State Street and Mendelsohn Avenue.

At the southeastern terminus in Clairton, you can take the Clairton Connector route (urban, on road) about 5 miles to McKeesport, which links to the 150-mile Great Allegheny Passage (see page 82).

CONTACT: montourtrail.org

DIRECTIONS

To reach the northern endpoint from I-79 N, take Exit 64 for PA 51 toward Coraopolis/McKees Rocks, and turn left onto PA 51 N/Coraopolis Road. Go 0.7 mile, and take a sharp right onto Montour Coketown Road. Go 0.1 mile, and look for parking on the right. To reach the trailhead, turn right, heading north along Montour Coketown Road, and turn left into the trailhead access point.

To reach the endpoint at Pittsburgh International Airport from downtown Pittsburgh, take I-376 W (follow signs to the airport). Take Exit 53, and follow the blue signs to the parking area. Take the exit for extended parking, just past the employee parking area. The trail endpoint is between the extended parking and long-term parking lots. Sharrows (shared-road arrows) will lead you through the parking lot to the northwest corner of the parking area.

To reach parking at the Westland trailhead from I-79, take Exit 43 for PA 519 toward Houston/Eighty Four. Turn left onto PA 519 N, and go 4.4 miles. Turn right onto Hornhead Road, and go 0.2 mile. Look for parking on the right.

To reach the western trailhead in Clairton from I-70, take Exit 27 toward Dunningsville. If you're coming from I-70 E, take a sharp left onto Brownlee Road, and go 0.4 mile; if you're coming from I-70 W, you'll turn right onto Brownlee Road. Take a slight right onto Church Road, and go 1.0 mile. Then take a slight right onto PA 136 E, and go 5.1 miles. PA 136 E turns slightly left and becomes PA 917 S. Follow it 0.4 mile, continue onto PA 136 E, and go 0.2 mile. Turn left to merge onto PA 43 N toward Pittsburgh, and go 8.7 miles. Continue onto Exit 54 (signs for PA 51/Pittsburgh/Elizabeth), and go 0.8 mile. Turn right onto Payne Hill Road, and go 1.0 mile. Turn right onto Clairton Road, go 1.2 miles. The road turns left and becomes Walnut Ave.; go 0.4 mile, and turn right onto N. State St. Go 0.3 mile, and turn left into the trailhead.

Although relatively short at 1.8 miles, the Muhlenberg Rail Trail extends the ability of residents to exercise or visit local parks, schools, and businesses under their own power. The asphalt trail that runs through a residential and light industrial area of Muhlenberg Township north of Reading is mostly flat and partially covered by a tree canopy that provides welcome shade in the summer.

The path uses the former corridor of the busy East Penn Branch of the Reading Railroad that ran between Allentown and Reading beginning in the 19th century. The rail line fell into disuse in the 1980s, and Muhlenberg Township acquired the right-of-way in 2003 for the trail.

The trail runs between Mt. Laurel Road in the north to Montrose Avenue in the borough of Laureldale in the south. The trail crosses three streets: two at grade and one via an underpass. It also parallels a former electric trolley line that ran along Rosedale Avenue and 11th Avenue on the west side. Overhead power lines mark its former course today.

The paved trail ducks under trees for a brief respite from the summer sun.

County
Berks

Endpoints
Mt. Laurel Road and Furnace Road (Temple) to Montrose Ave. and Prince St. (Laureldale)

Mileage
1.8

Type
Rail-Trail

Roughness Index
1

Surface
Asphalt

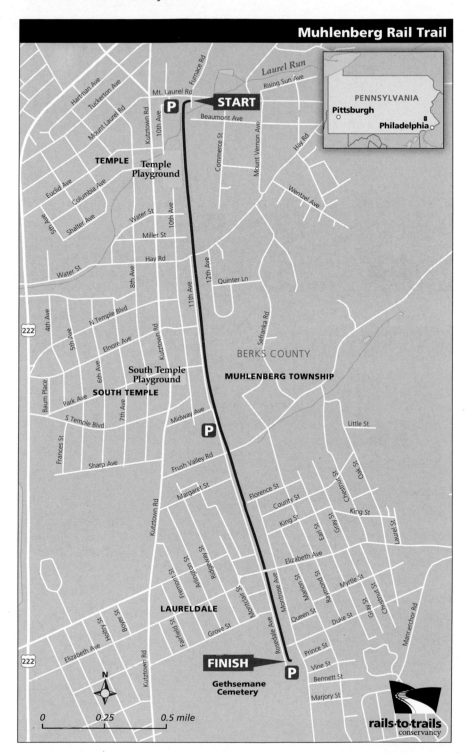

The northern trailhead at Mt. Laurel Road posed a challenge for trail builders. The railroad spanned the road on a bridge about 25 feet overhead, but that bridge had been removed in the 1970s. A wheelchair-accessible path was installed that gradually slopes to the trail from the parking lot below.

For the next 0.5 mile to Hay Road, you'll pass an old commercial area east of the trail, and mixed business, residential, and park space on the west. Temple Playground is adjacent to the trail; access the playground from the trailhead by heading west on Mt. Laurel Road 0.1 mile. Turn left onto Kutztown Road, go 0.2 mile, and then turn left onto Euclid Avenue and go about 190 feet. Turn left onto 10th Avenue, go 295 feet, and turn right into the playground parking lot.

From Hay Road, the next 0.3 mile of trail is bordered by housing before you reach the sprawling site of the 24-acre Empire Steel Castings, which has been mothballed. Its towering steel structures make this an industrial landmark on the route.

The remainder of the trail passes through Laureldale. The 0.4-mile segment from Frush Valley Road to Elizabeth Avenue is bordered by housing and a small sports field. The trail goes beneath Elizabeth Avenue on an underpass and then ends 0.3 mile later at a parking lot on Montrose Avenue. Gethsemane Cemetery is located just west of the trail, and the 38-acre Bernhart Reservoir Park is about 0.5 mile south. There are several cafés and taverns along this last segment.

CONTACT: muhlenbergtwp.com

DIRECTIONS

To reach the northern trailhead from the intersection of US 222 and US 422 northwest of Reading, take US 222 N for 5.6 miles. Exit at PA 61 S toward Tuckerton. Turn right onto PA 61 S, and go 0.6 mile. Turn left onto Tuckerton Road, go 0.5 mile, and turn right onto US 222 Bus./N. Fifth St. Go about 440 feet, and turn left onto Mt. Laurel Road. Go 0.6 mile, and turn right into the trailhead parking lot on Railroad Ave.

To reach the northern trailhead from the intersection of US 222 and US 22 Bus. in Reading, continue south on US 222 Bus. S, and go 1.2 miles. Turn left onto Kutztown Road, and go 0.3 mile. Turn left onto Mt. Laurel Road, and go 0.1 mile. Turn right into the trailhead parking lot on Railroad Ave.

To reach the southern trailhead from the intersection of US 222 and US 422 northwest of Reading, take US 222 N for 5.6 miles. Exit at PA 61 S toward Tuckerton. Turn right onto PA 61 S, go 1.8 miles, and turn left onto E. Bellevue Ave. Go 0.4 mile, and turn right onto US 222 Bus. S. Then go 0.1 mile, and turn left onto Elizabeth Ave. Go 0.7 mile, and turn left onto Montclare St. Immediately turn right onto Elizabeth Ave., go 0.1 mile, and turn right at the second cross street onto Montrose Ave. Go 0.3 mile, and turn right into the trailhead parking lot.

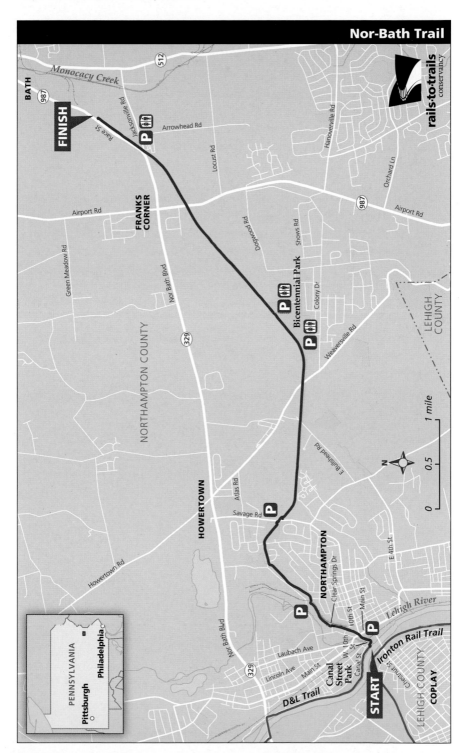

In 2017 the borough of Northampton added a single mile of asphalt to the nearly 6-mile Nor-Bath Trail, effectively extending the use of the trail by more than 100 miles in eastern Pennsylvania by connecting it to the D&L Trail (Delaware & Lehigh National Heritage Corridor) (see page 53), which winds through the Delaware and Lehigh Valley for more than 140 miles.

The Nor-Bath Trail follows the corridor of the Northampton and Bath Railroad, a short-line rail line that ran 8.5 miles between those towns for 77 years to serve the local cement industry's connection to larger rail carriers. Northampton County acquired the corridor after it fell into disuse in 1979 and built the trail to encourage self-propelled travel between parks, schools, and historic centers along the way.

Northampton is part of a populated area that stretches down the Lehigh River to Allentown and Easton. Until 1982, it was home to Atlas Portland Cement, which was used in building the Panama Canal. The trail—mostly asphalt in Northampton and crushed stone elsewhere— passes through residential neighborhoods and a wooded

County
Northampton

Endpoints
D&L Trail at Canal St. and W. 10th St. (Northampton) to PA 987/Race St., 0.6 mile northeast of Jacksonville Road (Bath)

Mileage
5.9

Type
Rail-Trail

Roughness Index
1

Surface
Asphalt, Crushed Stone

The crushed-stone surface creates a smooth ride for cyclists.

corridor that soon crosses farmland on the way to Bath, originally a Scotch-Irish settlement founded in 1737 that's now home to a cement company of its own.

Starting on the bank of the Lehigh River, the Nor-Bath Trail shares a trailhead with the D&L Trail at the southern tip of Canal Street Park. From the trailhead, turn right onto Canal Street, which curves left onto West 10th Street, to pick up the paved trail in 0.1 mile at Main Street.

It passes the government center that includes the Atlas Cement Co. Memorial Museum, the Northampton Recreation Center, and Atlas Sports Complex before crossing Clear Springs Drive and entering a wooded area. You'll pass through outlying suburbs of Northampton and open farmland before you arrive at Bicentennial Park in about 3.3 miles, where you'll find restrooms, pavilions, playgrounds, tennis courts, and athletic fields.

The trail takes you across more open farmland for another 1.9 miles to Jacksonville Road. The trail dead-ends about 0.7 mile ahead near the Keystone Cement quarry. A shoulder along PA 987/Race Street goes into Bath, 1.7 miles from the Jacksonville Road crossing. A right turn onto Jacksonville Road goes 0.6 mile to the Wolf Academy Historic Site, a stone-built school that dates to the 1700s.

A renovation of the trail and its amenities began in the spring of 2019. Plans also call for extending the trail 0.8 mile to Mill Street in Bath, with construction due to take place between 2020 and 2021.

CONTACT: www.northamptoncounty.org/pubwrks/parkrec/pages /nor-bath-trail.aspx

DIRECTIONS

To reach the Northampton trailhead from I-78 E, take Exit 59, and turn left onto W. Rock Road. In 0.2 mile turn left onto PA 145, and go 2.0 miles. Continue straight another 2.1 miles, as the road changes names from S. Fourth St., Basin St., S. Third St., and finally American Pkwy. Turn left onto Sumner Ave., and go 0.8 mile. Turn right onto N. Sixth St., which merges into Mac-Arthur Road in 0.2 mile. Continue on MacArthur, which rejoins PA 145, for 2.7 miles. Turn right onto Lehigh St., go 1.2 miles, and then continue onto Eugene St., which turns into Cypress St. Turn left onto Fourth St., and go 1.3 miles (note that Fourth St. turns right and becomes Main St.). Turn left onto W. 10th St., which turns right and becomes Canal St. Look for parking at the endpoint, to your left. Another larger parking lot is 0.3 mile farther along Canal St., to your left.

To reach the Northampton trailhead from I-78 W, take Exit 60B to merge onto PA 145 N. In 2.8 miles, continue straight onto S. Fourth St., and follow the directions above from there.

To reach the trailhead in Bath from I-476, take Exit 53, and keep right to merge onto US 22/ Lehigh Valley Thwy. Go 11.1 miles, take the PA 512 exit, and turn right onto PA 512/Bath Pike. Go 3.3 miles, and turn left onto Jacksonville Road. Go 0.6 mile, and look for parking on the right. The trail is straight ahead. Turn right on the trail to dead end in 0.7 mile, or turn left to go to Northampton.

The Northwest Lancaster County River Trail follows the route of the historic Pennsylvania Main Line Canal, tracing the Susquehanna River northwest from Columbia to Falmouth. While the majority of the trail is paved, the northern segment from Bainbridge to Falmouth is largely undeveloped and best suited for walking, hiking, or mountain biking. In season, cross-country skiers and snowshoers can also enjoy the trail.

Begin your journey at the southern trailhead, where the Columbia Crossing River Trails Center offers exhibits, restrooms, and information about the trail and nearby attractions. Though the trail starts out on road, it transitions within a mile to the scenic Chickies Rock County Park just north of Columbia. Here, you'll pass through the abandoned (and allegedly haunted) Point Rock Tunnel, also known as Chickies Rock Tunnel. The unlined 180-foot-long tunnel

Point Rock Tunnel, also known as Chickies Rock Tunnel, highlights the trail's railroad history.

County
Lancaster

Endpoints
Columbia Crossing River Trails Center at N. Front St. and Walnut St. (Columbia) to Falmouth Boat Launch on Collins Road and PA 441/River Road (Bainbridge)

Mileage
14.1

Type
Rail-Trail

Roughness Index
1, 3

Surface
Asphalt, Crushed Stone, Dirt

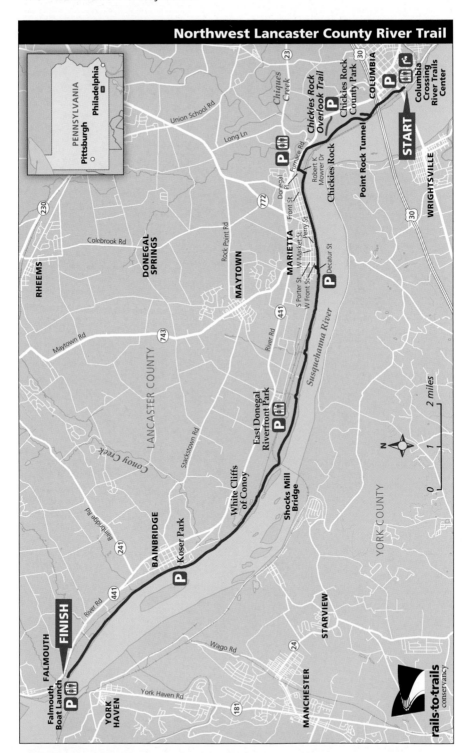

Northwest Lancaster County River Trail

was blasted through solid rock when it was built in the 1850s for the Pennsylvania Railroad. A mile from the tunnel, you may see rock climbers scaling the craggy face of Chickies Rock via the 0.5-mile Chickies Rock Overlook Trail.

The trail crosses over Chiques Creek before continuing along Furnace Road. From here, you can take either an undeveloped portion of trail along the Susquehanna River or a route through the town of Marietta. To take the more direct, undeveloped route, take the first left off Furnace Road onto Robert K. Mowrer Drive, heading toward the river. In about 500 feet, you'll come to a parking lot alongside the river that ends in a 0.2-mile dirt path leading to the main trail. Bicyclists may prefer to walk their bikes along the dirt path. For information on fishing in this area, visit **fishandboat.com.**

To get onto the route through Marietta, take the second left off Furnace Road onto Donegal Place. After a brief crushed-stone section, you'll continue on Front Street through the downtown area about 1.4 miles, and then turn right onto Perry Street. Go 0.1 mile, and turn left onto West Market Street. Then go about 0.3 mile, and turn left onto South Porter Street. In a little more than 450 feet, the road cuts right and turns into West Front Street. Go about 450 feet, and turn left onto Decatur Street. The main trail resumes about 400 feet ahead on Decatur Street, at a parking lot under the train tracks.

The Northwest Lancaster County River Trail offers great views of the Susquehanna River on its journey from Columbia to Falmouth.

This route passes several taverns, pubs, and other dining options. It is also rather winding, with vegetation creating blind spots around every corner in the summer. Use extra caution if bicycling, and keep to the right if walking.

Leaving Marietta, the path becomes straighter, occasionally exiting the tree cover to travel along cornfields. At 7 miles, East Donegal Riverfront Park offers covered picnic tables and a great view of the Susquehanna River. In another 1.5 miles, you'll pass under the brick-arch Shocks Mill Bridge of the Norfolk Southern Railway and then alongside the White Cliffs of Conoy in another mile. This unique landmark was formed over time by the waste products of a limestone quarry, creating a hilly area of limestone "cliffs" on the shores of the Susquehanna.

In another 1.6 miles the path reaches Koser Park in Bainbridge. A 3-mile section of trail that extends to the Falmouth Boat Launch at Fisherman's Wharf is scheduled to be paved in 2020.

CONTACT: nwrt.info

DIRECTIONS

To reach the trailhead at Columbia Crossing River Trails Center from I-83 S, take Exit 19B, and merge onto E. Philadelphia St. Immediately turn left onto N. Yale St., go 770 feet, and turn left onto PA 462/E. Market St. Go 0.2 mile, turn left onto N. Hills Road, and follow the directions below. From I-83 N, take Exit 19, and continue straight onto N. Hills Road. In 0.6 mile turn right onto US 30 E, and go 10.8 miles. Take the exit toward PA 441 in Columbia, turn right onto Linden St., and go 0.2 mile. Turn left onto N. Second St., and go 0.2 mile. Turn right onto Bridge St., go 0.1 mile, and then turn left onto N. Front St. Go 0.1 mile, and turn right at the first crossing onto Walnut St., heading toward the river. Turn right into the parking lot, and look for parking in the back of the lot.

To reach the trailhead at Columbia Crossing River Trails Center from the intersection of US 222 and US 30 in Lancaster, head west on US 30, and go 1.4 miles. Keep right to stay on US 30, and go 10.7 miles. Take the exit for PA 441 toward Columbia/Marietta, continue straight onto PA 441 S, and go 0.7 mile. Turn right onto Walnut St., heading toward the river, and turn right into the parking lot. Look for parking in the back of the lot.

To reach parking at Koser Park in Bainbridge, follow the directions above from US 30 W to the PA 441 exit toward Columbia/Marietta. Turn right onto PA 441 N, and go 9.8 miles. Turn left onto Race St., go 0.4 mile, and look for the parking lot straight ahead beside the Susquehanna River.

To reach parking at Koser Park in Bainbridge from I-83, follow the directions above to US 30 E. Go 10.8 miles, and take the PA 441 exit. Turn right onto Linden St., and go 0.2 mile. Turn right onto N. Third St., and go 0.2 mile. Then continue on PA 441 N, and go 9.8 miles. Turn left onto Race St., go 0.4 mile, and look for the parking lot straight ahead on the Susquehanna River.

I t's hard to believe that the world's first oil boom occurred along the path of what's now the Oil Creek State Park Trail. The park's forests, beaver ponds, and trout streams were once the site of oil derricks, boomtowns, pipelines, refineries, and a railroad that served the nation's first oil patch.

In 1859 Edwin Drake was the first to strike oil after months of difficult drilling at a site along Oil Creek known since pre-Colonial times for its oil seepages. Oil was mainly used as a substitute for whale oil in lamps and patent medicines; such uses as fuels, plastics, and fertilizers all came later. Soon oil boomtowns popped up along Oil Creek, and railroads began serving them in 1862.

The trail runs on the corridor of the first railroad to reach Titusville, the Oil Creek Rail Road, which ran to a main rail line in Corry. It later ran the length of Oil Creek to Petroleum Centre and merged to become the Oil Creek and Allegheny River Railway in 1868, and still later became part of the Pennsylvania Railroad.

Travelers will find the Petroleum Centre Train Station at the southern end of Oil Creek State Park Trail.

County
Venango

Endpoints
Queen City Trail at Drake Well Road near Museum Lane (Titusville) to McClintock Trail near Petroleum Center Road and Russell Corners Road/Oil Creek State Park (Oil City)

Mileage
9.7

Type
Rail-Trail

Roughness Index
1

Surface
Asphalt

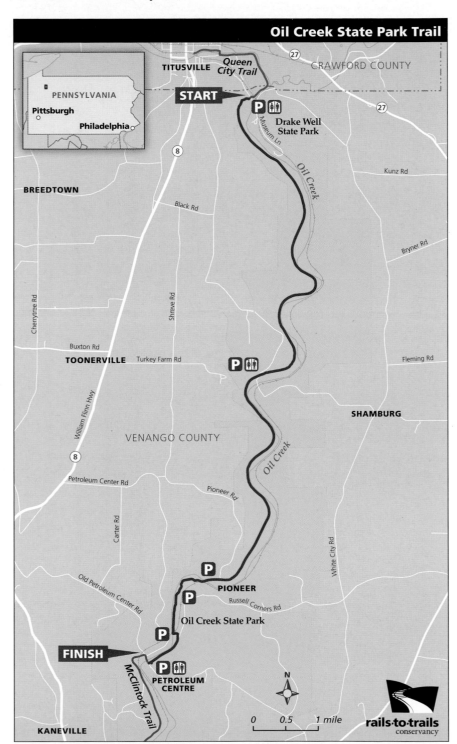

Oil Creek State Park Trail

The trail passes through Oil Creek State Park for 9.7 miles; the 1.5-mile Queen City Trail (see page 205) connects it to Titusville. In addition to the frequent bicyclists and hikers, the path—open daily, sunrise–sunset—is also popular among those who enjoy fishing for bass and trout.

The trail is part of the future 270-mile Erie to Pittsburgh Trail, which will connect with the Great Allegheny Passage (see page 82). At its southern endpoint, it connects to the 9.4-mile McClintock Trail, which heads south to Oil City and provides further connections to the 3-mile Oil City Trail and 6-mile Samuel Justus Recreation Trail (see page 215). The trail is also part of the Industrial Heartland Trails Coalition's developing 1,500-mile trail network through Pennsylvania, West Virginia, Ohio, and New York.

The main trailhead is at the Jersey Bridge Parking Area at Oil Creek State Park, which is also the southern endpoint for the Queen City Trail. For a 0.3-mile side trip to the informative Drake Well Museum, which includes a replica of that first oil well, turn right from the parking lot and cross Oil Creek, and then turn right onto Museum Lane.

A replica of Edwin Drake's first oil well lies just 0.3 mile from the trail at the Drake Well Museum.

Otherwise, turn left from the parking lot and head south along the west shore of Oil Creek. The trail follows the twists and turns of Oil Creek through a mostly hardwood forest, which provides good shade in the summer and good views across the gorge that Oil Creek and the trail runs through. There also are numerous historical sites along the trail, as well as some still-working oil and gas wells.

You'll pass the locations of such boomtowns as Boughton, Millers Farm, Shaffer Farm, Pioneer, and Funkville as you head south. Crossing the river at 7.9 miles past the trailhead, you'll come in contact with rails of the Oil Creek & Titusville Railroad, a tourist train that has been running on the east side of Oil Creek from Titusville since 1986.

The Oil Creek State Park Trail continues on the east side of Oil Creek and then follows a park road for its last 0.5 mile, ending at the site of the most notorious of the boomtowns, Petroleum Centre. Today the area has shelters, restrooms, parking, and a boat launch; the ranger station here also rents bicycles, or you can take a self-guided walking tour of the "wickedest town east of the Mississippi," according to the state park's brochure. A depot for the Oil Creek & Titusville Railroad is here.

At the terminus, you can make a seamless connection with the McClintock Trail by following Petroleum Center Road to your right and then Number Five Power Road, which curves left and then south toward Oil City.

CONTACT: dcnr.pa.gov/stateparks/findapark/oilcreekstatepark/pages/default.aspx or friendsocsp.org/trails/biking/ocbiketrail.html

DIRECTIONS

To reach parking at the northern trailhead at the Jersey Bridge Parking Area, which is shared with the Queen City Trail, from I-79, take Exit 141, turn right onto PA 285 E, and go 7.4 miles. Turn left onto PA 173 N, and go 8.0 miles. Turn right onto PA 27 E, and go 15.7 miles. Take a slight right onto W. Spring St., and go 0.2 mile; then turn right onto S. Perry St., and go 0.3 mile, crossing Oil Creek. Turn left onto W. Bloss St./Allen St./Drake Well Road, and go just more than 1 mile. Turn right into the trailhead parking lot, just before Drake Well Road crosses Oil Creek.

To reach the southern trailhead at Petroleum Center Road from I-80, take Exit 29. Head north on PA 8, go 16.3 miles, and turn right onto Liberty St. Then go 0.2 mile, and turn left onto 13th St./Meadville Pike. Go 0.5 mile, and bear right onto PA 417/Rocky Grove Ave. Go 12.1 miles, and turn left onto PA 8 N/PA 417/William Flinn Hwy. Go 0.3 mile, and turn right onto Old Petroleum Center Road. Go 2.6 miles, and take a slight left onto Petroleum Center Road. Go 0.1 mile, and turn left into the parking lot.

The Panhandle Trail offers the most direct and scenic route for self-propelled travel between the Pittsburgh suburbs and West Virginia. Although the trail follows an old railroad grade through the hilly terrain, there was only so much the railroad builders could do to flatten the route. Expect a steady climb to the town of Midway, the high point on the rural journey.

The Panhandle Trail is a host trail for the 3,700-plus-mile Great American Rail-Trail—which will one day form a seamless connection between Washington, D.C., and Washington State—and is part of the Industrial Heartland Trails Coalition's developing 1,500-mile trail network through Pennsylvania, West Virginia, Ohio, and New York.

This route was made famous by the merger of several railroads in the 1860s to create the Pittsburgh, Cincinnati, Chicago and St. Louis Railway (PCC&StL), or simply the Panhandle Route. It was named for the sliver of northern West Virginia it crossed on the way to Ohio. The Pennsylvania Railroad leased the route in the 1920s, and the line later became part of the Penn Central and Conrail systems until it fell into disuse in 1991.

The 29-mile trail is maintained by several communities and organizations along the way. Starting at the old Walkers Mill station about 10 miles west of Pittsburgh, the trail passes through a succession of small towns that become farther apart as you head west. The Panhandle Trail crosses the 61.5-mile Montour Trail (see page 157), which links to the 150-mile Great Allegheny Passage (see page 82) and the 184.5-mile C&O Canal Towpath for an off-road connection to Washington, D.C. Horseback riding is allowed in the corridor in Pennsylvania, but not on the trail itself.

At Walkers Mill Road, the trail starts with a crushed-limestone surface as it heads west across the Allegheny Plateau through a hardwood forest alongside Robinson Run. A quarry at 0.3 mile is a scenic picnic spot, and the site of the annual Rock the Quarry fundraiser held in August for Collier Friends of the Panhandle Trail. A side

Counties
Allegheny and Washington (PA); Brooke and Hancock (WV)

Endpoints
Walkers Mill Road/ SR 3028 and Scott Al (Oakdale, PA) to 0.8 mile west of Police Lodge Road and US 22 (Colliers, WV)

Mileage
29.2

Type
Rail-Trail

Roughness Index
2

Surface
Asphalt, Crushed Stone

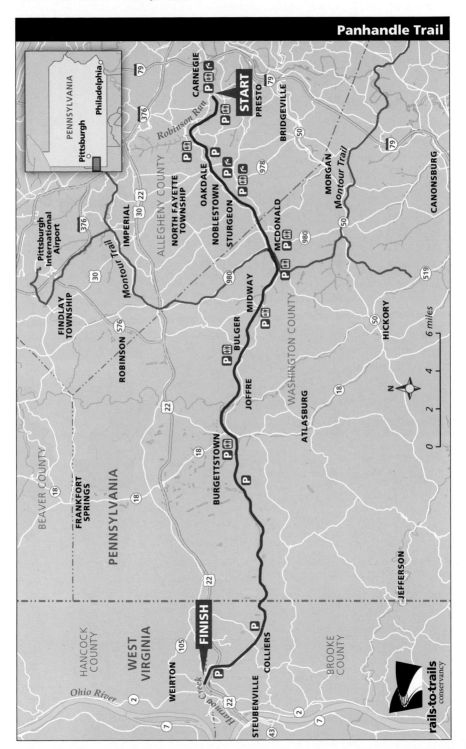

Panhandle Trail

path another 0.3 mile up the trail visits Fossils Cliff, where rock hounds can find fossilized fern leaves.

The trail passes through Oakdale at 3.7 miles, where thirsty travelers will find a brewery next to the trail and a market and diner down the street. A TNT explosion near the rail line here in 1918 killed 200 people. Over the next 3.5 miles, the trail passes three more towns—Noblestown, Sturgeon, and McDonald—which provide trailhead picnic tables (some covered) and opportunities for buying food in town.

The trail becomes paved asphalt as you enter Washington County just before McDonald. The substantial brick buildings in McDonald are evidence of the oil boom that struck in the late 1800s; coal is still mined in the area. A visitor center, located at the South McDonald Street trailhead, is the start for the annual Tour de Panhandle bike ride in June.

At 8 miles, you'll pass beneath a 1913 railroad trestle on the Montour Trail that crosses the Panhandle Trail and Robinson Run. You can turn onto the Montour Trail at a nearly mile-long side trail that connects the two about 0.4 mile ahead.

At 10.6 miles, you'll reach Midway. Although you've only completed a third of the trail's distance, the town was the railroad's halfway point between Pittsburgh and Steubenville, Ohio. Nearly a mile west of town, you'll pass a small airfield and the highest point on the trail. Heading downhill, you'll find that the next two towns, Bulger (13.5) and Joffre (14.5), won't offer much in the way of services. You'll encounter another uphill grade on the way to Burgettstown, which offers a food stop at a market, diner, or pizza parlor.

The Panhandle Trail passes beneath a 1913 railroad trestle on the Montour Trail.

It's all downhill to the finish, with few services along the way. You'll cross into West Virginia in 7.3 miles, where the trail becomes crushed limestone again. This final leg meanders through coal country to Weirton, West Virginia, once home to the giant Weirton Steel Corporation. The path runs along Harmon Creek, known for its catfish and carp.

CONTACT: panhandletrail.org or cityofweirton.com/363/northern-panhandle -rail-trail

DIRECTIONS

To reach the eastern trailhead in Oakdale from I-79, take Exit 57 toward Carnegie, and head west on W. Main St./SR 3048. Go 0.5 mile, and turn right onto First St., and then immediately bear right onto Dorrington Road. Go 0.8 mile, and turn right onto Hilltop Dr./SR 3052, and then go 1.6 miles, and turn right on Boyds Run Road/SR 3028. Go 0.5 mile, and look for trailhead parking on the left.

To reach the western trailhead in Colliers, West Virginia, from I-376, take Exit 60A and merge onto US 22/US 30 W. Go 3.9 miles, and stay straight to continue on US 22. Go 18.5 miles, and take Exit 3 for WV 1/Harmon Creek Road/Cove Road toward WV 507, and turn left onto Harmon Creek Road. Go 0.2 mile, and turn right onto Worthington Lane. Then go 100 feet, and turn right onto McColl Road. Go 0.2 mile, and turn right into the parking lot. Facing the trail, turn left to go 1.5 miles to the western endpoint.

The Path of the Flood Trail might be unique among rail-trails for being named after a tragedy, the Johnstown Flood of 1889, considered the nation's worst catastrophe of the 19th century. Some 2,200 people lost their lives when the South Fork Dam failed and 20 million tons of water washed down the narrow Little Conemaugh River Valley for 14 miles to Johnstown, destroying everything in its path.

The trail is paired with the Staple Bend Tunnel Trail, which preserves a tunnel finished in 1833 as the nation's first railroad tunnel. The National Park Service operates the 901-foot-long tunnel and associated trail. Both trails are part of the Trans Allegheny Trail System, comprised

An overlook of the Conemaugh Viaduct features a marker that tells the history of the Johnstown Flood of 1889.

County
Cambria

Endpoints
Johnstown Flood Museum at Washington St. and Walnut St. (Johnstown) to Ehrenfeld Park at Penn St. and Mt. Carmel St. (Ehrenfeld)

Mileage
11.8

Type
Rail-Trail

Roughness Index
1–2

Surface
Asphalt, Ballast, Crushed Stone

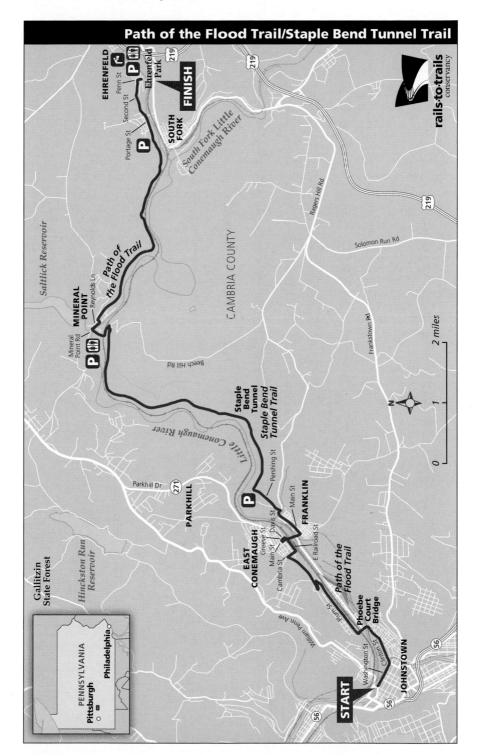

Path of the Flood Trail/Staple Bend Tunnel Trail

of several trails in western Pennsylvania. The Path of the Flood Trail is also part of the September 11th National Memorial Trail that connects the 9/11, Flight 93, and Pentagon Memorials, as well as the Industrial Heartland Trails Coalition's developing 1,500-mile trail network through Pennsylvania, West Virginia, Ohio, and New York.

Together, they follow the course of the Allegheny Portage Railroad. Built in the 1830s, the railroad carried barges across Allegheny highlands, connecting the eastern and western segments of the Pennsylvania Canal. Eventually becoming obsolete, the portage railroad was acquired in 1857 by the Pennsylvania Railroad, which discontinued using some segments (it never used the tunnel) and upgraded others.

Including on-road sections, the two trails run 11.8 miles along the Little Conemaugh River. Given the nature of the Allegheny Portage Railroad—level sections paired with steep inclines, rather than the gradual slopes associated with most railroads—the Staple Bend Tunnel Trail has a short, steep grade in each direction. The off-road trail comprises mostly crushed stone, with a 0.5 mile of aggregate stone surfacing near the Staple Bend Tunnel.

The route starts at the Johnstown Flood Museum (**jaha.org**) at 304 Washington St. The trail is mostly on sidewalks and city streets in this 4.2-mile segment to the Staple Bend Tunnel Trail. Follow the bike route signs on Washington and Clinton Streets; turn left on the Phoebe Court Bridge, then use the tunnel under the railroad tracks. The trail continues right on Plum Street to a short trail that follows switchbacks on an old trolley line. Emerging in East Conemaugh, turn right onto Cambria Street and left onto East Railroad Street. You'll then need to make a series of three lefts onto Davis, Greeve, and Main Streets, respectively. Take the PA 271/Main Street bridge across the river to Franklin, and then turn left onto Main Street for 0.5 mile.

Turn left onto Pershing Street, and take the right fork to the parking area at Franklin Borough Ball Field. In about 1 mile, the surface changes to a bikeable aggregate stone surface for 0.5 mile to the Staple Bend Tunnel, which carried barge traffic over the mountains via rail. Note that this section, while maneuverable by wheelchair and bike, contains some challenging hills. Entering the tunnel, notice the ornamental stonework at the west portal, which was designed to impress users; a similar portal on the east side was removed in 1907. A flashlight isn't absolutely necessary, but it would allow you to closely examine the workmanship inside the tunnel.

Back to crushed stone, the tunnel trail continues 2 miles to the Beech Hill Road trailhead. Turn left and cross the bridge to Mineral Point, and then turn right onto Mineral Point Road and right onto Reynolds Lane to pick up the Path of the Flood Trail. The trail follows a bench overlooking the Little Conemaugh River, the surrounding forest, and the tracks of the Norfolk Southern Railroad.

Following a slight uphill grade for the next 2 miles, you'll see the borough of South Fork across the river and its confluence with the South Fork Little Conemaugh River, which carried the deluge from the failed dam. Signs mark historic points on this segment.

The off-road trail ends just ahead at Portage Street. Continue on Portage Street 0.4 mile, and then on Second Street another 0.4 mile to Penn Street. Turn right onto Penn Street, and go a little less than 0.1 mile to the Ehrenfeld Park trailhead, where you'll find parking, a drinking fountain, and restrooms.

Note that to avoid the hilly section near the Staple Bend Tunnel in Johnstown, some trail users opt to do an out-and-back trip to the tunnel beginning at the Ehrenfeld Park or Beech Hill Road trailheads.

Plans call for extending the trail across the river in South Fork, and then along the South Fork Little Conemaugh River to about 0.2 mile away from the dam and the Johnstown Flood National Memorial (**nps.gov/jofl**).

CONTACT: cambriaconservationrecreation.com/path-of-the-flood-trail

DIRECTIONS

To reach the western endpoint at the Johnstown Flood Museum from I-76, take Exit 110 toward US 219/Somerset/Johnstown. Continue on PA Turnpike Access Road for 0.3 mile, and then continue on N. Pleasant Ave. 0.4 mile. Turn left onto PA 281/Stoystown Road, go 1.9 miles, and exit right onto US 219. Go 23.8 miles, and take the PA 56/Johnstown Expy. exit. Go 5.3 miles, and turn right onto Walnut St. Then go 0.3 mile, and turn right onto Washington St. The museum is located at this intersection at 304 Washington St. Look for on-street parking.

To reach the eastern trailhead at Ehrenfeld Park from I-76, follow the directions above to US 219. Go 31 miles, and exit toward South Fork, turning left onto PA 53 N/Railroad St. Go 0.8 mile, and turn right onto Oak St. Then go 0.1 mile, turn right onto Portage St., and go 0.1 mile. Take a slight right onto Second St., and go 0.4 mile. Turn right onto Penn St., and then turn right onto Mt. Carmel St. Look for parking immediately to your left at Ehrenfeld Park.

A renovated former railroad tunnel that features a separate entrance for bats is a highlight of the Penns Creek Path. The path is a relatively flat segment of the 328-mile Mid State Trail that runs across the ridge and valley section of Central Pennsylvania. Visitors can easily traverse the 2.7-mile trail through hardwood forest overlooking Penns Creek by bicycle, on horseback, or on foot.

The Lewisburg, Centre and Spruce Creek Railroad left behind the railroad grade that the trail follows. Pitched as an east–west route across the mountains in the late 1850s to link with larger rail lines and to haul lumber out of the mountains, the railroad had difficulties building across the mountains and didn't finish the Penns Creek section until 1877. It became the Lewisburg and Tyrone Railroad after bankruptcy in 1879, and the Pennsylvania Railroad acquired it in 1915. Trains stopped using it in 1968.

In winter, bats enter the renovated Poe Paddy Tunnel, a former railroad tunnel, through a specially constructed gate.

Counties
Centre, Mifflin

Endpoints
Tunnel Spur Road between Poe Paddy Dr. and Stewart Lane at Poe Paddy State Park (Woodward) to the Fish Commission parking lot, 0.5 mile west of Cherry Run Road/SR 3002 and Weikert Road (Cherry Run)

Mileage
2.7

Type
Rail-Trail

Roughness Index
2

Surface
Crushed Stone

Penns Creek Path (Mid State Trail)

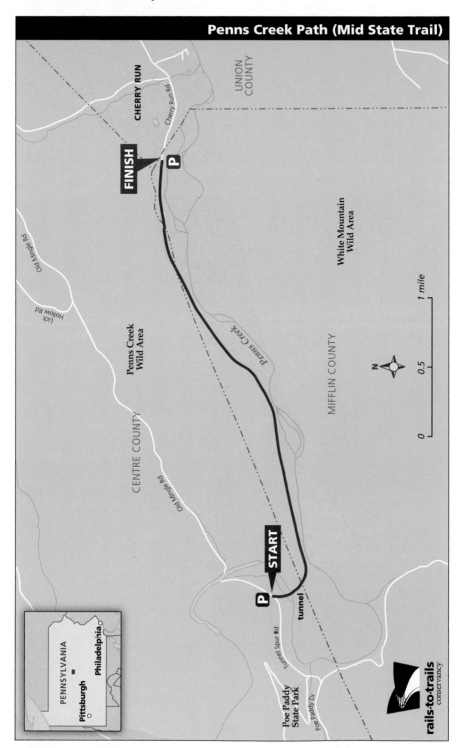

You won't find towns or services along the trail, although pit toilets and drinking water are available at campgrounds in Poe Paddy State Park near the western trailhead. A state project to renovate the previously closed almost-300-foot tunnel in 2015 had the side benefits of shoring up the eastern 2 miles of trail for construction traffic, as well as redecking a pedestrian bridge over Penns Creek. While birding is a popular pastime along the trail, you might encounter other wildlife on the trail, such as black bears, bobcats, and timber rattlers. It's best to review the proper options for dealing with these wildlife before setting out in their habitat.

Heading east from the Tunnel Spur Road trailhead at Poe Paddy State Park, named for an old lumbering town here, you'll soon come to a pedestrian bridge crossing Penns Creek. If you're here in late May or June, you'll likely see fly-fishers hoping to catch brown trout with green drake flies.

Soon after crossing the bridge you'll encounter the entrance to a tunnel blasted through West Paddy Mountain. Closed because of safety concerns for two years, the tunnel reopened in 2016 with a new wall lining and trail surface. Take a flashlight, because a curve prevents light from passing through the tunnel. Above the east entrance, you'll see a bat gate where winged mammals can come and go. The bats generally find other places to roost in the spring and summer and retire here in the winter to hibernate.

Exiting the tunnel, you'll experience a pleasant trek through the designated 6,000-acre Penns Creek Wild Area for the next 2.4 miles to the Cherry Run parking lot. Several overlooks provide views of Penns Creek in the valley below, and hardwoods provide a colorful palette in the fall.

CONTACT: hike-mst.org

DIRECTIONS

To reach the western trailhead at Poe Paddy State Park from I-99/US 322, take Exit 73 to merge onto US 322 E. Go 16.7 miles, and turn left onto Sand Mountain Road. Go 3.6 miles, and turn right to stay on Sand Mountain Road. Go 2.5 miles, and bear left onto Siglerville Millheim Pike. Go 1.0 mile, and take the right fork onto Poe Valley Road. Go 3.3 miles, and take the right fork onto Poe Paddy Dr. Go 2.5 miles, and turn left to stay on Poe Paddy Dr. Go 0.1 mile, and take the right fork onto Tunnel Spur Road. Go 0.5 mile, and look for the trailhead parking lot on the right.

To reach the eastern endpoint from I-99/US 322, take Exit 81 for PA 26 S/PA 64 S toward Pleasant Gap. Turn right onto PA 26 S, go 0.9 mile, and turn left onto S. Harrison Road. Go 0.5 mile, and turn left onto PA 144 S/S. Main St. Go 4.7 miles, and turn left onto PA 45 E. Go 17.9 miles, and turn right onto Woodward Gap Road. In 3.3 miles continue onto Cherry Run Road, go 3.7 miles, and turn right onto Cherry Run Road/SR 3002. Go 0.5 mile, and look for the parking on the left.

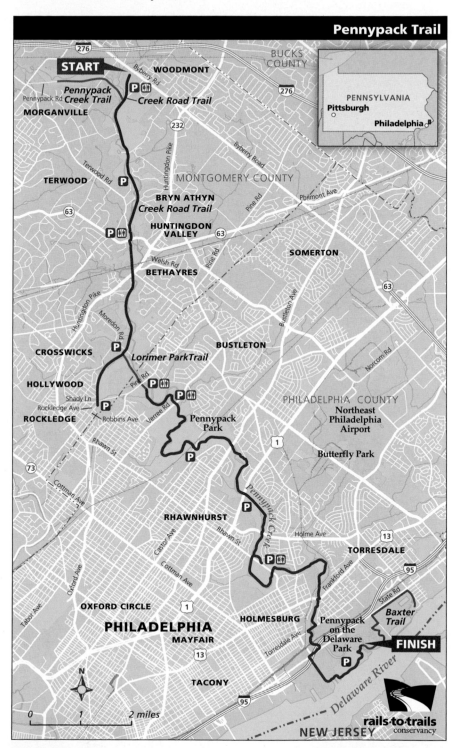

The Pennypack Trail travels through wooded parks in Philadelphia and Montgomery Counties along Pennypack Creek, which derives its name from a local American Indian term for a slow-moving creek. History comes alive along the packed-cinder and asphalt trail as the route passes the remains of 19th-century mills and the site of a 1920s head-on train crash. The pleasant creekside views culminate in a broad vista across the Delaware River.

The northern section of the Pennypack Trail follows an old Southeastern Pennsylvania Transportation Authority (SEPTA) commuter line that got its start as the Philadelphia & Montgomery County Railroad Company in the 1860s. It later became the Philadelphia, Newtown and New York Railroad and then the Newtown branch of the Reading Railroad. SEPTA acquired the line in 1976 but suspended service in 1983. Montgomery County leased

Counties
Montgomery, Philadelphia

Endpoints
Byberry Road between Reading Way and Pioneer Road (Woodmont) to Rockledge Ave. and Robbins Ave. (Rockledge); Pennypack Park at Pine Road between Longmead Lane and Shady Lane to Baxter Trail, 1.2 miles west of Pennypack Path and State Road at Pennypack on the Delaware Park (Philadelphia)

Mileage
16.0

Type
Rail-Trail

Roughness Index
1

Surface
Asphalt, Cinder

Be courteous to other trail users; equestrians have the right-of-way.

the corridor for $1 and opened the first section of trail in 2009. The southern section of trail traces the winding creek through Pennypack Park, which the city created as one mill after another closed in the early 1900s.

Open sunrise–sunset, the path follows a steady downhill course through wooded parkland, carved out of dense neighborhoods, to the Delaware River. Horseback riding is allowed on the Montgomery County segment between Byberry Road and Robbins Avenue. The trail is part of the Circuit Trails, a developing 800-mile urban network of trails in Greater Philadelphia, of which about 350 miles are currently complete. A short section along the Delaware River is part of the East Coast Greenway that stretches 3,000 miles from Maine to Florida.

Stretching from Byberry Road to near Rockledge Avenue, the 5.4-mile-long Montgomery County section of trail is packed cinder and passes through the Pennypack Ecological Restoration Trust, where native plants and animals are preserved. In 0.4 mile you'll reach Creek Road Trail, where you can take a sharp right and then another sharp right onto the 1.9-mile Pennypack Creek Trail, a

The trail travels through wooded parks in Philadelphia and Montgomery Counties along Pennypack Creek.

footpath that leads northwest through the woods and onto Pennypack Road toward Davisville Road/State Route 2042.

About 0.6 mile past Byberry Road, you'll pass through an area known locally as Death Gulch, where two trains collided in 1921, resulting in 27 deaths. In another 1.4 miles, you'll find a weekend food truck at the Bryn Athyn Post Office (a former train station) and picnic area. In 0.7 mile the Welsh Road trailhead provides a midpoint location for exploring both ends of the Montgomery County section.

Upon approaching the Moredon Road trailhead, you can opt to take a 0.6-mile gravel path called the Lorimer Park Trail to the southern section of the Pennypack Trail in Philadelphia County. The Montgomery County section of the Pennypack Trail ends a little more than 1 mile farther south at Rockledge Avenue.

The southern segment of the trail begins on Pine Road at the edge of Pennypack Park, which the city started acquiring in 1905. The wooded route trends downhill toward the river, though some short hills are steep. The woods make this section of trail seem remote, although users will pass beneath multiple bridges carrying traffic overhead. One notable bridge you'll cross comes 7.6 miles past Pine Road at Frankford Avenue; the stone-arch bridge built in 1697 is considered the oldest surviving road bridge in the United States. Side trails connect with adjacent neighborhoods along the route.

The last 2 miles of trail pass two prisons, Holmesburg Prison (closed) and Philadelphia House of Correction (slated for closure in 2020). Entering Pennypack on the Delaware Park, you'll find a fishing pier as the river comes into sight. You'll ride along the Delaware River for 0.8 mile until the trail ends at the 0.6-mile Baxter Trail, which crosses the creek toward Pleasant Hill Park and connects with bike lanes on State Road.

CONTACT: friendsofpennypackpark.org or montcopa.org/922/pennypack-trail

DIRECTIONS

To reach the northern endpoint from I-95, take Exit 35 toward PA 63 W/Woodhaven Road. Merge onto PA 63 W/Woodhaven Road, and go 3.2 miles; then continue straight on Woodhaven Road another 0.2 mile. Turn left onto Evans St., and go 0.2 mile. Turn right onto Byberry Road. Go 0.9 mile, and veer left to stay on Byberry Road. Go 4.4 miles, and turn left into the parking lot.

To reach the southern endpoint from I-95, take Exit 30 toward PA 73/Cottman Ave. From I-95 S turn right onto Bleigh Ave., go 420 feet, and then turn right onto State Road. From I-95 N continue onto Cottman Ave. about 390 feet, and turn right onto State Road. Go about 0.5 mile, and turn right onto Pennypack Path. Go about 0.8 mile to the parking lot. Take a spur path toward the Delaware River; it will intersect with the Pennypack Trail. Turn right to head northward. The endpoint is located about 1.3 miles farther east along the trail.

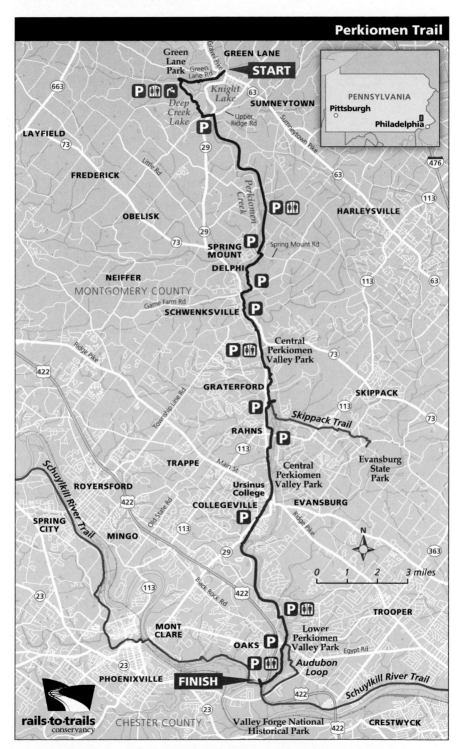

Perkiomen Trail

START — GREEN LANE

Green Lane Park

Green Lane Rd

Gravel Pike

Knight Lake

Deep Creek Lake

663

LAYFIELD

73

FREDERICK

OBELISK

Little Rd

29

SUMNEYTOWN

Upper Ridge Rd

Summneytown Pike

63

Perkiomen Creek

29

73

SPRING MOUNT

DELPHI

NEIFFER

MONTGOMERY COUNTY

Game Farm Rd

SCHWENKSVILLE

Spring Mount Rd

HARLEYSVILLE

113

113

63

Central Perkiomen Valley Park

73

Ridge Pike

422

Township Line Rd

GRATERFORD

RAHNS

113

TRAPPE

Main St

Ursinus College

COLLEGEVILLE

29

Old State Rd

SPRING CITY

ROYERSFORD

MINGO

422

SKIPPACK

113

Skippack Trail

73

Evansburg State Park

Central Perkiomen Valley Park

EVANSBURG

Ridge Pike

N

0   1   2   3 miles

363

23

113

Black Rock Rd

422

TROOPER

Lower Perkiomen Valley Park

Egypt Rd

MONT CLARE

OAKS

Audubon Loop

Schuylkill River Trail

23

PHOENIXVILLE

FINISH

422

Schuylkill River Trail

CRESTWYCK

CHESTER COUNTY

Valley Forge National Historical Park

422

23

PENNSYLVANIA

Pittsburgh

Philadelphia

rails·to·trails
conservancy

The Perkiomen Trail provides so many interesting historical and natural sites along its 20.6-mile length that visitors may have to ignore some of the trailside distractions to reach the other end.

Created in 2003, the trail rolls down the valley of Perkiomen Creek, which may have been a reference by local American Indians to the surrounding cranberry bogs. The trail is part of the Circuit Trails, a developing 800-mile urban network of trails in Greater Philadelphia, of which about 350 miles are complete.

The Perkiomen Trail passes through numerous parks that feature side trails, historical buildings, museums, and periodic festivals, and it ends at a junction with the Schuylkill River Trail (see page 221) near Valley Forge. There's a short climb in the vicinity of a ski resort, but otherwise the path is flat. Plenty of services are available along the route, which is open dawn–dusk. Most of the trail is crushed stone, though about 6 miles are paved at the southern end.

The Perkiomen Railroad gained popularity soon after it opened in 1868 from Oaks to Green Lane, and later to Allentown. Development surged along the line, and vacationers hopped trains bound for tourist destinations. The Reading Railroad bought the line in 1944, but passenger trains ceased running by 1955. Conrail later acquired the line, and Montgomery County bought the land in 1978.

Start your journey in the north at Morrow Pavilion in Green Lane Park, where you'll find parking and restrooms. The trail passes Knight and Deep Creek Lakes, two of the reservoirs in this 3,400-acre park that supply water to the region. The park features 25 miles of equestrian, mountain biking, and hiking trails.

The trail leaves the park, travels alongside Deep Creek Road for 0.1 mile, crosses the creek on a stone-arch bridge that dates to 1839, and then rejoins the trail after 500 feet on Upper Ridge Road.

The path travels through forests and alongside some farm lots for the next 3 miles to the site of the Philadelphia

County
Montgomery

Endpoints
Gravel Pike and Lumber St. (Green Lane) to Station Ave., 0.1 mile north of Pawlings Road (Oaks)

Mileage
20.6

Type
Rail-Trail

Roughness Index
1

Surface
Asphalt, Crushed Stone

Folk Festival (**pfs.org/philadelphia-folk-festival**), which takes place each August in Harleysville. In another mile, you'll reach Spring Mount, home to a ski resort. The trail crosses the creek on a separated path on Spring Mount Road, passes through more than a mile of woods, and crosses the creek again just before Schwenksville, which dates to the 1680s. Many services and old homes are located on Main Street, which runs next to the trail through town; the Pennypacker Mills historical site across the creek features a mansion restored to the early 1900s.

The trail enters the 800-acre Central Perkiomen Valley Park about a mile later and crosses the creek twice within the next 2 miles—first about 0.5 mile after crossing Plank Road, and the second about 1.8 miles farther (0.5 mile after passing Graterford Road). Note that at the second crossing, the Perkiomen Trail makes a sharp 90-degree turn left, followed by a sharp 180-degree turn right, to take you over the waterway. Optionally, you can continue southeast immediately before the second river crossing on the 3.3-mile Skippack Trail to Evansburg State Park.

The Perkiomen Trail then passes through Rahns and Collegeville, the latter named for the Pennsylvania Female College that closed in 1880, although Ursinus College remains today.

The calm waters of Perkiomen Creek border the rail-trail.

The route continues south through residential and commercial areas, which are screened by vegetation along the railroad grade for 4.5 miles to Lower Perkiomen Valley Park. In 0.2 mile inside the park, the trail joins the Audubon Loop, which travels 2.5 miles and visits the former home and museum dedicated to famed naturalist and artist John James Audubon. The route ends in another mile, where it intersects with the Schuylkill River Trail near the confluence of Perkiomen Creek and the Schuylkill River. The Valley Forge National Historical Park is about 3 miles away by trail.

CONTACT: montcopa.org/1153/perkiomen-trail

DIRECTIONS

To reach the trailhead at Green Lane Park from I-476 N, take Exit 31 to PA 63 W/Sumneytown Pike. Go 9.6 miles, and turn right onto PA 29/Gravel Pike. Go 0.2 mile, and turn left onto Hill Road. Then go 0.3 mile, and turn left onto Green Lane Road. Go 0.5 mile, and turn left onto the park access road. Go 0.1 mile to the parking lot, straight ahead. To find the northern endpoint, backtrack to the lot's entrance and turn right; the endpoint is 0.7 mile farther ahead along the trail.

To reach the trailhead at Green Lane Park from I-476 S, take Exit 44 toward PA 663/Quakertown/Pottstown. Turn right onto PA 663 (signs for Pottstown/Pennsburg), and go 3.4 miles. Turn left onto Geryville Pike, and go 1.7 miles. Then turn left to stay on Geryville Pike, and go 2.2 miles. Turn right onto Hoppenville Road, go 1.4 miles, and continue onto Lumber St. Go 0.2 mile, and turn right onto PA 29 S/Gravel Pike; then turn left onto Hill Road. Go 0.2 mile, and take a slight left onto Green Lane Road. Go 0.5 mile, and turn left onto the park access road. Go 0.1 mile to the parking lot, straight ahead. To find the northern endpoint, backtrack to the lot's entrance and turn right to go 0.7 mile farther north along the trail.

To reach the southern trailhead in Oaks from I-76, take Exit 328A toward US 202/US 422 W. Merge onto US 422 W. Go 5.3 miles, exit toward Oaks, and turn right onto Egypt Road/SR 4002. Immediately turn right onto New Mill Road, go 0.2 mile, and turn left into the trailhead parking lot. Take the Audubon Loop Trail spur at the southern side of the parking lot to the Perkiomen Trail. To find the southern endpoint, turn right and go 2 miles farther south along the trail (the creek will be on your left).

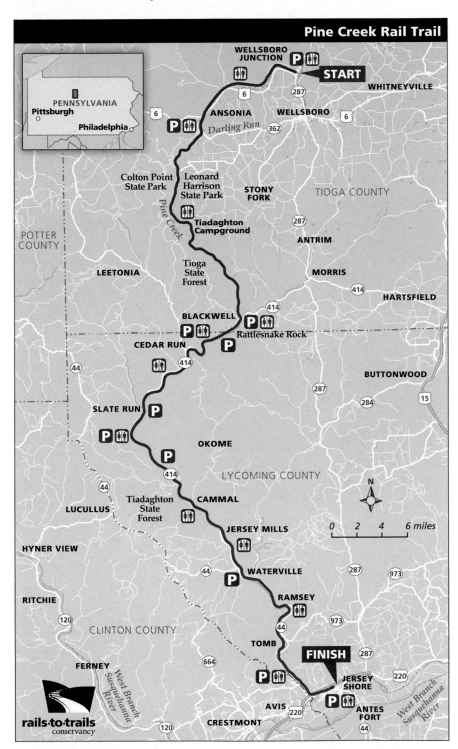

Pine Creek Rail Trail

The Pine Creek Rail Trail is one of Pennsylvania's destination trails, and for good reason. The 62-mile well-maintained trail runs at the bottom of überscenic Pine Creek Gorge, commonly called the Grand Canyon of Pennsylvania. Small towns along the route cater to trail visitors, and numerous trailheads, comfort stations, campgrounds, and lodging make extended stays possible. The finely crushed limestone surface is best suited for hybrid bikes; a service road next to the trail from Ansonia to Tiadaghton Campground (just northwest of where the trail intersects T357/Tiadaghton Road) is open to equestrians as well. It's a good trail for families, but remember that bicyclists age 12 and under must wear a helmet.

Melting glaciers carved the gorge, which runs 800–1,400 feet deep and a mile wide. A natural travel route through northern Pennsylvania for American Indians, the gorge in 1883 became the route of the Jersey Shore, Pine Creek and Buffalo Railway—later named Pine Creek Railway—that served lumber companies that clear-cut the mountainsides. The last freight passed through in 1988, and the trail was born in 1996 and extended to its present length in 2012.

The trail slopes imperceptibly downhill alongside Pine Creek, from Wellsboro Junction in the north to Jersey Shore in the south. Pines and hardwoods now carpet the

Counties
Lycoming, Tioga

Endpoints
Butler Road just south of Lower Marsh Creek Road (Wellsboro Junction) to Seminary St. between McClintock Alley and Fountain St. (Jersey Shore)

Mileage
62.0

Type
Rail-Trail

Roughness Index
1

Surface
Crushed Stone

Vistas such as this portray the beauty of Pine Creek Gorge, known as the Grand Canyon of Pennsylvania.

bare slopes left behind by loggers. Deer, elk, wild turkeys, and black bears inhabit the area bound by the Tioga and Tiadaghton State Forests, and you might see river otters or beavers in the water and bald eagles or ospreys above. The northern section is bound by state parks, and more food and lodging are available in the south. Visitors can use bike rental and shuttle services, as well as canoe and kayak liveries, and horse-drawn wagon rides are available on some sections.

The trailhead at Wellsboro Junction is the northern starting point (plans are underway for a 3-mile trail connection—the Marsh Creek Greenway—to Wellsboro that will provide more services to visitors). The Tioga Central Railroad station 0.5 mile east hosts an excursion train that runs north.

The first 7 miles to Ansonia are fairly wide open, but the gorge begins forming soon after the trail joins Pine Creek. The route passes between Colton Point State Park on the right and Leonard Harrison State Park on the left. Take the Turkey Path trail at 3.5 miles past the Darling Run trailhead to enjoy waterfall views.

The next 12.5 miles to a store at Blackwell travel through the most remote section of the gorge, passing only the Tiadaghton Campground. After Blackwell, PA 414 follows the trail south as the surroundings become more populated. A good swimming hole lies at Rattlesnake Rock, 1.8 miles past Blackwell, and in another 4 miles, Cedar Run has a popular café.

You'll encounter numerous trailheads and towns along the final 33 miles to Jersey Shore (the name refers to an early family from New Jersey) on the West Branch Susquehanna River. There's a store at Slate Run and services at Cammal and Jersey Mills. PA 44 arrives at Waterville, 1,450 feet below the surrounding ridgetops. The trail runs alongside PA 44 into Jersey Shore. Long-range plans call for extending the trail to Williamsport.

CONTACT: pinecreekvalley.com/Pine_Creek_Rail_Trail_About.asp or rtc.li/Pine_Creek_Rail_Trail

DIRECTIONS

To reach the northern trailhead at Wellsboro Junction from I-180 W, take Exit 29 to merge onto US 15 N. Go 27.6 miles, and turn left onto PA 414. Go 9.8 miles; stay straight on PA 287 N. Go 11.7 miles, and turn right onto PA 287/Main St. Go 0.3 mile, and stay straight on US 6/PA 287/Roosevelt Hwy. Go 2.5 miles, and bear right to stay on PA 287. Go 0.4 mile; turn left onto Lower Marsh Creek Road. Go 0.1 mile, and turn left onto Butler Road. Go 0.1 mile; turn right into the parking lot.

To reach the southern trailhead in Jersey Shore from I-180 W, stay on US 220 as I-180 ends in Williamsport (past mile marker 29). Go 13.3 miles, take the Thomas St. exit, and turn left onto Thomas St. Go 0.2 mile, and turn right onto Railroad St. Go 0.2 mile, and turn left into the parking lot. The endpoint is about 0.9 mile east along the trail at Seminary St. (facing the railroad tracks, turn left along the Pine Creek Rail Trail).

You've heard of the Steel Belt and the Sun Belt. The 6.7-mile Plainfield Township Recreation Trail passes through an area known as the Slate Belt. The quantity and quality of local slate made this part of Northampton County the world's largest slate producer for a time and prompted construction of a railroad that later became the rail-trail.

An immigrant from Wales started the first local slate quarry in nearby Bangor in 1848. The popularity of the blue-gray slate soon grew, and others began mining. The Bangor and Portland Railway was created to serve the quarries in 1879. After 1909, a series of railroads operated it until Conrail sold it to the township in 1987. The trail was completed in 1991.

The trail crosses Little Bushkill Creek five times on scenic wooden bridges from West Pen Argyl to the outskirts of Stockertown on a slight downhill grade. All but the northern segment is paved. The trail is open dawn–dusk.

Starting at the trailhead in West Pen Argyl, you begin at the foot of Blue Mountain, which carries the Appalachian Trail across its summit. A neighboring community, Pen Argyl—where Jayne Mansfield, a Hollywood actress

County
Northampton

Endpoints
Buss St. just south of PA 512/Pennsylvania Ave. (West Pen Argyl) to PA 191/Main St. between Sullivan Trail and Dogwood Lane (Stockertown)

Mileage
6.7

Type
Rail-Trail

Roughness Index
1–2

Surface
Asphalt, Ballast, Grass, Gravel

This eastern Pennsylvania trail begins at the base of Blue Mountain and winds through lush forest for much of its route.

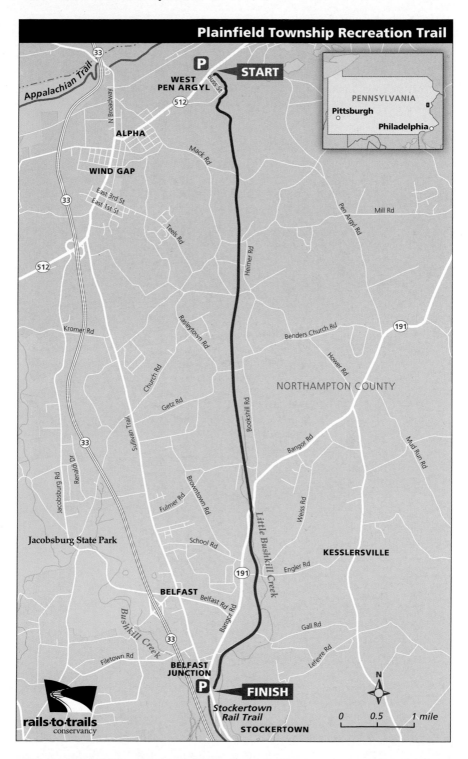

Plainfield Township Recreation Trail

of the 1950s and 1960s, now rests beneath a heart-shaped tombstone—is about a mile east of the trail. Pen Argyl is also home to the 1923 vintage Weona Park Carousel, which is ringed with three rows of horses and is listed in the National Register of Historic Places.

Passing through a wooded area, you'll see a large slate refuse pile like many that dot the landscape here. More than two-thirds of the mined slate was considered unfit for use and was discarded in slag piles like these. The useful slate found its way onto houses and buildings as slate roofs, which still abound in older parts of Philadelphia and other Eastern Seaboard cities. Single quarries are still operating in nearby Wind Gap, Pen Argyl, and Bangor.

The route heads south past farms, though the surroundings can be difficult to discern in the summer because of the dense forest bordering the path. You'll likely see horses grazing in pastures when you pass some clearings.

The trail ends just past the Belfast Junction trailhead off Main Street on the outskirts of Stockertown, home to a large cement factory. The trailhead for Stockertown Rail Trail is just across Main Street, and the trail goes 1.1 miles into town, where you'll find a mini-mart and tavern.

Plans are underway to build a trail to improve safety between the Plainfield Township Recreation Trail and Stockertown Rail Trail. The 1.6-mile connector trail will also link trails in Jacobsburg State Park. The project will take place in two phases, with work anticipated to be completed in Bushkill Township in 2019–2020 and in Plainfield Township in 2020–2021.

CONTACT: rtc.li/Plainfield_Township_Trail or plainfieldtownship.org/parks -and-recreation

DIRECTIONS

To reach the northern trailhead in West Pen Argyl from I-80 W, take Exit 304 for US 209 S toward Snydersville/PA 33 S. Merge onto US 209 S, go 6.2 miles, and then continue onto PA 33 S. Go 5.4 miles, and take the exit toward Wind Gap. Turn left onto PA 115, and go 0.1 mile. Then continue onto N. Broadway, and go 0.4 mile. Turn left onto Alpha Road, go 0.4 mile. Then turn left onto PA 512 N/N. Lehigh Ave., and go 0.8 mile. Turn right onto Buss St., and take an immediate left into the trailhead parking lot.

To reach the northern trailhead in West Pen Argyl from I-80 E, take Exit 302A to merge onto PA 33 S toward US 209 S/Snydersville in 3.2 miles. PA 33 S turns slightly right and becomes PA 33 S/US 209 S. Go 2.2 miles. Continue onto PA 33 S, and go 5.4 miles. Take the exit toward Wind Gap, and follow the directions above from Wind Gap to the trailhead parking lot.

To reach the southern trailhead in Stockertown from I-78, take Exit 71 for PA 33 N toward US 22/Stroudsburg. Merge onto PA 33 N, go 8.5 miles, and then take the PA 191 exit toward Stockertown/Bangor. Turn right onto PA 191 N/Industrial Blvd. Go 0.1 mile, and turn left onto PA 191 N/Main St. Go 0.7 mile, and turn right into the trailhead parking lot.

Power Line Trail

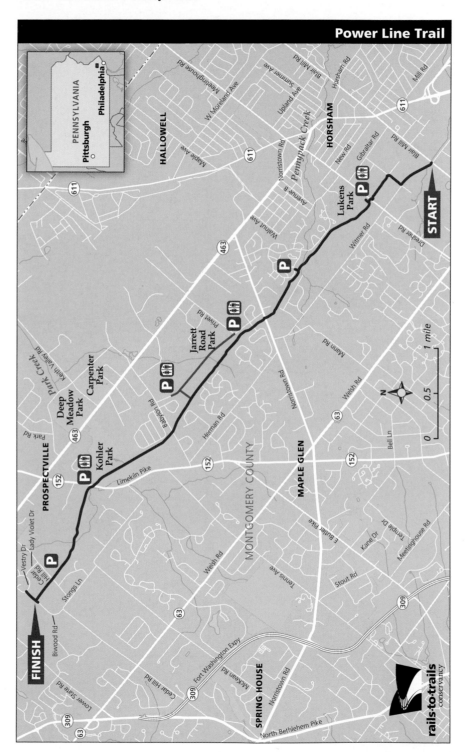

The paved Power Line Trail carries its users between residential neighborhoods, parks, schools, and other destinations in Horsham Township. The 5.5-mile utility-easement trail also heads north to green open spaces, a rare delight in the northern Philadelphia suburbs. The trail crosses about a half dozen roads, some of which were laid out by original settlers in early Colonial times.

The township, established in 1717 and settled mainly by Quakers, is named for a town in England. Today, it's home to corporate offices as well as the Pennsylvania Air National Guard's sprawling Horsham Air Guard Station, which got its start as a grass airstrip opened by pioneering aviator Harold Pitcairn in 1926.

As the trail's name implies, it shares a corridor with a power line operated by PECO Energy. Those overhead power lines mean that the trail is exposed its entire length. There's very little shade from adjacent trees, even as the route passes parks or open space. The trail is part of the Circuit Trails, a developing 800-mile urban network of trails in Greater Philadelphia, of which about 350 miles are complete. There are plans for connecting other Circuit

Traveling through the wide power line corridor, the trail makes its way to a number of parks alongside Park Creek.

County
Montgomery

Endpoints
Blair Mill Road and Witmer Road (Horsham) to Vestry Dr. near Biwood Road (Prospectville)

Mileage
5.5

Type
Greenway/Non-Rail-Trail

Roughness Index
1

Surface
Asphalt

Trails by extending the rail-trail northwest to the 202 Parkway Trail and south-east to the Pennypack Trail (see page 188).

A convenient starting place to explore the Power Line Trail is Lukens Park, where you'll find restrooms and plenty of parking off Dresher Road. Open dawn–dusk, the trail ends in a commercial center about a mile southeast at Blair Mill Road via a short off-road path and sidewalk adjacent to Witmer Road. A gravel trail through Lukens Park connects with housing beyond.

Heading northwest under transmission lines, you'll pass several side trails that lead to neighborhoods near the path. At 0.8 mile beyond Lukens Park, the path crosses the upper reaches of Pennypack Creek, which meanders 22 miles through northern Philadelphia suburbs before it drains into the Delaware River.

The trail crosses Norristown Road and passes through Jarrett Road Park before entering a 0.7-mile segment bordered by cropland on the east and hous-ing on the west. (If you turn right onto Privet Road at the north end of the park, then left onto Jarrett Road, you can travel through this agricultural zone on a road that's been converted to a gated trail and connects to Horsham Township Library and the Jarrett Nature Center.)

The power line corridor cuts a wide swath between subdivisions for 0.8 mile past the farmland to a cluster of parks alongside Park Creek. A paved side trail to the right, just before a small bridge, links to a trail network connecting Horsham Dog Park, Kohler Park, Deep Meadow Park, and Carpenter Park. Most of the parks are dedicated as sports fields, though Kohler has a fishing pond.

Past the parks, the utility corridor passes between woodlots and cropland for another 1.2 miles to a residential neighborhood. There are trail connections to a golf course and Cedar Hill Road Park at this end of the trail.

CONTACT: horshamrec.com/info/dept/details.aspx?deptinfoid=1049

DIRECTIONS

To reach Lukens Park in Horsham from I-276, take Exit 343. After the toll plaza, go 0.3 mile, and turn right to merge onto PA 611 N/Easton Road. Go 0.4 mile, and turn left onto Blair Mill Road/SR 2026. Go 0.2 mile, and turn right onto Gibraltar Road. Go 0.6 mile, and turn left onto Dresher Road. Go 0.2 mile, and turn right at the sign for Power Line Trail parking. Go 0.3 mile left on Power Line Trail, cross Prudential Road, and turn right on the sidewalk. Go 0.1 mile, and turn left at the sidewalk alongside Witmer Road. Go 0.3 mile to the trail end at Blair Mill Road.

To reach parking in Prospectville from I-276, take Exit 339. Take the first exit past the toll plaza; merge right onto PA 309/Fort Washington Expy. Go 5.4 miles, and turn right onto PA 63. Go 0.9 mile, and turn left onto Cedar Hill Road. Go 0.8 mile; turn right to stay on Cedar Hill Road. Go 0.1 mile; turn left to stay on Cedar Hill Road. Go 0.2 mile, and turn right into the trailhead park-ing. Turn right onto the trail, and go 0.4 mile to the end of the trail at Vestry Dr. in Squires Knoll.

Running 1.5 miles, the Queen City Trail serves as a community connector for the small city of Titusville, where the American oil industry began in 1859. The trail provides a short, paved connection between the downtown area and the city's sports complex.

The Queen City Trail also represents a vital link in the developing Erie to Pittsburgh Trail, which also includes 9.7-mile Oil Creek State Park Trail (see page 173) at the Queen City Trail's southern end. The Oil Creek State Park Trail also connects to multiple other trails in the network heading south to Pittsburgh, including the 9.4-mile McClintock Trail, 3-mile Oil City Trail, and 6-mile Samuel Justus Recreation Trail (see page 215). Eventually, the Queen City Trail will be extended northwest an additional 6 miles to Hydetown, further advancing the goal of a connected long-distance trail from Erie to Pittsburgh. The Queen City Trail is also part of the Industrial Heartland

Counties
Crawford, Venango

Endpoints
Oil Creek State Park Trail at Drake Well Road, just north of Museum Lane, to S. Martin St. and E. Mechanic St. (Titusville)

Mileage
1.5

Type
Greenway/Non-Rail-Trail

Roughness Index

Surface
Asphalt

Though the Queen City Trail is short at 1.5 miles, it connects with other trails to provide a longer journey for more-ambitious riders.

Queen City Trail

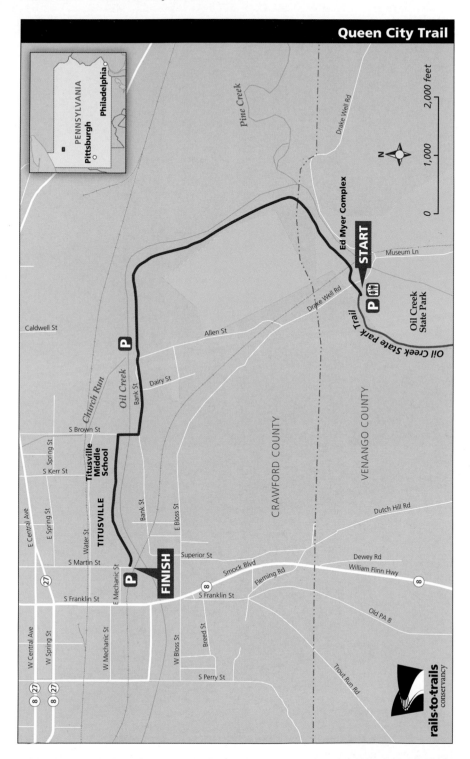

PENNSYLVANIA

Pittsburgh

Philadelphia

Pine Creek

Drake Well Rd

2,000 feet

1,000

0

N

Ed Myer Complex

START

Museum Ln

Oil Creek State Park

P

Caldwell St

Allen St

Drake Well Rd

Oil Creek State Park Trail

CRAWFORD COUNTY

VENANGO COUNTY

Church Run

Oil Creek

Dairy St

Bank St

P

S Brown St

S Spring St

S Kerr St

Titusville Middle School

TITUSVILLE

Dutch Hill Rd

E Central Ave

E Spring St

Water St

Bank St

E Bloss St

Superior St

Smock Blvd

Fleming Rd

Dewey Rd

William Flinn Hwy

8

S Martin St

P

FINISH

8

S Franklin St

S Franklin St

Old PA 8

27

E Mechanic St

W Central Ave

W Spring St

W Mechanic St

W Bloss St

Breed St

S Perry St

Trout Run Rd

8   27

8   27

rails·to·trails
conservancy

Trails Coalition's developing 1,500-mile trail network through Pennsylvania, West Virginia, Ohio, and New York.

Begin your journey at the shared trailhead with the Oil Creek State Park Trail just south of Titusville on Drake Well Road. Unlike its longer neighbor, the Queen City Trail is a greenway, though it is just as flat as a rail-trail. Heading north from Drake Well Road, watch the low clearance as you pass almost immediately under an active rail line. With Oil Creek to your right, follow the trail along the edge of the Ed Myer Complex, a park property managed by the City of Titusville, where you might see soccer, baseball, or softball games in action.

In just under 1 mile, shortly after leaving the sports complex, you'll merge seamlessly onto Bank Street, a low-stress residential road. This on-road portion of trail, marked with signage, continues over Oil Creek via South Brown Street before the trail resumes to the left behind Titusville Middle School. The remainder of the trail follows the northern bank of the creek before ending at the intersection of South Martin and East Mechanic Streets.

Downtown Titusville, with shops, restaurants, and a couple of breweries, is just a short trek up South Franklin Street (one block west from the endpoint), with the creek behind you.

CONTACT: trailsofnwpa.com/queen-city-trail or rtc.li/Queen-City-Trail

DIRECTIONS

To reach parking at the southeastern trailhead at the Jersey Bridge Parking Area, which is shared with the Oil Creek State Park Trail, from I-79, take Exit 141, turn right onto PA 285 E, and go 7.4 miles. Turn left onto PA 173 N, and go 8.0 miles. Turn right onto PA 27 E, and go 15.7 miles. Take a slight right onto W. Spring St., and go 0.2 mile; then turn right onto S. Perry St., and go 0.3 mile, crossing Oil Creek. Turn left onto W. Bloss St./Allen St./Drake Well Road, and go just more than 1 mile. Turn right into the trailhead parking lot, just before Drake Well Road crosses Oil Creek.

To reach parking at the northwestern endpoint near downtown Titusville from I-79, follow the directions above to W. Spring St. Go 0.4 mile, continue onto Diamond St., and take the first right onto S. Martin St. Go 0.2 mile, and turn left into the parking lot, just before S. Martin St. dead-ends.

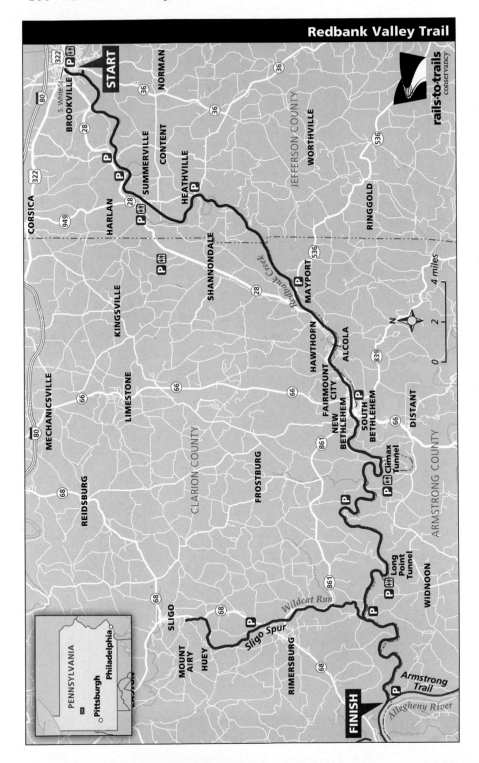

Redbank Valley Trail

The Redbank Valley Trail follows a rail corridor developed by the Allegheny Valley Railroad in 1872 to carry passengers, coal, and lumber to Pittsburgh and beyond. Passenger service along the line stopped in the 1940s, while freight continued until the rails were removed in 2007. The corridor now carries trail users along the forested banks of Redbank Creek for more than 41 miles to the Allegheny River and along a 9-mile perpendicular spur to Sligo. The trail is part of the Industrial Heartland Trails Coalition's developing 1,500-mile trail network through Pennsylvania, West Virginia, Ohio, and New York.

Grades along the pathway are around 1%, making for a pleasant journey. Cellular service is somewhat limited along the mostly rural trail, and there are long stretches

Counties
Armstrong, Clarion, Jefferson

Endpoints
Depot St. Spur trailhead, just southwest of PA 36/S. White St. and Madison Ave. (Brookville), to the Armstrong Trail at the confluence of Redbank Creek and the Allegheny River, just north of Redbank Creek and SR 1002, 1.2 miles north of Scenic Road (Templeton); **Sligo Spur:** Lawsonham Road and Montgomery Road (Rimersburg) to Walker Farm Road just west of PA 68 (Sligo)

Mileage
51.0

Type
Rail-Trail

Roughness Index
2

Surface
Ballast, Crushed Stone

Remnants of the Allegheny Valley Railroad can be found along the Redbank Valley Trail, which now traverses the corridor.

without drinking water or restrooms, so be sure to carry plenty of water with you. You'll also want to bring a good light if you plan on visiting the Climax or Long Point Tunnels.

Brookville to Rimersburg/Sligo Spur: 36.2 miles

You can begin your journey in Brookville at a parking lot just off of PA 36/South White Street, across from a grocery store. From the parking lot, the short Depot Street Spur will bring you to the main railway corridor in less than a mile. Here, you'll bear right onto a well-maintained crushed-limestone surface along Redbank Creek. To the left, a short, currently closed, segment of trail heads over a bridge to a closed tunnel and portion of trail that will eventually extend to Second Street in Brookville. There are currently no plans to reopen this trail; please do not enter the tunnel for your own safety.

Summertime heat is greatly reduced as the trail heads through a cut into a limestone hill just past mile 5.5. Thermometers here and at a bridge just a few hundred yards away indicate the difference in temperature. In 2 miles, the Summerville trailhead—the site of the town's old railroad station—offers parking, a portable toilet, and a map kiosk. The trail meanders mostly through forested and rural areas for the next 8 miles, after which you'll pass through the small communities of Mayport, Hawthorn, and Alcola. In Fairmount City, in the spring of 2019, the trail managers reopened a 0.4-mile section of trail between Middle Run Road and Fairmount Avenue, which had been closed for redevelopment.

Continuing 4 miles on the trail along the creek, you'll travel through New Bethlehem and then more woods before entering the impressive 517-foot Climax Tunnel, built in 1872 and renovated and reopened to the public in 2018. As the trail meanders back to the east, you'll pass a large sculpture of a hand with two bright-red cardinals. Just past mile 33, you'll reach a camp shelter featuring a sheltered picnic table, permanent pit toilet, and bike repair station. Dubbed Ray's Place, the Adirondack shelter was established in 2016 as a memorial to one of the trail's dedicated volunteers. Just beyond lies the entrance to the 640-foot Long Point Tunnel. As the tunnel has yet to be reinforced or improved, travelers are advised to use good lights.

Sligo Spur: 9.0 miles

At mile 36 in Rimersburg, you'll come to the 9-mile Sligo Spur. Take a right to follow the spur north alongside Wildcat Run for the first 3 miles. Continue north to Walker Farm Road just south of Sligo. This spur features a more challenging 3% grade. Check the trail's website for more information on current conditions of this segment at **redbankvalleytrails.org/access-limitations**.

Sligo Spur to Templeton: 5.8 miles

From the Sligo Spur intersection, the main trail continues just under 6 miles heading west, following the meandering creek and ending at the Allegheny River. Here, the trail meets the 35.5-mile Armstrong Trail (see page 12), which follows the Allegheny River south to Ford City. Cross Redbank Creek to access a parking area for the trail.

CONTACT: redbankvalleytrails.org

DIRECTIONS

To reach the Depot St. trailhead in Brookville from I-80, take Exit 78 for PA 36 toward Sigel/Brookville. Head south on PA 36 S/Allegheny Blvd., and go 0.4 mile. Turn left onto Main St., go 0.8 mile, and turn right onto PA 36/S. White St. Go 0.1 mile, and turn right onto the short access road just before Redbank Creek, where a sign points you to the Depot Street trailhead.

To reach the endpoint in Templeton, also an access point for the Armstrong Trail, from I-80, take Exit 64. Head south on PA 66 toward Clarion/New Bethlehem, and go 0.3 mile. Go 13.0 miles, and turn right onto Broad St. Then go 0.6 mile, and continue left onto PA 28 S/PA 66 S/North St. Go 2.4 miles, and continue straight onto Madison Road. Go 4.7 miles, and turn right onto State Route 1004/Kellersburg Road. Go 4.0 miles, turn right onto SR 1002, and go 3.0 miles. Turn left into the parking lot, located at the confluence of Redbank Creek and the Allegheny River. Access the Red Bank Valley Trail by turning right onto the Armstrong Trail, crossing Redbank Creek, and taking a sharp right onto the Redbank Valley Trail. You can also take a hard left to head south on the Armstrong Trail toward Ford City.

To reach parking in Rimersburg on the Sligo Spur from I-80 E, take Exit 45 for PA 478 toward St. Petersburg/Emlenton. (From I-80 W, take Exit 45, and turn left onto PA 208. Go 0.2 mile, and turn left onto PA 478.) Turn right onto PA 478 E, go 2.0 miles, and turn left onto PA 58 E/E. Main St. Go 2.9 miles. Turn right to stay on PA 58 E, and go 5.3 miles. Then turn left to stay on PA 58 E, and go 3.5 miles. Turn left onto Bald Eagle St., and turn right onto PA 68 W/Colerain St. Go 4.0 miles, and turn right into the parking lot. To access the trail, head south 0.2 mile down PA 68. The endpoint is located 4.2 miles farther north along the trail.

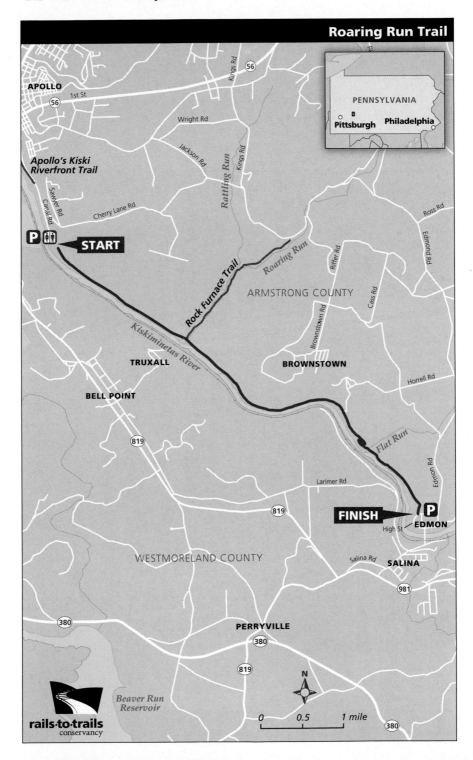

Roaring Run Trail

PENNSYLVANIA

Pittsburgh   Philadelphia

APOLLO

1st St

Kings Rd

56

Wright Rd

Jackson Rd

Kings Rd

Apollo's Kiski Riverfront Trail

Rattling Run

Sawyer Rd

Canal Rd

Cherry Lane Rd

Ross Rd

Edmond Rd

P

START

Rock Furnace Trail

Roaring Run

Riffer Rd

ARMSTRONG COUNTY

Cass Rd

Kiskiminetas River

Brownstown Rd

TRUXALL

BROWNSTOWN

Horrell Rd

BELL POINT

819

Flat Run

Edmon Rd

Larimer Rd

819

FINISH

P

EDMON

High St

WESTMORELAND COUNTY

Salina Rd

SALINA

981

380

PERRYVILLE

380

819

N

Beaver Run
Reservoir

0   0.5   1 mile

380

rails-to-trails
conservancy

Evidence of the Roaring Run Trail's past lives are readily visible all along the 4.8-mile corridor in western Pennsylvania. Stone remains in the Kiskiminetas River (Kiski for short) mark the site of a canal lock left over from the 1820s to 1860s when the route served as a towpath on the cross-state Main Line Canal system. Mileage markers and a bridge are remnants of the Pennsylvania Railroad, which bought the canal system in 1857 and converted it to rail. Here the railroad hauled coal from nearby mines and iron from local furnaces.

After it fell into disuse, the corridor was acquired by the Kovalchick Salvage of Indiana, Pennsylvania, which donated the right-of-way to the Roaring Run Watershed Association. The group formed in 1982 to help preserve this historic area and clean up pollution flowing from former mines. In addition to the Roaring Run Trail, the nonprofit also maintains the 1.5-mile Apollo's Kiski Riverfront Trail to the north and the 1.5-mile Rock Furnace Trail.

The name of the Roaring Run Trail belies the calm waters of the Kiskiminetas River.

County
Armstrong

Endpoints
Canal Road, 0.4 mile south of Kiski Ave. (Apollo), to High St., just west of Gartley St. (Edmon)

Mileage
4.8

Type
Rail-Trail

Roughness Index
1

Surface
Crushed Stone

The trail runs along the eastern shore of the Kiskiminetas River from south of the borough of Apollo to Edmon. There are no services between the two communities. About the first 4 miles of trail follows the railroad grade upriver from Apollo on a crushed-stone surface; the last mile is marked by a climb, a dip, and then a steeper climb on tar and chip asphalt to the Edmon trailhead. The trail is open dawn–dusk.

Starting at the trailhead south of Apollo, the trail cuts a wooded course along the river for 1.5 miles to the confluence of Roaring Run. If the river isn't running high, you can see the remnants of a canal lock here. You'll also meet the Rock Furnace Trail that climbs 1.5 miles from here to a trailhead in Brownstown. The Rock Furnace Trail features a suspension bridge over cascading waterfalls in the creek and the piled ruins of the Biddle Iron Furnace that dates back to the canal era. A huge stone hanging over the trail here is called the Camel Rock.

Back on the Roaring Run Trail, in another 1.8 miles a mountain bike single-track heads up the slope, where the remains of an old coal washing and loading operation is disappearing into the vegetation. Other mountain biking tracks are on the hillside as well.

You'll want to take the right fork in another 0.5 mile to go the remaining mile, mostly uphill, to the trailhead in Edmon. The left fork pays a visit to Flat Run, where a hiking path continues to a falls.

Roaring Run Trail is one of the Trans Allegheny Trails, a system of trails in western Pennsylvania. The trail is also part of the Industrial Heartland Trails Coalition's developing 1,500-mile trail network through Pennsylvania, West Virginia, Ohio, and New York.

CONTACT: roaringrun.org

DIRECTIONS

To reach the northern trailhead in Apollo from Pittsburgh, take I-376 E to its end (near mile marker 85) and continue onto US 22 E/William Penn Hwy. Go 10.1 miles on US 22, and exit onto PA 66 N toward Delmont. Turn left onto PA 66, and go 11.6 miles. Take a slight right to stay on PA 66 N, go 2.6 miles, and turn right onto Kiski Ave. Go 0.8 mile, and keep right to continue onto Canal Road. Go 0.5 mile, and turn right into the trailhead parking lot.

To reach parking near the southern endpoint in Edmon from Pittsburgh, take I-376 E to its end (near mile marker 85) and continue onto US 22 E/William Penn Hwy. Go 18.4 miles on US 22, and turn left onto PA 981 in New Alexandria. Go 11.9 miles, and turn right onto Main St./Walnut St. Go 0.5 mile, turn left onto Bridge St./State Route 1060, and go 0.2 mile. Turn left onto High St./SR 2047, go 0.2 mile, and then turn left to stay on High St. Go 0.2 mile, and look for trailhead parking on the left.

Oil flows through the veins of the Samuel Justus Recreation Trail. Its northern departure point is Oil City, which was founded during the 1860s oil boom and became the headquarters for several petroleum corporations. The route follows the unused corridor of the Allegheny Valley Railroad, whose trains carried crude away from the oil fields to the refineries. It's even named for an oil baron, Samuel Justus, who used his fortune to create a trust fund for widows and children.

The paved trail rolls 6 miles along a wooded route overlooking the Allegheny River between Oil City and Franklin. The 8-foot-wide paved surface parallels a dirt access road suitable for horses. Its southern trailhead connects to the Allegheny River Trail (see page 8) that runs another 30 miles south from Franklin to Parker. Its northern trailhead links with the 3-mile Oil City Trail, which crosses the Petroleum Street Bridge and joins the 9.4-mile McClintock Trail to Oil Creek State Park. Horse

The Samuel Justus Recreation Trail begins where the Oil City Trail ends.

County
Venango

Endpoints
Oil City Marina near Wyllis St. and W. Front St. (Oil City) to Allegheny River Trail at US 322/ Lakes to the Sea Hwy. and Bredinsburg Road (Franklin)

Mileage
6.0

Type
Rail-Trail

Roughness Index
1

Surface
Asphalt

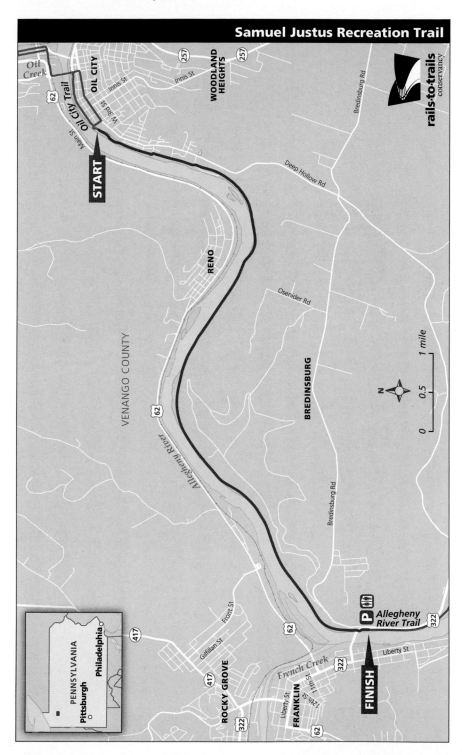

Samuel Justus Recreation Trail

riding is allowed on an adjacent gravel road, though horses are not permitted on the trail itself.

The trail is part of the future 270-mile Erie to Pittsburgh Trail, which will incorporate several trails stretching from Presque Isle State Park on Lake Erie to the Steel City, and the Industrial Heartland Trails Coalition's developing 1,500-mile trail network through Pennsylvania, West Virginia, Ohio, and New York.

Starting at a boat launch site on the south side of Oil City, the path rolls along the base of a bluff alongside the Allegheny River. You'll enjoy views of the river the entire way. After passing a sewage treatment plant in a mile, you'll pass a half dozen pumps over the next couple of miles that still bring up oil or natural gas.

About 4.5 miles down the trail, you'll pass the large stone gate for River Ridge Farm, built in 1913 for Joseph C. Sibley, who made his money in the oil refining and animal breeding businesses. He later became a five-term congressman, first as a Democrat and then as a Republican. The mansion, still standing, is owned by Life Ministries and commands a view of the river and surroundings.

In about a mile you'll start seeing commercial businesses across the river in Franklin, soon after which you'll pass underneath the US 322 bridge and arrive at the southwestern trailhead. A visitor center is located here, housed in a saltbox-style house identified by the roof that slopes lower in back than the front.

CONTACT: avta-trails.org/allegheny-samuel-trails.html

DIRECTIONS

To reach the northern trailhead in Oil City from I-80, take Exit 29, and head north on PA 8/ Pittsburgh Road. Go 16.4 miles, and turn right onto Liberty St. Go 0.7 mile (Liberty St. curves right at 12th St.), and turn left onto US 62 N/Allegheny Blvd. Go 7.5 miles. Turn right onto Petroleum St., go 0.3 mile, and turn right onto W. First St. Go 0.5 mile, turn right onto Wyllis St., and go about 0.1 mile. Take the access road straight ahead, which dead-ends at the Allegheny River and then curves left into the Oil City Marina parking lot.

To reach the southern trailhead in Franklin from I-80, follow the directions above to Liberty St. Go 1.1 miles (Liberty St. curves right at 12th St.), and turn left onto US 322 E/Eighth St. Go 0.5 mile, and turn right at the trailhead (a sign says SAMUEL JUSTUS RECREATION TRAIL). The trail is accessible at the north end of the parking lot.

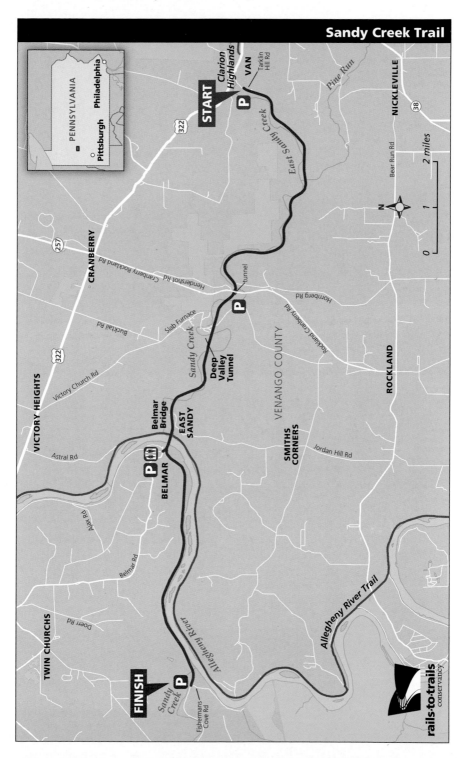

Sandy Creek Trail

You'll want to pack water, food, and flashlights to travel the Sandy Creek Trail, as it crosses 12 miles of remote, but scenic, countryside in Northwestern Pennsylvania. Named for separate Sandy Creeks at each end, the paved trail passes through forests and a tunnel and makes seven stream or river crossings, including the spectacular Belmar Bridge spanning the Allegheny River. There are no services along the route or at either end. The path is part of the Industrial Heartland Trails Coalition's developing 1,500-mile trail network through Pennsylvania, West Virginia, Ohio, and New York.

Local oilman Charles Miller built the Jamestown, Franklin and Clearfield Railroad, a subsidiary of the New York Central Railroad, through here around 1907 to take advantage of the oil exploration and production. The corridor mostly carried passengers and coal, however, and later became part of the Penn Central Railroad, before the line eventually fell into disuse.

From the east, the trail trends downhill to the Allegheny River crossing and then follows the river downstream almost to the trail's end. A short gap exists

This wooden bridge travels over one of the Sandy Creeks for which the trail is named.

County
Venango

Endpoints
Tarklin Road near US 322/ Lakes to the Sea Hwy. (Van) to Fishermans Cove Road and T370 (Polk)

Mileage
12.0

Type
Rail-Trail

Roughness Index
1

Surface
Asphalt

between it and the 8-mile Clarion Highlands trail in the east, and it crosses the 30-mile Allegheny River Trail (see page 8) spanning from Franklin to Parker.

Starting on Tarklin Hill Road a couple miles north of the crossroads community of Van, the trail begins its descent through evergreens before it emerges into a hardwood forest. The path keeps to the ridge south of East Sandy Creek (also known as Turkey Run) until a high crossing just before Cranberry Rockland Road.

At 5.6 miles past the trailhead, the path crosses the creek on another high bridge and enters a tunnel—known variously as the Mays Mill or Deep Valley Tunnel—that's 967 feet long. The 100-year-old railroad tunnel, suffering from a crumbling ceiling, has been improved by building a smaller tunnel inside and filling the gap with concrete and recycled rubber tires.

Once outside the chilly tunnel, the trail continues to descend and crosses the creek three more times before reaching the 1,385-foot-long Belmar Bridge. You'll have unfettered views up and down the Allegheny River from the wooden deck of the through-truss bridge. This section of river is a national wild and scenic river. Below, you can see the paved Allegheny River Trail. A stairway connects with the trail.

After the bridge, the path runs along a hillside above the river for 4 miles. Then the trail crosses another Sandy Creek and veers inland for 0.2 mile to the trailhead on Fishermans Cove Road. The railroad grade (not part of the trail) continues another 3 miles on the dirt road until it reaches Old PA 8 in Polk.

CONTACT: avta-trails.org/sandy-creek-trail.html

DIRECTIONS

To reach the eastern trailhead in Van from I-80 E, take Exit 45 to PA 478 W toward St. Petersburg/Emlenton. Turn left onto PA 478 W, and go 0.3 mile. Turn right onto PA 208/PA 38, and go 10.1 miles. Turn left onto US 322/Lakes to the Sea Hwy., and go 1.4 miles. Turn left onto Tarklin Hill Road, go 0.3 mile, and look for trailhead parking on the left. As you face the trail at the back of the lot, the Sandy Creek Trail heads right.

To reach the eastern trailhead in Van from I-80 W, take Exit 53, and turn right onto T385/Canoe Ripple Road. Go 0.5 mile, and turn right onto PA 338. Go 7.6 miles, and turn left onto US 322. Go 4.9 miles, and turn left onto Tarklin Hill Road. Go 0.3 mile, and look for trailhead parking on the left. As you face the trail at the back of the lot, the Sandy Creek Trail heads right.

To reach the western endpoint in Polk from I-80, take Exit 29, and head north on PA 8/Pittsburgh Road. Go 5.1 miles, and exit and turn left onto PA 308 N. Go 0.3 mile, and turn right onto Old PA 8/State Route 3013. Go 5.1 miles, and take a slight left at the exit (sign for SENECA HILLS BIBLE CAMP). Turn right onto Fishermans Cove Road (passing underneath Old PA 8). Go 2.8 miles, and find parking along the road at the endpoint.

At one time an important thoroughfare for commerce carried by canal barges and railroad cars in southeastern Pennsylvania, the Schuylkill River corridor now accommodates walkers, bicyclists, and others on the Schuylkill River Trail. Projected to stretch 120–130 miles when complete, the trail forms the backbone of the five-county Schuylkill River Greenways National Heritage Area.

The trail, now covering about 71 miles, follows the route of old canals and the Pennsylvania Railroad that hauled resources out of the anthracite coalfields. Planning for the trail began in the late 1960s, with construction starting in the 1990s and continuing today. Check the website (**schuylkillrivertrail.com**) before setting out for information on closures or trail gaps.

The trail helps make up part of the Circuit Trails, a developing 800-mile urban trail network in Greater Philadelphia, of which 350 miles are currently complete. It's also

Counties
Berks, Chester, Montgomery, Philadelphia, Schuylkill

Endpoints
S. 56th St. near Eastwick Ave. at Bartram's Garden (Philadelphia) to Main St. and S. Greenview Road (Landingville)
Note: This developing route is not yet fully contiguous; please refer to **schuylkillrivertrail.com** to bridge the gaps.

Mileage
71.7

Type
Rail-Trail/Rail-with-Trail

Roughness Index
1–2

Surface
Asphalt, Boardwalk, Concrete, Crushed Stone, Dirt, Gravel

Philadelphia's Schuylkill Banks Boardwalk extends 50 feet from the shoreline over the Schuylkill River.

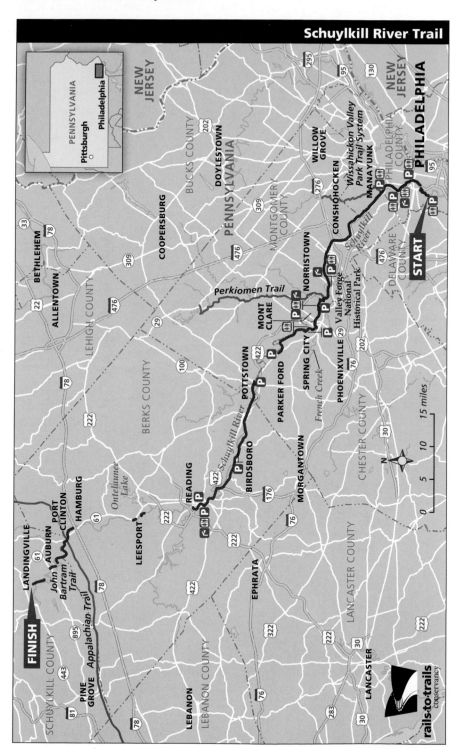

Schuylkill River Trail

included in the East Coast Greenway, which one day will span 3,000 miles from Maine to Florida. The Schuylkill River Trail links with other trails as it heads deep into Pennsylvania, and it's a component of the September 11th National Memorial Trail that connects the 9/11, Flight 93, and Pentagon Memorials.

Philadelphia to Valley Forge: 25.9 miles

Beginning on the west bank of the Schuylkill River in southwest Philadelphia, the trail traverses Bartram's Garden, the oldest botanical garden in North America. Resuming on the eastern riverbank as a paved trail, it passes through an old industrial area—Grays Ferry Crescent—that's now a park. A pedestrian bridge to connect both sections of trail is scheduled to open in 2020.

Another paved trail segment begins about 0.5 mile upriver and continues along the Schuylkill Banks Boardwalk that runs out over the river about 50 feet from the shoreline. Future plans call for extending the boardwalk downriver to the Grays Ferry Crescent segment.

At the northern end of the boardwalk, you can hop onto one of the Schuylkill River Trail's most popular sections, the nearly 30-mile stretch from downtown Philadelphia to Valley Forge National Historical Park. Along this segment, which is nearly all paved, you'll pass many attractions, such as the Philadelphia Museum of Art, Boathouse Row, Fairmount Water Works, Lemon Hill Mansion, and the 2,000-acre Fairmount Park, a premier outdoor Philadelphia destination. Vendors often sell snacks along this section of trail.

A part of the 8.5-mile Wissahickon Valley Park Trail System (see page 269) connects with the trail about a mile north of Falls Bridge. Beyond are the former industrial towns of Manayunk, Conshohocken, and Norristown, where you'll pass redbrick mills and old factories tucked alongside modern office buildings and restaurants. The Southeastern Pennsylvania Transportation Authority (SEPTA) commuter rails parallel the Schuylkill River Trail here. Nearby SEPTA regional rail stations create an opportunity to travel by train.

Valley Forge to Parker Ford: 14.3 miles

About 4 miles north of Norristown, you'll arrive at Valley Forge National Historical Park, the winter encampment of the Continental Army in 1777–78. You can visit the museum and historical structures by crossing the newly opened pedestrian bridge that spans the river parallel to US 422. Just north of the park, the Schuylkill River Trail offers a direct connection to the Perkiomen Trail (see page 192), which follows the creek more than 20 miles north to the borough of Green Lane.

To stay on the Schuylkill River Trail, head west toward Phoenixville on a mostly crushed-stone section. In 3.6 miles, you'll reach the village of Mont Clare,

crossing the river on PA 29/Bridge Street to enter Phoenixville and Chester County. For the next 8 miles, the trail continues through town along French Creek, heads northwest through Spring City, and ends in the community of Parker Ford.

Pottstown to Reading: 20.3 miles

After a 5.5-mile gap, the trail resumes on the eastern shore of the river in Pottstown. The 20.3-mile Pottstown to Reading section, which includes a section known as the Thun Trail, is well shaded. Leaving Pottstown's Riverfront Park as a paved trail, it switches to crushed stone entering Berks County. A 5.8-mile section beginning in Birdsboro is on road. Back on the trail, the route arrives in Reading after crossing the Schuylkill River three times.

Reading to Landingville: 11.2 miles

A 20-mile gap between Reading and Hamburg must be navigated by following a signed on-road route. A short stretch of gravel exists between Ontelaunee Township and Leesport Borough.

The final leg of the Schuylkill River Trail is known as the John Bartram Trail. Horseback riding is allowed on three disconnected gravel sections between

The Schuylkill River Trail runs past the Fairmount Water Works, a National Historic Landmark dating back to the early 19th century.

Hamburg and Pottsville, which will be the trail's future terminus. The longest section runs 6 miles from Hamburg to Auburn. Along the way, the scenic trail enters Schuylkill County and crosses the Appalachian Trail south of the village of Port Clinton. Another piece of trail spans 0.75 mile through a heavily wooded area east of Auburn between River Road and Market Street. The last segment of completed trail runs through Landingville, paralleling Tunnel Road and Canal Street.

CONTACT: schuylkillrivertrail.com

DIRECTIONS

To reach parking for the southern trailhead at Bartram's Garden from I-76 W, take Exit 347 for Passyunk Ave. Turn right onto W. Passyunk Ave., and go 0.2 mile. Take a slight right onto W. Passyunk Ave., and go 1.1 miles. Turn right onto S. 61st St., and go 0.8 mile. Turn right onto Lindbergh Blvd., and go 0.5 mile. Turn right onto S. 56th St., and go 0.3 mile. The road dead-ends into the trailhead parking lot.

To reach parking for the southern trailhead at Bartram's Garden from I-95 N, take Exit 13 to merge onto PA 291 W/Penrose Ave., and go 1.4 miles. Turn right onto Island Ave., and go 0.4 mile. Stay straight to continue on Island Ave., and go 0.5 mile. Take a slight right to stay on Island Ave., and go 0.1 mile. Turn right onto Lindbergh Blvd., and go 2.3 miles. Turn right onto S. 56th St., and go 0.3 mile. The road dead-ends into the trailhead parking lot.

To reach the Sullivans Lane trailhead at Valley Forge National Historical Park from I-76, take Exit 328A for US 202 S/US 422 W/Swedesford Road toward W. Chester/Pottstown. Follow signs for US 422 W, merge onto US 422 W, and go 2.0 miles. Take the PA 363 N/S. Trooper Road E exit toward Audubon/Trooper. Take a sharp left onto SR 3051/S. Trooper Road, go 420 feet, and take a slight left to stay on SR 3051/S. Trooper Road. Go 0.2 mile, and turn right onto Sullivans Lane. Turn right into the trailhead parking lot. A spur in the back of the parking lot leads to the trail. Turn left to head north toward Parker Ford. Turn right to head south toward Philadelphia.

To reach parking in Reading from I-76, take Exit 286 toward US 222/Reading/Ephrata, and continue onto Col. Howard Blvd. 0.7 mile. Turn right to merge onto US 222 N, and go 12.2 miles. Continue onto US 422 E, and go 0.3 mile. Take the exit to stay on US 422 E toward Pottstown, and go 1.6 miles. Exit onto Bus. US 422 E/Penn Ave. toward Penn St./Reading, and go 0.4 mile. Turn right onto S. Second St., and go 0.1 mile; then turn right onto Franklin St., and go about 0.1 mile. Turn right onto S. Front St., and go 0.2 mile. Turn left into the parking lot.

To reach the trailhead in Hamburg from I-78, take Exit 30 toward Hamburg. Head south on N. Fourth St. Go 0.3 mile, and turn right onto Franklin St. Go 0.2 mile, and look for parking straight ahead.

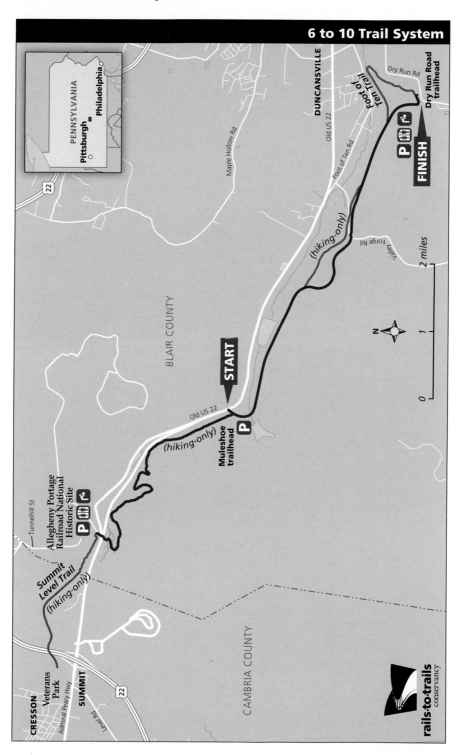

6 to 10 Trail System

PENNSYLVANIA

Pittsburgh
Philadelphia

Dry Run Rd

Foot of Ten Trail

Dry Run Road trailhead

DUNCANSVILLE

Old US 22

FINISH

Maple Hollow Rd

Foot of Ten Rd

(hiking-only)

Valley Forge Rd

2 miles

BLAIR COUNTY

N

START

1

Old US 22

Muleshoe trailhead

(hiking-only)

0

Tunnelhill St

Allegheny Portage
Railroad National
Historic Site

Summit
Level Trail
(hiking-only)

CAMBRIA COUNTY

CRESSON

Veterans
Park

SUMMIT

Admiral Peary Hwy

Level Rd

22

rails-to-trails
conservancy

Spurred by the success of New York's revolutionary Erie Canal, Pennsylvania started constructing its own canal system in 1826 to link Pittsburgh and Philadelphia. But the Allegheny Mountains complicated Pennsylvania's task.

In the years it took to establish Pennsylvania's canal system on either side of the Alleghenies, trains were coming into use. Forward-thinking engineers looked to these machines to traverse the final 40 miles of rugged terrain, but the primitive locomotives couldn't manage the mountain slopes. Pennsylvania's solution was the Allegheny Portage Railroad, a complex system that saw entire canalboats transferred from canals onto trains that, much like the canals themselves, ran over more or less level ground before coming to an elevation change. At each steep incline, the locomotive would be disconnected and

Look for wildlife along the 6 to 10 Trail, as much of the route is heavily forested.

County
Blair

Endpoints
Allegheny Portage Railroad National Historic Site at Tunnelhill St. south of US 22 (Gallitzin) to Dry Run Road between A T386 and Mill Road (Duncansville)

Mileage
10.3

Type
Rail-Trail

Roughness Index
1, 3

Surface
Crushed Stone, Dirt

its line of cars hoisted up the slope by a stationary steam engine at the top. The train cars would be connected to a new locomotive and transported to the next incline, where the process would be repeated. On the downhill side, the same machinery controlled the train cars' descent.

Ten such inclines brought canalboats and other cargo up and over the Alleghenies between Johnstown and Hollidaysburg—five each on the eastern and western slopes of the range. Once the barges had been portaged across the mountains, they were returned to canals to finish their journeys. It was a massive undertaking that reduced travel time between Philadelphia and Pittsburgh from about 23 days to just under 4. Officially opening in 1834, the system would run only for a little more than two decades before more powerful locomotives rendered it obsolete.

Today, the 10.3-mile route between inclines 6 and 10 has been converted into a rail-trail featuring both hiking and biking sections, with historical culverts (drainage structures) visible along the hiking-only route. The trail makes up a small part of the September 11th National Memorial Trail that connects the 9/11, Flight 93, and Pentagon Memorials.

Start your visit at the top of the mountain, where the National Park Service maintains a visitor center at the Allegheny Portage Railroad National Historic Site dedicated to the history of the railway, as well as restrooms, drinking fountains, and picnic areas. At the summit is a reproduction of an engine that lifted the train cars and a re-creation of the steep tracks of incline 6, as well as a tavern restored to its 1840s appearance. These buildings are open daily (9 a.m.–5 p.m.) in spring, summer, and fall, and weekends only in winter. This area also provides access to a hiking-only trail heading westward, the Summit Level Trail.

From the visitor center, hikers can tackle the 6 to 10 Trail as it heads east and downhill along the path of the Allegheny Portage Railroad; this twisting section is a steep and tricky descent recommended for capable hikers. Loops and spurs offer opportunities to extend the mileage a bit and to see additional historical artifacts. Bicycles are not allowed on this portion of the trail, so bikers will start about 3.3 miles farther along the route at the Muleshoe trailhead and follow the path of the railroad that supplanted the portage system.

From the Muleshoe trailhead, you'll roll about 4.2 miles downhill on limestone dust to the Dry Run Road trailhead, where restrooms and water fountains are available. Look for wildlife such as white-tailed deer, turkeys, pheasants, and chipmunks, as well as snakes and the occasional black bear. About halfway along this segment, you'll also come to another 1.2-mile hiking-only segment that extends past two historical culverts and then reconnects with the trail just southeast of Valley Forge Road and a third historical culvert.

As you near the southeast trailhead at Dry Run Road, the trail connects with the 1.6-mile Foot of Ten Trail, a hiking-only, somewhat triangular loop

that extends northeast toward the former site of an engine house and another historical culvert, after which it heads south (on a partially overgrown path) toward the Dry Run Road trailhead. The last 0.25 mile of the 6 to 10 Trail, leading to the trailhead, shares the same path as the southwest side of the Foot of Ten Trail loop.

Be aware that the biking portion of the trail contains steep grades and poor sight lines, and while it is wheelchair accessible, the Valley Forge Road crossing is not. State game land surrounds much of the trail (both hiking and biking sections), and users are advised to wear bright colors to alert hunters year-round, but particularly in the fall. The trail and parking areas are open sunrise–sunset.

CONTACT: nps.gov/alpo/planyourvisit/six-to-ten-inclines.htm

DIRECTIONS

To reach the endpoint at the Allegheny Portage Railroad National Historic Site visitor center from I-99, take Exit 28 to merge onto US 22 W. In about 7 miles, take the Gallitzin exit, and turn right onto Tunnelhill St. Go 0.7 mile south, following signs for the Allegheny Portage Railroad. The road terminates at the visitor center parking lot.

To reach the Muleshoe trailhead from the visitor center parking lot, take US 22 W 1.7 miles to the exit for Old US 22, following signs for Cresson/Summit. Turn left onto Old US 22/ Admiral Peary Hwy. In 3.0 miles, you'll find a parking area on the right, immediately before the curved stone archway of the Muleshoe Bridge; if that lot is full, another option is just 700 feet farther down the road on the left.

To reach the Dry Run Road trailhead from I-99, take Exit 28 for US 22 E. Keep right to immediately exit onto US 22 E, and go 1.5 miles. Turn right onto Old US 22 in Duncansville. Go 0.2 mile, and turn left onto Foot of Ten Road. Go 0.5 mile, and turn left onto Mill Road. Go 0.3 mile, and turn right onto Dry Run Road. Go 0.6 mile, and turn right into the trailhead parking lot.

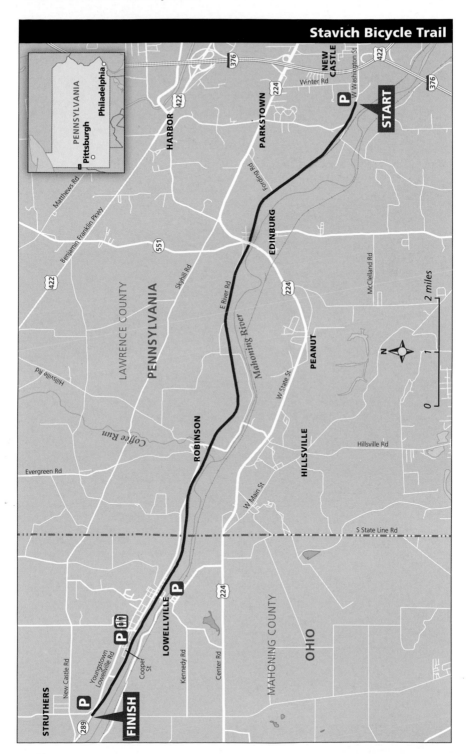

Fifty years after the last trolley cars ran on the Penn-Ohio Electric System between Youngstown, Ohio, and New Castle, Pennsylvania, in 1932, travelers on foot, bikes, and skates began using the corridor as the Stavich Bicycle Trail. Opened in 1983 with the help of donations from the local Stavich family and other individuals, the paved trail was an early example for rail-trails and is still somewhat uncommon, as it connects two states.

The trail doesn't go the entire distance of its streetcar predecessor. It runs from the Youngstown suburb of Struthers to the outskirts of New Castle. Running through the Mahoning River Valley, the route follows a more rolling terrain than you'd expect. The trolley line's builders were not so concerned as their counterparts in the railroad industry about dragging their cars over elevation changes.

The major donation for the trail came from a trust from the Stavich family, which made a fortune in processing aluminum in the Youngstown area. The trail named for them passes mainly through unshaded country alongside the active short-line railroad and pastureland. The 7 miles of asphalt in Pennsylvania are newer and smoother than the corresponding 3 miles in Ohio. Mileage markers count down to 0 at the Ohio line.

Counties
Lawrence (PA);
Mahoning (OH)

Endpoints
W. Washington St./
SR 3010 near Leasure
Valley Dr. (New Castle,
PA) to OH 289/Broad
St. and Coit Road
(Struthers, OH)

Mileage
10.0

Type
Rail-with-Trail

Roughness Index
1

Surface
Asphalt

The Stavich Bicycle Trail traverses both suburban areas and quiet countryside.

Starting at the trailhead parking on West Washington Street on the west side of New Castle, the trail actually heads east about 0.2 mile to the endpoint. Heading west on the trail, the route takes a downhill slope the first 2 miles to a trailside pond, where you may see some ducks paddling about. From here, you'll follow alongside the railroad toward Youngstown.

You'll cross under US 224 at 2.4 miles, and then cross Coffee Run on a bridge at 3.3 miles. The Ohio state line arrives in 6.8 miles past the parking lot.

In 0.6 mile, the trail portion ends at Liberty Street, which you'll take through Lowellville for 0.4 mile until the paved trail begins again.

The town is known as Little Italy because many Italians started settling here in the late 1800s, and today more than a third of its population claims Italian ancestry. An Italian society hosts a festival in July featuring Italian food, boccie ball tournaments, and a local band. Lowellville also has a long history in the steel industry, first with Ohio Iron & Steel Co. and then with Sharon Steel Corp., until it closed in the early 1960s. Antique cars are on display every Monday evening through the summer across the tracks on Water Street.

Returning to the trail, you'll pass the high school football stadium and baseball fields as you leave town. The trail ends on Youngstown Lowellville Road at 0.7 mile past the athletic fields.

CONTACT: co.lawrence.pa.us/departments/planning-community-development /recreational-facilities/stavich-bike-trail

DIRECTIONS

To reach parking near the eastern endpoint in New Castle, Pennsylvania, from I-376 E, take Exit 13A. Turn right onto US 224 W, and go 0.8 mile. Turn left onto W. Washington St., go 1.4 miles, and look for parking on the right. The endpoint is 0.2 mile east along the trail.

To reach parking near the eastern endpoint in New Castle, Pennsylvania, from I-376 W, take Exit 17. Turn left onto PA 108 W/Mt. Jackson Road, and go 0.5 mile. Turn right onto Cleland Mill Road/T378, go 1.4 miles, and keep left to continue onto Coverts Road/T378. Go 0.8 mile. Turn right onto Brewster St., and go 0.2 mile. Continue onto Covert Road; go 0.5 mile. Take a slight right onto W. Washington St., and go 0.1 mile. Look for parking on the right. The endpoint is 0.2 mile east along the trail.

To reach parking near the western endpoint in Struthers, Ohio, from I-680 N, take Exit 8. Turn right onto Shirley Road; go 0.2 mile. Turn right onto Poland Ave., go 1.5 miles, and continue onto State St. Go 0.9 mile, and turn left onto S. Bridge St. Go 0.4 mile, and turn right onto Broad St. Go 1.1 miles. Look for parking on the right by a sign that says STAVICH BIKE TRAIL WELCOMES YOU! From I-680 S, take Exit 8. Continue onto Cooper St. 0.3 mile, and turn left onto E. Indianola Ave. Go 0.3 mile, turn right onto Poland Ave., and follow the directions above.

Tucked into the Appalachian Ridge and Valley region, the Stony Valley Railroad Grade makes tracks through a state game land for nearly 20 miles past vanished coal boomtowns and tourist resorts. There are no services, but there is plenty of quietude for those who enjoy a forested reprieve from hustle and bustle.

Originally named St. Anthony's Wilderness by Moravian missionaries who arrived in the 1740s to convert the local American Indians, the Stony Creek Valley was a big draw for lumbering and coal mining companies in the 1820s due to its abundant natural resources. The Dauphin & Susquehanna Railroad entered the region in 1854 to haul coal to larger railroads, and it subsequently became the Schuylkill & Susquehanna Railroad in 1859, and then part of the Philadelphia & Reading Rail Road in 1872. The Reading pulled the plug on the money-losing line in 1939 after a bridge burned down.

It's hard to imagine that five towns once inhabited this valley, now a serene natural habitat.

Counties
Dauphin, Lebanon, Schuylkill

Endpoints
Ellendale Road, 1.5 miles east of Snyder Lane (Dauphin), to Lebanon Reservoir near Old Forge Road, 1.0 mile north of Oak Grove Road (Pine Grove)

Mileage
19.7

Type
Rail-Trail

Roughness Index
2

Surface
Dirt, Gravel

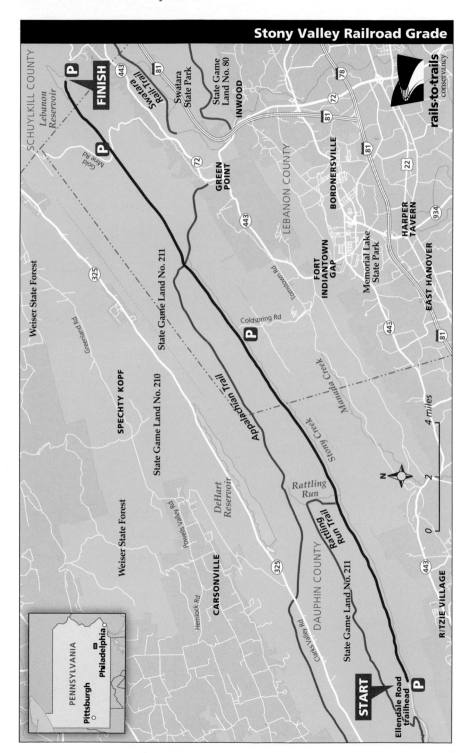

Stony Valley Railroad Grade

rails-to-trails
conservancy

SCHUYLKILL COUNTY

Lebanon Reservoir

443

81

Swatara Rail-Trail

Swatara State Park

State Game Land No. 80

78

72

INWOOD

81

FINISH

Gold Mine Rd

72

GREEN POINT

LEBANON COUNTY

BORDNERSVILLE

81

22

443

HARPER TAVERN

934

Weiser State Forest

325

State Game Land No. 211

Coldspring Rd

FORT INDIANTOWN GAP

Memorial Lake State Park

EAST HANOVER

Tomstown Rd

443

81

Greenland Rd

Appalachian Trail

Manada Creek

SPECHTY KOPF

State Game Land No. 210

Stony Creek

4 miles

Weiser State Forest

DeHart Reservoir

Rattling Run

N

2

Powells Valley Rd

325

Rattling Run Trail

DAUPHIN COUNTY

0

443

Hemlock Rd

CARSONVILLE

State Game Land No. 211

RITZIE VILLAGE

Clarks Valley Rd

PENNSYLVANIA

Philadelphia

Pittsburgh

START

Ellendale Road trailhead

The state game commission acquired the 44,000 acres in 1945 and later transformed the railroad corridor into a restricted road through State Game Land No. 211. Hunters come here for deer, squirrels, grouse, and turkeys. The route is closed to nonhunting bicyclists and equestrians in hunting season (the last Saturday in September through the third Saturday in January, and before 1 p.m. from the second Saturday in April through the last Saturday in May). Visitors must wear an orange vest during those periods. It is open one day a year to vehicles between the Ellendale Road and Gold Mine Road trailheads. The route can be susceptible to ravages of extreme weather, so be prepared for potholes and washouts.

Starting from the western trailhead, you'll experience a slight but steady grade for 13.0 miles, and then a downhill journey for the remainder of the route. You'll cross a bridge at 5.7 miles over Rattling Run, which shares its name with an old coal mining town up the hill. At 9 miles, a footpath on the right heads uphill to a deteriorating stone tower.

The Coldspring Road parking area at 11.2 miles marks the approximate location of a former 200-room tourist resort where visitors once soaked in spring waters. It was swept away by fire in 1900. About 2 miles later, the Appalachian Trail crosses the old railroad grade at 13.5 miles, also the site of the ghost town of Rausch Gap. Stone foundations, as well as a cemetery with a few headstones dating to the 1850s, are visible in the forest here.

The trail passes the Gold Mine Road trailhead in about 17.3 miles and then ends another 2.4 miles ahead, where it overlooks Lebanon Reservoir, which supplies drinking water to the town of Lebanon.

CONTACT: stonyvalley.com

DIRECTIONS

To reach the western endpoint on Ellendale Road from I-81, take Exit 67B, and merge onto US 22 W/US 322 W. Go 5.4 miles, and exit to Dauphin Borough/Stony Creek onto Allegheny St. Go 0.3 mile, and turn right onto Schuylkill St. Then go 250 feet, and turn right onto Erie St. Go 0.1 mile, and turn left onto Stony Creek Road. Go 4.9 miles, and Stony Creek Road becomes Ellendale Road at a traffic circle. Go 2.0 miles, and look for trailhead parking straight ahead at the gate.

To reach the Gold Mine Road trailhead from I-81, take Exit 100, and head west onto PA 443/Suedberg Road. Go 6.1 miles, and turn right onto Gold Mine Road. Go 2.8 miles, and look for trailhead parking on your right. The endpoint is located 2.4 miles farther east along the trail at the Lebanon Reservoir.

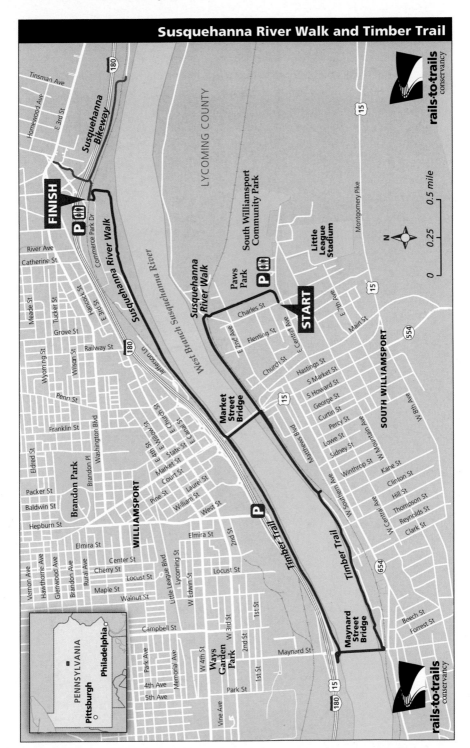

Susquehanna River Walk and Timber Trail

The Susquehanna River Walk and Timber Trail provide easy walking and biking experiences for all ability levels in the communities of Williamsport and South Williamsport. The trails are built primarily atop levees along the north and south shores of the West Branch Susquehanna River. Active freight railroads border both sides of the river, with the short-line Lycoming Valley Railroad to the north and the Norfolk Southern mainline to the south.

As you ride along the trail, it is easy to imagine the level of complex partnerships required to make the trail a reality. Tastefully engineered to incorporate electric utilities, sewage inlets, active railroads, highway bridges, and levee views, the trails appear seamlessly connected, providing a real-life inspiration for partnership in trail building. The local government and community advocates have much to be proud of here.

A surprising diversity of native plants, trees, and wildlife are consistent throughout the route. Especially wonderful views of the river and South Williamsport

Beautiful views can be had along this route, which follows both shores of the West Branch Susquehanna River.

County
Lycoming

Endpoints
Charles St. and E. Central Ave. (South Williamsport) to Susquehanna Bikeway at Commerce Park Dr. just south of S. Northway Road (Williamsport)

Mileage
4.2

Type
Rail-with-Trail

Roughness Index
1

Surface
Asphalt

add to the trail's simple beauty. Look out for a low dam between the Market Street and Maynard Street Bridges that provides a beautiful contrast to the relatively slow-moving Susquehanna. Also prevalent along the path is interpretive signage—not to mention lumber-themed public art—highlighting the importance of logging to the region.

Start your journey at the southeastern terminus of the Susquehanna River Walk portion of the trail in South Williamsport, passing Paws Park to your right. Follow the trail over a railroad crossing, then continue on the trail with the river to your right. At US 15/Market Street in South Williamsport, you can either turn right to cross the Market Street Bridge or continue on the Timber Trail to cross the Maynard Street Bridge. Both bridges feature a dedicated pedestrian-bicyclist portion on the west side to provide easy, protected access to both the north and south portions of the riverside trail. Gradual grades on the entrances and exits of ramps under the bridges provide easy access for all ability levels.

The C-shaped Timber Trail portion of the trail connects the southern and northern sections of the Susquehanna River Walk. Running west from the Market Street Bridge in South Williamsport, with the river to the right, the Timber Trail heads 1.3 miles to cross the Maynard Street Bridge. Loop beneath the bridge and follow the trail to Market Street in Williamsport, with the river to your right.

From here, the Susquehanna River Walk resumes, heading 1.5 miles to the northeastern endpoint at Commerce Park Drive, just south of I-180. The trail shares a parking lot with the Susquehanna Bikeway, which heads another 3.2 miles east along the river and then northeast into Montoursville. Lycoming County is working on a 3-mile extension from the Maynard Street Bridge west to Susquehanna State Park that would run entirely along the north side of the river. The project is estimated to be complete by the end of 2021.

CONTACT: Lycoming County Planning Commission, 570-320-2138, **rtc.li/Susquehanna-River-Walk-Timber-Trail**

DIRECTIONS

To reach the southeastern endpoint in South Williamsport from I-80, take Exit 210B to merge onto US 15 N. Go 15.5 miles, and turn right onto Fairmont Ave. Go 0.4 mile, and turn right onto E. Mountain Ave. Take the second left onto Charles St., and go 0.1 mile. Turn right onto E. Central Ave., and immediately turn left into the parking lot.

To reach the northern endpoint in Williamsport from I-180, take Exit 25 toward Faxon. (From I-180 E, turn right onto Commerce Park Dr. From I-180 W, keep left at the fork, and turn left onto S. Northway Road. Go 0.1 mile, and turn left onto Commerce Park Dr.) A parking lot for both the Susquehanna River Walk and Timber Trail and the Susquehanna Bikeway is located immediately over the railroad tracks to your right. The trail access point, marked with bike route signage, is located across Commerce Park Dr.

The Swatara Rail-Trail uses the corridors left behind by a canal and a railroad to snake around an Appalachian mountain in eastern Pennsylvania, passing through the forests of Swatara State Park most of the way.

The trail route got its start with the discovery of anthracite coal in nearby Tremont, prompting construction of the Pine Grove feeder canal in the early 1800s that ran along Swatara Creek and connected with the main Union Canal near Lebanon. In 1862 a flood wiped out the feeder canal, which was never rebuilt. In the meantime, the Reading Railroad had built several connecting lines along the canal that were consolidated as the Lebanon and Tremont Branch in 1871. The Union Canal closed 14 years later.

Operating under several subsequent owners, the rail branch closed in segments from 1965 to 1981. The state acquired the land and built the trail. The 10-mile trail begins in Lickdale, crosses a gap in Blue Mountain created

The Swatara Rail-Trail crosses several streams along its route.

Counties
Lebanon, Schuylkill

Endpoints
Lickdale Road near PA 72 (Lickdale) to Anspach Dr. near PA 443 (Pine Grove)

Mileage
10.0

Type
Rail-Trail

Roughness Index
2–3

Surface
Asphalt, Crushed Stone, Dirt, Grass

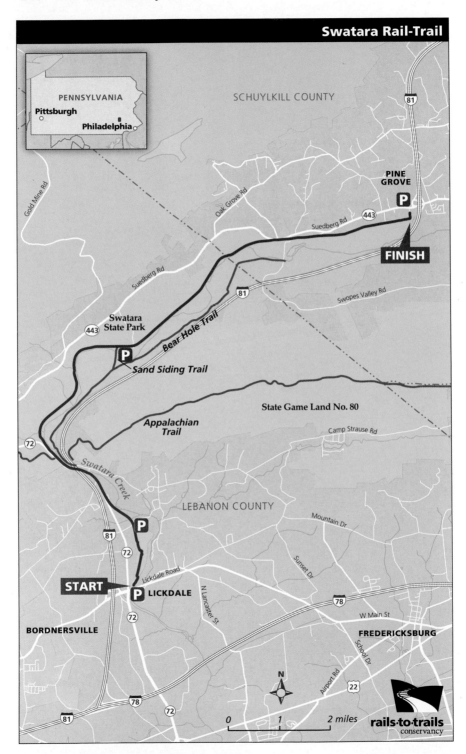

Swatara Rail-Trail

PENNSYLVANIA
Pittsburgh
Philadelphia

SCHUYLKILL COUNTY

81

Gold Mine Rd

Oak Grove Rd

PINE GROVE

P

Suedberg Rd

443

FINISH

Suedberg Rd

81

Swopes Valley Rd

Swatara State Park

443

Bear Hole Trail

P

Sand Siding Trail

State Game Land No. 80

Appalachian Trail

Camp Strause Rd

72

Swatara Creek

LEBANON COUNTY

Mountain Dr

P

81

72

Sunset Dr

Lickdale Road

START

P LICKDALE

N Lancaster St

78

W Main St

BORDNERSVILLE

72

FREDERICKSBURG

School Dr

N

Airport Rd

22

78

72

0   1   2 miles

81

rails·to·trails
conservancy

by Swatara Creek, and ends in Pine Grove. Much of the trail is crushed limestone and asphalt, although segments at either end are dirt and grass and may
be more conducive to mountain bikes than road and hybrid bikes. There are
several trail junctions, including one with the Appalachian Trail, along the way.
Future plans call for the Lebanon Valley Rail-Trail (see page 139) to meet up
with the Swatara Rail-Trail in Lickdale. Horseback riding is allowed from the
Sand Siding Trail east to Pine Grove. Cross-country skiing is permitted in the
park, although the trail is not groomed.

The southern trailhead begins in the vicinity of a commercial campground
in Lickdale, where you'll also find multiple restaurants, hotels, and an RV park.
Heading north toward Swatara State Park, you'll pass a small trail parking lot
and reach another trailhead on Monroe Valley Road in 0.8 mile. A historical
marker nearby shows the spot of Fort Swatara, a stockaded blockhouse built in
1755 to guard settlements against attacks through the Swatara Gap during the
French and Indian War.

In another 1.2 miles, the trail begins a narrow passage through the water
gap through Blue Mountain created by Swatara Creek. Here, you'll pass the 1890
vintage Waterville Bridge, a 221-foot steel bridge that was relocated here after
it was retired in the village of Waterville, more than 100 miles from here. The
bridge carries the Appalachian Trail across the creek and connects with the Bear

The 1890 Waterville Bridge, spanning 221 feet across Swatara Creek, provides a connection to Bear Hole Trail on the other side.

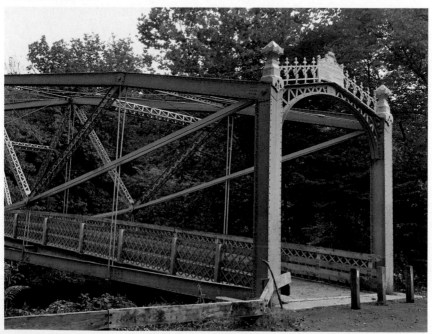

Hole Trail that runs 5 miles through the state park on the other side of the creek. Remains of seven locks and three dams, as well as sections of towpaths, are visible in the state park, and you'll spot the first ones in this gap if you cross to the Bear Hole Trail for a short distance.

Trending right after the water gap on the Swatara Rail-Trail, you'll pass six mountain bike singletrack runs to your left of about 1.5 miles each. About 4.3 miles from the Monroe Valley Road trailhead, you'll pass a pedestrian bridge for the 0.4-mile Sand Siding Trail. A side trip here crosses the creek and turns left for a mile on the Bear Hole Trail to an old log cabin built from on-site lumber and stone in 1939. The owner refused to leave when the park claimed the land, and the state let him live out his days here.

From the bridge, the trail runs another 2 miles through the park and then continues 3 miles through mostly wooded terrain to a truck stop and hotel in Pine Grove.

CONTACT: rtc.li/Swatara-Rail-Trail

DIRECTIONS

To reach the southern trailhead in Lickdale from I-81, take Exit 90 toward PA 72 N/Fisher Ave., and turn left onto Fisher Ave. Continue onto Lickdale Road, crossing over PA 72, and then turn left into the parking lot by the camping sign.

To reach the Monroe Valley Road trailhead from I-81, follow the directions above, but instead of continuing on Lickdale Road, turn left onto PA 72 N. Go 0.9 mile, and turn right onto Monroe Valley Road. Go 0.2 mile, and look for trailhead parking on the right. The endpoint is located 0.8 mile farther south along the trail.

To reach the northern endpoint in Pine Grove from I-81, take Exit 100, and head west onto PA 443/Suedberg Road. Go 2.3 miles, and look for roadside parking on the left. The endpoint is located 2.2 miles farther east along the trail at Anspach Dr. (facing the trail from the road, turn left to head east).

To reach a centrally located parking area in Swatara State Park from I-81, take Exit 100, and head west onto PA 443/Suedberg Road. Go 5.1 miles, and turn left at the entrance for Sand Siding Road. Go 0.6 mile, and look for parking straight ahead, where the road intersects with the trail. From the parking lot, turn left to head 5 miles toward the southern trailhead in Lickdale, or turn right to head 5 miles toward the northern trailhead in Pine Grove.

Three Rivers Heritage Trail features the best that the city of Pittsburgh has to offer, connecting major cultural venues, the downtown area, historical sites, and some of the city's most well-known neighborhoods and parks along more than 20 miles of riverfront trails. Extended outward in three major paved, connected segments from Point State Park, the urban trail parallels its namesake three rivers—the Allegheny, Ohio, and Monongahela—that helped lift the city into prominence as America's once industrial powerhouse.

Now, the pathway, which began as an idea nearly three decades ago and had its first groundbreaking in 1991—serves as an active-transportation and recreation asset, and major tourism destination, for more than a half million people each year.

Pittsburgh boasts more than 440 bridges, and several of the city's most iconic in this category serve as

Take the Duquesne Incline, a historical cable car, to behold a panorama of the city and its three rivers below.

County
Allegheny

Endpoints
W. Station Sq. Dr. and PA 837/Lincoln Hwy. to the Great Allegheny Passage at Haysglen St. near Baldwin Road; 43rd St. near Willow St. to 38th St. near Foster St.; 11th St. and Fort Duquesne Blvd. to Boundary St. and Junction Hollow Trail; Browns Hill Road and Homestead Grays Bridge to just south of Old Browns Hill Road and Second Ave.; 0.6 mile northeast of Millvale Riverfront Park at Riverfront Dr. and 40th St. to Ohio River at Westhall St. near Preble Ave. (Pittsburgh)

Mileage
20.5 (plus 0.7 mile of bridges)

Type
Rail-Trail

Roughness Index
1

Surface
Asphalt, Crushed Stone

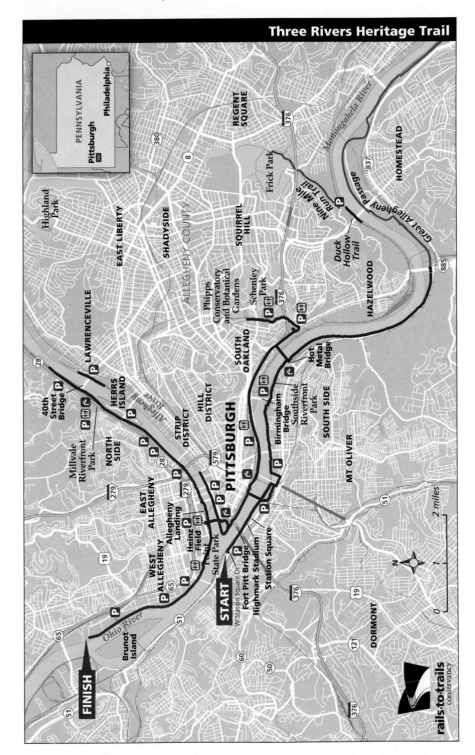

Three Rivers Heritage Trail

connectors for the trail's various segments. Managed by the nonprofit Friends of the Riverfront, the Three Rivers Heritage Trail also shares a corridor with, and links to, one of America's most well-known rail-trails, the 150-mile Great Allegheny Passage (see page 82).

The Three Rivers Heritage Trail is a host trail for the 3,700-plus-mile Great American Rail-Trail, which will one day form a seamless connection between Washington, D.C., and Washington State, and serves as a major spine for the Industrial Heartland Trails Coalition's developing 1,500-mile trail network through Pennsylvania, West Virginia, Ohio, and New York.

Southern Segment: Station Square to Great Allegheny Passage (Monongahela River–South): 6.9 miles

A great place to begin your journey is on West Station Square Drive on the southern side of the Monongahela River. Here the Duquesne Incline, one of Pittsburgh's two historical cable cars, travels up the steep hillside 400 feet on an 800-foot track to offer a panoramic view of Pittsburgh and the three rivers.

Heading east on a paved trail beneath the Fort Pitt Bridge, you'll travel by Highmark Stadium and the Gateway Clipper Fleet before reaching historic Station Square, built in the 1870s to greet passengers of the Pittsburgh & Lake Erie Railroad on their way from Youngstown. Ceasing all operations by 1970 and redeveloped in 1976, Station Square is now home to restaurants, bars, shops, and the Monongahela Incline, featuring extensive vistas of the city skyline.

Continuing along the river, you'll pass under the Smithfield Street Bridge—a spectacular structure completed in 1883 with sweeping blue arches of steel—and then beneath the Liberty Bridge and into an industrial area with a series of shared roadways. Turn right onto Second Street, left onto McKean Street, and left onto Fourth Street, where the off-road trail picks up again at about 1.7 miles from the starting point. Note the brightly colored trailside artwork created on the 2016 national Opening Day for Trails by the local community and overseen by former Pittsburgh Steeler Baron "The Artist" Batch.

In another mile, you'll approach the Southside Dog Park, just before the Birmingham Bridge. Here, you'll be greeted by the larger-than-life sculpture *The Workers* (2012), which was made from scrap metal from local steel mills and celebrates Pittsburgh's industrial past while embracing the present and future.

From the Birmingham Bridge, you'll go another 0.7 mile through Southside Riverfront Park and the SouthSide Works, a trendy shopping and restaurant area, where you can cross the river on the beautifully restored pedestrian/bicycle Hot Metal Bridge, a 1900 rail trestle that once transported hot iron to the South Side and steel ingots to the northern side of the river. Continuing southeast another 0.7 mile takes you past the practice field for the Pittsburgh Steelers and toward a more remote section of trail that leads to Haysglen Street and a continuous connection with the Great Allegheny Passage.

Middle Segment: Strip District to Schenley Park
(Allegheny River–South, Monongahela River–North): 6.8 miles

While the trail technically begins at 24th Street in the Strip District—an area known for its gourmet food and produce shops, eateries, and nightlife—the trail is closed to 11th Street due to nearby construction projects on this section.

A short 0.4-mile section of crushed-stone trail begins farther up the southern side of the Allegheny River in the Lawrenceville neighborhood, which begins at Bernard Dog Run, a local dog park, and ends at 43rd Street. Future plans call for eventually connecting this section of trail to the main section through the Strip District.

Begin your journey at 11th Street, which is also located one block from the Senator John Heinz History Center on Smallman Street. Heading west, you'll skirt the southern side of the Allegheny River about 1 mile to Point State Park, at the confluence of the city's famous river system, which marks the historical sites of Fort Duquesne and Fort Pitt—strongholds of France and Great Britain in the mid-1700s.

Along the way you'll pass by the Pittsburgh Convention Center and through the Cultural District, which houses several of the city's top performance venues. The trail then makes a hard left turn southwest from the Point, switching back over the Smithfield Street Bridge in about 0.7 mile to continue toward South Oakland. An awkward merge point for I-279 and I-376 used to require

The Fort Duquesne Bridge over the Allegheny River affords spectacular vistas of Pittsburgh.

an on-road detour, but the completion in 2018 of an off-road segment of trail, including the switchback ramp at the Smithfield Street Bridge, now allows a seamless trail experience to South Oakland.

Heading east, you'll pass a trailside bike shop two blocks after the Smithfield Street Bridge, and then the north side of the Hot Metal Bridge in about 2.4 more miles. The trail curves on a southward then northward trajectory for about 1.4 miles, terminating at Schenley Park, a 456-acre green space with a café and visitor center, golf course, sports plex and ice-skating rink, swimming pool, trails, playgrounds, and the 15-acre Phipps Conservatory and Botanical Gardens.

Navigate this section by going straight on Second Avenue 0.3 mile, taking a slight left onto Greenfield Avenue, and then taking an immediate left onto Saline Street. Go 0.3 mile, and turn left onto Boundary Street. Go about 300 feet, and turn right onto Junction Hollow Trail. Go 0.5 mile, and take a slight left to stay on Junction Hollow Trail, which ends at Boundary Street, adjacent to some railroad tracks and Panther Hollow Lake.

Extending southeast from the intersection of Second Avenue and Greenfield Avenue is a currently closed 0.7-mile section of trail that is within an active construction zone. As of early 2019, this section was scheduled to reopen in the next couple years.

South of Hazelwood, a 1.4-mile section—also known as the Duck Hollow Trail—extending from the Glenwood Bridge north to Old Browns Hill Road was closed for repairs at press time. This trail connects to the Nine Mile Run Trail, leading another 1.5 miles to the 106-acre Frick Park.

This section from Point State Park and over the Hot Metal Bridge to Homestead is also considered a shared corridor with the Great Allegheny Passage.

Northern Segment: Millvale Riverfront Park to Westhall Street (Ohio River–North, Allegheny River–North): 6.8 miles

The best place to begin your journey on the northern segment of the trail is at Millvale Riverfront Park, just west of the 40th Street Bridge. This paved segment of trail curves southwest and then northwest through Pittsburgh's North Side neighborhoods.

In about 0.9 mile from the parking lot at Millvale Riverfront Park, you can opt to take a sharp left onto Herrs Island (also known as Washington's Landing) via a historical rail trestle. This connector trail is mostly gravel and takes you along the island's quiet communities and waterfront. Trail users on bikes are asked to ride slowly on the narrow pathway and dismount in certain sections—especially near the waterfront restaurant patio and the marina, where heavy equipment operates.

Head south another 1.5 miles to Allegheny Landing, which is billed as one of the nation's first urban riverfront sculpture parks. For a side excursion, head

to nearby Sandusky Street for a museum dedicated to Pop Art phenomenon Andy Warhol. To reach the museum, head north through the park to Isabella Street, turn right onto Isabella Street, and then turn left onto Sandusky Street. Go one block to the museum, which will be on your left.

Over the course of about 1.1 miles, you'll pass a series of major venues in the North Side, including PNC Park, Heinz Field, and the Rivers Casino. The trail heads northwest another 2.1 miles, terminating at Westhall Street north of Brunot Island.

CONTACT: friendsoftheriverfront.org/trails/three-rivers-heritage-trail

DIRECTIONS

To reach the western endpoint on W. Station Square Dr. from I-376 E toward Pittsburgh, take Exit 69C to merge onto US 19 N/PA 51 N/Saw Mill Run Blvd., and go 0.1 mile. Take the PA 51/PA 837/McKees Rocks/West End exit, and then merge onto S. Main St. Turn right onto W. Carson St., go 0.5 mile, and turn left onto W. Station Square Dr. Go about 0.1 mile, and turn right into the parking lot.

To reach the Millvale Riverfront Park trailhead from I-279 S, take Exit 2B for E. Ohio St. toward PA 28 N. Continue onto East St., and go 0.1 mile. Turn left onto E. North Ave., and then continue onto Spring Garden Ave. Go 0.1 mile, and turn right onto Chestnut St. Go 0.2 mile, and turn left onto the PA 28 N ramp to Etna. Turn left to merge onto PA 28 N, go 2.0 miles, and then take Exit 3B toward Millvale. Go 0.1 mile, turn left onto E. Ohio St. (signs for Millvale), and then take a slight left to stay on E. Ohio St. Go about 410 feet, and turn left onto Riverfront Dr. Go 0.4 mile, and look for the large parking lot straight ahead.

To reach the parking lot at 11th St. from I-579, follow signs to take the Seventh Ave. exit toward the convention center. Head northeast on Seventh Ave., and immediately turn right onto Grant St. In 0.1 mile continue onto Liberty Ave., and immediately turn left onto 11th St. Go 0.2 mile. Turn right onto Waterfront Pl., and turn left into the parking lot.

The Trolley Trail uses a former interurban line to link several communities north of Scranton. The trail comprises two disconnected sections that total 4.7 miles, although the nonprofit Countryside Conservancy plans to extend the trail in its mission to preserve distinctive natural features and create a recreational trail.

The route uses the right-of-way of the former Scranton, Montrose, and Binghamton Railroad, also known as the Northern Electric trolley line, which carried passengers between Scranton and Dalton, and later to Montrose, from 1907 to 1932. A spur line from Clarks Summit ran west to Lake Winola, where the railroad company built a dance pavilion and amusement park that subsequently closed.

The southern section of the trail begins in Clarks Summit and runs north 2.5 miles to Dalton. Northeast of Dalton, a 1.8-mile segment runs through the Keystone College campus from La Plume to Factoryville. Most of the trail is crushed stone or packed dirt. The two sections of trail are connected by a two-lane road that lacks shoulders or sidewalks for its entire length.

Counties
Lackawanna, Wyoming

Endpoints
Old State Road and US 6/US 11/Lackawanna Trail (Clarks Summit) to S. Turnpike Road near Prospect St. (Dalton); SR 4016 near College Road (La Plume) to Riverside Dr./SR 2033 near Church St. (Factoryville)

Mileage
4.7

Type
Rail-Trail

Roughness Index
2

Surface
Boardwalk, Crushed Stone, Dirt, Grass

The northern segment of the Trolley Trail, between La Plume and Factoryville, winds through wooded environs.

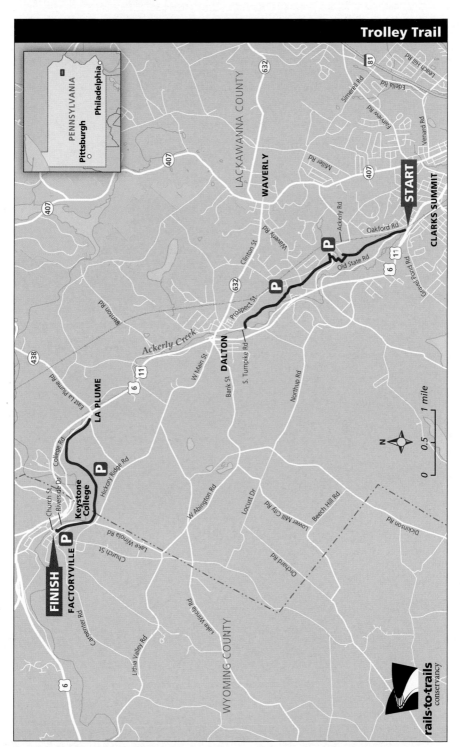

Beginning at US 6/US 11/Lackawanna Trail, the route passes rock outcrops before entering a densely wooded area for about a mile. Shortly thereafter, a left turn (off the original rail corridor) is required, which takes you on an earthen path leading to a small footbridge over Ackerly Creek. (Continuing straight takes you to a dead end at Arch Avenue.)

You'll pass through an opening in a chain-link fence to rejoin the old rail corridor, now with a crushed-stone surface (note the Abington Little League ball fields to your left), which detours right and then left around a missing bridge to cross Ackerly Road. Just after Ackerly Road, you can head right to a trailhead on South Waterford Road, or left and then right in quick succession back toward the rail corridor.

Here, the trail passes through a field for 0.5 mile to the Waverly Road crossing, where you'll ride on Pine Tree Drive for 0.2 mile. The trail then crosses Church Hill Road and passes through a parking lot before reentering wooded environs. A stretch of boardwalk carries you over wetlands before the path ends at South Turnpike Road in Dalton.

A newer segment starts on State Route 4016 in La Plume, just west of College Road. You'll note a similar surface on this stretch, as well as familiar wooded surroundings. Developed collaboratively with Keystone College, a private four-year institution, the trail winds through the college campus and offers access to hiking trails and the college's athletic fields. The trail ends in the borough of Factoryville, where you can find snacks or a meal.

CONTACT: countrysideconservancy.org/trolley-trail

DIRECTIONS

To reach the southern endpoint in Clarks Summit from I-81, take Exit 194 for US 6 W/US 11 toward Clarks Summit. Merge onto I-476 N, and immediately take the US 11 N/US 6 W/PA 407 N exit toward Binghamton/Towanda/Clarks Summit. Merge onto US 11 N/US 6 W, and immediately exit right onto PA 407 N/S. Abington Road. Go 1.3 miles, and take a slight left onto Glenburn Road. Go 1.2 miles, and turn left onto Oakford Road. Go 0.2 mile, and continue onto Ackerly Road/SR 4010. Go 0.3 mile, and turn right onto Waterford Road; then go 240 feet and turn left into the parking lot. To reach the southern endpoint, turn left from the trailhead, and head south about 1.1 miles.

To reach the northern trailhead in Factoryville from I-81, take Exit 194 toward US 6 W/US 11 toward Clarks Summit. Merge onto I-476 N, and immediately take the US 11 N/US 6 W/PA 407 N exit toward Binghamton/Towanda/Clarks Summit. Merge onto US 11 N/US 6 W, and go 8.3 miles. Turn left onto SR 1035, and go about 0.1 mile. Turn right onto College Ave., and go 0.2 mile. Turn left onto SR 2033, and go about 300 feet. Turn left onto Riverside Dr./SR 2033, and look for parking on the right in 220 feet.

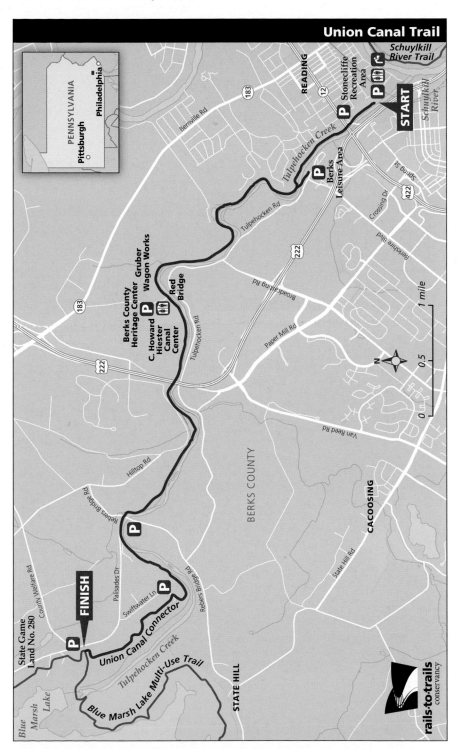

Union Canal Trail

Schuylkill
River Trail

READING

Schuylkill
River

Stonecliffe
Recreation
Area

START

183

12

Bernville Rd

Tulpehocken Creek

Berks
Leisure Area

Tulpehocken Rd

Crossing Dr

Berkshire Blvd

422

IS Buuds

Gruber
Wagon Works

Berks County
Heritage Center

222

Red
Bridge

Broadcasting Rd

222

Paper Mill Rd

C. Howard
Hiester
Canal
Center

183

Tulpehocken Rd

1 mile

N

0.5

0

Van Reed Rd

BERKS COUNTY

Hilltop Rd

Rebers Bridge Rd

State Hill Rd

CACOOSING

FINISH

Palisades Dr

Swiftwater Ln

Union Canal Connector

Rebers Bridge Rd

STATE HILL

State Game
Land No. 280

County Welfare Rd

Tulpehocken Creek

Blue Marsh Lake Multi-Use Trail

Blue
Marsh
Lake

rails·to·trails
conservancy

PENNSYLVANIA

Pittsburgh

Philadelphia

The Union Canal Trail runs along the Tulpehocken Creek from the city of Reading up to Blue Marsh Lake in Leesport. The trail makes up a segment of the 71.7-mile Schuylkill River Trail (see page 221) in southeastern Pennsylvania. The flat, crushed-stone trail surface makes for a comfortable journey on foot, bicycle, cross-country skis, or even snowshoes.

The Union Canal historically connected the Schuylkill River in Reading to the Susquehanna River in Middletown, creating a means to ship coal and lumber from the rest of Pennsylvania to Philadelphia. Construction began during George Washington's presidency but was not completed until 1828. The canal ran 82 miles and had 93 locks, the remnants of several of which are visible along the trail. The canal operated until the 1880s, when the combination of costly repairs and the emergence of the Lebanon Valley Railroad led to the canal ending service.

You'll cross several bridges as you follow the Union Canal Trail along Tulpehocken Creek.

County
Berks

Endpoints
Stonecliffe Recreation Area at Columbia St. and Montgomery St. (Reading) to Tulpehocken Road and Resh Ave. or to Blue Marsh Lake Multi-Use Trail at Palisades Dr. just south of County Welfare Road (Leesport)

Mileage
6.5

Type
Greenway/Non-Rail-Trail

Roughness Index
2

Surface
Crushed Stone, Gravel

Beginning in a public parking lot at the Stonecliffe Recreation Area in Reading, you'll head north along Tulpehocken Creek, a tributary of the Schuylkill River. About 0.8 mile into your ride, you'll pass a bridge across the creek that leads to the Berks Leisure Area of the Berks County Park Rangers. This area has a picnic pavilion and restrooms.

Crossing back over the bridge and continuing down the trail another 1.8 miles will bring you to the Berks County Heritage Center, a historical interpretive complex. Here you'll find the Gruber Wagon Works, a facility that made wagons from the 1880s to the 1950s. In the late 1970s, the building was relocated to its current location and designated a national historic landmark. The Heritage Center also includes the Red Bridge, originally known as Wertz's Bridge. The longest covered bridge in Pennsylvania, the Red Bridge crosses over the creek to provide trail access from its southern bank. Another site at the center is the C. Howard Hiester Canal Center, which details the history of the canal system in the United States and southeastern Pennsylvania.

Another 1.8 miles will take you to the end of the main portion of the trail at the intersection of Rebers Bridge Road. There is parking available just south of the creek across the bridge. This area is known for its fly-fishing. The remainder of the trail is also known as the Union Canal Connector, as it bridges the gap between the Union Canal Trail and the 28.6-mile Blue Marsh Lake Multi-Use Trail.

Lush vegetation decorates this summer scene along the Union Canal Trail.

The first leg of the connector has a similar surface to the previous section of trail, though it's slightly less developed. In about 0.8 mile from Rebers Bridge Road, you will encounter a fairly steep curved hill as you reach a parking lot at Swiftwater Lane/Palisades Road. For the remaining mile of the connector, you'll ride alongside fields and grassland. This portion of the trail's surface is less compact than the rest and includes rolling hills.

At this endpoint, the trail seamlessly connects with the Blue Marsh Lake Multi-Use Trail that forms a 28.6-mile loop around its namesake. The lake is a recreational hot spot offering picnic areas, concession stands, a small beach, and boat launches; it's a popular spot for bird-watching.

CONTACT: co.berks.pa.us/dept/parks/pages/unioncanaltowpathtrail.aspx

DIRECTIONS

To access the Stonecliffe Recreation Area trailhead in Reading from I-176, take Exit 11B to merge onto US 422 W. In 4.9 miles take the exit onto PA 12 E toward Pricetown. Go 0.5 mile, and turn right onto Chester St. Go 0.2 mile, and turn right at the second cross street (0.2 mile) onto Columbia St. Go 0.2 mile, and the road terminates at the Stonecliffe Recreation Area parking lot, to your left.

To access parking at the northern endpoint near Blue Marsh Lake from I-176, take Exit 11B to merge onto US 422 W. In 5.8 miles continue onto US 222 N. Go 1.1 miles, and take the Spring Ridge Dr. exit. Turn left onto Spring Ridge Dr., and go 0.1 mile. Turn right onto Paper Mill Road, go 0.3 mile, and turn left to stay on Paper Mill Road. Go 1.1 miles, turn right onto Rebers Bridge Road, and then go 0.6 mile. After you cross the creek, turn left onto Palisades Dr., and go 1.0 mile. Turn left onto the access road, and then take an immediate right into the parking lot.

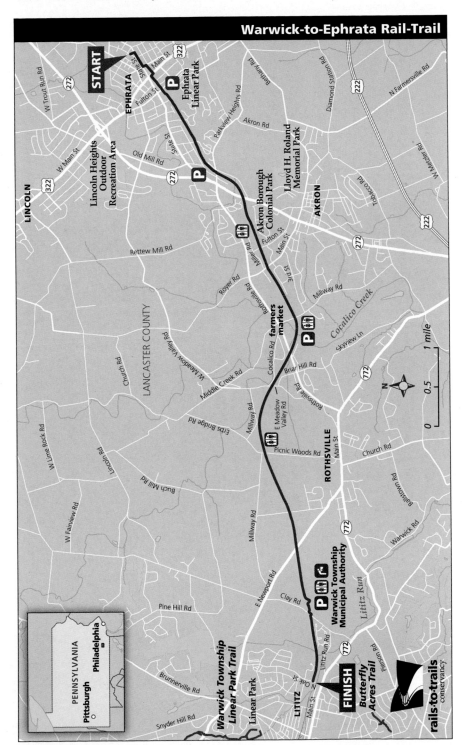

Warwick-to-Ephrata Rail-Trail

The 7.1-mile Warwick-to-Ephrata Rail-Trail runs from Ephrata west to Lititz in Warwick Township, following the former Reading and Columbia Railroad, which began service in 1863. The Lancaster Junction Trail is located farther down the same rail line on the route to Columbia. When the rail line was built during the Civil War, there was debate about whether the terrain was suitable for a rail line and if cutting a mere 25 miles off a trip from New York to Washington, D.C., was worth the investment, particularly when a rail line already existed through Harrisburg.

Though the easternmost endpoint is located a bit farther north, at Hazel Alley and Acorn Alley, it's best to begin your journey 0.5 mile along the trail at Ephrata Linear Park, where parking is available. From here, the trail takes you through downtown Ephrata before passing through mostly residential areas. This portion of trail is paved and lit. At Millway Road in about 2.7 miles, parking and a restroom are available. If you turn right here, go

Rolling hills and farmsteads contribute to the tranquility along the path.

County
Lancaster

Endpoints
Hazel Alley and Acorn Alley (Ephrata) to N. Oak St. between Front St. and PA 772/E. Main St. (Lititz)

Mileage
7.1

Type
Rail-Trail

Roughness Index
1–2

Surface
Asphalt, Crushed Stone

0.2 mile, and turn right again, you'll find a farmers market offering fresh fruits, vegetables, and baked goods.

In 2018 the 0.75-mile portion of trail in Warwick Township between a bridge at Cocalico Creek and East Meadow Valley Road was completed. From Millway Road, the trail crosses Cocalico Creek and heads to a trailhead on East Meadow Valley Road, between Cocalico and Briar Hill Roads. After this point, the trail becomes crushed stone and runs through farmland, though it still has some tree cover to keep your trip pleasant on a sunny day. Here, users are advised to be aware of farm equipment crossing the trail, stay a safe distance away, and observe posted rules and regulations.

In another 2.4 miles, you'll pass through the Warwick Township Municipal Authority on Clay Road. More than just an administrative building, this trailhead offers a 20-acre park with baseball fields, a playground, and a 0.6-mile trail encircling it. The Warwick Township Municipal Authority also includes restrooms and the closest trail parking to the Lititz terminus. Head another 0.7 mile west on trail that is once again paved and dead-ends at North Oak Street in Lititz.

From here, the southern endpoint of the 1.2-mile Warwick Township Linear Park Trail is just over a mile northwest, and the northern endpoint of the 0.5-mile Butterfly Acres Trail is less than a mile south.

On the western side of the Warwick-to-Ephrata Rail-Trail, Lititz Borough is working to extend the trail about 1 mile farther west in the future. On the eastern side, Ephrata Borough is in the planning stages for an extension north to West Pine Street, with an estimated completion date of 2020.

CONTACT: warwicktownship.org/regional-rails-to-trails

DIRECTIONS

To reach a parking lot at Ephrata Linear Park from I-76, take Exit 286 for US 222. Continue onto Col. Howard Blvd. 0.8 mile, and then turn left to merge onto US 222 S toward Lancaster. In 4.9 miles take the US 322 exit, and turn right onto US 322/Main St. in Ephrata. Go 1.8 miles, turn left onto S. State St., and go 0.2 mile. Turn left onto E. Fulton St. Take the second right (280 feet) onto Railroad Ave., and then take an immediate left into the parking lot at Ephrata Linear Park. The endpoint is 0.3 mile farther east along the trail.

To reach the Warwick Township Municipal Authority trailhead near the western endpoint from I-76, take Exit 286 for US 222. Continue onto Col. Howard Blvd. For 0.8 mile, and then turn left to merge onto US 222 S toward Lancaster. In 9.3 miles take the PA 772 exit toward Brownstown/Rothsville, and turn right onto PA 772 W. Go 2.8 miles, and continue straight onto E. Newport Road. Go 1.4 miles, and turn left onto Clay Road. Then go 0.2 mile, and turn left into the municipal authority parking lot. The endpoint is 0.7 mile farther west along the trail.

The West Creek Recreational Trail connects St. Marys and Emporium in a forested area of northern Pennsylvania known as elk country. The 19.5-mile trail follows the route of the Philadelphia and Erie Railroad that began serving the area in the 1860s. It was later acquired by the Pennsylvania Railroad and then became one of the many short-line railroads: the Allegheny and Eastern Railroad, owned by Genesee & Wyoming. In 2008 that company hammered out an agreement to deed the corridor to the West Creek Recreational Trail Association. Work on the trail proceeded in stages over the years until it was completed in 2017.

The crushed-stone trail loses about 600 feet from St. Marys to Emporium. Emporium's motto is Land of the Endless Mountains, but the trail only takes the one long grade along West Creek. Round-trip bicyclists like to start in Emporium to enjoy the long downhill on the return trip. In the wintertime, snowmobilers flock to the trail, groomed by the St. Marys Snowmobile Association.

In the west, the trail starts on the northern outskirts of St. Marys, the larger of the two towns, which were once

West Creek is not always visible from its eponymous trail, though it parallels the path for its entire length.

Counties
Cameron, Elk

Endpoints
West Creek Road and Wilson Road (St. Marys) to E. Second St. near PA 120/E. Allegany Ave. (Emporium)

Mileage
19.5

Type
Rail-Trail

Roughness Index
1

Surface
Crushed Stone

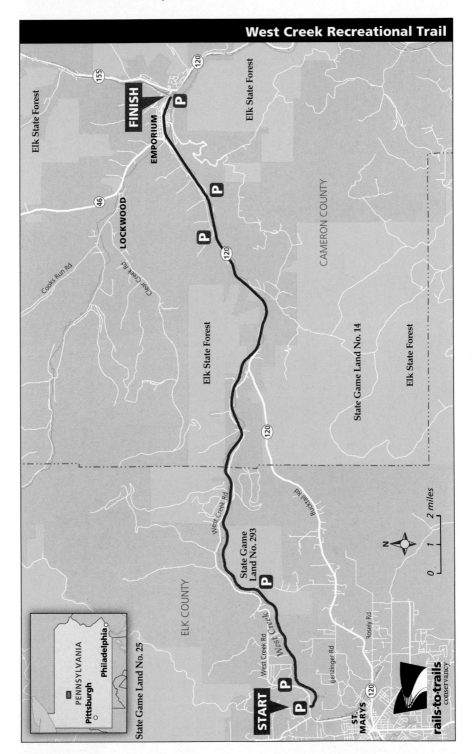

West Creek Recreational Trail

flourishing lumber and manufacturing centers. The trail leaving the parking lot at the West Creek Wetland Learning Center has some large stones and drainage issues. The trailhead 0.6 mile east on West Creek Road makes for a better start.

Elk and Cameron Counties are populated with elk, reintroduced in the early 20th century after native herds were hunted to oblivion by the 1870s. You might see them on your travels, although the prime viewing areas are the hills and valleys south of the trail. During the summer, the best viewing times are early morning and evening as the elk spend the days in the shade.

Following the meandering West Creek, you'll pick up the northern boundary of State Game Land No. 293 in 3 miles. Deer, turkeys, bears, beavers, bobcats, and coyotes inhabit the area. You'll leave the vicinity of the state game area about 4 miles down the trail as you cross West Creek Road.

In another 2.5 miles, you'll come to PA 120, which accompanies the trail for about 7 miles into Emporium. Use caution at occasional cross streets and driveways along this section. In 4.8 miles, you'll pass a valley on the right called Hercules Hollow, named for one of the seven dynamite factories based in the Emporium area that operated from the late 1800s to the 1950s.

As the trail approaches Emporium, you'll see more reminders of the manufacturing that once flourished here as you pass the old Sylvania plant, where incandescent light bulbs and radio tubes were once manufactured. The town, which serves as the county seat, is surrounded by hills. Trailside signs direct you to some of the restaurants, cafés, taverns, and ice cream shops that make this a good destination. An old red caboose marks the trail's end.

CONTACT: cameroncountychamber.org/trails

DIRECTIONS

To reach the endpoint in St. Marys from I-80, take Exit 97, and head north on US 219. Go 10.4 miles, and turn right onto US 219/Main St. Go 6.5 miles, and turn right onto Toby Road/SR 2003. Go 6.7 miles, and continue straight onto SR 2007. Go 0.8 mile, and turn left onto Irishtown Road/SR 2007. Go 1.2 miles, and stay straight on Old Kersey Road/SR 2007. Go 1.9 miles, and turn left onto PA 255/S. St. Marys Road/Million Dollar Hwy. Go 2.8 miles, and bear right onto PA 120/Railroad St. Go 200 feet, and bear left onto Lafayette St. Go 370 feet, and turn right onto Washington St. Go 1.9 miles, and go straight onto W. Creek Road. Go 0.3 mile, and turn right onto the access road for the West Creek Wetland Learning Center trailhead parking lot. Another trailhead is located 0.6 mile farther east on W. Creek Road.

To reach the endpoint in Emporium from I-80, take Exit 178, and head north on US 220. Go 7.1 miles. Take Exit 111, and turn left onto Paul Mack Blvd. Go 0.7 mile, and stay straight onto PA 120/N. Jay St. Go 0.2 mile, turn left onto PA 120/E. Water St., and go 1.1 miles. Bear right onto PA 120/Susquehanna Ave., and go 71.4 miles. Turn left to stay on PA 120 W/E. Allegany Ave. Go 0.1 mile, turn left onto E. Second St. at the caboose, and look for parking on the right.

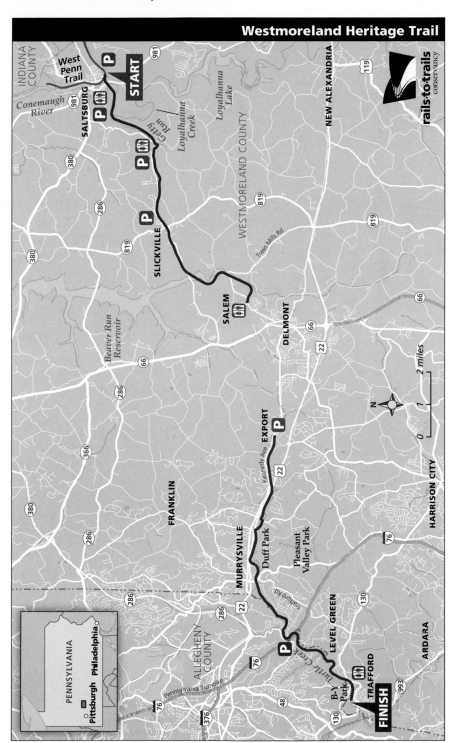

Westmoreland Heritage Trail

The 17.8-mile Westmoreland Heritage Trail, a family-friendly multiuse rail-trail, offers opportunities for recreation and connections to nature along its two separated segments between Saltsburg and Trafford. The pathway features reclaimed railroad bridges over the Conemaugh River and Loyalhanna Creek—affording great views of the river hydraulics below, as well as providing opportunities for bird-watching and wildlife spotting.

The trail inhabits a segment of the Turtle Creek Branch of the former Pennsylvania Railroad corridor, which was originally chartered in 1886 by George Westinghouse Jr. to connect Saltsburg and Export. The line transported both passengers and freight between the many towns along its route before it fell into disuse in 2009 (passenger service had ceased in 1936).

Saltsburg to Salem: 8.6 miles

Even on the hottest summer day, you will find yourself enveloped in a lush deciduous canopy on this scenic trail, a portion of which runs along a small tributary, where natural

County
Westmoreland

Endpoints
West Penn Trail junction at Water St. and Canal St. (Saltsburg) to Athena Dr. between Lauffer Mine Road and Brook Lane (Salem); Lincoln Ave. and Kennedy Ave. (Export) to just north of Seventh St. and Forest Ave. (Trafford)

Mileage
17.8

Type
Rail-Trail

Roughness Index
2

Surface
Crushed Stone

From Saltsburg, the Westmoreland Heritage Trail crosses the Conemaugh River on a reclaimed railroad bridge.

seeps can be seen in the limestone railroad cuts at various points. At its eastern end in Saltsburg, the Westmoreland Heritage Trail intersects with the 15-mile West Penn Trail (see page 265).

Heading west, you'll cross over the Conemaugh River and Loyalhanna Creek in quick succession, after which you'll enter a tree-canopied route that loosely follows Getty Run. The path has a distinct uphill grade along most of the nearly 5-mile length from Saltsburg to Slickville, offering an opportunity for a quick downhill ride back to Saltsburg. From Slickville to Salem, a 3.7-mile segment that opened in 2013 features a steep climb west of Slickville, leading to a rapid descent to Beaver Run Reservoir. The trail skirts the edge of the reservoir before reentering a peaceful, densely wooded landscape.

Export to Trafford: 9.2 miles

This segment of trail used to begin along US 22, just north of Duff Park at the Roberts Parcel trailhead in Murrysville, and ran 5.9 miles to B–Y Park in Trafford. However, a 2019 project extended the trail from Murrysville to Export and improved the small bridges along the route, for a total of 9.2 miles. The new eastern endpoint for this section, scheduled for public opening in mid-August 2019, begins at a small park with a restored caboose at Lincoln Avenue and Kennedy Avenue in Export. While there is no official parking lot at this endpoint, trail users will find surface parking lots, as well as several restaurants and eateries, just east of the endpoint in the small downtown area.

Heading west, the trail follows Turtle Creek and then veers away from the waterway to pass underneath the Pennsylvania Turnpike. It then picks up Turtle Creek again for most of its remaining alignment to B–Y Park.

CONTACT: westmorelandheritagetrail.com

DIRECTIONS

To reach the trailhead in Saltsburg from Pittsburgh, take I-376 E to its end (near mile marker 85) and continue onto US 22 E/William Penn Hwy. Go 18.4 miles on US 22, and turn left onto PA 981 N. Go 7.7 miles. Turn right onto PA 286 E, and take an immediate right onto Water St. Go 0.5 mile, and look for trailhead parking to your right (the parking lot abuts the Conemaugh River).

To reach the trailhead at B–Y Park in Trafford from I-76, take Exit 67 to merge onto US 30 W, and go 1.0 mile. Turn right onto Rocky Road, go 0.1 mile, and then turn left onto Old US 30/Pennsylvania Ave. Go 0.6 mile, turn right onto Brush Hill Road, and go 0.5 mile. Turn right onto PA 993 E, and go 0.8 mile. Turn left onto Manor Harrison City Road, go 0.2 mile, and turn left onto Sandy Hill Road. After 2.5 miles, turn left onto PA 130 W, and go 4.7 miles. Turn right onto the park access road, and go 0.1 mile into the parking lot. Head north into the park to access the trail, which begins 0.5 mile farther west.

The West Penn Trail is named for a branch of the Pennsylvania Railroad that paralleled the Western Division Canal of the cross-state Main Line of Public Works from Lockport to Freeport and then to Pittsburgh. Canal barges negotiated locks, aqueducts, and tunnels in this division to carry cargo between Pittsburgh and Johnstown. The Pennsylvania Railroad used the corridor until 1950, when a portion of tracks near Bow Ridge was moved to a less flood-prone route during the construction of the Conemaugh Dam.

Today, the trail, which is open dawn–dusk, extends from north of Saltsburg to just west of Blairsville, with plans to expand north to Avonmore and east to the Hoodlebug Trail (see page 95). The trail is part of the Industrial Heartland Trails Coalition's developing 1,500-mile trail network through Pennsylvania, West Virginia, Ohio, and New York. Along the way, you'll see remnants of the historic Main Line Canal that was replaced by railroads in the late 19th century, as well as rare rail-trail features, including switchbacks and a flight of stairs. Other than the middle sections, which are best suited to mountain or hybrid bikes with thicker tires, most of the rail-trail is accessible by wheelchair. Equestrian use is allowed west of Auen Road in Conemaugh Township.

Begin your journey at the northernmost endpoint by the Kiskiminetas River. Head south to cross Blacklegs Creek, and continue 1 mile to North Park on Salt Street, where parking can be found. Traverse historic Saltsburg along the canal path to a trailhead on the east end of town. For an alternate route along the Conemaugh River, turn right off the trail onto Point Street, take a left onto Water Street, and head 0.4 mile to the trailhead. At Canal and Water Streets, this trailhead also serves as the northernmost endpoint of the 17.8-mile Westmoreland Heritage Trail (see page 262). You'll then follow the river through wooded areas and beside an active rail line for the next few bends in the pathway.

About halfway through the route, the terrain becomes hilly, making for a challenging workout. Elders Run marks the start of the 2.2-mile Dick Mayer Section stretching to

Counties
Indiana, Westmoreland

Endpoints
Urban Road, 0.5 mile north of Nowrytown Road, near Kiskiminetas River (Saltsburg) to Newport Road near Blacklick Creek, 0.25 mile north of Lakeview Dr. (Blairsville)

Mileage
15.0

Type
Rail-Trail

Roughness Index
2–3

Surface
Asphalt, Crushed Stone, Gravel

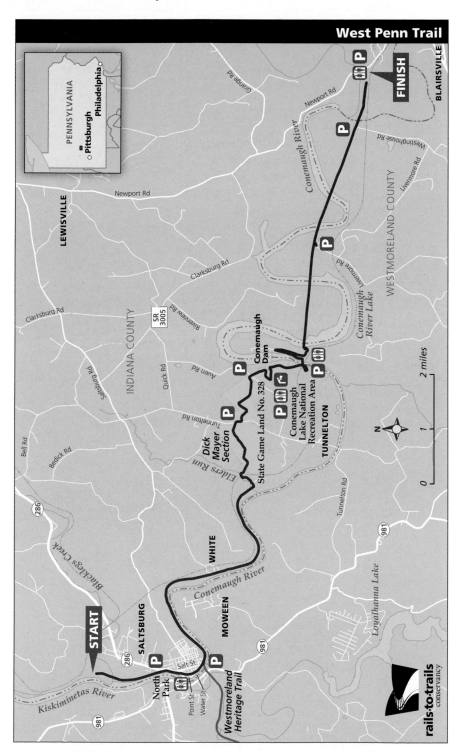

West Penn Trail

the Conemaugh Dam. Expect challenging uphill grades as you make your way up and across railroad tracks and through the forest, as well as a quick downhill stretch approaching State Route 3003/Tunnelton Road, less than a mile from Elders Run. Follow the steep zigzagging trail to the Conemaugh Lake National Recreation Area at 7.7 miles. To your left, the Conemaugh Dam offers beautiful views of the river. As portions of trail can be submerged east of the dam, especially in the spring, be sure to check the trail website for the latest conditions. Continue through the park past a visitor center, playground, parking lot, picnic area, water fountain, and restrooms.

The trail then diverges from the rail corridor onto a low-traffic shared roadway. Known as the Bow Ridge Switchback, this segment is the most challenging. Study the elevation graph provided along the path to gauge your abilities before continuing over an impressive stone-arch bridge that once carried the rail line over the Conemaugh River. After crossing the bridge and passing two sealed tunnels, the trail grows steep and rough. Continue uphill along loose gravel before switching back onto a rolling singletrack trail through wooded hillside.

In just under 0.5 mile, use extreme caution as the trail heads into a steep and narrow descent containing loose gravel and ruts. Be ready to dismount to use the staircase at the base of the hill with a side ramp for bikes. The trail continues east from the opposite end of the plugged railway tunnel across a small stone-arch bridge that is sometimes laced with flooding debris.

Although the Bow Ridge Switchback segment of the trail is challenging, the impressive views from the stone-arch bridge over the Conemaugh River are worth the effort.

The final portion of trail alternates between shady forested areas and river crossings on gravel-covered asphalt. The trail ends at a small parking area just west of a gravel access road leading to Newport Road, about 2 miles shy of cafés and refreshments in Blairsville.

CONTACT: conemaughvalleyconservancy.com/initiatives/west-penn-trail or transalleghenytrails.com/trails/west-penn-trail.aspx

---

DIRECTIONS

To reach parking near the western endpoint in Saltsburg from I-76, take Exit 57 for I-376 W/ US 22 W toward Pittsburgh. Keep right, following signs for US 22 E/Murrysville. Merge onto US 22 E, and go 1.7 miles. Take the PA 286 E/Golden Mile Hwy. exit, and go 17.4 miles. Veer right to remain on PA 286 E/Waukeena Road, which becomes PA 981 as it approaches the Kiskiminetas River. Go 1.9 miles, and turn left onto PA 286 E/Washington St. to cross the river. Go 0.2 mile, and turn left onto PA 286 E/Salt St. Parking at North Park is on the left, across from the fire department. The endpoint by Blacklegs Creek is located 1.0 mile farther north along the trail.

To reach parking at the Conemaugh Lake National Recreation Area from I-76, take Exit 57 for I-376 W/US 22 W toward Pittsburgh. Keep right, following signs for US 22 E/Murrysville. Merge onto US 22 E, and go 18.5 miles. Take a left onto PA 981 N, and follow it 4.7 miles. Turn right onto Tunnelton Road, and go just under 2 miles (the Conemaugh River will be on your left). Turn left to continue on Tunnelton Road/SR 3003, crossing the river. Go 1.0 mile, turn right onto Auen Road, and go 0.75 mile. Turn right onto the access road to the Conemaugh Lake National Recreation Area, and follow the roadway to the parking area.

To reach parking at the eastern endpoint in Blairsville from I-76, take Exit 57 for I-376 W/ US 22 W toward Pittsburgh. Keep right, following signs for US 22 E/Murrysville. Merge onto US 22 E, and go 27.4 miles. Take the exit toward PA 217/Blairsville, and turn right onto W. Ranson Ave. Go 0.2 mile, and turn right onto PA 217 N. Go 0.7 mile, and turn left onto Newport Road. After about 0.8 mile, as the roadway begins to bend north, turn left onto a small gravel driveway marked with a WEST PENN TRAIL sign. Slowly follow this gravel access road west 0.2 mile to a small parking area and trailhead.

Visitors to northwestern Philadelphia can acquaint themselves with the parks that surround Wissahickon Creek on a nearly 9-mile system of multiuse trails. In the north, the Wissahickon Trail (also known as the Green Ribbon Trail) passes along the quiet creek in Fort Washington State Park. Then a short section of roadside trail links to more dramatic scenery on the Forbidden Drive and Lincoln Drive Trails in Wissahickon Valley Park in the south. The trail ends near the creek confluence with the Schuylkill River and adjacent Schuylkill River Trail (see page 221).

The picturesque creek, whose name translates to either "catfish creek" or "stream of yellowish color" in local American Indian dialects, has been appreciated since its earliest visitors. A German immigrant and his followers came to the creek's gorge in the late 1690s to meditate and briefly set up residence in a hollow known today as Hermit's Cave. Later,

Counties
Montgomery, Philadelphia

Endpoints
E. Skippack Pike between Militia Way and Mathers Lane, State Park Road just south of SR 3005/Militia Hill Road, or 0.3 mile northeast of Valley View Road and W. Mill Road to W. Valley Green Road and Stenton Ave. (Fort Washington); W. Northwestern Ave. and Stenton Ave. to W. Northwestern Ave. and Germantown Pike (Philadelphia); Andorra Road and Thomas Road to Ridge Ave. and Lincoln Dr. (Philadelphia)

Mileage
8.5

Type
Greenway/Non-Rail-Trail

Roughness Index
1–2

Surface
Asphalt, Dirt, Gravel

Forbidden Drive was open to cars until 1920, which accounts for the wide path.

Wissahickon Valley Park Trail System

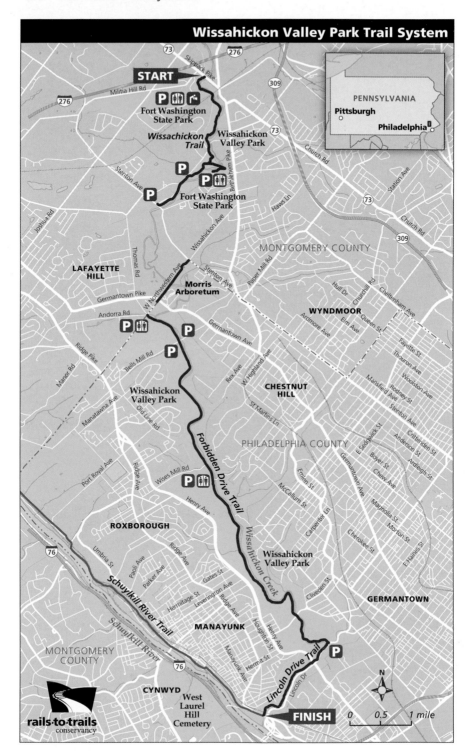

73

276

START

309

Militia Hill Rd

276

Fort Washington
State Park

PENNSYLVANIA

Pittsburgh

Philadelphia

Wissachickon Trail

Wissahickon
Valley Park

73

Church Rd

Stenton Ave

Fort Washington
State Park

Haws Ln

73

Joshua Rd

Station Ave

Church Rd

309

MONTGOMERY COUNTY

LAFAYETTE
HILL

Thomas Rd

Stenton Ave

Morris
Arboretum

Paper Mill Rd

Hull Dr

Churchill Rd

Cheltenham Ave

WYNDMOOR

Germantown Pike

Andorra Rd

Germantown Ave

Ardmore Ave

Elm Ave

Queen St

Fayette St

Thouron Ave

Woolston Ave

Ridge Pike

Bells Mill Rd

Rex Ave

W Highland Ave

CHESTNUT
HILL

Mansfield Ave

Rodney St

Stenton Ave

Manor Rd

Wissahickon
Valley Park

Old Line Rd

St Martins Ln

PHILADELPHIA COUNTY

Germantown Ave

E Sedgwick St

Boyer St

Chew Ave

Anderson St

Ardleigh St

Critterden St

Manatawna Ave

Port Royal Ave

Ridge Ave

Wises Mill Rd

Henry Ave

Forbidden Drive Trail

Emlen St

McCallum St

Carpenter Ln

Magnolia St

Cherokee St

Morton St

ROXBOROUGH

Ridge Ave

Wissahickon Creek

Wissahickon
Valley Park

Cliveden St

E Haines St

76

Umbria St

Paoli Ave

Parker Ave

Gates St

Leverington Ave

Ridge Ave

GERMANTOWN

Schuylkill River Trail

Hermitage Ave

Houghton St

Henry Ave

Hermit St

MANAYUNK

Manayunk Ave

Schuylkill River

76

MONTGOMERY
COUNTY

CYNWYD

West
Laurel
Hill
Cemetery

Lincoln Drive Trail

Lincoln Dr

N

FINISH

0   0.5   1 mile

rails·to·trails
conservancy

the creek valley underwent industrialization as entrepreneurs built dams and mills. The Philadelphia park commission began buying up sections of the valley in the late 1800s to preserve water quality downstream in the Schuylkill River, and the creek surroundings returned to a more natural state.

The Forbidden Drive and Lincoln Drive Trails are part of the Circuit Trails, a developing 800-mile urban network of trails in Greater Philadelphia, of which about 350 miles are currently complete.

The multiuse trail system starts in the north at Skippack Pike, where it enters Fort Washington State Park, named for a temporary military fortification during the Revolutionary War. Upstream, it's a walking trail that follows the creek for more than 15 miles nearly to North Wales. The 12-foot-wide multiuse trail in the state park is a combination of asphalt and gravel as it passes through lush woods laced with sunlit pockets where shrubbery thrives. Also known as the Green Ribbon Trail, it leaves the state park to travel a segment of Wissahickon Valley Park, and then returns to Fort Washington State Park–South to complete its 2.5-mile journey at Stenton Avenue.

Nearly a mile south on Stenton Avenue, another section of the trail follows alongside West Northwestern Avenue in front of the 92-acre Morris Arboretum of the University of Pennsylvania for 0.6 mile. It ends at Germantown Pike in Lafayette Hill. Montgomery County intends to extend this section another 0.2 mile to the Forbidden Drive Trailhead in Wissahickon Valley Park.

The Forbidden Drive Trail is a rare road-to-trail conversion that runs along the most spectacular section of Wissahickon Creek for 5.4 miles. Constructed in the mid-1800s as a turnpike, this roadway was renamed Forbidden Drive in 1920 when vehicles were banned from it. Today, the trail is open to walking, horseback riding, and bicycling, although the gravel and dirt surface is not suitable for bikes with skinnier tires.

A picturesque trail experience, Forbidden Drive Trail users will pass many interesting historical and natural features. Notably, the historical circa 1850 Valley Green Inn is a full-service restaurant and special events venue located 2.5 miles from the trailhead.

At the south end of the park, the 1.4-mile Lincoln Drive Trail runs on the opposite side of Wissahickon Creek from Lincoln Drive. The paved trail ends at a trailhead on Ridge Avenue, where it meets the Schuylkill River Trail.

The 2,000-acre Wissahickon Valley Park contains some 50 miles of trails. Hikers are allowed on any of them, but horseback riders, cyclists, and mountain bikers must get a special permit to use trails other than the Forbidden Drive and Lincoln Drive Trails. Permits are available at **phila.com** by searching "Natural Surface Trail Permit."

CONTACT: fow.org or montcopa.org/924/wissahickon-trail

DIRECTIONS

To reach the northern endpoint for the Wissahickon Trail in Fort Washington State Park from I-276, take Exit 339 for PA 309 S toward Philadelphia. Keep left, and follow signs for Fort Washington/Oreland. Go 0.1 mile, continue onto Pennsylvania Ave./SR 2027, and go 0.6 mile. Turn left onto S. Bethlehem Pike, go 1.0 mile, and turn right onto Mathers Lane. Go 0.1 mile, and turn right onto PA 73 W. Go 0.2 mile, and turn left onto Militia Hill Road. Go about 400 feet, and turn left onto State Park Road. Go 0.3 mile, and turn right into the parking lot. After parking, double back on State Park Road until you cross the trail in 0.2 mile.

To reach the northern endpoint for the Forbidden Drive Trail in Wissahickon Valley Park from I-476, take Exit 18A toward Conshohocken. Head southeast onto Ridge Pike. Go 3.6 miles, and turn left onto W. Northwestern Ave. Look for parking on the right in 0.7 mile. From I-76, take Exit 338. Head northeast on Green Lane to cross the Schuylkill River, and go 0.1 mile. Turn left onto Main St., and go 0.2 mile. Turn right onto Leverington Ave., and immediately turn left onto Umbria St. In 1.6 miles turn right to merge onto Shawmont Ave. Go 0.8 mile, and turn left onto Ridge Ave. In 0.5 mile keep right onto Ridge Ave. Connector, and go 0.2 mile. Turn slightly left onto Henry Ave. and continue onto Ridge Ave. Go 0.7 mile, and turn right onto W. Northwestern Ave. Look for parking on the right in 0.7 mile.

Index

Photo Credits

Page iii: TrailLink user psucsi; *page ix:* Jake Laughlin; *page x:* Milo Bateman; *page 7:* Anthony Le; *pages 9 and 10:* Tom Bilcze; *page 13:* Thomas Snow; *page 17:* TrailLink user mark.rutkowski; *page 21:* Milo Bateman; *page 22:* Vicki Schooley; *page 25:* James McGinnis; *page 27:* TrailLink user jwagner2_tl; *page 29:* James McGinnis; *page 31:* TrailLink user jdubohio; *pages 35 and 37:* Amy Kapp; *pages 39 and 40:* TrailLink user amosonu; *page 43:* Harvey Barrison; *page 44:* TrailLink user cdains; *page 47:* Jorge Brito; *page 49:* courtesy of Rail-Trail Council of NEPA; *pages 55 and 56:* Milo Bateman; *page 61:* TrailLink user peterm2413; *page 63:* Vicki Schooley; *page 67:* TrailLink user jnic; *page 68:* TrailLink user mtfuhrman; *page 71:* Vicki Schooley; *pages 75 and 76:* TrailLink user coach-anthony79; *page 79:* TrailLink user craignurmi; *pages 83 and 86:* Milo Bateman; *page 89:* Scott M. Jones; *page 91:* Jake Laughlin; *page 93:* John Gensor; *page 95:* TrailLink user amosonu; *pages 99 and 101:* courtesy of Rails to Trails of Bedford County; *pages 103 and 105:* Ken Bryan; *page 107:* TrailLink user lquinlan76; *page 112:* Nancy Kapp; *page 115:* Milo Bateman; *page 119:* TrailLink user case.gladwell; *page 121:* Anthony Le; *page 123:* Vicki Schooley; *page 127:* Anthony Le; *page 129:* Eli Griffen; *page 134:* Anthony Le; *page 137:* Jake Laughlin; *page 141:* Harvey Barrison; *page 145:* TrailLink user pgericson; *page 147:* Anthony Le; *page 151:* TrailLink user mark.rutkowski; *page 155:* TrailLink user dougel; *page 157:* Ken Bryan; *page 160:* Milo Bateman; *page 163:* Jake Laughlin; *page 167:* TrailLink user BlackCloud; *pages 169 and 171:* Jake Laughlin; *pages 173 and 175:* Yann C. Dexcoté; *page 179:* Milo Bateman; *page 181:* Harry Hunt; *page 185:* TrailLink user mkissinger07; *page 189:* TrailLink user rosetwig; *page 190:* TrailLink user trishalynn; *page 194:* TrailLink user rcpat; *page 197:* TrailLink user mkissinger07; *page 199:* TrailLink user frau blucher; *page 203:* James McGinnis; *page 205:* Suzanne Matyas; *page 209:* Ryan Cree; *page 213:* TrailLink user waterfall seeker; *pages 215 and 219:* Vicki Schooley; *pages 221 and 224:* TrailLink user rcpat; *page 227:* courtesy of the National Park Service; *page 231:* TrailLink user orangedoug; *page 233:* TrailLink user clifford.w.oliver; *page 237:* Anthony Le; *page 239:* Bob Youker; *page 241:* TrailLink user dlwertz57; *page 243:* Amy Kapp; *page 246:* Milo Bateman; *page 249:* Eli Griffen; *pages 253, 254, and 257:* Jake Laughlin; *page 259:* Eli Griffen; *pages 263 and 267:* Milo Bateman; *page 269:* TrailLink user popsknox.

Support Rails-to-Trails Conservancy

The nation's leader in helping communities transform unused rail lines and connecting corridors into multiuse trails, Rails-to-Trails Conservancy (RTC) depends on the support of its members and donors to create access to healthy outdoor experiences.

Your donation will help support programs and services that have helped put more than 24,000 rail-trail miles on the ground. Every day, RTC provides vital assistance to communities to develop and maintain trails throughout the country. In addition, RTC advocates for trail-friendly policies, promotes the benefits of rail-trails, and defends rail-trail laws in the courts.

Join online at **railstotrails.org,** or mail your donation to Rails-to-Trails Conservancy, 2121 Ward Court NW, Fifth Floor, Washington, D.C. 20037.

Rails-to-Trails Conservancy is a 501(c)(3) nonprofit organization, and contributions are tax deductible.

Find your next trail adventure on TrailLink

Visit TrailLink.com today.

TrailLink
by Rails-to-Trails Conservancy

Table of Contents

PENNSYLVANIA 7

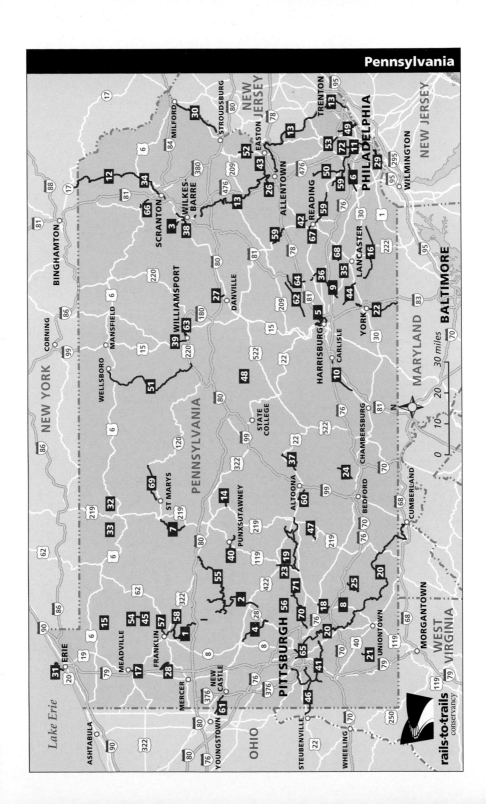

Pennsylvania

About Rails-to-Trails Conservancy

Headquartered in Washington, D.C., Rails-to-Trails Conservancy (RTC) is a nonprofit organization dedicated to creating a nationwide network of trails from former rail lines and connecting corridors to build healthier places for healthier people.

Railways helped build America. Spanning from coast to coast, these ribbons of steel linked people, communities, and enterprises, spurring commerce and forging a single nation that bridges a continent. But in recent decades, many of these routes have fallen into disuse, severing communal ties that helped bind Americans together.

When RTC opened its doors in 1986, the rail-trail movement was in its infancy. Most projects focused on single, linear routes in rural areas, created for recreation and conservation. RTC sought broader protection for the unused corridors, incorporating rural, suburban, and urban routes.

Year after year, RTC's efforts to protect and align public funding with trail building created an environment that allowed trail advocates in communities across the country to initiate trail projects. These ever-growing ranks of trail professionals, volunteers, and RTC supporters have built momentum for the national rail-trails movement. As the number of supporters multiplied, so did the rail-trails.

Americans now enjoy more than 24,000 miles of open rail-trails, and as they flock to the trails to connect with family members and friends, enjoy nature, and get to places in their local neighborhoods and beyond, their economic prosperity, health, and overall well-being continue to flourish.

A signature endeavor of RTC is **TrailLink.com,** America's portal to these rail-trails as well as other multiuse trails. When RTC launched TrailLink.com in 2000, our organization was one of the first to compile such detailed trail information on a national scale. Today, the website continues to play a critical role in both encouraging and satisfying the country's growing need for opportunities to ride, walk, skate, or run for recreation or transportation. This free trail-finder database—which includes detailed descriptions, interactive maps, photo galleries, and firsthand ratings and reviews—can be used as a companion resource to the trails in this guidebook.

With a grassroots community more than 1 million strong, RTC is committed to ensuring a better future for America made possible by trails and the connections they inspire. Learn more at **railstotrails.org.**

Rail-Trails: Pennsylvania

Maps: Lohnes+Wright; map data © OpenStreetMap contributors
Cover design: Scott McGrew
Book design and layout: Annie Long

Library of Congress Cataloging-in-Publication Data

Names: Rails-to-Trails Conservancy, author.
Title: Rail-trails : Pennsylvania : the definitive guide to the state's top multiuse trails /
　Rails-to-Trails Conservancy.
Other titles: Rail trails Pennsylvania
Description: First Edition. | Birmingham, Alabama : Wilderness Press, an imprint of
　AdventureKEEN, [2019] | Series: Rails-to-Trails Conservancy guidebook | "Distributed
　by Publishers Group West"—T.p. verso. | Includes index.
Identifiers: LCCN 2018061563| ISBN 9780899979670 (paperback) | ISBN 9780899979687
　(ebook)
Classification: LCC GV199.42.P4 R35 2019 | DDC 796.5109748—dc23
LC record available at https://lccn.loc.gov/2018061563

Manufactured in China

Published by: 🐾 **WILDERNESS PRESS**
　　　　　　　An imprint of AdventureKEEN
　　　　　　　2204 First Ave. S, Ste. 102
　　　　　　　Birmingham, AL 35233
　　　　　　　800-678-7006; fax 877-674-9016

Visit wildernesspress.com for a complete listing of our books and for ordering information. Contact us at our website, at facebook.com/wildernesspress1967, or at twitter.com
/wilderness1967 with questions or comments. To find out more about who we are and
what we're doing, visit blog.wildernesspress.com.

Distributed by Publishers Group West

Front cover: Montour Trail (see page 157), photographed by Milo Bateman; *back cover:*
D&L Trail (see page 53), photographed by Milo Bateman

SAFETY NOTICE: Although Wilderness Press and Rails-to-Trails Conservancy have
made every attempt to ensure that the information in this book is accurate at press time,
they are not responsible for any loss, damage, injury, or inconvenience that may occur to
anyone while using this book. You are responsible for your own safety and health while in
the wilderness. The fact that a trail is described in this book does not mean that it will be
safe for you. Be aware that trail conditions can change from day to day. Always check local
conditions, know your own limitations, and consult a map.

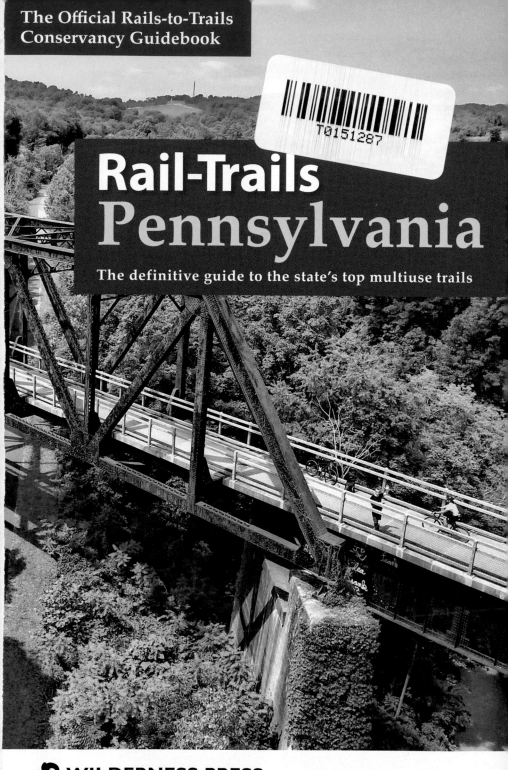

The Official Rails-to-Trails
Conservancy Guidebook

Rail-Trails
Pennsylvania

The definitive guide to the state's top multiuse trails

T0151287

🐃 **WILDERNESS PRESS** ... *on the trail since 1967*

CONTENTS

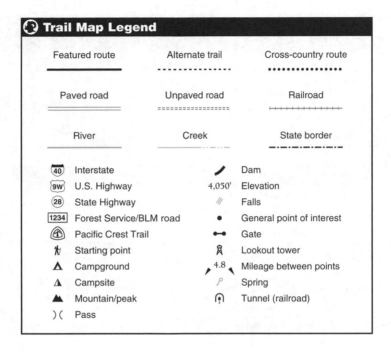

FEATURED TRIPS SUMMARY CHART

RATINGS (1–10)			LENGTH IN		ELEVATION	SHUTTLE
SCENERY	SOLITUDE	DIFFICULTY	DAYS	MILES	GAIN	MILEAGE
10	5	4	3–6	40	3,700'	43
7	6	3	3–5	47	1,626'	36
10	7	8	4–5	41	6,000'	n/a
10	8	8	5–8	63	14,900'	46
9	10	8	2–3	17	3,500'	n/a
8	8	5	5–7	53	7,400'	63
10	8	9	2–4	26	4,200'	n/a
8	9	7	2–3	22	6,500'	20
8	7	5	4	37	8,400'	25
8	6	5	3–4	27	3,500'	n/a
7	6	6	4–5	47	6,800'	34
9	6	7	4	35	7,600'	31
9	6	6	3	27	3,000'	35
7	6	7	3–6	35	5,300'	n/a
8	8	8	3–6	39	6,300'	n/a
9	6	8	4–5	40	9,400'	42
10	4	6	5–6	39	7,900'	n/a
6	7	6	3–5	29	6,000'	n/a
10	2	7	3–5	42	8,600'	n/a
10	3	6	4–6	44	6,400'	76
10	2	6	5–6	55	8,200'	n/a
6	7	6	4–6	42	4,700'	n/a
7	4	5	3–4	31	3,600'	41
9	4	6	4–6	43	8,700'	n/a
10	2	7	4–5	36	7,100'	n/a
7	4	3	3	24	1,600'	16

PREFACE

Guidebook authors face a dilemma. Without dedicated supporters, the wilderness wouldn't be protected in the first place. The best and most enthusiastic advocates are those who have actually visited the land, often with the help of a guidebook. On the other hand, too many boots can be destructive. It is the responsibility of every visitor to tread lightly on the land and to speak out strongly for its preservation.

Even land officially protected as wilderness needs continued citizen involvement. Use restrictions, grazing rights, mining claims, horse damage, and entry fees all continue to present challenges. Remember that you own this land. Treat it with respect and get involved in its management.

Almost every agency official who reviewed this material stressed the need for hikers to leave no trace of their visit. The authors believe the time has come for us to go beyond the well-known Leave No Trace principles. It must be our goal to leave behind a landscape that not only shows no trace of our presence but is also in better shape than before we arrived. Here are some guidelines:

- Leave no litter of your own. Even better, remove any litter left by others (blessedly little these days).

- Do some minor trail maintenance as you hike. Kick rocks off the trail and remove limbs and debris. Major trail maintenance problems, such as large blowdowns or washouts, should be reported to the land managers, so they can concentrate their limited dollars where those are most needed.

- *Always* camp in sites that either are compacted from years of previous use or can easily accommodate a tent without being damaged (sand, gravel bars, and densely wooded areas are best). Never camp on fragile meadow vegetation or beside lakes or streams. If you see camps being established in inappropriate places, be proactive. Place a few limbs or rocks over the area to discourage further use, scatter horse apples, and remove fire-scarred rocks. Report those who ignore the rules to rangers (or offer to help the offenders move to a better location).

- *Never* feed wildlife, and encourage others to do likewise.

- Do *not* build campfires. This holds doubly true for desert areas, where there is little fuel anyway. You don't need a fire to have a good time, and it is damaging to the land. When you discover a fire ring in an otherwise pristine area, scatter the rocks and cover the fire pit to discourage its use.

- Leave *all* of the following at home: soap (even biodegradable soap pollutes); pets (even well-mannered pets are instinctively seen as predators by wildlife); anything loud; and any outdated attitudes you may have about going out to "conquer" the wilderness.

- For environmentally conscious backpackers, one good solution to the old dilemma of how to dispose of toilet paper is to find a natural alternative. Two excellent options are the large, soft leaves of thimbleberry at lower elevations and the light green lichen that hangs from trees at higher elevations. They're not exactly Charmin soft, but they get the job done.

A WORD ABOUT THE THIRD EDITION

Thanks to the enthusiastic response of hikers in every corner of the state, *Backpacking Oregon* now goes proudly into its third edition. Fans of the first and second editions will recognize the familiar user-friendly format as well as most of the trips, but we've made a handful of changes.

All but four of the outstanding trips described in the second edition have been retained. The two extended backpacking trips on the coast that were in the previous edition have become difficult to reasonably recommend, due to parking problems, beach closures, and perilous river crossings. The Eagle Creek Fire of 2017 forced the closure of several trails in the Columbia River Gorge, including much of the loop described in the previous edition. Some of the trails in that area have reopened, but at press time, the main Eagle Creek Trail was still closed, with no time line for reopening. Similarly, massive wildfires in the Wenaha River Canyon destroyed much of that hike's scenery and appeal. We've extended our coverage of the quiet, woodsy North Umpqua Trail to make it a featured trip. In addition, the original hikes have been carefully updated to reflect changes in trail conditions, roads, phone numbers, administrative rules, and the like.

We invite all readers, whether new to hiking and this book or already wearing boots worn ragged from years of backpacking, to use this third edition as a guide to many years of great adventures in the wildlands of Oregon. We hope you enjoy touring these trails as much as we did. Please feel free to contact us, in care of Wilderness Press at the address listed on the copyright page, with your suggestions and updates, so that this book can continue to be the best and most accurate backpacking guide to the Beaver State.

INTRODUCTION

There are many ways to see and appreciate the beauty of Oregon. Many parts of the state can be seen just as easily (sometimes more efficiently) via day hikes, rafting trips, bicycle tours, or even from your car. This book, however, focuses on the best ways for backpackers to see the state. After many years and tens of thousands of trail miles, the authors have listed what they believe to be Oregon's very best backpacking trips. The emphasis is on longer trips—from three days to two weeks. These are beyond a simple weekend outing, but they make terrific vacations and give you enough time to fully appreciate the scenery. Best of all, you'll have the chance to get to know and love the country.

HOW TO USE THIS GUIDE

Each featured trip begins with an information box that provides a quick overview of the hike's vital statistics and important features. This lets you rapidly narrow down your options based on your preferences, your abilities, how many days you have available, and the time of year.

Scenery This is the authors' subjective opinion of the trip's overall scenic quality, on a 1 (an eyesore) to 10 (drop-dead gorgeous) scale. This rating is based on the authors' personal biases in favor of flowers, photogenic views, and clear streams. If your tastes run more toward lush forests or good fishing, then your own rating may be quite different. Also keep in mind that the rating is a *relative* one. All the featured trips are beautiful, and if they were somehow transplanted to, say, Nebraska, they would justifiably draw crowds of admirers.

Opposite: Toketee Falls (see Trip 11, page 74)
photographed by Becky Ohlsen

Solitude Because solitude is one of the things backpackers are seeking, it helps to know roughly how much company you can expect. This rating is also on a 1 (bring stilts to see over the crowds) to 10 (just you and the juncos) scale. Of course, even on a trip rated as a 9 or 10, there's always an outside chance that you'll end up plagued by a pack of wild Cub Scouts.

Difficulty This is yet another subjective judgment by the authors. The rating is intended to warn you away from the most difficult outings if you're not in shape to try them. The scale is only *relative to other backpacking trips*. Most Americans would find even the easiest backpacking trip to be a very strenuous undertaking. So this scale of 1 (barely leave the La-Z-Boy) to 10 (the Ironman Triathlon) is only for people already accustomed to backpacking.

Miles This item lists the total mileage of the recommended trip in its *most basic form* (with no side trips). For most trips, however, a *second* mileage number (in parentheses below) includes distances for recommended side trips. These side trips are also shown on the maps and included in the "Possible Itinerary" section. (*Note:* Some exact mileages were not available, especially for cross-country routes. The mileage shown may be only an approximation—based on extrapolation from maps or the authors' own pedometer readings.)

Elevation Gain For many hikers, how far *up* they go is even more important than the distance. This entry shows the trip's *total* elevation gain, not the *net* gain. As with the mileage section, a second number (in parentheses below the first number) includes the elevation gain in recommended side trips.

Days This is a *rough* figure for how long it will take the average backpacker to do the trip. It is based on traveling about 10 miles per day. Also considered were the spacing of available campsites and the trip's difficulty. Hard-core hikers may cover as many as 25 miles a day, while others saunter along at 4 or 5 miles per day, a good pace for hikers with children. Most trips can be done in more or fewer days, depending on your preferences and abilities.

Shuttle Mileage This is the shortest one-way driving distance between the beginning and ending trailheads. Be sure to schedule enough time at both ends of your trip to complete the necessary car shuttle.

Maps Every trip includes a sketch map that is as up-to-date and accurate as possible. As every hiker knows, however, you'll also need a good contour map of the area. This line identifies the best available map(s) for the described trip. All references to USGS maps are for the 7.5-minute series.

Usually Open This entry tells you when a trip is usually snow-free enough for hiking (which can vary considerably from year to year).

Best This note lists the particular time(s) of year when the trip is typically at its best (when the flowers peak, the fall colors are at their best, or the mosquitoes have died down,

Previous page: *Three-Fingered Jack from the Pacific Crest Trail (Trip 5)*
photographed by Douglas Lorain

Above left: *The view north from South Sister (Trip 6)*
photographed by Douglas Lorain

Left: *Duffy Lake (Trip 5)*
photographed by Becky Ohlsen

Above: *Rogue River Ranch (Trip 1)*
photographed by Becky Ohlsen

Right: *Wildflowers along the Rogue River Trail (Trip 1)*
photographed by Becky Ohlsen

Above: *Eagle Cap from Carper Pass Trail (Trip 17)*
photographed by Douglas Lorain

Left: *Diamond Peak reflected in Mountain View Lake (Trip 9)*
photographed by Douglas Lorain

Right: *Battle Ax over Elk Lake (Trip 3)*
photographed by Douglas Lorain

Above left: *The North Umpqua Wild and Scenic River (Trip 11)*
photographed by Becky Ohlsen

Left: *Himmelwright Meadow (Trip 21)*
photographed by Douglas Lorain

Above: *East Eagle Falls below Prospect Lake (Trip 20)*
photographed by Douglas Lorain

Right: *The shady, well-marked North Umpqua Trail (Trip 11)*
photographed by Becky Ohlsen

Above: *Standley Cabin (Trip 16)*
photographed by Douglas Lorain

Left: *Meadow below High Lake (Trip 13)*
photographed by Douglas Lorain

Right: *Meadow at south end of Swamp Lake (Trip 17)*
photographed by Douglas Lorain

Above left: *The Bench Trail above Pleasant Valley (Trip 23)*
photographed by Douglas Lorain

Left: *The scene from Hells Canyon Overlook (Trip 21)*
photographed by Becky Ohlsen

Above: *Owyhee Reservoir (Trip 26)*
photographed by Becky Ohlsen

Right: *Peak 9,775 over Ice Lake (Trip 18)*
photographed by Douglas Lorain

Above: *Mules hauling a wagon at Red's Horse Ranch (Trip 15)*
photographed by Douglas Lorain

Left: *Lemolo Falls (Trip 10)*
photographed by Douglas Lorain

Right: *Red's Horse Ranch (Trip 15)*
photographed by Douglas Lorain

Above left: *Bald Mountain and Washboard Ridge (Trip 16)*
photographed by Douglas Lorain

Left: *Mount Thielsen (Trip 10)*
photographed by Douglas Lorain

Above: *Red Indian paintbrush in the Honeycombs (Trip 26)*
photographed by Douglas Lorain

Right: *Swamp Lake (Trip 17)*
photographed by Douglas Lorain

Following page: *Mount Hood near Cairn Basin (Trip 4)*
photographed by Douglas Lorain

and so on). Unfortunately, the best season may also be the most crowded, so you may prefer to visit when conditions aren't as good, but you'll enjoy more solitude.

Permits Several areas require backpackers to obtain and carry permits, and other areas restrict the number of hikers allowed into traditionally crowded locations. Most of these permits are free, but a few agencies charge for them (and some are technically free but include a processing or reservation fee). Generally, you should obtain backcountry permits from the nearest U.S. Forest Service ranger station. It is always advisable to call ahead and ask about current restrictions and the need for reservations because the regulations are constantly changing.

Rules This section lists any restrictions on fires, camping, or the number of people in your party, as well as other regulations for the area.

Contact This item includes the phone number and website for the local land agency responsible for this area. Be sure to check on road and trail conditions, as well as any new restrictions or permit requirements, before your trip.

Special Attractions This section focuses on attributes of this trip that are rare or outstanding. For example, almost every trip has views, but some have views that are *especially* noteworthy. The same is true of areas with a good chance of seeing wildlife, with excellent fishing, and so on.

Challenges This is the flip side to the "Special Attractions" section. It lists the trip's special or especially troublesome problems. Expect to see warnings about areas with particularly abundant mosquitoes, poor road access, or limited water.

How to Get There This section includes driving directions to the trailhead(s), as well as GPS coordinates.

Tips, Warnings, and Notes Throughout the text are numerous helpful hints and ideas. These all result from the authors' experiences. By relying on the hard-won experience of others, these prominently labeled Tips, Warnings, and Notes will hopefully make your trips safer and more enjoyable the *first* time through.

Possible Itinerary This is listed at the *end* of each trip. To be used as a planning tool, it includes daily mileages and total elevation gains, as well as recommended side trips. Your own itinerary is likely to be different. Though the authors have hiked all the listed trips, most were not done quite as written here. If the authors were to rehike the trip, however, they would follow the improved itineraries here.

WILD AREAS OF OREGON

What follows is a general overview of the principal remaining wild areas in the state of Oregon. All of these have at least one backpacking trip in the featured trips section. Thus, whether you're a desert rat, a mountain man, or a canyon lover, there's a choice of outstanding trips for you.

It is appropriate here to say a few words about Crater Lake, probably the best-known scenic attraction in the state. It is also the only major natural wonder for which there is no recommended trip. Construction of the rim road around the lake created one of the most spectacular drives in North America and simultaneously eliminated any chance for developing what would have been one of the most spectacular *hikes* on the continent. Today the national park features only short (but very scenic) day hikes. The only backpacking is through generally viewless forests, well away from the lake, with little to recommend it other than solitude. The best plan is to visit the park (it really is too good to miss), take a day hike or two, and then head for the longer trails in the nearby Mount Thielsen, Rogue River, or Sky Lakes area.

Similarly, the Oregon coast is world-famous and unmissable, but a few recent developments have made it difficult to backpack here. As with Crater Lake, your best bet is to explore the coast via day hikes, then continue inland for extended backpacking trips. Countless tourists drive up and down this shoreline enjoying some of the continent's best scenery. The coastal highway has also become a popular bicycle tour. Hikers are also drawn to the coast's abundant and diverse wildlife. Long before we *Homo sapiens* built summer homes at the beach, it attracted numerous other species. Keep an eye out for whales, harbor seals, and sea lions. Tidepools teem with life in a dizzying array of forms and colors. The Oregon coast is especially popular with our feathered friends. The cliffs and offshore rocks here support some 1.3 million nesting birds—more than the coasts of California and Washington *combined*, even though the total shorelines of those two states is almost five times longer. Nesting bird numbers peak from about mid-May to the end of June.

NOTE: All offshore rocks are part of a protected wildlife refuge and are strictly off-limits to people. Bring binoculars to get a close-up view.

Visiting midweek will help you avoid crowds, but the best plan is to hike in the off-season. The beach is a great place to visit during a patch of good weather in the winter and is equally scenic in fall (after Labor Day) or spring (before Memorial Day). Whenever you visit, remember to prepare for the notoriously volatile Oregon weather.

KLAMATH AND SISKIYOU MOUNTAINS

Most of southwestern Oregon is a jumbled mass of ancient mountains cut by scenic river canyons. These mountains are much older than the better-known Cascades or Wallowas, and their peculiar geology and botany are a large part of their charm. Unique soils and millions of years of isolation have resulted in Oregon's greatest concentration of rare and unusual plants. This region is truly a botanist's paradise.

The higher Siskiyou Mountains to the east are friendlier terrain for hikers. They feature less steep trails, small lakes, diverse forests, and cooler summer temperatures. Both ranges provide lots of solitude, wildflowers, and surprisingly abundant wildlife.

WESTERN "OLD" CASCADES

Only a couple of generations ago, the Western "Old" Cascades were still a vast forested wilderness. Huge old-growth forests, crystal-clear streams, rugged ridges, and small mountain lakes were just some of the treasures that have now been largely replaced by clear-cuts and logging roads. Only tiny fragments of the old forests remain, either in isolated preserves or as forested strips near highways or rivers. Exploring the Old Cascades now is best done in the form of day hikes. Backpackers have the option of hiking longer river trails (usually paralleling roads) or seeking out one of the larger preserves that still have a good sampling of what's left. Two such areas are the Bull of the Woods and Middle Santiam Wildernesses.

Elevations are lower here than in the nearby High Cascades, so the trails are free of snow sooner and stay open later. The most attractive times to visit are from mid-June to mid-July, when the rhododendrons bloom, and autumn, with its sprinkling of color and mushrooms. There are no spectacular jagged peaks to admire, but this country is ideal for the spiritual renewal you get from a cathedral-like forest, clear fishing streams, uncrowded trails, and lush vegetation.

Generally off-trail travel is difficult to impossible, though the occasional elk or deer path can be followed. Stick to the maintained routes or follow streambeds during the lower water of autumn. Finally, you'll need to bring a good up-to-date map to find trailheads amid the maze of logging roads.

HIGH CASCADES

Many of the trips in this guide are in the High Cascades—centered on well-known volcanic peaks like Mount Hood, Mount Jefferson, and the Three Sisters. These are the signature mountains of the state, and they deserve their popularity. All feature excep-

Mount Yoran over Divide Lake
(see Trip 9, page 61)
photographed by Douglas Lorain

tional scenery, wildflower-filled meadows, and miles of trails. Even backpacking snobs who avoid any trail with the slightest whiff of popularity can't resist doing a classic trip like the Timberline Trail at least once in a lifetime. The peaks in the south part of the range are lower and lack glaciers, but they are also less crowded. Between these peaks, the High Cascades showcase great expanses of forests and numerous lakes. Fortunately, most of the best areas have been set aside as wilderness, so backpackers can enjoy many days of scenic travel without the intrusion of roads, chain saws, or motorbikes.

The ultimate way to experience these mountains is to hike from one end of the state to the other along the Pacific Crest Trail. A total of 380 trail miles (excluding side trips) extend from Fish Lake (east of Medford) to the Columbia River at Cascade Locks. Most people have neither the time nor the energy to tackle this monthlong excursion. A few well-chosen backpacking vacations of 4–10 days, however, can hit all the highlights and provide enough memories to last a lifetime.

Summer in the Oregon Cascades is just about ideal. While you should come prepared for rain, your chances of encountering endless days of wetness are actually rather small, despite all those stories we tell out-of-staters in an effort to keep them out. You should expect rain perhaps one day in four, and it is even possible to go weeks without any rain. Temperatures are usually in the comfortable range (both day and night) with low humidity. Flowers bloom in profusion, and the quiet hiker has a good chance of seeing wildlife. There are no dangerous animals to worry about because rattlesnakes are found on the east side only at lower elevations, and grizzly bears have been gone for more than a century. Even horse flies and deer flies—so abundant in other parts of North America—are rarely a problem in these mountains. The only issues worth mentioning are mosquitoes (particularly in the lake country) and the need to get permits for some areas, as land managers slowly try to reduce the impact of too many visitors.

BLUE MOUNTAINS

For the most part, northeastern Oregon's Blue Mountains are a gentle region of rolling mountains, open forests, and enticing meadows. In places, however, subranges with snowy crags and sparkling lakes reach dramatically skyward. Elsewhere, rivers have cut impressive canyons into the lava tablelands. At these special places, backpackers can savor not only grand scenery but also lightly traveled trails.

The Wallowas (see the subsection below) are the best-known mountains in this area, but the Strawberry Mountains and the Elkhorn Range have very similar scenery with only a fraction of the people. Like the Wallowas, these smaller and more compact ranges showcase craggy granite peaks, sparkling lakes, meadows ablaze with wildflowers, and wildlife such as elk, bighorn sheep, and mountain goats. *Unlike* in the Wallowas, hikers won't have to face trails pounded to dust by heavy horse use or compete with hundreds of other hikers for a campsite.

A big advantage for hikers accustomed to the jungles of the Western Cascades is the open nature of the forests here. The drier climate means less undergrowth, so cross-country travel is much easier. The weather is also generally better, except for afternoon thunderstorms. Mosquitoes present the usual problems near lakes in July, and rattlesnakes are common in the lower canyons.

WALLOWA MOUNTAINS

Though billed as America's Little Switzerland, the Wallowa Mountains of northeastern Oregon are actually more similar to California's Sierra Nevada. (That comparison, however, apparently doesn't carry the same marketing appeal.) The mountains are a stunningly beautiful mix of white granite peaks, shimmering lakes and streams, alpine meadows, and attractive forests. Even better, God seemingly designed this paradise with backpackers in mind. The bulk of the most scenic country is beyond the range of day hikers. For long-distance hikers, however, the Eagle Cap Wilderness is laced with hundreds of miles of interconnecting trails. Because more than 75% of all visits are to the Lakes Basin, Aneroid Lake, and Glacier Lake areas, there are many miles of lonesome trails in other areas to explore.

Relative to the region's attributes, the downsides are so minor that only a true pessimist could dwell on them. Nonetheless, you should be prepared for crowds in a few areas, mosquitoes near the lakes in July, afternoon thunderstorms, and dusty (and aromatic) trails due to fairly heavy horse use.

Most of the range's many highlights are within the areas of the described trips. If, like the authors, you develop a love for this country and want to see more, there are dozens of additional places to explore. Almost any chosen destination will reward you with beautiful scenery and wonderful memories.

HELLS CANYON

The vastness of Hells Canyon is impossible to describe. Neither words nor photographs seem able to capture it adequately. One must personally experience the area to properly appreciate it. Unlike the heavily forested trails familiar to most Oregonians, the mostly treeless routes here present nonstop great views. The gaping chasm, backed by the snow-capped peaks of Idaho's Seven Devils Mountains, presents an incredible expanse of jaw-dropping scenery. The canyon is also one of the best areas for viewing wildlife in the state. Elk, deer, black bears, coyotes, bighorn sheep, mountain goats (on the Idaho side), numerous birds, and various reptiles are all common.

Like the canyon itself, the problems associated with backpacking in Hells Canyon are also on a grand scale. Summer's heat in the shadeless lower canyon is unbearable. Rattlesnakes, ticks, and black widow spiders are all common, and the canyon supports large populations of black bears and mountain lions. Though no one has been attacked, hikers have reported being stalked by lions. Thickets of poison ivy crowd the lower-elevation trails near water. Even the main trails are often rough, steep, and hard to follow, and lesser-used paths may be nothing more than rumors. Access roads (when they exist at all) are typically long, rough, dirt roads that may be impassable for passenger cars and should generally not be attempted when wet. This is truly the realm of the dedicated adventurer.

Three roughly parallel trails travel the entire north-south length of the canyon. Each is described in the text. Because they are at different elevations, they have different peak seasons. Numerous connecting paths allow for loop trips of almost any length.

SOUTHEAST OREGON MOUNTAINS

Oregon is famous for its dense green forests, rain-soaked valleys, and glacier-clad peaks. Not so well known is that fully one-third of the state is desert. Brown, not green, is the predominant color of southeastern Oregon. Trees are either scarce or nonexistent. Rain falls infrequently, and glaciers are just a distant memory.

Though the landscape differs from western Oregon, it is at least as scenic. The country is especially appealing to those who prefer open views to the claustrophobic feel of dense forests, and dry weather to overcast and drizzle. The principal attractions for backpackers are the mountain ranges that rise dramatically from the sagebrush plains. These spectacular mountains have water (due to more precipitation at higher elevations), lots of flowers, and vistas that seem to stretch to eternity. Most of the mountains also have few (if any) people. Wildlife is no more abundant here than elsewhere in Oregon, but the lack of dense vegetation makes it much easier to actually *see* the animals.

The best known and most spectacular mountain is Steens Mountain, with its great glacial gorges and towering snowy cliffs. Other nearby ranges like the Pueblo, Hart, and

Trout Creek Mountains provide more solitude for those who want to gain a more meaningful distance from the world of crowds and machines. To truly get away from it all, just head off into the seemingly endless sagebrush. A few of the more interesting areas to consider are Beatys Butte, Orejana Canyon, Coyote Lake, Hawk Mountain, Oregon End Table, and Diablo Peak. If you can even find these places on the map, you'll be well on your way to your own desert adventure.

Those unaccustomed to desert travel must beware of some unique hazards. Expect rattlesnakes, ticks (*extremely* abundant in spring), long distances between water sources, poorly maintained roads, and few (if any) established trails.

OWYHEE COUNTRY

Hidden in southeastern Oregon near the Idaho border is a land that looks more typical of southern Utah than Oregon. Several spectacularly deep slot canyons and colorful rock formations cut into the sagebrush plains and mountains of this region. The cliffs host bighorn sheep, while pronghorns and wild horses roam the plateaus. It all adds up to a stunningly scenic land, with the added advantage of being a great place to go for solitude. There are *no* crowds here; in fact you are unlikely to see another human being in weeks of hiking.

The isolation creates unique problems requiring extra precautions. The only trails are those traveled by deer or cattle, so at least one group member must be very good with a map and compass (you might consider bringing a GPS device). Many of the "roads" here are very poor, especially if wet, and rarely traveled. Carry plenty of emergency gear in your car—extra food, *lots* of extra water, spare parts and tools, and so on. Bring along an especially well-stocked first aid kit (and, of course, you *are* up-to-date on your first aid methods and skills, right?). Except for the bottoms of major river canyons, water is very scarce. In addition, the canyon country throughout southeastern Oregon gets extremely hot during the summer season (June–mid-September). Carry *at least* 3 gallons of water in your car, and a gallon per day when hiking. You should always assume water sources are badly polluted by livestock—*double treat* all water. The authors' preference is to first use iodine, wait, and then filter it.

The above precautions aside, this area is well worth the extra effort to explore. Spring (late April–May) is especially nice, with wildflowers, cooler temperatures, and more water. To hike the canyons, however, fall is usually better because water levels are lower and you won't have to do as much wading.

SAFETY NOTICE

The trips described in this book are long and often difficult, and some go through remote wilderness terrain. In the event of an emergency, supplies and medical facilities may be several days away. Anyone who attempts these hikes must be experienced in wilderness travel, properly equipped, and in good physical condition. While backpacking is not inherently dangerous, the sport *does* involve risk. Because trail conditions, weather, and hikers' abilities all vary considerably, the authors and the publisher cannot assume responsibility for the safety of anyone who takes these hikes. Use plenty of common sense and a realistic appraisal of your abilities so you can enjoy these trips safely.

References to water in the text attest only to its availability, not its purity. All backcountry water should be treated before drinking.

POISONOUS PLANTS

Recognizing poison ivy and oak and avoiding contact with them are the most effective ways to prevent the painful, itchy rashes associated with these plants. Poison ivy ranges from a thick, tree-hugging vine to a shaded ground cover, 3 leaflets to a leaf; poison oak occurs as either a vine or shrub, with 3 leaflets as well. Urushiol, the oil in the sap of these plants, is responsible for the rash. Usually within 12–14 hours of exposure (but sometimes much later), raised lines and/or blisters will appear, accompanied by a terrible itch. Refrain from scratching because bacteria under fingernails can cause infection. Wash and dry the rash thoroughly, applying a calamine lotion or other product to help dry out the rash. If itching or blistering is severe, seek medical attention. Remember that oil-contaminated clothes, pets, or hiking gear can easily cause an irritating rash on you or someone else, so wash not only any exposed parts of your body but also clothes, gear, and pets.

MOSQUITOES

Mosquitoes are common in Oregon, especially spring–midsummer. Though it's very rare, individuals can become infected with the West Nile virus by being bitten by an infected mosquito. Culex mosquitoes, the primary varieties that can transmit West Nile virus to humans, thrive in urban rather than natural areas. They lay their eggs in stagnant water and can breed in any standing water that remains for more than five days. Most people infected with West Nile virus have no symptoms of illness, but some may become ill, usually 3–15 days after being bitten.

Anytime you expect mosquitoes to be buzzing around, you may want to wear protective clothing, such as long sleeves, long pants, and socks. Loose-fitting, light-colored clothing is best. Spray clothing with insect repellent. Remember to follow the instructions on the repellent and to take extra care to protect children against these insects.

SNAKES

In some of the regions described in this book, you may encounter venomous rattlesnakes. They like to bask in the sun and won't bite unless threatened. Hibernation season is typically October–April. Most of the snakes you will see while hiking, however, will be non-venomous species and subspecies. The best rule is to leave all snakes alone, give them a wide berth as you hike past, and make sure any hiking companions (including dogs) do the same. When hiking, stick to well-used trails, and wear over-the-ankle boots and loose-fitting long pants. Do not step or put your hands beyond your range of detailed visibility, and avoid wandering around in the dark. Step onto logs and rocks, never over them, and be especially careful when climbing rocks. Always avoid walking through dense brush or willow thickets.

TICKS

Ticks are often found on brush and tall grass, where they seem to be waiting to hitch a ride on a warm-blooded passerby. Adult ticks are most active April–May and again October–November. Among the varieties of ticks, the black-legged tick, commonly called the deer tick, is the primary carrier of Lyme disease, but documented cases of Lyme in Oregon are uncommon. Ticks here are more a nuisance than a serious health risk (though tick bites always carry the risk of infection, so properly disinfecting the area is key). Wear light-colored clothing to make it easier for you to spot ticks before they migrate to your skin.

At the end of the hike, visually check your hair, back of neck, armpits, and socks. During your posthike shower, take a moment to do a more complete body check. For ticks that are already embedded, removal with tweezers is best. Grasp the tick close to your skin, and remove it by pulling straight out firmly. Do your best to remove the head, but do not twist. Use disinfectant solution on the wound.

BLACK BEARS

Though attacks by black bears are uncommon, the sight or approach of a bear can give anyone a start. If you encounter a bear while hiking, remain calm and avoid running in any direction. Make loud noises to scare off the bear, and back away slowly. In primitive and remote areas, assume bears are present. Most encounters are food related, as bears have an exceptional sense of smell and not particularly discriminating tastes. Hang all food (and anything else with an odor) at night and any time you leave your camp unattended; consider renting a bear canister—it adds weight but also convenience. Several campsites have bear boxes or electric fences; take advantage of these.

GENERAL TIPS ON BACKPACKING IN OREGON

This book is not a how-to guide for backpackers. Anyone contemplating an extended backpacking vacation will (or at least *should*) already know about equipment, Leave No Trace principles, conditioning, selecting a campsite, first aid, and all the other aspects of this sport. Myriad excellent books cover these subjects. It is appropriate, however, to discuss some tips and ideas that are specific to Oregon and the Pacific Northwest.

1) Most national forests in Oregon require a trailhead parking pass (Northwest Forest Pass). In general, a windshield sticker or pass is required for cars parked within 0.25 mile of major developed trailheads. As of 2018, daily permits cost $5, and an annual pass, good in all the forests of Oregon and Washington, was $30 (actually a pretty good deal). The fees are used for trail maintenance, wilderness rangers' pay, and trailhead improvements. You can order the passes online at discovernw.org or buy them at ranger stations and many outdoors stores.

2) The winter's snowpack has a significant effect not only on when a trail opens but also on peak wildflower times, peak stream flows, and how long seasonal water sources will be available. You can check the snowpack around April 1 and note how it compares to normal. This information is available through the local media or by contacting the Oregon Snow Survey office in Portland (503-414-3271; nrcs.usda.gov/wps/portal/nrcs/main /or/snow). If the snowpack is significantly above or below average, adjust the trip's seasonal recommendations accordingly.

3) When driving on Oregon's forest roads, keep a wary eye out for log trucks. These scary behemoths often barrel along with little regard for those annoying speed bumps known as passenger cars.

4) The Northwest's frequent winter storms create annual problems for trail crews. Early-season hikers should expect to crawl over deadfall and search for routes around landslides and flooded riverside trails. Depending on current funding and the trail's popularity, maintenance may not be completed until several weeks after a trail is snow free and officially open. Unfortunately, this means that trail maintenance is often done well after the best time to visit. On the positive side, trails are usually less crowded before the maintenance has been completed.

5) Mid-August is usually the best time for swimming in mountain lakes. Water temperatures (while never exactly tropical) are at their warmest, and the bugs have decreased enough to allow you to dry off in relative peace. A swimsuit makes a good addition to your gear for any trip to the mountains at this time of year, or you can go with a birthday suit in less popular areas.

6) General deer-hunting season in Oregon runs from the first weekend of October to the end of the month or early November. Also, for a week in early to mid-September, Oregon holds a High Cascades deer hunt in the wilderness areas of the Cascade Mountains. For safety, anyone planning to travel in the forests during these periods (particularly those doing any cross-country travel) should carry and wear a bright red or orange cap, vest, pack, or other conspicuous article of clothing.

7) Elk-hunting season is in late October or, more often, early November. The exact season varies in different parts of the state.

8) Mushrooms are an Oregon backcountry delicacy. Though our damp climate makes it possible to find mushrooms in any season, late August–November is usually best. Where and when the mushrooms can be found varies with elevation, precipitation, and other factors.

> **WARNING:** Make absolutely sure that you know your fungi. Several poisonous species exist in our forests, and you do not want to make a mistake.

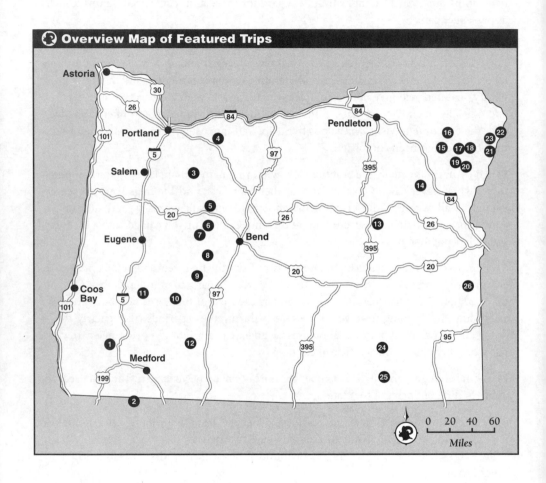

Astoria

30

26

101

Portland

84

Pendleton

84

4

97

16

23 22

15 17 18

21

5

Salem

3

395

19 20

14

5

20

Bend

26

7

13

26

8

395

20

9

26

Coos
Bay

11

10

97

20

101

5

95

1

12

Medford

395

24

199

25

2

0 20 40 60

Miles

Opposite: Three-Fingered Jack above Santiam Lake
(see Trip 5, page 37)

FEATURED TRIPS

1

ROGUE RIVER TRAIL

RATINGS: Scenery 10   **Solitude** 5   **Difficulty** 4

MILES: 40

ELEVATION GAIN: 3,700'

DAYS: 3–6

SHUTTLE MILEAGE: 43

MAPS: USFS *Rogue River National Forest Oregon* and *Powers and Gold Beach Ranger Districts;* USGS *Mount Reuben* and *Bunker Creek*

USUALLY OPEN: Year-round (may be unhikable in some winters)

BEST: Late April–May and late October–early November

PERMITS: None

RULES: Fires within 400 feet of the river must use a raised fire pan. Check for current fire regulations with the Smullin Visitor Center at Rand, 541-479-3735, or the Gold Beach Ranger District, 541-247-3600, before you start your trip.

CONTACT: Grants Pass Office, Bureau of Land Management, 541-471-6500, blm.gov/office/grants-pass-interagency-office; Gold Beach Ranger District, Rogue River–Siskiyou National Forest, 541-247-3600, www.fs.usda.gov /rogue-siskiyou

SPECIAL ATTRACTIONS ●

Outstanding river and canyon scenery, whitewater rafters to watch, waterfalls, wildlife, fall colors

Above: Quail Creek Bridge
photographed by Becky Ohlsen

CHALLENGES

Profuse poison oak, rattlesnakes, ticks, summer heat, camp-raiding black bears

HOW TO GET THERE

To reach the Grave Creek (upstream) trailhead, take I-5 N to Exit 76. Take a left and then an immediate right onto Old OR 99, and go 0.5 mile. Turn left onto Front Street; Front Street turns left and becomes Lower Wolf Creek Road in 0.1 mile. Then follow the directions below. From I-5 S, take Exit 76, and turn right onto Old OR 99. In 0.2 mile, turn right onto Front Street; Front Street turns left and becomes Lower Wolf Creek Road in 0.1 mile.

Continue another 5.6 miles on Lower Wolf Creek Road, and go straight on Lower Grave Creek Road. Drive 8.9 miles west to the Grave Creek Bridge. Parking is available on the north shore at the signed trailhead and boat ramp, but cars left there overnight may be ticketed. You're allowed to park overnight along the road on the other side of the river, but rangers warn of rockslides and vandalism. A better option may be to park overnight ($5 daily fee) at Almeda Campground, 5 miles upriver along Galice Road (open April–November).

To reach the lower (downstream) trailhead from Gold Beach along US 101, just south of the Rogue River, drive northeast on County Road 595 (variously Jerrys Flat Road and Rogue River Road) for 9.8 miles. Continue straight on what is now Agness Road/Forest Service Road 33 for 20.9 miles. Turn right onto CR 375 just after the bridge over the river, and drive 3.5 miles to the Foster Bar trailhead. Overnight parking is free at the Foster Bar trailhead/boat launch.

GPS TRAILHEAD COORDINATES:

(Grave Creek) N42° 38.892' W123° 35.034'

(Foster Bar) N42° 38.306' W124° 03.344'

INTRODUCTION

Southern Oregon's Rogue River has earned a special place in the hearts of whitewater rafters. The 40-mile float trip from Grave Creek to Illahe is one of the most popular in the country, and it's easy to understand why. This wild canyon provides continuously spectacular scenery, waterfalls, unusually abundant wildlife, and plenty of thrilling rapids. The Bureau of Land Management (BLM) has a lottery system in place to regulate the number of people on the river. For backpackers there is an equally scenic way to see this roadless canyon. The Rogue River Trail has no crowds and requires no permits. The route parallels the north bank of the river for the entire distance. It is unquestionably one of Oregon's most exciting long backpacking trips.

WARNINGS: While the hike is undeniably outstanding, there are more than a few difficulties to keep in mind. Refer to pages 9–10 for more information about poison oak, ticks, rattlesnakes, and bears.

Poison oak is profuse along the entire length of the trail, and it can be difficult to avoid. Ticks and rattlesnakes are also fairly common.

ⓡ **Rogue River Trail**

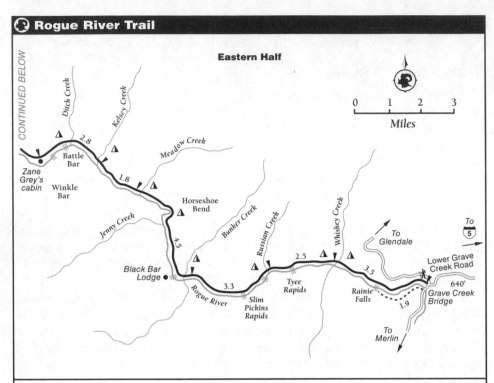

Eastern Half

CONTINUED BELOW

Ditch Creek
Kelsey Creek
Meadow Creek

0   1   2   3
Miles

Zane
Grey's
cabin

2.8
Battle Bar
Winkle Bar

1.8

Jenny Creek

Horseshoe
Bend

4.5

Black Bar
Lodge

Bunker Creek
Russian Creek
Whiskey Creek

Rogue River

3.3

Slim
Pickins
Rapids

Tyee
Rapids

2.5

Rainie
Falls

1.9

3.5

To
Glendale

To
5

Lower Grave
Creek Road

640'
Grave Creek
Bridge

To
Merlin

Western Half

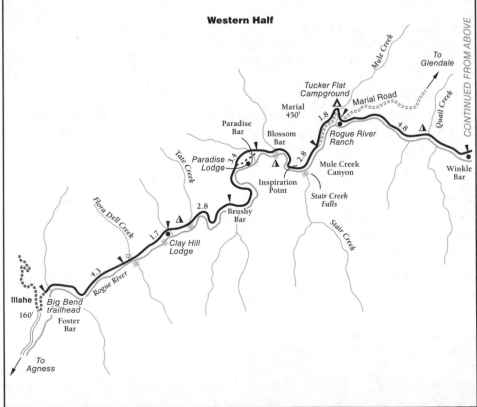

Mule Creek

To
Glendale

Tucker Flat
Campground

Marial
450'

Paradise
Bar

Blossom
Bar

Marial Road

1.8

Rogue River
Ranch

4.8

Quail Creek

CONTINUED FROM ABOVE

Tate Creek

Paradise
Lodge

3.4

Inspiration
Point

2.8

Mule Creek
Canyon

Stair Creek
Falls

Winkle
Bar

Flora Dell Creek

2.8

Brushy
Bar

Stair Creek

1.7

Clay Hill
Lodge

4.3

Rogue River

Illahe
160'

Big Bend
trailhead

Foster
Bar

To
Agness

Black bears have become used to raiding the camps of river rafters for food. The bruins are more of a problem here than anywhere else in the state. Several of the campsites have bear boxes or electric fences; take advantage of these.

Avoid this trail in midsummer—the heat can be unbearable. Most of the trail is on sunny south-facing slopes, so bring a hat and plenty of sunscreen.

Probably the best way to see and enjoy the canyon is to hike upstream from Illahe to Grave Creek and then float down the river back to your car. The logistics of this plan, however, are rather complicated. For those who just want to hike the trail, an excellent option is to hike downstream and then use a shuttle service to take you back to your car. Make arrangements with any of several commercial operators.

TIP: Many shuttle services will both drive you to the starting trailhead and pick you up at the end. This way you can leave your car at a safer location near the operator's business rather than the trailhead parking lot; prices start around $125.

DESCRIPTION

From the Grave Creek trailhead, the hiker-only trail starts with an easy stroll over mostly open slopes well above the river. Twisted oak trees provide frames for canyon photographs. You pass frothing Grave Creek Rapids and then, at the 1.9-mile mark, reach Rainie Falls. Most rafters avoid running this dangerous section by using ropes to walk their boats over a fish-diversion channel. A short side path leads to the base of this cascade. The main trail continues downstream, passes a nice sandy beach (a popular campsite for boaters), and then goes inland to the footbridge over Whiskey Creek. A short spur trail to the right leads to a historical cluster of mining machinery and an old cabin—well worth exploring. There are good camps near here for hikers setting a leisurely pace. The best camps are on a bench 0.4 mile west of Whiskey Creek.

To continue your tour, keep going west along the well-graded up-and-down trail, generally staying on slopes 50–100 feet above the river. Pass Russian Creek's camps 2.5 miles from Whiskey Creek and then Slim Pickins Rapids in a narrow section of the canyon. After crossing Bunker Creek on a large bridge (good camp here) and passing Black Bar Lodge, the trail begins to climb and enters a thicker forest of firs and maples on its way to Horseshoe Bend, where there are nice camps and a good view of this large loop in the river. More good camps tempt the hiker at Meadow Creek, but the ones just before the bridge over Kelsey Creek are even better. After passing Ditch Creek (a small camp here) and Battle Bar, the trail traverses an open grassy bench at Winkle Bar. Here you can take a peek into a log fishing cabin and a few outbuildings once owned by Zane Grey (1872–1939), the famous Western author. The cabin, listed on the National Register of Historic Places, is managed by the BLM, but hikers are asked to refrain from camping or backpacking there.

Near Quail Creek (nice campsite here) the trail returns to river level at a sandy beach.

The path now climbs back up the slope to detour around a slide and then passes through a 1970 burn area before reaching Rogue River Ranch, 23 miles from Grave Creek. This historic home, located in a pretty valley and now a museum, is listed on the National Register of Historic Places. It is accessible by car via Marial Road, so don't expect to be lonesome. Normally drinking water is available at the ranch, but on a recent hike the filtration system was being upgraded, and no potable water was available until further notice, so plan ahead.

TIP: Be sure to schedule some time to tour the restored ranch and nearby exhibits, which include a blacksmith shop and tack house.

The Rogue River "Trail" now follows roads for a short distance as it climbs to Marial Road, crosses a bridge over Mule Creek near the six-spot Tucker Flat car campground, and then follows the deteriorating dirt road to its end and the resumption of trail.

The lower canyon section from Marial to Illahe is even more dramatic and interesting than the upper canyon. In addition to the improved scenery, two trailside lodges welcome hungry hikers.

WARNING: Jet boats use this section of the river (at least as far up as Paradise Bar), so hikers can expect the tranquility to be interrupted occasionally by the roar of powerboats.

You reach one of the major highlights of the lower river not long after the Marial trailhead. Beyond a short stretch through forests, you break out and follow a trail that has been blasted into the cliffs above very narrow Mule Creek Canyon. At aptly named Inspiration Point, savor a breathtaking view of this slot canyon. Adding even more to an already tremendous scene is Stair Creek Falls, dropping into the river across from you. After rounding this dramatic section, the trail reenters forests and then drops a bit to Blossom Bar.

TIP: Be sure to visit the river here, as these rapids are challenging for rafters. It's great fun to watch them run the whitewater. Nice camps are near Blossom Bar Creek.

Continuing the trip, you soon reach Paradise Lodge on a large meadowy flat above the river. Hikers can stop for lunch or even spend the night—but you'll need to make reservations *well* in advance by calling 888-667-6483 or visiting paradise-lodge.com. Jet boats make scheduled stops here May 1–October 31. If you choose not to visit Paradise Lodge, the official trail detours around the meadow, staying in the perimeter forest.

TIP: Watch and listen for wild turkeys in this area.

After Paradise Lodge the trail follows the river around a prominent bend as the path cuts across a ridge called Devils Backbone, which provides lots of good canyon views. The trail then crosses Brushy Bar—a forested flat that includes a ranger cabin, a creek, and several good campsites.

WARNING: Black bears are numerous in this area.

From Brushy Bar the trail climbs to a historic high point signed CAPTAIN TICHENOR'S DEFEAT. In 1856 Takelma Indians overwhelmed a group of Army soldiers under the captain's command by simply rolling rocks down the steep slopes onto the troops. Drop to Solitude Bar, another good place for viewing rafters, and then continue to the bridge over Tate Creek. Just below the bridge is a lovely waterfall. You will find good camps here and 0.1 mile farther at Camp Tacoma. For more luxurious accommodations, try Clay Hill Lodge (reservations are crucial: 503-859-3772; clayhilllodge.com) about 0.5 mile ahead.

The trail crosses a long, sparsely forested section with plenty of river views on its way to Flora Dell Creek. Twenty-foot-high Flora Dell Falls has created an idyllic little fern-lined grotto and swimming hole just above the trail. Plan on spending extra time here to cool off and enjoy the scenery. The falls is a common day hike goal for people coming upriver from the Foster Bar trailhead.

The final stretch of trail remains very scenic as it crosses open slopes with nice river views, especially of Big Bend. The trail climbs some 350 feet to make a detour around a landslide, but otherwise the hiking is easy. Impressive old-growth forests and several splashing side creeks add to the scenery. The last 0.5 mile passes an old apple orchard near the former Billings homestead. You may have to walk down the road a bit to reach the Foster Bar boat ramp, where commercial float-trip operators take out their rafts for the shuttle back to Grave Creek.

POSSIBLE ITINERARY

	CAMP	MILES	ELEVATION GAIN
Day 1	Russian Creek	6.0	500'
Day 2	Battle Bar/Ditch Creek	10.8	2,000'
Day 3	Blossom Bar	10.3	1,700'
Day 4	Out	12.9	900'

Zane Grey's cabin
photographed by Becky Ohlsen

SISKIYOU–BOUNDARY TRAIL

RATINGS: Scenery 8   **Solitude** 7   **Difficulty** 5

MILES: 37 (41)

ELEVATION GAIN: 8,400' (10,000')

DAYS: 4 (4–5)

SHUTTLE MILEAGE: 25

MAPS: USFS *Red Buttes Wilderness;* USGS *Grayback Mountain*

USUALLY OPEN: Mid-June–October

BEST: Late June–mid-July

PERMITS: None

RULES: Maximum group size of 8 people/12 stock; no camping within 100 feet of lakes; no camping or fires within the boundaries of the Azalea Lake Loop Trail

CONTACT: Siskiyou Mountains Ranger District, Rogue River–Siskiyou National Forest, 541-899-3800, www.fs.usda.gov/rogue-siskiyou

SPECIAL ATTRACTIONS •

Solitude, expansive views, wildlife, unusual geology and botany

CHALLENGES •

Black bears are common (hang all food and avoid areas with recent signs of bears); cattle

Above: Lonesome Lake
photographed by Douglas Lorain

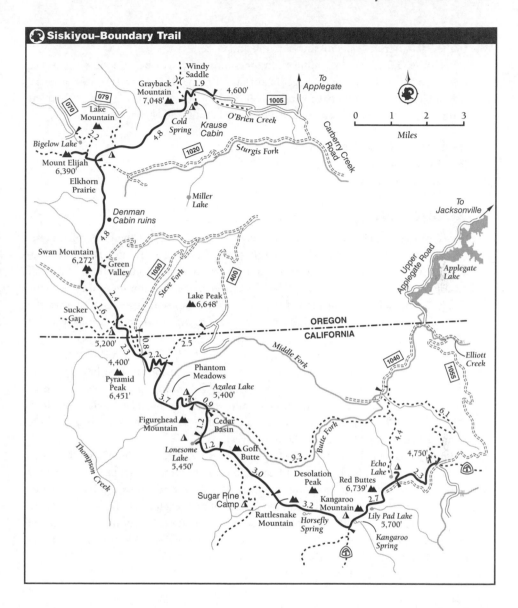

HOW TO GET THERE ●

To reach the east trailhead from I-5, take Exit 30 in Medford, and head west on OR 62, which becomes OR 238. In 5.5 miles turn right in Jacksonville to remain on OR 238; continue 7.8 miles to Ruch. Turn left (south) onto Upper Applegate Road, and follow the paved road 18.8 miles to Applegate Lake and a junction at the south end of the lake. Turn left and 1.3 miles later keep straight on gravel Forest Service Road 1050, which goes up

Elliott Creek. At a fork in 0.8 mile, turn right onto FS 1055, which climbs 9.5 miles all the way to the Pacific Crest Trail crossing at Cook and Green Pass.

To reach the O'Brien Creek trailhead, the recommended exit point, follow the directions above to the south end of Applegate Lake and turn right (northwest) onto Carberry Creek Road. Follow this good paved and gravel road for about 9 miles to a pass. Turn left on FS 1005 for 4 sometimes rocky miles to the hiker's trailhead at road-end.

GPS TRAILHEAD COORDINATES:

(**Cook and Green Pass**) N41° 50.511' W123° 08.705'

(**O'Brien Creek**) N42° 06.641' W123° 17.243'

INTRODUCTION •

The Siskiyou Mountains are unique. Nowhere else in the world is there a similar combination of converging climatic zones, merging geographic regions, and rare soils. The unusual east-west orientation of the range also helps to create a peculiar pattern of rainfall and ecologic zones. The result is one of the most diverse plant communities on the continent. There are both dry-zone plants and rainforest ferns; odd-looking endemic species live beside familiar favorites; alpine wildflowers grow next to sagebrush; and more species of conifers live here than almost anywhere else on the planet.

But this area has more to offer than just unique flora. There is also a fascinating and highly scenic assortment of rocks. Shining white marble intrusions mix with gray granite and green-black serpentinite, while in other places reddish-orange peridotite turns whole mountains its own special color. Small lakes and frequent vistas also enchant visitors. Even the wildlife seem to agree about the attributes of these mountains, as they live here in an abundance unusual for the Pacific Northwest.

As the observant reader will note, a large part of the suggested route actually lies in California. The trip has been included here in a book of *Oregon* backpacking trips for two reasons: First, it really is too good to leave out, and second, from a practical standpoint, this truly is an *Oregon* hike. Road access is almost exclusively from the Oregon side, and the short car shuttle is almost entirely in that state. In addition, the nearest population center is Oregon's Rogue River Valley, where the Siskiyous are familiar landmarks. The hike is equally attractive in either direction but is described here from east to west, as this involves less elevation gain.

DESCRIPTION •

From Cook and Green Pass, your route, the Pacific Crest Trail (PCT), heads southwest on a south-facing slope above a jeep road. South-facing slopes in these mountains tend to have only scattered trees but are choked with heavy brush. North-facing slopes have thicker forests with much less undergrowth. Excellent views extend toward the mountainous country to the south. At a pass covered with manzanita bushes is a junction, and to the right is a steep but worthwhile 0.5-mile downhill side trip to Echo Lake.

The PCT continues west, crosses the end of the jeep road, and contours around a ridge to Lily Pad Lake. Grazing cattle and exposed terrain make this otherwise attractive pool unsuited for camping. Instead, continue hiking to the scenic basin holding Kangaroo

Spring. The massive double summit of Red Buttes dominates the skyline. Rare Brewer's weeping spruce is found near the PCT as you hike. The hulking form of reddish-colored Kangaroo Mountain serves as the backdrop for the lush meadow at Kangaroo Spring, which features a small pond and good camps.

TIP: The next several trail miles have little or no water. Fill your bottles here.

As you climb away from Kangaroo Spring, the trail passes a particularly good example of white marble intermixed with the other assorted rocks of these mountains. At a ridgetop junction, the PCT heads south on its way to Devils Peak and the Klamath River canyon. Your route, however, turns right and contours across the south side of the main ridge for the next few miles. The trail passes beneath or beside ominously named places such as Desolation Peak, Horsefly Spring, and Rattlesnake Mountain (none of which lives up to its name) before dropping to a saddle and a junction. The trail to the left goes down to Sugar Pine Camp. The more scenic alternative stays with the Boundary Trail as it closely follows the up-and-down ridgetop to Goff Butte. You pass on the south side of this peak and then climb over another high point in the ridge. Now drop to a small creek and look for the possibly unsigned junction with the trail to Lonesome Lake. The short side trip to this irregularly shaped pool is highly recommended due to its scenic setting, nice camps, and the reasonable chance of solitude.

To continue your tour, return to the main trail and follow the lake's outlet creek. The path goes up and down along the side of a mostly wooded ridge. You reach a marshy area with a nice view up to Figurehead Mountain and then drop to a junction in Cedar Basin. A fine collection of old-growth incense cedars accounts for the name of this place. The basin also has good camps, a wildflower meadow, and a pleasant stream.

Turn left at the junction in Cedar Basin and climb beside the creek to shallow but good-sized Azalea Lake. A trail circles this fairly popular lake, passing designated camping areas for both horses and hikers. Craggy Figurehead Mountain looms above the southern shore. Mid-June–July the air is filled with the sweet, pungent aroma of blooming mountain azalea—one of nature's most powerful and lovely perfumes. Of course, the colorful flowers also provide a treat for the eyes. There can be no question that Azalea Lake earns its name.

As you switchback out of this basin, the trail ascends through an open forest of lodgepole pine (unusual for these mountains) to a pass. The route then cuts across a rocky, view-packed slope to a saddle, where knobcone pine and Brewer's weeping spruce dominate. You loop north around the basin that holds Phantom Meadows and gradually descend a brushy sidehill with numerous views. Turn left at a junction and make a quick climb to a saddle with an excellent perspective of Pyramid Peak to the west before descending a series of long switchbacks into Steve Fork Canyon.

Just after crossing the creek reach a junction. Turn left, make a switchback, and then begin a long, gradual, and usually dry climb northwest. Shortly after crossing a creekbed, you'll pass into Oregon (the occasion apparently not worthy of a sign).

TIP: At a sharp right turn about 2 miles from Steve Fork Creek, look for a short, unsigned, unmaintained path that leads west to a scenic lake in a cliff-walled little basin—well worth a visit.

The trail then climbs to a four-way junction at grassy Sucker Gap. The Boundary Trail turns to the right, but you first veer left for about 100 yards and then scramble down a steep trail to the lovely meadow beside Sucker Creek shelter. This meadow features a spring, lots of wildflowers, old-growth cedar trees, and welcome campsites. What may or may not be welcome are the black bears that seem to favor this basin. Hang all food, and camp away from the shelter, where bruins have become accustomed to finding bits of food. Deer are also common.

To continue your tour on the Boundary Trail, return to Sucker Gap and head north. The well-graded trail gradually climbs along the west side of a wooded ridge, eventually reaching a saddle with good views.

> **TIP:** For an outstanding side trip, climb cross-country 0.5 mile northwest along a narrow brushy ridge to the top of Swan Mountain. The scramble is made easier by pieces of an old trail through the brush. At 6,272 feet, Swan Mountain provides an exceptional vantage point, particularly of the Oregon part of this range and the distant Cascade peaks to the east. To the north you can pick out Craggy Mountain, Mount Elijah, Lake Mountain, and Grayback Mountain—the string of scenic peaks that will occupy your attention for the next several miles.

From the saddle, follow the main trail north as it slowly descends the east side of a ridge. You pass an unmarked junction in a sloping meadow, appropriately called Green Valley, and then climb back to another saddle. Now the trail loops around the west side of a hill and reaches a pass on the south flank of aptly named Craggy Mountain.

> **TIP:** It is possible to scramble to the top of this peak, but the going is much steeper and more difficult than the route up Swan Mountain.

Continuing to alternate between the east and west sides of the ridge, the trail leads around the east side of Craggy Mountain, passes below the remains of hard-to-find Denman Cabin, and then crosses a saddle back to the west. Shortly after the saddle, two springs just below the trail provide water. As you continue north, the path alternates between forest and open areas with nice views and lots of wildflowers.

Your trail now returns to the ridgecrest and crosses spacious Elkhorn Prairie. From

Pacific Crest Trail below Red Buttes
photographed by Douglas Lorain

this sloping meadow, the trail descends to a junction in a forested saddle and then climbs briefly to a second junction. There is a nice sheltered campsite at this junction, with water from a spring 0.2 mile northeast along the Boundary Trail.

TIP: A worthwhile side trip goes left (west) from here to the top of Mount Elijah, overlooking the Oregon Caves area. From partway along this side trail, you can also take a trail down to the wildflower meadow holding Bigelow Lake.

The main trail turns right at the junction, cuts across the south face of Lake Mountain, and then traces a tiring up-and-down course along the ridge to the northeast. Water is limited or nonexistent, but there are some nice views.

At a forested saddle on the south side of hulking Grayback Mountain (the tallest peak along this ridge), the trail turns east and loops around the south side of this lofty summit. You round a ridge and pass just below the wooded area holding Cold Spring (good camps), from which an abandoned trail drops steeply to Krause Cabin. The main trail goes north across a large sloping meadow with several springs, wildflowers, and a sweeping look up at Grayback Mountain. Determined scramblers can reach the summit of this peak with its expected great vistas by making their way up steep meadows and then a rocky ridge. An easier side trip climbs the moderately steep trail to the north for 0.5 mile to the grassy pass called Windy Saddle, with exceptional views of its own.

To complete your tour, turn right at a junction with the O'Brien Creek Trail and descend a series of switchbacks to a junction just before the trail crosses O'Brien Creek.

TIP: Be sure to make a quick side trip to the right from here to visit a snow shelter and historic Krause Cabin. The view up the sloping wildflower meadow from this cabin is excellent.

Back on the main trail, cross O'Brien Creek and complete the hike with a moderately steep descent through forest to the trailhead.

POSSIBLE ITINERARY

	CAMP	MILES	ELEVATION GAIN
Day 1	Kangaroo Spring (with side trip to Echo Lake)	5.6	1,700'
Day 2	Azalea Lake (with side trip to Lonesome Lake)	9.9	2,400'
Day 3	Sucker Gap	8.4	1,800'
Day 4	Bigelow Lake junction (with side trips up Swan Mountain and Mount Elijah)	9.9	2,700'
Day 5	Out	6.7	1,400'

3

BULL OF THE WOODS LOOP

RATINGS: Scenery 6   **Solitude** 7   **Difficulty** 6
MILES: 29
ELEVATION GAIN: 6,000'
DAYS: 3–5
SHUTTLE MILEAGE: n/a
MAP: Green Trails *Battle Ax (#524)*
USUALLY OPEN: Mid-June–October
BEST: Late August–mid-September
PERMIT: None (just sign the trailhead register)
RULES: Maximum group size of 12 people and/or stock
CONTACT: Clackamas River Ranger District, Mount Hood National Forest, 503-630-6861, www.fs.usda.gov/mthood

SPECIAL ATTRACTIONS ●●●●●●●●●●●●●●●●●●●●●●●●●●●●●●●●●●

Small, scenic lakes with good fishing; lovely forests

CHALLENGES ●●

Irregular trail maintenance, mosquitoes in early summer

Above: Mount Beachie over Elk Lake
photographed by Douglas Lorain

Bull of the Woods Loop

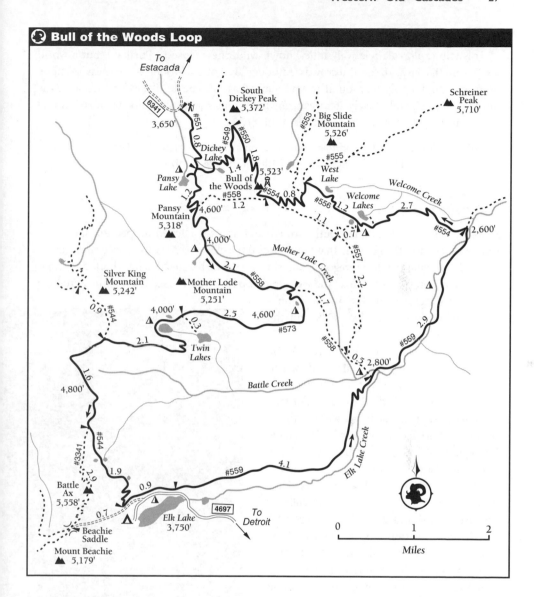

HOW TO GET THERE •••

From I-205, take Exit 12 or 12A in Clackamas and head east on OR 212. In 3.2 miles, turn right to head south on OR 224. In 40.3 miles continue straight (slight right) onto Forest Service Road 46, and go 3.7 miles to a prominent junction with FS 63. Turn right, following signs to Bagby Hot Springs, and proceed 5.6 miles to a fork. Turn right onto gravel FS 6340. Stay on the main road at several minor intersections for 7.7 miles to a major fork, where you bear right, now on FS 6341, and continue 3.6 miles to the Pansy Lake Trailhead. Parking is on the right; the trail is on the left.

GPS TRAILHEAD COORDINATES: N44° 53.995' W122° 06.982'

INTRODUCTION •

This trip explores a relatively little-known wilderness close to Portland, but a world away from that city's traffic and crowds. Although Bull of the Woods Wilderness has none of the eye-popping scenery found around major Cascades peaks like Mount Hood or the Three Sisters, it is still a lovely area, featuring numerous small lakes suitable for swimming or fishing, lots of huckleberries, and beautiful forests.

> **NOTE:** Unlike other trips in this book, the trails here are also identified by number because most of the trail junction signs in this wilderness only use trail numbers.

DESCRIPTION •

Pansy Lake Trail #551 goes south through an impressive lichen-draped forest of western hemlocks and Douglas firs that tower over the usual western Cascades understory of sword ferns, vine maples, Oregon grape shrubs, huckleberries, Pacific rhododendrons, and various forest wildflowers. The well-graded path steadily ascends 0.8 mile, crossing several tiny creeks along the way, to a junction with Dickey Lake Trail #549 and the start of the loop.

For the recommended counterclockwise circuit, go right on the main trail, which goes up and down for 0.2 mile to a poorly signed junction with the 120-yard spur trail to Pansy Lake. This side trip is well worth the minimal effort for the view of this shallow but scenic lake backed by the steep slopes and ridges radiating from Pansy Mountain.

The main trail bears left at the Pansy Lake junction and then makes two switchbacks up rocky slopes and through open forest for 1 mile to a junction atop a wooded ridge. Go straight and descend Mother Lode Trail #558, mostly in forest but with occasional glimpses through the trees of pointed Mount Jefferson to the southeast. A few irregularly spaced switchbacks help you descend to a low point at a campsite beside the trickling headwaters of Mother Lode Creek. Unfortunately, this creek is often dry by late summer and cannot be relied upon for water. Beyond this campsite, another 1.1 miles of up-and-down hiking leads to the next junction.

Bear right (uphill) on Twin Lakes Trail #573 and gradually climb, still in forest, for 0.4 mile to a good and very scenic campsite on a

Bull of the Woods Fire Lookout
photographed by Douglas Lorain

small knoll above a pair of pretty, lily pad–filled ponds. More climbing follows before you level off, finally losing about 500 feet to reach the Twin Lakes, 6.6 miles from the trailhead. An unsigned but obvious side trail goes sharply left to Lower Twin Lake. The upper lake, however, is more scenic and has better campsites, so stick with the main trail for 0.3 mile to the fine camps at that lake's west end. A rocky but delightful little swimming beach is nearby with easy access to the deep, clear water. It is usually comfortable enough for swimming from about late July to mid-September.

To exit the Twin Lakes Basin, follow the trail as it loops around the west end of Upper Twin Lake and then angles southeast, climbing a low ridge. Near the top of this ridge, the trail winds its way back to the west and then continues gradually climbing. The forest here is dominated by higher-elevation species like mountain hemlock and western white pine, with frequent openings providing nice views of pyramid-shaped Battle Ax to the southwest. About 1.7 miles from Upper Twin Lake is a junction. Turn left (south) on Bagby Hot Springs Trail #544 and go up and down (mostly up) along an attractive ridge for 1.6 miles to a fork and a choice of trails.

The longer uphill trail switchbacks to the summit of Battle Ax, where you will enjoy fine views up and down the Cascades and eastward over the drainage of Battle Creek. From there the trail switchbacks steeply downhill to the jeep road at Beachie Saddle, where you turn left and follow this rocky road downhill 0.7 mile to a reunion with the lower trail.

If you prefer the easier and shorter trail, turn left at the fork north of Battle Ax, cross a rockslide, and then come to a small meadow with a fine view of Battle Ax. Just beyond here you pass two shallow ponds (no good campsites). The trail then crosses a brushy slope before passing another pond and descending four switchbacks to a junction with the jeep road coming down from Beachie Saddle, and a reunion with the upper trail.

Walk east on the jeep road, and go straight at a junction with a better road coming in from a car campground on the right. Then walk through the forests north of large, tranquil, and very scenic Elk Lake. Near the western end of this lake, the road comes very close to the water and passes several excellent walk-in campsites that are well suited for backpackers.

TIP: The farther east you go, the better the views will be from your campsite across the lake to craggy Mount Beachie and towering Battle Ax.

Just before the road curves right to cross the lake's outlet, look for a sign identifying Elk Lake Creek Trail #559. Turn left onto this path, which, despite its name, goes nowhere near Elk Lake Creek for its first 4 miles. Instead, the trail contours for about 2 miles through relatively open old-growth forest—some of which was scarred by wildfire in 2011—and then gradually descends 2.1 miles to a junction at a spacious camping area near the site of the old Battle Creek Shelter (now long gone).

Go straight at the junction here, still on Trail #559, and 0.1 mile later cross clear Battle Creek—an easy ford in early summer or a dry-footed rock hop by late summer. The up-and-down path then follows Elk Lake Creek through a lovely Douglas fir and western hemlock forest, with an understory featuring an unusual abundance of vine maples and Pacific yews. About 1.1 miles from Battle Creek is a bridgeless crossing of Elk Lake Creek. This ford is not dangerous, but you should expect your ankles and calves to get wet. The trail goes another 0.6 mile and then passes above a terrific (but chilly) swimming and fishing hole with deep clear water and lots of rising trout. There is a small but very good campsite on the opposite side of the creek, reachable by scrambling down to the stream and then crossing the flow on a large log.

The trail now goes downstream another 0.9 mile, fords the creek a second time, and then climbs 0.2 mile to a junction. Turn left on Welcome Lakes Trail #554 and begin a long, steady climb, always in forest and often through a jungle of tall Pacific rhododendron bushes. After climbing 1,600 feet in 2.5 miles, you come to an unsigned junction with a 0.1-mile spur trail that goes downhill to the right to brush-lined Lower Welcome Lake. The main trail continues uphill another 0.2 mile to a good campsite and a junction just below small, lily pad–filled Upper Welcome Lake.

Here you have another choice of trails. The slightly longer but more scenic recommended trail (West Lake Way Trail #556) goes to the right through open forests and rocky areas, where you will find a particular abundance of huckleberries—deliciously ripe in late August. The route also has pleasant views and passes above small and easy-to-miss West Lake. About 1.2 miles from Upper Welcome Lake is a ridgetop junction. Turn left on Schreiner Peak Trail #555, almost immediately pass a muddy pond, and soon come to another junction. Turn left again and then steeply ascend 18 short switchbacks to a junction with the optional trail from Upper Welcome Lake. Veer right, walk 0.3 mile, and reach another fork.

To finish your trip with the area's best viewpoint, bear right (slightly uphill) on Trail #554 and climb seven switchbacks in 0.7 mile to the boarded-up fire lookout atop Bull of the Woods. On a clear day this lofty grandstand provides views stretching from Mount Rainier to the Three Sisters, as well as over the entire route of this trip.

From the summit of Bull of the Woods, go north (downhill) on Bull of the Woods Trail #550, which leaves just a few yards below the fire lookout. This scenic trail descends intermittently along a ridge for 1.1 miles past rocky overlooks and through forest to a junction. Turn sharply left on Trail #549 and steeply descend 0.9 mile to an unsigned junction with a 50-yard spur trail that goes to brushy Dickey Lake, which is set in a forested basin (no camps). The main trail goes right and continues downhill 0.5 mile back to the junction with Trail #551 and the close of the loop. Turn right and retrace your steps 0.8 mile to your car.

POSSIBLE ITINERARY

	CAMP	MILES	ELEVATION GAIN
Day 1	Upper Twin Lake	6.9	1,800'
Day 2	East end of Elk Lake	6.2	900'
Day 3	Upper Welcome Lake	9.7	2,000'
Day 4	Out	6.0	1,300'

4

TIMBERLINE TRAIL LOOP

> **RATINGS: Scenery** 10   **Solitude** 2   **Difficulty** 7
> **MILES:** 42 (62)
> **ELEVATION GAIN:** 8,600' (15,000')
> **DAYS:** 3–5 (5–7)
> **SHUTTLE MILEAGE:** n/a
> **MAPS:** Green Trails *Government Camp (#461)* and *Mount Hood (#462)*
> **USUALLY OPEN:** Mid-July–October
> **BEST:** Early to mid-August
> **PERMITS:** Yes (required May 15–October 15; free at trailhead)
> **RULES:** Horses banned, except on the Pacific Crest Trail; no camping or fires
>   in meadows, within 500 feet of Ramona Falls, or within the tree-covered
>   islands of Elk Cove and Elk Meadows; no camping within 200 feet of lakes
>   or streams; no fires in Paradise Park or within 500 feet of McNeil Point
> **CONTACT:** Mount Hood Information Center, 503-622-7674; Hood River Ranger
>   District, Mount Hood National Forest, 541-352-6002; Zigzag Ranger District,
>   Mount Hood National Forest, 503-622-3191, www.fs.usda.gov/mthood

SPECIAL ATTRACTIONS •

Great mountain scenery, wildflowers

Above: Mount Adams and Mount Rainier from the Timberline Trail
photographed by Douglas Lorain

⟳ Timberline Trail Loop

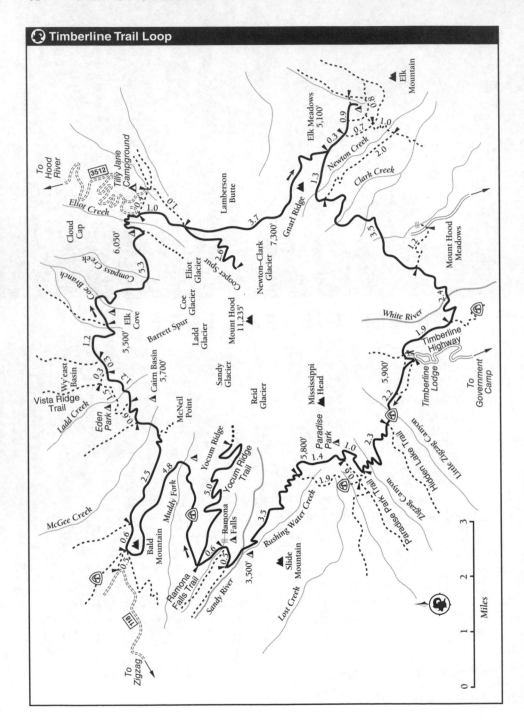

CHALLENGES

Crowded; steep snowfields; unbridged glacial streams

HOW TO GET THERE

From I-205, take Exit 12 or 12A in Clackamas and head east on OR 212. In 3.2 miles, turn right to head south on OR 224. In 9.7 miles, in Eagle Creek, turn left to head northeast on OR 211. In 6.1 miles turn right onto US 26. Go 28.7 miles to Government Camp, and turn left onto Timberline Highway. Go 5.5 miles to Timberline Lodge.

> **TIP:** *Spacious* is hardly an adequate word to describe the acres of parking here. Don't forget to take a photo of where you parked, or you might face hours of embarrassment trying to locate your vehicle when you return.

GPS TRAILHEAD COORDINATES: N45° 19.870' W121° 42.678'

INTRODUCTION

The Timberline Trail circling Mount Hood is probably the most famous footpath in the state. Guidebooks describing the finest hiking trails in the nation often include this spectacular route, so Oregonians must share the trail with people from all over the country (and even international travelers). Even before the official trail was built by Civilian Conservation Corps workers in the 1930s, this round-the-mountain tour had many admirers—and justifiably so. The mountain views are stunning, wildflowers choke many of the meadows, and exceptional side trips abound. Day hikers, who have access to every corner of the mountain, dominate the enormous trail population. Because horses are banned from most of the route, the trails and meadows are still in good shape, despite the number of hikers.

It is traditional to start this hike at Timberline Lodge and travel clockwise. Almost all the backpackers who do the circuit choose this course, even though the trip is equally scenic in either direction and can be begun at any of several trailheads. (Note that a few of the other trailheads require a Northwest Forest Pass for parking; if you choose an alternative starting point, be sure to check the requirements before you set out.)

DESCRIPTION

From the back side of Timberline Lodge, follow a paved route signed TIMBERLINE TRAIL to a junction with the Pacific Crest Trail (PCT) and turn left. The scenic path gradually loses elevation through flowery meadows and then crosses Little Zigzag Canyon. Keep right at the Hidden Lake Trail junction and continue losing elevation. The trail rounds a narrow ridge, where you will enjoy a fine view of Zigzag Canyon before dropping in long switchbacks to its bottom.

> **WARNING:** The Zigzag Creek crossing has no bridge and may be wet.

Climb back up the west side of this gorge to a junction. The horse route below Paradise Park goes left, while the more scenic hiker's trail goes right and continues its long climb out of Zigzag Canyon.

In a sloping meadow covered with blossoms is a junction with the Paradise Park Trail. Keep right to reach the remains of an old trail shelter, near which are many good but heavily used camps (please use a designated site). Although the camps are pleasant, trees and a small ridge block the sight of Mount Hood from here. You'll get better vistas as you continue hiking northwest on the up-and-down route for another 0.6 mile, with flowers and unrestricted views, before dropping back down to a reunion with the horse trail.

Brace your knees for a long series of downhill switchbacks as the trail descends 2,200 feet on its way into the Sandy River canyon. Along the way are excellent views of the eroding cliffs of Slide Mountain.

TIP: Shortly before crossing the Sandy River is a nice, uncrowded camp beside Rushing Water Creek on the left. (Be sure to camp at least 200 feet from the creek.)

You ford the Sandy River and climb a bench on the far side to a junction with the popular Ramona Falls Trail coming in from the west. Make a sharp right turn and climb gradually 0.5 mile to Ramona Falls—a lovely curtain of water that cascades over a basalt cliff. Camps must be made at least 500 feet from the falls. A designated camping area is located to the south.

If the weather is good, we *strongly* recommend that you spend an extra day here with a long side trip up Yocum Ridge. The trail leaves the PCT at a ridgecrest 0.6 mile northwest of Ramona Falls and makes a long but moderately graded climb through mostly viewless forests. Eventually the trail breaks out into wildflower meadows with a *terrific* perspective of Reid Glacier. By continuing on the trail another mile and scrambling up a ridge, you can also get up close and personal with the Sandy Glacier—*wow!*

Back on the main circuit, from the junction with the Yocum Ridge Trail, the PCT makes a long up-and-down traverse along the side of Yocum Ridge to a crossing of accurately named Muddy Fork Sandy River.

WARNING: The ford of this multibranched stream is a potentially cold, or even dangerous, adventure—especially on hot afternoons with lots of snow and/or ice melting above.

TIP: A clear stream a little north of the third branch of the Muddy Fork Sandy River has a good campsite and water that won't clog your filter.

A long, mostly uphill segment takes you up to Bald Mountain. The scene as you look back to Mount Hood from the steeply sloping wildflower meadows below Bald Mountain is outstanding. Now the trail loops back into the forest and soon reaches a major junction. The PCT heads off to the northwest, but our trail (Timberline Trail) turns to the right (east). You hike through a viewless forest, pass a trail junction, and then begin a steady climb along a ridge. Eventually the trail breaks out into ridgetop meadows with flowers and terrific vistas of Mount Hood. Make four switchbacks and encounter an unmarked but obvious side trail that climbs very steeply over loose rocks and roots to McNeil Point shelter (a tiring but worthwhile side trip).

Stick with the Timberline Trail and cross a basin with two small ponds.

TIP: Photographers will want to climb the small hill south of these ponds to a fine photo opportunity of the top one-third of Mount Hood.

The route climbs briefly over a ridge and then contours to the excellent camps in scenic Cairn Basin. This area shows evidence of the massive Dollar Lake Fire of 2011 (including a couple of damaged campsites in Cairn Basin), but the trail is in good shape despite the swath of dead trees, and plenty of campsites in the vicinity remain undamaged. The trail here provides an excellent opportunity for an up close look at just how much destruction a wildfire can cause and how quickly new undergrowth moves in as the forest starts to recover. Burn-zone pioneers include fireweed, bear grass, and huckleberries (happy about the extra sunlight).

If you're camped at Cairn Basin and have time for some exploring, there are several possible options. You can make a lovely loop trip by dropping to the wildflower gardens of Eden Park, going east to Wy'east Basin, and returning to Cairn Basin via the Timberline Trail.

WARNING: The loop requires two crossings of Ladd Creek, not always easy.

Ambitious hikers should also consider making the trailless scramble up Barrett Spur. Leave the Timberline Trail near the junction with the Vista Ridge Trail and climb through meadows and over rocky slopes for about 1.5 miles to the summit viewpoint. The jumbled ice masses of Ladd and Coe Glaciers are especially impressive.

The main Timberline Trail goes through continuously spectacular terrain on an up-and-down course to the east. Shortly before it drops down a sidehill ridge, an unmarked side trail goes right to tiny Dollar Lake, which has camps but only limited views. Just ahead is Elk Cove, one of the mountain's most impressive beauty spots. The cove has a particularly striking view of the north face of Mount Hood and the white mass of Coe Glacier. Wildflowers choke the meadow and a clear brook provides water. Camps here must be made in the trees below the fragile meadow.

The magnificent circle route continues with a loss of elevation to the crossing of Coe Branch above two towering waterfalls (which you can hear but not see) and then climbs back to higher-elevation meadows. Look for frequent scenes north to Mount Adams and Mount Rainier. At the crossing of Compass Creek are views of two waterfalls—a short one near the trail and a taller one a bit farther downstream.

TIP: From a ridge just west of Eliot Creek, an unmarked path climbs the moraine beside Eliot Glacier to some great observation points above the ice.

Severe flood damage closed the Timberline Trail at Eliot Creek in 2006, but in 2016 the trail was rerouted downstream of the original crossing, making it passable once more. The reroute adds just over a mile of steep switchbacks to the hike, but it's a much safer and more stable option than the do-it-yourself crossing many hikers had been using.

Make your way across raging Eliot Creek and then climb a bit to the road and campground at Cloud Cap.

The old inn at Cloud Cap is usually closed to the public (though you can sign up in advance for one of the U.S. Forest Service's occasional tours), but this is still a popular trailhead with a campground to accommodate both car campers and backpackers. Tilly Jane Campground, 0.5 mile east, is another option for spending the night.

From Cloud Cap the Timberline Trail turns sharply southward, and skyward, as it climbs toward the highest part of the circuit. After 1 mile is a junction near a shelter.

TIP: An outstanding side trip from here climbs southwest in long switchbacks over talus slopes and snowfields to the viewpoint atop Cooper Spur. Before taking this side trip, keep in mind that it involves a round-trip distance of 5.2 miles and an elevation gain of 1,900 feet.

The main trail goes south, climbing above timberline and crossing some steep snowfields.

WARNING: These snowfields are dangerously icy on cold mornings.

Expect plenty of wind near the trail's high point on Gnarl Ridge before beginning a long descent into more friendly terrain. Above Lamberson Butte there are some great views across Newton Creek canyon and up to Mount Hood. The massive Newton-Clark Glacier fills most of the mountain's east face.

The trail continues its long descent back into forests and meadows to a junction with the trail dropping to Elk Meadows. This large, popular meadow is well worth the 700-foot elevation loss and gain to make a visit. Highlights include an old shelter, excellent camps, marvelous views back up to Mount Hood, and a notorious population of gray jays that will happily eat from your hand (or steal your unguarded breakfast). To reduce damage here, the U.S. Forest Service asks that you camp in the trees around the perimeter of the meadow.

Back on the Timberline Trail, the route sidehills down to Newton Creek, which you can sometimes hop across, but a wet crossing is usually required. Pass a trail junction and then contour around a ridge before coming to Clark Creek, an easier crossing. The tour now passes through a surprisingly scenic area of wildflowers in the Mount Hood Meadows ski area. Ski areas are usually eyesores in summer, but this one isn't bad. There are even occasional views up to Mount Hood.

Leave the ski area and start a long 1,000-foot descent into the bouldery wasteland of the White River valley. This stream has no bridge and is the last potentially difficult crossing. The trail crosses this unattractive valley and then climbs a long switchback up the far side back into meadows. In a particularly nice meadow is a junction with the PCT. Turn right and climb this often-sandy route 2 miles back to your car (*somewhere in that huge parking lot*).

POSSIBLE ITINERARY

	CAMP	MILES	ELEVATION GAIN
Day 1	Ramona Falls	10.9	1,400'
Day 2	Day trip up Yocum Ridge (return to Ramona Falls)	11.8	3,400'
Day 3	Cairn Basin	9.1	2,900'
Day 4	Cloud Cap Camp	8.0	1,500'
Day 5	Elk Meadows (with side trip up Cooper Spur)	11.3	3,400'
Day 6	Out	10.5	2,400'

MOUNT JEFFERSON
WILDERNESS TRAVERSE

RATINGS: Scenery 10   **Solitude** 3   **Difficulty** 6
MILES: 44
ELEVATION GAIN: 6,400'
DAYS: 4–6
SHUTTLE MILEAGE: 76
MAP: USFS *Detroit Ranger District: Willamette National Forest*
USUALLY OPEN: Mid-July–October
BEST: Late July–mid-August
PERMITS: Yes, self-issued at trailhead; Northwest Forest Pass required at trail-heads; limited-entry permits also required for the Pamelia Area (reserve in advance, $10 reservation fee, available at recreation.gov or 877-444-6777).
RULES: No fires at Rockpile Lake or Jefferson Park; designated campsites at Wasco Lake and lakes in Jefferson Park
CONTACT: Detroit Ranger District, Willamette National Forest, 503-854-3366, www.fs.usda.gov/willamette

SPECIAL ATTRACTIONS •

Views and mountain scenery; Jefferson Park—*wow!*

Above: Marian Lake in the Mount Jefferson Wilderness
photographed by Becky Ohlsen

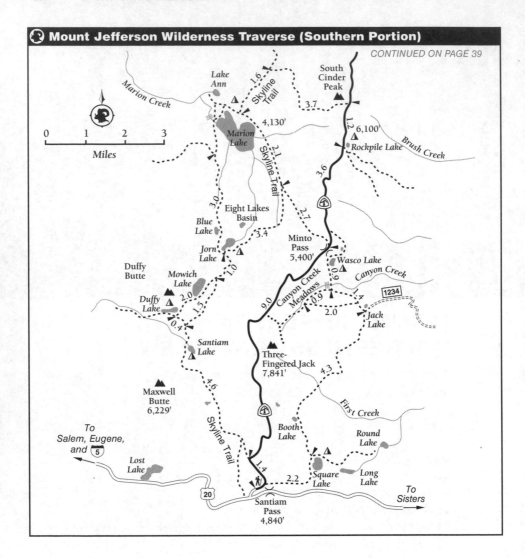

Mount Jefferson Wilderness Traverse (Southern Portion)

CONTINUED ON PAGE 39

CHALLENGES

Permits and access restrictions; long stretches without water; crowds; snowfields; crossing of Russell Creek; mosquitoes (especially in the Olallie Scenic Area) mid-July–mid-August

HOW TO GET THERE

From I-5, take Exit 228 (about halfway between Salem and Eugene), and head east on OR 34. In 7.9 miles, take a right onto North Second Street, and in 0.1 mile turn right onto US 20. In 67.1 miles, you will find the well-marked Pacific Crest Trailhead at Santiam Pass on your left.

The north trailhead is reached by taking I-5 to Exit 253 in Salem. Head east on OR 22, and go 48.5 miles to Detroit. Turn left onto Forest Service Road 46, heading northeast from Detroit. Go over a pass after 16 miles, descend north another 7 miles, and then turn

Mount Jefferson Wilderness Traverse (Northern Portion)

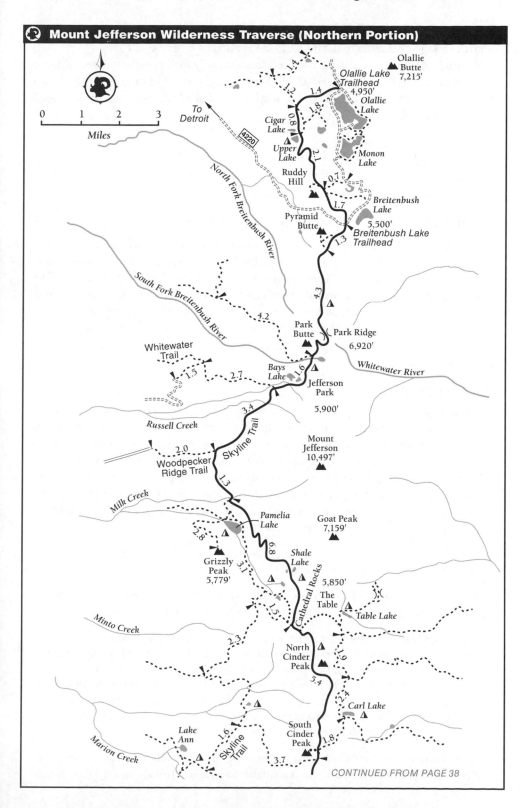

0 1 2 3
Miles

To Detroit

North Fork Breitenbush River

South Fork Breitenbush River

4220

Olallie Butte 7,215'

Olallie Lake Trailhead 4,950'

Olallie Lake

1.4

1.2 1.4

1.8

0.8

Cigar Lake

Upper Lake

7.2

Ruddy Hill

Monon Lake

0.7

Breitenbush Lake

1.7

Breitenbush Lake Trailhead 5,500'

Pyramid Butte

1.3

4.3

4.2

Park Butte

Park Ridge 6,920'

Whitewater Trail

1.5 2.7

Bays Lake

1.6

Whitewater River

Jefferson Park 5,900'

3.4

Skyline Trail

Russell Creek

2.0

Woodpecker Ridge Trail

Mount Jefferson 10,497'

1.3

Milk Creek

2.8

Pamelia Lake

Goat Peak 7,159'

6.8

Grizzly Peak 5,779'

3.1

Shale Lake

Cathedral Rocks 5,850'

The Table

Table Lake

Minto Creek

1.5

2.3

North Cinder Peak

1.9

5.4

2.4

Carl Lake

Lake Ann

1.6

Skyline Trail

South Cinder Peak

1.8

Marion Creek

3.7

CONTINUED FROM PAGE 38

right (east) on one-lane, paved FS 4690. After 4.5 miles turn right onto gravel FS 4220 and continue another 5.2 miles to the trailhead at the north end of Olallie Lake.

To reach the Breitenbush Lake trailhead (suitable only for four-wheel drive vehicles) from Detroit, take FS 46 northeast. Go 16.5 miles, and turn right onto FS 4220. Go 6.5 miles to reach the trailhead. (You can also reach it via Olallie Lake, but that section of road is notoriously bad.)

GPS TRAILHEAD COORDINATES:
(Santiam Pass) N44° 25.365' W121° 51.307'
(Olallie Lake) N44° 51.467' W121° 46.396'
(Breitenbush Lake) N44° 45.888' W121° 47.126'

INTRODUCTION •

The Pacific Crest Trail (PCT) traces the entire mountainous backbone of Oregon. Along the way it visits most of the scenic highlights of the Cascade Range. Most hikers rank the section through the Mount Jefferson Wilderness as the best part of the PCT's route through Oregon, and it would be difficult to argue with them. The trail stays high for most of its length here, providing memorable vistas at nearly every turn. Continuing the trip north through the Olallie Scenic Area adds even more lovely meadows and lakes. Hiking this additional section also eliminates the need to drive the *very* poor road to the Breitenbush Lake trailhead.

DESCRIPTION •

From the large trailhead parking lot at Santiam Pass, follow a short spur trail east to a junction with the PCT and turn left. Climb gradually through forest for 1.5 miles, passing a few stagnant ponds, to a junction with the Oregon Skyline Trail. Keep right and climb more steadily along the southern ridge of Three-Fingered Jack. The woods become more open and the scenery improves as you climb, but the views of Three-Fingered Jack remain limited until you round a ridge and, rather suddenly, the trees break for a full frontal view of this craggy mountain. The trail crosses a talus slope and probably a few lingering snow-fields as it traverses the west and north faces of this peak.

TIP: Shortly after a small pass north of the peak, look back for a final close-up view of Three-Fingered Jack's northeast cliffs.

The PCT then descends through forest and recovering burn areas to a junction at Minto Pass. Several designated camps are at Wasco Lake a short distance southeast of the pass.

TIP: A highly scenic alternate cross-country route to Wasco Lake drops steeply from the pass north of Three-Fingered Jack to spectacular Canyon Creek Meadows. These meadows have a terrific view of Three-Fingered Jack and support a riot of wildflowers in late July. Visit this popular spot on a weekday, and be extra careful not to trample the flowers. To exit the meadows, hike the access trail to the northeast. Keep left at a fork (now paralleling Canyon Creek) and reach a small waterfall near a trail junction. Turn left (north) for another 0.7 mile to Wasco Lake.

Continuing north from Minto Pass on the PCT, slowly climb a heavily burned ridge and cross an open slope with fine vistas south back to jagged Three-Fingered Jack. Round a ridge and then reach the bowl holding Rockpile Lake. Fires are prohibited here. This small lake marks the beginning of an extended ridge walk, featuring more great scenery. The only significant drawback to this terrific stretch is a lack of water.

Only 1.4 miles north of Rockpile Lake is an open pass beside the reddish-colored summit of South Cinder Peak.

TIP: Don't miss the easy scramble to the top of this cinder cone for an excellent viewpoint.

The PCT continues its scenic route in and out of trees as it leads north toward the sharp spire of Mount Jefferson.

TIP: At a small meadow, shortly after rounding the west side of North Cinder Peak, the trail passes an unseen shallow pond on the right, with water and a few camps. This is the only reliable trailside water between Rockpile and Shale Lakes—a total distance of 8.8 miles.

Not far beyond the pond is the first of several dramatic clifftop overlooks of Mount Jefferson and the diverse volcanic landscape below. This display of volcanism includes cinder cones, lava flows, and a basalt-rimmed mesa called The Table. Only the Three Sisters area showcases a more interesting and scenic variety of the volcanic forces that shaped this landscape.

The trail drops a bit to the west and reaches a junction. Turn right (sticking with the PCT) and hike along the western side of the impressively rugged Cathedral Rocks. Next on the list of wonders is a partially forested plateau supporting several small lakes, of which only Coyote, Shale, and Mud Hole Lakes are near the trail.

TIP: These lakes are the jumping-off point for excellent cross-country explorations to Goat Peak, to The Table, and, for the truly ambitious, up the long, steep south ridge of Mount Jefferson. Strong scramblers can get all the way to a point a little below the summit, where a dangerously exposed traverse stops those not equipped with climbing gear.

The PCT gradually descends from the lovely high country on a series of long switchbacks to a junction with a trail coming up from popular Pamelia Lake. Nearby is a sweeping view up the steep canyon of Milk Creek to the top of Mount Jefferson. You step across Milk Creek and gradually climb to a junction with the little-used Woodpecker Ridge Trail. Continue on the PCT, which passes a small, narrow lake with an unattractive campsite as it makes its way across the northwest side of Mount Jefferson.

Now you confront a potential problem—the crossing of Russell Creek. As with most glacial streams, this creek's volume increases significantly on hot summer afternoons due to the melting of snow and glacial ice above. Try to cross in the morning, and expect a cold, possibly dangerous crossing—made worse by the brown glacial water obscuring possible footholds.

Not long after the crossing is a junction with the overly popular Whitewater Trail from the west. Keep right and follow the crowds to Jefferson Park, a nationally famous spot that should be seen by every Oregon outdoors lover. It is the perfect blend of alpine meadows, scattered trees, wildflowers, and lakes. Overlooking this scene is the snowy crown of Mount Jefferson. Camping near lakes is restricted to designated sites, and fires are prohibited.

Once you manage to drag yourself away from this paradise, the PCT climbs through more great scenery to the top of Park Ridge. Allow plenty of extra time here to gaze in amazement upon what many believe to be the best view in Oregon. The scene back down across the lovely expanse of Jefferson Park and sweeping up to the top of Mount Jefferson is impossible to describe.

To continue your trip, hike (or *slide*) down the huge semipermanent snowfield on the north side of Park Ridge. Relocate the trail and tour a scenic area of ponds, small trees, and heather meadows. Your route goes through a low pass and then turns northeast across a slope with views of prominent Pyramid Butte. Leave the wilderness and reach the trailhead near Breitenbush Lake on dirt FS 4220—an alternate stopping point for those with less time for hiking and a vehicle they don't mind driving up this rough road.

The *recommended* exit point lies another 6 miles to the north at Olallie Lake. The route is continuously beautiful, if not as grandly scenic as the areas you've already seen. Go north around a shallow lake surrounded by meadows, wildflowers, and heather and then lose elevation past two quick junctions with trails from the east. Look for a short side path to the left up Ruddy Hill—well worth the 15-minute detour. The trail gradually descends to good camps beside shallow Upper Lake, backed by a scenic rockslide, and continues to Cigar Lake, with its nearby ponds, meadows, and huckleberries. Continue north 0.5 mile to a four-way junction. Here you keep straight on the PCT for a final 1.4 scenic miles to the northern trailhead at Olallie Lake.

WARNING: The lakes and ponds of the Olallie Scenic Area support a voracious population of mosquitoes. If you visit in July or early August, come prepared with a head net, insect repellent, and a willingness to do some swatting.

NOTE: For loop lovers, the best option here is to follow the PCT to Milk Creek; take a day or two for a side trip to Jefferson Park; then return via the forested Oregon Skyline Trail past Pamelia Lake, Marion Lake, and Eight Lakes Basin.

POSSIBLE ITINERARY

	CAMP	MILES	ELEVATION GAIN
Day 1	Wasco Lake	10.6	1,900'
Day 2	Shale Lake	12.2	1,500'
Day 3	Jefferson Park	9.9	1,800'
Day 4	Upper Lake	9.5	1,100'
Day 5	Out	2.2	100'

THREE SISTERS LOOP

RATINGS: Scenery 10   **Solitude** 2   **Difficulty** 6

MILES: 55 (75)

ELEVATION GAIN: 8,200' (10,600')

DAYS: 5–6 (6–10)

SHUTTLE MILEAGE: n/a

MAP: National Geographic Trails Illustrated *Bend/Three Sisters*

USUALLY OPEN: Mid-July–October

BEST: August

PERMITS: Yes, self-issued at trailhead; Northwest Forest Pass required; limited-access permit required for the Obsidian area (reserve in advance, $10 reservation fee, available at recreation.gov or 877-444-6777)

RULES: No fires at Chambers, Eileen, Golden, Green, Moraine, or Sisters Mirror Lake, nor at Park Meadow; no camping within 100 feet of trails or water in Linton Meadows and around Eileen Lake; designated camps at Green, Moraine, and Matthieu Lakes

CONTACT: Sisters Ranger District, Deschutes National Forest, 541-549-7700, www.fs.usda.gov/deschutes; and McKenzie River Ranger District, Willamette National Forest, 541-822-3381, www.fs.usda.gov/willamette

SPECIAL ATTRACTIONS ••••••••••••••••••••••••••••••••••

Terrific mountain scenery, interesting volcanic geology

Above: South Sister over Camp Lake
photographed by Douglas Lorain

Three Sisters Loop

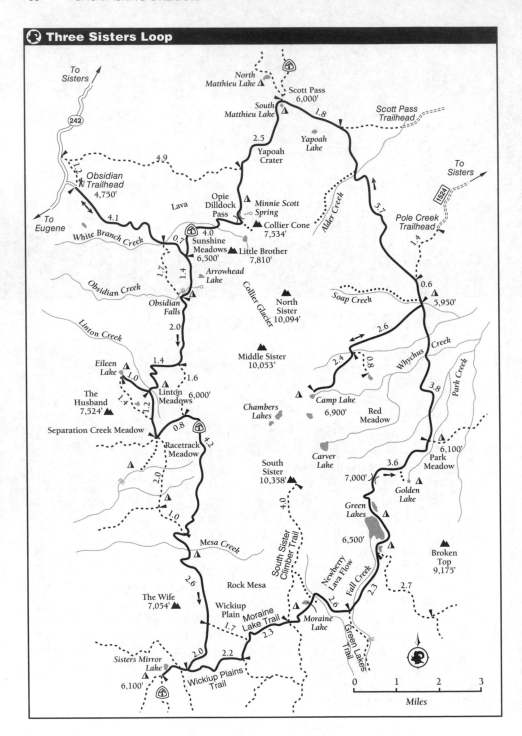

To Sisters

North Matthieu Lake ▲

Scott Pass 6,000'

South Matthieu Lake

Scott Pass Trailhead

242

4.9

2.5

Yapoah Crater

Yapoah Lake

1.8

To Sisters

Obsidian Trailhead 4,750'

2.2

Lava

Opie Dilldock Pass

Minnie Scott Spring

Collier Cone 7,534'

5.7

Alder Creek

1524

Pole Creek Trailhead

To Eugene

4.1

White Branch Creek

0.7

4.0

Sunshine Meadows 6,500'

Little Brother 7,810'

1.4

Park Creek

1.7

1.4

Arrowhead Lake

North Sister 10,094'

Soap Creek

0.6

5,950'

Obsidian Creek

Obsidian Falls

Collier Glacier

2.0

Linton Creek

2.6

2.4

0.8

Whychus Creek

Eileen Lake

1.0

1.4

1.6

Middle Sister 10,053'

The Husband 7,524'

1.2

Linton Meadows 6,000'

Camp Lake 6,900'

Red Meadow

3.8

Separation Creek Meadow

0.8

Chambers Lakes

6,100'

Park Meadow

Racetrack Meadow

4.2

Carver Lake

3.6

2.0

South Sister 10,358'

7,000'

Golden Lake

1.0

Green Lakes

Mesa Creek

4.0

6,500'

Broken Top 9,175'

2.6

Rock Mesa

The Wife 7,054' ▲

South Sister Climber Trail

Newberry Lava Flow

Fall Creek

2.3

2.7

Wickiup Plain

Moraine Lake Trail

1.7

Moraine Lake

2.6

Sisters Mirror Lake

2.0

2.2

2.3

Green Lakes Trail

6,100'

Wickiup Plains Trail

0   1   2   3

Miles

CHALLENGES

Crowds, permit and access restrictions

HOW TO GET THERE

From I-5, take Exit 194A in Eugene, and head east on OR 126. Go 6.3 miles and turn left to remain on OR 126. Go 48.4 miles, and turn right onto OR 242/McKenzie Highway (closed November–July). In 15.3 miles the well-marked Obsidian Trailhead will be on your right, just 0.5 mile south of the Scott Lake turnoff.

From the intersection of US 20 and US 97 in Bend, head northwest on US 20 toward Sisters, and go 19.2 miles. Turn left onto West Hood, and almost immediately, turn right onto OR 242/McKenzie Highway. The Obsidian Trailhead will be on your right in 21 miles.

GPS TRAILHEAD COORDINATES: N44° 12.228' W121° 52.522'

WARNING: This is a popular trailhead leading to an overly populated area (the Sunshine Meadows), so don't expect to be lonesome.

INTRODUCTION

One of Oregon's greatest long backpacking trips, this route completely circles the Three Sisters, providing ever-changing views of these beautiful siblings. It also visits lesser-known family members (Little Brother, The Husband, and The Wife)—and craggy Broken Top, an apparent outcast without family ties. The basic loop is unsurpassed, and countless side trips visit even more lakes, high meadows, and viewpoints. A hiker could spend weeks here and never tire of the scenery or run out of places to explore. So get your permit and savor this area.

Volcanic features dominate the landscape. In addition to rugged lava flows, cinder cones, and glasslike obsidian, you'll also see pumice meadows. Formed when enormous quantities of pumice bury an area, these meadows have sparse vegetation and no surface water. Examples of this geologic oddity include Racetrack Meadow and Wickiup Plain.

DESCRIPTION

The Obsidian Trail starts by climbing gradually through thick forests, which show some evidence of the Horse Creek Complex Fire that swept through in 2017, causing several temporary closures. After 3.5 sometimes dusty miles the trail crosses a lava flow for 0.6 mile and comes to White Branch Creek. This stream often runs dry as the water percolates into the porous volcanic soils. On the far side is a junction. To the right is the most direct route to pick up the main loop trail, but any hiker not suffering from "destinationitis" should turn left. Although this route is 0.4 mile longer, it is much more scenic.

Choosing the left course, you climb fairly steeply through a mountain hemlock forest before arriving at the open expanse of Sunshine Meadows and a four-way junction with the Pacific Crest Trail (PCT). To the left is the return route of the loop, to the right (south) is your current route, and straight ahead is an old trail that goes through a lovely meadow topped by the summits of North and Middle Sisters. Because the mountain views from this meadow are partially obstructed, consider making a fun side trip on this old trail, past campsites and up a steep rocky slope, to a small plateau featuring tiny Arrowhead Lake and more open views.

As you head south on the PCT, a quick examination of the rocks underfoot reveals why the entry route is called the *Obsidian* Trail and why walking barefoot here is not recommended. The black glass rock chips can be razor-sharp.

You hike past a gushing spring and then drop to joyful Obsidian Falls (which makes for a *very* cold shower) and a junction. Keep left (south) on the PCT and soon leave the day hikers behind.

After 2 miles from Obsidian Falls, turn right (west) at a junction and descend sometimes steeply to the north end of beautiful Linton Meadows. This large wildflower garden is one of the trip's many highlights. A lovely clear creek cascades down from springs and then crosses this grassy expanse. Middle Sister, South Sister, and The Husband surround the basin, providing unequaled mountain scenes. The meadow is popular with backpackers, so consider hiking 1 mile northwest to tiny Eileen Lake for the night.

TIP: The best views from Eileen Lake are from the trailless northwest shore.

To continue your tour, pass the south end of Linton Meadows with its unique view of Middle Sister (a nearly perfect, unbroken cone from this angle) before reaching rather barren Racetrack Meadow and a five-way junction.

TIP: A nice side trip from here goes down a gully to the south on an unmarked, unmaintained, but easy-to-follow use path for 0.8 mile to large Separation Creek Meadow, with another nice creek and more views.

The main route goes sharply left through Racetrack Meadow, sometimes following posts, back to the PCT. Turn south as the PCT gradually climbs through an attractive mix of open woods and small, rolling meadows with occasional views. You pass a seasonal pond on the left, then continue on a rolling descent to Mesa Creek (good camps).

TIP: As you switchback up the slope south of this stream, be sure to look back for a nice view of redheaded South Sister—the mountain is topped by reddish cinders.

Top out at a saddle and then pass through a barren flat nestled between Rock Mesa lava flow and the remains of a craggy mountain called The Wife. Eventually our trail reaches the edge of Wickiup Plain, a large, flat, almost treeless expanse of volcanic pumice. As you continue south, enjoy ever-improving vistas across Wickiup Plain and Rock Mesa up to shining South Sister.

Near the south end of Wickiup Plain is a junction. Turn right and go 0.8 mile to reach the nearest camps with water at popular Sisters Mirror Lake. The trees here have obviously grown since this lake was named, although the top of South Sister can still be seen.

TIP: Several small off-trail lakes are nearby and provide more private camping.

Returning to the Wickiup Plain junction, go east on Wickiup Plains Trail (also called Devils Lake Trail on some maps) along the meadow's south edge for 1.7 miles, and then turn north and climb back into forest on the path to Moraine Lake.

NOTE: Several old trails and jeep roads cross Wickiup Plain, but unless it's foggy, it would be difficult to become lost.

At a junction, you'll cross the South Sister Climber Trail coming from the Devils Lake Trailhead 2 miles south. Energetic hikers have the option to make a difficult but highly rewarding 8-mile (round-trip) side trip to the top of South Sister, Oregon's third-highest mountain. To do so, turn left (north) at this junction and follow a well-used boot path that climbs the mountain's south side. The route requires no technical climbing equipment or experience but should be attempted only in good weather.

Continuing on the main loop, you go straight and pass Moraine Lake (which has fair camps) and then drop through woods beside a lava flow to Fall Creek and a junction. Turn left on the popular Green Lakes Trail (sometimes called Fall Creek Trail), which parallels Fall Creek across from the jumbled Newberry Lava Flow. After 2 miles you top out at the magnificent plain containing the Green Lakes. Nestled between South Sister and Broken Top, this basin of lakes, springs, and wildflowers is one of the most beautiful places in Oregon. Judging by the number of hikers and backpackers here, a lot of people share this opinion. Try to avoid camping here. You will, however, want to linger long enough to soak in the views and make a loop of the largest Green Lake.

Continuing north, pass to the left of the final Green Lake and begin climbing out of the basin, still on Green Lakes Trail. A long switchback and well-graded trail lead to a high, windy saddle and the start of a long drop to the east.

TIP: A worthwhile but easy-to-miss side trip is the 0.6-mile unsigned path leading south to Golden Lake. This little jewel sits in a beautiful meadow basin and features a superb view of Broken Top. The route starts about 0.9 mile beyond the pass.

The descent ends at Park Meadow, yet another remarkable spot in this wilderness. A clear creek runs through this meadow, with its picturesque islands of trees, its small ponds, and its particularly photogenic view of Broken Top.

WARNING: Horse packers commonly use this meadow, so the drinking water is polluted.

TIP: The best photograph here is about 100 yards upstream from the trail crossing of Park Creek.

There are numerous camps here, although they are overused, and fires are prohibited.

To continue your loop trip, stay on Green Lakes Trail and head north from the meadow, following signs to Pole Creek.

TIP: Shortly after crossing the west fork of Park Creek, look for an unsigned side path to the left that goes to Red Meadow. Although not as scenic as Park Meadow, it is less crowded and well worth a visit.

You top a small rise and then drop through forest to a fork of Whychus Creek (formerly Squaw Creek). Over the next low ridge is another branch of Whychus Creek—this one dirty with glacial silt.

After another 0.7 mile of uneventful hiking, you reach the welcome banks of Soap Creek and a trail junction. Good campsites are available in the nearby trees.

Two outstanding side trips leave the main loop at this point. If the weather is good, try to make time for both of them. The first climbs the 5-mile trail to Camp Lake and the Chambers Lakes.

WARNING: Beware of a tricky crossing of Whychus Creek along the Camp Lake Trail—particularly on warm afternoons with lots of glacial ice melting above.

A night spent at popular Camp Lake is likely to be cold and windy, but it will be richly rewarded with terrific scenery. If the weather is good, we highly recommend carrying your gear up here and spending the night. From Camp Lake you could also take an extra day to scramble up the steep, rocky south slope of Middle Sister to its summit. This climb is recommended only for confident and experienced hikers.

The second side trip from the Soap Creek crossing is less crowded, and it doesn't visit any lakes, but it is still glorious. Follow an unmarked use path going west up the north bank of Soap Creek. After about 3 miles you'll reach a large, flat pumice meadow beneath the towering cliffs on the east face of North Sister. This is a spectacular spot, although, like Camp Lake, it's too exposed for comfortable camping in bad weather.

The sometimes dusty main loop trail continues north from Soap Creek for 0.6 mile to a junction with the Pole Creek Trail (keep left, staying on the Green Lakes Trail), and then takes a rather monotonous course through dry, mostly viewless terrain for 5.7 miles to a junction with the Scott Trail.

TIP: A fine way to break up this segment is to follow a faint use path up splashing Alder Creek to its highly scenic headwaters beneath the northeast side of North Sister.

Turn left at the Scott Trail junction and climb 1.8 miles to Scott Pass, where there is a junction with the PCT beside tiny South Matthieu Lake. The three designated camps here are justifiably popular with both weekend backpackers and PCT thru-hikers.

TIP 1: Excellent short evening strolls lead to high points both north and south of this pool. Both are wonderful places to watch the sunset.

South Sister over pond near Green Lakes
photographed by Douglas Lorain

TIP 2: If the weather is threatening, more-sheltered camps are available at North Matthieu Lake.

Your loop trip is nearly complete now, but the remaining hike is *not* anticlimactic. Ahead lie still more grand scenery and the most interesting geology of the tour. Walk south on the PCT, cross a short section of lava, and then round the slopes of a relatively recent cinder cone called Yapoah Crater. Another 0.6 mile leads to a junction in a meadow, which is filled with blue lupine blossoms in early to mid-August. You continue straight (south) and gradually climb past tiny Minnie Scott Spring (which has fair camps) and then go back into the lava to oddly named Opie Dilldock Pass. From here a not-to-be-missed side trip climbs to Collier Cone and Collier Glacier viewpoint. As the name advertises, this spot provides an excellent overlook of this massive ice sheet, one of the largest in Oregon.

Back on the PCT, travel south through a lava flow to a crossing of White Branch Creek, the outflow of Collier Glacier. An up-and-down hike, mostly in forest, leads to the junction in Sunshine Meadows that you hit on day one. Turn right and follow the Obsidian Trail 4.8 miles back to your car. The hike may now be behind you, but expect the memories to last forever.

POSSIBLE ITINERARY

	CAMP	MILES	ELEVATION GAIN
Day 1	Eileen Lake	10.6	2,100'
Day 2	Sisters Mirror Lake	12.3	1,500'
Day 3	Park Meadow	12.9	1,700'
Day 4	Camp Lake	8.8	1,800'
Day 5	Soap Creek (with side trip up Soap Creek)	11.6	1,300'
Day 6	South Matthieu Lake	7.5	1,300'
Day 7	Out	11.3	900'

7

SEPARATION CREEK LOOP

RATINGS: Scenery 6   **Solitude** 7   **Difficulty** 6
MILES: 42 (44)
ELEVATION GAIN: 4,700' (5,200')
DAYS: 4–6 (4–6)
SHUTTLE MILEAGE: n/a
MAP: National Geographic Trails Illustrated *Bend/Three Sisters*
USUALLY OPEN: Mid-July–October
BEST: Mid-July–October
PERMIT: Yes (free at the trailhead)
RULES: Maximum group size of 12 people; no fires near Eileen, Husband, or Sisters Mirror Lake; no camping within 100 feet of trails or water in Linton Meadows and around Eileen and Husband Lakes
CONTACT: McKenzie River Ranger District, Willamette National Forest, 541-822-3381, www.fs.usda.gov/willamette

SPECIAL ATTRACTIONS ·····················

Solitude, wildflowers, mountain meadows

CHALLENGES ·····························

Mosquitoes until about mid-August

Above: Separation Creek along the shore of Horse Lake
photographed by Douglas Lorain

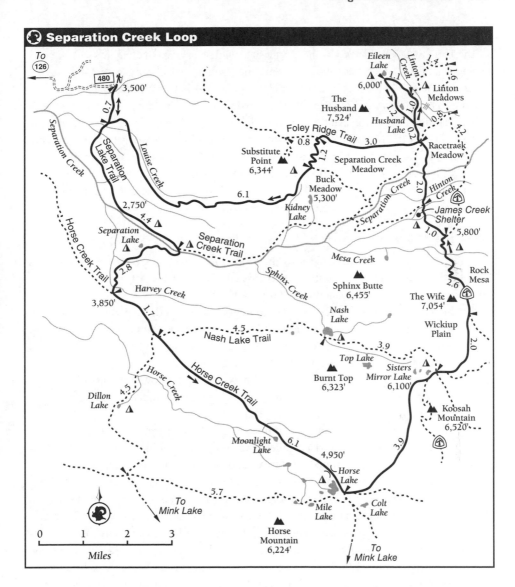

HOW TO GET THERE ●

From I-5, take Exit 194A in Eugene, and head east on OR 126. Go 6.3 miles and turn left to remain on OR 126. Drive 46.8 miles east on OR 126 to a junction with Forest Service Road 2643 (Foley Ridge Road), exactly 0.6 mile past the McKenzie River Ranger Station. Turn right (south) and go 7.7 miles on this one-lane paved road to a junction where the pavement ends. Veer right, drive 0.6 mile, and then bear right onto FS 480 and proceed 1.2 miles to the Separation Lake Trailhead.

GPS TRAILHEAD COORDINATES: N44° 08.196' W121° 58.395'

INTRODUCTION •

The Three Sisters Wilderness is the most visited wilderness area in Oregon, so it's not surprising that hikers sometimes have a hard time finding uncrowded trails. But solitude-loving pedestrians need not fear because such trails do exist. The key to finding them is realizing that the vast majority of visitors to this huge wilderness concentrate on a handful of very popular destinations. If you avoid these areas, there is a good chance that you will have the trail all to yourself. This loop takes you through some of the quietest parts of the preserve as it makes a long, woodsy approach to the more crowded high country. In addition to providing solitude, this warm-up period helps build anticipation for the great scenery to come, and if you start your trip on a Saturday, as most people do, it won't be until the quieter days of midweek that you reach the popular meadows and lakes around timberline.

DESCRIPTION •

The trail begins in a stately old-growth forest dominated by western hemlocks and Douglas firs mixed with a few western red cedars and Pacific yews. After 0.7 mile of minor ups and downs, you reach a junction and the start of the loop.

For the recommended counterclockwise tour, go straight on the Separation Lake Trail, which over the next mile crosses two branches of Louise Creek, then larger George Creek on a convenient log. The sometimes brushy trail then contours through viewless but attractive woods for about 1 mile before gradually descending to the bottom of the heavily forested canyon of Separation Creek. From here, the trail follows this cascading creek upstream 1.2 miles to an excellent campsite and then gradually ascends another 0.8 mile to a second campsite and a junction.

Turn right, cross the creek on a flat-topped log, and then traverse the slope on the south side of the stream. The next 1.1 miles take you gently uphill to lily pad–filled Separation Lake, which is surrounded by skunk cabbage bogs and dense forests and has a good campsite above its southeastern shore. About 0.5 mile beyond Separation Lake, you cross an unnamed creek and then make a very steep 700-foot climb of a wooded slope. At the top of the climb you step over tiny Harvey Creek and come to a junction. Turn left on Horse Creek Trail and ascend this gently graded route 1.6 miles to an easily missed junction. For a really long loop you could turn right, walk past seldom-visited Dillon Lake, and then continue about 12 miles south to the Mink Lake Basin. From there, you would head north on the Pacific Crest Trail (PCT) and return to the main loop near Horse Lake.

Instead, the recommended trail goes straight at the faint junction and, 0.1 mile later, reaches a fork and another choice of routes. The shorter option goes left on the Nash Lake Trail, which passes its namesake lake after 4.5 miles and then climbs to a junction with the PCT near Sisters Mirror Lake. The other option is slightly longer but is recommended because it is more scenic. For this alternative, go right at the fork and begin a mostly forested climb. After 3.5 pleasant but uneventful miles, the trail levels off near small Moonlight Lake. The trail then contours for 2 miles along a ridge on the north side of the Horse Creek valley. Shortly after it goes through an indistinct pass, the trail reaches a series of excellent campsites beside large and popular Horse Lake.

TIP: For even better campsites, take the rugged angler's path that loops around the west side of this scenic lake.

WARNING: In July, the mosquitoes are voracious around Horse Lake and often seem to rival the lake's namesake animal in size.

At the east end of Horse Lake is a junction. Bear left on a dusty trail and walk uphill 0.2 mile to a second junction. Turn left (north) and go steadily uphill through viewless forest for 3 rather monotonous miles to a group of small lakes and ponds on the meadowy Sisters Mirror Plateau. Several enchanting heather-rimmed pools here feature good campsites, though fires are prohibited. In the middle of this plateau you merge with the PCT just before reaching Sisters Mirror Lake. Trees now mostly obstruct the view from here of South Sister, which the lake once mirrored, but this popular lake is still very beautiful.

TIP: The campsites at Sisters Mirror Lake are often crowded. For more privacy, consider going to any of several off-trail lakes to the west.

A little past Sisters Mirror Lake is a junction with the Nash Lake Trail, where you connect with the shorter loop option discussed earlier. Go straight and walk 0.3 mile to the next junction, where you bear left, staying on the PCT. From here, make a brief traverse through woods before crossing the west side of Wickiup Plain, a large and sparsely vegetated pumice-covered meadow. This plain provides excellent vistas of bulky South Sister and the large obsidian, lava, and pumice flow called Rock Mesa spread out at the mountain's base. To the northeast is Middle Sister, a sharp pyramid that rises a little to the left of her taller southern sibling. In keeping with the area's family theme, the small rocky peak on the left (northwest) side of Wickiup Plain is called The Wife.

At the north end of Wickiup Plain is a junction. Go straight, traverse a waterless depression just below the edge of Rock Mesa, and then descend two switchbacks to an excellent campsite near the second of two branches of spring-fed Mesa Creek. The trail almost immediately climbs away from Mesa Creek, gaining about 200 feet to a junction. The PCT goes straight, but for this trip turn sharply left, following signs to Linton Meadows, and wander up and down on the James Creek Trail through open forest and past small meadows for 0.8 mile to James Creek Shelter. This well-maintained wooden structure is a wonderful place to camp because it has water and boasts a fine view of the top third of South Sister over a lush little meadow.

About 0.2 mile past the shelter, you hop over a tiny creek and immediately reach a junction. Go straight, soon cross Separation Creek on a log, and then make a 2-mile traverse that ends at a confusing junction at the southwestern tip of pumice-covered Racetrack Meadow. The unsigned trail that goes sharply left leads in less than 1 mile to Separation Creek Meadow, a worthwhile side trip for its flowers and nice view of Middle Sister. The main trail, however, goes straight at the Separation Creek Meadow junction and, 20 yards later, reaches a signed four-way junction.

The Foley Ridge Trail, which goes left here, is the return route of this loop. Before going that way, however, take the scenic side trip to Linton Meadows and Eileen Lake. So go straight, walk 0.2 mile across the west side of Racetrack Meadow, and then come to a fork. This junction is the start of a very scenic loop. Bear right (slightly downhill) and descend past great viewpoints of Middle Sister's nearly perfect pyramid to the green, flowery wonderland of Linton Meadows. The beauty of this oasis is enhanced by spring-fed Linton Creek, which tumbles down a tiered waterfall to the east before meandering across the meadow. Towering above the flower-studded grassland are Middle Sister, South Sister, and The Husband, all vying for the title of being the most beautiful member of their extended family. It's a tough contest to judge, and one on which you can spend several happy hours trying to make up your mind. Camping is not allowed within 100 feet of water or trails in Linton Meadows.

At the north end of Linton Meadows are some possible campsites and a junction. Bear left and make a scenic 1.1-mile jaunt to spectacular Eileen Lake. This small meadow-rimmed gem has very scenic (but overused) campsites and, from the northwestern shore, views of the Three Sisters that will take your breath away. Fires are prohibited within 0.25 mile of this lake as well as at nearby Husband Lake.

From the outlet of Eileen Lake, the trail turns south and goes gradually uphill to Husband Lake. From the east (nontrail) side of this shallow lake, there are stunning reflections of (appropriately enough) The Husband. A little beyond Husband Lake you close the side-trip loop when you reach the junction with the trail to Linton Meadows. Go straight to return to the junction with the Foley Ridge Trail at the southwest corner of Racetrack Meadow.

Go right (west) on the Foley Ridge Trail and travel gently up and down for 3 miles through forest and past several stagnant ponds to a junction. Turn left and descend a half dozen switchbacks to a junction at the north end of long and narrow Buck Meadow. The well-used trail that goes straight dead-ends after 100 yards at a leaky wooden shelter and a possible campsite.

WARNING: The tiny creek here usually dries up by late summer.

Your trail, which is very faint at first, veers right at the junction and travels along the west side of grassy, 0.5-mile-long Buck Meadow. From the south end of the meadow, the trail makes a brief climb to the west and then begins a long descent. The entire route is through forest, which becomes increasingly lush with a denser understory as you lose elevation. A little over 6 miles from Buck Meadow is the junction with the Separation Lake Trail and the close of the loop. Turn right and thus back to your car.

POSSIBLE ITINERARY

	CAMP	MILES	ELEVATION GAIN
Day 1	Separation Lake	6.2	200'
Day 2	Horse Lake	9.4	1,800'
Day 3	James Creek Shelter	9.6	1,700'
Day 4	Eileen Lake (with side trip to Separation Creek Meadow)	6.3	800'
Day 5	Out	12.4	700'

8

MINK LAKE AREA

RATINGS: Scenery 7   **Solitude** 4   **Difficulty** 3
MILES: 24 (38)
ELEVATION GAIN: 1,600' (3,300')
DAYS: 3 (3–5)
SHUTTLE MILEAGE: 16
MAP: National Geographic Trails Illustrated *Bend/Three Sisters*
USUALLY OPEN: July–October
BEST: Late August–September
PERMITS: Yes, self-issued at trailhead; Northwest Forest Pass required
RULES: No camping or fires within 100 feet of lakes
CONTACT: Bend–Fort Rock Ranger District, Deschutes National Forest, 541-383-4000, www.fs.usda.gov/deschutes

SPECIAL ATTRACTIONS •

Fishing and swimming lakes, relatively easy hiking

CHALLENGES •

Mosquitoes in July and early August, crowded in spots

Above: Campsite at Snowshoe Lake
photographed by Becky Ohlsen

🔵 Mink Lake Area

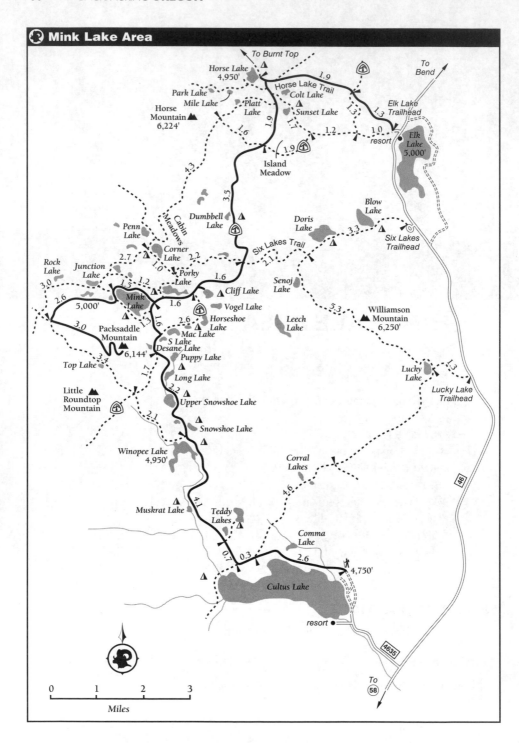

HOW TO GET THERE ●●

For a south-to-north tour, start from the east end of Cultus Lake. From I-5, take Exit 188A in Goshen, and head southeast on OR 58. In 72.5 miles turn left onto Cascade Lakes National Scenic Byway/Forest Service Road 61, and go 3.2 miles. Turn left to remain on Cascade Lakes National Scenic Byway/FS 46 (closed in winter; usually open by Memorial Day). Go 24.5 miles, and near the north end of Crane Prairie Reservoir, turn left (west) onto FS 4635 to Cultus Lake. At a fork in 2 miles, keep right toward the campground, and in 0.5 mile keep right again on dirt FS 100 to its end at the trailhead.

To reach the north trailhead, from the intersection of US 20 and US 97 in Bend, head south on US 20 and take Exit 138 to Downtown/Mount Bachelor. Turn right (east) onto Colorado Avenue, and go 1.6 miles. At the second traffic circle, take the third exit to head left onto Southwest Century Drive. Go 5.3 miles and continue straight onto Cascade Lakes National Scenic Byway/FS 46. Drive 25 miles, then turn right at signs for Elk Lake Resort and the trailhead, at the end of Elk Lake Resort Loop.

GPS TRAILHEAD COORDINATES:
(Cultus Lake) N43° 50.387' W121° 50.042'
(Elk Lake) N43° 59.043' W121° 48.666'

INTRODUCTION ●●

The south half of the Three Sisters Wilderness has a totally different character than the north. There are no tall peaks, no glaciers, few meadows, and only limited views. What the hiker will discover, however, are miles of pleasant forest trails and enough lakes to impress even Minnesota natives. Every turn of the trail seems to reveal another lovely mountain pool, ranging from a small pond to a large lake. Each is distinct enough that lovers of fishing, swimming, rafting, or just sightseeing can stay happy for weeks. Another nice thing about this country is the easy hiking. Because almost everything is at roughly the same elevation, extended ups and downs simply don't exist—which means a lot less work for tired backpackers. This trip is perfect for hikers of advancing years with knees that suffer on long downhills or as a first long backpack for younger travelers. Easy trails and numerous lakes allow for short hiking days and lots of time for lazy afternoons.

All that water, of course, has one big drawback—*mosquitoes!* The clouds of flying bloodsuckers here are thicker than a Dairy Queen milkshake. In July your essential gear should include repellent, a head net, and an extra pint or two of blood to replace that stolen by the bugs. Fortunately, by mid-August or so the number of invertebrates has dropped dramatically, and by September you can comfortably travel without repellent or even a tent—the rain gods permitting, of course.

DESCRIPTION ●●

From the Cultus Lake Trailhead, hike west along the lakeshore path, passing several good swimming beaches with views across this large lake. The trail veers away from the lake after 1.7 miles and leads northwest for 0.9 mile to a junction with the trail to Corral Lakes. Go straight here, and 0.3 mile farther turn right at a second junction. After 0.7 mile, you pass the side trail to Teddy Lakes (which has good camps). Another 1.4 miles of

Cabin beside Muskrat Lake
photographed by Becky Ohlsen

easy walking leads to a lovely meadow, which contains lily pad–filled Muskrat Lake and its quaint little cabin. If the ground isn't too swampy, take time to visit this cabin; it was once a nice first-come, first-served overnight shelter for backpackers, but it has deteriorated a bit too much to be tempting. Better camps are available in the woods at the lake's north end near the inlet creek.

Muskrat Lake is an inviting camp spot, but you probably won't be tired when you get there, since in 5 miles the elevation gain has been only 200 feet. With all that extra energy, you might prefer to continue north to equally scenic Winopee Lake. The route gradually gains a bit of elevation as it parallels a small creek (usually nothing more than a trickle by late summer). About 2 miles from Muskrat Lake is the south shore of large, irregularly shaped Winopee Lake. The trail works around the east shore of this lake, mostly in viewless forest, to a lovely meadow at the north end. This meadow is well worth exploring, though it's rather boggy.

At the trail junction beside Winopee Lake, keep right, and in rapid succession reach Snowshoe Lake (with a good campsite or two on rocky outcrops) and two smaller, unnamed lakes as you *slowly* climb on this attractive route. Upper Snowshoe Lake is the next highlight, with its excellent camps and lunch spots. Here, as at all the larger lakes along this tour, hikers should look for goldeneyes (ducks), ospreys, and bald eagles—all common in the area. Continuing your hike north, the seemingly endless parade of lovely lakes continues with Long Lake and Puppy Lake. At a meadow holding Desane Lake is a junction with the Pacific Crest Trail (PCT). Turn right on the PCT to reach the shores of S Lake and another junction.

The PCT keeps right here, passing yet another string of attractive lakes. The recommended route, however, turns left, climbs a low ridge, and then drops fairly steeply into the basin containing popular Mink Lake. Dozens of excellent camps surround this scenic 360-acre lake. The best views are from the northeast shore near an old shelter. Good camps and worthwhile day hike destinations are found in almost every direction. Our favorite camps are a little to the east at Porky Lake, but other nearby lakes (some off-trail) provide more private locations. For those with enough time, consider setting up a base camp at Porky Lake and exploring in various directions from there.

One highly recommended day hike side trip is the path from Mink Lake to the top of Packsaddle Mountain, the area's highest viewpoint. The climb is fairly long but worthwhile, and the tired hiker can look forward to returning to a lakeside camp and a pleasant swim. The path starts near Junction Lake west of Mink Lake. Some of the less strenuous day hike options include Corner Lake, Junction Lake, and Cabin Meadows.

To continue the recommended trip, hike along the south side of Porky Lake and then climb out of the lakes basin back to the PCT. Turn north and after about 100 yards reach the possibly unsigned 0.1-mile side trail to Cliff Lake.

TIP: Be sure to visit this scenic lake—it features good camps, a trail shelter, and great rocks along the north shore.

The PCT continues north and east through forests and meadows. You pass several small rock formations on the way to a four-way junction with the Six Lakes Trail. Keep straight (north) on the PCT along an easy route through rolling mountain hemlock forests. The trail passes tiny Island Lake and larger Dumbbell Lake (good camps) and then drops over a gentle saddle to a four-way junction west of Island Meadow. If the weather is bad, turn right here for a quick exit back to the Elk Lake Trailhead. Otherwise, veer left to reach Horse Lake—just 2 miles away.

Horse Lake is the largest and prettiest of another cluster of lakes. Excellent campsites abound near Horse Lake, but for more privacy try nearby Mile or Park Lake—any of which would make another good base camp for further explorations.

TIP 1: The best lunch spot at Horse Lake is on the rock peninsula on the lake's west shore—reached by an angler's path around the lake. The view from here includes a nice perspective of Mount Bachelor.

TIP 2: If you have an extra day and good route-finding skills, consider visiting Burnt Top. Take the trail going northwest from Horse Lake for about 1.8 miles and then hope to find the unmaintained 3.5-mile route to the right leading to Burnt Top's summit views.

To reach the exit point, head due east from Horse Lake on well-used Horse Lake Trail #3516. You gradually climb to a viewless pass and a junction with the PCT. Keep straight on a dusty trail, and in 1.3 miles reach civilization, in the form of the Elk Lake Trailhead.

NOTE: For loop lovers, this area provides several possible options. One alternative is to start your trip at the Lucky Lake Trailhead. Hike southwest via Corral Lakes to Cultus Lake, turn north past Winopee and Mink Lakes to the Six Lakes Trail, and then return via Senoj Lake and Williamson Mountain.

POSSIBLE ITINERARY

	CAMP	MILES	ELEVATION GAIN
Day 1	Mink Lake	11.5	500'
Day 2	Day trip up Packsaddle Mountain (return to Mink Lake)	14.0	1,700'
Day 3	Horse Lake	8.8	700'
Day 4	Out	3.4	400'

Winopee Lake
photographed by Becky Ohlsen

9

DIAMOND PEAK LOOP

RATINGS: Scenery 8   **Solitude** 6   **Difficulty** 5
MILES: 27 (36)
ELEVATION GAIN: 3,500' (4,300')
DAYS: 3–4 (4–5)
SHUTTLE MILEAGE: n/a
MAP: USFS *Middle Fork Ranger District*
USUALLY OPEN: July–October
BEST: Mid- to late July
PERMITS: Yes, self-issued at trailhead
RULES: Maximum group size of 12 people
CONTACT: Crescent Ranger District, Deschutes National Forest, 541-433-3200,
www.fs.usda.gov/deschutes

SPECIAL ATTRACTIONS •

Relative solitude, scenic lakes, relatively easy loop

CHALLENGES •

Mosquitoes

Above: Lakeview Mountain over Stag Lake
photographed by Douglas Lorain

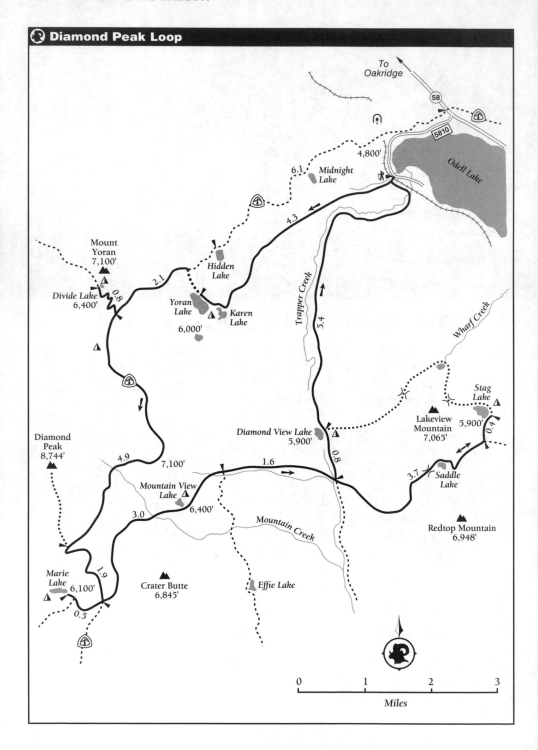

Diamond Peak Loop

To Oakridge

58

5810

4,800'

Odell Lake

6.1

Midnight Lake

4.3

Trapper Creek

Wharf Creek

Mount Yoran
7,100'

Hidden Lake

2.1

0.8

Divide Lake
6,400'

Yoran Lake

Karen Lake

6,000'

5.4

Stag Lake

0.4

Diamond Peak
8,744'

Diamond View Lake
5,900'

Lakeview Mountain
7,065'

5,900'

4.9

7,100'

1.6

0.8

3.7

Saddle Lake

Mountain View Lake

6,400'

3.0

Mountain Creek

Redtop Mountain
6,948'

Marie Lake

6,100'

1.9

Crater Butte
6,845'

Effie Lake

0.5

0   1   2   3

Miles

HOW TO GET THERE ●

From I-5, take Exit 188A in Goshen, and head southeast on OR 58 for 62.1 miles to Willamette Pass. Just east of the pass, turn right onto Odell Lake Road/Forest Service Road 5810. Follow this paved route 1.8 miles to the well-marked Yoran Lake Trailhead.

GPS TRAILHEAD COORDINATES: N43° 34.970' W122° 02.729'

INTRODUCTION ●

The high, snowy ridge of Diamond Peak rises impressively over the lush forests and quiet lakes south of Willamette Pass. Despite easy access and beautiful scenery, the wilderness surrounding this mountain receives less use than other areas. Like a neglected stepchild, Diamond Peak is ignored by most Oregonians in favor of the Three Sisters to the north or Mount Thielsen to the south. Diamond Peak, however, provides scenery to rival any other major Cascade peak—and this trip proves it.

DESCRIPTION ●

To hike this loop counterclockwise, take the trail to Yoran Lake. Climb gradually through generally viewless forests for 4 miles to irregularly shaped Karen Lake and larger Yoran Lake just beyond. Good campsites can be found at both lakes, but Yoran Lake has the edge in scenery because it boasts a forested island and a good, if partly obstructed, view of Diamond Peak.

Hike around to the north end of Yoran Lake and then break out the compass and climb cross-country on a northwest course through forests for about 0.4 mile to the Pacific Crest Trail (PCT). Turn left and follow this well-graded route to a junction with the trail to Divide Lake. For a side trip and campsite turn right, climb over a low saddle, and switchback down to Divide Lake. The towering double summits of Mount Yoran loom over the north shore of this deep little pool.

TIP: Don't forget your wide-angle lens.

Nearby small ponds and heather meadows add to the magic of this scene. The best camps here are at the west end of the lake.

TIP: A superior late-afternoon or evening stroll follows the trail along a ridge northwest of Divide Lake. An incredible perspective of Diamond Peak appears in about 0.5 mile.

Now return to the PCT and turn south. This route soon passes a pair of lovely ponds with a nearby campsite, climbs a bit, and then begins a long contour across the view-packed meadows and talus slopes on the east shoulder of Diamond Peak. The route is very scenic and very high. Be prepared to cross snowfields here through July.

An exceptional side trip for fit and experienced hikers is the steep cross-country scramble to the summit of Diamond Peak. After the trail begins to descend from the high country, leave the PCT just before a switchback on the south side of the peak and scramble up the long south ridge. The rocky, exposed route should be attempted only in good weather, but it does not require technical climbing skill or equipment. On a clear day the view from atop Diamond Peak may be the best in Oregon. From here you can see all the way from Mount Hood to California's Mount Shasta. To the east stretch the seemingly endless forests and deserts of eastern Oregon.

Back on the trail, you drop through open forests to a four-way junction. To reach the good camps at quiet Marie Lake, turn right and hike 0.5 mile through a pumice meadow with nice views of Diamond Peak.

Return to the PCT junction and go straight (traveling north and east) on a sketchy route that climbs through open mountain hemlock forests.

TIP: Watch for tree blazes to help you navigate this trail.

After 1.6 miles is a beautiful meadow where you cross Mountain Creek and then hike downhill through forest another 0.7 mile to reach shallow Mountain View Lake. The mosquitoes here are particularly fierce in July, so camping is not recommended, but the reflected view of the long, snowy ridge of Diamond Peak is exceptional. Unfortunately, later in the season—when the bugs are gone—the snow on the mountain has melted and the lake's level is lower, so the view isn't as good. Continue hiking east 2.4 forested miles to a possibly dry creekbed and a four-way junction. Turn left and hike 0.8 mile to aptly named Diamond View Lake. Several good camps exist at this popular and scenic lake. The bugs here are less numerous than at Mountain View Lake, but you'll still be glad you brought repellent and a tent with mosquito netting.

A highly recommended side trip starts from the junction south of Diamond View Lake. Go east and climb gradually to a pass containing appropriately named Saddle Lake, and then continue another 1.3 miles to reach the side trail to Stag Lake. Turn left to reach this shallow pool, with its excellent camps and a superb view of the cliffs on the east face of Lakeview Mountain. Hikers accomplished with a map and compass can scramble steeply over a pass west of Stag Lake and drop to a secluded pool north of Lakeview Mountain. There are great views of this craggy butte from the pool's north shore. Now you travel southwest past another pond and through yet another saddle before striking off west by southwest to reach the trail near Diamond View Lake. The entire circuit of Lakeview Mountain makes for a challenging but highly satisfying day trip from a base camp at Diamond View Lake.

To complete the trip, hike north from Diamond View Lake through monotonous lodgepole pine forests. On the left, rushing Trapper Creek plays hide-and-seek with the trail for a few miles before you finally cross it and make the short jog back to your car.

POSSIBLE ITINERARY

	CAMP	MILES	ELEVATION GAIN
Day 1	Divide Lake	7.3	2,100'
Day 2	Marie Lake	8.1	800'
Day 3	Diamond View Lake	5.9	500'
Day 4	Day trip to Stag Lake (return to Diamond View Lake)	9.8	800'
Day 5	Out	5.4	100'

10

NORTH UMPQUA–
MOUNT THIELSEN TRAILS

RATINGS: Scenery 7   **Solitude** 6   **Difficulty** 6
MILES: 47 (49)
ELEVATION GAIN: 6,800' (8,700')
DAYS: 4–5 (4–6)
SHUTTLE MILEAGE: 34
MAP: USFS *Umpqua Divide Wilderness: Boulder Creek Wilderness, Rogue–*
Umpqua Divide Wilderness, Mount Thielsen Wilderness, Oregon Cascades
Recreation Area
USUALLY OPEN: Late June–October
BEST: July
PERMITS: Overnight parking fee $5 at Toketee Lake Campground; Northwest
Forest Pass required at North Crater Trailhead
RULES: Maximum group size of 12 people; no camping within 100 feet of lakes
CONTACT: Diamond Lake Ranger District, Umpqua National Forest, 541-498-
2531, www.fs.usda.gov/umpqua

SPECIAL ATTRACTIONS ●

Waterfalls, mountain scenery, diverse landscapes, easy road access

Above: Mount Thielsen and Cottonwood Creek
photographed by Douglas Lorain

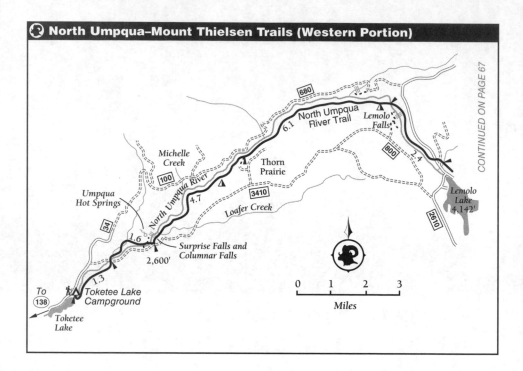

North Umpqua–Mount Thielsen Trails (Western Portion)

CONTINUED ON PAGE 67

CHALLENGES

Less-attractive section near Lemolo Lake; mosquitoes at higher elevations in July; long stretches without water; inconvenient parking

HOW TO GET THERE

Due to persistent overuse problems at Umpqua Hot Springs, overnight parking is no longer allowed at the hot springs trailhead (formerly our recommended entry point). Instead, you can leave your car at the nearby Toketee Lake Campground. From I-5, take Exit 124 in Roseburg. Turn right (east) onto Harvard Avenue, which becomes Oak Avenue. In 0.6 mile turn left (north) onto Southeast Stephens Street. In 0.3 mile turn right onto OR 138, and go 58.8 miles. Turn left (north) onto paved Forest Service Road 34, signed as Toketee-Rigdon Road. After about 200 yards keep left and cross the North Umpqua River, staying on FS 34. Drive 1.5 miles to the Toketee Lake Campground entrance on the right.

TIP: Be especially careful to leave nothing of value in your car. The proximity to the hot springs means that this area gets a lot of traffic and seems to attract burglars.

The end of this hike is easier to locate. Follow the directions above to OR 138, and go east 86.6 miles, 1 mile from the north entrance to Crater Lake National Park, and turn left (north) at the sign for the North Crater Trailhead/Sno-Park. Signs in the parking area point you to the Pacific Crest Trail.

North Umpqua–Mount Thielsen Trails (Eastern Portion)

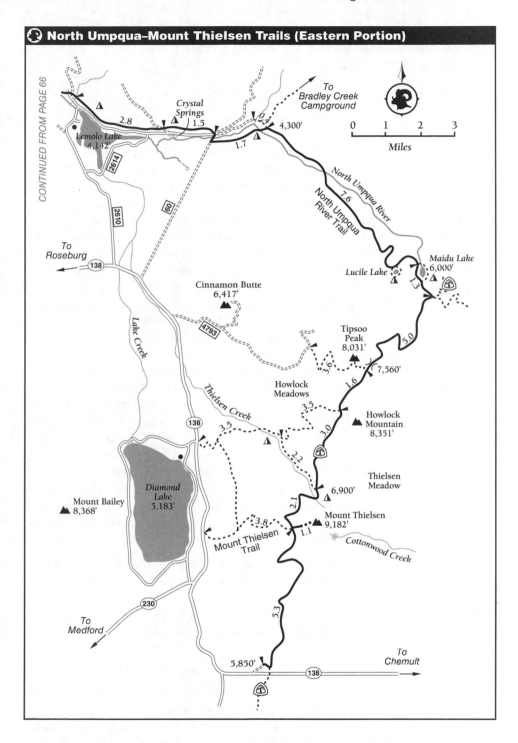

CONTINUED FROM PAGE 66

Crystal
Springs
1.5

To
Bradley Creek
Campground

4,300'

Lemolo Lake
4,142'

2.8

1.7

2614

2610

60

North Umpqua River

North Umpqua
River Trail

7.6

To
Roseburg

138

Maidu Lake
6,000'

Lucile Lake

1.3

Cinnamon Butte
6,417'

4793

Tipsoo
Peak
8,031'

5.0

7,560'

Howlock
Meadows

1.6

3.6

Thielsen Creek

3.5

Howlock
Mountain
8,351'

138

3.5

3.0

2.2

Diamond
Lake
5,183'

Thielsen
Meadow

Mount Bailey
8,368'

6,900'

2.1

Mount Thielsen
9,182'

3.8

1.1

Cottonwood Creek

Mount Thielsen
Trail

5.3

230

To
Medford

5,850'

To
Chemult

138

0   1   2   3
Miles

GPS TRAILHEAD COORDINATES:
(Toketee Lake Campground) N43° 16.417' W122° 24.233'
(North Crater) N43° 05.552' W122° 05.642'

INTRODUCTION ••

This wonderful hike has a split personality. The first part travels through the wild canyon of the North Umpqua River, where the highlights include old-growth forests, towering waterfalls, columnar basalt formations, and a lovely stream. The second half of the hike climbs to the Cascade crest and explores the scenic meadows, crags, and views around Howlock Mountain and Mount Thielsen. Few people hike these two trails in one outing because they are separated by a less attractive area around busy Lemolo Lake. Done in combination, however, they are a great experience. This is one of the few places in Oregon where it is still possible to take the long, respectful trail approach to the high country that was formerly the only way to visit it. By starting from low-elevation riverside forests and gradually working up to the high volcanic peaks, the hiker gets a complete sampling of the Cascade Mountains' many environments and charms. It is, of course, possible to do this trip from high to low (which would mean less elevation gain), but going from low to high saves the climactic scenery for the end.

Altitude is not the only difference between the two trail sections. The canyon section is a celebration of water—both in its many forms and of the beautiful things it creates. The trail passes countless large and small springs, mossy cliffs, several waterfalls, and, of course, always the enchanting river. Lush old-growth forests here feature specimens of Douglas fir, western hemlock, cedar, big-leaf maple, and Pacific yew. Ferns, mosses, and other water-loving species crowd the forest floor. In contrast to the virtual rainforest below, the high-country section of this route is amazingly dry. There is very little surface water and limited ground cover, and the forests consist of water-starved lodgepole pine and mountain hemlock. There is, of course, a reason for the striking difference between these two neighboring environments. Porous volcanic soils around Mount Thielsen allow most of the water to percolate into the ground rather than flowing on top. This water later feeds the many springs in the lower canyon. Lemolo Lake marks the dividing point between the two environments, and the change from one to the other is remarkably sudden.

NOTE: If you choose to hike the trails separately, note that the peak seasons are late May–mid-June for the lower canyon and mid- to late July for the high country.

WARNING: The lower part of this trail is shared with mountain bikers. In theory, hikers have the right-of-way, but always stay alert for other trail users.

DESCRIPTION ••

Catch the North Umpqua Trail at the southwest side of the campground, near the parking area, and follow it northeast about 1.3 miles to the Umpqua Hot Springs trailhead.

If you start your hike on a weekday, when the hot springs are much less crowded, consider taking the steep 0.3-mile trail to the springs. Here you can relax and soak your muscles in the 100+°F waters. You might also elect to save this experience for when you return after the hike.

WARNING: Nude bathing is the norm here. Leave your modesty at home.

The North Umpqua Trail picks up again about 100 yards up the road from the hot springs parking area and drops to the left into the trees. You cross Loafer Creek and soon reach aptly named Surprise Falls, which leaps out of the ground from a large spring directly beneath the trail. Just ahead is even more impressive Columnar Falls, where smaller springs feed a lacy waterfall that drops over a moss-covered basalt cliff. At the base of this cliff, the water simply disappears back into the ground. A third waterfall, this one on a more conventional side stream, is 0.2 mile beyond Columnar Falls.

As the trail continues up the canyon, it zigzags around numerous landslides and the remnants of downed trees. Storms do a number on the trail every winter; early season hikers should check the status of the trail before setting out, as the spring recovery process takes longer in some years.

In the wettest sections, plank boardwalks provide a dry passage for hikers. Though the trail closely parallels the river, it is rarely level, as it seems to go constantly up and down between marshy river flats and cliffs above the water. The wonderful scenery amply compensates for the sweat.

NOTE: Most of the North Umpqua River's water flows in a diversion canal and pipeline rather than the natural streambed. The water is taken out upstream at Lemolo Lake and feeds several electric power stations. Hikers can only imagine how beautiful this canyon must have been with a full stream.

Just 1.5 miles from the hot springs is Michelle Creek, where the trail cuts across a series of mossy rocks, springs, and small waterfalls. Another 0.5 mile of hiking takes you to three large nurse logs that have fallen with their upended root systems exposed. Signs identify these giants as the Sleeping Stooges, and each log is marked with the name of one of the famous comics. ("Larry" actually bridges the river.) Continuing upstream, several river flats make nice camps for those who got a late start.

Keep straight at the junction with the Thorn Prairie connector trail, which makes a short climb to a spur road. The main trail continues upstream through more forests. On the opposite side of the river, an unobtrusive gravel road follows a section of the diversion canal. About 4.5 miles from the Thorn Prairie connector, a set of power lines leads from Lemolo generator #1 on the opposite bank. The trail continues 1.4 miles beyond the generator to a river crossing.

The roar coming from up the canyon is Lemolo Falls. At 169 feet this enormous waterfall is one of the trip's scenic highlights.

TIP: The best views are from the south. Take the time to scramble up this bank for a few hundred yards to a trail that comes down from the right. You can follow this trail upstream to reach some wonderful photo opportunities of the falls' sheer drop.

Now cross the river on a log and begin to climb. Near the top of the ascent are some partly obstructed views of the falls.

Once above the falls, the trail closely follows the river as the water cascades along and drops in a series of small but attractive falls. The forests here support lots of wildflowers in May and June. The trail slowly climbs to meet the pipes and canals of the water diversion system on the left. Small leaks give the impression of natural springs, especially since water-loving plants have colonized these human-made creeklets. Where the path leaves the canyon, there is a trailhead and a bridge over the canal to a paved road.

The trail resumes on the opposite side of the road and immediately enters a different environment. Open lodgepole pinewoods replace the lush canyon forests. These trees are smaller and straighter and provide less shade than the Douglas fir forests below. The ground cover is also sparser and has changed from rhododendrons and ferns to huckleberries and manzanita.

The trail crosses a gravel road and a creek and then begins its long eastward course paralleling the paved road on the north side of Lemolo Lake. Occasional breaks in the trees provide views of Lemolo Lake and distant Mount Thielsen to break up the monotony. Fortunately, the trail is nearly level, so the miles go by quickly.

TIP 1: Try to do this stretch on a weekday when the road is less busy.

TIP 2: If you need water or a place to camp, simply scramble down to the lake, where numerous possible sites exist.

Mount Thielsen over Thielsen Creek
photographed by Douglas Lorain

Presently you cross another gravel road and shortly thereafter a sometimes dry creekbed.

TIP: A short side trip to the main road from here leads to a fine camp—complete with a picnic table—beside large Crystal Springs.

In another mile the trail drops to a road junction. To continue your tour, veer right, follow the road over the sparkling stream, and look for a sign on the left marking the resumption of trail. The route immediately enters wilder, more attractive terrain.

The path continues upstream almost 2 miles before crossing the river (possible camps). Shortly thereafter is a junction with a spur trail from the Bradley Creek Campground and Trailhead. The North Umpqua Trail turns right and begins a long, mostly viewless climb to the high country. As you gain elevation, the ground cover gets lusher and the trees slowly change over to mountain hemlock. The remnants of the North Umpqua River (now only a small creek) splash along on the right. Cross the flow and begin a long sidehill climb. The well-graded trail is mostly in shade, so the climb is not difficult. Eventually the trail turns south up a ridge, crosses a dry creekbed, and soon reaches a poorly marked trail junction.

To the right is forest-rimmed Lucile Lake. A pleasant trail circles this mountain pool; the best camps are on its southwest shore. About 0.5 mile from the Lucile Lake junction, the main trail passes an excellent high viewpoint before making a short, mostly level jog to Maidu Lake. Forests and excellent campsites surround this popular lake. As always, camp well away from fragile lakeshore locations.

WARNING: Be prepared for lots of mosquitoes here in July.

This lake is the source of the North Umpqua River, which you have now followed upstream all the way from Toketee Lake.

TIP: Fill your water bottles here. The only trailside water for the next 11 miles is from lingering snowfields.

To continue your tour, pass the lake and take the trail from its south end that climbs to a forested pass and a junction with the Pacific Crest Trail (PCT). Turn right (south) and begin a long, viewless climb through mountain hemlock forests. After 2.2 miles the trail reaches a marvelous viewpoint atop a rocky promontory. Rest and enjoy the scenery, and then reshoulder your pack and resume climbing. The trail circles around the remains of a flattened volcanic butte, passes another viewpoint, and comes to a saddle on the northeast side of Tipsoo Peak. Ice age glaciers obviously ripped deeply into this reddish-colored peak's north side, though no ice remains today. You continue climbing beside a gully and then come to a meadow leading to another broad pass, where posts mark the way across a pumice-covered flat. Tired hikers rejoice—this 7,560-foot pass is the highest point on the PCT in Oregon!

TIP: Don't miss the relatively easy scramble to the excellent overlook atop Tipsoo Peak.

From the pass your trail returns to the trees and begins a gradual descent. Now you round a ridge and begin to enjoy occasional views of craggy Howlock Mountain. Shortly after you pass a junction, the PCT skirts around the left side of a large pumice flat called Howlock Meadows.

> **TIP:** For an exceptionally scenic vista of Howlock Mountain, take the time to visit the middle of this meadow. From here it's easy to see how this section of the Cascade crest got the name Sawtooth Ridge.

Although camping here seems inviting, lingering snowfields provide the only water. Forced, therefore, to continue south, you can look for intermittent views of Diamond Lake and Mount Bailey to the west as you make a long, irregular descent. About 3 miles from Howlock Meadows is Thielsen Meadow and the welcome waters of Thielsen Creek. Please camp back in the trees, well away from the fragile meadows.

Thielsen Meadow is a popular place for several reasons. Water from the spring-fed stream attracts PCT hikers. Abundant wildflowers provide delicate beauty and draw their share of admirers. Most outstanding of all, however, is the jaw-dropping view of the north face of Mount Thielsen. The towering cliffs rise almost 2,300 feet above the meadow to the mountain's famous pointed summit. The incredible scenery has earned this spot a place on our list of Oregon's most spectacular locations.

> **TIP:** Photographers will need an extrawide-angle lens to capture this scene.

You could easily spend an extra day here just gazing up in amazement. For more exercise, venture out on any of several highly rewarding day hikes. Nearby are the boulder field and springs at the head of Thielsen Creek and the small glacier at the base of the cliffs on the north face of Mount Thielsen. More ambitious hikers can scramble up an unnamed high point northeast of Mount Thielsen, where an outstanding overlook of the peak and surrounding country awaits. A final option is to scramble over a bouldery pass to the east and then drop steeply to the huge pumice flat at the head of Cottonwood Creek, directly beneath the steep east face of Mount Thielsen.

The PCT continues south from Thielsen Creek, making a long, gradual climb to a ridge, where you are treated to a frontal view of the colorful scree slopes on Mount Thielsen's northwestern face. The mountain's impressive summit spire is prominently displayed. This pinnacle is a favorite target of Mother Nature's wrath, earning Mount Thielsen the nickname Lightning Rod of the Cascades. The trail cuts across a scree slope to a second ridge, where there is a junction with the Mount Thielsen Trail from Diamond Lake.

If the weather is good, strong hikers who aren't afraid of heights should take the time to climb Mount Thielsen. The unofficial trail is easy to follow as it winds through twisted mountain hemlocks and whitebark pines and passes numerous delicate rock gardens. Views of distant peaks and lakes improve with every heart-pounding step. Above the treeline the "trail" charges up a supersteep slope of scree and loose rocks, eventually topping out on a small ledge at the base of the summit pinnacle. The world-class landscape from here includes most of the state of Oregon, as well as parts of California. A sharp eye will even be able to see over the rim of Crater Lake not far to the south. The final 100 feet or so to the top of the mountain is definitely not for everyone. While not technically difficult, it requires using handholds and footholds to crawl carefully up the rock face. To the north and east sheer cliffs drop 2,000–3,000 feet, so vertigo is a real concern.

WARNING: Given this mountain's nickname, hikers should avoid this climb when there is any threat of a thunderstorm.

After returning to the PCT, continue south and make a long, gradual, and rather uneventful descent around forested ridges to a dirt road. Cross the road and shortly thereafter turn right at a junction with the 0.2-mile trail that drops down a forested gully to the official Pacific Crest Trailhead and your car.

POSSIBLE ITINERARY

	CAMP	MILES	ELEVATION GAIN
Day 1	Below Lemolo Falls	10.6	1,100'
Day 2	North Umpqua River crossing	9.0	900'
Day 3	Maidu Lake	7.7	2,100'
Day 4	Thielsen Creek	10.9	2,100'
Day 5	Out (with side trip up Mount Thielsen)	9.6	2,500'

Dodger Point lookout
photographed by Douglas Lorain

11

NORTH UMPQUA TRAIL

RATINGS: Scenery 7   **Solitude** 6   **Difficulty** 3

MILES: 47

ELEVATION GAIN: 1,626'

DAYS: 3–5

SHUTTLE MILEAGE: 36

MAP: USFS *North Umpqua Ranger District*

USUALLY OPEN: March–November

BEST: April and May

PERMITS: None

CONTACT: Roseburg Office, Bureau of Land Management, 541-440-4930, blm
.gov/office/roseburg-district-office; Umpqua National Forest, 541-672-6601,
www.fs.usda.gov/umpqua (North Umpqua Ranger District, 541-496-3532;
Diamond Lake Ranger District, 541-498-2531)

SPECIAL ATTRACTIONS •

Whitewater rafters; beautiful river and canyon scenery; wildlife; waterfalls; fishing

CHALLENGES •

Poison oak; nearby major highway; ticks

Above: North Umpqua River
photographed by Becky Ohlsen

North Umpqua Trail (Western Portion)

CONTINUED ON PAGE 76

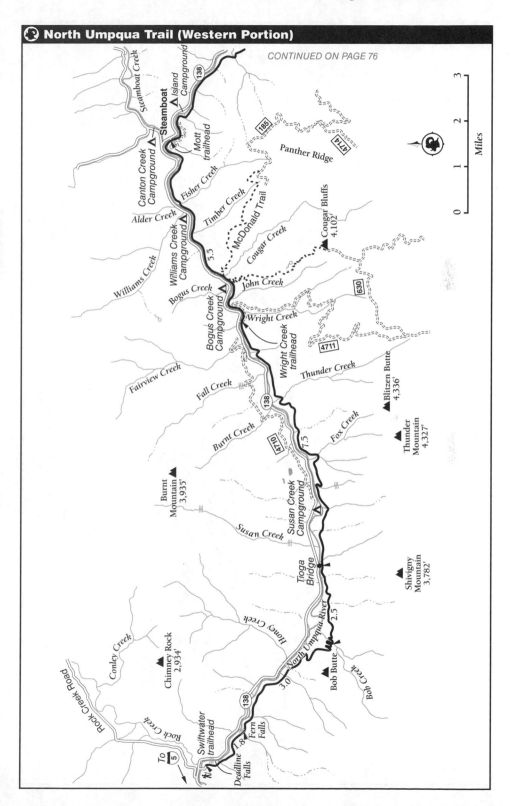

North Umpqua Trail (Eastern Portion)

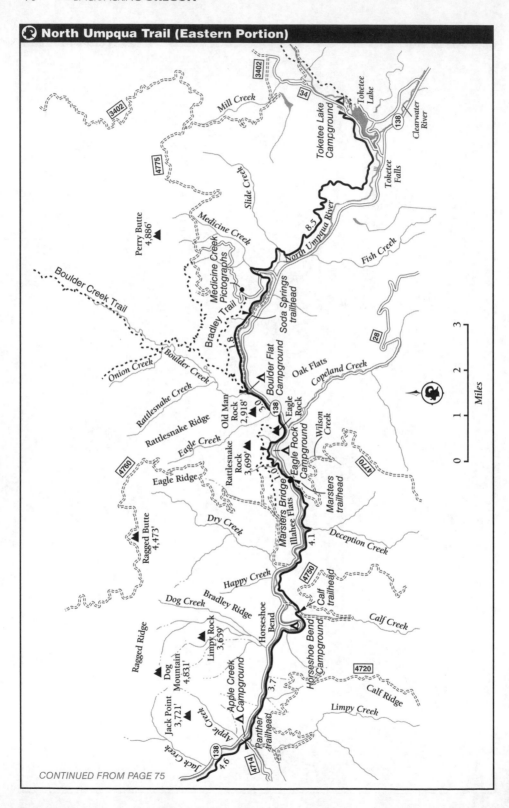

CONTINUED FROM PAGE 75

HOW TO GET THERE •

To reach the Swiftwater trailhead, take Exit 124 from I-5 in Roseburg. Turn right (east) and cross the South Umpqua River. In 0.5 mile turn left (north) onto Southeast Stephens Street, and go 0.3 mile. Turn right onto OR 138, and go 22 miles to a well-marked day-use area; the trail starts just across the bridge.

The Toketee Lake trailhead is just as easy to reach: it's an additional 36.7 miles east along OR 138, and it's also well marked. Turn left onto Toketee-Rigdon Road, veer left to cross the river, and turn left immediately after the crossing to reach the trailhead.

GPS TRAILHEAD COORDINATES:
(Swiftwater) N43° 19.902' W123° 00.304'
(Toketee Lake) N43° 16.347' W122° 24.348'

INTRODUCTION •

The North Umpqua Trail, completed in 1997, follows the beautiful North Umpqua River from Idleyld Park all the way to the river's source. Even though the trail parallels busy OR 138, it has a surprisingly wild character. A series of bridges and road crossings allows for one-way trips of 5–70 miles; access points are easy to find all along OR 138.

A shady path along the North Umpqua River
photographed by Becky Ohlsen

Another advantage of this hike: there's no shortage of water sources, as you follow the river the entire way, and smaller creeks fan out from the path every couple of miles.

The best early-season choice is the section described here, from Swiftwater Park to Toketee Lake. The upper part of the trail, going east from Toketee Lake, is described in Trip 10. Given enough time, you could easily combine the two into one longer trip.

DESCRIPTION • • • • • • • • • • • • • • • •

From the Swiftwater trailhead, follow the clear and well-established footpath along the river through deep, quiet, old-growth forest of sugar pine, hemlock, and Douglas fir. In just 0.25 mile you'll reach Deadline Falls, where May–October you can observe salmon and steelhead jumping the falls on the way to their spawning grounds. Another mile and a half down the trail, you reach Fern Falls. About 5 miles in, the trail climbs to Bob Butte, a popular goal for day hikers.

Two miles farther along is the start of the Tioga segment, marked by the Tioga Bridge—it was built in 2013 over the ruins of an old bridge that washed out in 1964. The Tioga segment is 8 miles of mostly dense old-growth forest. At several points you can see the burned-out area left behind by the 2009 Williams Creek Fire. There are no official campgrounds in this segment, but it's possible to find sites off the trail. A developed campground is located at Bogus Creek, near the Wright Creek trailhead.

Next up is the Mott segment, 5.3 miles of riverside trail that makes the transition from old-growth forest to wildflower meadows. It's followed by the almost 5-mile Panther segment, which goes through riverside gravel bars and high rocky bluffs. Near the Panther segment trailhead, you will find a developed campground at Apple Creek.

The path goes back down to the river to start the Calf segment, which borders the results of yet another fire, the 17,000-acre Apple Fire of 2002. The river stopped the fire's progress northward.

WARNING: The fire also created some unstable areas along the trail, leading to occasional washouts; be sure to check conditions before you go, especially early in the season. Call the North Umpqua Ranger District at 541-496-3532.

You climb away from the river again for the 3.6-mile Marsters segment, which winds through mossy rocks and forests and offers good views of the river below. Near the Marsters Bridge is a Chinook salmon spawning bed, where you can see the fish returning from the ocean in the fall. Just beyond the Marsters segment trailhead is another developed campground at Eagle Rock.

The trail meets a roadbed that goes through a canyon on the Jessie Wright segment (named for an early homesteader). A number of side trails branching off from this segment—especially the Boulder Creek and Bradley Trails—give you the option of making a side-trip loop (with a bonus: the side trails are closed to mountain bikes).

The Deer Leap segment takes you high again, along the rim of a canyon. Don't miss the side trip to Medicine Creek Pictograph, a mile up on Forest Service Road 4775. You soon reach Toketee Lake and the spectacular double-tiered Toketee Falls. A campground and trailhead here mark the end of the recommended route (though not the end of the trail).

POSSIBLE ITINERARY

	CAMP	MILES	ELEVATION GAIN
Day 1	Wright Creek	15.8	200'
Day 2	Apple Creek	9.2	300'
Day 3	Eagle Rock	8.0	200'
Day 4	Out	14.0	846'

12

SKY LAKES TRAVERSE

RATINGS: Scenery 7 **Solitude** 4 **Difficulty** 5
MILES: 31 (45)
ELEVATION GAIN: 3,600' (5,200')
DAYS: 3–4 (4–6)
SHUTTLE MILEAGE: 41
MAP: USFS *Sky Lakes Wilderness*
USUALLY OPEN: July–October
BEST: Mid-August–early September
PERMITS: None
RULES: Maximum group size of 8 people/12 stock; near lakes, camping is allowed only at designated sites
CONTACT: Klamath Ranger District, Fremont–Winema National Forest, 541-883-6714, www.fs.usda.gov/fremont-winema

SPECIAL ATTRACTIONS •

Huckleberries; swimming and fishing lakes

CHALLENGES •

Mosquitoes (through mid-August); crowded in spots

Above: Devils Peak over Cliff Lake
photographed by Douglas Lorain

79

Sky Lakes Traverse

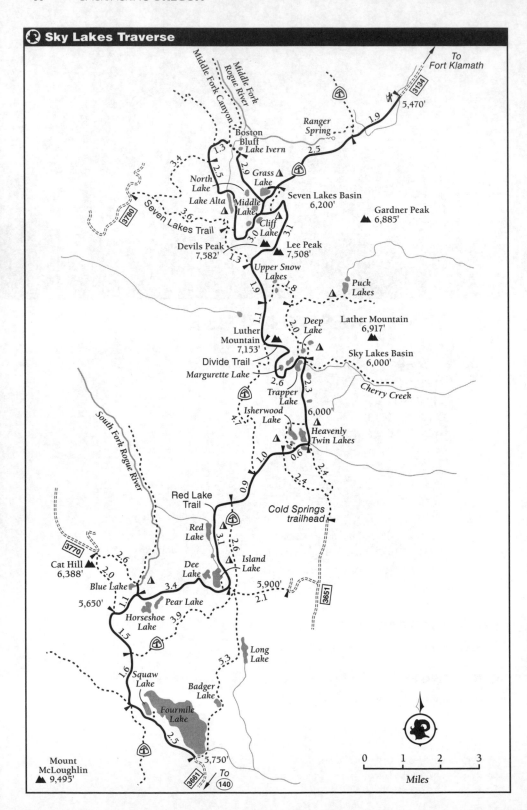

To Fort Klamath

3134
5,470'

1.9

Middle Fork Rogue River

Middle Fork Rogue Canyon

Ranger Spring

Boston Bluff
Lake Ivern

1.3   2.5

2.5   2.9

Grass Lake △

3.4

North Lake

Lake Alta △

Middle Lake

Seven Lakes Basin
6,200'

Gardner Peak
▲ 6,885'

Seven Lakes Trail

3780

3.6

Cliff Lake △

3.0   3.1

Devils Peak
7,582'   1.3

Lee Peak
7,508'

Upper Snow Lakes

Puck Lakes △

1.9   1.8

1.1

Deep Lake

Lather Mountain
6,917'

Luther Mountain
7,153'

2.0

Divide Trail

Sky Lakes Basin
6,000'

Margurette Lake

2.6

2.3

Trapper Lake

Cherry Creek

South Fork Rogue River

Isherwood Lake

.4.7   △

6,000'

Heavenly Twin Lakes

△

1.0   0.6

2.4

0.9   2.4

Red Lake Trail

Cold Springs trailhead

3770

2.6

Red Lake △

3.1   2.6

Island Lake △

3651

Cat Hill ▲
6,388'

2.0

Dee Lake △

5,900'

Blue Lake

1.1   3.4

2.1

5,650'

Pear Lake

Horseshoe Lake

3.9

1.5

Long Lake

5.3

1.6   Squaw Lake

Badger Lake

Fourmile Lake

Mount McLoughlin
▲ 9,495'

2.5

5,750'

3661   To
140

0   1   2   3

Miles

HOW TO GET THERE ●

To reach the north trailhead from the intersection of US 97 and OR 140 in Klamath Falls, head 4.7 miles north on US 97. Continue on US 97 N another 20.9 miles. Turn left (west) onto OR 62, and go 13.7 miles. In Fort Klamath, turn right (north) to continue on OR 62, and go 0.3 mile. Turn left (west) onto Nicholson Road, and go 3.9 miles. Nicholson Road becomes Forest Service Road 33; continue another 0.4 mile. Turn right onto FS 3134 (also labeled FS 3334 on some maps), following signs to Sevenmile Marsh Trailhead, and drive 5.5 miles to the road's end.

To reach the Fourmile Lake Trailhead, take I-5 to Exit 30 in Medford. Head northeast on OR 62, and go 5.6 miles to OR 140. Turn right (east) on OR 140 toward Klamath Falls, and drive 35.6 miles. Then turn left at a sign for Fourmile Lake, and follow gravel FS 3661/ Fourmile Lake Road. Go 5.7 miles to the trailhead.

NOTE: Another recommended option is to turn this traverse into a figure eight hike that starts and concludes at the Cold Springs Trailhead. To get here, take OR 140 as above, but continue 5.2 miles farther east beyond the Fourmile Lake turnoff. Then turn left (north) onto FS 3651, and drive 10 miles to the road's end (look for signs to Cold Springs Trailhead). There are also many possibilities for side trips along the described route.

GPS TRAILHEAD COORDINATES:
(Sevenmile Marsh) N42° 41.963' W122° 08.896'
(Fourmile Lake) N42° 27.329' W122° 15.019'
(Cold Springs) N42° 32.582' W122° 10.850'

INTRODUCTION ●

South of Crater Lake, the Cascade Range narrows somewhat, but packed tightly into this mountainous strip is a beautiful land of open forests, deep canyons, craggy mountains, and countless lakes. Such features long ago made the Sky Lakes Wilderness a popular destination for local outdoor lovers. Now, as word of the area's beauty spreads, hikers from other regions are increasingly discovering this private hideaway. This highly attractive point-to-point hike samples most of the charms of this wilderness and is equally scenic in either direction. It is described here from north to south, so you can enjoy a gradual approach to Mount McLoughlin, the area's principal landmark.

WARNING: The numerous lakes and ponds of the Sky Lakes Wilderness are a nursery for a tremendous population of invertebrate vampires (mosquitoes). If you come in July—when the crags are streaked with snow and pictures are at their prettiest—be prepared with repellent, a head net, and a well-enclosed tent. Otherwise, consider visiting mid-August—early September, when the bugs are mostly gone and the huckleberries are ripe.

DESCRIPTION ●

From the Sevenmile Marsh Trailhead, follow the dusty but mostly level Seven Lakes Trail past a marshy area and through a forest of lodgepole pines to a junction with the Pacific Crest Trail (PCT).

TIP: An interesting side trip from here goes north and then west to gushing Ranger Spring—the source of the Middle Fork Rogue River.

Continue south on the PCT 2.5 miles to aptly named Grass Lake. A short side trail leads to a camping area on the lake's northeast shore and the first good view of craggy Devils Peak. From Grass Lake your route veers right, away from the PCT, and follows the southeast shore of the lake to a junction near Middle Lake. All the nearby lakes, including Middle Lake, have good to excellent camps.

From a base camp at any of the scenic lakes in this area, an outstanding day hike turns north at Middle Lake. The path travels past North Lake on its way to tiny Lake Ivern.

TIP: A few hundred feet north of this pool is Boston Bluff and an outstanding viewpoint of the impressive glacial canyon of the Middle Fork Rogue River.

From Lake Ivern set a northwest course and walk cross-country 0.4 mile to reach a trail coming up from the Middle Fork Canyon. Turn left and follow this trail to a junction, where you turn left again and climb a ridge to narrow and remarkably straight Lake Alta, a nice place for a swim. Continue south to a junction with the western access trail for the Seven Lakes Basin and turn left. This path drops into the basin, first visiting South Lake, before arriving at Cliff Lake—most dramatic of all. Cliff Lake sits directly beneath the towering north face of Devils Peak, so you should allow time to admire this spectacular spot. To close the loop, continue north a short distance back to Middle Lake.

To continue your trip, exit the basin by heading south on the PCT as it climbs the northeast shoulder of Devils Peak to a saddle beside Lee Peak.

TIP: It is easy, and highly rewarding, to climb the ridge from here to the summit of Devils Peak.

The PCT goes west across an open slope to a junction with the trail coming up from Lake Alta. Turn left and hike south along a very scenic ridge with excellent views to distant Mount McLoughlin. After 1.9 miles a trail goes northeast to nearby Upper Snow Lakes before dropping into the Sky Lakes Basin. A more scenic approach to the Sky Lakes heads south on the PCT another mile and then turns left on the spectacular Divide Trail. This route descends past ponds and viewpoints to lovely Margurette Lake, which offers excellent camps.

TIP: A nice side trip from here goes north about 1.3 miles to Lower Snow Lakes, directly below the cliffs of Luther Mountain. Return via a short loop around quiet Deep and Donna Lakes.

To continue your hike, go south past Trapper Lake and then through generally viewless forests for 2.1 miles to the two Heavenly Twin Lakes—the largest of another attractive cluster of lakes, though these lack mountain views.

The trail crosses a narrow, forested peninsula between North and South Heavenly Twin Lakes, and then it continues 1.5 miles southwest to a junction with the PCT, which has made a mostly forested descent from Luther Mountain to this point. You now follow the PCT 0.9 mile to another junction and once again turn off the main path, this time to the right on the Red Lake Trail. You pass the shores of the trail's namesake before reaching appropriately named Island Lake. In addition to a forested island, this lake features a nice vista of Mount McLoughlin from a camp on its northeast shore. The path then works southeast away from the lake to a junction. Turn right and pass near the southern shore of Island Lake and an interesting historical landmark. In 1888 Judge John B. Waldo, for whom Waldo Lake in Willamette National Forest was named, carved his name in a tree here during his epic exploration of the Cascade Range.

Leaving Island Lake and the Waldo Tree behind, go west and make a forested descent into a fifth lake basin. This one features Pear and Horseshoe Lakes, both barely touched by the trail, and several off-trail pools. The prettiest, and most popular, of the lakes here is Blue Lake, backed by a 300-foot cliff. You reach this lake via a short side trip to the north at a junction west of Horseshoe Lake. There are plenty of options for campsites throughout this basin.

To complete your journey, turn southwest from Blue Lake and climb 1.1 miles to a ridgetop junction. Turn left here and travel over Cat Hill, where an opening in the trees provides a nice if partly obstructed view of Mount McLoughlin.

When you yet again reach the PCT, turn right (south) and gradually go up and down, mostly in forest, to a saddle with a four-way junction. Turn left and soon reach shallow Squaw Lake.

TIP: Don't miss taking a short side trip up the trailless east shore of Squaw Lake. Photographers will especially like the excellent reflection of Mount McLoughlin in the tranquil early morning waters.

The trip ends with an almost level forest walk to the south end of Fourmile Lake (actually a human-made reservoir).

POSSIBLE ITINERARY

	CAMP	MILES	ELEVATION GAIN
Day 1	Cliff Lake	5.2	800'
Day 2	Day hike loop around Lake Ivern (return to Cliff Lake)	9.8	1,400'
Day 3	Margurette Lake	11.0	1,600'
Day 4	Blue Lake	11.7	500'
Day 5	Out	6.9	900'

13

STRAWBERRY MOUNTAINS TRAVERSE

RATINGS: Scenery 9   **Solitude** 6   **Difficulty** 7
MILES: 35 (52)
ELEVATION GAIN: 7,600' (11,700')
DAYS: 4 (5–6)
SHUTTLE MILEAGE: 31
MAP: USFS *Strawberry Mountain and Monument Rock Wilderness*
USUALLY OPEN: Late June–early November
BEST: Early to mid-July and mid-October
PERMITS: None
RULES: No camping within 100 feet of lakes or streams; maximum group size of 12 people/18 stock
CONTACT: Prairie City Ranger District, Malheur National Forest, 541-820-3800, www.fs.usda.gov/malheur

SPECIAL ATTRACTIONS

Mountain scenery; views; fall colors; solitude (for most of the trip); wildlife

CHALLENGES

Long stretches without water; several burn areas

Above: Strawberry Mountain from ridge near Indian Creek Butte
photographed by Douglas Lorain

Strawberry Mountains Traverse

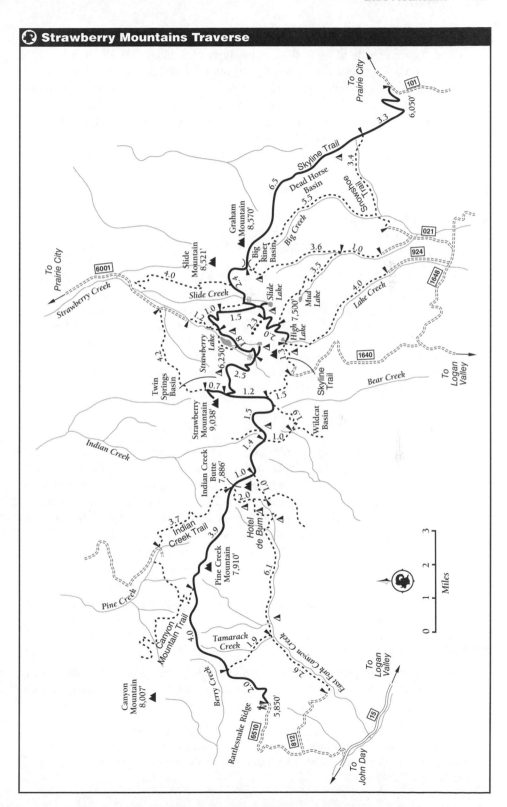

HOW TO GET THERE •

To find the west trailhead, from the intersection of US 26 and US 395 in John Day, head south on US 395. In 8 miles, turn left (east) onto paved Canyon Creek Road/Forest Service Road 15, and go 4 miles. Turn left onto gravel FS 1510, which becomes FS 6510, and follow it 4.9 miles to its end at the Joaquin Miller Trailhead.

To reach the east trailhead, follow the directions above to Canyon Creek Road/FS 15. Turn left (east) onto FS 15, and go 13.7 miles to FS 16. Turn left (northeast) onto FS 16, and drive 13.8 miles, through Logan Valley to Summit Prairie. Turn left (north) onto Summit Prairie Road/FS 14/County Road 62 and go 3.2 miles; then turn left (west) onto rough gravel FS 101. Drive 1.4 miles to the Skyline Trailhead.

GPS TRAILHEAD COORDINATES:

(Joaquin Miller) N44° 17.361' W118° 53.556'

(Skyline) N44° 14.385' W118° 32.280'

NOTE: In 1996 the Wildcat Fire swept through a large section of the Strawberry Mountain Wilderness. On this hike, the still-obvious affected area extends from Indian Creek Butte in the west to Twin Springs Basin on the east side of Strawberry Mountain. You'll also see damage from the 2015 Canyon Creek Complex Fire, especially around Indian Creek Butte. In places, blowdown from the fire has made the trail faint, so be sure to carry a good map and compass. While flowers and grasses tend to benefit from wildfires, the larger trees have yet to fill in, and many views still include snags and blackened timber. Shade is at a premium on this section of the trail.

INTRODUCTION •

The narrow spine of the Strawberry Mountains packs a lot of scenic punch in a small package. Its snowy line of peaks provides a lovely backdrop, seen both from the north over the upper John Day River Valley near Prairie City and from the south over Logan Valley. Happily, the backcountry trails deliver scenery at least as good as that seen from a distance. Views are spectacular throughout, flowers are abundant, and wildlife is unusually common. The range is crowded only near the few lakes in it, so there are miles of rarely traveled trails. For those who do make the scenic traverse of the Strawberries, most begin at the Canyon Mountain Trailhead near Iron King Mine. The route described here is shorter, involves less climbing, and has better road access. It also passes through some of the range's best wildlife habitat, so your chances of seeing elk, bighorn sheep, and other animals are significantly improved.

DESCRIPTION •

This trip starts with a short climb along Rattlesnake Ridge, followed by three long downhill switchbacks to a saddle. Now you contour around two hills and then drop a bit to another saddle and a junction with the Tamarack Creek Trail, where you go left.

TIP: This is one of the best areas in Oregon to spot bighorn sheep. Keep your binoculars handy for the next few miles. If you're really lucky, you may also see black bears or the elusive mountain lion. Watch for movement on the steep canyon walls of Berry and Tamarack Creeks.

From the junction your trail climbs steeply along a ridge and then contours around the head of Tamarack Creek.

TIP: At a saddle on the side of this ridge, be sure to visit a small rise south of the trail to check out the view and look for animals.

The climb eases somewhat as you approach a pass along the high ridge of the Strawberry Mountains. For the next several miles the route follows this view-packed ridge. Water is scarce except for a few snow patches into July.

Keep right at a junction with the Canyon Mountain Trail and then cut across the steep north face of Pine Creek Mountain. Snow lingers here for much of the season. Your route climbs to a pass on the east slopes of Pine Creek Mountain and then makes a long traverse along the south side of the ridge. The trail remains on the south side as it makes a gradual descent to a four-way junction, immediately north of prominent Indian Creek Butte.

TIP: Camps in this area are best made near the previous crossings of two small creeks, or turn right and drop 500 feet in 1.5 miles to a spring with a good campsite. The as-fancy-as-it-sounds Hotel de Bum, a small camp at the headwaters of the East Fork of Canyon Creek, offers good views of Indian Creek Butte.

NOTE: From this point to a little beyond Strawberry Mountain, wildfires have made great changes to the landscape, still starkly in evidence along the trail.

The main trail stays straight at the four-way junction and cuts across the east face of Indian Creek Butte. To the east, across the deep canyon of Indian Creek, rises Strawberry Mountain, the highest point in this range. The trail contours through a low saddle to a junction. Turn left and travel east along the ridge to a large meadow, which supports scattered wildflowers in July and has an exceptionally picturesque view of Strawberry Mountain. From here the trail drops to a junction where there is a choice of trails. To the right, the main trail drops to the wildflowers of Wildcat Basin (decent camps) before climbing through an interesting eroded "badlands" back up to the ridge. A shorter but equally scenic route, described here, from the junction goes left, passes a junction with the Indian Creek Trail, and soon reaches a beautiful little meadow at the head of Indian Creek. This marshy basin holds lots of wildflowers, provides a fine vista of the cliffs to the south, and has good camps.

WARNING: This boggy area supports a healthy mosquito population through July.

From Indian Creek you make several switchbacks up to a ridge and then reunite with the main trail climbing from Wildcat Basin. Hike east and climb to the end of a closed jeep road that now serves as a trail. You turn left here and follow this exposed and rocky path north, passing several exceptional vistas to the west.

At a ridgetop junction, drop your heavy pack, pick up a camera, and then head north for an excellent side trip to the summit of Strawberry Mountain. The route first cuts across the rocky east face of the peak, where you'll enjoy terrific scenes to the east. A short side trail climbs the northeast ridge to the top. On a clear day there seems to be no end to the views from this overlook. The John Day River Valley lies to the north. To the west is the crumpled spine of the Strawberry Range, with the Aldrich and Ochoco Mountains in the distance. On very clear days even the snowy peaks of the Cascades can be seen. To the south are the forested Blue Mountains and distant Steens Mountain. Turning east you will see the scenic

Strawberry Lake
photographed by Douglas Lorain

peaks, cliffs, and lake basins that will occupy your attention for the next couple of days. A sharp eye will even be able to spot the Elkhorn Range and part of the Wallowa Mountains to the northeast.

After absorbing the views, return to your pack and begin the long descent east toward Strawberry Lake. The highly scenic trail goes through Twin Springs Basin (good camps) and then rounds a ridge with excellent vistas of Strawberry Lake and the cliffs surrounding this basin. About 1,000 feet farther down, you reach a crossing of Strawberry Creek and a junction. To the right is a highly recommended 0.6-mile side trip to beautiful Little Strawberry Lake. The lake sits at the base of 1,500-foot cliffs, so bring an extrawide-angle lens for photographs. There are good camps at both Little Strawberry Lake and Strawberry Creek.

TIP: These camps are generally less crowded than those farther down the trail at popular Strawberry Lake.

To continue your trip, return to the main trail and switchback down the forested slope to the north, stopping along the way to enjoy Strawberry Falls. At the south end of 31-acre Strawberry Lake is a junction. The trail along the west shore is more scenic, but the shorter route along the east side is the usual choice.

TIP: At the north end be sure to take a short detour along the lake's northwest shore to enjoy a classic scene across the lake of the jagged snowy ridge above. Afternoons provide the best lighting for photographs. Because the lake's water level fluctuates considerably, early summer is best.

Camps (and people) are abundant near Strawberry Lake, so if you camp here, expect plenty of company and heed all U.S. Forest Service restrictions on where to set up your tent.

Keep right at two junctions not far below the lake's outlet, following signs to Slide Lake. The trail climbs steadily to a junction at a flat spot on the ridge. The quickest exit goes left, but taking it would bypass too much great scenery, so keep right and make a long up-and-down traverse across an open slope. The distinctive peak to the east is Slide Mountain. Reenter woods and keep right at a junction before climbing to a second junction. To the left a short side trail leads to pretty Slide Lake, which has excellent camps.

Slide Lake makes an outstanding base camp for day hikes. Possible hikes range from the short stroll to Little Slide Lake, a small pool about 0.2 mile south of Slide Lake, to the long scramble up Slide Mountain. The two spectacular destinations could be combined in one rugged day. Begin by climbing the trail heading southwest from the Slide Lake junction. Leave the trail near the base of a steep talus slope and scramble up the ridge to the northwest. The climb ends at the top of the high cliffs above Little Strawberry Lake.

To continue your day hike excursion, return to the trail, turn right, and climb across a steep, rocky slope to a pass.

WARNING: This slope is usually covered with steep snowfields until about mid-July.

Keep right at a junction and travel along the top of an open ridge, where windswept trees and small alpine wildflowers enhance the wonderful scenery. The path now makes a long descent to High Lake—a spectacular pool backed by high cliffs and ridges. Once you've had your fill, return to Slide Lake the way you came.

At the junction north of Slide Lake, turn right. As the trail drops to a junction, look for fine views up to Slide Mountain. Turn right and continue downhill to a creek crossing.

TIP: Impressive Slide Falls is a short bushwhack upstream.

The trail now makes a long 1,200-foot climb out of Slide Basin. Along the way you turn right at a junction with the Slide Basin Shortcut Trail and then complete your climb to a pass with another trail junction. South of the pass is Big Riner Basin (good campsites) and to the left is Graham Mountain.

Turn left at the junction, staying on the Skyline Trail as it makes a long traverse across the southwest slopes of Graham Mountain. You reach a saddle and begin following a scenic up-and-down ridge. To the east, across the forested upper John Day River Valley, are Lookout and Glacier Mountains. As the route loops south around Dead Horse Basin, it stays on the west side of the ridge and passes two welcome springs. Views to the west are superb.

The trail returns to the increasingly forested ridgecrest and eventually meets the Snowshoe Trail coming up from a fire-scarred area to the west. The Skyline Trail continues straight, staying along the ridge for another mile before dropping in very long switchbacks to the eastern trailhead on FS 101.

POSSIBLE ITINERARY

	CAMP	MILES	ELEVATION GAIN
Day 1	Spring below Indian Creek Butte	11.4	3,000'
Day 2	Twin Springs Basin (with side trip up Strawberry Mountain)	9.6	3,100'
Day 3	Slide Lake (with side trip to Little Strawberry Lake)	7.3	1,300'
Day 4	Day hike to High Lake and Strawberry Ridge (return to Slide Lake)	11.0	2,400'
Day 5	Out	12.5	1,900'

14

ELKHORN CREST TRAIL

RATINGS: Scenery 9   **Solitude** 6   **Difficulty** 6
MILES: 27 (32)
ELEVATION GAIN: 3,000' (5,700')
DAYS: 3 (3–4)
SHUTTLE MILEAGE: 35
MAP: USGS *Elkhorn Peak, Bourne,* and *Anthony Lakes*
USUALLY OPEN: July–October
BEST: Mid-July
PERMITS: None
RULES: Maximum group size of 12 people/18 stock; no camping within 100
   feet of lakes and streams.
CONTACT: Whitman Ranger District, Wallowa-Whitman National Forest,
   541-523-6391 or 541-742-7511, www.fs.usda.gov/wallowa-whitman

SPECIAL ATTRACTIONS ●

Views; granite peaks, cirque lakes, and generally excellent mountain scenery; relative
solitude; mountain goats

CHALLENGES ●

Poor road access to southern trailhead; motorbikes

Above: Dutch Flat Lake
photographed by Douglas Lorain

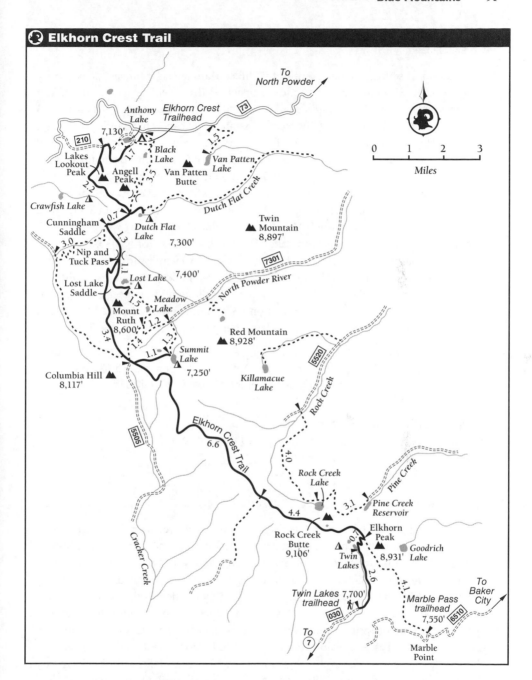

Elkhorn Crest Trail

To North Powder

Elkhorn Crest Trailhead
Anthony Lake 7,130'
73
210
Lakes Lookout Peak
Angell Peak
Black Lake
Van Patten Lake
Van Patten Butte
Crawfish Lake
Dutch Flat Creek
Cunningham Saddle
0.7
Dutch Flat Lake 7,300'
Twin Mountain 8,897'
Nip and Tuck Pass
7301
Lost Lake 7,400'
North Powder River
Lost Lake Saddle
1.5
Meadow Lake
Mount Ruth 8,600'
1.2
Red Mountain 8,928'
3.4
1.4
1.3
5520
Columbia Hill 8,117'
1.1
Summit Lake 7,250'
Killamacue Lake
Rock Creek
5505
Elkhorn Crest Trail 6.6
4.0
Rock Creek Lake
Pine Creek
3.1
Pine Creek Reservoir
4.4
Rock Creek Butte 9,106'
0.7
Elkhorn Peak
Goodrich Lake
Cracker Creek
Twin Lakes
8,931'
2.6
4.1
To Baker City
Twin Lakes 7,700' trailhead
Marble Pass trailhead 7,550'
6510
030
To 7
Marble Point

0 1 2 3
Miles

HOW TO GET THERE

To reach the north trailhead at Anthony Lake, take I-84 to Exit 285 for North Powder. Head west on River Lane, and go 4 miles. Turn left (south) onto Ellis Road, and go 0.7 mile. Turn right (west) onto Anthony Lakes Highway, and go 8.2 miles. Anthony Lakes Highway becomes Forest Service Road 73. Follow signs to Anthony Lakes as you climb paved FS 73 for 7 miles to the Anthony Lake Campground.

TIP: The best place to park is a bit east of the campground at the well-marked Elkhorn Crest Trailhead.

The traditional southern entry point to this hike, Marble Pass trailhead, is extremely difficult to reach without a high-clearance, four-wheel drive vehicle. (That said, if you have the vehicle for the job, starting at Marble Pass saves you significant initial climbing.) From I-84, take Exit 302 in Baker City. Head west on OR 86, and go 0.8 mile. Turn right (west) onto Hughes Lane, and drive 1.2 miles. Continue straight onto Pocahontas Road, and go 7.2 miles (making a right turn and then a left turn to stay on Pocahontas). Turn left (west) onto Marble Creek Road, and in 0.3 mile, turn left (south) to stay on Marble Creek. Go 3.7 miles, and continue straight on FS 6510, which enters national forest land and passes the Marble Creek Picnic Area. In 3.7 miles from the beginning of FS 6510, you top out at a pass and the (signposted) Marble Pass Trailhead.

For an easier drive, start at the Twin Lakes Trailhead, at the end of FS 030. From I-84, take Exit 304 in Baker City. Head west on Campbell Street. In 0.9 mile turn left (south) onto Main Street, and go 0.5 mile. Continue straight on OR 7 S for 22.5 miles. Make a right turn (north) onto Deer Creek Road/FS 6550, continue 3.3 miles, and then veer right (northwest) onto FS 6540. In 0.6 mile keep straight on FS 030. In 2.5 miles the road becomes a hikable track at a trailhead entrance sign, and another parking area is 0.5 mile farther.

TIP: For around $80, local shuttle services (try Range Tour & Shuttle Co.: 541-519-8028; rangetour.com) will pick you up at the Anthony Lake boat launch ($4 parking fee), where you leave your car, and drop you at the Marble Pass trailhead.

GPS TRAILHEAD COORDINATES:
(Anthony Lake/Elkhorn Crest) N44° 57.797' W118° 13.505'
(Marble Pass) N44° 46.402' W118° 02.631'
(Twin Lakes) N44° 46.780' W118° 05.518'

INTRODUCTION ●

The jagged spine of the Elkhorn Range rises dramatically above Baker City and the Powder River Valley. Strangely, although countless people drive past these impressive peaks on I-84, relatively few stop to explore. This narrow range hides many of the same treasures that make the nearby Wallowa Mountains so popular (granite peaks, glacial lakes, and clear streams), but for some reason it receives only a tiny fraction of the publicity. Lovers of solitude would prefer it if it stayed that way. Unfortunately, most of this range is unprotected and therefore open to mining (once an important business in these mountains), logging, and motorbikes. A trip along the view-packed Elkhorn Crest Trail is the ideal way for backpackers to enjoy this lovely range and learn what is at stake. This relatively easy trail closely follows a high ridge for its entire length. Side trails drop to numerous lakes and meadows with scenic campsites. The trip is beautiful in either direction, but south to north is marginally easier because the start is some 400 feet higher.

WARNING: The southern half of this trail is open to motorbikes. Be prepared to have the quiet disrupted on occasion.

DESCRIPTION ●

Your route climbs gradually (if you start from Marble Pass) or steeply (if you start from the Twin Lakes Trailhead) along a mostly open ridge to the northwest. Views here, as well as along most of this route, are superb, as they alternate between the forested Blue Mountains and Sumpter Valley to the southwest, and the Powder River Valley and the distant Wallowa Mountains to the northeast. For most of the trip the trail stays on the west side of the Elkhorn Crest, so vistas west dominate.

The outstanding scenery—particularly of the picturesque basin holding the Twin Lakes, with brown and reddish peaks all around—continues along the next stretch of trail. The high point on the east side of this basin is Elkhorn Peak, an inviting mountain with reasonably easy access up its south ridge. The crest trail continues its scenic course— sometimes on the ridge's west side, sometimes at or near the crest—another 3 miles to a trail junction in a saddle. If you started the hike at the Twin Lakes Trailhead, you'll have come up this way; if not, don't miss this excellent side trip, which turns left and drops 0.7 mile in a series of long switchbacks to Lower Twin Lake—backed by rugged cliffs. Smaller Upper Twin Lake is also worth exploring, though there is no official trail. The lower lake is prettier and has better camps.

Fill your water bottles (there is precious little of the stuff along the ridge), climb back to the crest trail, turn left, and round the head of the Twin Lakes Basin.

> **TIP:** An outstanding cross-country side trip climbs moderately steep slopes to the summit of Rock Creek Butte. At 9,106 feet this is the highest point in the range, and it commands a breathtaking view in all directions. Most impressive of all is the look down to sparkling Rock Creek Lake, which sits in a stark basin beneath sheer cliffs. Bring binoculars to check for what appear to be small moving snowfields, but are actually mountain goats.

After another 0.7 mile on the crest trail, scramble up to a second cliff-edge viewpoint, this time of tiny Bucket Lake. Mountain goats are common here as well.

The delightful and gently graded trail passes a junction with a rarely used path from the west and then continues another 6.6 joyous miles of open ridges and views. Notice how the rock changes from reddish volcanic rocks to predominantly white granite. The soils also become more suitable for forests, and the trees grow thicker and healthier than in the sparsely vegetated Twin Lakes Basin. The only blemish on the landscape is the remains of mining activity along Cracker Creek. In a saddle about 0.5 mile northeast of prominent Columbia Hill is a trail junction. From here a worthwhile side trip goes east to popular Summit Lake. This is a large, beautiful lake with good fishing, several excellent campsites, and photogenic granite cliffs above its southwest shore.

From the Summit Lake junction, go west and quickly reach a four-way junction with a jeep track (still in use), where you go straight and soon reach a pass beside Columbia Hill. Your route goes north, sticking to the Elkhorn Crest Trail (#1611). The trail gradually climbs toward Mount Ruth and soon enters the North Fork John Day Wilderness, so the motorbikes are finally left behind.

> **TIP:** The summit view from Mount Ruth amply rewards the scrambler.

The path skirts the west side of this peak before dropping first to Lost Lake Saddle and then Nip and Tuck Pass and a junction. A highly recommended side trip drops southeast from this junction across a rocky slope and then loops around the basin holding Lost Lake (1 of at least 14 lakes in Oregon holding this unimaginative name). An easy walk through open woods and meadows leads to the lake's southeast shore with views back up to Mount Ruth. Several good camps are located around this lake.

Back at Nip and Tuck Pass, the crest trail continues to Cunningham Saddle and a junction with a path coming up from the west. To the north are terrific vistas of spacious Crawfish Meadows backed by a jagged ridge. Now you cross a slope, with intermittent views of this spectacular basin, to a pass and a junction. To the right a recommended side trail drops 600 feet to small but pretty Dutch Flat Lake, with good views and nice camps. From the pass, the official Elkhorn Crest Trail climbs north to a saddle beside Angell Peak, then drops past Black Lake on its way to the trailhead on FS 73. This scenic route is the quickest way out for those in a hurry.

There is another alternative, however, that allows you to savor still more of this country. Turn left and drop about 400 feet before contouring across the slope on the north side of Crawfish Basin. You round another ridge and then climb to a junction with the 0.7-mile trail to the top of Lakes Lookout Peak. This peak provides a particularly good perspective of the Anthony Lakes area, so the side trip is well worthwhile. A short distance north is the end of FS 210 coming up from the west, as well as the top of several ski lifts for the Anthony Lakes ski area.

Keep right and descend on a road/trail that makes a long switchback. At the second switchback, keep straight on a trail leading to the small but very scenic Hoffer Lakes. Finally, drop steeply to busy Anthony Lake with its mountain views, campground, and, of course, your waiting vehicle.

POSSIBLE ITINERARY

	CAMP	MILES	ELEVATION GAIN
Day 1	Lower Twin Lake	4.8	800'
Day 2	Summit Lake	12.8	1,300'
Day 3	Dutch Flat Lake (with side trip to Lost Lake)	9.8	1,800'
Day 4	Out (with side trip to Lakes Lookout Peak)	6.1	1,800'

MINAM RIVER LOOP

> **RATINGS: Scenery** 7   **Solitude** 6   **Difficulty** 7
> **MILES:** 35 (41)
> **ELEVATION GAIN:** 5,300' (5,900')
> **DAYS:** 3–6 (4–6)
> **SHUTTLE MILEAGE:** n/a
> **MAP:** Green Trails *Wallowa Mountains*
> **USUALLY OPEN:** July–October
> **BEST:** July
> **PERMIT:** Yes (free at the trailhead)
> **RULES:** Maximum group size of 12 people
> **CONTACT:** Wallowa Mountains Office, Wallowa-Whitman National Forest, 541-426-4978, www.fs.usda.gov/wallowa-whitman

SPECIAL ATTRACTIONS

Diverse scenery, including deep canyons, high ridges, and fine viewpoints; solitude

CHALLENGES

Confusing junctions with unmapped trails; faint trails; heavy horse use

Above: View from a cabin at Minam River Lodge
photographed by Douglas Lorain

Minam River Loop

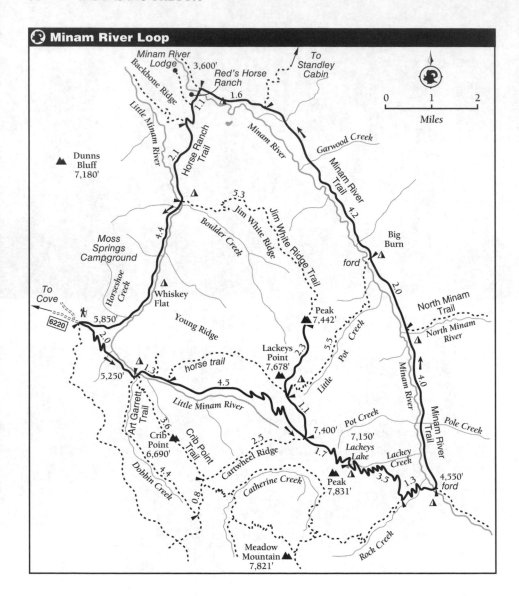

HOW TO GET THERE •

From I-84 take Exit 261 in La Grande, and turn right (northeast) onto OR 82. Drive 1.5 miles to a major junction. Go straight (east) on OR 237 and proceed 13.5 miles to Cove. One block after the road makes a 90-degree turn to the right (west), turn left (south) onto French Street, which soon becomes Mill Creek Lane. Remain on this road, which turns to gravel after 2.1 miles and becomes Forest Service Road 6220, and drive another 4.3 miles to the trailhead at the east end of horse-oriented Moss Springs Campground.

GPS TRAILHEAD COORDINATES: N45° 16.517' W117° 40.799'

INTRODUCTION •

Although this western third of the Eagle Cap Wilderness is easier to reach for most Oregonians, who drive from the populous Willamette Valley, it receives far fewer visitors than the central portion of the preserve. The reason for this seeming incongruity is that this part of the wilderness has none of the fish-filled lakes or high granite peaks that draw crowds to other parts of the Wallowa Mountains. Nonetheless, there is still plenty of great scenery, most notably high alpine ridges that boast terrific views, plenty of wildflowers, and the remarkably clear Minam River, which flows through an impressive 3,500-foot-deep forested canyon. In addition, while you probably won't have the trails all to yourself, you also won't have to fight off other backpackers for a good campsite, which is sometimes a problem in the more popular areas to the east.

DESCRIPTION •

Start by walking east from the trailhead and soon pick up a dusty, horse-pounded trail that goes through a pleasant forest of western larches, mountain hemlocks, Engelmann spruces, lodgepole pines, and subalpine firs. After only 70 yards, the trail splits at the start of the loop.

A counterclockwise tour is preferable because it avoids a long climb out of the Minam River Canyon, so bear right, following signs to Upper Little Minam River. For 1.5 miles you gradually lose elevation in four lazy switchbacks to the bottom of the canyon of the Little Minam River. Here you hop over a tiny creek and then walk 0.5 mile through an open lodgepole pine forest to a junction with the Art Garrett Trail. Go straight and, 100 yards later, make a log crossing of clear Dobbin Creek. Just 50 yards later is a nice campsite and another junction, this time with Crib Point Trail. Veer left and immediately cross the gravel-strewn Little Minam River on a log.

The route now goes upstream, gradually gaining elevation through a mix of forest and small meadows. In early July these meadows are filled with tall wildflowers, including false hellebores, mariposa lilies, horsemint, sunflowers, pink geraniums, and bluebells. About 0.8 mile from the crossing of the Little Minam River, go straight at a confusing and unmapped junction with an unofficial horse trail that goes uphill to the left. Just 0.5 mile farther, go straight again at a junction with another unmapped equestrian trail, this one an unofficial shortcut to Jim White Ridge.

WARNING: These are only the first of many unofficial horse trails that you will encounter on this trip. Confusingly, many of these paths appear to get more use than the official U.S. Forest Service trails. Keep your map handy and consult it often to ensure that you are headed in the proper direction.

After these junctions, the trail gradually pulls away from the river (now just a creek), ascending at a steady but moderate grade on a partly forested hillside. Several tiny side creeks provide water on this long 2,200-foot climb. About one-third of the way up, you enter the Little Minam Burn, a decades-old blaze that left many snags but opened up fine views of the high ridges flanking this canyon. The most interesting of these ridges lies straight ahead to the southeast, tempting hikers with its open, rounded slopes that promise fine views. This enticing ridge is your goal, but it is still a long way up, so settle in for a lengthy trudge. Six switchbacks add variety along the way, but the increasingly excellent scenery is what really keeps you going. Vistas of the nearby ridges and the distant Grande Ronde Valley and Elkhorn and Blue Mountains are more impressive with each upward step. In July wildflowers compete with the views for your attention. Expect colorful displays of Sitka valerian, Indian paintbrush, buckwheat, lupine, and scarlet gilia. The large sloping meadows here seem even more expansive because many of the trees were burned in the Little Minam Fire. At 7.8 miles from the trailhead, you reach a four-way junction marked by a prominent post just below the top of Cartwheel Ridge.

Here you have a choice. The recommended longer trail goes straight, heading for Lackeys Lake and the Minam River. If you prefer a shorter, 21-mile loop that skips the Minam River, you can take the Jim White Ridge Trail to the left. Even if you choose the longer loop, however, take a day to explore the first few miles of Jim White Ridge because this area features terrific wildflower displays and outstanding views. So turn left (north) and ramble up and down through rolling alpine meadows that feature the usual assortment of high-elevation flora and fauna. Of the latter, look for elk lounging in the meadows, coyotes trotting by in search of ground squirrels, and mountain bluebirds and Clark's nutcrackers flying overhead. Plant life here includes pink heather, whitebark pines, and numerous grasses and small wildflowers. At 1.1 miles from the four-way junction, there is a signed junction with the Little Pot Creek Trail.

> **TIP:** Just 0.1 mile down the Little Pot Creek Trail is an excellent campsite on a scenic little bench beside a small spring. This makes a good base camp for exploring Jim White Ridge.

> **WARNING:** If you look at the map, the Little Pot Creek Trail appears to be a good shortcut to the Minam River. This route, however, is often sketchy and involves a tricky ford of the river at the end. The longer trail via Lackeys Lake, described below, is a much better option.

About 100 yards past the Little Pot Creek junction, the Jim White Ridge Trail comes to a fork at a cairn. The unofficial horse trail to the left is the route mentioned earlier that drops to the Little Minam River Trail at the unsigned junction 1.3 miles from the crossing of that stream. The less obvious and lesser-used official trail goes right (uphill) from the cairn. This sketchy but wildly scenic path soon climbs to nearly the top of 7,678-foot Lackeys Point and then drops briefly but steeply on a rocky trail (not recommended for livestock) before going up and down along the ridge to the north. There are acres of flowers here in July and terrific views in all directions. You can hike for several miles, but a logical turnaround point is a high viewpoint about 2 miles past Lackeys Point.

Returning to the four-way junction on Cartwheel Ridge, those taking the recommended loop should go southeast and, 0.1 mile later, top the rounded ridge at a point featuring fine vistas southwest down to the forests and meadows beside Catherine Creek, some 2,000 feet below. The often narrow but mostly level trail then cuts across the steep slopes on the southwest side of a ridge for 0.7 mile before crossing over to the northeastern side of this ridge. Here views shift to the high snowy peaks of the central Wallowa Mountains towering above the deep chasm of Minam River Canyon. From here four downhill switchbacks and a gently descending traverse of a mostly wooded slope take you down to a small saddle over a spur ridge. You then drop briefly in one switchback to a crossing of Lackey Creek just below marshy and hard-to-see Lackeys Lake. Nice camps can be found above the east side of this pretty little lake, but the water is too shallow for fish.

From the lake the path goes steadily downhill, losing 2,600 feet on its way to the bottom of the Minam River Canyon. Fortunately, the route is well graded, but anyone taking this loop in the opposite direction will find the climb very tiring. Initially, the descent is through a sloping meadow immediately below the lake. Then the trail crosses Lackey Creek a couple of times and enters forest. A dozen switchbacks over the next 3.5 miles take you to an unsigned junction with the lightly used trail to Meadow Mountain and North Catherine Creek. Go left (downhill) and make 19 short switchbacks in 1.1 miles to an aging wooden bridge over Rock Creek. Another 0.2 mile of downhill leads to a small meadow with an inviting campsite just before a ford of the crystal-clear Minam River. The water here is usually over knee-deep and quite cold, but the ford is not dangerous. Just 75 yards after the ford is a junction with the Minam River Trail.

Turn left and walk downstream on a trail that includes some minor uphills but that is generally a long, gradual descent that never strays far from the winding Minam River. The forest and shrubbery near the water are surprisingly lush and include ponderosa pines, Pacific yews, and thimbleberries, all species that prefer these lower elevations to the high ridges. After crossing Pole Creek on a log, you continue descending, mostly in forest, but with many lovely views of the river with high ridges rising in the background. At 4 miles from where you started on the Minam River Trail is a good camp below the trail, just before a sturdy wooden bridge over North Minam River. About 100 yards later is a junction with the North Minam Trail, where you go straight.

About 2 miles past the North Minam junction, you come to a lovely meadow named, for no obvious reason, Big Burn, with nice camps and a cairn marking the junction with the Little Pot Creek Trail. The tread of this side trail is so faint that it is hard to locate. Go straight and, for the next 4.2 miles, spend most of your time well away from the river and, illogically, seeming to go uphill. The forest scenery is rather mundane, though it is more varied as large cottonwoods now grow in the bottomlands near the river. At the end of this section, go straight at a junction with a faint trail to Standley Cabin and then return to the banks of the now quite large Minam River.

TIP: A couple of very nice, secluded camps are along the river here, which you can reach via unsigned use paths that drop down to the left.

About 1.6 miles from the Standley Cabin junction is an intersection with the Horse Ranch Trail. Turn left, immediately cross an elaborately large wooden bridge over the river, and then climb briefly to the huge meadow holding the buildings, fences, and corrals of historic Red's Horse Ranch (now run by the U.S. Forest Service). The trail goes through a gate (cleverly latched in place with horseshoes) and then across a large pasture, part of which is mowed and used as a wilderness airstrip.

NOTE: Be sure to close all gates behind you to keep the horses from straying.

At the west end of the meadow, or pasture, you go through another gate and immediately come to a junction with a spur trail to privately owned Minam River Lodge. This rustic but very comfortable facility offers cabin accommodations, hearty homemade meals, and a variety of outdoor-oriented activities. If you are interested in staying here as part of your trip, contact the lodge at minam-lodge.com (booking ahead is essential).

After the Minam River Lodge junction, you return to the forest, some of which has been partially burned, and begin a 700-foot climb to the top of narrow Backbone Ridge. Most of this climb is a long traverse, though there are two switchbacks as you approach the top. Just 0.1 mile past the top of the ridge is a junction with the Little Minam River Trail, which goes downhill and sharply to the right. You go straight and continue uphill, now on the west side of the ridge, before finally leveling off and then contouring until you meet up with the Little Minam River. About 2.1 miles from the last junction is a spacious but horsey campsite at the junction with the Jim White Ridge Trail. This is where you rejoin the main route if you took the shorter, 21-mile loop mentioned earlier.

Go right at the junction, crossing the Little Minam on a wooden bridge, and then follow that sparkling river upstream. This clear, rushing stream is a haven for dippers, chunky little gray birds that live along mountain streams and sing all year long. About 2.2 miles after the bridge is an excellent campsite on your left at a place called Whiskey Flat. From here, you follow the river another 0.7 mile before crossing Horseshoe Creek on a bridge and then climbing away from the water across open, sunny slopes with blooming snowberry bushes in July and nice views up the Little Minam River's canyon. After 1.5 miles of climbing, you return to the Moss Springs Trailhead and your car.

POSSIBLE ITINERARY

	CAMP	MILES	ELEVATION GAIN
Day 1	Little Pot Creek Camp	8.9	2,400'
Day 2	Minam River (after day hike out Jim White Ridge)	12.3	900'
Day 3	Minam River before Red's Horse Ranch	11.2	200'
Day 4	Out	8.2	2,400'

16

BEAR CREEK LOOP

RATINGS: Scenery 8   **Solitude** 8   **Difficulty** 8
MILES: 39 (40)
ELEVATION GAIN: 6,300' (6,800')
DAYS: 3–6 (4–6)
SHUTTLE MILEAGE: n/a
MAP: Green Trails *Wallowa Mountains*
USUALLY OPEN: July–October
BEST: Mid-July
PERMIT: Yes (free at the trailhead)
RULES: Maximum group size of 12 people; no camping within 50 yards of spring by Standley Cabin
CONTACT: Wallowa Mountains Office, Wallowa-Whitman National Forest, 541-426-4978, www.fs.usda.gov/wallowa-whitman

SPECIAL ATTRACTIONS

Spectacular alpine ridge; wildlife; solitude

CHALLENGES

Faint trail that often disappears; rugged hiking

Above: Minam River above Red's Horse Ranch
photographed by Douglas Lorain

Bear Creek Loop

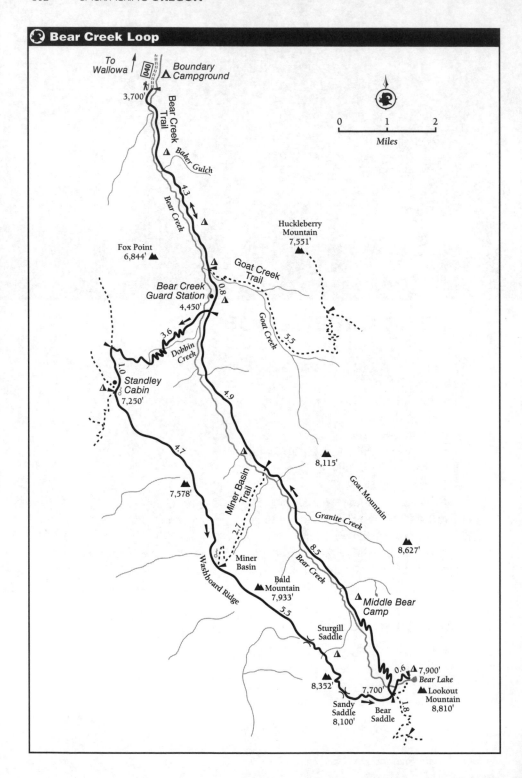

To Wallowa

040

Boundary Campground

3,700'

Bear Creek Trail

Baker Gulch

4.3

Bear Creek

Fox Point 6,844'

Huckleberry Mountain 7,551'

Goat Creek Trail

Bear Creek Guard Station 4,450'

0.8

Goat Creek

5.5

3.6

Dobbin Creek

1.0

Standley Cabin 7,250'

4.9

4.7

7,578'

8,115'

Goat Mountain

Miner Basin Trail

2.7

Granite Creek

8,627'

Washboard Ridge

Miner Basin

Bald Mountain 7,933'

Bear Creek

8.5

Middle Bear Camp

5.5

Sturgill Saddle

0.6   7,900'
Bear Lake

8,352'

7,700'

Sandy Saddle 8,100'

Bear Saddle

1.8

Lookout Mountain 8,810'

0   1   2
Miles

HOW TO GET THERE •

From I-84 take Exit 261 in La Grande, and turn right (east) onto OR 82. In 1.4 miles turn left (north) to remain on OR 82. Go 17.7 miles and turn right (east) to again remain on OR 82. Drive 25.8 miles to the town of Wallowa. Turn right (west) onto West Fifth Street, following signs for Boundary Campground, and drive 0.3 mile. Turn left (south) onto Bear Creek Road. Follow this paved then good gravel road, which becomes Forest Service Road 8250, for 7.5 miles, then turn right (south) onto FS 040 and follow it 0.8 mile to the trailhead at the south end of Boundary Campground.

GPS TRAILHEAD COORDINATES: N45° 28.288' W117° 33.565'

INTRODUCTION •

Tucked away in a lesser used corner of the Wallowa Mountains, this loop provides an excellent opportunity for experienced hikers to explore some outstanding country, see plenty of wildlife, and enjoy lonesome trails. Though there is only one lake along the way, anglers have ample opportunity to try their luck in catching Bear Creek's many brook and rainbow trout. (Artificial flies or lures are required, and any bull trout must be released unharmed.) The hike also features two historical log cabins, both of which are worth exploring. This trip's main attraction, however, at least from a scenery standpoint, is the spectacular hike along Washboard Ridge, one of the most outstanding ridge walks in Oregon. Although the vistas are awe inspiring, the hike is quite rugged, so only fit hikers should consider this trip.

DESCRIPTION •

The well-used Bear Creek Trail goes south, paralleling the cascading waters of boulder-strewn Bear Creek through an open forest of western larches, Engelmann spruces, grand firs, ponderosa pines, and Douglas firs. A few stately black cottonwoods—along with several shrubs, including wild rose, thimbleberry, snowberry, alder, birch, and vine maple—grow near the stream. After 0.2 mile cross the creek on a bridge beneath moss-draped cliffs. The trail then closely follows the stream almost 1 mile through dense riparian vegetation. The path next climbs a bit to a cliff-edged bluff overlooking the stream before dropping to a pleasant creekside campsite at 1.8 miles.

At 2.1 miles you hop over the trickle of water in Baker Gulch, after which you gradually ascend in open forest with occasional glimpses of the wooded ridges to the south and west. By 3.3 miles you drop back down to Bear Creek and pass two good campsites. Then it's another mile to a large meadow with a cluster of landmarks: first a junction with the Goat Creek Trail (go straight), then a bridge over that trail's namesake creek, and finally a spacious and inviting camping area in the trees at the meadow's south end. Just 0.4 mile past this camp is an unsigned but obvious spur trail that goes right 150 yards to the beautifully built log structure of the old Bear Creek Guard Station. This historical cabin is now locked, but good camps are nearby, and use trails lead to Bear Creek for water.

Back on the Bear Creek Trail, it's another 0.4 mile before you come to a junction at the start of the loop. Turn right and, 120 yards later, encounter an easy ford of Bear Creek, which after mid-July probably won't even get your ankles wet.

To this point the hike has been very easy, but the gentle creekside ramble is now over, as you rapidly ascend the western side of Bear Creek Canyon. The mostly open slopes here are surprisingly dry, hosting both western juniper and mountain mahogany, species that are normally found in the desert mountains of southeastern Oregon, not in the relatively wet Wallowa Mountains. In addition to botanical interest, these slopes provide nice views of the Bear Creek drainage and the high peaks at the stream's headwaters.

The first mile of steady uphill includes six switchbacks to ease the steepness somewhat, but the ascent is still a challenge for both thighs and calves. At 1.4 miles from the Bear Creek ford, you cross Dobbin Creek, whose cool, rapidly falling waters are a welcome relief from the heat of the climb. The next mile uses numerous short switchbacks to climb through a shady forest, where the trail is often overgrown with a mix of thimbleberry, gooseberry, currant, bracken fern, tall larkspur, coneflower, cow parsnip, bluebell, false Solomon's seal, and (beware) stinging nettle. The uphill is unrelenting, but the shade makes things more comfortable. That shady comfort comes to an abrupt halt at 2.4 miles from Bear Creek when you enter an area still scarred by the old Fox Point Fire.

Look for abundant July blossoms of false hellebore, aster, Lewis's monkeyflower, penstemon, pearly everlasting, and Indian paintbrush, among other wildflowers taking advantage of the sunshine here. After a little less than 1 mile of uphill walking through the burn, you pass a marshy pond backed by a red-tinged ridge. You then climb a bit more before finally returning to unburned forest shortly before a junction.

Turn left on a well-used trail and go grad-ually uphill 1 mile through forest and rolling ridgetop meadows to Standley Cabin. This quaint log cabin, which formerly served as a U.S. Forest Service guard station, is now locked, but it is fun to poke around the outside and take pictures. A tiny but reli-able spring nearby feeds a creek that flows through a lush green meadow. Camping is prohibited within 50 yards of the spring, but plenty of legal sites are nearby.

About 0.1 mile south of Standley Cabin the trail forks. Bear left, following signs to Upper Bear Creek, and begin what is perhaps the most magnificent ridge walk in Oregon. Fol-lowing Washboard Ridge for its entire length, the route starts high and remains so, never dipping below 7,300 feet and topping out at more than 8,000. The views are tremendous, especially west across the great depths of the Minam River Canyon to the distant Elkhorn Mountains, and southeast to the highest

Dramatic clouds over a meadow west of Standley Cabin
photographed by Douglas Lorain

peaks of the Wallowa Mountains. Trees rarely block the vista, with only a few scattered whitebark pines, subalpine firs, and mountain hemlocks. Gentle breezes (and occasionally strong winds) help to keep you comfortable in the hot sun and create waves in the acres of grasses and wildflowers. And there are plenty of wildflowers to blow around, with fine displays of lupine, Cusick's speedwell, buckwheat, penstemon, campion, yarrow, orange mountain dandelion, and other blossoms that usually peak in mid-July. All in all it is great fun. But that fun is reserved for hardy and experienced backpackers because the trail is often very faint—frequently disappearing in the meadows—and Washboard Ridge is true to its name, with lots of ups and downs. The trail is also steep and narrow in places, making it dangerous for stock, though horses sometimes use it.

The first mile is all uphill on the west side of the ridge, as the trail ascends a huge meadow where the tread soon disappears. A few large cairns guide you, but they are surprisingly hard to find. The best plan is to angle uphill to the southeast until you meet the tread again just below the ridgecrest. Now on clearer trail, descend a steep section with impressive views of the knife-edge ridge ahead and the Minam River Canyon below. Wildlife frequent this area. Two common species to look for include Rocky Mountain elk and calliope hummingbirds—the first is one of Oregon's largest wild mammals and the latter its smallest bird. You can also expect families of blue grouse to suddenly flush up from your feet, often in a startling flurry of activity.

The next 2 miles stay almost exclusively on the west side of the ridge, with easterly views only at the few places where you hit saddles. The most notable feature of this section, however, is that it can be rather scary for hikers who are afraid of heights. In several places, the rocky and dangerously sloping trail cuts across dizzying ledges that are frequently no more than a foot across. So even though the views are distracting, keep a close eye on your footing. After negotiating this section, an easier (but no less scenic) segment follows as the path goes through long grassy saddles and rolling ridgetop meadows.

At 4.8 miles from Standley Cabin, you pass 50 feet above a tiny spring (the first potential water along the ridge) and, 30 yards later, come to a junction with the Miner Basin Trail. Go straight and then cut across the steep slopes of Bald Mountain before traversing a large sloping meadow, where, once again, the tread fades away. The proper route goes downhill and then traverses a long basin on the west side of Washboard Ridge. If you lose the tread, simply head toward Sturgill Saddle, an obvious low point in the ridge a little more than 1 mile to the southeast. Once you are there, the tread becomes obvious again as it drops into an exceptionally scenic alpine basin beneath an unnamed 8,352-foot peak. Alpine buttercup, Cusick's speedwell, pink heather, and other alpine wildflowers seem to be everywhere, and small creeks provide much-needed water. There are several places to camp here, and you will probably have the basin all to yourself.

From the south end of this basin, the trail climbs 500 feet to 8,100-foot Sandy Saddle and then turns left (east) and follows a ridge. The route initially contours but soon begins descending, steeply at times, to a meadow-filled saddle. This place has no official name, but it is locally referred to as Bear Saddle. Though the trail disappears here, it is easy to make your way east across the meadow to an obvious cairn marking the junction with Bear Creek Trail.

Several trails converge at this remote location. To the right (south), hikers with extra time could spend several days exploring such worthwhile destinations as Wilson Basin and North Minam Meadows. Another option is to go straight (east) on an initially promising use path that heads uphill toward Bear Lake. Unfortunately, this trail soon disappears, forcing hikers to make a rather rugged scramble to that lake. Two trails go to the left at Bear Saddle, neither of which is initially easy to see. The one angling slightly left is the official trail to Bear Lake. The tread of this path becomes obvious about 100 feet from the junction as it contours and then climbs sharply for 0.6 mile to the shores of clear, 20-foot-deep Bear Lake. This lovely 10-acre pool is ideal for fishing (it's filled with hungry brook trout), swimming (if you don't mind chilly water), and camping (with a good site above the north side of the outlet creek).

The return route of the recommended loop goes sharply left at the Bear Saddle junction. The tread is initially hidden in meadow but becomes obvious after about 50 yards. After 0.2 mile the trail crosses the outlet of Bear Lake and then descends 15 well-graded switchbacks through an area covered with white granite boulders to the bottom of Bear Creek Canyon. For the next 1.5 miles the trail stays on the forested hillside above the stream, though from time to time you can see meadows below you beside the creek.

TIP: Look for herds of elk in these meadows, especially early in the morning.

After this traverse, four lazy switchbacks take you down to the creek and, at 4.5 miles from Bear Saddle, to Middle Bear Camp, a nice spot in the trees at the south end of a small but particularly inviting meadow.

Below Middle Bear Camp the hiking is easy and enjoyable, though views are infrequent through the forest. Occasional meadows provide westward vistas to Washboard Ridge, the rugged high points of which you will recognize from earlier in the trip. A little more than 2 miles below Middle Bear Camp is a rock-hop crossing of Granite Creek, after which you continue mostly downhill, often in large sloping meadows. Deer frequently browse in these meadows, and ground squirrels squeak loud alarms at your passing. In the forested sections between the meadows, look for snowshoe hares bounding away with their summer-brown bodies and flashing white back feet.

At 8.5 miles from Bear Saddle, you pass two small cairns on your left that mark the junction with Miner Basin Trail. Go straight on the main trail, and a little less than 1 mile later, pass two unsigned trails that drop to pleasant campsites near Bear Creek. At 13.4 miles from Bear Saddle, though the distance seems less than that with all the easy downhill, you return to the junction with the trail to Standley Cabin and the close of your loop. Go straight and retrace your steps back to your car.

POSSIBLE ITINERARY

	CAMP	MILES	ELEVATION GAIN
Day 1	Standley Cabin	9.6	3,700'
Day 2	Basin below Sturgill Saddle	8.0	1,800'
Day 3	Middle Bear Camp (with side trip to Bear Lake)	8.0	1,000'
Day 4	Out	14.0	300'

17

LOSTINE–MINAM LOOP

RATINGS: Scenery 9 **Solitude** 4 **Difficulty** 6
MILES: 43 (52)
ELEVATION GAIN: 8,700' (11,000')
DAYS: 4–6 (5–8)
SHUTTLE MILEAGE: n/a
MAP: Green Trails *Wallowa Mountains*
USUALLY OPEN: July–October
BEST: Late July–September
PERMITS: Yes (free and unlimited); Northwest Forest Pass required at Two Pan
Trailhead
RULES: No fires within 0.25 mile of Chimney, Laverty, Mirror, Moccasin,
Steamboat, or Swamp Lake; maximum group size of 6 people/9 stock in
Lakes Basin and at Minam and Blue Lakes
CONTACT: Wallowa Mountains Office, Wallowa-Whitman National Forest,
541-426-4978, www.fs.usda.gov/wallowa-whitman

SPECIAL ATTRACTIONS

Great mountain scenery

CHALLENGES

Crowded in spots; short road walk; unbridged stream crossings; thunderstorms

Above: Lostine River Trail at Two Pan Trailhead
photographed by Becky Ohlsen

Lostine–Minam Loop

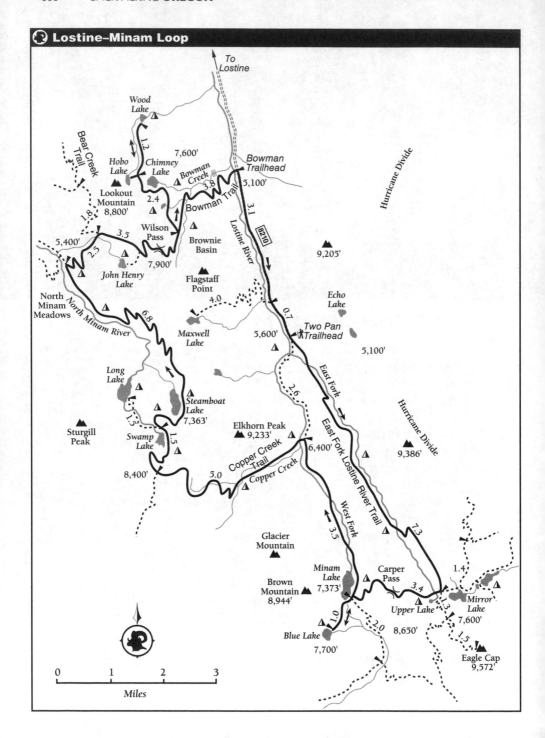

To Lostine

Wood Lake

Bear Creek Trail

1.2

7,600'

Hobo Lake

Chimney Lake

Bowman Creek

Bowman Trailhead

5,100'

Hurricane Divide

Lookout Mountain 8,800'

2.4

3.8

Bowman Trail

8210

3.1

Lostine River

9,205'

1.8

Wilson Pass

Brownie Basin

Echo Lake

3.5

2.5

5,400'

John Henry Lake

7,900'

Flagstaff Point

North Minam Meadows

North Minam River

6.8

Maxwell Lake

4.0

0.7

5,600'

Two Pan Trailhead

5,100'

Long Lake

Steamboat Lake 7,363'

East Fork

2.6

Hurricane Divide

9,386'

Sturgill Peak

Swamp Lake

1.5

1.5

Elkhorn Peak 9,233'

6,400'

East Fork Lostine River Trail

8,400'

5.0

Copper Creek Trail

Copper Creek

7.3

Glacier Mountain

West Fork

3.5

Brown Mountain 8,944'

Minam Lake 7,373'

Carper Pass

1.4

3.4

Mirror Lake 7,600'

Upper Lake

1.3

1.0

2.0

8,650'

1.5

Blue Lake 7,700'

Eagle Cap 9,572'

0   1   2   3

Miles

HOW TO GET THERE ●

From I-84 take Exit 261 in La Grande, and turn right (east) onto OR 82. In 1.4 miles turn left (north) to remain on OR 82. Go 17.7 miles and turn right (east) to again remain on OR 82. Drive 34.2 miles to the town of Lostine. Continue straight (south) on Lostine River Road, signed LOSTINE RIVER CAMPGROUNDS. The road turns to gravel after 7 miles and becomes Forest Service Road 8210/Upper Lostine Road. The route gets rougher and bumpier as it goes up the canyon but remains passable for passenger cars. Reach the Bowman Trailhead 7.7 miles after the road turns to gravel. If you have two cars, leave one here and the other 3.3 miles farther south at the spacious Two Pan Trailhead.

GPS TRAILHEAD COORDINATES:
(Two Pan) N45° 15.018' W117° 22.571'
(Bowman) N45° 17.639' W117° 23.681'

INTRODUCTION ●

This is one of several classic loop hikes in the Wallowa Mountains. Like the others, this one includes all the major attractions of this wonderful range. There are mountain lakes, alpine passes, wildflower-filled meadows, clear streams, and granite peaks. These features make this hike fairly popular, but it's not as crowded as the Wallowa River Loop (Trip 18). For those with less time or ambition, this route lends itself nicely to a shorter version. In fact, the most common way this trip is done skips East Lostine Canyon and Minam Lake and heads directly up the West Lostine River to the Copper Creek Trail. Without side trips this alternate loop is only about 32 miles long. Don't forget your fishing gear (lots of lake and stream fishing is available), binoculars (to search for elk, bighorn sheep, and mountain goats), swimsuit, and, most of all, your camera (the scenery is terrific).

DESCRIPTION ●

From Two Pan Trailhead hike up the trail 0.1 mile to a junction. The short version of this loop goes to the right. For a longer, more satisfying trip, keep left on the popular East Fork Lostine River Trail. The wide path makes a moderately steep climb through forests for the first 2.5 miles as it ascends toward the stream's high glacial valley. Views become more impressive near the top of the climb, especially of imposing Hurricane Divide to the east. All that climbing is rewarded when you enter the impressive glacier-carved upper East Lostine River Valley. Jagged ridges rise steeply on either side, while the crystalline river flows lazily through wildflower meadows on the valley floor. At the 3.2-mile point a large, swampy, wide spot in the stream goes by the name of Lost "Lake."

For the next few miles the path remains nearly level as it wanders up this beautiful valley.

TIP: Look for elk, deer, and mountain goats in this area, especially in the early morning and evening.

You are walking through a classic U-shaped glacial canyon, which adds geologic interest to the fine scenery. The trail travels through a delightful mix of open forests, meadows, and boulder fields. At the head of the valley looms the distinctive shape of Eagle Cap.

Cross the stream near the head of the valley and increase the rate of your climb as you switchback through open forests to a four-way junction. Most visitors turn left here to visit lovely Mirror Lake—well worth a side trip. Your route, however, turns right, passing below Upper Lake and providing excellent views down the East Lostine Canyon. If you choose to camp in this popular but fragile basin, be even more careful than usual to leave no trace. The trail now begins a moderately steep climb toward Carper Pass. Frequent views of Eagle Cap, resembling Yosemite's Half Dome from this angle, make the climb more of a joy than a strain. As expected, the views from the pass are exceptional. From the high point the trail makes a rolling descent before dropping more consistently to the south end of large Minam Lake.

An earthen dam blocks this lake's former outlet to the south, so it now drains principally north into the West Lostine River. Aptly named Brown Mountain dominates the skyline to the west.

> **TIP:** To visit lovely Blue Lake, cross the dam and follow a trail 1 mile to this round jewel below a serrated ridge of granite peaks. The lake's outlet is the source of the Minam River.

To continue your tour, turn north as the trail loops around the east shore of Minam Lake and then gradually descends to the valley of the West Lostine River. If the scenery in the East Lostine Valley rates a 10, then the West Lostine has to be a 9.9. You cross the stream twice as you wind down through the meadows and forests of this lovely valley. Not all the crossings have bridges, so be prepared to wade (chilly but not dangerous).

About 3.5 miles from Minam Lake is a poorly marked junction at a talus slope. Turn left on the Copper Creek Trail to a ford of the West Lostine River. Good camps are in the meadows nearby. The trail then begins to climb through the valley of Copper Creek, crossing the stream four times along the way.

> **WARNING:** Through July these crossings will be wet and sometimes treacherous.

Though the climb is moderate in grade, it seems to go on forever. However, the excellent scenery is ample compensation. Camps are abundant in this section of bouldery areas and meadows, with a terrific variety of wildflowers throughout the summer.

Eventually the trail veers away from the creek and climbs to a high, sandy plateau. Swamp Lake lies in the basin to the right. More distant views extend to the Matterhorn, Eagle Cap, and the other distinctive peaks of this range. Now the trail gradually loses a bit of elevation to a junction, where you turn right. This route makes a long, switchbacking descent into the meadowy basin holding Swamp Lake, which has good camps near the north end. The south end of this irregularly shaped pool is an intricate mix of meadows, creeks, and small ponds that looks like a Japanese garden.

> **TIP:** A side trail drops from here to large Long Lake, which features secluded camps and good fishing but has only limited views.

To continue your tour, top a low saddle near two small ponds (good camps) and enjoy a nice view down to Steamboat Lake. The route makes a series of switchbacks down a mostly open slope to the south end of this lake, where the best camps are along the east shore. A large rock island apparently looked like a steamboat to imaginative early travelers. The trail veers away from Steamboat Lake over a low rise before descending through a meadow to an overlook of the North Minam River Canyon. For the next few miles the trail leads down into this canyon in a series of irregular switchbacks over semi-open terrain. Numerous side creeks provide ample water. Several good campsites highlight the last couple of miles of the descent as the trail follows an attractive stream to spacious North Minam Meadows.

TIP: Though the trail skirts this large meadow, it is worthwhile to walk over for a visit.

Near the north end of the meadow, you turn right at a junction with the Bowman Trail. Climb in a series of moderately steep switchbacks, enjoying several nice views down to North Minam Meadows along the way. You pass an unseen waterfall and then reach a junction with the Bear Creek Trail. Keep right, and 1.2 miles later look for the unsigned and unmaintained path to John Henry Lake. The lake, 0.5 mile away, features nice camps.

The main trail climbs to Wilson Pass, which offers an excellent view to the east of Twin Peaks and the Hurricane Divide. Your route then switchbacks down to the trees above Brownie Basin, a long, scenic meadow with a lovely setting that is well worth a visit. The trail goes north along the slope above the meadow to a junction. Here you have the option of either heading directly out to your car or investing a bit more time and energy in the worthwhile side trip to Chimney and Hobo Lakes.

To do the side trip, keep left at the junction, traverse a view-packed slope to Laverty Lake, and then round a ridge to large and beautiful Chimney Lake. Granite peaks rise to the west, and two small islands add to the scene. To reach the more alpine setting of Hobo Lake, climb above Chimney Lake to a saddle. From here turn left at a junction and climb over rocky meadows to the high basin holding Hobo Lake.

TIP: Ambitious hikers can also make the cross-country scramble to overlooks atop Lookout Mountain and take the trail down to the lovely meadow basin holding Wood Lake.

Back at Brownie Basin, the well-graded trail crosses Bowman Creek and then drops in long gentle switchbacks to FS 8210/Upper Lostine Road. Near the bottom, a nice sloping waterfall on the creek adds scenic interest. From the Bowman Trailhead it's an easy 3.8-mile walk up the road to Two Pan Trailhead and your car. (So easy, in fact, that you may be able to talk your companion into doing the extra walk while you volunteer for the "difficult" task of guarding the packs and daydreaming about this wonderful trip.)

POSSIBLE ITINERARY

	CAMP	MILES	ELEVATION GAIN
Day 1	Mirror Lake	7.3	2,100'
Day 2	Minam Lake (with side trip to Blue Lake)	5.4	1,500'
Day 3	Swamp Lake	10.0	2,200'
Day 4	John Henry Lake	11.1	2,000'
Day 5	Brownie Basin (with side trip to Chimney, Hobo, and Wood Lakes)	9.7	2,600'
Day 6	Out (with road walk to Two Pan Trailhead)	7.6	600'

18

WALLOWA RIVER LOOP

RATINGS: Scenery 10 **Solitude** 2 **Difficulty** 7
MILES: 36 (54)
ELEVATION GAIN: 7,100' (11,700')
DAYS: 4–5 (5–10)
SHUTTLE MILEAGE: n/a
MAP: Green Trails *Wallowa Mountains*
USUALLY OPEN: July–October
BEST: Late July and August
PERMITS: Yes (free and unlimited)
RULES: No fires within 0.25 mile of Glacier, Mirror, Moccasin, or Upper Lake;
    maximum group size of 6 people/9 stock in Lakes Basin and at Ice Lake
CONTACT: Wallowa Mountains Office, Wallowa-Whitman National Forest,
    541-426-4978, www.fs.usda.gov/wallowa-whitman

SPECIAL ATTRACTIONS ●

Stunning mountain scenery

CHALLENGES ●

Crowded; thunderstorms; horse-pounded trails

Above: Wallowa Lake
photographed by Becky Ohlsen

⊕ Wallowa River Loop

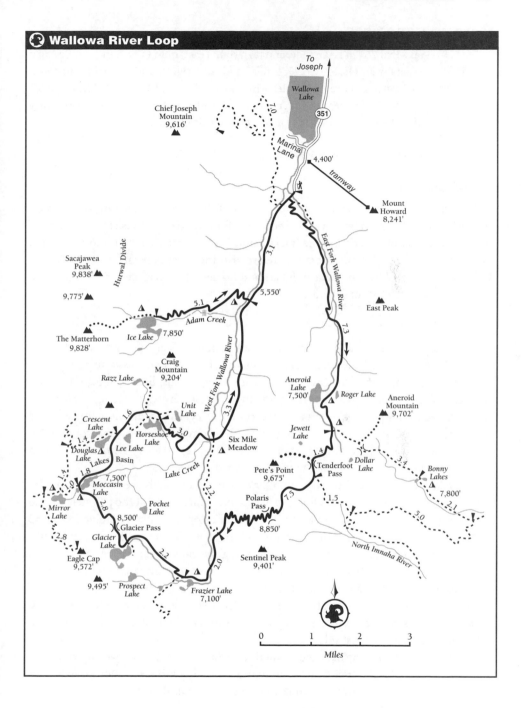

To
Joseph

Wallowa
Lake

351

Chief Joseph
Mountain
9,616'

7.0

Marina
Lane

4,400'

tramway

Mount
Howard
8,241'

East Fork Wallowa River

3.1

5,550'

East Peak

Sacajawea
Peak
9,838'

Hurwal Divide

9,775'

5.1

Adam Creek

7.3

Ice Lake 7,850'

The Matterhorn
9,828'

Craig
Mountain
9,204'

Razz Lake

West Fork Wallowa River

Aneroid
Lake
7,500'

Roger Lake

Aneroid
Mountain
9,702'

3.3

Unit
Lake

Jewett
Lake

Crescent
Lake

1.6

3.0

Horseshoe
Lake

Six Mile
Meadow

1.4

1.4

Douglas
Lake

Lee Lake

Lakes
Basin

Lake Creek

Pete's Point
9,675'

Tenderfoot
Pass

Dollar
Lake

3.4

Bonny
Lakes

7,800'

1.4

7,500'

1.8

Moccasin
Lake

Polaris
Pass

7.5

1.5

5.0

2.1

1.0

Mirror
Lake

2.8

Pocket
Lake

8,500'

2.2

8,850'

North Imnaha River

2.8

Glacier Pass

Glacier
Lake

2.2

2.0

Sentinel Peak
9,401'

Eagle Cap
9,572'

9,495'

Prospect
Lake

Frazier Lake
7,100'

0   1   2   3
Miles

HOW TO GET THERE •

From I-84 take Exit 261 in La Grande, and turn right (east) onto OR 82. In 1.4 miles turn left (north) to remain on OR 82. Go 17.7 miles and turn right (east) to again remain on OR 82. Drive 44.2 miles to the town of Enterprise. Turn right (south) onto OR 82, and go 6.3 miles to Joseph. OR 82 becomes OR 351; continue 6.9 miles past the south end of Wallowa Lake to the end of the road. Parking is available on the side of the road.

GPS TRAILHEAD COORDINATES: N45° 16.034′ W117° 12.765′

INTRODUCTION •

This trip features the best scenery in the most beautiful mountains in Oregon. Crystal-clear lakes and streams, meadows filled with wildflowers, glacier-polished white granite peaks . . . the list of joys excites the imagination, and the reality lives up to those high expectations. Unfortunately, the trails here are also the most popular in the Eagle Cap Wilderness, traveled by thousands of hikers and horses. However, the beauty more than compensates for the lack of solitude.

DESCRIPTION •

Go left on the East Fork Wallowa River Trail, following signs to Aneroid Lake. You switchback up the mostly forested hillside, and after 1.6 miles you pass a small waterfall and a diversion dam. The trail enters the official wilderness just beyond this point. Continue climbing at a gentler pace and enter the stream's more level upper valley. As the path leads upstream, views of meadows and the surrounding peaks become more frequent and enticing. Cross the stream on a footbridge 3.9 miles from the trailhead and continue up its east bank, eventually reaching the shores of large and very scenic Aneroid Lake. Good though sometimes crowded camps abound in the woods nearby.

This lake makes an excellent base camp for exploring the highly scenic terrain nearby. Don't miss the easy stroll around the lake itself—including a stop at the privately owned cabins at the lake's south end. A much more strenuous option is the scramble to the top of Aneroid Mountain (a long, tiring, trailless climb, but *what a view!*). Another worthwhile trip is Dollar Lake and the easy climb along the ridge behind it. Jewett Lake, on a bench southwest of Aneroid Lake, is also worth a visit. Highly recommended are the lovely Bonny Lakes and a magnificent 15-mile wildflower loop around a ridge south of these lakes. Finally, the climb to the summit of Pete's Point is extremely rewarding. This peak is most easily reached by a sketchy boot path that climbs steeply on the exposed ridge on the peak's northeast side.

Once you've sampled the day hike possibilities from Aneroid Lake, pack up your gear and continue south. The trail climbs through a typically glorious Wallowa Mountains meadow on the way to exposed Tenderfoot Pass. The trail then traverses a slope and climbs to the fine view from Polaris Pass.

WARNING: The trail to Polaris Pass receives only irregular maintenance.

The landscape west from this overlook is stunning, as most of the rugged Wallowa Mountains spread out in front of you. From the pass the trail drops almost 2,000 feet in a seemingly endless series of very gradual switchbacks all the way to the bottom of the valley. There is no water on the long descent, which explains why this loop is less attractive in the opposite direction.

Once you reach the bottom, turn left (upstream) at the junction with the West Fork Wallowa River Trail and soon enter the highly scenic upper valley of this stream. Cross the creek—there is no bridge, so expect a chilly wade—and continue another mile to the good camps at pretty Frazier Lake.

TIP: A nice side trip from Frazier Lake leads south past beautiful Little Frazier Lake to the view from Hawkins Pass–2.3 miles from Frazier Lake.

The trail now climbs a series of meadowy benches beside the waterfalls and cascades of the West Fork Wallowa River to Glacier Lake—one of the classic beauty spots in the state of Oregon. Camping here is *not* recommended due to the fragile alpine terrain and the exposed nature of camps.

WARNING: The water of this aptly named lake is bone-chillingly cold even on the hottest days of summer.

TIP: While views across any part of Glacier Lake are terrific, perhaps the best is from the east shore looking toward Eagle Cap and Glacier Peak. Reach this viewpoint by crossing the outlet creek and following a use path beside the lake for a few hundred yards.

Once you manage to pull yourself away from the beauty of Glacier Lake, climb in a series of short switchbacks to the tremendous vista from windswept Glacier Pass. Spread out to the north are the forested Lakes Basin and myriad distant peaks. Spend some time here to rest and pick out the many landmarks.

The path now drops 1,200 feet into the Lakes Basin, a heavily used area that consists of a series of large, beautiful lakes that seem to pop up at every turn in the trail. Every lake features a different scene of the surrounding peaks. The first one you'll reach is Moccasin Lake, perhaps the prettiest of all, where numerous excellent camps can be found (as is the case at all of the lakes). Side trips abound, but the easy stroll to Mirror Lake and tiny Upper Lake should be

Peak 9,505 over Ice Lake
photographed by Douglas Lorain

included in any itinerary. More ambitious hikers can follow exposed but view-packed routes to Carper Pass or even the top of Eagle Cap.

TIP: A superior but unmarked and hard-to-find side trail leads from the east end of Moccasin Lake to the austere setting of Pocket Lake.

To continue the loop trip, turn right at Moccasin Lake and take Moccasin Trail #1810A. Pass Douglas Lake, with an unnamed but spectacular granite ridge for a backdrop, and then Lee and Horseshoe Lakes as you slowly descend through the Lakes Basin. Side trips from Horseshoe Lake lead to forest-rimmed Unit Lake or lovely Razz Lake (the trail to the latter is not marked or maintained). Reluctantly, you must now leave the Lakes Basin and descend through forest to the West Fork Wallowa River. Several moderate switchbacks eventually lead down to a stream crossing just before you enter Six Mile Meadow (good camps). Turn left at the trail junction here and follow the river downstream as you gradually leave the high country behind. There are several nice cross-canyon views, and small side creeks provide water.

If time and energy allow, a highly recommended side trip switchbacks up to Ice Lake—located in a high basin on the Hurwal Divide to the west. This large, scenic lake provides a good base camp for scrambles up the Matterhorn and Sacajawea Peak, the highest summits in the Wallowa Mountains. Other rewarding pursuits there include angling, scanning for the area's mountain goats, and simply sitting and enjoying the landscape. To reach Ice Lake, leave the main trail 3.3 miles north of Six Mile Meadow and turn left on a path that climbs a seemingly endless series of switchbacks to the lake. The tedium of this climb is broken by ever-improving views and a terrific look at a long waterfall on Adam Creek.

Once you convince yourself to leave this paradise, return down all those switchbacks to the West Fork Wallowa River Trail. Turn north and follow this woodsy path back down to your car.

POSSIBLE ITINERARY

	CAMP	MILES	ELEVATION GAIN
Day 1	Aneroid Lake	6.3	3,200'
Day 2	Day hike up Pete's Point (return to Aneroid Lake)	8.0	2,300'
Day 3	Frazier Lake	11.8	2,200'
Day 4	Horseshoe Lake	8.5	1,500'
Day 5	Ice Lake	11.1	2,400'
Day 6	Out	8.2	100'

19

SOUTHERN WALLOWAS TRAVERSE

RATINGS: Scenery 9   **Solitude** 6   **Difficulty** 8

MILES: 40 (55)

ELEVATION GAIN: 9,400' (13,400')

DAYS: 4–5 (6–8)

SHUTTLE MILEAGE: 42

MAP: Green Trails *Wallowa Mountains*

USUALLY OPEN: July–October

BEST: Mid-July–early August

PERMITS: Yes (free and unlimited); Northwest Forest Pass required at Main Eagle trailhead

RULES: No fires within 0.25 mile of Eagle Lake; maximum group size of 12 people/18 stock

CONTACT: Wallowa Mountains Office, Wallowa-Whitman National Forest, 541-426-4978, www.fs.usda.gov/wallowa-whitman

SPECIAL ATTRACTIONS •

Mountain landscapes; relative solitude

Above: Needle Point over Cached Lake
photographed by Douglas Lorain

Southern Wallowas Traverse

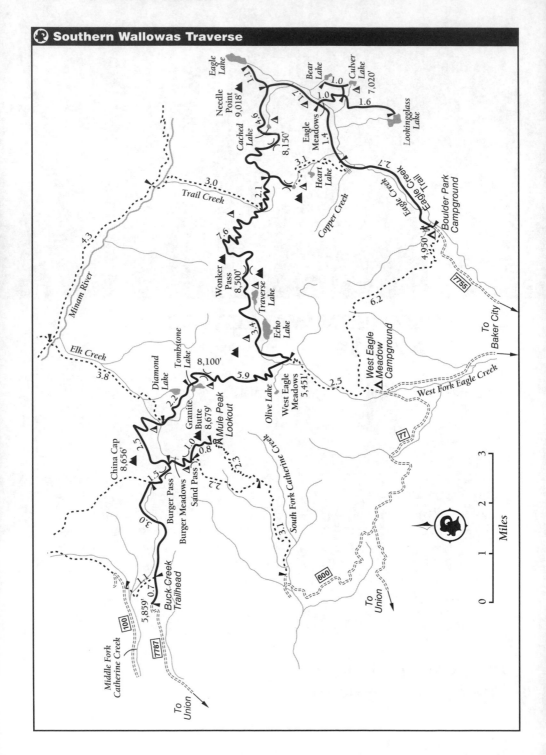

Eagle Lake

Needle Point 9,018'

Bear Lake

1.0

Culver Lake 7,020'

1.1

1.0

1.6

1.1

Cached Lake 8,150'

8.6

Eagle Meadows

1.4

Lookingglass Lake

3.1

Heart Lake

Copper Creek

2.7

Eagle Creek

Eagle Creek Trail

Boulder Park Campground

3.0

Trail Creek

2.1

4,950'

7755

4.3

7.6

6.2

Minam River

Wonker Pass 8,500'

Traverse Lake

To Baker City

Echo Lake

3.4

Elk Creek

3.8

Tombstone Lake 8,100'

5.9

West Eagle Meadows 5,451'

West Eagle Meadow Campground

2.5

West Fork Eagle Creek

Diamond Lake

2.2

Olive Lake

77

China Cap 8,656'

2.5

Granite Butte 8,679'

Mule Peak Lookout

South Fork Catherine Creek

1.5

1.0

0.8

Burger Pass

Burger Meadows

Sand Pass

2.3

2.2

3.0

3.1

600

Buck Creek Trailhead

1.1

0.7

To Union

5,859'

Middle Fork Catherine Creek

100

7787

To Union

Miles

0   1   2   3

To Union

CHALLENGES •••

Rugged up-and-down hike; thunderstorms

HOW TO GET THERE •••••••••••••••••••••••••••••••••••

The east trailhead is at Boulder Park, a former horse-outfitting ranch on Eagle Creek. From I-84 take Exit 298, and head east on OR 203 N. Go 18.2 miles to the village of Medical Springs, and turn right (south) onto Big Creek Road, following signs for Tamarack Campground. After 1.7 miles keep left on Forest Service Road 67. In 13.9 miles, just before a bridge over Eagle Creek, turn left onto FS 77/Eagle Creek Road. After another 0.7 mile keep right at a fork and travel on FS 7755 for 3.5 miles to the road-end Main Eagle trailhead.

The west trailhead is reached by taking I-84 to Exit 265 near La Grande. Turn right to head southeast on OR 203 S. In 10.8 miles turn left (east) onto East Beakman Street/ OR 203. Go 11.3 miles, and turn left (east) onto FS 7785/Catherine Creek Lane, about 8 miles north of Medical Springs. This gravel road follows the North Fork of Catherine Creek 4.1 miles to a fork. Turn right (southeast) onto FS 7787 and go 3.7 miles. Turn left (east) and go 0.3 mile to the Buck Creek Trailhead.

GPS TRAILHEAD COORDINATES:

(Main Eagle) N45° 03.936' W117° 24.614'
(Buck Creek) 45° 08.899' W117° 34.356'

INTRODUCTION ••

The southern Wallowa Mountains are both very similar to and quite different from the northern part of the range. As in the areas to the north, the scenery is spectacular, with the same enchanting combination of granite peaks, alpine lakes, and wildflowers. The southern part, however, has a very different character. First of all, the trail population is smaller. While you won't be lonesome, longer road access and more rugged trails mean that far fewer people choose to hike in this region. The terrain also differs from the northern Wallowas. Granite peaks are still found in abundance, but the geology here is more varied, with many prominent peaks being more reddish than white. Finally, the forests are more open and the meadows more expansive, so vistas are wider and more common. This attractive but difficult hike traces a rugged up-and-down route as it alternates between the high passes and deep canyons that characterize the southern Wallowas. For the fit hiker who longs for the beauty of the Wallowas without the crowds, this is a wonderful choice. The hike is described here from east to west.

DESCRIPTION ••

Begin by hiking northeast up an abandoned jeep road across the remains of a landslide to a bridged crossing of Eagle Creek. Now a pleasant footpath, the route climbs through forests as it closely parallels the stream. You recross Eagle Creek and soon reach the ford of Copper Creek—expect to get your feet wet until late summer—just downstream from impressive Copper Creek Falls.

TIP: For the best photo opportunity of this falls, take a short spur trail north of the creek.

Keep straight at a trail junction a little past Copper Creek, sticking with the Eagle Creek Trail. The trail gets rougher, but the terrain is more open, with meadows and views of the surrounding peaks. At 4.1 miles is large Eagle Meadows, with good camps. There is also a junction here with the route to Lookingglass Lake.

To visit the lovely lakes in the high cirques to the south and east, ford Eagle Creek and climb a fairly steep trail along the canyon wall. Views to the north of Needle Point and the basin of Eagle Lake improve as you ascend to a trail junction near the base of a meadow. To the right, a 1.6-mile path climbs over a mostly open ridge before dropping a bit to large Lookingglass Lake. This deep lake has good fishing but is artificially dammed, so when the water is lower, it resembles a bathtub. The rocky terrain around the lake makes for generally poor camping, but the views are excellent. Back at the last junction, the left fork quickly enters the basin holding very scenic Culver Lake. Towering cliffs behind the east shore of this lake present a challenge for even the widest-angle camera lens. The trail continues north another mile to Bear Lake. This pool is attractive but less spectacular than Culver or Lookingglass Lake.

TIP: The best plan is to camp down at Eagle Meadows and day hike up to these lakes.

Continuing north on the Eagle Creek Trail, wildflowers brighten the canyon ascent as the landscape changes from meadows and open slopes back into forest. Not long after the trail begins to make a switchbacking climb is a rock cairn (and possibly a sign) marking the junction with the trail to Eagle Lake. Though Eagle Lake is artificially dammed and has generally poor campsites, it's still well worth the side trip. The last 0.3 mile of the trail to this lake goes up a steep granite ridge with stunted whitebark pines, framing excellent views back down the canyon. The lake itself sits in a spectacular alpine basin rimmed by 9,000-foot granite peaks. There are few trees in this high bowl, but the scenery is impressive.

For better camps, return to the main trail and climb to the meadow flat holding tiny Cached Lake. Nice sheltered camps are in the trees on this pool's north side.

TIP: Be sure to walk around to the lake's southwest shore for some excellent views across Cached Lake to Needle Point—dominating the local skyline.

As is true in many parts of the Wallowas, friendly deer are likely to visit your camp in the evening.

TIP: Peak baggers will want to make the steep, but not technically difficult, scramble to the top of Needle Point. The vistas from the summit are truly outstanding, especially of the deep, curving Minam River Canyon to the north.

From Cached Lake your trail makes a long looping climb to a windswept pass and then descends back into forest to a meadow with a trail junction. An excellent side trip turns left here, climbs steeply over a rocky pass, and drops to the alpine cirque holding tiny Arrow Lake. With a high granite peak, small islands, and a rocky wildflower meadow, Arrow Lake is a magical place. Now you return to the main trail and switchback steadily downhill to Trail Creek. You'll have to get used to this pattern of alternating between high passes and deep canyons because that pretty much describes the rest of this trip. There are precious few stretches of level trail. Fortunately, frequent lakes and views provide ample compensation. A break in the trees partway down this particular descent offers an excellent glimpse of the peaks to the west.

At the bottom of the canyon, you go left at a junction and then cross Trail Creek. Rest awhile and refill your water bottle before tackling the long 2,300-foot climb to Wonker Pass. The well-graded trail climbs gradually for 1 mile to a nice meadow with a good campsite. From here you ascend through forest and then up a series of airy switchbacks on an exposed talus slope with increasingly good views to the pass.

From Wonker Pass it's only a short descent to the alpine basin holding beautiful Traverse Lake, with excellent camps. The lake has an idyllic setting in a large meadow surrounded by scattered islands of trees. The most impressive view is from the northwest shore looking back toward a prominent granite monolith beside Wonker Pass—outstanding!

To continue your tour, head away from the waters of Traverse Lake and soon reach a grand overlook of Echo Lake and the canyon below. (Yes, you're going *all the way down there*.) Walk past a nice spring and then drop to Echo Lake, which can be reached by any of several short side trails. A serrated ridge south of this lake makes a nice backdrop.

WARNING: Later in the summer, the water level drops in this artificially controlled lake, making it much less attractive.

Copper Creek Falls
photographed by Douglas Lorain

You continue downhill, making a few switchbacks, and then cross a marshy area near a small pond. Switchbacks resume as the trail crosses semi-open slopes with high peaks on either side.

In a brushy area, long before the switchbacks end, is a junction. Turn right, cross the West Fork Eagle Creek, and brace yourself for the next big climb, as the trail regains all the previously lost elevation on a long and rather uneventful ascent toward the pass above Tombstone Lake. There are nice views as you climb but only intermittent shade. It's all worthwhile once you top out at a high pass because the vistas, as usual, are superb. From the pass the trail contours along a ridge for a bit then drops to the shores of Tombstone Lake, which has several choice camps for the weary hiker. The lake's name comes from a large pinnacle rising from the southwestern shore. With some imagination, it might be said to resemble a tombstone.

The path continues to the northwest, traveling above the basin holding woodsy Diamond Lake, which can be reached by steep side trails, and then continues to lose elevation to a trail junction beside Elk Creek.

Turn left and cross the stream to an excellent campsite where two creeks meet. The meadow here is a lovely foreground for craggy Granite Butte to the south, and trees provide welcome shade.

WARNING: Bugs can be an annoyance here because the meadow is rather boggy.

Leaving this meadow basin, you'll notice an older trail that climbs steeply along a slope to the left, but the well-graded newer trail climbs gradually to the right in two very long switchbacks with several good views along the way. Near the top of this climb, the trail contours around sloping Burger Meadows and then climbs another hillside to a junction in the trees. For a quick exit, turn right, but keep straight for a terrific side trip.

The side trip first visits a beautiful meadow with a fine campsite, wildflowers, and small ponds. The view across this meadow toward prominent China Cap is particularly fetching. Leaving this meadow, you travel up very steep, sandy switchbacks to aptly named Sand Pass, often snowbound until late summer. Turn left at Sand Pass and follow a more gently graded trail that climbs through semi-open forest on a ridge east of Sand Pass. The route traverses an open slope a few hundred feet below the summit of Granite Butte and then crosses a saddle and goes up the spine of a narrow ridge to Mule Peak Lookout. This is one of Oregon's least-visited fire lookouts, but the lack of visitors is due only to its isolation because outstanding panoramas extend in all directions. Fire-scarred forests below the peak testify to the need for this facility; the 2016 Mule Peak Fire even caused the lookout to be evacuated.

Back at the junction above Burger Meadows, turn west and climb to Burger Pass. The peaks on either side are not the typical white granite of the Wallowas but are reddish summits instead.

TIP: For those with energy to burn, the scramble up China Cap to the north is particularly rewarding.

The trail drops a few hundred feet to a junction below the pass. To the right is a long, view-packed ridge walk, but keep left to reach your car.

The final part of the hike is a pleasant downhill stretch, mostly in forest, along Middle Fork Catherine Creek. Keep straight at a trail junction near the bottom and soon reach the Buck Creek Trailhead—the end of an exhausting but glorious hike.

POSSIBLE ITINERARY

	CAMP	MILES	ELEVATION GAIN
Day 1	Eagle Meadows (with side trip to Lookingglass and Bear Lakes)	11.3	2,700'
Day 2	Arrow Lake (with side trip to Eagle Lake)	9.6	3,000'
Day 3	Traverse Lake	10.8	2,400'
Day 4	Tombstone Lake	9.3	2,200'
Day 5	Meadow below Sand Pass (with side trip to Mule Peak Lookout)	7.8	2,500'
Day 6	Out	5.7	600'

20

EAST EAGLE–IMNAHA LOOP

RATINGS: Scenery 10   **Solitude** 4   **Difficulty** 6
MILES: 39 (46)
ELEVATION GAIN: 7,900' (10,400')
DAYS: 5–6 (5–7)
SHUTTLE MILEAGE: n/a
MAP: Green Trails *Wallowa Mountains*
USUALLY OPEN: Mid-July–October
BEST: Mid-July–August
PERMITS: Yes (free and unlimited)
RULES: No fires within 0.25 mile of Glacier, Mirror, Moccasin, or Sunshine Lake;
    maximum group size of 6 people/9 stock in Lakes Basin and at Frazier and
    Glacier Lakes
CONTACT: Wallowa Mountains Office, Wallowa-Whitman National Forest,
    541-426-4978, www.fs.usda.gov/wallowa-whitman

SPECIAL ATTRACTIONS •

Great mountain scenery; wildlife

CHALLENGES •

Crowded in spots; thunderstorms

Above: Eagle Cap over upper Moccasin Lake
photographed by Douglas Lorain

🌎 East Eagle–Imnaha Loop

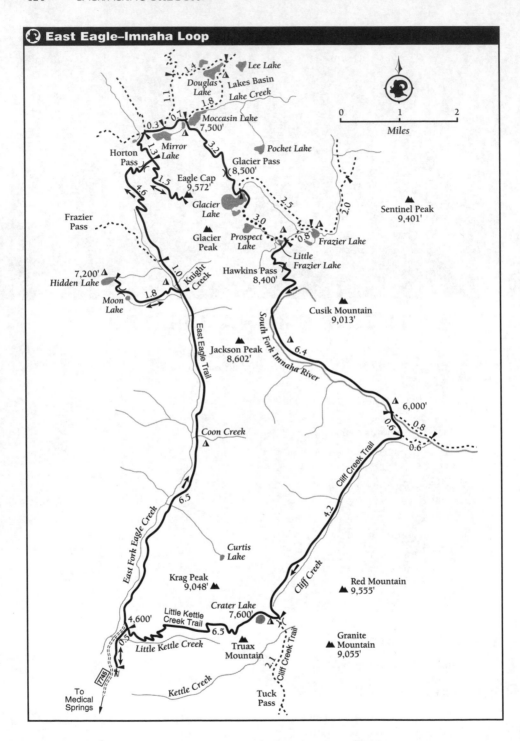

Lee Lake

1.4

Douglas
Lake   Lakes Basin

1.8   Lake Creek

0.7

0.3   Moccasin Lake
7,500'

1.3   Mirror
Horton   Lake   3.2
Pass

1.5   Pocket Lake

4.6   Eagle Cap   Glacier Pass
9,572'   8,500'

Frazier   Glacier   2.5
Pass   Lake   2.0

3.0   Sentinel Peak
9,401'

Glacier   Prospect   0.8   Frazier Lake
Peak   Lake

Little
Frazier Lake

1.0   Knight   Hawkins Pass
Creek   8,400'

7,200'   Cusik Mountain
Hidden Lake   1.8   9,013'

Moon
Lake   East Eagle Trail   South Fork Imnaha River

Jackson Peak
8,602'   6.4

6,000'

0.6   0.8

Coon Creek   0.6

6.5   Cliff Creek Trail   4.2

Curtis
Lake   Cliff Creek

East Fork Eagle Creek   Krag Peak   Red Mountain
9,048'   9,555'

Crater Lake
7,600'

4,600'   Little Kettle
Creek Trail   Granite
Mountain
9,055'

0.5   6.5

Little Kettle Creek   Truax
Mountain   Cliff Creek Trail

7745   2.1

To
Medical
Springs   Kettle Creek   Tuck
Pass

0   1   2
Miles

HOW TO GET THERE •

To reach the start of this adventure, from I-84 take Exit 298, and head east on OR 203 N. Go 18.2 miles to the village of Medical Springs, and turn right (south) onto Big Creek Road, following signs for Tamarack Campground. After 1.7 miles keep left on Forest Service Road 67. Drive 14 miles, cross a bridge over Eagle Creek, and then go another 0.6 mile to Tamarack Campground. The road turns right and becomes FS 77. After another 5.8 miles turn left onto FS 7745, following signs to the East Eagle Trailhead. Drive this gravel route 5.6 miles to a trailhead parking area on the right.

GPS TRAILHEAD COORDINATES: N45° 03.448' W117° 19.398'

INTRODUCTION •

Here is yet another remarkably beautiful loop hike through the spectacular Wallowa Mountains. The focus here is on the southeast part of the range. As is true everywhere in these mountains, this trip features a wealth of breathtaking mountain scenery. My vocabulary of adjectives is simply inadequate to convey the glories.

DESCRIPTION •

From the trailhead the path wanders through an attractive forest of beautiful old-growth ponderosa pine, grand fir, and western larch. You cross Little Kettle Creek, and 0.5 mile from the trailhead, you reach a junction with the Little Kettle Creek Trail, the return leg of your loop. You go straight as the trail drops to creek level near the old trailhead. From here the route makes a gradual up-and-down climb with frequent views extending up 4,000-foot canyon walls. Your path alternates among forests, brushy slopes, and meadows. Look for views of Krag Peak and several waterfalls across the canyon. Water from tributary creeks is abundant. The lower canyon offers limited camping opportunities, though comfortable camps are possible a little south of Coon Creek and near Eagle Creek a bit farther along.

At 7 miles, a little before the waterfall on Knight Creek, is a possibly unsigned junction with the trail to Hidden Lake. To make this excellent side trip, turn left and drop to a fairly easy ford of East Eagle Creek. A good campsite is a bit farther up the far bank. The trail climbs fairly steeply about 1 mile before leveling off below Moon Lake. You climb over a low ridge and then drop down the other side to large and beautiful Hidden Lake. There are numerous excellent camps here, as well as views of the craggy granite peaks circling the meadowy basin. The lake also offers good fishing and swimming.

TIP: Some of the best vistas are from the lake's trailless north shore.

After returning to the East Eagle Trail, turn upstream and continue climbing. Keep right at the Frazier Pass junction as the trail gets narrower and rockier. Several long switchbacks moderate the climb. Cross East Eagle Creek and enter the high meadows of the headwall basin. Watch for deer and elk in this area. A long climb is required to exit this lovely basin as the trail winds up moderately steep granite slopes to Horton Pass.

WARNING: Snow often obscures this high route well into summer, so navigate carefully.

A cairn marks the top of windswept Horton Pass with its excellent views.

The outstanding side trip to the summit of Eagle Cap should not be missed. The summit trail begins beside a pond below the north side of Horton Pass.

TIP: It's easier to simply walk up the rocky ridge directly from the pass for about 0.4 mile to where you meet the official path.

The trail climbs steadily over rocks and snowfields, eventually switchbacking up the exposed slopes to the top. From here the rugged topography of the entire Wallowa Range spreads out in all directions. There are especially good views down the huge U-shaped gorges of East Eagle Creek and East Lostine River. To the east, Glacier Lake shimmers in its basin, and granite peaks rise in all directions. *Wow* pretty much sums it up.

From Horton Pass the main trail crosses meadows and semipermanent snowfields and then drops to tiny Upper Lake at the head of East Lostine Canyon. You turn right at a junction and right again just 100 yards later to reach popular Mirror Lake. On a calm morning or evening, this lake lives up to its name, with fine reflections of towering Eagle Cap. Continue down the trail to the east to reach deep and beautiful Moccasin Lake (excellent camps), and turn right at the junction at the lake's west end.

The trail now makes a long, strenuous climb to Glacier Pass, traveling first through forest, then meadows, and finally alpine terrain. Once again the views from the pass are terrific, but even better scenery is just ahead at Glacier Lake. On my personal list of Oregon's most spectacular lakes, this large alpine jewel ranks second only to incomparable Crater Lake, in the southern Cascades. When free of ice (only about two or three months out of the year), this clear pool, surrounded by white granite peaks and permanent snowfields, is unbelievably beautiful. Camping here is not recommended due to the fragile terrain and cold nights.

From Glacier Lake the easiest route to continue your trip drops 2.5 miles to Frazier Lake, where the trail turns right and climbs to Little Frazier Lake and on to Hawkins Pass. For hikers who don't mind some steep cross-country travel, a more scenic alternative crosses the outlet creek of Glacier Lake and follows a boot-beaten path along the lake's east shore. Look carefully for an unmarked route that goes by a smaller upper lake, continues south over a saddle, and then drops to Prospect Lake. The stark granite basin holding this deep lake is only slightly less spectacular than the setting for Glacier Lake, and it is much more private. Unfortunately, the camps here are rocky and exposed. Reaching Little Frazier Lake requires a steep downhill scramble following the outlet creek of Prospect Lake.

TIP: In general the right (south) side of the creek provides more manageable trail conditions, but you'll still have to crawl around some boulders and small cliffs.

The creek itself is a joyful series of cascades and waterfalls with lots of flowers. At the bottom, go left along the north shore of Little Frazier Lake to pick up the trail.

Turn right and follow the path as it makes a moderately steep climb in several small switchbacks to Hawkins Pass.

WARNING: Snow remains on the north side of Hawkins Pass practically all summer.

The trail then drops into the basin at the head of the South Fork Imnaha River, which features outstanding views and acres of wildflowers. The prominent pinnacle to the southwest is Jackson Peak. There are several inviting camps both here and a bit below a lovely waterfall about 0.4 mile past where the trail crosses the stream. Farther down the canyon the views become more restricted as the forests grow thicker, but it's still a pleasant walk. Near the junction with Cliff Creek Trail, about 4.5 miles from the headwall basin, are some clearings with more nice camps.

Turn south on Cliff Creek Trail and immediately face a chilly ford of the Imnaha River. The path then climbs steadily through forests and brushy meadows on its way up Cliff Creek. Wildflowers add color in summer, and larch trees make October equally attractive in this area. Look for deer in the meadows—and often in your camp at night. Aptly named Red Mountain towers to the east, adding to the excellent scenery. You top out at a forested pass and then turn right at a junction to reach Crater Lake, which has good camps in the trees above the north shore. Unlike most lakes in the Wallowas, this one does not fill a glacial cirque but sits in a low saddle near the pass. The lake's water level fluctuates considerably during the year. The high water of early summer is more attractive. Distant Krag Peak, Red Mountain, and Granite Mountain provide lovely backdrops.

TIP: If you have an extra day, spend it on an easy flower walk to Tuck Pass and the Pine Lakes to the southeast.

To complete the loop trip, you hike west through a low saddle past a couple of shallow ponds and then make a long, fairly steep descent along the brushy avalanche slopes beside Little Kettle Creek. A seemingly endless series of switchbacks eases the grade. The trail ends at the junction with the East Eagle Trail just 0.5 mile from your car at the trailhead.

POSSIBLE ITINERARY

	CAMP	MILES	ELEVATION GAIN
Day 1	Hidden Lake	8.8	2,800'
Day 2	Mirror Lake (with side trip up Eagle Cap)	12.0	3,500'
Day 3	Upper Imnaha Basin	10.0	2,500'
Day 4	Crater Lake	8.4	1,500'
Day 5	Out	6.7	100'

21

HELLS CANYON WESTERN RIM "SUMMIT" TRAIL

RATINGS: Scenery 8 **Solitude** 8 **Difficulty** 5
MILES: 53 (66)
ELEVATION GAIN: 7,400' (9,300')
DAYS: 5–7 (6–9)
SHUTTLE MILEAGE: 63
MAP: USFS *Hells Canyon National Recreation Area and Wilderness*
USUALLY OPEN: Late May–November
BEST: Early to mid-June
PERMITS: None
RULES: Private land along Cow Creek—no public traffic on road; close any gates you open
CONTACT: Wallowa Mountains Office, Wallowa-Whitman National Forest, 541-426-4978, www.fs.usda.gov/wallowa-whitman

SPECIAL ATTRACTIONS ·

Views; wildlife; solitude; wildflowers

CHALLENGES ·

Limited water sources; some road walking; large burned areas; ticks

Above: The scene from Hells Canyon Overlook
photographed by Becky Ohlsen

HOW TO GET THERE •

Reach the south starting point by taking I-84 to Exit 302 in Baker City. Head east on OR 86, and go 60.2 miles. Turn left (north) onto North Pine Road, and go 14.3 miles. Turn right onto the paved Wallowa Loop Road/Forest Service Road 39 (closed late October–early May or early June due to snow), and go 5.1 miles. Turn right (east) onto FS 490, and drive 5.5 miles, passing Hells Canyon Overlook. Continue straight on FS 3965, a rough gravel road. Drive 7.3 miles, past the turnoff to McGraw Lookout and a gate, to the developed south trailhead.

There are two options for exiting this hike. The first is Dug Bar (see below for directions). A slightly shorter option is to exit via Cow Creek. This route crosses private land and follows a road closed to public traffic, but hikers are allowed to walk through. This exit avoids the final steep 10 miles of Dug Bar Road, so it is easier for those with a typical passenger car. From I-84 take Exit 261 in La Grande, and turn right (east) onto OR 82. In 1.4 miles turn left (north) to remain on OR 82. Go 17.7 miles and turn right (east) to again remain on OR 82. Drive 44.2 miles to the town of Enterprise. Turn right (south) to continue another 6.3 miles on OR 82 to Joseph. Turn left (east) onto OR 350, and go 29.4 miles. After crossing the Imnaha River, turn left (north) onto Lower Imnaha Road. In 6.3 miles make a slight right (northeast) onto Dug Bar Road/FS 4260. In 6.8 miles turn left (north) to remain on Dug Bar Road. Go 6.5 miles, and the Cow Creek trailhead is on the left just before you cross a bridge over the Imnaha River again. (For the Dug Bar trailhead, cross the bridge over the Imnaha River, and turn left to stay on FS 4260. Go 10.7 miles to the end of the road and the trailhead.)

TIP: To avoid the time-consuming and tedious car shuttles in Hells Canyon, consider employing a shuttle service. Originally designed for rafters, these services also assist hikers by moving your vehicle between trailheads while you spend more time hiking. Fees vary, and you'll have to make arrangements in advance. One such service is Hells Canyon Shuttle (800-785-3358; hellscanyonshuttle.com).

GPS TRAILHEAD COORDINATES:
(south) N45° 13.818' W116° 46.514'
(Dug Bar) 45° 48.277' W116° 41.207'
(Cow Creek) N45° 45.822' W116° 44.900'

INTRODUCTION •

Of the three long trails in Hells Canyon described in this guide, the Western Rim Trail is the most comfortable for backpackers. This trip has comparatively few steep ups and downs because the path follows the surprisingly gentle Summit Ridge. The unbearable heat of the lower canyon is replaced by higher-elevation temperatures that are 20 or more degrees cooler. Nights are also more comfortably cool for sleeping. There is also plenty of shade among the rim's evergreen forests. On the other hand, the rim route has fewer water sources, so camping choices are limited.

(continued on page 132)

🌐 Hells Canyon Western Rim "Summit" Trail

CONTINUED ON PAGE 131

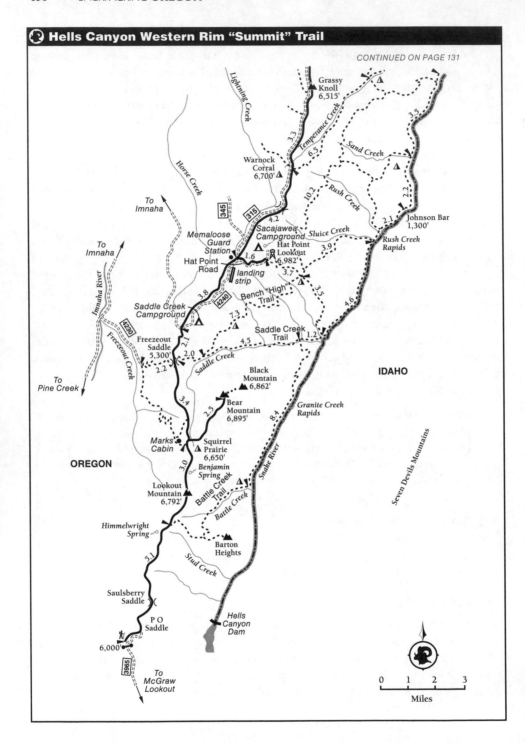

Lightning Creek

Grassy Knoll
6,515'

3.3

Temperance Creek

6.5

Sand Creek

3.5

Warnock Corral
6,700'

2.2

Horse Creek

10.2

Rush Creek

Johnson Bar
1,300'

2.1

To Imnaha

345

315

4.2

Sacajawea Campground

Sluice Creek

Rush Creek Rapids

2.1

To Imnaha

Memaloose Guard Station

Hat Point Lookout
6,982'

3.9

Hat Point Road

1.6

Imnaha River

landing strip

3.7

Bench "High" Trail

3.5

4240

3.8

3.5

4.6

Saddle Creek Campground

7.3

4230

Freezeout Creek

2.1

Saddle Creek Trail

1.2

2.0

4.5

Saddle Creek

Freezeout Saddle
5,300'

2.2

Black Mountain
6,862'

IDAHO

To Pine Creek

3.4

2.5

Bear Mountain
6,895'

Granite Creek Rapids

8.4

Marks Cabin

Squirrel Prairie
6,650'

Shake River

OREGON

3.0

Benjamin Spring

Seven Devils Mountains

Lookout Mountain
6,792'

Battle Creek Trail

Battle Creek

Himmelwright Spring

Barton Heights

5.1

Stud Creek

Saulsberry Saddle

P O Saddle

Hells Canyon Dam

6,000'

3965

To McGraw Lookout

0   1   2   3

Miles

🐏 Hells Canyon Western Rim "Summit" Trail (Northern Portion)

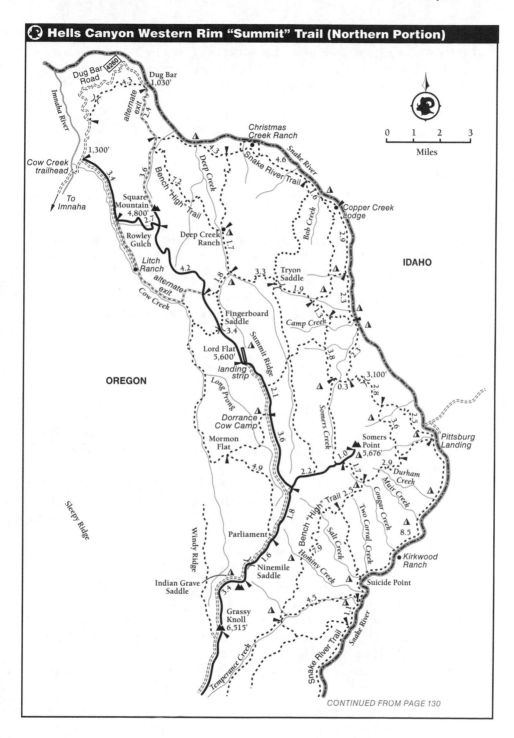

Dug Bar Road 4260

Dug Bar
1,030'

alternate exit

4.3

2.4

Imnaha River

1,300'

Cow Creek trailhead

To Imnaha

3.4

3.6

Christmas Creek Ranch

4.3

Deep Creek

Snake River Trail

4.6

Snake River

.6

Bench "High" Trail

7.2

Square Mountain
4,800'

2.7

Rowley Gulch

Litch Ranch

4.2

alternate exit

Cow Creek

Deep Creek Ranch

1.7

1.8

3.3

Tryon Saddle

1.9

2.3

Bob Creek

Copper Creek Lodge

2.9

IDAHO

Fingerboard Saddle

3.4

Summit Ridge

Camp Creek

1.3

Lord Flat
5,600'

landing strip

2.1

3.8

2.3

3,100'

0.3

2.8

Long Prong

Dorrance Cow Camp

3.6

Somers Creek

3.6

2.5

OREGON

Mormon Flat

4.9

2.2

1.0

Somers Point
5,676'

Pittsburg Landing

2.9

Durham Creek

Muir Creek

1.7

Cougar Creek

Sleepy Ridge

1.8

Bench "High" Trail

2.5

Two Corral Creek

8.5

Windy Ridge

Parliament

1.6

Salt Creek

Kirkwood Ranch

Indian Grave Saddle

3.4

Ninemile Saddle

Hominy Creek

7.9

Suicide Point

Grassy Knoll
6,515'

4.5

1.7

Temperance Creek

Snake River Trail

Snake River

CONTINUED FROM PAGE 130

0   1   2   3
Miles

(continued from page 129)

TIP 1: For more solitude, hike this route before Hat Point Road opens to traffic (usually around the second week of June, but call ahead to confirm). You will have to walk over a few snowfields, but the joy of having the terrific view from Hat Point all to yourself is well worth it.

TIP 2: Don't forget to bring binoculars; wildlife is abundant.

DESCRIPTION

From the south trailhead, the Western Rim Trail follows a gravel road that drops to P O Saddle.

NOTE: From about mid-June to mid-September this road is open to cars for the first 1.5 miles, to Saulsberry Saddle. At this point it temporarily enters the wilderness, so the U.S. Forest Service has blocked the road with a berm.

The road continues to Saulsberry Saddle, where it crosses under a set of power lines and reverts to a dirt jeep track. The jeep road climbs a wide gully to a large flat area with a mix of forests and meadows.

TIP: Two springs can be found to the west of the trail for those in need of water.

The route continues northeast along the ridge and then breaks out of the trees at the expansive meadows near Himmelwright Spring. In June this meadow is a flower bonanza, choked with the large white blossoms of Wyethia, as well as yellow balsamroot and a smattering of other species. Views extend to the snowy peaks of the distant Wallowa Mountains. Unfortunately, cows often trample the whole area, so the trail can be smelly and muddy, and camping is problematic.

After descending from Himmelwright Meadow, the old jeep road climbs a bit and then comes to a junction with the Battle Creek Trail. This route veers off to the right on its way down to the Snake River. Continuing north, your trail makes a gradual ascent, sometimes in a tunnel of trees, to Lookout Mountain. Trees partly obscure the views, but the open area on top supports a wealth of wildflowers.

The old road pretty much ends at Lookout Mountain, though a jeep track continues as far as Squirrel Prairie. You drop a bit to Benjamin Spring, which may run dry by mid- to late summer, and continue the moderate descent to a junction. To the left is the trail to Marks Cabin and a spring. The Western Rim Trail goes right and drops to the sloping meadow and the (usually) year-round creek in Squirrel Prairie. This is an excellent place to camp, though the presence of a healthy bear population makes it prudent to hang your food. (So far, the bears in Hells Canyon have not presented a problem for campers. Proper food storage will help keep it that way.)

TIP: A superb side trip from here follows the Bear Mountain Trail east through meadows and a once-burned forest. The trail climbs a bit and then follows a wide ridge all the way to the outstanding overlook atop Bear Mountain. The perspective of the snowy Seven Devils Mountains, appearing deceptively close across the gaping chasm, is particularly noteworthy.

Back on the Western Rim Trail, the route soon becomes a footpath, but travel remains easy, with only modest ups and downs. More burned and regrowing trees provide further evidence of old fires. Views alternate between the Freezeout and Imnaha Canyons to the west and Hells Canyon and the peaks in Idaho to the east. You may even spot the lookout tower on Hat Point in the distance to the north. About 3.7 miles from Squirrel Prairie is Freezeout Saddle, where the Bench and Saddle Creek Trails cross our route.

The Western Rim Trail goes straight and makes a well-graded climb along a rocky ridge covered with wildflowers, bunchgrass, and a few evergreens. Excellent views provide interest and variety as the trail shifts from one side of the ridge to the other. A little before the final switchbacks are two (usually flowing) creeklets.

TIP: Stock up on water here because this is the last opportunity for several miles.

At the top of the climb is the gravel Hat Point Road/Forest Service Road 4240, which serves as the trail for the next several miles. If your trip is in early June, the road walk should be pleasantly quiet; otherwise you must share the route with cars.

Turn right on the road and soon reach walk-in Saddle Creek Campground, which supplies picnic tables, campsites, and breathtaking sights but no water. The road makes a series of ups and downs through subalpine fir forests and burned areas as it tours the top of the ridge overlooking Hells Canyon. Several viewpoints along the way will keep your camera busy. The road eventually works away from the ridge, passes some buildings beside the Memaloose helitack (for helicopter-transported wildfire crews) and airstrip, and reaches the junction with FS 315 to Hat Point. This entire area (and for many miles to come) was burned by the Summit Fire in 1989, which left behind a seemingly endless silver ghost forest that is interesting but provides little shade and is rather monotonous. Lodgepole pines and a mixture of undergrowth have sprouted a new forest, but they are still fairly sparse and short.

The quickest way to continue the Western Rim Trail is to go straight on the road toward Warnock Corral, but to come this far and skip Hat Point would be absurd. So turn right and make the moderate 1.7-mile climb along the road to the Hat Point Lookout. This 90-foot tower is staffed in summer, and the person assigned here enjoys views that defy description. The look down to the Snake River, flowing more than a vertical mile below, is amazing. Even more thrilling, however, are the seemingly endless vistas of canyon slopes, the mountains in Idaho, and the distant Wallowa Mountains in Oregon. In early July the meadows provide gorgeous foregrounds with a colorful array of wildflowers. A picnic area and a short interpretive trail surround the lookout, providing information as well as scenic lunch spots.

TIP: To spend the night at Hat Point, continue north another 0.3 mile to Sacajawea Campground with its year-round spring.

To continue on the Western Rim Trail, return to FS 4240 and turn right. The road immediately passes the Memaloose Guard Station, then slowly descends beside the headwaters of Lightning Creek. At a gate, the road changes from gravel to dirt and then continues down to a nice view from Sluice Creek Saddle before climbing a bit to the Warnock Corral Trailhead in a small meadow. Camping here is pleasant (especially before the road is open), with a spring and small creek for water and a few green trees providing shade amid the fallen snags of the burned area. The Temperance Creek Trail drops to the northeast from here on its way to the Snake River.

From Warnock Corral the Western Rim Trail follows a four-wheel drive road that winds north through more of the slowly recovering burn area from the 1989 fire. The road is used primarily by hunters in the fall, so early-summer hikers should have it all to themselves. There is neither water nor much shade on this rather dull segment, so it can get surprisingly hot for this elevation. The road/trail passes a marked side route to Sleepy Ridge and, 0.5 mile later, finally leaves the ghost forest and enters more attractive terrain. You keep straight at the junction with a jeep road to Windy Ridge and then climb briefly to the overlook atop aptly named Grassy Knoll.

From this high point the route cuts through a nearly pure stand of even-age lodgepole pines (the legacy of a fire several decades ago) for 2 miles to a fence line. Beyond this the terrain becomes more diverse and interesting, with better views but also several steep ups and downs—a rarity for this hike. After about 1 mile you reach a low point called Indian Grave Saddle, where you will find an excellent camp and a spring with a pipe and horse trough. Refill your water bottles here. The road now enters another recovering burn area and makes a quick climb to a ridge.

TIP: A worthwhile side trip goes south from here to an unnamed open knoll with terrific views.

The Western Rim Trail goes north along the rim before dropping to Ninemile Saddle (more views). Shortly beyond the next hill an unmarked jeep trail to the west goes 0.2 mile to a spring and an old cabin (possible camps here).

Atop the next hill is a junction and a large meadow area identified on maps as Parliament. No other legislature on the planet could possibly have enjoyed a better view! To the east drops the enormous gorge of Hells Canyon, while to the west is a gentler slope of forests that drop off into the canyons and ridges of Imnaha River country. Elk are generally the only legislators likely to be present. Leaving "Capitol Hill," so to speak, the road remains easy walking as it gradually descends past viewpoints for 1.8 miles to a junction.

Veering off to the right is the highly recommended up-and-down route to Somers Point. Views along this path—especially the jaw-dropper from Somers Point itself—are among the most memorable on this trip. The first 200 yards follow a jeep road, but the route soon becomes a pleasant footpath. The trail passes some nice camps in a saddle after 1.1 miles. You keep right at a junction just west of an unobtrusive radio tower and then descend through attractive forests. The last mile to Somers Point goes over a wide and spectacular meadowy ridge with lots of vistas and wildflowers.

You'll enjoy an outstanding view from the end of Somers Point. The river can be seen in two different directions, contorted canyon walls stretch for miles, and the snowy peaks of Idaho provide a fine backdrop. Pittsburg Landing, with its boat ramp and campground, lies directly below on the Idaho side of the river. Fires over the years have left some snags, but these can't diminish the scene.

TIP: Binoculars will come in handy to spot wildlife and rafters.

A view like this is hard to leave; fortunately, an inviting camp is nearby. A spring with a pipe and horse trough sits 200 yards north of and below the trail, 0.2 mile west of Somers Point. Excellent camps are found another 200 yards west of the spring in a strip of trees.

WARNING: If you leave camp, and at night, be sure to hang your food. Curious bears have been known to come sniffing around campsites in the area.

Back at the Somers Point junction, the Western Rim Trail continues to follow the road on its gentle course to the north. After curving left, the route heads back toward the ridge but generally remains in the trees. After making a long, fairly gradual descent, the road starts to break out into more open country. A short side trail goes left near here to Dorrance Cow Camp, where a cabin and some good camps are located. The main trail continues north over a grassy hill and drops through view-packed bunchgrass meadows to the south end of the Lord Flat landing strip. Despite its remote location, this airstrip's grassy 2,000-foot "tarmac" gets a surprising amount of use by U.S. Forest Service personnel, hunters, and others. Water is also available here.

From the landing strip the Western Rim Trail veers left on a jeep track and gradually drops down open slopes. Look for wildlife such as elk and black bears here. The jeep road finally ends near a tiny pond, after which the trail descends 19 switchbacks as it closely follows the Summit Ridge. To your immediate right lies Deep Creek Canyon, while to the left is Cow Creek's rugged defile. Your route switchbacks down to a saddle and a junction, with sketchy use paths heading both left and right. Continue straight and trace an up-and-down route along the ridge for about 2 miles to Fingerboard Saddle.

Pittsburg Landing from Somers Point
photographed by Douglas Lorain

A good trail crosses our route here, providing a possible exit to Cow Creek Road and back to the trailhead. This is the shortest way out for hikers in a hurry. To exit from here, turn left, drop to Cow Creek, and follow the road downstream through Litch Ranch and eventually out to your car.

If you decide to stick with the Western Rim Trail, keep straight from Fingerboard Saddle and follow a roller-coaster route along the ridge. The north end of Summit Ridge is much narrower and more rugged than the south end, but it also has more continuous views and fewer trees. The trail is often indistinct, but because it closely follows the ridgeline, you shouldn't get lost.

WARNING: Water along the ridge is scarce to nonexistent—carry extra.

Loop around the headwaters of Little Deep Creek to the east and make a sometimes steep descent from a high point on the ridge to a saddle. The trail goes over another hill before facing the final short climb to Square Mountain. The Rowley Gulch Trail goes left and makes a steep switchbacking descent from the saddle just south of Square Mountain. Having come this far, however, you really should make the climb to Square Mountain to enjoy its views all the way to the Snake River near Dug Bar.

If Dug Bar is your chosen exit, follow the Western Rim Trail north from Square Mountain as it follows Dug Creek through a mix of forests and meadows to a junction first with the Bench Trail and then with the Snake River Trail (beware of poison ivy near here). The trail goes over a small rise with excellent views down to Dug Bar Ranch and drops down to the river-level trailhead.

To exit via Rowley Gulch, the steep route (often easy to lose) switchbacks down a ridge and then goes over to a side canyon before paralleling the seasonal creek in Rowley Gulch to Cow Creek Road. Turn right and follow this road through attractive, mostly open country, usually well above the stream, back to your car.

NOTE: Please be respectful of the private land here by keeping gates open or closed as you found them and by not camping.

NOTE: The three trips described in Hells Canyon are all one-way, point-to-point hikes. For those unable to arrange a car shuttle, it is also possible to devise several long and spectacular loop trips in the canyon. One of the best begins at Dug Bar, goes up the Snake River Trail to Somers Creek, and then returns to Dug Bar via the Bench Trail over Tryon Saddle. This 42-mile trip is at its best in early to mid-May. A second trip—which peaks in early June, though with some snow at the highest elevations—begins at the Freezeout Trailhead and follows the Bench Trail to Kneeland Place. The route then climbs steeply to Somers Point and returns to the Freezeout Trailhead via the Western Rim Trail. The total distance for this loop is 58 miles. With some creativity and a good map, many other loop trips of various lengths can be planned.

WARNING: Less-used connecting trails are often faint and difficult to find on the ground. Also, the canyon's great changes in elevation create radically different environments. Therefore, while one part of your planned loop is cool, green, and beautiful, the lower part of the same trip may be hot, dry, and brown. Prepare accordingly.

POSSIBLE ITINERARY

	CAMP	MILES	ELEVATION GAIN
Day 1	Squirrel Prairie (with side trip to Bear Mountain)	13.1	2,200'
Day 2	Sacajawea Campground (Hat Point)	11.4	2,300'
Day 3	Indian Grave Saddle	12.2	1,100'
Day 4	Somers Point	6.6	1,200'
Day 5	Lord Flat	8.9	1,000'
Day 6	Out	13.7	1,500'

22

SNAKE RIVER TRAIL

RATINGS: Scenery 10 **Solitude** 7 **Difficulty** 8
MILES: 41
ELEVATION GAIN: 6,000'
DAYS: 4–5
SHUTTLE MILEAGE: n/a
MAP: USFS *Hells Canyon National Recreation Area and Wilderness*
USUALLY OPEN: Year-round
BEST: Mid-April–early May
PERMITS: None
RULES: No fires within 0.25 mile of the Snake River
CONTACT: Wallowa Mountains Office, Wallowa-Whitman National Forest, 541-426-4978, www.fs.usda.gov/wallowa-whitman

SPECIAL ATTRACTIONS •

Whitewater rafters to observe; historical sites; wildlife; great canyon scenery

CHALLENGES •

Complicated and expensive boat transportation; rattlesnakes, ticks, and black widow spiders (especially in the spring and early summer); no shade—it can be extremely hot; lots of poison ivy

Above: View below Suicide Point
photographed by Douglas Lorain

Snake River Trail

HOW TO GET THERE •

The logistics of starting this hike are unusually complicated. A very long and tedious car shuttle from Hells Canyon Dam to Dug Bar is one option. This would allow you to enjoy the trail's entire length, but it also would require making arrangements for a short boat ride downstream to Battle Creek, where Oregon's river trail starts.

For Hells Canyon Dam, take I-84 to Exit 302 in Baker City. Head east on OR 86 for 67 miles. At Copperfield, go straight for 0.5 mile onto Hells Canyon Road (also known as Forest Service Road 454), crossing into Idaho, then turn left. Follow Hells Canyon Road 22 miles to the dam.

To reach the Dug Bar trailhead, from I-84 take Exit 261 in La Grande, and turn right (east) onto OR 82. In 1.4 miles turn left (north) to remain on OR 82. Go 17.7 miles and turn right (east) to again remain on OR 82. Drive 44.2 miles to the town of Enterprise. Turn right (south) to continue another 6.3 miles on OR 82 to Joseph. Turn left (east) onto OR 350, and go 29.4 miles. After crossing the Imnaha River, turn left (north) onto Lower Imnaha Road. In 6.3 miles make a slight right (northeast) onto Dug Bar Road/FS 4260. In 6.8 miles turn left (north) to remain on Dug Bar Road. Go 6.6 miles, cross the Imnaha River again, and turn left to stay on FS 4260. Go 10.7 miles to the end of the road and the trailhead. The drive is long and sometimes rough but incredibly scenic.

WARNING: The last 8 miles are especially steep and difficult. When the road is wet, a four-wheel drive vehicle is highly recommended.

A second option (with a much shorter car shuttle) is to start the trip from the Freeze-out Trailhead (see Trip 23). This requires a climb over Freezeout Saddle, where there is likely to be some snow through April. The route then descends the Saddle Creek Trail to reach the Snake River Trail about 8 miles downstream from Battle Creek. To reach Freezeout Trailhead, from I-84 take Exit 302 in Baker City, and head east on OR 86. Go 60.1 miles, and in Halfway turn left onto North Pine Road. Drive 14.3 miles, and turn right onto Forest Service Road 39/Wallowa Mountain Loop. In 8.8 miles turn right onto FS 39/Upper Imnaha Road. Go 2 miles and turn right onto Wallowa Mountain Loop/FS 3955/Upper Imnaha Road. Drive 18 miles, cross the Imnaha River, and turn right onto FS 4230 (marked SADDLE CREEK TRAIL). Keep left at the first fork, and continue 2.7 miles to the Freezeout Trailhead at the road's end.

WARNING: The Saddle Creek Trail includes several stream crossings that in the spring can be cold and rather treacherous.

Still another plan (and the one recommended here) necessitates only one car, but you must make arrangements at least two weeks in advance with a jet boat operator to pick you up at Dug Bar and drop you off upstream. The larger companies are happy to help, but you'll have to work around their regular tour schedules. Expect to pay between $80 and $160 for boat transport from Dug Bar to about Johnson Bar. Reliable operators include Hells Canyon Adventures (800-422-3568; hellscanyonadventures.com) and Snake River Adventures (800-262-8874; snakeriveradventures.com).

A final option, which avoids bad roads altogether, is to leave your car in Lewiston, Idaho; take the jet boat upstream to your chosen drop-off; and then arrange for the boat to pick you up for the ride back down to Lewiston at the end of the hike. This option requires that you stick with a set schedule on the trail to make the prearranged pickup time, and you'll probably have to pay for two boat trips.

TIP: See the note in Trip 21 concerning car-shuttle services for hikes in Hells Canyon.

NOTE: While jet boats are recommended here as the most convenient transportation for backpackers, they are not necessary for this hike. If you are morally opposed to the use of jet boats, do not avoid this outstanding trip as a result. Use one of the other options noted above.

GPS TRAILHEAD COORDINATES:
(Dug Bar) N45° 48.277' W116° 41.207'
(Freezeout) N45° 22.548' W116° 45.715'
(Hells Canyon Dam) N45° 14.493' W116° 42.190'

INTRODUCTION •

Two words sum up the experience of hiking Oregon's Snake River Trail: *spectacular* and *exhausting*. With all due respect to the marvelous canyon scenery found along the Rogue River, the Owyhee River, and many other Oregon streams, they all pale in comparison to the vastness of Hells Canyon. The Snake River Trail provides perhaps the ultimate backpacking experience in the canyon. Only the most jaded traveler will fail to return with a sore neck from so much time spent looking up to the canyon's rim thousands of feet above. More serious threats than a sore neck, however, are rattlesnakes and poison ivy, so you must spend at least as much time looking down as up.

TIP I: Summer days are blisteringly hot and nights are uncomfortably warm. Dress accordingly and be prepared to sleep on top of your bag.

TIP 2: In many places poison ivy is so abundant that you simply cannot avoid the stuff. Try using a shielding product, applied before contact, and/or a special soap to wash off the toxins afterward. People who are particularly allergic should probably avoid this hike altogether.

DESCRIPTION •

Pick up your prearranged boat ride at Dug Bar and plan on a long, exciting, and informative trip upriver to the recommended drop-off opposite Johnson Bar. The larger companies typically stop along the way at Kirkwood Ranch, an interesting museum that is well worth a visit. It will be early afternoon by the time you disembark. You must scramble up the bank a bit to reach the trail.

TIP: Before starting the downstream trek, consider a short exploration upstream. Rush Creek Rapids is a good nearby goal and logical turnaround point.

Downstream from Johnson Bar, the wildly scenic route stays close to the river and soon comes to a fine camp at (probably dry) Yreka Creek—obtain water from the Snake River. The path then crosses a huge rock shelf called Eagle's Nest, where the trail has been blasted into the side of the rock. Take a moment to marvel at the work involved—not to mention the quantity of dynamite it must have taken. Civilian Conservation Corps workers did an admirable job building this path in the 1930s. About 2.2 miles from the takeout point is the Sand Creek game warden's cabin. Farther downstream, at Alum Bed Rapids, the Idaho side boasts a colorful area of exposed yellow cliffs.

The trail works around a bend in the river and then tours a grassy bench above the stream. You pass a marked junction with a very sketchy "trail" up Dry Gulch and then go around a large, fenced meadowy flat. In a confusing section near the north end of this pasture, the trail crosses the fence and goes down to Temperance Creek Ranch. You make a bridged crossing of Temperance Creek and come immediately to a junction in the trees. You can camp upstream amid this creek's lush riparian vegetation.

Now the Snake River Trail goes north, passes the massive cliffs of Suicide Point (across the river in Idaho), and reaches good camps and a cabin at the flats of Salt Creek.

TIP: A possible side trip climbs the steep Salt Creek Trail to a series of excellent overlooks above the river.

Continuing on the Snake River Trail, cross Two Corral Creek, briefly follow close to the river, and then go across a large, sloping bench. Near the north end of this bench is Slaughter Gulch (often dry). The trail now drops to the riverside and hugs the shore beside steep cliffs. The route is chiseled into the canyon walls and, despite staying close to river level, is constantly making tiny ups and downs. The crossing of Cougar Creek offers good views across the river to the meadowy flat holding Kirkwood Ranch.

The rugged trail continues to hug the cliffs on the Oregon side for the next mile or two before breaking out onto a meadowy bench across from Idaho's Kirby Bar. Muir Creek supplies water and some possible spots to eat lunch or camp. The alternating pattern of steep slopes and river benches continues as you cross a set of cliffs and reach the bench at Durham Creek (more potential camps). For the next 2 miles the trail goes through a narrow section of the canyon, where both the Oregon and Idaho trails have been carved out of the hillsides and cliffs. You are likely to see far more people on the Idaho side's trail because that popular route has easy access for day hikers from Pittsburg Landing.

NOTE: Geography buffs may be interested to note that, as the trail rounds the slopes of Robertson Ridge, it crosses the easternmost point in Oregon.

Landmarks, mainly on the opposite shore, include the trailhead at Upper Pittsburg Landing and, later, the car campground at Lower Pittsburg. On the Oregon side, the trail crosses an arid bench to a junction with a steep path going up Robertson Gulch and then continues to the Pittsburg Guard Station.

In the miles ahead the Snake River cuts through a particularly narrow and steep-walled part of Hells Canyon. To avoid this difficult section, you are forced to make a long, sometimes rugged, but highly scenic detour. First your path climbs inland to the Bench Trail, some 1,500 feet above. The climb is steep in places and, as is true on the entire trail, exposed to the sun. Start with full water bottles and carry your own shade—a hat. The route contours away from Pittsburg and climbs a draw to a point about 500 feet above the river. Near the head of this draw is a spring with possible water. The trail then traces an up-and-down course about 1 mile to the crossing of Pleasant Valley Creek, with water and some shade. Now the climb really gets under way as the rocky path leads up a small ridge, gaining a little more than 1,000 feet in 1 mile. Just short of the high point is a junction with the Bench Trail in a large meadow with terrific views up to Somers Point.

The two trails follow the same route north for the next 2.8 miles. After 1.5 beautiful ridge-and-meadow miles, the fun abruptly ends as the trail steeply climbs a shadeless gully to a pass. Take a well-deserved rest at the top to enjoy the panoramas. As the trail descends toward Somers Creek, you will have some fine views down to the Snake River.

At a junction near the rounded summit called Englishman Hill, the Bench Trail goes left a short distance to Somers Creek (good camps), while the Snake River Trail (our route) turns right and continues its descent back to the river. After you make a couple of quick switchbacks, the often-steep route follows a tributary canyon of Somers Creek down to the main stream. A pleasant riparian zone of dense deciduous vegetation and a few ponderosa pines accommodates the trail as it parallels the rushing stream. The route requires three creek crossings that may get your feet wet but aren't difficult.

WARNING: Be particularly alert for poison ivy and rattlesnakes through this section.

Where you return to the Snake River, there are good campsites near an old cabin. At Camp Creek, a short distance farther north, are more camps and a junction with a trail that climbs back to the Bench Trail near Tryon Creek Ranch.

To continue your tour, closely follow the banks of the Snake River as it cuts a surprisingly straight path north for the next few miles. Steep cliffs on both sides of the canyon

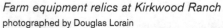

Farm equipment relics at Kirkwood Ranch
photographed by Douglas Lorain

provide exciting scenery. The Idaho side no longer has a trail, as that path's northern terminus was Pittsburg Landing. About 0.4 mile north of Camp Creek, Tryon Creek furnishes a good camp and a chance to refill your water bottles. If this spot doesn't suit you, more camps are located at Lookout Creek just over 1 mile farther north. After Lookout Creek the trail passes along the base of some impressive cliffs, and in places it has been blasted right into the side of them.

After a junction with a sketchy trail just before Lonepine Creek (usually dry), your trail leads well above the raging Snake River as it cuts through a particularly narrow segment of the canyon. Near Highrange Rapids an old mine shaft, just above the trail, is protected as a nursery for bats. The trail then works back down to river level and returns to its pattern of miniature ups and downs blasted into the cliffs.

Just past a second mine tunnel, the trail splits. The official trail climbs to the left, while to the right are a boat landing and the lush oasis of Copper Creek Lodge, a modern facility run by a commercial boat operator. In fact, you may have stopped here on the boat ride up. It includes several modern cabins, manicured lawns and shade trees, running water, gift items and souvenirs, and dining facilities. Hikers need reservations to spend the night or eat here; call 800-522-6966 or visit hellscanyontours.com. Day hikers from Copper Creek Lodge use the trails near here, so this is one of the few areas where you can expect company on this trip.

Shortly beyond the lodge you cross a wide bench where there is a junction near Bob Creek.

TIP: Shortly after crossing this creek, look for a short spur trail that goes upstream to a small waterfall.

Several trees on the flat meadow area near Bob Creek make this a particularly good campsite. As you leave the day hikers behind, the Snake River Trail remains close to the river until Cat Creek, where it detours around an abandoned ranch. A sketchy trail ascends the slopes south of here on its way to Tryon Saddle.

To continue your tour, traverse a large meadowy bench above Roland Bar Rapids and then arrive at Roland Creek. This small creek usually flows all year, so stock up on water here. For the next several miles the Snake River Trail travels a rugged up-and-down course well away from the river over terrain that will keep your heart pounding, from both the exertion and the views.

TIP: Elk are common. Keep an eye out for wildlife.

The detour away from the river starts with a sometimes steep and rocky 600-foot climb from Roland Creek to a saddle. The trail then follows a less strenuous up-and-down course to the buildings of abandoned Dorrance Ranch. Just past the ranch the trail splits. To the right, a path drops back down to the Snake River and then continues to Christmas Creek Ranch. The official Snake River Trail keeps left, crosses Bean Creek (usually flowing), and then drops a bit around a ridge to Christmas Creek. Shortly beyond this small stream is the junction with the return loop of the trail to Christmas Creek Ranch. Next is yet another climb, though this time at a fairly moderate grade, along a view-packed slope to a junction with the spectacular path to Deep Creek Ranch.

TIP: If you have an extra day, this trail is well worth taking as a long side trip.

After crossing Thorn Spring Creek near an old cabin, the trail climbs a bit more and then begins the steep 1,100-foot descent back to the Snake River.

The trail returns to the river just above Deep Creek Bar. There is plenty of water here, as well as a collection of interesting shacks and old machinery from Chinese miners. Several luxurious camps in the vicinity cater to whitewater rafters and feature such amenities as picnic tables and an outhouse.

WARNING: You must ford Deep Creek here, which can be a bit tricky in the spring, so use caution.

To complete your adventure, continue along the Snake River another 1.1 miles to Dug Creek. You turn up this side stream and travel through the dense grasses and vegetation along the creek.

WARNING: The stinging nettles and poison ivy in this section are so thick that they are impossible to avoid.

The trail crosses and recrosses the creek, sometimes making it easy to lose. Often the easiest alternative is to simply walk up the streambed itself. After about 0.8 mile the trail finally works away from the creek (though the poison ivy remains in force) and reaches a junction. Turn right and climb a bit to reach a great view overlooking Dug Bar, and then drop steeply to the ranch. The well-marked public trail goes to the right around the ranch area.

TIP: Don't miss the short side trail to a sign referencing the Nez Perce Indians' crossing of the Snake River near this location in 1877. The courageous band of American Indians led by Chief Joseph traveled through here on a heroic (and ultimately futile) journey in search of freedom.

From here it is only a few hundred yards to the parking area near the boat ramp at the trailhead.

POSSIBLE ITINERARY

	CAMP	MILES	ELEVATION GAIN
Day 1	Temperance Creek	6.8	500'
Day 2	Pittsburg	8.5	500'
Day 3	Bob Creek	13.2	2,600'
Day 4	Out	12.5	2,400'

23

HELLS CANYON BENCH "HIGH" TRAIL

RATINGS: Scenery 10   **Solitude** 8   **Difficulty** 8

MILES: 63

ELEVATION GAIN: 14,900'

DAYS: 5–8

SHUTTLE MILEAGE: 46

MAP: USFS *Hells Canyon National Recreation Area and Wilderness*

USUALLY OPEN: April–November

BEST: Early to mid-May

PERMITS: None

RULES: No fires within 0.25 mile of Snake River

CONTACT: Wallowa Mountains Office, Wallowa-Whitman National Forest, 541-426-4978, www.fs.usda.gov/wallowa-whitman

SPECIAL ATTRACTIONS

Views; abundant wildlife; wildflowers; solitude

CHALLENGES

Rattlesnakes; poor road access; poison ivy; often very hot; rough trail; several burn areas; ticks (especially in the spring)

Above: Wisenor Place
photographed by Douglas Lorain

🌐 Hells Canyon Bench "High" Trail (Southern Portion)

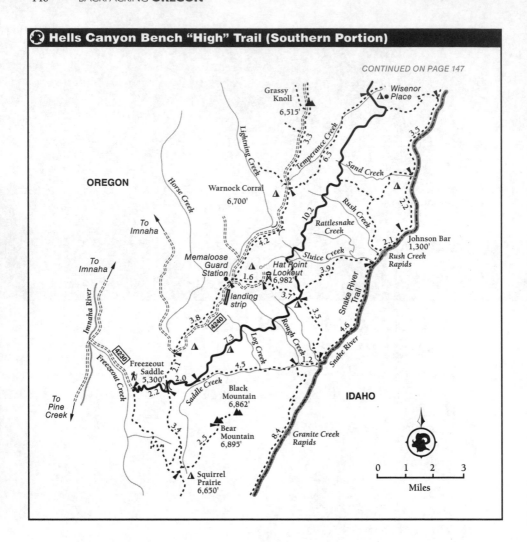

CONTINUED ON PAGE 147

HOW TO GET THERE ●●●

To reach the north trailhead of this hike, drive to the end of Dug Bar Road. The Freeze-out Trailhead is the south trailhead for this hike. See page 139 of Trip 22 for directions to both trailheads.

TIP: See the note in Trip 21 on page 129 concerning car-shuttle services for hikes in Hells Canyon.

GPS TRAILHEAD COORDINATES:
(Dug Bar) N45° 48.277' W116° 41.207'
(Freezeout) N45° 22.548' W116° 45.715'

Hells Canyon Bench "High" Trail (Northern Portion)

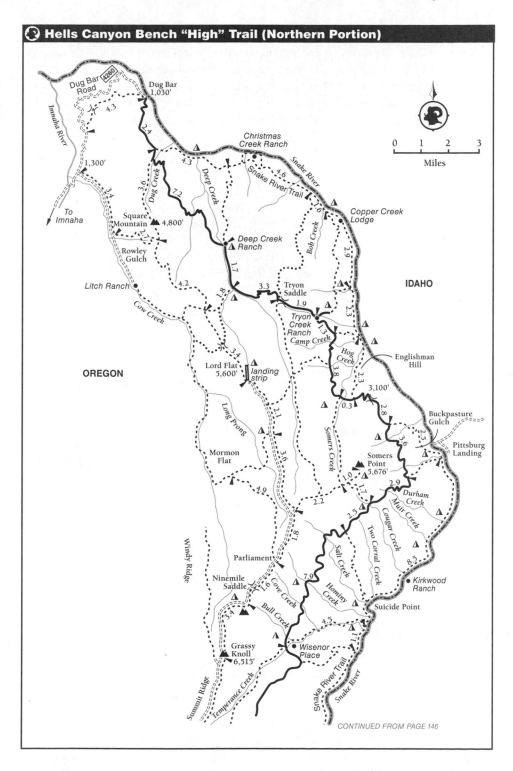

Dug Bar Road
4260
Dug Bar
1,030'

4.3

2.4

Christmas
Creek Ranch

Snake River

Imnaha River

1,300'

3.6

4.3

Snake River Trail

4.6

3.4

To Imnaha

Square Mountain

4,800'

7.2

Deep Creek

Bob Creek

1.6

Copper Creek Lodge

2.7

Deep Creek Ranch

2.9

Rowley Gulch

1.7

IDAHO

Litch Ranch

4.2

Cow Creek

1.8

3.3

Tryon Saddle

1.9

2.3

Tryon Creek Ranch

Camp Creek

1.3

3.4

Lord Flat
5,600'

landing strip

Hog Creek

3.8

Englishman Hill

OREGON

2.3

3,100'

Long Prong

2.1

Somers Creek

0.3

2.8

Buckpasture Gulch

2.5

Mormon Flat

3.6

Pittsburg Landing

3.6

Somers Point
5,676'

4.9

2.2

1.0

2.9

Durham Creek

8.1

1.7

2.5

Muir Creek

Windy Ridge

Parliament

Cougar Creek

Two Corral Creek

8.5

Ninemile Saddle

1.6

7.9

Salt Creek

Kirkwood Ranch

3.4

Cove Creek

Bull Creek

Hominy Creek

Suicide Point

4.5

1.1

Grassy Knoll
6,515'

Wisenor Place

Summit Ridge

Temperance Creek

Snake River Trail

Snake River

0   1   2   3
Miles

CONTINUED FROM PAGE 146

INTRODUCTION

For lovers of canyon scenery and wildflowers, the Bench Trail through Hells Canyon is the experience of a lifetime. Following a mid-canyon route about halfway between the Snake River and the Summit Ridge, this spectacular tour provides a greater variety of scenery than any other long trail in the canyon. In addition to offering vistas across the canyon to the peaks in Idaho, the area delivers views down into the depths below, up to the contorted canyon walls above, and, often most impressive of all, of the scenic meadows right at the hiker's feet. Photographers must become very choosy to avoid running out of storage space (bring extra memory cards!). This trail also travels through the finest examples of native bunchgrass in Oregon—a plant community lost elsewhere to the hooves of cattle and introduced plant species. In season, wildflowers and wildlife are perhaps more abundant here than on any other long trail in the state.

Despite the awesome scenery, the great distances and rugged terrain keep out all but the best-conditioned backpackers. Horse packers are much more common, though even they are rather few and far between. You'll probably have most of this wonderful hike all to yourself.

NOTE: Trail signs usually identify this as the High Trail. Users, however, more often refer to it as the Bench Trail, as this is a better description of the terrain.

WARNING: Those who choose to come here must be prepared for the rigors of this place. The second half of this hike is particularly rugged, with numerous steep climbs and descents over sunbaked slopes. (Fortunately, unlike on the Snake River Trail, there are usually enough trees to provide shade at rest stops.) At lower elevations you may encounter poison ivy. Rattlesnakes inhabit the entire length of the trail. Temperatures, while more comfortable than at the bottom of the canyon, can be very hot on sunny afternoons. In a few places, where game and livestock trails veer off in all directions and grasses obscure the path, the route is easy to lose—good route-finding instincts will come in handy.

TIP: Fans of watching wildlife should carry binoculars. Use them in the early morning and evening to scan the grassy slopes and rock ledges. You have a good chance of spotting elk, deer, bighorn sheep, black bears, coyotes, and maybe even a mountain lion. As you sit quietly and continue to search, more animals inevitably seem to come into view. It's great fun!

DESCRIPTION

Your route begins with a long series of moderately steep switchbacks up a grassy slope to Freezeout Saddle. (Odds are very good that you will be hot and sweaty after the 1,700-foot climb, and "freezing" will be the last thing on your mind.) In many ways Freezeout Saddle is the focal point of hiking in Hells Canyon. In addition to the Bench Trail, the Western Rim Trail (see Trip 21) cuts through here on its way south to McGraw Lookout and north to Hat Point, and the Saddle Creek Trail grants access to the Snake River. Finally, this is one of the few locations in the canyon with reasonable access for day hikers to such landmarks as Bear Mountain.

To hike the Bench Trail, go straight from the saddle and descend a mostly open slope with several exceptional views of smooth-sided Bear Mountain and craggy Black Mountain to the south. The trail passes through an old burn area—the first of many on this trip—whose snags provide habitat for a large population of Lewis's and other wood-peckers. After 2 miles you turn left at a junction with the Saddle Creek Trail.

As the Bench Trail goes north, several patterns that will hold true for most of this trip soon become apparent. For the most part, the trail is gently graded, following the canyon slopes at elevations between 3,500 and 4,500 feet. To allow this, it contours out across the ridges and into the creek canyons in a seemingly endless series of zigzags. Large mead-owy benches sometimes provide a platform for the trail, but the in-out pattern predom-inates. The river, flowing some 3,000 feet below, is rarely visible. The vegetation provides another interesting pattern. Surprisingly lush forests of Douglas fir and ponderosa pine, along with numerous shrubs and ground cover plants, grow on the north-facing slopes. On drier, south-facing slopes only the occasional ponderosa pine survives amid rocky meadows sprinkled with wildflowers. The meadowy benches and ridges are perhaps most scenic of all, with breathtaking views and thousands of flowers. Look for balsamroot, lupine, phlox, wallflower, yarrow, Indian paintbrush, Lomatium, gilia, brodiaea, and countless others.

With these patterns in place, your route begins with a long, undulating approach to a prominent ridge about 5 miles northeast. The trail has only moderate ups and downs, and numerous small creeks provide water, so the hiking is easy and enjoyable. Log Creek has the first good campsites. Upon finally reaching the ridge, you are rewarded with a large grassy area and excellent views of the cliffs above. Shortly beyond the ridge, the route crosses Rough Creek above a small falls and then continues through forest to crossings of the several branches of Hat Creek.

About 100 feet after the last branch of Hat Creek, a sheepherder's cabin appears on the right, and just beyond is a junction with the trail from Hat Point. The cabin, usually open, is a good shelter if it rains.

WARNING: Lots of mice inhabit this cabin. Hang your food and be prepared for a long night of listening to the sounds of scurrying rodents.

Keep straight at the junction with the Hat Point Trail, and drop another 100 yards to a second junction; the trail to the right goes past a corral on a grassy bench before descend-ing to the Snake River.

TIP: This bench area is a wonderful place to camp, with nearby creek water, shade, and truly outstanding cross-canyon vistas.

Now the Bench Trail goes north 0.2 mile to yet another junction. You turn left and immediately enjoy terrific views of the impressive cliffs below Hat Point—still sporting plenty of snow in early May.

Continuing on the Bench Trail, the route traces a surprisingly gentle course as it cir-cles the headwaters of Sluice Creek. The awesome cliffs and rock pinnacles of Hat Point tower above. At the final branch of Sluice Creek the route passes below an impressive waterfall—the best on the entire trip. The trail then continues to crossings of Rattlesnake Creek (a reminder to keep an eye out for these creatures) and Rush Creek. A little beyond Rush Creek is the simple grave site of Charlie Gordon (1901–1918) for whom there is no epitaph, but the years indicate that he died far too young. A little farther along is a junction with a faint trail to Sand Creek and the Snake River.

Continuing north, the rambling route passes through scattered decades-old burn areas as it gradually gains elevation and works toward the top of the rugged divide separating Temperance Creek from the main canyon. The trail reaches the top of this wide and very beautiful meadowy ridge and then follows it about 1 mile. You pass a fenced corral and then go around the right side of a grassy knoll to a saddle with a junction. Turn left and descend very steeply on a rocky trail (watch your step), losing 1,200 feet to a ford of Temperance Creek. The old Wisenor Place homestead is on the opposite bank. There are excellent camps here—some of the best along the entire trail.

TIP: The Wisenor Place's porch is a comfortable place to hole up during a thunderstorm or rainy night.

The Temperance Creek Trail meets the Bench Trail here. To continue your tour, keep right and contour 0.2 mile to a crossing of Bull Creek (more camps). The trail then makes a series of ups and downs as it traverses open, grassy ridges and canyons. After crossing Cove Creek (beware of poison ivy) the trail makes a determined assault up a side canyon on its way to Hominy Saddle, almost 1,000 feet above. From the saddle the trail turns left and follows a fence line up the ridge before dropping to Hominy Creek (good camps).

Returning to its familiar "into canyon; out ridge" course, the 8-mile tour between Hominy Creek and Kneeland Place is easy, mostly level hiking over open, view-packed slopes. The only problem may be losing the sometimes overgrown path as your attention turns to the view rather than the trail. The Salt Creek Trail intersects your route at one of the many meadowy ridges. Watch for elk in this area. Cross Two Corral Creek and continue to Cougar Creek at the site of the old Kneeland Place (long gone). Lots of ponderosa pines and riparian shrubs make this a choice campsite—though horse packers seem to think so too, so you may be crowded out.

TIP 1: The best camps are about 200 yards upstream near a spring.

TIP 2: An excellent but steep side trip from here climbs to the outstanding overlook at Somers Point, though this high ridge may still have some snow in May.

Not far beyond the Kneeland Place, the previously gentle character of the Bench Trail begins to change as the canyon's topography requires the trail to go more radically up and down. After contouring around a ridge and crossing South Durham Creek, the path drops in a series of short, steep switchbacks to North Durham Creek (water, but no camps). The path then contours out to a ridge, where a confusing ditch trail goes straight, while the Bench Trail switchbacks to the left and drops to a junction. The road and developed area visible on the Idaho side of the canyon are at Pittsburg Landing. The trail drops into Buckpasture Gulch before crossing yet another view-packed ridge and descending steeply to Pleasant Valley. Look for bears and some excellent campsites in this aptly named location.

Now the Bench Trail climbs gradually through a large meadow to a junction with the Snake River Trail. In a rugged detour around river-level cliffs, this lower trail has been forced to climb to meet the Bench Trail at this point. The two trails follow the same route north for the next 2.8 miles.

WARNING: Beware of poison ivy in this section.

After about 1.5 joyful ridge-and-meadow miles, the fun is over because the trail climbs a shadeless gully *steeply* to a pass. Take a well-deserved rest at the top to enjoy the great panoramas. As the trail descends toward Somers Creek, you will have some fine views down to the Snake River.

At a junction near the rounded summit called Englishman Hill, the Snake River Trail departs to the right while the Bench Trail makes a short jog left to Somers Creek at the site of burned-down Somers Ranch. This is a fine spot for lunch or to camp for the night. After passing a junction with a trail to Somers Point, the Bench Trail climbs gradually along grassy slopes and through lush riparian areas to Hog Creek. Keep right at a junction and then cross some beautiful grassy terraces before dropping very steeply over loose, boot-skidding rocks to splashing Camp Creek (which, despite its name, has no decent flat spot to camp). Climb to a grassy saddle and then traverse an open terrace dotted with bushes on the way to inviting Tryon Creek Ranch. This ranch house and its outbuildings are still used by U.S. Forest Service crews, so the area is well maintained. A hose provides a steady flow of water from an unseen spring.

TIP: If you have some extra energy in the evening, invest it in the fine side trip out to Tryon Viewpoint—0.6 mile northeast along the trail to Lookout Creek.

From Tryon Creek Ranch the Bench Trail makes a long, wickedly steep 2,000-foot climb to Tryon Saddle.

TIP: Try to tackle this section in the shade of evening or the cool of the morning.

Views from the windswept saddle are outstanding, especially of Deep Creek Canyon to the west. Elk populate the nearby slopes. Low-growing phlox and other flowers help to give this treeless pass an alpine feeling.

To continue your tour, keep right at the saddle, contour around a basin, and then begin the long descent to Deep Creek. The route drops through a mix of rocky areas and trees before following a small creek for the final 0.5 mile. An excellent camp is located in the trees next to Deep Creek at the bottom of the descent.

The trail turns north and takes a joyful course as it follows the clear, rushing waters of Deep Creek. You pass through a surprisingly lush and shady forest of ponderosa pine, Douglas fir, grand fir, and mixed deciduous trees. The hiking is easy and beautiful through this environment, which is unusual for Hells Canyon—it more closely resembles the higher-elevation forests of the Blue Mountains. Familiar forest residents like red-breasted nuthatches, porcupines, Douglas squirrels, and chipmunks find good habitat here. In early May look for huge serviceberry bushes, some as big as trees, putting on a showy display of white blossoms.

You pass the junction with a trail headed for Cow Creek before reaching a nice campsite. Continue straight to Deep Creek Ranch, which marks the end of the easy creekside forest walk.

TIP: A little downstream from the ranch is a nice flat area where backpackers can make a comfortable camp.

You ford Deep Creek next to the ranch house and then begin to climb a mostly open slope above the cliffs lining lower Deep Creek's canyon. The climb tops out several hundred feet above Deep Creek Ranch, where you can savor terrific views of the lower canyon. Sadly, the trail now loses virtually all of that hard-won elevation as it drops to Little Deep Creek. This area would make a good campsite if it weren't so badly churned to dust and used as a toilet by cattle.

The trail climbs gradually away from Little Deep Creek along an open grassy slope. Eventually you'll come to a fence line at a high pass, which delivers outstanding views. From this vantage point you can see all the way to Dug Bar Ranch, the end point of your hike. The path makes a long descent to Dug Creek and to a junction with the trail to Lord Flat.

WARNING: Beware of poison ivy near Dug Creek. The thickets here are the worst on the entire trip.

A short distance farther is a second junction, this one with the Snake River Trail coming up from the right. Keep straight, climb a bit to reach a great view overlooking Dug Bar, and then drop steeply to the ranch. The well-marked public trail goes to the right around the ranch area.

TIP 1: Don't miss the short side trail to a sign referencing the Nez Perce Indians' crossing of the Snake River near here in 1877. While crossing the flooding river as they did is not advisable, it does feel great to jump in briefly, both to cool down and to wash off a few layers of dirt before hiking the last few hundred yards to your car.

TIP 2: Don't forget to allow plenty of time for the long, slow drive back out Dug Bar Road to Imnaha.

POSSIBLE ITINERARY

	CAMP	MILES	ELEVATION GAIN
Day 1	Hat Creek	11.5	3,700'
Day 2	Temperance Creek	10.2	2,100'
Day 3	Kneeland Place	10.4	2,300'
Day 4	Tryon Creek Ranch	14.7	2,800'
Day 5	Little Deep Creek	9.3	2,800'
Day 6	Out	7.2	1,200'

24

STEENS MOUNTAIN GORGES LOOP

RATINGS: Scenery 10   **Solitude** 8   **Difficulty** 9
MILES: 26 (28)
ELEVATION GAIN: 4,200′ (5,400′)
DAYS: 2–4 (3–4)
SHUTTLE MILEAGE: n/a
MAPS: USGS *Fish Lake* and *Wildhorse Lake*
USUALLY OPEN: Mid-June–October
BEST: Late June and late September
PERMITS: None
RULES: Fires strongly discouraged
CONTACT: Burns District, Bureau of Land Management, 541-573-4400,
   blm.gov/office/burns-district-office

SPECIAL ATTRACTIONS ●

Solitude; incredible scenery; fall colors; wildflowers

Above: Alvord Desert and Steens Rim from Steens Summit
photographed by Douglas Lorain

🌀 Steens Mountain Gorges Loop

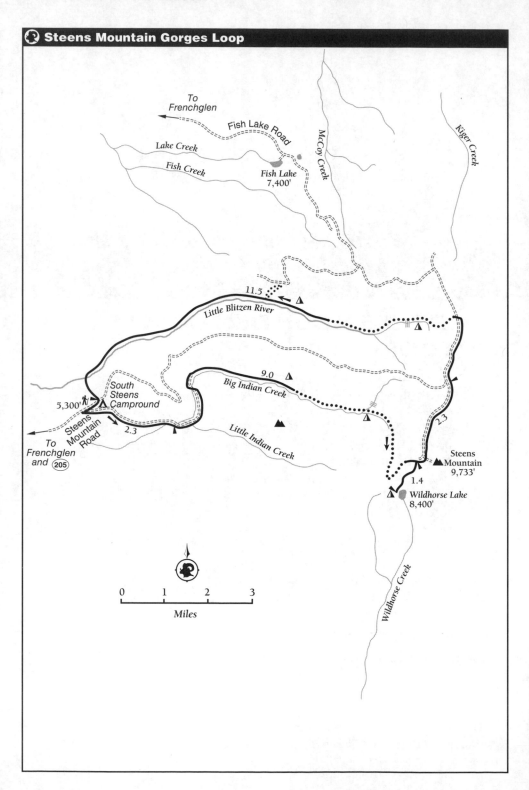

To
Frenchglen

Fish Lake Road

Lake Creek

Fish Creek

McCoy Creek

Kiger Creek

Fish Lake
7,400'

11.5

Little Blitzen River

9.0

Big Indian Creek

South
Steens
Campround

5,300'

Steens
Mountain
Road

2.3

To
Frenchglen
and (205)

Little Indian Creek

2.3

Steens
Mountain
9,733'

1.4

Wildhorse Lake
8,400'

Wildhorse Creek

0   1   2   3

Miles

CHALLENGES ••

Steep and very difficult scrambles up and down canyon headwalls; difficult stream crossings; thunderstorms; early season snowfields; limited shade; ticks (especially in spring and early summer); rattlesnakes

HOW TO GET THERE ••••••••••••••••••••••••••••••••••••••

From the intersection of US 20 and US 395 in Burns, head south on OR 205, and go 60 miles to Frenchglen. Continue another 9 miles to a junction with a well-marked gravel road. This is the southern end of Steens Mountain Loop. Ominous signs here warn of possible blizzards. (When completely open, this is the highest road in Oregon, so they're not kidding.) Drive east on this decent gravel road about 17 miles to Blitzen Crossing. About 2.2 miles beyond the bridge is the South Steens Campground. Turn into this campground and park near the marked trailhead.

GPS TRAILHEAD COORDINATES: N42° 39.404' W118° 43.708'

INTRODUCTION ••

Steens Mountain dominates the landscape of southeastern Oregon. At 9,733 feet it towers over the hills and marshes of the surrounding desert, and it can be seen for hundreds of miles in all directions. People are drawn to this landmark for many reasons, not least of which is the scenery.

The majestic beauty of this desert mountain has no equal in Oregon or, arguably, anywhere else in North America. The cliffs on the mountain's eastern escarpment drop more than 5,500 feet to the flat expanse of Alvord Desert. On the gently sloping west side of the mountain, ice age glaciers carved immense U-shaped gorges that are among the most impressive in the world. In most of North America, forests now obscure the evidence of past glaciation. Here, however, the only trees are scattered mountain mahogany and a few aspen groves near the bottom of canyons. Thus, the geologic history is spectacularly displayed for all to see. Waterfalls stream down steep walls that rise thousands of feet above the canyon floor. Clear, rushing streams flow through meadows sprinkled with wildflowers. Wildlife, including bighorn sheep, badgers, coyotes, bobcats, and the occasional rattlesnake (especially in the lower parts of the canyons), is plentiful. Best of all, the isolation and the lack of official trails mean that there's plenty of solitude—except, perhaps, during the fall hunting season. If you do this hike just before the higher parts of the loop road open to cars, you may have the entire trip to yourself. The road's lower elevations usually open in May (but call ahead to be sure).

NOTE 1: The snowpack on Steens Mountain is extremely variable. The highest parts of the loop road typically open around July 1; therefore, the last week of June is ideal for this trip. Call ahead to the Bureau of Land Management office in Burns for the latest conditions.

NOTE 2: Steens Mountain is a fragile island in a desert. Leave No Trace techniques are especially critical here. Fires in particular should be avoided. The country is dry and wood is scarce, so bring a backpacking stove.

DESCRIPTION •••

Walk east to the small parking area for the family campground, and pick up an old jeep track here. Follow this jeep track east as it gains elevation and then drops steeply to a berm, beyond which all vehicles (including bicycles) are prohibited. The route now crosses Indian Creek.

WARNING: In spring or early summer, this can be a cold and potentially difficult ford.

TIP: A sturdy walking stick and wading shoes will come in handy.

On the opposite side, continue on the abandoned jeep track and quickly reach a crossing of Little Indian Creek (possibly wet but not a problem). This side creek flows down from its own scenic gorge—a worthwhile day hike if you have the time. Your route now goes north, following the main canyon of Big Indian Creek. Less than 1 mile beyond the first crossing is the second ford of the creek. This time the streambed is a bit wider, so the crossing is easier.

The old road provides easy walking as it slowly gains elevation. Springs and small tributaries provide ample water early in summer. The mostly flat canyon bottom and the nearby stream mean that you can camp almost anywhere. The canyon turns east and grows ever more dramatic, with continuous and awe-inspiring views of the high peaks and cliffs. Sagebrush and juniper give way to more frequent meadows and occasional groves of aspen, and wildflowers become more numerous. Patches of snow from the previous winter add to the scenery.

TIP: Photographers will need an extrawide-angle lens to capture the vastness of this gorge.

About halfway up the canyon, the route fades out in a meadow. A large grove of aspen trees makes this a particularly inviting campsite. Though the road disappears, a sketchy trail continues up the canyon. It is sometimes lost amid sagebrush, aspens, or lush meadows, but the trail isn't really necessary. Be sure to look downstream from time to time to enjoy ever-improving views of this huge gorge. The relatively easy hiking ends at the sloping basin beneath the canyon headwall, one of Oregon's most spectacular locations. Flowers bloom in abundance, waterfalls cascade down the lava walls, and the surrounding cliffs rise almost 2,000 feet. There are plenty of possible campsites but not much shade.

Up to this point the going has been fairly easy, but sturdy boots and strong lungs are needed for the next section. Exiting the basin requires a steep uphill scramble over sometimes loose rocks. There is no single "best" route, but the recommended way turns south, following the left side of one of the creek's larger branches. Scramble up the grassy and rocky slopes toward the base of a pinnacle of pitted rock. You pass to the left of this pinnacle and soon reach a small upper basin where the terrain flattens out again. Continue to travel south over grassy alpine terraces to a saddle with a view of Little Wildhorse Lake, in the next drainage to the south. Turn left (east) and scramble past some rock outcrops to a cliff-edge vista of large Wildhorse Lake. This basin often remains snow-covered into July, but later in the season the lake sits in a lovely meadow filled with wildflowers. Follow the ridgeline first north, then east around the head of this basin. As you approach the end of a spur road, a path leads down to Wildhorse Lake—a highly recommended side trip if the basin isn't filled with snow and ice.

Hike 0.2 mile up the spur road to a road junction, where you should turn right for the short uphill side trip to the highest point on Steens Mountain. A radio tower and buildings intrude on the wilderness setting, but the panorama is amazing! Even the peaks of the Cascade Range are visible on clear days. Best of all, though, is the view east to the large playa called Alvord Desert, more than a vertical mile below.

TIP: Bring binoculars to look for bighorn sheep here and at other spots overlooking the eastern cliffs.

If the Steens Mountain Loop Road is not yet open to traffic, you should have this overlook all to yourself. The trade-off for solitude is the need to walk over some large snowfields.

Walk north along the summit spur road for 2.5 miles past a remarkable overlook of Big Indian Gorge to a junction with the main loop road. The high alpine grasslands in this area are alive with wildflowers in early August. Continue north along the road to the overlook of massive Little Blitzen Gorge.

Brace your knees because the next obstacle is a very steep scramble down the headwall cliffs of Little Blitzen Gorge. The cliffs directly below the overlook are ridiculously steep, so try the slopes either 0.5 mile farther north or about 0.3 mile south for a marginally easier route. It's about 1,600 feet down to the floor of the canyon, and there is no trail, so carefully pick your way down the rocky terrain. This effort is amply rewarded because the large, boggy basin below the headwall is only slightly less impressive than the one in Big Indian Gorge. Here you will enjoy more of the cliffs, wildflowers, clear streams, and generally outstanding scenery characteristic of Steens Mountain. There are numerous possible campsites to spend a night amid this grandeur.

From the top of a small waterfall that drops from the headwall basin, you'll enjoy a marvelous view down the canyon. Now a sketchy trail follows the north bank of the stream. This path, which is worth following, improves and becomes a reasonably good trail as it continues downstream.

Your route travels past a second waterfall and through lovely meadows filled with grasses, wildflowers, and pungent sage. Near the creek, aspens provide frames for photographs, as well as welcome shade. Dark canyon walls rise on either side. About 4 miles down the canyon, a sketchy pack trail meets our route from the north. This little-used path switchbacks steeply up the north wall to a jeep track south of Fish Lake. The canyon floor is wide and almost level near this junction, with several nice meadows and good campsites. A few old cabins and stock corrals add historical interest.

The Little Blitzen River Canyon slowly angles southwest as the stream's descent gets a bit steeper. The sage, mountain mahogany trees, and brush get thicker at lower elevations, so views are somewhat limited the rest of the way. After passing a massive buttress on the south wall, the river and the trail begin to angle a little more to the south before breaking out into the rolling sagebrush country at the mouth of the canyon. At a fence line, the trail turns left and fords the river.

WARNING: This crossing can be waist deep in early summer.

The trail continues south, away from the river, as it climbs over a low ridge and gradually descends to the loop road at a signed trailhead. An easy 0.5-mile walk down the road leads back to your car and the close of an incredibly scenic trip.

POSSIBLE ITINERARY

	CAMP	MILES	ELEVATION GAIN
Day 1	Big Indian Gorge	8.3	1,700'
Day 2	Little Blitzen Gorge (with side trips to Wildhorse Lake and Steens Mountain summit)	9.0	3,200'
Day 3	Out	8.4	500'

DESERT TRAIL: PUEBLO MOUNTAINS SECTION

RATINGS: Scenery 8   **Solitude** 9   **Difficulty** 7

MILES: 22 (29)

ELEVATION GAIN: 6,500' (8,200')

DAYS: 2–3 (3–4)

SHUTTLE MILEAGE: 20

MAP: Oregon Natural Desert Association *Oregon Desert Trail Region 3 (Section 16: Fields to Denio Creek)* (available as a free download at onda.org/discover-oregons-desert/trail-resources)

USUALLY OPEN: Mid-May–November

BEST: Mid-June and September–October

PERMITS: None

RULES: Fires strongly discouraged (check locally for seasonal fire bans)

CONTACT: Burns District, Bureau of Land Management, 541-573-4400, blm.gov/office/burns-district-office; Oregon Natural Desert Association, 541-330-2638, onda.org

SPECIAL ATTRACTIONS ··

Expansive views; solitude; wildflowers

Above: Star of Bethlehem alongside the Desert Trail
photographed by Douglas Lorain

Desert Trail: Pueblo Mountains Section

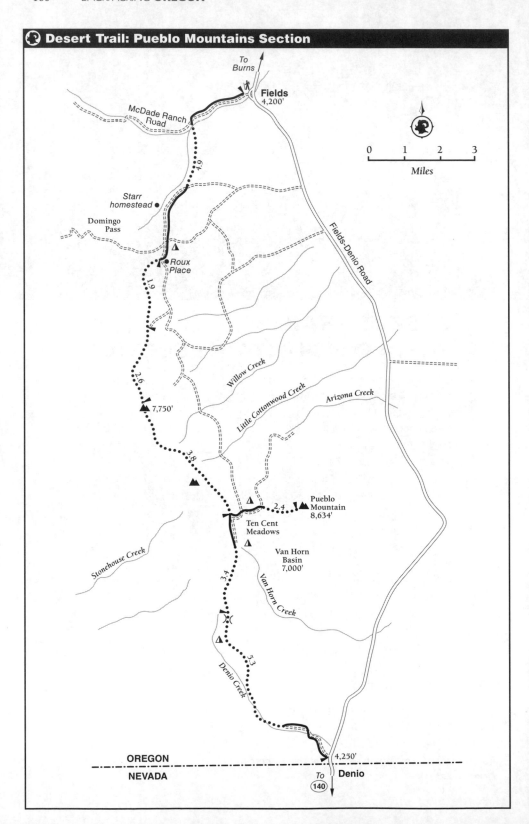

To
Burns

Fields
4,200'

McDade Ranch
Road

4.9

Starr
homestead •

Domingo
Pass

Roux
Place

1.9

Fields-Denio Road

Willow Creek

Little Cottonwood Creek

Arizona Creek

2.6

7,750'

3.8

2.4

Pueblo
Mountain
8,634'

Ten Cent
Meadows

Van Horn
Basin
7,000'

Stonehouse Creek

3.4

Van Horn Creek

5.3

Denio Creek

4,250'

OREGON

NEVADA

To
140

Denio

0   1   2   3
Miles

CHALLENGES ●

Route-finding difficulties; no shade; limited water; rattlesnakes

HOW TO GET THERE ●

Both ends of this trip are on a good paved highway with an easy car shuttle between them—a real blessing in an area where road access is typically over poor dirt tracks. Start from the tiny town of Fields. To reach it, from the intersection of US 395 and US 20 in Burns, head south on OR 205 (which becomes Fields–Denio Road) and go 120 miles to the Fields General Store, where you can also get a famously excellent milkshake and good advice on camping and travel in the area.

The south trailhead is at the small town of Denio on the Oregon–Nevada border, only 21 miles farther south.

GPS TRAILHEAD COORDINATES:
   (Fields) N42° 15.854' W118° 40.520'
   (Denio) N41° 59.267' W118° 38.296'

INTRODUCTION ●

Until recently, almost no one in Oregon had heard of the Pueblo Mountains. If you told someone you were going to "the Pueblos," they assumed that you were driving to the American Southwest to check out old American Indian dwellings. Even today, despite a good paved road along their base and a segment of the Desert Trail running through them, the Pueblos remain isolated and receive relatively little use. But this desert range has a great deal to offer. Views seem to stretch to eternity. There are permanent streams and springs (rare for southeastern Oregon). Enough snow falls that the high cliffs and peaks are picturesquely streaked with white into June, and spring wildflowers put on a beautiful show. Don't expect much shade, however, as trees are limited to a few mountain mahogany and aspen.

The Oregon Desert Trail is largely conceptual—that is, unmarked and stitched together from an evolving network of existing trails, dirt roads, and cross-country routes. It's possible, but challenging, to thru-hike the length of the trail.

For this segment, you'll want to download a copy of the Oregon Natural Desert Association's (ONDA's) guidebook, carry a GPS device, and have good way-finding skills using a map and compass. Through this range the Desert Trail is marked by large cairns that set only a general course through the terrain without a defined footpath. Hikers must pick their own way from one distant pile of rocks to the next.

WARNING: Bring a good map, a compass, and binoculars to help locate each cairn. The ONDA's downloadable maps and guidebook include detailed directions and way-points for each cairn, making them indispensable.

WARNING: In places, magnetism in the rocks can throw off compass readings. Make sure that you actually see the next cairn before proceeding.

DESCRIPTION ••

From the north end of "downtown" Fields (that is, the single building that serves as store, post office, and gas station), hike 2 miles west on McDade Ranch Road and then turn south at a cattle guard. Cross a (usually dry) creek and follow a fence line 0.5 mile. Head briefly west about 100 yards along another fence to reach a jeep road and once again turn south. Stick with this jeep road about 2 miles (with a short detour around the Starr homestead) to Domingo Pass Road. Shortly thereafter, head southwest along a fence line. Follow this fence to its end, then continue southwest about another 100 yards to a grove of aspens at Roux Place Springs, the first reliable water.

> **NOTE:** The springs are on private land. If you wish to camp, do so on public land, 200 yards or more to the south.

Continue south and contour at a roughly constant elevation around two hills to a jeep track that comes up from the east. Here you should find the first in the series of cairns that you'll be following for the remainder of this trip. Ahead is a long and difficult climb along a steep gully and hillside. Views to the north of distant Alvord Desert and Steens Mountain steadily improve as you climb. Closer at hand are the crags of the Pueblos, as well as small flowers and colorful lichens on the rocks underfoot.

> **WARNING:** The route often crosses areas of loose rocks, so exercise caution.

> **TIP:** Be sure to check out an interesting rock with a large hole in it near cairn #7.

Reach the ridgecrest near cairn #8 and enjoy grand sights in all directions—particularly to the west over the Rincon Valley and beyond. Stick with the up-and-down ridgecrest, often on game trails, to the top of a mountain. The bulk of your climbing is now complete, so congratulate yourself and enjoy the hard-won view. Reshoulder your pack and drop down the east side of the ridge. You pass a welcome spring and then contour around the cliffs above the head of Willow Creek.

Now you round a ridge at a saddle near cairn #22 and turn south. Towering cliffs rise

The ridge of the Pueblos from the east
photographed by Douglas Lorain

to the west for the next 2 miles, and twisted mountain mahogany adds to the scenery. Cross a small tributary of Cottonwood Creek and then pass a grove of stunted aspen trees on the way to Ten Cent Meadows, set in a mile-wide saddle between the main ridge of the Pueblos on the west and hulking Pueblo Mountain on the east. There are possible campsites here, with nearby spring water.

You meet a jeep road coming up from Arizona Creek and follow it south 1.2 miles as it drops into beautiful Van Horn Basin. There are many possible places to camp near Van Horn Creek, with aspen groves providing shade.

TIP 1: The morning view over the creek and the aspen groves of Van Horn Basin to the snow-streaked ridge of the Pueblos is a photographer's dream.

TIP 2: Don't miss the side trip from here to the summit of Pueblo Mountain. It's about 2.5 miles to the top, and the route often travels over steep and loose rocks, but the view is well worth the effort. There is, of course, no trail, but you don't really need one.

To continue your tour, leave the jeep road at cairn #32 and climb, often steeply, along a sidehill. You walk on top of a long rock ledge as the route works toward the pass between Van Horn and Denio Basins. The sights, as expected, are outstanding, especially to the east of massive Pueblo Mountain and of Van Horn Basin with its many aspen groves. After a well-deserved stop at the pass, proceed south into the Denio Creek drainage as you rapidly lose elevation. Wildflowers are particularly abundant here. At a large aspen grove, there is room to make a pleasant camp beneath the trees, with nearby water.

Now the route makes a long, poorly marked detour to the east around a parcel of private land in Denio Basin. You cross a fence line marking the end of private property and meet a jeep road as you continue to descend the canyon of Denio Creek.

TIP: Cattle trails through here are often confusing, but they provide easier walking through the sagebrush.

Cross the creek a couple of times and then reach an interesting old stone cabin. For the final 1.8 miles the route follows a jeep road down to Denio.

POSSIBLE ITINERARY

	CAMP	MILES	ELEVATION GAIN
Day 1	Roux Place Springs	5.2	1,100'
Day 2	Van Horn Basin	9.2	3,600'
Day 3	Denio Basin (with side trip up Pueblo Mountain)	9.5	3,200'
Day 4	Out	5.0	300'

26

HONEYCOMBS LOOP

RATINGS: Scenery 9   **Solitude** 10   **Difficulty** 8

MILES: 17 (29)

ELEVATION GAIN: 3,500' (6,400')

DAYS: 2–3 (3–4)

SHUTTLE MILEAGE: n/a

MAPS: USGS *Three Fingers Rock* and *Pelican Point*

USUALLY OPEN: April–November

BEST: Early May and September

PERMITS: None

RULES: Fires strongly discouraged (and periodically banned; check regulations in advance); camping in Leslie Gulch is allowed only at Slocum Creek Campground

CONTACT: Vale District, Bureau of Land Management, 541-473-3144, blm.gov/office/vale-district-office

SPECIAL ATTRACTIONS ●

Colorful rock formations; solitude

CHALLENGES ●

Limited water; poor road access (or complicated boat transport); no trails; rugged hiking; rattlesnakes

Above: A delicate little arch on the ridge above Honeycombs
photographed by Douglas Lorain

Honeycombs Loop

To
Succor Creek
Road

Sheepshead Ridge

Sheepshead
Basin

Sage Creek

Juniper Ridge

1.0

4,250'

4,771'

7307-0-00

McIntyre Spring Road

Bensley
Flat

5.8

Honeycombs

2.8

Painted Canyon

7306-0-00

Three Fingers
Rock
4,828'

Saddle Butte
3,653'

3.1

3.0

Carlton Canyon

To
Succor
Creek
Road

2,635'

Three Fingers Gulch

3.1

Owyhee Reservoir

1.6

1.5   1.3

Long Gulch

Atkins Butte
4,117'

0.8

Shadscale Flat

Craig Gulch

To
Leslie Gulch
Road

0   1   2   3
Miles

HOW TO GET THERE

For those without boat transportation, access to the closest roads is easier from the south. Drive north from Jordan Valley on US 95 for 18.2 miles, and turn left onto gravel Succor Creek Road. Follow this route 8.5 miles, and turn right to remain on Succor Creek Road. Go another 6.6 miles (5 miles north of the well-marked Leslie Gulch Road turnoff), and turn left onto McIntyre Spring Road. The driving difficulties start here. With mud, rocks, and little or no maintenance, this road will never be mistaken for a superhighway. On the positive side, the drive provides wonderful views of cliff-edged McIntyre Ridge and the chance to see wild horses.

In 4 miles, drive over a saddle about 1 mile east of prominent Three Fingers Rock (well worth the relatively short walk to explore), and continue north another 3.5 miles. Turn left in a grassy little valley holding Sage Creek, which is dry by early summer. This road, even worse than the one you've been on, climbs about 2.8 miles to a junction.

> **TIP:** If this road is too rough, an alternate approach is to continue 1 mile north from the valley junction, turn left onto Forest Service Road 7307-0-00, and go 2 miles. Turn south onto FS 7306-0-00, and drive 1.5 miles to the previously mentioned junction with the road up Sage Creek.

In a low pass 0.2 mile south of this junction, park beside a livestock watering tank.

GPS TRAILHEAD COORDINATES: N43° 28.653' W117° 14.143'

INTRODUCTION

A land of striking beauty lies on the east side of the Owyhee Reservoir. In the dry canyons of this desert country, you will discover a collection of oddly shaped rock pinnacles, towers, and cliffs painted in a colorful array of browns, reds, and oranges. In spring, especially after a wet winter, the sagebrush and grasses turn green, and wildflowers like balsamroot and Indian paintbrush add yellows, reds, and other colors to the scene. Hikers familiar with the canyon lands of southern Utah will feel right at home.

Actually getting there, however, is not easy. A good gravel road goes down Leslie Gulch, so this canyon has become popular with hikers, photographers, and other admirers. Stretched out to the north are several equally spectacular canyons whose remoteness provides much more solitude. For the backpacker, the best access is either by boat from Owyhee Reservoir or over rough and poorly marked dirt roads that are torture on cars. Boat access requires finding someone willing to shuttle you down the reservoir about 25 miles to Bensley Flat and then return to pick you up after your trip. There is no commercial service, and relatively few private boaters go this far down the lake. As for the roads, after it rains, only high-clearance four-wheel drive vehicles should try them. One option is to park on one of the area's good roads (through Leslie Gulch or Succor Creek Canyon) and then take a mountain bike to the starting point for your hike.

> **WARNING:** Water ranges from scarce to nonexistent. The only reliable year-round source is Owyhee Reservoir, and this should be treated with both chemicals and filtering before drinking. On the other hand, beware of occasional thunderstorms that may cause flash floods.

DESCRIPTION

Having survived the drive, strap on a pair of sturdy boots (good ankle support is essential in this steep, rocky, trailless terrain), and head northwest on a jeep track. You top a low hill and then turn south and drop to a gully at the head of Painted Canyon. Hike down this ravine as it grows narrower and more spectacular. In places you may be forced to make rugged detours around cliffs and dry waterfalls.

TIP: Bring a rope to lower your pack over especially steep and dangerous sections before climbing down yourself.

The long, steep descent ends as the canyon bottom widens and levels out. Multicolored cliffs and spires rise on both sides, and as you continue down the canyon, the geologic scenery does nothing but improve. Near the mouth of Painted Canyon, the walls narrow considerably before breaking out into Carlton Canyon.

TIP: To see more towers and cliffs, drop your pack and explore east into upper Carlton Canyon for 0.5 mile.

Turning west, you'll find that the scenery remains good, though not as continuously dramatic as Painted Canyon.

TIP: After about 1 mile look for a side canyon to the north that is well worth exploring.

About 2 miles from Painted Canyon and 1 mile from the mouth of Carlton Canyon, you'll reach some high buttresses on either side that are especially dramatic. You can make camp in the flats where the canyon widens near Owyhee Reservoir—just don't count on any shade.

You can make an excellent but rugged day trip to Three Fingers Gulch from a base camp at the mouth of Carlton Canyon. Pack some water and hike south along the up-and-down slopes beside Owyhee Reservoir. After about 2 miles, cross the mouth of a good-sized canyon and then climb along this canyon's south ridge for 1.5 miles to where it levels out. From here you turn south up a second ridge, bordered on the west by cliffs and pinnacles.

NOTE: These cliffs go steeply down to the reservoir, which explains why you had to make this detour. Access beside the water is not feasible.

Descend east to a saddle, then *carefully* scramble down a *very* steep and narrow gully between two cliffs. You should reach the base of Three Fingers Gulch near a fork in the canyon at Shadscale Flat, where a very faint jeep road approaches from the south. Be sure to explore downstream through this scenic, narrow gulch to the Owyhee Reservoir.

WARNING: The last 0.2 mile to the reservoir requires some tough scrambling.

TIP: If you're really ambitious, scramble up the canyon's steep south slope to enjoy clifftop views of Three Fingers Gulch. Once on top, turn west and go about 0.5 mile to reach the terrific overlook atop the impressive cliffs rising directly from the waters of Owyhee Reservoir.

Turning east (upcanyon), keep left at the forks where you entered Three Fingers Gulch, and travel between two impressive cliffs. After about 0.8 mile you'll reach the mouth of Long Gulch at a point distinguished by a tall pinnacle. Keep left, following Three Fingers Gulch, and 0.3 mile later turn left again into a small canyon. You can climb this canyon all the way to the top of the ridge that you came in on earlier in the day, and retrace your route back to Carlton Canyon.

To complete the recommended backpack loop, go north from the mouth of Carlton Canyon along the sagebrush-covered hills beside Owyhee Reservoir. After about 1 mile you'll reach the base of Saddle Butte. Scramble over the pass on the east side of this landmark, and then drop down a ravine to the large expanse of Bensley Flat. You can comfortably camp almost anywhere on this bench. There are even a few boaters' cabins and willow trees near the reservoir's shore.

Tall reddish-brown cliffs rise to the east of Bensley Flat.

TIP: These cliffs are best photographed in the low light of late evening.

From the south end of the cliffs, you walk up a scenic draw that heads initially south and then loops around to the northeast. This gulch goes through the heart of the Honeycombs—a spectacular region with a dizzying display of colorful rock formations, many pockmarked with holes and small caves. The north side of the canyon is particularly impressive.

About 2 miles from the canyon's mouth, you pass to the left of a large rock monolith and then continue to follow the canyon bottom as it climbs and turns east. At the head of the canyon, scramble very steeply to the right to reach the top of long, rolling Juniper Ridge, where the walking is much easier as you follow game and cattle trails.

WARNING: The crisscrossing trails along this ridge can be confusing. The correct route follows a generally northeast course along the top of this wide ridge.

After about 2 miles turn east, drop down a gully, and look for the jeep track coming down to the head of Painted Canyon.

TIP: If Juniper Ridge reaches a little saddle and starts to climb moderately steeply toward a 4,500-foot high point, then you've gone about 0.5 mile past the proper turnoff.

Pick up the jeep route and follow it back to your vehicle (either car or mountain bike).

POSSIBLE ITINERARY

	CAMP	MILES	ELEVATION GAIN
Day 1	Mouth of Carlton Canyon	6.8	200'
Day 2	Day trip to Three Fingers Gulch (return to mouth of Carlton Canyon)	12.0	2,900'
Day 3	Out (via Honeycombs)	9.9	3,300'

OTHER BACKPACKING OPTIONS

Though this book includes what the authors consider to be the *best* long backpacking trips in Oregon, there are many other options for the adventurous backpacker. With some creativity and a good set of contour maps, a backpacker could easily spend a lifetime in this diverse state. What follows is an overview of some additional recommended trips, with just enough description to whet the appetite. Because many of these hikes are in lesser-known areas, they are excellent options for solitude lovers. (Unless specifically noted, none of these trips requires a permit.)

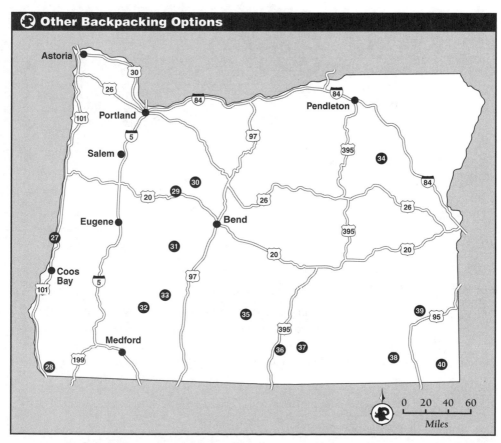

27

OREGON DUNES LOOP

RATINGS: Scenery 7 **Solitude** 3–8 **Difficulty** 5
MILES: Varies
DAYS: Varies
MAP: USFS *Oregon Dunes National Recreation Area*
USUALLY OPEN: Year-round
BEST: Winter and mid-May

SPECIAL ATTRACTIONS ·

Extensive sand dunes

CHALLENGES ·

Summer crowds; quicksand in winter

GPS TRAILHEAD COORDINATES:
(Siltcoos River) N43° 52.512' W124° 09.396'

Though this area is crowded in summer, it is blessedly quiet in winter. Mid-May features blooming rhododendrons in the forests. Backpackers have several options, but your best choice is some combination of beach and inland dune hiking south from the Siltcoos River, past Tahkenitch Creek, to Umpqua Spit, and back.

Above: Oregon's coastal landscape
photographed by Hills Outdoors/Shutterstock

28

SOUTH COAST

RATINGS: Scenery 10   **Solitude** 4   **Difficulty** 5
MILES: Varies
DAYS: Varies
MAP: USGS *Brookings, Gold Beach,* and *Cape Sebastian*
USUALLY OPEN: Year-round
BEST: Mid-April–May

SPECIAL ATTRACTIONS •

Spectacular coastal scenery

CHALLENGES •

Very limited camping options; some road walking

GPS TRAILHEAD COORDINATES: (Brookings) N42° 03.898' W124° 18.205'

Between Gold Beach and Brookings, the Oregon coast is at its most spectacular. By connecting beach walks with trail segments, a *stunningly* scenic hike is possible. Lack of campsites, proximity to the highway, and sometimes-crowded trails make this area more popular with day hikers than backpackers. Hike north from Brookings through Samuel H. Boardman State Scenic Corridor as far as time and ambition allow. Two possible stopping points are Arch Rock and Cape Sebastian.

Rocks near Thunder Rock in Samuel H. Boardman State Scenic Corridor
photographed by Douglas Lorain

29

OLD CASCADES LOOP

RATINGS: Scenery 4 **Solitude** 9 **Difficulty** 5
MILES: 42
DAYS: 4–5
MAP: USFS *Willamette National Forest: Sweet Home Ranger District*
USUALLY OPEN: June–November
BEST: Late June–July

SPECIAL ATTRACTIONS

Solitude; old-growth forests

CHALLENGES

High elevation gain; mountain bikes

GPS TRAILHEAD COORDINATES: N44° 25.758' W122° 01.815'

The star attraction of this route is the old-growth forest. Several sloping wild-flower meadows and ridgetop viewpoints add variety and scenic interest. You start from the Maude Creek (also known as Crescent Mountain South) Trail-head; from Bend, take US 20 northwest about 49 miles, past its junction with OR 22, then turn right (north) onto Forest Service Road 2067. Climb over Crescent Mountain and the Three Pyramids and then loop counterclockwise via Scar Mountain, Knob Rock, Donaca Lake, and Pyramid Creek back to Crescent Mountain and your car.

Above: Mount Jefferson over cliffs of Scar Mountain
photographed by Douglas Lorain

30

TABLE LAKE LOOP

RATINGS: Scenery 9 **Solitude** 5 **Difficulty** 7
MILES: 25+
DAYS: 3–5
MAP: National Geographic Trails Illustrated *Mount Jefferson/Mount Washington*
USUALLY OPEN: Mid-July–October
BEST: Late July–August

SPECIAL ATTRACTIONS ·

Diverse volcanic scenery; great views

CHALLENGES ·

Mosquitoes

GPS TRAILHEAD COORDINATES: N44° 34.949' W121° 40.655'

This hike tours the scenic east part of the Mount Jefferson Wilderness. The route includes many outstanding views, a lava flow, lakes, and plenty of room for exploring. Start from the Jefferson Creek Trailhead, reached from the lower Metolius River near Sisters on Forest Service Road 1292/Candle Creek Road, and follow the Jefferson Creek Trail to Table Lake.

TIP: Schedule extra time for spectacular day hikes to The Table and Hole-in-the-Wall Park.

Return by the Sugar Pine Ridge Trail to the south. Permits are required.

Above: Mount Jefferson from Sugar Pine Mountain
photographed by Douglas Lorain

31

WALDO LAKE LOOP

RATINGS: Scenery 6   **Solitude** 5   **Difficulty** 3
MILES: 21+
DAYS: 2–6
MAP: USFS *Willamette National Forest: Middle Fork Ranger District*
USUALLY OPEN: Mid-June–late October
BEST: Mid-August–September

SPECIAL ATTRACTIONS

Easy trail; good swimming; scenic lake vistas; huckleberries

CHALLENGES

Mosquitoes (through early August); poor fishing (the lake is too pure to support many fish)

GPS TRAILHEAD COORDINATES: N43° 43.473' W122° 04.381'

Large, beautiful, and incredibly clear Waldo Lake is the only major lake in Oregon with a shoreline trail good for backpackers. (Other lakes all have too many roads, people, and/or speedboats.) In addition to having pleasant scenery, the loop trail is also relatively easy, making this trip ideal for families with children. Excellent side trips to places like Black Meadows, Waldo Mountain Lookout, the Eddeeleo Lakes, and the Rigdon Lakes are fine for those looking for more exercise. The lake is north of OR 58 east of Oakridge.

32

ROGUE–UMPQUA DIVIDE

RATINGS: Scenery 7   **Solitude** 7   **Difficulty** 5
MILES: 27
DAYS: 3
MAP: USFS *Boulder Creek Wilderness, Rogue–Umpqua Divide Wilderness, Mount Thielsen Wilderness, Oregon Cascades Recreation Area*
USUALLY OPEN: Late May–November
BEST: Mid- to late June

SPECIAL ATTRACTIONS

Wildflowers; rock formations; views; solitude

CHALLENGES

Long car shuttle

GPS TRAILHEAD COORDINATES: (Abbott Butte) N42° 55.160' W122° 35.087'

This little-known wilderness is a pleasant surprise to most Oregon hikers. The hike features meadows filled with a stunning array of wildflowers, subalpine lakes, fascinating rock formations, and expansive views. The best tour of the area starts in the south at a pass on gravel Forest Service Road 68 northwest of Prospect. Hike north past Abbott Butte, Elephant Head, Anderson Butte, and Hershberger Mountain.

TIP: Don't miss the short side trip to the Hershberger Lookout.

Continue along spectacular Rocky Ridge, descend to Fish Lake, and exit at the Fish Lake Creek Trailhead off FS 2840 in Umpqua National Forest. Side trips abound.

33

UPPER ROGUE RIVER

RATINGS: Scenery 6   **Solitude** 4   **Difficulty** 3
MILES: Varies
DAYS: Varies
MAP: USFS *Rogue River National Forest*
USUALLY OPEN: Late May–November
BEST: Late October

SPECIAL ATTRACTIONS

Beautiful river and canyon scenery; fall colors; waterfalls

CHALLENGES

Some crowded areas; nearby major highway

GPS TRAILHEAD COORDINATES: N43° 05.449' W122° 13.290'

Although it's never far from a busy highway, this long river path is a real treat. While a few of the more geologically interesting attractions, such as the Natural Bridge, are crowded with tourists, other areas are quiet. Late October brings few people and exceptional fall colors. Start from the Crater Rim viewpoint along OR 230 west of Diamond Lake, and hike downstream past waterfalls, past campgrounds, and through attractive old-growth forests all the way to Prospect (48 miles). Numerous access points allow for shorter options.

34

NORTH FORK JOHN DAY RIVER

RATINGS: Scenery 6   **Solitude** 8   **Difficulty** 4
MILES: 25
DAYS: 3–6
MAP: USFS *North Fork John Day Ranger District*
USUALLY OPEN: June–November
BEST: June–October

SPECIAL ATTRACTIONS ·

Excellent fishing; canyon scenery

CHALLENGES ·

Some burned areas

GPS TRAILHEAD COORDINATES: N44° 54.935' W118° 24.272'

This forested canyon hike is especially appealing to anglers. Opportunities to try your luck in the rushing waters of the North Fork John Day River are found around every bend. Several historical old cabins are also interesting. For a one-way downhill hike, start from the North Fork Trailhead along paved Forest Service Road 73 northwest of Sumpter. The trail stays close to the stream's north bank for its entire length. The lower trailhead is on dirt FS 5506, most easily reached from Ukiah to the west.

35

FREMONT NATIONAL RECREATION TRAIL

RATINGS: Scenery 7   **Solitude** 10   **Difficulty** 5
MILES: Varies
DAYS: Varies
MAP: USFS *Fremont National Forest: Paisley Ranger District, Silver Lake Ranger District,* and *Lakeview Ranger District*
USUALLY OPEN: Mid-June–November
BEST: Late June–July

SPECIAL ATTRACTIONS

Views; solitude; bighorn sheep

CHALLENGES

Limited water in places

GPS TRAILHEAD COORDINATES:

(Fremont Point Day-Use Area) N42° 51.806' W120° 50.249'

Fremont National Forest is developing an excellent new long trail that connects nearly all parts of this little-known but scenic forest. Consisting of three segments, northern, middle, and southern, this trail explores the high peaks of the Warner Mountains, travels along a remote ridge west of Valley Falls, crosses the Chewaucan River, and then follows Winter Ridge for views of Summer Lake. Parts of the trail are still primitive and may be hard to discern. Eventually plans call for the trail to connect all the way west to the Pacific Crest Trail and east to the Desert Trail. Early summer provides the best conditions, when seasonal water sources are available and the area supports lots of wildflowers.

36

ABERT RIM

RATINGS: Scenery 9   **Solitude** 10   **Difficulty** 7
MILES: 24
DAYS: 3
MAP: USGS *Little Honey Creek* and *Lake Abert South*
USUALLY OPEN: June–November
BEST: June

SPECIAL ATTRACTIONS

Bighorn sheep; views!

CHALLENGES

No trail; almost no water

GPS TRAILHEAD COORDINATES: N42° 23.292' W120° 14.051'

Abert Rim is the tallest and perhaps the most impressive fault scarp in the world. An extended backpacking trip is the ideal way to appreciate the vastness of this scenic rim. Off OR 140 northeast of Lakeview, go north on Forest Service Road 3615 and then dirt FS 377 to the Abert Rim overlook. Walk cross-country north along the view-packed rim's edge. Exit either at Mule Lake (poor road access) or via the steep use path down to US 395 at Poison Creek.

37

HART MOUNTAIN–POKER JIM RIDGE

RATINGS: Scenery 8   **Solitude** 10   **Difficulty** 8
MILES: 30
DAYS: 3
MAPS: USGS *Hart Lake, Warner Peak, Campbell Lake,* and *Bluejoint Lake East*
USUALLY OPEN: Mid-May–November
BEST: June

SPECIAL ATTRACTIONS

Wildlife; views; solitude

CHALLENGES

Poor road access; no trails; rugged route; ticks; very limited water

GPS TRAILHEAD COORDINATES: N42° 23.589' W119° 49.772'

This is a long but very scenic hike along Hart Mountain's desert escarpment. From Plush (northeast of Lakeview) drive south along the rough, narrow, dirt track beside Hart Lake's east shore for about 4 miles and park. You start with a difficult scramble up to the high plateau of Hart Mountain. Turn north to Warner Peak and Rock Creek and then cross the refuge access road and continue along Poker Jim Ridge to the recommended exit at Bluejoint Lake. Wildlife and views are abundant throughout. Except for Rock Creek, water is nonexistent. Permits are required.

38

TROUT CREEK MOUNTAINS LOOP

RATINGS: Scenery 8   **Solitude** 9   **Difficulty** 8
MILES: 44
DAYS: 4–6
MAPS: USGS *Doolittle Creek* and *Little Whitehorse Creek*
USUALLY OPEN: Mid-May–October
BEST: June and early October

SPECIAL ATTRACTIONS •

Solitude; fishing; wildlife; fall colors (especially aspens); wildflowers

CHALLENGES •

Poor roads; no trails; private land to circumvent

GPS TRAILHEAD COORDINATES:
(Sweeney Ranch) N42° 15.043' W118° 10.709'

These little-known desert mountains near the Nevada border are a real treat for hikers. One of several possible trips is a long loop hike that starts near privately owned Sweeney Ranch and goes up scenic Whitehorse Creek Canyon. Turn west along a jeep road on the high ridge of the Trout Creeks and then return via Little Whitehorse Creek Canyon.

Confluence of Whitehorse and Cottonwood Creeks
photographed by Douglas Lorain

39

LOWER OWYHEE CANYON RIM

RATINGS: Scenery 9   **Solitude** 10   **Difficulty** 6
MILES: 44
DAYS: 4–6
MAPS: USGS *Lambert Rocks* and *Rinehart Canyon*
USUALLY OPEN: April–November
BEST: May

SPECIAL ATTRACTIONS

Wildlife; magnificent canyon scenery

CHALLENGES

Awful road access; very limited water; poison ivy near the river; rattlesnakes

GPS TRAILHEAD COORDINATES: N42° 52.039' W117° 43.328'

The *best* way to experience the wild and scenic canyon of the Owyhee River is to float the stream. The *next* best way is to backpack the rim—a highly rewarding adventure, despite the lack of trails.

WARNING: The "roads" here are passable only to high-clearance four-wheel drive vehicles.

From the tiny community of Rome, go northwest on gravel and then dirt county roads through a private ranch (leave all gates the way you found them) to the start of public land near Crooked Creek. Park and walk east and then north along the canyon rim.

TIP: Don't miss exploring Chalk Basin and the side trip to the vista from Iron Point.

Exit at Rinehart Canyon "Road" (more of a jeep track) northwest of Jackson Hole.

40

LOUSE CANYON

RATINGS: Scenery 8   **Solitude** 10   **Difficulty** 10
MILES: 50
DAYS: 4–7
MAPS: USGS *Rawhide Springs, Drummond Basin,* and *Three Forks*
USUALLY OPEN: May–October
BEST: September

SPECIAL ATTRACTIONS

Solitude; desert canyon scenery

CHALLENGES

Poor road access; very rough scrambling required; rattlesnakes; lots of wading (or even swimming)

GPS TRAILHEAD COORDINATES: N42° 07.839' W117° 18.958'

This is an *extremely* remote and rugged hike down the canyon of the West Little Owyhee River. The canyon features towering cliffs, colonnades and pinnacles, pools of water reflecting canyon walls, and wildlife. The hike is *extraordinarily* rough and should be contemplated only by very experienced and well-equipped hikers willing to expend an enormous amount of both physical and mental energy to enjoy this adventure. Start from Anderson Crossing at the mouth of Massey Canyon and end near Three Forks—both reached by very poor dirt roads. Good maps are essential.

Above: Formation near mouth of Massey Canyon
photographed by Douglas Lorain

Wild horses along the Honeycombs Loop (see Trip 26, page 164)
photographed by Douglas Lorain

INDEX